OFFICIAL
(ISC)² GUIDE TO
THE SSCP® CBK®

OTHER BOOKS IN THE (ISC)²® PRESS SERIES

Building and Implementing a Security Certification and Accreditation Program: Official (ISC)²® Guide to the CAPᶜᵐ CBK®
Patrick D. Howard
ISBN: 0-8493-2062-3

Official (ISC)²® Guide to the SSCP® CBK®
Diana-Lynn Contesti, Douglas Andre, Eric Waxvik,
Paul A. Henry, and Bonnie A. Goins
ISBN: 0-8493-2774-1

Official (ISC)²® Guide to the CISSP®-ISSEP® CBK®
Susan Hansche
ISBN: 0-8493-2341-X

Official (ISC)²® Guide to the CISSP® CBK®
Harold F. Tipton and Kevin Henry, Editors
ISBN: 0-8493-8231-9

OFFICIAL
(ISC)² GUIDE TO THE
SSCP® CBK®

Diana-Lynn Contesti, Douglas Andre,
Eric Waxvik, Paul A. Henry, and Bonnie A. Goins

SECURITY TRANSCENDS TECHNOLOGY®

Auerbach Publications
Taylor & Francis Group
Boca Raton   New York

Auerbach Publications is an imprint of the
Taylor & Francis Group, an informa business

Auerbach Publications
Taylor & Francis Group
6000 Broken Sound Parkway NW, Suite 300
Boca Raton, FL 33487-2742

© 2007 by Taylor & Francis Group, LLC
Auerbach is an imprint of Taylor & Francis Group, an Informa business

International Standard Book Number-10: 0-8493-2774-1 (Hardcover)
International Standard Book Number-13: 978-0-8493-2774-2 (Hardcover)

Library of Congress Cataloging-in-Publication Data

Official (ISC)2 guide to the SSCP CBK / Diana-Lynn Contesti ... [et al.].
   p. cm. -- ((ISC)2 press series)
  Includes index.
  ISBN 0-8493-2774-1 (978-0-8493-2774-2 : alk. paper)
  1. Computer networks--Security measures--Examinations--Study guides. 2. Electronic data processing personnel--Examinations--Study guides. I. Contesti, Diana-Lynn.

TK5105.59.O44 2007
005.8--dc22   2007011467

Visit the Taylor & Francis Web site at
http://www.taylorandfrancis.com

and the Auerbach Web site at
http://www.auerbach-publications.com

Contents

Domain 2
Security Operations and Administration **43**
Bonnie Goins, CISSP

Foreword to the Offical (ISC)²® Guide to the SSCP® CBK®

Information Security is an increasingly important and critical component in the preservation, progress and stability of business in today's world. Never have the pressures on corporations, governments and militaries been so widespread and multifaceted. While consumers and citizens are looking for the delivery of new and faster services, the legislatures of the world are placing more restrictions and oversight on the secure handling of information.

The SSCP® is an exciting and practical solution for many organizations today. The SSCP provides a solid foundation of understanding of information security concepts and issues for many people throughout the organization. Whether as a system or network administrator, information systems auditor, computer programmer or systems analyst, or database administrator, the SSCP is an excellent introduction to beginning and advanced concepts in information security and is sure to be of benefit to many people throughout the organization.

Information Security is a field of many opinions and perspectives; and the road to secure systems is often littered with tales of failures and unexpected lapses in security. All too often these failures are linked to a lack of understanding of the field of information security. This book will provide an excellent source of information, best practices, advice, and guidance that may prove invaluable in helping an organization to prevent errors, avert security breaches, and experience the loss of trust of consumers and officials.

(ISC)²® has become recognized as the leader in the fields of information security and management. It is with great pleasure and respect that we provide you with this reference and welcome you to be a part of this fast moving and growing field. Whether as a new person in the field or looking to expand your knowledge, you will be sure to find the SSCP to be a practical, informative, and challenging step in your development. As you study this book and possibly prepare to sit for the SSCP (Systems Security Certified Practitioner) examination you are almost certain to venture into new areas of understanding or places that were formerly unfamiliar. This often leads the SSCP to pursue even more learning and development opportunities and we hope that you will consider contacting (ISC)$^{2®}$ for the opportunity to assist on volunteer and research projects. As a not-for-profit organization, (ISC)^2 has been pleased to provide examinations and educational events, and to promote the development of information security throughout the world. You too can be a part of this by contacting us at www.isc2.org.

Thank you for your interest in the field of information security and for purchasing this book. Welcome to an open door of opportunity and exciting new challenges.

Tony Baratta, CISSP-ISSAP®, ISSMP®, SSCP

Director of Professional Programs

(ISC)$^{2®}$

Introduction to the (ISC)²® SSCP® CBK®

This first edition of the "Official (ISC)²® Guide to the SSCP® CBK®" marks an important milestone for (ISC)². It acknowledges the important role that implementers of information security policy, procedures, standards, and guidelines play in an organization's overall information security management infrastructure. Tacticians who implement technical countermeasures like firewalls, intrusion prevention systems, anti-virus software, access control technologies, cryptography, and a wide array of physical security measures are the real warriors on the front lines defending an organization's digital assets. The (ISC)² SSCP certification is the internationally recognized credential that allows those warriors to demonstrate their information security expertise, experience, and professionalism.

The SSCP Credential

The (ISC)² Systems Security Certified Practitioner (SSCP) certification is today's most important certification for information security practitioners. An SSCP has a demonstrated level of competence and understanding of the seven domains of the compendium of topics pertaining to the information systems security practitioner, the (ISC)² SSCP CBK. The SSCP credential is ideal for those working toward or who have already attained positions such as systems or network administrator, senior network security engineer, senior security systems analyst, or senior security administrator. In addition, the SSCP has proven to be one of the best introductions to security principles for personnel that work in a role where security is not one of their primary responsibilities, such as application or Web programmers, information systems auditors, network, system and database administrators, and risk managers.

The seven domains of the SSCP CBK include:

- Access Controls
- Security Operations and Administration

- Analysis and Monitoring
- Risk, Response, and Recovery
- Cryptography
- Networks and Telecommunications
- Malicious Code

The SSCP is awarded by (ISC)² to information security practitioners who successfully pass the comprehensive examination based on the (ISC)² SSCP CBK®, a compendium of global information security topics, possess at least one year of cumulative work experience in the field and subscribe to the (ISC)² Code of Ethics. Once certified, the SSCP must maintain his or her certification through gathering Continuing Professional Education credits (CPEs).

As a SSCP, you gain access to (ISC)² services and programs that serve to support and enhance your growth throughout your information security career. These services and programs include:

- Ongoing education
- Peer networking
- Forums
- Events
- Job postings
- Industry communications
- Speaking and volunteer opportunities

Global Recognition

(ISC)²'s commitment to developing global information security credentials was recognized in December 2005 by the representative for the International Organization for Standardization's (ISO) in the United States, the American National Standards Institute (ANSI). ANSI accredited (ISC)²'s SSCP credential under ISO/IEC Standard 17024:2003 in the area of information security. The ISO/IEC 17024 standard is a new benchmark for general requirements for organizations that provide for certification of personnel. This certification helps verify that individuals in a particular field have the necessary knowledge, skills, and abilities to perform their work.

The ANSI/ISO/IEC 17024 standard extends global recognition and acceptance of the SSCP, adding value to SSCP credential holders as they continue to be one of the most sought-after information security practitioners in the global market. The ANSI/ISO/IEC 17024 accreditation serves as a discriminator as employers and business partners seek the most qualified information security practitioners who hold accreditation credentials. Earning ISO/IEC 17024 ensures employers, customers, and citizens that information security practitioners holding the SSCP credential have proven quality assurance skills and the global mobility so necessary in today's marketplace.

Educated, qualified, and certified information security practitioners are the key to protecting the critical infrastructure on which businesses and governments around the world operate. Employers in the public and private sectors can be confident that information security practitioners holding the (ISC)² SSCP credential possess the necessary skills and experience to effectively manage and deploy information security programs and policies anywhere in the world.

For SSCPs, this means their credential is recognized as an international standard in nearly 150 countries around the world as meeting a rigorous standard for qualifying and validating the skills and knowledge of information security practitioners. In today's global economy and its continuing transformation by the information technology infrastructure and the Internet, accreditation means SSCPs can more easily traverse international boundaries and be recognized for their knowledge.

The (ISC)² SSCP CBK

The (ISC)² SSCP CBK is a taxonomy — a collection of past, present, and future topics relevant to information security professionals around the world. The (ISC)² CBK establishes a common framework of information security terms and principles that allows information security practitioners worldwide to discuss, debate, and resolve matters pertaining to the profession with a common understanding.

The (ISC)² SSCP CBK, like the other (ISC)² CBKs, is continuously evolving. Every year the (ISC)² SSCP CBK Committee, an international assembly of subject matter experts, reviews the content of the SSCP CBK and updates it with a list of topics from an in-depth job analysis survey of information security practitioners from around the world. These topics may address implementing new technologies, dealing with new threats, incorporating new security tools, and, of course, managing the human factor of security.

The following are the seven domains of the SSCP CBK:

- Access Controls — Access controls permit managers to specify what users can do, which resources they can access, and what operations they can perform on a system. Access controls provide systems managers with the ability to limit and monitor who has access to a system and to restrain or influence the user's behavior on the system. Access control systems define what level of access that individual has to the information contained within a system based upon predefined conditions such as authority level or group membership. Access control systems are based upon varying technologies including passwords, hardware tokens, biometrics, and certificates, to name a few.

- Security Operations and Administration — Security operations and administration entails the identification of an organization's information assets and the documentation required for the implementations of policies, standards, procedures, and guidelines that ensure confidentiality, integrity, and availability. Working with management, information owners, custodians, and users, the appropriate data classification scheme is defined for proper handling of both hardcopy and electronic information.
- Analysis and Monitoring — Monitoring is an activity that collects information and provides a method of identifying security events, assigning a priority to these events, taking the appropriate action to maintain the security of the system, and reporting the pertinent information to the appropriate individual, group, or process.

  The analysis function provides the security manager with the ability to determine if the system is being operated in accordance with accepted industry practices, and in compliance with any specific organization policies and procedures.
- Risk, Response, and Recovery — Risk management is the identification, measurement, and control of loss associated with adverse events. It includes overall security review, risk analysis, selection and evaluation of safeguards, cost benefit analysis, management decisions, safeguard implementation, and effectiveness review.

  Incident handling provides the ability to react quickly and put highly trained people at the forefront of any incident, and allows for a consistently applied approach to resolving the incident. Investigations include data collection and integrity preservation; seizure of hardware and software; evidence collection, handling, and storage; and reporting.

  Business Continuity Planning is planning that facilitates the rapid recovery of business operations to reduce the overall impact of the disaster, through ensuring continuity of the critical business functions. Disaster Recovery Planning includes procedures for emergency response, extended backup operations, and post-disaster recovery when the computer installation suffers loss of computer resources and physical facilities.
- Cryptography — The ability of any organization to protect its information from unauthorized access or modification has become a major concern in recent years. The application of cryptography for the storage and transmission of information attempts to address these concerns. Cryptography is concerned with the protection of information by modifying the information to ensure its integrity, confidentiality, authenticity, and non-repudiation. Cryptanalysis is the opposite of cryptography, concerned with defeating the cryptosystem and violating the confidentiality or integrity of the protected data.
- Networks and Telecommunications — In today's global market place,

the ability to communicate with others is a mandatory requirement. The networks and telecommunications domain encompasses the network structure, transmission methods, transport formats, and security measures used to maintain the integrity, availability, authentication, and confidentiality of the transmitted information over both private and public communications networks.

- Malicious Code — The number and types of attacks using malicious code is increasing. The requirement for an individual or organization to protect themselves from these attacks is extremely important. The malicious code domain addresses computer code that can be described as being harmful or destructive to the computing environment. This includes viruses, worms, logic bombs, the Trojan horse, and other technical and non-technical attacks. While there are a variety of methods available to build a virus, many viruses are still targeted to a specific computing platform. With the availability of platform independent languages such as Perl, Active-X, and Java, it is becoming easier to write malicious code that can be run across different platforms.

Organization of the Book

The organization of this book follows the seven domains of the (ISC)² SSCP CBK. The domains are represented in this book as seven chapters. Each chapter is followed by a series of self-assessment questions based upon the content of the preceding chapter. This book also follows the organization of the official (ISC)² SSCP CBK Review Seminar. For candidates who choose to attend an official (ISC)² SSCP CBK Review Seminar, this book should be used as supplementary material in conjunction with the SSCP CBK Review Seminar Student Manual, which is provided to all attendees.

Although this book includes a broad range of important information security topics related to the SSCP CBK, the information security profession is so vast that candidates are advised to review other references as well. A list of (ISC)² recommended reading for the SSCP CBK can be found at http://www.isc2.org.

The Official (ISC)² SSCP CBK Review Seminar

For candidates who are studying for the SSCP examination, (ISC)² offers an official (ISC)² SSCP CBK Review Seminar. The seminar is designed as an in-depth review of all seven domains of the SSCP CBK. It serves as an excellent tool by which candidates can review and refresh their knowledge of information security.

During the three-day program, SSCP candidates will:

- Complete a high-level overview of the seven SSCP CBK domains.

- Identify areas for further self-study.
- Survey the spectrum of understanding that distinguishes a certified IT security practitioner.

The SSCP CBK Review Seminars are three-day, instructor-led, classroom-based events held worldwide on a regular basis. Official (ISC)² SSCP CBK Review Seminars are only conducted by (ISC)² Authorized Instructors, each of whom is up-to-date on the latest information security-related developments and is an expert in the SSCP CBK domains. For more information, visit http://www.isc2.org.

SSCP Examination

The SSCP examination consists of 125 multiple choice questions. Candidates are given three hours to complete the examination. The questions are product-neutral and are designed to test a candidate's understanding of information security fundamentals. Examination questions are written by professionals who have already obtained the SSCP certification. On an annual basis, (ISC)² offers approximately 500 opportunities to take the examination in some 50 countries around the world.

Acknowledgments

(ISC)² would like to thank the authors who contributed to this book, as well as the efforts of the many people who made this effort such a success. We trust that you will find this book to be a valuable reference that leads you to a greater appreciation of the important field of information security.

Authors

Doug Andre, CISSP, SSCP is a security program manager and has over 15 years of information security and law enforcement experience. He has a proven track record assisting federal departments and agencies and private-sector clients with all phases of information security efforts.

Diana-Lynn Contesti, SSCP, CISSP-ISSAP®, ISSMP® is the information security officer for DOFASCO Inc., in Hamilton, Ontario. This role involves the development and implementation of various security architectures, corporate security policy development, and implementation of virus and incident detection and response programs. Prior to working in information security, Diana-Lynn was involved in business continuity planning.

Bonnie A. Goins, M.A. BS7799 Lead Auditor, CISSP, CISM, GIAC, ISS, NSA IAM, NSA IEM, ITIL Foundations is a nationally recognized subject matter expert in regulatory compliance consulting and crossmapping, information security management, and business continuity/disaster recovery planning. Her compliance, security, and business expertise has been put to use by many organizations to enhance, or to develop, world-class operations. She has over 17 years of experience in management consulting, information technology and security. Goins is called upon by executive management in global and national companies for her depth of knowledge and experience in information technology, regulatory compliance and security strategy development/refinement; business continuity, disaster recovery, and incident response planning; risk and security assessment methods; security program design, development and implementation; regulatory compliance initiatives, such as HIPAA, Sarbanes-Oxley, GLBA, NERC/FERC, FISMA, VISA CISP (PCI-DSS) and others; policy, procedure, and plan creation; technology and business process reengineering; secure network infrastructure design and implementation; and application security methods; and security/technology/regulatory training. She is the coauthor of the *Digital Crime Prevention Lab*, has authored chapters on security and regulatory compliance for national publications, and has been recognized in the *Who's Who in Information Technology*.

Paul A. Henry, MCP+I, MCSE, CCSA, CCSE, CFSA, CFSO, CISSP, CISM, CISA, ISSAP, CIFI Vice President, Strategic Accounts, Secure Computing® is one of the world's foremost global information security experts, with more than 20 years experience managing security initiatives for Global 2000 enterprises and government organizations worldwide.

At Secure Computing, Henry plays a key strategic role in launching new products and retooling existing product lines. In his role as vice president strategic accounts, Henry also advises and consults on some of the world's most challenging and high-risk information security projects, including the National Banking System in Saudi Arabia, Department of Defense's Satellite Data Project, USA, and NTT Data in Japan.

Henry is a frequently cited by major and trade print publications as an expert on both technical security topics and general security trends, and serves as an expert commentator for network broadcast outlets such as NBC and CNBC. In addition, Henry regularly authors thoughtful leadership articles on technical security issues, and his expertise and insight help shape the editorial direction of key security publications such as the *Information Security Management Handbook*, where he is a consistent contributor.

Henry serves as a featured and keynote speaker at network security seminars and conferences worldwide, delivering presentations on diverse topics including network access control, cyber crime, DDoS attack risk mitigation, firewall architectures, computer and network forensics, enterprise security architectures, and managed security services.

Eric Waxvik has been in the IT industry for 17 years, the majority of which have been in the computer security arena. As the former chief of the Information Assurance Defense for the Automated System Security Incident Support Team (ASSIST), now know as the Department of Defense Computer Emergency Response Team (DoD CERT), he was responsible for conducting and overseeing the Vulnerability Analysis and Assistance Program (VAAP), the Virus Team, and the Incident Response Team, which were responsible for investigations for the entire Department of Defense. He has since moved on to the private sector, where he consults with Fortune 500 companies and the federal government on the latest security recommendations and solutions.

Domain 1
Access Controls
Paul A. Henry, CISSP

Introduction

Access controls are those systems that provide for the ability to control "who" can do specifically "what" with respect to data, applications, systems, networks and physical spaces. In the simplest of terms (and in a perfect world), an access control system grants system users only those rights necessary for them to perform their respective jobs. The term "access controls" is very broad in nature and can include everything from a simple password authentication that allows a user to access an e-mail account to a biometric retina scanner that unlocks the door to a critical data center.

There are three principle components of access control:

1. Access control systems
   - Policies that define the access control rules
   - Procedures that determine how the rules will in fact be enforced
   - Technologies that actually accomplish the enforcement objectives
2. Access control subjects
   - Authorized users
   - Unauthorized users
   - Applications
   - Processes
   - Systems
   - Networks
3. Access control objects
   - Data
   - Applications
   - Systems
   - Networks
   - Physical space (i.e., the data center)

In the simplest of terms, access control systems control how an access control subject may interact in some manner with an access control object.

In order for any access control subject to obtain access to an access control object, there are typically three steps that must accomplished (shown in Figure 1.1).

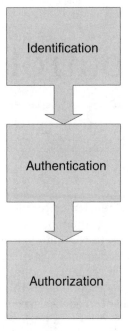

Figure 1.1

Identification

Identification asserts a unique user or process identity and provides for accountability. Identification of an access control subject is typically in the form of an assigned username. This username could be public information whether intentional or not. For example, in most networks the username that identifies the user for network access is also the identification used as the e-mail account identifier. Hence, all one would have to do to determine the account holder's username would be to know the account holder's e-mail address. An access control that relied on the username alone to provide access would be an ineffective access control. In order to prove that the individual who presented the username to the access control is the individual that the username was assigned to, a secret is shared between the access control system and the respective user. This secret is the user's password and is used to authenticate that the user that is trying to gain access is in fact the user that owns the rights associated with the respective identification.

Authentication

Authentication is the process of verification that the identity presented to the access control system belongs to the party that has presented it. In network authentication the identification of the user is authenticated using a secret password that only the user would know. This would be referred to as simple authentication. There are more complex authentication methodologies, such as "dual factor authentication," that not only require the secret that the user knows but also requires another layer of authentication in the form of something the user "has" in his or her possession — such as a security token or something the user "is" as in the case of biometric authentication a finger print or retina scan. We will discuss complex authentication methodologies such as dual factor later in this chapter. Again, the objective of authentication is to prove the identity of the user that is asking for some type of access from the access control system.

Authorization

Authorization is granted to the access control object only after the access control subject has been properly identified and authenticated. The access control system determines what specific access rights are granted to the access control subject based upon the rules within the access control system. Typically, the rules that are applied are directly related to the identification of the individual requesting access. Authorization can be as simple as allowing access to a specific account in an email application after the access control subject has been properly authenticated. In more complex access control system rules the authorization of access may also take time into consideration, i.e., the subject is allowed access to the e-mail application for his account but only during normal office hours. Another complex example access control rule could take the user's physical location at the time of authentication into consideration and require that the user authenticates from an IP address or location inside of the network during normal working hours using a username and password, but, when access is requested by the access control subject from outside of the network across the public Internet, the access control rules could require the use of two factor authentication before permitting access to the user's e-mail account.

Logical Access Controls in Terms of Subjects

Requirements

An access control subject is an active entity and can be any user, program, or process that requests permission to cause data to flow from an access control object to the access control subject or between access control objects. The authorization provided to the access control subject by an access control system can include but is not limited to the following considerations:

- Access control subject
  - Temporal — time of day, day of request
  - Locale from where the access control subject authenticated

3

— Inside or outside of the network
— Password or token utilized
— An individual access control subject may have different rights assigned to specific passwords that are used during the authentication process
- Access control object
  — Data content of the object
  — The access control subject may be restricted from accessing all or part of the data within the access control object because of the type of data that may be contained within the object
  — Transaction restrictions may also apply

The attributes of a subject are referred to as privilege attributes or sensitivities. When these attributes are matched against the control attributes of an object, privilege is either granted or denied.

In a typical access control system, additional subject specific requirements may include:

- A secure default policy should be applied to any newly created subject.
- The attributes of the subject should not be expressed in terms that can easily be forged such as an IP address.
- The system should provide for a default deny on all permissions for the subject, thereby requiring access to any object be explicitly created by an administrator.
- In the absence of policy for a given subject, the default policy should be interpreted as default deny.
- A user ID should remain permanently assigned to a subject.

Group Profiles

The configuration of privileges in access control for an individual subject affords maximum granularity. In systems with perhaps hundreds or thousands of users, this granularity can quickly become a management burden. By incorporating multiple subjects with similar permissions (e.g., job titles) within a group, the granularity is thereby coarsened and the administration of the access control system is simplified.

User Account Maintenance

Password Administration The selection, management, and auditing of passwords are critical components of the access control system. Current technology access control systems provide for automated password administration to reduce the managerial burden associated with password administration.

Password selection is typically based on the following criteria:

- Minimum password length
- Required usage of letters, case, numbers, and symbols in the makeup of the password
- Password expiration (typically 90 days)
- Restrictions on the reuse of a user's previous passwords

The regular auditing of passwords can provide for increased security by reducing the potential for unauthorized access.

Many legacy access control systems that are still in use today provide little password administration automation. Often, this results in high administrative workload or, when neglected, in unauthorized access.

Account Administration The account administration of an access control system is a complex task that includes setting the rights and or privileges of all user, system, and services accounts. Typical account administration tasks include, but are not limited to:

- Account creation
  - Authorizations, rights, and permissions
- Maintenance
  - Resetting of locked out accounts
  - Auditing of passwords to validate adherence to policy
- Account termination
- Disabling account
  - Temporary renaming of the account to allow for limited management access
  - Final closure of the account

Access Rights and Permissions It is most common for the owner of the data (object) to determine the permissions and access rights to the data for a specific account (subject).

The principle of least privilege is most often used in configuring the rights and permissions for an account. Effectively, only those rights and privileges necessary for the account owner to perform their respective duties are assigned. The use of least privilege in the assignment of access rights and permissions can contribute to a higher level of security by mitigating the risk of abuse of authorized access.

Monitoring All changes to accounts within the access control system should be logged and reviewed on a regular basis. Particular attention should focus on any newly created accounts as well as any escalation of the privileges for an existing account to make certain that the new account or the increased privileges are authorized. The regular monitoring of changes to accounts can help to mitigate the risk of misuse or unauthorized access.

Logical Access Controls in Terms of Objects

Requirements

An access control object is a passive entity that typically receives or contains some form of data. The data can be in the form of a file, a program, or may be resident within system memory.

Typical access control object considerations can include but are not limited to the following:

- Restrict access to operating system configuration files and their respective directories to authorized administrators.
- Disable write/modify permissions for all executable files.
- Ensure that newly created files inherit the permissions of the directory in which they were created.
- Ensure that subdirectories cannot over ride the permissions of parent directories unless specifically required by policy.
- Log files should be configured to only permit appending data to mitigate the risk of a log file's contents being purposely deleted or overwritten by a malicious user or process.
- Encryption of data at rest can afford additional security and should be a consideration in the determination of the policies for access control objects.

Object Groups

The configuration of privileges to access an individual object affords maximum granularity. It is not uncommon today for the number of objects within an access control system to number in the tens or even hundreds of thousands. While configuring individual objects affords maximum control, this granularity can quickly become an administrative burden. It is a common practice to assign the appropriate permissions to a directory, and each object within the directory inherits the respective parent directory permissions. By incorporating multiple objects with similar permissions or restrictions within a group or directory, the granularity is thereby coarsened and the administration of the access control system is simplified.

Authentication Implementation

Authentication Methods

Authentication validates the identity of the access control subject. It does so by using something unique that the access control subject either knows, has, or is. Authentication can be implemented in many ways but there are three basic types of authentication:

- Knowledge-based — something that you know
  — Password or passphrase
- Token-based — something that you have
  — Synchronous or asynchronous Token
  — Smartcard
- Characteristic-based — something that you are
  — Biometric
  — Behavioral

As you move down the list of available techniques, security assurance is increased. Simply put, knowledge-based devices can be more easily defeated than characteristic-based devices.

Multi-Factor Authentication

For many years knowledge-based authentication in terms of passwords was the most common methodology in use in access control systems. Improved Brute Force and Dictionary attacks against passwords has effectively rendered these knowledge based methodologies obsolete.

In October 2005 the Federal Financial Institutions Examination Council (FFIEC) provided a recommendation (http://www.ffiec.gov/pdf/authentication_guidance.pdf) to U.S. banks that included, in part, a requirement to replace passwords — single factor authentication with multifactor authentication. The recommendation clearly pointed out that passwords alone were simply no longer a secure methodology for authenticating users in the current Internet environment.

The best practice in access control is to implement at least two of the three common techniques for authentication in your access control system:

- Knowledge-based
- Token-based
- Characteristic-based

Common Authentication Methodologies

Static Passwords and Passphrases Static passwords/passphrases are still the most common authentication methodology in use today. Unfortunately for the community at large, they have also proven to be one of the weakest links in network security. Lists of default static passwords for network and security products are freely downloadable on the public Internet. Furthermore hackers no longer have to take the time to brute force (guess) static passwords because tools such as Rainbow Tables (precomputed hash database) have made determining passwords as simple as looking up the respective hash in a database to determine the underlying password.

The weaknesses in passwords/passphrases are many and include but are not limited to:

- Leakage during use
  — Stolen by Spyware
  — Stolen with key logger
  — Stolen by malicious fake Web site (phishing)
- Leakage during login
  — Password sniffing — i.e., Cain & Able or LophtCrack are able to sniff passwords on the wire during login
- Leakage during password maintenance
  — While password is being generated
  — While password is being distributed
  — While password is in storage

In the opinion of this author, the use of static passwords/passphrases as a security mechanism has been rendered obsolete.

One-Time Password Token One-time password methodologies are typically implemented utilizing hardware or software token technology. The password is changed after each authentication session. This effectively mitigates the risk of shoulder surfing or password sniffing as the password is only valid for the one session and cannot be reused.

Asynchronous A popular event driven — asynchronous token — from Secure Computing called SafeWord provides a new one-time password with each use of the token. While it can be configured to expire on a specific date, its lifetime depends on its frequency of use. The token can last from five to ten years and effectively extend the time period typically used in calculating the total cost of ownership in a multifactor authentication deployment. In the use of an asynchronous one-time password token, the access control subject typically executes a five-step process to authenticate identity and have access granted:

1. The authentication server presents a challenge request to the access control subject.
2. The access control subject enters the challenge into his or her token device.
3. The token device mathematically calculates a correct response to the authentication server challenge.
4. The access control subject enters the response to the challenge with a password or PIN number.
5. The response and password or PIN number is verified by the authentication server and, if correct, access is granted.

Synchronous In the use of a synchronous token, time is synchronized between the token device and the authentication server. The current time value is enciphered along with a secret key on the token device and is presented to the access control subject for authentication. A popular synchronous token from RSA called SecureID provides for a new 6–8 digit code every 60 seconds; it can operate for up to four years and can be programmed to cease operation on a predetermined date. The synchronous token requires fewer steps by the access control subject to successfully authenticate:

1. The access control subject reads the value from his or her token device.
2. The value from the token device is entered in the log-in window along with the access control subject's PIN.
3. The authentication server calculates its own comparative value based on the synchronized time value and the respective access control subject's PIN. If the compared values match, access is granted.

The use of a PIN together with the value provided from the token helps to mitigate the risk of a stolen or lost token being used by an unauthorized person to gain access through the access control system.

Smart Card   Smart cards are another form of "what-you-have" security devices. Smart cards employ a microprocessor that contains detailed information about the access control subject that is accessible (readable) with a proximity or contact device. Currently there are two types of smart cards:

- Proximity (RF based) smart cards
  —Use an RF device to read the access control subject's smart card data whenever the card is within proximity of the reader
- Contact based smart cards
  —Require the cardholder to insert the card into a card reader to obtain the access control subject's smart card data

Memory Card technology today is being used primarily to secure physical access to a facility. The memory card can allow the access control system to trace an individual's movement throughout a secured facility.

Benefits of Smart Cards

- Can securely and portably store personal information
- Critical computations are isolated and performed within the card
- Can offer authentication across a large enterprise
- Can securely store encryption keys
- Able to execute encryption algorithms within the card
- User authentication is done within the card reader thereby mitigating the risks associated with a nontrusted path log-in transmission

Biometrics   Biometrics, "what-a-person-does" or "what-a-person-is," allows for the confirmation of an individual's identity based on either a physiological condition such as a fingerprint, retina scan, or a behavioral characteristic, such as keystrokes, speech recognition, or signature dynamics.

Types of biometric devices include those that recognize:

- Physical traits
  — Fingerprints
  — Hand geometry
  — Eye features — retina scan or iris scan
  — Facial recognition
- Behavioral traits
  — Voice pattern
  — Signature dynamics
  — Keystroke dynamics

Fingerprint Verification Technology Fingerprint verification typically requires seven characteristics or matching points in order to either enroll a new access control subject or to verify an existing access control subject. The task is not as difficult as it may seem as the human finger contains 30–40 characteristics or matching points. The fingerprint reader does not store an image of the fingerprint. Rather, it creates a geometric relationship between the characteristics or matching points and stores and then compares that information.

Hand Geometry Technology Hand geometry verification is typically accomplished by building a five-element array of finger lengths determined from scanned matching points at the base and end of each finger. The stored five-element array is compared to a new hand scan and a mathematical calculation is performed to determine the geometric distance between the respective arrays.

Eye Features — Retina Scan The retina scan is one of the oldest and most accurate biometric authentication methodologies. Dating back to 1930, it was recognized that each human retina had unique characteristics; however, it was 1984 before the first commercial retina scanner was released to the public. Traditionally, the retina scan has been reserved only for the most secure application of physical access control systems. The retina scan simply maps the blood vessels in the back of the eye and only requires ten or so seconds to complete a scan. There is no known technology that can forge a retina scan signature and, as the blood vessels quickly decay upon death, a retina scan on a dead individual will not create the same signature as that of the live individual. Hence, a retina scan prevents unauthorized access.

Eye Features — Iris Scan Iris scanning is based upon scanning the granularity of the richly detailed color bands around the pupil. The color bands are well defined at birth and change little over the subject's lifetime. The typical iris scanner maps nearly 247 variables in the iris and can do so at a distance of 19 to 20 inches. This makes the iris scanner potentially more accurate than a fingerprint (with only 40 to 80 characteristics) and is less obtrusive than a retina scanner as it does not require the same close proximity to the reading device or a light shining into the eye.

Facial Recognition   Like the fingerprint reader and hand geometry devices, facial recognition uses a mathematical geometric model of certain landmarks of the face such as the cheekbone, tip of the nose, and eye socket orientation and measures the distance between them. There are approximately 80 separate measurable characteristics in the human face, but most facial recognition systems only rely upon 14 to 22 characteristics to perform their recognition.

Voice Recognition   Voice recognition works by creating a database of unique characteristics of the access control subject's voice. The access control subject then simply speaks at or near a microphone and the access control device compares the current voice pattern characteristics to the stored characteristics to determine if access is to be granted. Biology, not technology, is the issue with voice recognition. As the subject ages, the characteristics of the voice naturally change. Voice characteristics can change under stress, and during an emergency situation the access control subject could be denied access simply because of the stress he or she was under at that moment. Further, it is possible to create an error simply by altering the inflection of a given phrase. Voice recognition is an inexpensive methodology to implement, but, because of the high probability of error, it is best used to compliment another more accurate technology such as iris scanning and not to be relied upon as a primary access control device.

Signature Analysis   The handwritten signature is unique to each individual. Most access control signature analysis access devices use a 3D analysis of the signature that includes both the pressure and form of the signature. Signature analysis dynamically measures the series of movements that contain biometric characteristics, such as acceleration, rhythm, pressure, and flow. Signature analysis access control devices have become popular with credit card merchants for authorization of credit card transactions.

Keystroke Dynamics   Keystroke dynamics, like the other forms of authentication devices mentioned above, rely upon characteristics that are unique to an individual. In the case of keystroke dynamics, it is the characteristics of the access control subject as the username and password (actually passphrase) is typed on the key board. The normal characteristics of the individual are learned over time and typically can be enrolled with six or eight samples. The individual characteristics used by the typical keystroke analysis device include, but are not limited to:

- Length of time each key is held down
- Length of time between keystrokes
- Typing speed
- Tendencies to switch between a numeric keypad and keyboard numbers
- Keystroke tendencies involved in capitalization

The accuracy of keystroke dynamics can be easily impacted by hand injuries, fatigue, arthritis and perhaps temperature. Hence, while keystroke dynamics is regarded as the lowest cost authentication mechanism it cannot yet be used reliably in a single factor or perhaps two factor (using passphrase) authentication methodology and is better suited to compliment another technology such as iris scanning in a two factor authentication scheme.

Biometric Accuracy   Biometric accuracy is measured by two distinct rates:

- Rate of false acceptance — false acceptance rate (FAR)
  — Referred to as type two error
- Rate of false rejection — false rejection rate (FRR)
  — Referred to as type one error

The actual methodologies of the measurement of accuracy may differ in each type of biometric device, but you can obtain a good comparative accuracy factor by looking at the intersection point at which the type one error rate equals the type two error rate as shown in Figure 1.2. This value is commonly referred to as the cross-over error rate (CER). The biometric device accuracy increases as the cross over value becomes smaller as shown in Figure 1.3 (derived from a report on the comparison of biometric techniques by Thomas Ruggles http://www.bio-tech-inc.com/bio.htm).

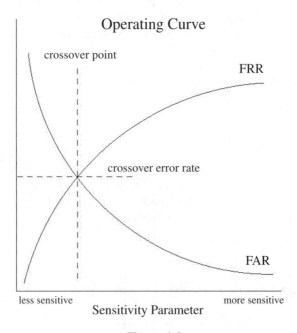

Figure 1.2

Biometric Cross Over Accuracy	
Retinal Scan	1:10000000
Iris Scan	1:131,000
Fingerprint	1:500
Hand Geometry	1:500
Signature Dynamics	1:50
Voice Dynamics	1:50

Figure 1.3

Comparison of Biometrics							
Characteristic	Fingerprints	Hand Geometry	Retina	Iris	Face	Signature	Voice
Ease of Use	High	High	Low	Medium	Medium	High	High
Error incidence	Dryness, dirt, age	Hand injury, age	Glasses	Poor Lighting	Lighting, age, glasses, hair	Changing signatures	Noise, colds, weather
Accuracy	High	High	Very High	Very High	High	High	High
User acceptance	Medium	Medium	Medium	Medium	Medium	Medium	High
Required security level	High	Medium	High	Very High	Medium	Medium	Medium
Long-term stability	High	Medium	High	High	Medium	Medium	Medium

Figure 1.4

A further comparison of biometric technologies is provided in Figure 1.4, which has been derived from data contained within an article entitled "A Practical Guide to Biometric Security Technology" by Simon Liu and Mark Silverman (IEEE 2005).

In reusable password authentication, the access control subject had to remember a perhaps difficult password, in token based authentication the access control subject had to retain possession of the token device. In biometric characteristic based authentication, the actual access control subject is the authentication device.

Remote Access Protocols and Applications Access control system authentication is typically accomplished in either one of two architectures:

- Decentralized
  - The access control subject credentials are stored on the local device. This architecture is common on stand alone devices such as a home PC or some physical access control devices.
  - While local authentication offers easy system maintenance in comparison to a centralized authentication methodology, it can be difficult to add additional access control objects, therefore, it is most often regarded as not scalable.
- Centralized
  - The access control subject credentials are stored on a central server. This architecture is common in network environments.

— The centralized server can be positioned within a protected network and, therefore, offers additional security.
— Centralized authentication allows both additional access control subjects and access control objects to be added, thereby making this methodology more scalable.
— Popular centralized implementations are RADIUS, TCACS+, and Kerberos.
— Strength is consistent administration of creating, maintaining, and terminating credentials, but weaknesses include credentialing delays and single point of failure.

It must be noted that in either architecture, physical access to the server or device that stores the access control subject's credentials is a common goal of a malicious hacker or insider and can be disastrous.

Indirect Access and Authentication Indirect access and authentication occurs when the user is not directly authenticating to a given application. The user authenticates to a middle tier such as a RADIUS server or a firewall that is effectively used as an authentication proxy. The middle tier then acts on the user's behalf to impersonate the user when authenticating to protected applications.

Indirect access authentication is commonly used in providing authentication services for both internal users within a large enterprise as well as remote clients connecting to the internal network. It is important to define the terminology used in describing some the inherent threats to indirect access and authentication prior to our discussion of the access control technologies used for indirect access and authentication.

Remote threats to indirect access and authentication include:

• War dialing
  — Sequential dialing of multiple (or all of the) telephone numbers within in a telephone exchange in an effort to find telephone numbers that offer modems
• Brute force attacks
  — Trying combinations of usernames and passwords from a dictionary or list in an effort to obtain unauthorized access
• Sniffing
  — Gaining physical access to the internal network and using a sniffer to collect usernames and user passwords or to record authentication sessions as they authenticate remotely
• Replay attacks
  — Using the play back of a previously recorded authentication session in an attempt to gain unauthorized access
• Compromised host
  — Gaining access to a remote laptop or workstation and using it to log into a network

Indirect Access and Authentication Technologies   While there are many technologies for providing indirect access and authentication, for the purposes of this chapter we will limit our discussion to:

- Single Sign-On (SSO)
- Terminal Server Controller Access Control System (TACACS)
- Extended Terminal Server Controller Access Control System (XTACACS)
- Terminal Server Controller Access Control System Plus (TACACS+)
- Remote Authentication Dial-In User Services (RADIUS)
- X.509
- Kerberos
- Secure European System for Application in a Multi-Vendor Environment (SESAME)
- Remote Terminal Solution — Secure Shell (SSH)

Single Sign-On (SSO)   SSO can best be defined as an authentication mechanism that allows a single identity to be shared across multiple applications. It allows the user to authenticate once and gain access to multiple resources.

The primary purpose of SSO is for the convenience of the user. With that in perspective SSO can also help in mitigating some of inherent risks of access control subjects using a different password or authentication mechanism for each of the many systems they access in a large network. Simply put, the chances of a security breach naturally increase as the number of passwords and or authentication mechanisms increase. This must, of course, be balanced against the additional risk of using SSO in that once implemented a malicious hacker now only has to obtain a single set of authentication credentials and then has access to all of the systems that the respective access control subject was permitted to access.

The following advantages and disadvantages of SSO must also be considered:

Advantages of SSO

- More efficient log-on process
- Easier administration
  - When a new employee is hired, all of the accounts on all of the systems that the new employee needs to access can be quickly added from a single administration point.
  - When an existing employee is terminated, all access can be quickly and simultaneously restricted at a single administration point.
  - If an existing user loses his token or forgets his password, the administrator can quickly update the user's authentication credentials from a single administration point.
- Mitigates some security risks
  - Reduces the inherent risk of a user having to remember multiple passwords for multiple systems within the enterprise.

— Because only a single password is used, the user is more apt to use a much stronger password.

— Timeout and attempt thresholds are enforced consistently across the entire enterprise.

- SSO generally offers a good return on investment for the enterprise. The reduced administrative costs can often pay for the cost of implementing SSO in a short period of time. However, it should be noted that if scripting is used to facilitate the implementation of SSO, the typical reduced administration costs associated with SSO could be negated.

Disadvantages of SSO

- Difficult to implement across the enterprise
  — Many systems use proprietary authentication systems that will not work well with standard SSO systems.
- Time consuming to implement properly
  — Many underestimate the amount of time necessary to properly implement SSO across all systems in the enterprise.
- Expensive to implement
  — Because of the difficulty and time involved to properly implement SSO, it is expensive. A redundant authentication server is required to avoid a single point of failure.
  — Proprietary authentication systems may need expensive custom programming in order to be used in an SSO implementation and more often than not this cost is not considered in the original estimates and results in SSO implementation cost overruns.
- Can increase security risks
  — Once SSO is implemented, a malicious hacker only has to compromise a user's single authentication credentials and then has access to all of the systems that the user had rights to. This makes it essential to employ 2 factor authentication.
  — In some cases, the original authentication system for a difficult to implement system has to be weakened in an effort to get it to work reliably in an SSO system.

Terminal Server Controller Access Control System (TACACS) TACACS is an older and once popular remote access authentication system and protocol that allows one or more remote access servers to send identification information to a TACACS authentication server for authentication and authorization. The implementation of TACACS provides indirect authentication technology that can be divided into three functional areas known as AAA (triple A):

1. Authentication
2. Authorization
3. Accounting

Simplicity was one of the reasons TACACS was once so popular:

1. The user attempts to log in on the remote access server.
2. The remote access server forwards the user's identification information to the TACACS authentication server.
3. After receiving the identification information from the remote access server, the authentication server either returns authorization information or it denies any access for the user.

Simplicity was perhaps involved in a serious security issue that was built into TACACS by design. The communications between the remote access server and the authentication server is performed unencrypted — in clear text. Hence, it is a simple matter for a malicious hacker to see the user's identification information as well as the returned authorization information thereby dramatically simplifying the potential compromise of the user's account.

Because it is a centralized access control architecture, it offers a single point of administration thereby reducing the effort and associated costs when compared to administering multiple separate authentication systems in decentralized architecture.

Extended Terminal Server Controller Access Control System (XTACACS) A second version of TACACS, called XTACACS, provided extensions to the original TACACS protocol for the support of both SLIP/PPP and CHAP/ARAP authentication.

Terminal Server Controller Access Control System Plus (TACACS+) TACACS+ is a later version of TACACS that, among other enhancements, is best known for solving the original TACACS communications security issues by encrypting the communications between the remote access server and the authentication server.

Remote Authentication Dial-In User Services (RADIUS) RADIUS is popular Internet Engineering Task Force (IETF) implementation of an indirect authentication service. It is similar to TACACS in that it uses a remote access server to forward the access control subject's information to an authentication server, the authentication server either returns the user's associated rights or denies access. Another common feature is that RADIUS centralizes and reduces administrative work load. However, unlike TACACS and XTACACS, the RADIUS implementation of indirect authentication used encryption by design not as an afterthought.

RADIUS in an IETF configuration offers a set of 255 standard attributes that are used to communicate AAA information between a client and a server. RADIUS in a Vendor Specific Attributes (VSA) implementation can extend the standard IETF attributes to an additional 255 VSA attributes. RADIUS is used by a number of network product vendors and is regarded as a de facto industry standard for indirect authentication.

X.509 X.509 is an International Telecommunications Union–Telecommunications Standardization Sector (ITU-T) recommendation originally issued in 1998 for indirect authentication services using public keys.

X.509 is commonly used to secure authentication and communications for Secure Socket Layer (SSL) over the Hypertext Transfer Protocol (HTTP) basing its authentication on a digitally signed public key issued by a Certificate Authority (CA). The use of the digital certificate in authentication also affords X.509 the ability to provide nonrepudiation.

X.509 allows an access control subject to establish multiple connections after properly authenticating only once, thereby offering SSO-like capabilities.

Because X.509 is a recommendation and not necessarily a standard, there can be issues with its implementation across different vendors, i.e., a certificate created for a Netscape browser may not necessarily work for a Microsoft browser.

Kerberos Kerberos, described in RFC 1510, was originally developed by the Massachusetts Institute of Technology (MIT) and has become a popular network authentication protocol for indirect authentication services. It is designed to provide strong authentication using secret-key cryptography. It is an operational implementation of key distribution technology and affords a key distribution center, authentication service and ticket granting service. Hosts, applications, and servers all have to be "Kerberized" to be able to communicate with the user and the ticket granting service.

Like the previously discussed indirect authentication technologies, Kerberos is based on a centralized architecture, thereby reducing administrative effort in managing all authentications from a single server. Furthermore, the use of Kerberos provides support for:

- Authentication
  — You are who you say you are.
- Authorization
  — What can you do once you are properly authenticated.
- Confidentiality
  — Keeps data secret.
- Integrity
  — The data received is the same as the data that was sent.
- Non-repudiation
  — Determines exactly who sent or received a message.

The process in the use of Kerberos is substantially different from those indirect authentication technologies we have previously reviewed and is considerably more complex. The following is a simplified explanation of the Kerberos process that was adapted for use here from *Applied Cryptography: Protocols, Algorithms, and Source Code in C* by Bruce Schneier (Wiley 1993):

1. Before an access control subject can request a service from an access control object, it must first obtain a ticket to the particular target object, hence the access control subject first must request from the Kerberos Authentication Server (AS) a ticket to the Kerberos Ticket Granting Service TGS. This request takes the form of a message containing the user's name and the name of the respective TGS.

2. The AS looks up the access control subject in its database and then generates a session key to be used between the access control subject and the TGS. Kerberos encrypts this session key using the access control subject's secret key. Then it creates a Ticket Granting Ticket (TGT) for the access control subject to present to the TGS and encrypts the TGT using the TGS's secret key. The AS sends both of these encrypted messages back to the access control subject.

3. The access control subject decrypts the first message and recovers the session key. Next, the access control subject creates an authenticator consisting of the access control subject's name, address, and a time stamp, all encrypted with the session key that was generated by the AS.

4. The access control subject then sends a request to the TGS for a ticket to a particular target server. This request contains the name of the server, the TGT received from Kerberos (which is already encrypted with the TGS's secret key), and the encrypted authenticator.

5. The TGS decrypts the TGT with its secret key and then uses the session key included in the TGT to decrypt the authenticator. It compares the information in the authenticator with the information in the ticket, the access control subject's network address with the address the request was sent from, and the time stamp with the current time. If everything matches, it allows the request to proceed.

6. The TGS creates a new session key for the user and target server and incorporates this key into a valid ticket for the access control subject to present to the access control object-server. This ticket also contains the access control subject's name, network address, a time stamp, and an expiration time for the ticket — all encrypted with the target server's secret key — and the name of the server. The TGS also encrypts the new access control subject-target session key using the session key shared by the access control subject and the TGS. It sends both messages to the access control subject.

7. The access control subject decrypts the message and extracts the session key for use with the target access control object-server. The access control subject is now ready to authenticate himself or herself to the access control object-server. He or she creates a new authenticator encrypted with the access control subject-target session key that the TGS generated. To request access to the target access control object-server, the access control subject sends along the ticket received from Kerberos (which is already encrypted with the target

access control object-server's secret key) and the encrypted authenticator. Because this authenticator contains plaintext encrypted with the session key, it proves that the sender knows the key. Just as important, encrypting the time of day prevents an eavesdropper who records both the ticket and the authenticator from replaying them later.

8. The target access control object-server decrypts and checks the ticket and the authenticator, also confirming the access control subject's address and the time stamp. If everything checks out, the access control object-server now knows the access control subject is who he or she claims to be, and the two share an encryption key that they can use for secure communication. (Since only the access control subject and the access control object-server share this key, they can assume that a recent message encrypted in that key originated with the other party.)

9. For those applications that require mutual authentication, the server sends the access control subject a message consisting of the time stamp plus 1, encrypted with the session key. This serves as proof to the user that the access control object-server actually knew its secret key and was able to decrypt the ticket and the authenticator.

In order to provide for the successful implementation and operation of Kerberos, the following should be considered:

- Overall security depends on a careful implementation.
- Trusted and synchronized clocks are required across the enterprise network.
- Enforcing limited lifetimes for authentication based on time stamps reduces the threat of a malicious hacker gaining unauthorized access using fraudulent credentials.
- The Key Distribution Server must be physically secured.
- The Key Distribution Server must be isolated on the network and should not participate in any non-Kerberos network activity.
- The Authentication Server can be a critical single point of failure.

Kerberos is available in many commercial products and a free implementation of Kerberos is available from the Massachusetts Institute of Technology.

Secure European System for Application in a Multi-Vendor Environment (SESAME) SESAME is similar to Kerberos and can be accessible through the Kerberos version 5 protocol. SESAME offers SSO with additional distributed access controls using symmetric and asymmetric cryptography (eases key management) to protect interchanged data. Promulgation, protection and the use of Privileged Attribute Certificates (PACs) are central features. The organization of a PAC is shown in Figure 1.5.

Field	Description
Issuer domain	Name the security domain of the issuer
Issuer identity	Name the PAS in the issuer's domain
Serial number	A unique number for this PAC, generated by the PAS
Creation time	UTC time when this PAC was created
Validity	Time interval when this PAC is valid
Time periods	Additional time periods outside which the PAC is invalid
Algorithm ID	Identifier of the algorithm used to sign this PAC
Signature value	The signature placed on the PAC
Privileges	A list of (attribute, value)-pairs describing privileges
Certificate information	Additional information to be used by the PVF
Miscellaneous	Currently used for auditing purposes only
Protection methods	Fields to control how the PAC is used

Figure 1.5

The architecture of a SESAME implementation requires numerous components:

- Client side components
  - User sponsor
  - Client application
  - APA client
  - Security manager
- Domain security server
  - Authentication server
  - Privilege attribute server
  - Key distribution server
  - Security information management base
- Server side components
  - PAC validation facility
  - Security manager
  - Server application

The following is a simplified explanation of the SESAME process:

1. The user contacts the authentication server.
2. The user receives an authentication certificate.
3. The certificate is delivered to a privilege attribute server.
4. The user receives a privilege attribute certificate.
5. The certificate is presented to the target that is to be accessed.
6. An access control decision is made based on the certificate presented, as well as the access control list attached to the resource.

Remote Terminal Solution — Secure Shell (SSH) SSH is an indirect authentication service (among other things) that was designed to replace earlier rlogin, telnet, and rsh protocols to provide secure encrypted communications between two un-trusted clients over an un-trusted network. It was originally released in 1995 by Tatu Ylonen as free software with source code. Shortly thereafter, Tatu Ylonen formed the SSH Communications company in an effort to commercialize SSH and to provide a mechanism to support the growing number of SSH users worldwide.

Typical SSH authentication methodologies that are supported:

- Host-based trust files
  — /etc/hosts.equiv
  — rhosts
- RSA-based user authentication
  — The user creates public/private keys using ssh-keygen.
  — The pubic key is placed in the user /.ssh/authorized_keys file.
  — When initiating connection, the username and chosen public key are sent to the remote host. Remote host sends a random sequence session key encrypted with the user's public key.
  — The session key is decrypted with the user's private key and is sent back to the remote host.
  — User is now authenticated.
- rhosts along with RSA-based authentication
  — Uses RSA key exchange
  — Consults host-based trust file
- Authentication using password
  — Since all traffic is encrypted, the password is not "in the clear."
- Kerberos
- Tokens such as SecureID

The typical encryption ciphers provided with the various SSH distributions may include:

- AES128
- AES256
- DES
- 3DES
- Blowfish
- Twofish
- ArcFour
- CAST

The current vendors/implementations of SSH or SSH clients now include:

- Lsh, the GNU Project's implementation of SSH
- OpenSSH, an open source implementation of SSH.
- PuTTY
- SSH Tectia
- PenguiNet

- SSHDOS
- WinSCP
- JavaSSH
- Dropbear
- Idokorro Mobile SSH
- Corkscrew (enables a user to run SSH over HTTPS proxy servers)

Several early vendor implementations of SSH (SSH-1) had numerous security vulnerability issues as reported by CERT/CC. A newer version has been released called SSH-2 that solves these issues and provides for several enhancements and/or improvements over SSH-1 including but not limited to:

- Security enhancements
  — Diffie-Hellman key exchange
  — Message Authentication Code
- Feature enhancements
  — Ability for multiple SSH shell sessions over a single SSH connection

SSH-2 is endorsed and is in the process of being standardized by Internet Engineering Task Force (IETF).

Access Control Concepts

Access Control Formal Models

There are three formal models for access control systems:

1. Bell–LaPadula
2. Biba
3. Clark–Wilson

These models are theoretical in nature offering guidelines but no specific examples of their use. Further, they are not well suited for use within a dynamic enterprise environment that is constantly changing due to their inherent management overhead.

Bell–LaPadula Formal Model The Bell–LaPadula formal model was written by David E. Bell and Len J. LaPadula in 1973 and is the basis for the confidentiality aspects of the mandatory access control model. In the simplest of terms, this model specifies that all access control objects be assigned a minimal security level and that access to the object is denied for any access control subject with a lower security level. We will discuss the aspects of the Bell–LaPadula formal model further and how it relates to mandatory access controls later in this chapter.

Biba Formal Model The Biba formal model was written by K. J. Biba in 1977 and is the basis for the integrity aspects of the mandatory access control model. The Biba formal model provides for three primary rules:

1. An access control subject cannot access an access control object that has a lower integrity level.
2. An access control subject cannot modify an access control object that has a higher integrity level.
3. An access control subject cannot request services from an access control object that has a higher integrity level.

We will discus the aspects of the Biba formal model further and how it relates to mandatory access controls later in this chapter.

Clark–Wilson Formal Model The Clark–Wilson formal model was written by Dr. David D. Clark and David R. Wilson in 1987, was updated in 1989 and, like the Biba formal model, it addresses integrity. However, unlike the Biba formal model, the Clark–Wilson formal model extends beyond limiting access to the access control object by adding integrity considerations to the processes that occur while using the access control object.

The Clark–Wilson formal model effectively provides for the integrity of the access control object by controlling the process that can create or modify the access control object.

The Clark–Wilson formal model also provides for the separation of duties. This aspect of the Clark–Wilson formal model establishes guidelines that require that no single person should perform a task from beginning to end and that the task should be accomplished by two or more people to mitigate the potential for fraud in one person performing the task alone.

Access Control Evaluation Criteria — Orange Book The U.S. Department of Defense has published a series of books (the rainbow series), which have historically reigned as an authoritative reference for computer security. Some of the books are considered out dated as they primarily addressed only standalone computers and did not work well with current technology — client server computing. However, the first access controls systems implemented were based on these books, hence the relevance to this chapter. The books are divided up by subject matter and each one has a different color spine. The book that addresses access controls related to confidentiality has an orange spine and is most often referred to as the "Orange Book." The official title is Department of Defense — Trusted Computer System Evaluation Criteria (TCSEC). While the subject matter for this chapter only references the Orange Book and Red Book, the listing of the complete series of books can be found in Figure 1.6. Online versions of the rainbow series of books can be found at: http://www.radium.ncsc.mil/tpep/library/rainbow. The complete historical reference of evaluated products can be found at http://www.radium.ncsc.mil/tpep/epl/historical.html.

The Orange Book defines a set of guidelines that classify the security rating of a system as well as the respective level of trust. The security classifications provide for four classification levels A, B, C and D. Each level is

Document	Spline Color	Book Title
5200.28-STD	Orange	DoD Trusted Computer System Evaluation Criteria, 26 December 1985 (Supercedes CSC-STD-001-83, dtd 15 Aug 83).
CSC-STD-002-85	Green	DoD Password Management Guideline, 12 April 1985.
CSC-STD-003-85	Light Yellow	Computer Security Requirements -- Guidance for Applying the DoD TCSEC in Specific Environments, 25 June 1985 (Light Yellow Book).
CSC-STD-004-85	Yellow	Technical Rational Behind CSC-STD-003-85: Computer Security Requirements -- Guidance for Applying the DoD TCSEC in Specific Environments, 25 June 1985.
NCSC-TG-001 Ver. 2	Tan	A Guide to Understanding Audit in Trusted Systems 1 June 1988, Version 2.
NCSC-TG-002	Blue	Trusted Product Evaluations - A Guide for Vendors, 22 June 1990.
NCSC-TG-003	Neon Orange	A Guide to Understanding Discretionary Access Control in Trusted Systems, 30 September 1987.
NCSC-TG-004	TeaGreen	Glossary of Computer Security Terms, 21 October 1988.
NCSC-TG-005	Red	Trusted Network Interpretation of the TCSEC (TNI), 31 July 1987.
NCSC-TG-006	Amber	A Guide to Understanding Configuration Management in Trusted Systems, 28 March 1988.
NCSC-TG-007	Burgundy	A Guide to Understanding Design Documentation in Trusted Systems, 6 October 1988.
NCSC-TG-008	Dark Lavender	A Guide to Understanding Trusted Distribution in Trusted Systems 15 December 1988.
NCSC-TG-009	Venice Blue	Computer Security Subsystem Interpretation of the TCSEC 16 September 1988.
NCSC-TG-010	Aqua Blue	A Guide to Understanding Security Modeling in Trusted Systems, October 1992.
NCSC-TG-011	Red	Trusted Network Interpretation Environments Guideline - Guidance for Applying the TNI, 1 August 1990.
NCSC-TG-013 Ver.2	Pink	RAMP Program Document, 1 March 1995, Version 2
NCSC-TG-014	Purple	Guidelines for Formal Verification Systems, 1 April 1989.
NCSC-TG-015	Brown	A Guide to Understanding Trusted Facility Management, 18 October 1989
NCSC-TG-016	Green	Guidelines for Writing Trusted Facility Manuals, October 1992.
NCSC-TG-017	Light Blue	A Guide to Understanding Identification and Authentication in Trusted Systems, September 1991.
NCSC-TG-018	Light Blue	A Guide to Understanding Object Reuse in Trusted Systems, July 1992.
NCSC-TG-019 Ver. 2	Blue	Trusted Product Evaluation Questionaire, 2 May 1992, Version 2.
NCSC-TG-020-A	Silver	Trusted UNIX Working Group (TRUSIX) Rationale for Selecting Access Control List Features for the UNIX® System, 7 July 1989.
NCSC-TG-021	Purple	Trusted Database Management System Interpretation of the TCSEC (TDI), April 1991.
NCSC-TG-022	Yellow	A Guide to Understanding Trusted Recovery in Trusted Systems, 30 December 1991.
NCSC-TG-023	Bright Orange	A Guide to Understanding Security Testing and Test Documentation in Trusted Systems.
NCSC-TG-024 Vol. 1/4	Purple	A Guide to Procurement of Trusted Systems: An Introduction to Procurement Initiators on Computer Security Requirements, December 1992.
NCSC-TG-024 Vol. 2/4	Purple	A Guide to Procurement of Trusted Systems: Language for RFP Specifications and Statements of Work - An Aid to Procurement Initiators, 30 June 1993.
NCSC-TG-024 Vol. 3/4	Purple	A Guide to Procurement of Trusted Systems: Computer Security Contract Data Requirements List and Data Item Description Tutorial, 28 February 1994.
NCSC-TG-024 Vol. 4/4	Purple	A Guide to Procurement of Trusted Systems: How to Evaluate a Bidder's Proposal Document - An Aid to Procurement Initiators and Contractors.
NCSC-TG-025 Ver. 2	Forest Green	A Guide to Understanding Data Remanence in Automated Information Systems, September 1991, Version 2.
NCSC-TG-026	Hot Peach	A Guide to Writing the Security Features User's Guide for Trusted Systems, September 1991.
NCSC-TG-027	Turquose	A Guide to Understanding Information System Security Officer Responsibilities for Automated Information Systems, May 1992.
NCSC-TG-028	Violet	Assessing Controlled Access Protection, 25 May 1992.
NCSC-TG-029	Blue	Introduction to Certification and Accreditation Concepts, January 1994.
NCSC-TG-030	Light Pink	A Guide to Understanding Covert Channel Analysis of Trusted Systems, November 1993.

Figure 1.6

Grade	Level	Definition	Example Evaluated Products
A	A1	Verified Protection	Boeing - MLS LAN, Gemini - Gemini Trusted Network Processor
B	B1,B2,B3	Mandatory Access Controls	Trusted IRIX, Harris (CyberGuard) CX/SX, Top Secret, ACF2, RACF
C	C1, C2	Discretionary Access Controls	Windows NT, DEC VMS, Novell NetWare, Trusted Solaris
D	None	This class is reserved for those systems that have been evaluated but that fail to meet the requirements for a higher evaluation class.	Fischer International - Watchdog PC Data Security, Okiok Data Ltd - RAC/M and RacMll

Figure 1.7

further divided to varying levels using numeric designations as shown in Figure 1.7. Within the Orange book, access controls are addressed in levels B — Mandatory Access Controls and C — Discretionary Access Controls.

Orange Book B Level — Mandatory Access Control Mandatory access control (MAC) is typically used in environments requiring high levels of security such as government or military systems. In mandatory access controls, the inherent problems of trying to rely upon each system owner to properly control access to each access control object is eliminated by having the system participate in applying a mandatory access policy (the system owner applies the "need-to-know" element). This policy affords three object classification levels; top secret, secret, and confidential. Each access control system subject (users and programs) are assigned clearance labels and access control system objects are assigned sensitivity labels. The system then automatically provides the correct access rights based upon comparing the object and subject labels. Mandatory access controls allow multiple security levels of both objects and subjects to be combined in one system securely.

A common theme among applications of mandatory access control is the "No read up — No write down" policy applied to each subject's sensitivity level. This is the "mandatory" part of mandatory access control. It is the implementation of the Bell–LaPadula security model:

- The Bell–LaPadula Model addresses confidentiality
  — Simple Security Property
  — The subject cannot read information from an object with a higher sensitivity level than the subject's.
- Star Property
  — The subject cannot write information to an object with a sensitivity level that is lower than the subject's.

The Bell–LaPadula confidentiality model provides the mandatory access control system with the following mandatory access control parameters:

- Top Secret level subjects
  — Can create as well as write only top secret level objects
  — Can read top secret level objects as well as lower sensitivity level objects — secret and confidential
  — Cannot write "down" to lower sensitivity level objects — secret and confidential
- Secret level subjects
  — Can create as well as write secret level objects and top secret level objects
  — Cannot read "up" in top secret level objects
  — Can read secret level objects as well as lower sensitivity level objects — confidential
  — Cannot write "down" to lower sensitivity level objects — confidential
- Confidential level subjects
  — Can create as well as write confidential level objects as well as secret and top secret level objects
  — Can read only confidential level objects
  — Cannot read "up" in top secret or secret level objects

The respective system owners have a limited amount of discretionary control in that they can restrict access to individual or groups of access control objects within the realm of their sensitivity level on a "need to know" basis.

Orange Book C Level — Discretionary Access Control In discretionary access control (DAC), the owner of the access control object would determine the privileges (i.e., read, write, execute) of the access control subjects. This methodology relies upon the discretion of the owner of the access control object to determine the access control subject's specific rights in order to afford the security of the access control object. Hence, security of the object is literally up to the discretion of the object owner. Discretionary access controls are not very scalable, rely upon the decisions made by each individual access control object owner, and it can be difficult to find the source of access control issues when problems occur.

The primary difference between MAC and DAC other then the labeling associated with MAC is that MAC requires both the access control object owner and the system's permission while DAC only requires the access control object owner's permission.

The implementation of discretionary access controls typically rely upon the use of access control lists (ACL) to determine the rights/permissions for access control subjects. In most implementations, every access control object has a default ACL defined upon creation. The object owners can modify the default ACL at their discretion to define a specific security policy. Simply put, the ACL defines "who" can do "what." The "who" refers to what are commonly referred to as "host entry types" as shown in Figure 1.8. The

Type	Permissions Apply To
user	Access control subject, whose name is to be specified in the key field
group	Group Access control subject, whose name is to be specified in the key field
host	Host systems (target agents acting on behalf of Access control subject for install or copy)
other	Access control subject with no matching user and group entries
any_other	Access control subject not matching any other entry
object_owner	Access control subject-owner of the object
object_group	Members of the group to which an Access control subject - object belongs

Figure 1.8

"what" refers to the typical rights and or permissions for respective access control subjects as shown in Figure 1.9.

Discretionary access controls are common in most commercially available operating systems. Systems utilizing discretionary access controls

Permission	Definition
Read	Permits the access control subject to read the data contained within the access control object
Write	Permits the access control subject to write data to the access control object
Create	Permits the access control subject to create a new access control object
Execute	Permits the access control subject to execute the code contained within the access control object
Modify	Permits the access control subject to Read, Write, Create and Execute the access control object
Delete	Permits the access control subject to delete the access control object
Rename	Permits the access control subject to rename the access control object
List	Permits the access control subject to list the contents of an access control object when it is a directory
No Access	Explicetly denies the access control subject any access to the access control object
Full Control	Permits the access control subject to change permissions, take ownership and grants all other access control permissions for the access control object

Figure 1.9

can only qualify for Orange Book C level certification. Discretionary access controls are not eligible for A level or B level evaluation and certification.

To overcome the issue of the Orange Book only addressing confidentiality and stand alone systems, the Red book, otherwise known as the *Trusted Network Interpretation of the TCSEC* (TNI) was introduced in 1987. The Red Book provides for the networking aspects that were absent in the Orange Book as well as addressing integrity and availability. In 2003 both the Orange Book and Red Book were superseded by the Common Criteria Evaluation and Validation Scheme (CCEVS). Further information on the CCEVS can be found at: http://niap.nist.gov/cc-scheme/index.html.

Other Discretionary Access Control Considerations

Authorization Table   An authorization table is a matrix of access control objects, access control subjects and their respective rights as shown in Figure 1.10. The authorization table is used in some discretionary access control systems in order to provide for a simple and intuitive user interface for the definition of access control rules. While an authorization table provides for an increase in ease of use, it does not solve the inherent issue of discretionary access control in that you are still relying upon the access control object owner to properly define the access control rules. Further, the use of an authorization table does not decrease the instance of errors or violations that may occur when changes are made within the authorization table.

Access Control Matrix   An access control matrix is used in a discretionary access control system to provide for a simple user interface to implement an ACL. The access control matrix determines the access rights for access control objects to access control subjects as shown in Figure 1.11. Like the authorization table previously mentioned, the access control matrix does not decrease the instance of errors or violations that may occur when changes are made within the access control matrix.

Time-Based ACL Rules   The capabilities of ACL rules in some access control mechanisms have been extended to include temporal (time)

Access Control Subjects	\multicolumn{6}{Access Control Objects}
	Procedure "A"	Procedure "B"	File "A"	File "B"	File "C"	File "D"
Bob	Execute		Read	Read/Write		Read
Tom		Execute			Read	
Mary		Execute			Read	
Process "A"			Read/Write			Write
Process "B"			Write			Read/Write

Figure 1.10

Access Control Subject	Access Control Objects															
	1	2	3	4	5	6	7	8	9	10	11	12	13	14	15	16
1	X		X		X	X		X					X	X		
2	X		X	X						X	X					
3	X	X				X	X	X						X		X
4			X	X	X											
5		X			X		X	X	X					X	X	
6												X				
7						X	X	X	X	X	X					
8		X	X								X			X		

Figure 1.11

considerations. The ACL rule can be configured to only be effective for a given time period.

Non-Discretionary Access Control The following is a definition of non-discretionary access control from the National Institute of Standards and Technology (NIST, May 19, 2006). "Most OSs provide what is called discretionary access control. This allows the owner of each file, not the system administrator, to control who can read, write, and execute that particular file. Another access control option is called non-discretionary access control. Non-discretionary access control differs from discretionary access control in that the definition of access rules are tightly controlled by a security administrator rather than by ordinary users."

Role-Based Access Control (RBAC) Role-based access control is generally considered to be discretionary because the owner determines which roles have access. RBAC is also discretionary because the owner determines the rules. While there are several different implementations of non-discretionary access controls, most implementations work on the principle of RBAC. RBAC works by assigning roles to access control subjects as well as labels to the access control objects that specify which roles are permitted access to the respective access control objects. Within an RBAC implementation, the ability to permit or deny the inheritance of roles within a given hierarchy is commonly available.

RBAC in many respects is similar to a well- managed work environment. Each employee has an assigned role and job function; they are only permitted access to the information necessary to accomplish their job function. The inheritance aspects of RBAC can be thought of like the organization chart at a well managed company where-by roles can be inherited across employees at the same organizational level or downward in the organizational chart but perhaps not permitting inheritance of a role moving up the organizational chart to levels above the current assigned role.

Rule Set-Based Access Control (RSBAC) A Linux specific open source initiative known as Rule Set-Based Access Control (RSBAC) has been in development since 1996 and in stable production since January 2000. RSBAC is based on the Abrams and LaPadula Generalized Framework for Access Control (GFAC). RSBAC works at the kernel level and affords flexible access control based on several modules:

- Mandatory Access Control module (MAC)
- Privacy module (PM)
- Function Control module (FC)
- File Flag module (FF)
- Malware Scan module (MS)
- Role Compatibility module (RC)
- Function Control module (FC)
- Security Information Modification module (SIM)
- Authentication module (Auth)
- Access Control List module (ACL)

All security relevant system calls in the Linux kernel are extended by RSBAC security enforcement code. The RSBAC security enforcement code calls the central decision component, which then calls all active decision modules (see above listing) and generates a combined decision. This decision is then enforced by the RSBAC system call extensions.

One of the original goals of RSBAC was to achieve Orange book B1 certification.

Content Dependent Access Control Content dependent access control (CDAC) is most commonly used to protect databases containing sensitive information; hence CDAC can be thought of as mechanism for privacy enforcement. CDAC is commonly based on the Abrams and LaPadula Generalized Framework for Access Control (GFAC). CDAC works by permitting or perhaps denying the access control subjects access to access control objects based upon the explicit content within the access control object. A timely example is with CDAC in a medical records database application. A healthcare worker may have been granted access to blood test records; however, if that record contains information about an HIV test, the healthcare worker may be denied access to the existence of the HIV test including the results. Only specific hospital staff would have the necessary CDAC access control rights to view blood test records that contain any information about HIV tests.

While high levels of privacy protection are attainable using CDAC, it comes at the cost of a great deal of labor in defining the respective permissions. Further, it should be noted that CDAC comes with a great deal of overhead in processing power as it must scan the complete record in order to determine if access can be granted to a given access control subject. This scan is done by an arbiter program to determine if access will be allowed.

Context-Based Access Control Context-based access control (CBAC) is primarily used in firewall applications to extend the firewalls decision-making process beyond basic ACL decisions to decisions based upon state as well as application-layer protocol session information:

- A static packet filtering firewall is a good example of a firewall that does not use CBAC. It looks at each and every packet and compares the packet to an ACL rule base to determine if the packet is to be allowed or denied.
- A stateful inspection firewall is a good example of a firewall that uses CBAC. The firewall also considers the "state of the connection," i.e., if a packet arrives, that is part of a continuing session that had previously been permitted to pass through the firewall. As a result, subsequent packets that are part of that session are allowed to pass without the overhead associated with comparing the packet to the ACL rules. CBAC affords a significant performance enhancement to a firewall.

CBAC is often confused with CDAC but they are two completely different methodologies. While CDAC makes decisions based upon the content within an access control object, CBAC is not concerned with the content it is only concerned with the context or the sequence of events leading to the access control object being allowed through the firewall.

In the example of blood test records for CDAC above, the access control subject would be denied access to the access control object because it contained information about an HIV test. CBAC could be used to limit the total number of requests for access to any blood test records over a given period of time. Hence, a healthcare worker may be limited to accessing the blood test database more than 100 times in a 24-hour period.

While CBAC does not require that permissions be configured for individual access control objects, it does require that rules be created in relation to the sequence of events that precede an access attempt.

View-Based Access Control   View-Based Access Control (VBAC) is also known as a type of Constrained User Interface and it is used in database applications to control access to specific parts of a database. VBAC restricts or limits an access control subject's ability to view or perhaps act upon "components" of an access control object based upon the access control subjects assigned level of authority. Views are dynamically created by the system for each user authorized access.

VBAC separates a given access control object into subcomponents and then permits or denies access for the access control subject to view or interact with specific subcomponents of the underlying access control object.

VBAC example in a medical records database:

- A billing clerk (access control subject) would be able to view the procedures, supplies, and related costs in a database (access control object) to be billed to a patient and would be restricted from seeing the result of any of the underlying tests and perhaps the doctors notes contained within the same database (access control object).

- A nurse (access control subject) would be able to view the results of procedures and tests as well as the doctor's notes but would be restricted from seeing the costs for the procedures and supplies.

VBAC example in a firewall administrator's management console:

- A firewall user administrator (access control subject) would be able to add new users and reset user passwords in the firewalls database (access control object) but would be restricted from seeing alerts or altering the firewall ACL rules within the same database.
- A firewall monitor (access control subject) would be able to see alerts in the firewall database (access control object) but would not be able to see or alter any information in the database relating to users or ACL rules.
- A firewall VPN administrator (access control subject) would have the ability to enter VPN related rules into the firewall database (access control object) to facilitate creating a point to point VPN tunnel or perhaps to permit a client to server VPN connection. However, the users would have to already exist in the firewall database (access control object) and the VPN administrator (access control subject) would be restricted from seeing alerts and access control rules that did not specifically relate to the VPN operations within the database.
- A firewall security officer (access control subject) would have full access to all information within the firewall database (access control object).

While the view that is given to an access control subject may only be a partial view of the information available from the access control object, it is important in the proper application of VBAC that the views presented to the access control subject appear normal complete and in context - without revealing signs of any missing information.

Temporal Isolation (Time-Based) Access Control Temporal Isolation (Time-Based) Access Control is commonly used to enhance or extend the capabilities of (Role-Based Access Control) RBAC implementations. This combined methodology is often referred to as Temporal Role-Based Access Control (TRBAC). Effectively, TRBAC applies a time limitation to "when" a given role can be activated for a given access control subject.

- A high level "top secret" role would be assigned to a given access control subject during the normal 8:00 a.m. to 5:00 p.m. working hours.
- A lower level "confidential" role would be assigned to the same access control subject during the 5:00 p.m. to 8:00 a.m. nonworking hours.

To decrease the labor of assigning TRBAC rules to each of many individual access control subjects, most implementations of TRBAC assign the temporal based classification levels to the perhaps lower number of access control objects rather than to the access control subject. Hence, a given access control object would have a temporal based classification level that is effective against all access control subjects.

Temporal extensions are also used to enhance other access control methodologies. It is common today to find access control devices that support time-based access control rules. The temporal enhancement of the access control rule only allows the rule to be effective during the specified time period.

Other Access Control Considerations

Capability Tables   A capability table provides the definition of the access control rights for a given access control subject to a given access control object within an access control system. The capability tables also include the authorization rights of the access control subject such as read, write, execute, delete, and so forth, thereby detailing the explicit access control subject's privileges. The access control right from the capability table for the respective access control object is referred to as a "ticket." This ticket can grant the access control subject access to the specified access control object for a given period. Access to a protected access control object is only granted if the access control subject possesses a capability ticket for the access control subject.

In closing our discussion of access control methodologies, it is important to note that there are several other methodologies to control access to and from both access control objects and access control subjects. These methodologies range from individual or combined criteria that can be enforced across tables, roles, time, and other constraints that are either at the data owner's discretion or defined within the system in a mandatory manner without the discretion of the access control subject.

Operating System Hardening

One of the most misunderstood terms in network security today is *OS (operating system) hardening* or *hardened OS*. Many vendors claim their products are provided with a "hardened OS." What you will find in virtually all cases is that the vendor simply turned off or removed unnecessary services and patched the operating system for known vulnerabilities. Clearly, this is not a "hardened OS" but really a "patched OS."

A "real" hardened OS is one in which the vendor has modified the kernel source code to provide for a mechanism that clearly supplies a security perimeter between the nonsecure application software, the secure application software, and the network stack. One common method of establishing a security perimeter is to write a label embedded within each packet as it enters the server. The label determines specifically what permissions the packet has and which applications can act upon the packet. If the packet's label does not afford the necessary permissions, then the packet is dropped

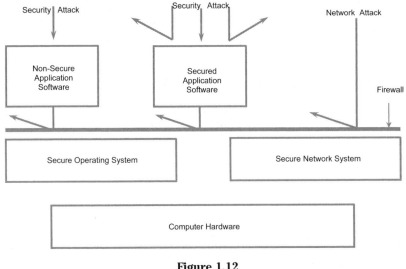

Figure 1.12

as shown in Figure 1.12. While this methodology provides tight control over which packets can be acted upon by both secure and nonsecure applications, it also affords a security perimeter in that external packets can be rejected if they attempt to act upon the secure operating system kernel, secure network, and underlying hardware. This reduces the risk of the exploitation of a service running on the hardened OS that could otherwise provide root level privilege to the hacker.

The security perimeter is typically established using one of two popular methodologies: Multi-Level Security and Compartmentalization. MLS establishes a perimeter using labels assigned to each packet and applies rules for the acceptance of said packets at various levels of the OS and services.Not to be confused with a mere CHROOT Jail , compartmentalization goes well beyond that of just a traditional sandbox approach — strong CHROOT Jail, whereby an application runs in a dedicated kernel space with no path to another object within the kernel. Compartmentalization includes a full MAC implementation and several other kernel level hardening features:

- Network stack separation
- Triggers for intrusion detection
- Control of "super user" privileges
- Principle of least privilege

What is a "patched" OS? A patched OS is typically a commercial OS from which the administrator turns off or removes all unnecessary services and installs the latest security patches from the OS vendor. A patched OS has had no modifications made to the kernel source code to enhance security.

Is a patched OS as secure as a hardened OS? No. A patched OS is only secure until the next vulnerability in the underlying OS or allowed services is discovered. An administrator may argue that, when he has completed installing his patches and turning off services, his OS is secure. The bottom-line question is: With more than 70 new vulnerabilities being posted to Bug Traq each week, how long will it remain secure?

How do you determine if a product is provided with a hardened OS? If the product was supplied with a commercial OS, you can rest assured that it is not a hardened OS. The principal element here is that, in order to harden an OS, you must own the source code to the OS so that you can make the necessary kernel modification to harden the OS. If you really want to be sure, ask the vendor to provide third-party validation that the OS is, in fact, hardened at the kernel level (see http://www.radium.ncsc.mil/tpep/epl/historical.html).

Why is OS hardening such an important issue? Too many in the security industry have been lulled into a false sense of security. Decisions on security products are based primarily on popularity and price with little regard to the actual security the product can provide. With firewalls moving further up the OSI model, more firewall vendors are providing application proxies that operate in kernel space. These proxies, if written insecurely, could provide a hacker with root access on the firewall itself. This is not a "What if?" proposition; it just recently happened with a popular firewall product. A flaw in their HTTP security mechanism potentially allows a hacker to gain root access to the firewall, which runs on a commercial "patched" OS.

Where can you find additional information about OS vulnerabilities?

- http://www.securiteam.com
- http://www.xforce.iss.net
- http://www.rootshell.com
- http://www.packetstorm.securify.com
- http://www.insecure.org/sploits.html

Where can I find additional information about patching an OS?
- More than 40 experts in the SANS community worked together over a full year to create two elegant and effective scripts:
  — For Solaris: http://yassp.parc.xerox.com/
  — For Red Hat Linux: http://www.sans.org/newlook/projects/bastille_linux.htm
- Lance Spitzner has written a number of great technical documents (http://www.enteract.com/~lspitz/pubs.html):
  — Armoring Linux
  — Armoring Solaris
  — Armoring NT

- Stanford University has also released a number of excellent technical documents (http://www.stanford.edu/group/itss-ccs/security/Bestuse/ Systems/):
  — Red Hat Linux
  — Solaris
  — SunOS
  — AIX 4.x
  — HPUX
  — NT

Patch Management

With over 70 new vulnerabilities being reported in operating systems and applications each week, it is not difficult to understand the importance of patch management. Even in a relatively small organization, patch management can be a full-time effort. For large enterprises that span multiple locations and with the added complexity of remote users, patch management can be a daunting task.

Patch management is not as simple as scanning servers and desktops and deploying the necessary patches. History has shown us that vendor patches often break applications and in some cases either reintroduce legacy vulnerabilities or introduce new vulnerabilities. Hence, patches should always be first tested in a lab environment to address security and stability concerns and be approved by an administrator before mass deployment across the enterprise.

Several vendors now offer comprehensive automatic patch management solutions. Key components of current technology offerings afford the following capabilities:

- Support for applications across multiple operating systems
- Both ad hoc and automatic recurring scheduled scanning of computers individually or in user definable groups
  — Facilitates staged scanning to minimize bandwidth impact
- WAN wide scan for installed patches and missing patches — including that date and time that a respective patch was deployed
- Provides for any required patch file configuration options and reboot notifications and actions
- Provides for administrator configurable patch file locations
- Allows the administrator to approve or deny selected patches
  — If a patch is currently being analyzed within the organizations lab environment, the patch management system can scan for and identify all computers that may be subject to a potential vulnerability. This can be useful in determining if any security policy changes are necessary to protect the organization pending patch approval and deployment.

- Deploy patches in ad hoc mode or in administrator configured groups.
— Supports staged deployment to minimize bandwidth impact

Vulnerability Management

Vulnerability management has become a necessity in today's Internet environment where vendors unfortunately often claim that hackers are lazy and wait for the vendor to release a patch for a vendor-discovered vulnerability and then reverse engineer the patch to create an exploit.

All too often we find that it was, in fact, actually a hacker that found the vulnerability and had actually created the exploit and circulated it across the Internet long before the vendor knew of any problem at all. The Windows Metafile (WMF) vulnerability is but one of many examples of this problem. Code for the actual WMF exploit was being sold by the Blackhat community on the Internet months before Microsoft even acknowledged that the vulnerability existed. A third party created a patch and it was endorsed by several industry experts as necessary to deploy immediately, while Microsoft was still considering if the exploit warranted a patch at all.

Vulnerability management is similar to patch management in that with current technology offerings it can automatically scan and compile a WAN wide database of all applications and the current revision and patch levels. Vulnerability management differs from patch management in that it utilizes third party — vendor neutral data sources in an effort to be fully aware of current vulnerabilities.

Another issue comes into play when multiple vulnerability research organizations separately perform analysis on the same vulnerability and use a different naming convention when reporting the vulnerability publicly. Those organizations that perform vulnerability research now typically adhere to the Common Vulnerability and Exposures (CVE) dictionary. The CVE dictionary is a resource to standardize the naming conventions of known vulnerabilities and security exposures. CVE provides a listing of CVE compliant services and products at http://www.cve.mitre.org/compatible/product.html.

Armed with the knowledge in the database of current assets, their respective version numbers and patch levels on each and every one of the computers across the enterprise and the real-time vulnerability subscriber data, the administrator is better able to manage risk. Simply put, vulnerability management systems provide the information necessary to allow the administrator to make timely/informed decisions regarding changes to security posture in response to known threats.

Because of their many similarities, it could be safely assumed that there will eventually be a convergence of patch management and vulnerability management in a single product offering.

Sample Questions

1. What are the three principle components of access control systems?
   a. Access control objects
   b. Biometrics
   c. Access control subjects
   d. Access control systems

2. Which of the following are behavioral traits in a biometric device?
   a. Voice Pattern
   b. Signature Dynamics
   c. Keystroke Dynamics
   d. All of the above

3. In the measurement of biometric accuracy which of the following is commonly referred to as a "type two error"?
   a. Rate of false acceptance — False Acceptance Rate (FAR)
   b. Rate of false rejection — False Rejection Rate (FRR)
   c. Cross over error rate (CER)
   d. All of the above

4. The three functional areas of TACACS known as AAA (triple A) are?
   a. Authentication
   b. Authorization
   c. Availability
   d. Accounting

5. Which of the following is an International Telecommunications Union — Telecommunications Standardization Sector (ITU-T) recommendation originally issued in 1998 for indirect authentication services using public keys?
   a. Radius
   b. X.509
   c. Kerberos
   d. SESAME

6. Which of the following is NOT one of the three primary rules in a Biba formal model?
   a. An access control subject cannot access an access control object that has a higher integrity level.
   b. An access control subject cannot access an access control object that has a lower integrity level.
   c. An access control subject cannot modify an access control object that has a higher integrity level.
   d. An access control subject cannot request services from an access control object that has a higher integrity level.

7. Which of the following is an example of a firewall that does not use Context Based Access Control?
   a. Application Proxy
   b. Static Packet Filter
   c. Stateful Inspection
   d. Circuit Gateway

8. In consideration of the three basic types of authentication which of the following is incorrect:
   a. Knowledge based = Password
   b. Token based = Smartcard
   c. Characteristic based = Biometric
   d. None of the above

9. In the authorization provided to the access control subject by an access control system, which of the following is not a consideration for an Access Control Subject?
   a. Temporal — Time of day, day of request
   b. Password or token utilized
   c. False Rejection Rate
   d. Locale from where the access control subject authenticated

10. Password selection is typically based on which of the following criteria?
    a. Minimum password length
    b. Authorizations, rights, and permissions
    c. Required usage of letters, case, numbers, and symbols in the makeup of the password
    d. All of the above

11. Which of the following should be considered in the routine monitoring of an access control system?
    a. The regular monitoring of changes to accounts can help to mitigate the risk of misuse or unauthorized access.
    b. All changes to accounts within the access control system should be logged and reviewed on a regular basis.
    c. Particular attention should focus on any newly created accounts as well as any escalation of the privileges for an existing account to make certain that the new account or the increased privileges are authorized.
    d. All of the above

12. Which of the following is not true in the consideration of object groups?
    a. It is a common practice to assign the appropriate permissions to a directory, and each object within the directory inherits the respective parent directory permissions.

b. Although configuring individual objects affords maximum control, this granularity can quickly become a administration burden.

c. By incorporating multiple objects with similar permissions or restrictions within a group or directory, the granularity is thereby coarsened and the administration of the access control system is simplified.

d. Configuring individual objects affords maximum control, this granularity can reduce administration burden.

13. In the three basic types of authentication, which of the following are related to "something you have"?
    a. Synchronous or asynchronous token
    b. Biometric
    c. Smartcard
    d. All of the above

14. Which of the following is an asynchronous device?
    a. Time-based token
    b. Event-based token
    c. All of the above

15. Which of the following are characteristics in biometric behavioral-keystroke dynamics?
    a. The length of time each key is held down
    b. Tendencies to switch between a numeric keypad and keyboard numbers
    c. Acceleration, rhythm, pressure, and flow
    d. All of the above

Domain 2
Security Operations and Administration

Bonnie Goins, CISSP

A key area for the security practitioner in which to develop strong skills is the area of security administration. This chapter discusses the aspects of the secure administration of an enterprise. It provides definitions for common security terms the practitioner will use in day-today work; discusses information critical to the understanding of information security fundamentals; and covers the personnel and technical aspects of securing an environment.

What Is "Security Administration"?

As defined in (ISC)²'s® SSCP® Review Seminar, "security administration encompasses the concept of identification, authentication and accountability of an enterprise's information assets." It includes the development of policies, procedures, guidelines and standards, as well as mechanisms for traceability in the event of disaster.

Fundamentals of Information Security

The A-I-C Triad

Central to the concept of security is the A-I-C triad. Some practitioners have also heard it referred to as the C-I-A. These three tenets are Availability, Integrity, and Confidentiality.

Availability

Availability is the assurance that resources can be successfully accessed by authorized users when they are needed and in the form needed. Availability may be provided for an organization through: appropriate business continuity, incident response and disaster recovery planning; redundant network architecture; redundant power generation and surge protection; data storage (both electronic and paper data storage) and the ability to access online data through more than one data path; and other mechanisms designed to overcome denial of service to authorized users. Denial of service can be precipitated in a completely innocent fashion (i.e., hardware is made "unavailable" due to a malfunction of components; personnel inadvertently cause an outage) or can occur through malfeasance. An example of this type of denial of service would include a deliberate attack of a network or its resources by an internal or external attacker. The attacker floods the network resources in question with bogus requests, until the bandwidth is saturated and the network can no longer respond to users at all.

Integrity

Integrity is the assurance that data stored, processed and transmitted has not been modified or destroyed in an inappropriate manner, either inadvertently or maliciously, from its original and correct state. That is, only authorized users are able to modify data, and then through appropriate means. Verification of both paper and electronic data must be performed by systems and personnel in order to determine that there are no data integrity issues.

Fortunately, there are safeguards that can be taken to assist an organization with the provision of data integrity; these include appropriate control of the physical environment within the organization.

No unauthorized individuals should ever be granted access to critical systems. In the case of physical control, only network administrators, system administrators, or privileged (authorized) users should be granted access to the systems and the data that resides on, is processed or is transmitted by them. It is essential that an organization maintains a current accounting of privileges provided to users to ensure that authorization continues to be appropriate. This can be done by verifying a user's role in the organization, the minimal set of data that is required for successful completion of tasks for this role (this is the concept of "least privilege") and the data's location (i.e., system location).

Monitoring and Maintenance of Appropriate Environmental Controls over Data and Systems This activity would include monitoring of humidity, temperature, pollutants, and other environmental concerns, as they relate to the protection of critical systems and data. Some organizations also monitor air quality for biological and other hazardous contaminants, in accordance with emergency management concepts that have been presented by federal and state governmental agencies.

Policies and Procedures An important part of maintaining data integrity in an organization is to create, implement, maintain, monitor, and enforce appropriate organizational and information security policies and procedures that set expectations for the personnel within the organization, as well as its business partners, contractors and vendors. Given that issues with data integrity may revolve around appropriate data input and validation of data pre- and post-processing, communicating to authorized users expected practices that may assist to safeguard data is crucial.

Business continuity and incident response plans also assist in the protection of the integrity of data within the organization. Data can be modified or lost during a calamity or an intrusion; therefore, having formally documented practices available to be used during these highly charged times is critical to performance during the emergency or intrusion.

Infrastructure Public Key Infrastructure (PKI) also assists an organization in protecting its data integrity. It does so through the use of digital signatures. These electronic signatures are used for a number of purposes, including the signing of developed computer code, the protection of e-mail, and for the signing of electronic documents.

Confidentiality Confidentiality may be defined as limiting access to protected data or systems to only those personnel, business partners, contractors, or vendors who are authorized (or have "need-to-know," in a properly secured environment). Like integrity, confidentiality refers to data and systems. Confidentiality is often confused with "privacy," which is an individual's right regarding hihe or sher data. Confidentiality's main tenet is authorization; that is, restriction of resources to authorized personnel or systems.

Confidentiality is also a primary tenet in regulatory compliance. In HIPAA, Sarbanes-Oxley, GLBA, NERC/FERC, FISMA, and other regulations, confidentiality must be maintained in order to meet compliance objectives. This puts an additional burden on administrators of systems on which critical data resides. It also puts additional burden on authorized users in an organization to meet expectations surrounding acceptable system use and appropriate data handling.

What are the consequences in the event of a breach of confidentiality? Clearly, as stated above, inappropriate disclosure of confidential information can result in a breach of compliance with regulatory objectives. This can mean fines, lawsuits and litigation by those compromised (to include individuals, organizations, and others, potentially including government entities, depending upon the type of information collected), which might also bring with it a jail term, as can be evidenced by recent litigation against corporate malfeasance. There can also be intangible effects that directly affect the bottom line of an organization, such as loss of prestige or public support, perhaps resulting in a decrease in an organization's net worth through reduction in its stock price.

Confidentiality can be promoted through correct identification of each authorized user, proper access control mechanisms for sensitive data that is stored on an organization's systems, and the use of appropriate encryption techniques for sensitive data that is in transmission.

Compliance with Policy Infrastructure

Building a policy infrastructure within an organization is useless unless there is a solid and effective effort to enforce that infrastructure. Enforcement ensures that the organization and its staff meet, or are "in compliance with," the expectations as set forth in the policy deliverables that make up the policy infrastructure.

Determination of compliance is aided through both technological and human means. Examples of activities designed to measure and promote compliance are presented below.

Security Event Logs

Monitoring of security in an automated fashion is common among most organizations. Security automation, such as intrusion detection/prevention systems, generate system logs (syslogs). These logs can be reviewed by security administrators to observe where deviations from stated policy occur. Examples of deviation from stated policy can include inappropriate use (such as surfing prohibited Web sites) and unauthorized access (such as using another's credentials to obtain increased access).

A good method for reviewing event logs is to aggregate and run them from a single syslog server. An advantage is that data can be viewed as a pool rather than through separate efforts. A disadvantage is that aggregated syslogs must be tuned so that the data is not overwhelming to the security administrator. Significant expertise is required to properly tune the logs so that important information for review is not lost or overlooked during log review.

It is important to note that logs should be reviewed daily for anomalies. If logs are only reviewed sporadically, it may be impossible to determine when, and under what conditions, security expectations have been violated within the organization. Upon completion of the log reviews, the security administrator must formally "sign off" and retain the signature for future auditing purposes. Logs should be saved in a secured location, such as an offsite storage facility or a secured warehouse. Archive requirements vary by legislation, but can span from three to six years or more. Logs that are not bound by legislation should be archived as long as business reasons dictate. An average archive length approximates three years.

Information Security Compliance Liaison

Many business units require some assistance in interpreting, implementing, and monitoring security compliance. It is useful to assign a compliance coach (liaison) to business units to facilitate the incorporation of security into daily operation. Coaches may be assigned either from the information security discipline or from the business unit, but must be dedicated, so as to promote continuity. Coaches must receive periodic training in both security and compliance issues that face the organization. Coaches assigned from the information security area must also receive training in the department's operations.

Remediation

When issues are discovered, it is important for the organization to determine whether the root cause must be fixed, or remediated. Remediation must be undertaken relative to risk; that is, high-risk issues must be addressed prior to lower-risk issues. Remediation ranges from the human to the technical, and can include everything from hardware or software implementation to security awareness education. In a compliance-driven environment, threats to compliance are always considered high risk.

Security Administration: Data Classification

Data classification is a necessary security activity within organizations looking to protect their assets. Classifying data by its level of sensitivity allows an organization to communicate expectations regarding how that data is labeled and handled by authorized users.

Data classification often commences after an organization has accounted for all its assets, perhaps documenting them in an asset inventory. This asset inventory may be the output of the organization's Business Impact Analysis (BIA) and is also used as an input to the risk assessment process.

Data classification typically begins by creating a "data classification scheme," or a framework for communicating labeling and handling instructions to employees, contractors, business associates, vendors or other authorized personnel. Examples of a data classification scheme can include:

- Restricted — this label is reserved exclusively for the organization's most sensitive data. An example would be compliance-oriented data, such as electronic personally identifiable healthcare information (ePHI).
- Confidential — this label is reserved for data that has a very limited distribution among authorized personnel, limited to only those with need-to-know. An example would be intellectual property that has a group distribution.

- Internal Use Only — this label is reserved for data that can be disseminated throughout the organization. An example would be the corporate information security policy.
- Public — this label is reserved for data that can be freely distributed both internal and external to the organization. An example would be information contained within the nonrestricted part of an organization's Web site.

The United States Department of Defense, along with other government and military organizations, implements a data classification scheme that includes the following categories:

- Top Secret
- Secret
- Confidential
- Sensitive but Unclassified
- Unclassified

In order for data to be classified, it requires an "owner." A data owner reviews the data to determine whether it is sensitive. A data owner may also determine whether the data is critical to the organization's functions, although criticality is typically determined by senior executives, who may or may not be data owners, but are responsible for the organization's continuing operations.

A data owner also determines permission levels and facilitates access control by identifying those individuals or groups with need-to-know and by assigning them to the appropriate permission levels. The data owner is also responsible for periodically reviewing access and updating that access, along with permissions, as required.

Data "custodians" must also be considered in the data classification scheme. Custodians handle and protect data, but do not "own" it. A good example of a data custodian is an Information Systems department within an organization. Network administrators protect the data as it is stored and transmitted; system administrators protect the data while it is being processed. Another good example of a data custodian could be an end user that has a need to work with the data to fulfill a job function, such as a Compliance Officer at a hospital (provider).

Given the number of individuals or groups that may be owners or custodians of data, it is clear that expectation must be communicated for the data is to be handled in a consistent and secure manner. Creation, implementation, maintenance, monitoring, and enforcement of appropriate data classification, labeling and handling policies, procedures and standards facilitates this goal.

The formal documentation listed above should also incorporate the following aspects as part of the classification:

- Exclusive possession — this encompasses intellectual property held by the organization
- Utility — this aspect discusses how the classification, and the formal documentation surrounding classification, will be used within the organization
- Cost of creation/recreation — this aspect discusses creation and replacement cost, as it relates to both data, documentation, backup and BCP
- Liability — this aspect discusses the organization's liability with regard to its critical and sensitive data, as well as its proper labeling and handling
- Operational Impact — this aspect discusses the impact that proper classification, labeling and handling of the data has on the organization
- Sanitation and media disposal — Instructions relative to appropriately scrubbing media (or shredding paper media) must also be included as part of the data classification effort

Marking and Labeling

Once the data classification scheme has been developed and approved by management, it is time for the organization to begin the job of marking and labeling data assets. Data in all its forms must be marked, including any magnetic and optical media, such as data tapes, audio and videotapes, diskettes, CDs, DVDs, and so on, as well as all paper documents. It is not sufficient to simply mark the first page of a document; the cover and all pages must be marked with the proper classification, in the event the document is disassembled. Where possible, data should also be labeled for access control permissions. This can be seen in software, with the labeling of field level, file level and directory level access permissions.

Labels

What do data labels look like? If magnetic media is being labeled, a standard label may be applied to the permanent tape housing. The classification must be visible to any authorized user who would handle the media. An internal system readable label is applied to the first section of the tape or magnetic media. In the case of paper documents, a stamp or watermark with the proper classification is acceptable. It is highly advisable that the organization create appropriate documentation templates with the classification automatically generated either in the header, the footer, or as a watermark across the page.

Assurance and Enforcement

It is crucial for the organization to continually monitor compliance with the classification scheme. This monitoring creates awareness to support successful control and handling of information. Should there be a lapse, the organization could potentially be jeopardized through loss or exposure of sensitive data. Below are some methods that could be utilized to assure the organization that there is compliance with the data classification policies, procedures, and standards:

- Walking through the organization and spot checking for data left in open view, such as on desks, printers, faxes, in mailboxes, and so on can expose lapses in properly securing sensitive information.
- Undertaking a review of the organization's data dictionary, if one exists, as well as a review of metadata, reporting formats, and the asset inventory itself can assist.
- Spot-checking for proper disposal of all types of media may assure the organization that proper disposal is occurring. Make sure to check hard drives in computer and multifunction machines, such as printers and copiers, as well, to ensure that they are properly scrubbed prior to disposal or reallocation.
- Periodically conducting access control authorizations reviews, in a formal way, by data owners.

Identity Management

Identification is the process of claiming an individual's, group, or system's identity. Authentication is the process of verifying identity claims. The discipline of "identity management" is central to an organization's access control objectives. It includes: identification of each of the individual components of the organization or "system" (such as a user, network, departments, and so on); the identification of users within the organization or system; identification of appropriate access rights (typically based on role; see the concept of "least privilege"); and using these identifications to limit access to the organization's resources based on the rights and restrictions that are "identified" as belonging to that component or system.

A good example of identity management is the use of an ID badge that allows access to an organization's data center. Not everyone in an organization can enter the data center; only those authorized or have the access rights associated with their roles, are typically allowed in.

Access control in a computer network typically centers on credentials, such as user IDs and passwords. Should a user forget a credential, there is a mechanism that can be employed to reset the password; this mechanism can be performed manually or in an automated fashion. Software used for identity management may save an organization time and money if it is used to allow users to reset their own passwords. Alternatively, perhaps an organization wishes to synchronize user passwords across both applications and systems. This is a part of the concept of "single sign-on," or one login attempt that, when successful, grants access to the user across all authorized applications and systems.

Security Administration: Configuration Management

What Is Configuration Management (CM)?

As stated in the Trusted Computer Systems Evaluation Criteria (TCSEC), a configuration management system maintains control of a system throughout its life cycle, ensuring that the system in operation is the correct system, implementing the correct security policy. The Assurance Control Objective as it relates to configuration management leads to the following control objective that may be applied to configuration management: "Computer systems that process and store sensitive or classified information depend on the hardware and software to protect that information. It follows that the hardware and software themselves must be protected against unauthorized changes that could cause protection mechanisms to malfunction or be bypassed completely. Only in this way can confidence be provided that the hardware and software interpretation of the security policy is maintained accurately and without distortion."

Why Is CM Important?

Given that one of the primary tenets of configuration management is to keep assets free from unauthorized modification, it is clear that configuration management may assist an organization through its contribution to baseline data surrounding the asset, which may in turn assist the organization in recovery of the asset post-incident.

As stated in the SSCP Administrative Domain course, configuration management consists of four separate tasks:

- Identification
- Control
- Status Accounting
- Auditing

When a change is initiated in an automated system, its business requirements and design input to the new system must be formally identified and documented. Additionally, the change, as well as the asset resulting from the change, must be approved by an appropriate third party, typically a Change Control Board. Once the approval is obtained, the change is implemented.

The process must be documented and progress reported to senior management. Post-implementation, appropriate testing for both functionality and quality must be undertaken. Once testing is completed, a configuration audit must be undertaken and compared with the security policy(ies) relevant to that system.

Change Control Roles in CM

The practice of configuration management is multidisciplinary. The participants, along with their responsibilities, are listed below.

- Senior Management
  - Responsible for approval for CM projects and staffing
  - Responsible for oversight of the CM plan to ensure it meets business objectives
  - Responsible for status reviews and approval of CM project or plan changes
- Configuration Management Unit
  - Responsible for identification or approval of the asset characteristics affected by CM
  - Responsible for assigning CM asset characteristics to a custodian
  - Responsible for creation and update (as appropriate) of CM baselines
  - Responsible for implementation of the authorized changes to the configurations
  - Responsible for status reporting to senior management
  - Responsible for the implementation of the CM
- Change Control Board
  - Responsible for review, approval and oversight of change requests to CM projects
  - Responsible for review of CM for determination that the final product functions as advertised
- Quality Assurance
  - Responsible for oversight relative to the conformance to the organization's policies, procedures and standards, as well as for conformance to the CM project plan
  - Responsible for ensuring that deliverables produced during the CM meet customer requirements, quality requirements and all organizational standards for delivery

Baselines

Baselines are measurements of the current state, or a "point in time," for use as a benchmark as an asset, such as a system, an application, or a policy, evolves. Functional baselines are measures to ensure that the asset adheres to design requirements. Once the functional baseline is set, any changes to that asset must be authorized and formally documented. Product baselines reflect the finalized state of the asset to be used for testing. At this point a "product" has been developed and is ready for implementation.

Baseline Measurements

There are many aspects by which a baseline can be measured, some of which are business- and not technology-oriented. The following metrics represent some of the measurements which one might expect to be included in an appropriate baseline state:

- Network utilization
- Server utilization
- The extent to which proper security contributes to the organization ensuring it retains its assets
- IDS measurements that indicate security function is appropriately implemented and is operating efficiently

Change Management Process

The following are elements within the process of change management:

- Establish baseline
- Create formal, documented procedures for facilitating changes to systems
- Implement any changes required and approved in a formal and controlled fashion
- Formally update the current baseline
- Monitor the current baseline for any unexpected events, incidents or issues

Change Control Board   The Change Control Board (CCB) is a multidisciplinary steering committee within an organization, assigned the task of oversight of CM. The members of the CCB meet regularly (in person, by conference, or video call) to discuss all relevant CM topics that might occur within an organization. These might include requested changes, status reporting, issues, and quality control. The board also ensures that only approved changes are implemented into the asset, after formally reviewing, as well as documenting the review, of all requested changes.

CCB Charter   The CCB constructs its charter, or the rules it operates by within the organization. A typical charter consists of, at least, the following elements:

- Responsibilities of the CCB
- Purpose for the CCB function

- The CCB's Scope of Authority
- Membership requirements for CCB
- The CCB's operating procedures
- The CCB's decision-making process
- Process for communication of findings to senior management and the board of the organization, as well as to stakeholders (which may fall outside senior management and the board)

Concept of Risk-Based, Cost-Effective Controls

Controls, or measures taken in an environment to protect its critical assets (which include people, processes, data, technology, and facilities), are implemented to have the greatest impact on higher risk areas within the organization. Tactically, this makes the most sense from a cost-effective perspective, as it is nonsensical to apply significant controls around any issue that is of little consequence to the organization. Controls must be evaluated for their effectiveness against their cost to the organization in terms of loss of the asset, resourcing costs, and so on. High cost, low impact controls should be avoided.

Validation of Security Controls

Prior to the implementation of a new or updated security control in the production environment, the control must be properly validated in a test environment that is separate from the production environment. In order to correctly assess whether the security control functions effectively, the test environment must reasonably approximately the production environment. It is advisable to construct a formal test plan, which includes all aspects of the control that are being tested. The test plan must be "signed off" once testing is completed, regardless of whether the testing was successful. All notes taken during testing must be saved as work product and attached to the test plan.

Configuration Management Plan Development and Implementation

Because configuration management is so integral to the proper operation of a secure environment, a formalized and documented plan must be developed, implemented, and monitored for successful completion. A configuration management plan consists of the following characteristics:

- The plan must be actionable.
- The plan must be achievable in an appropriate time frame.
- The plan must account for sufficient resources to complete the tasks detailed in the plan.

- The plan must detail sufficient security controls around the configuration management process.
- The plan must include implementation specifics.
- The plan must include a proper sampling plan, if staged configuration management is proposed.
- The plan must include an appropriate and formalized testing plan, complete with a process for reporting results.
- The plan must detail the process for enforcement and monitoring of activities in contained within the plan.
- The plan must specify the chain of approvals for contents the plan itself, up to and including successful completion of the plan elements.

Once the plan has been approved, it can be implemented into the environment. Affected business units must be notified and advised how the change will affect operations, prior to its implementation. Business units may have concerns that can be addressed in the current configuration plan. Post-implementation, the plan must be enforced and monitored to ensure it is operating effectively.

Impact of Security Environment Changes

Implementing changes to the security environment within an organization can bring about both positive and negative impact to operations and the business units that perform them. Prior to implementation of, or any change to, security controls within the organization, an impact analysis must be performed to determine whether there are any serious consequences and whether these consequences can be mitigated either through the use of an alternative security control. It is important to remember that impact is related to risk; that is, a high risk-high impact change to the environment must be evaluated closely and blessed by senior management prior to its implementation.

It is advisable to lessen impact to the organization through the use oʲ proper security education surrounding the change. This will facilitate its incorporation into daily operations and will speed staff in making the tranˌition to the new environment.

Patches, Fixes, and Updates Validation

Patching is typically incorporated into the general configuration management plan; however, it is also acceptable to create a separate plan for patching and general system remediation and changes. Regardless of whether a separate plan is used, validation of these activities must also be formally documented, as presented above in the section on configuration management.

Secure System Development Life Cycle

Introduction

In the past, technical security considerations have been the domain of the network or system administrator. However, with the publicizing of the detrimental effects that "bad code" can have on the technical environment within the organization, it has become apparent that application development personnel must be trained, and subsequently must code, to security standards.

This chapter discusses the secure system life-cycle design, including information surrounding applications and secure enterprise architecture design that can contribute to an organization's security assurance. As such, four contributing factors must be taken into account: the Development Life Cycle, Systems Acceptance, Systems Accreditation, and Systems Certification. All will be discussed within this section.

The System Development Life Cycle

The System Development Life Cycle is used to provide a foundation for each phase of an application development project. Many professionals, such as application developers, security personnel, database or system analysts, end users, and management are included as stakeholders in this life-cycle. Because the life cycle is a formal and documentable method for performance of secure application development, it may also serve, to some extent, as a project management tool.

The difference between "system life cycle" and "system development life cycle" is that we as security professionals are concerned not only with the development phases but also with the operation and maintenance phases (after the application has been developed) as well. The system development life cycle is really only the development project; it does not include operations and maintenance.

Most standards and regulations make mention of the requirement for a "formal software (or systems) development life-cycle (SDLC)." The requirement is based on the notion that application development (and indeed, the development of entire information systems) should be conducted in a standardized and structured way. Successful implementation of this life cycle will provide a framework for security, infrastructure and development professionals to proceed from prototype to completed project in an organized and documentable (i.e., formal) fashion.

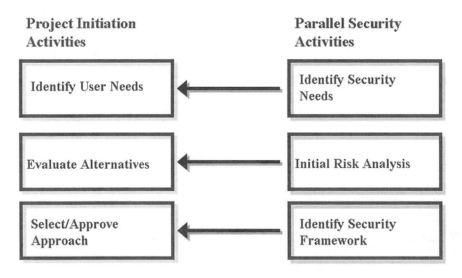

Project Initiation Activities

Parallel Security Activities

Identify User Needs ← Identify Security Needs

Evaluate Alternatives ← Initial Risk Analysis

Select/Approve Approach ← Identify Security Framework

Figure 2.1 Project Planning and Initiation

According to (ISC)², there are eight stages to the system life cycle. They are:

Project Initiation and Planning, Function Requirements Design, System Design Specifications, Develop and Document, Acceptance Testing, Implementation, Operations and Maintenance Support, and Disposal.

Figures 2.1 through 2.4 demonstrate security focus that is required as part of the process for appropriate system development, testing, and implementation. It is important to note that security requirements are considered from the beginning of development and progress apace with development, testing and implementation of the finalized product.

During project initiation, three steps are performed.

- Identification of user needs
- Evaluation of alternatives for system development
- Selection of an appropriate approach to perform the system development

During the identification of user needs, the development team works with the affected business unit(s) and, as required, management, to ensure that the system developed will address user needs. Post needs identification, the development team identifies alternative methods for the building of an appropriate system for the affected unit(s). Once all alternative approaches have been identified, an approach is selected that will meet the approval of the affected unit(s).

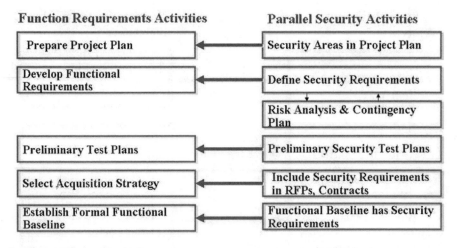

Figure 2.2 Define Function Requirements

This preparatory phase must also include security analogs to each of the steps in order to "bake in" security considerations for the system. When business unit needs are identified, security needs should be identified along with them so they can be addressed at the same time. Likewise, as alternative development approaches are being evaluated, the risks inherent to that approach must also be identified, in order to facilitate successful completion, implementation and functionality of the end product.

When an approach is approved and selected, it is important to build the security framework upon which subsequent development efforts will be built. Standards, such as the ISO17799 and ISO20000, and best practice frameworks and methods, such as the Capability Maturity Model for Integration (CMMI) and the Information Technology Infrastructure Library (ITIL) can be leveraged during the creation of the security framework.

When an appropriate approach has been selected, it is time to prepare the project plan for the development of the system. It is important to ensure that security considerations are also included in the project plan so they are addressed during development. The development team then conducts sessions with the affected unit(s) and management, as appropriate, to define the requirements of the system to be developed. During this requirements analysis activity, risk and contingency analyses should also be performed, in order to provide the development team with information about potential risks to functionality and development. When risks and contingencies have been identified, a testing strategy can be developed, along with security

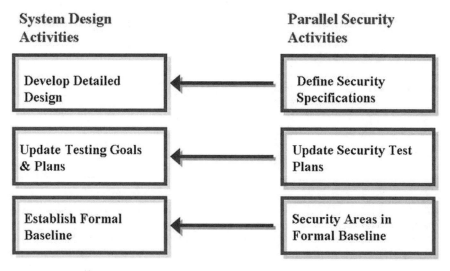

System Design Activities	Parallel Security Activities
Develop Detailed Design	Define Security Specifications
Update Testing Goals & Plans	Update Security Test Plans
Establish Formal Baseline	Security Areas in Formal Baseline

Figure 2.3 System Design Specifications

testing. This provides evidence that functionality is appropriate and controls are implemented and operating effectively in the system and its environment.

At this time, strategies for acquiring product can also be developed. Security requirements for the product can be detailed in any documentation produced, such as requests for proposals, service level agreements and so forth. At the conclusion, a formal baseline can be established, both for system development and security requirements present in that development.

When the preliminary system planning is completed, the design specifications can be formalized. This includes: developing a complete and detailed design, including appropriate security specifications; reviewing the test plan and updating it as required to meet both functional and security requirements; and establishing a documented and formal baseline, including security components, for measurement.

When the design and test plans are completed, system components can be tested using the plan. This includes the testing of security-related components, as identified in the test plan. The development and testing teams use this information to validate both the system performance and the security components that have been built into the system. If the tests prove that additional work is necessary, this work will be completed by the development team and resubmitted for testing. Once the testing is successfully completed, the system can be installed, complete with the controls identified as

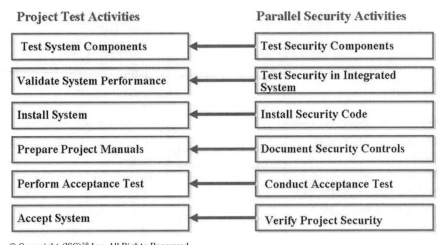

Project Test Activities   Parallel Security Activities

| Test System Components | ◄── | Test Security Components |

| Validate System Performance | ◄── | Test Security in Integrated System |

| Install System | ◄── | Install Security Code |

| Prepare Project Manuals | ◄── | Document Security Controls |

| Perform Acceptance Test | ◄── | Conduct Acceptance Test |

| Accept System | ◄── | Verify Project Security |

Figure 2.4 System Acceptance Process

required within the system design. At this time, manuals for the system can also be completed. Post-completion of the documentation and installation, acceptance testing occurs. Should the testing prove successful, the system is accepted; if it is not successful, remedial work is completed by the development team to ensure system acceptance. As part of the completion of the project, the security components and controls are reviewed again to ensure proper implementation and operating effectiveness.

Risk Assessment

It is typical for an organization to conduct a "risk assessment" prior to, or sometimes during, application development, in order to evaluate:

- Threats to its assets
- Vulnerabilities present in the environment
- The likelihood that a threat will "make good" by taking advantage of an exposure (or probability and frequency when dealing with quantitative assessment)
- The impact that the vulnerability being realized has on the organization
- The risk associated with each threat successfully exploiting a vulnerability

Why perform a risk assessment? Without knowing what assets are critical and, likewise, those that are most at risk within an organization, it is not possible to protect those assets appropriately. For example, if an organization is bound by Sarbanes-Oxley regulations, but does not know how financial reporting may be at risk, the organization may make significant mistakes such as neglecting to protect against certain risks or applying too much protection against low-level risks.

Qualitative Risk Assessments Organizations have the option of performing a risk assessment in one of two ways; either "qualitatively" or "quantitatively." Qualitative risk assessments produce valid results that are descriptive versus measurable. A qualitative risk assessment is typically conducted when:

- The risk assessors available for the organization have limited expertise.
- The time frame allotted for risk assessment is short duration.
- The organization does not have trend data readily available that can assist with the risk assessment.

Analysis of risk can include matching a threat to a vulnerability, matching threats to assets, determining how likely the threat is to exploit the vulnerability, and determining impact to the organization in the event the exploit is successful. Analysis also includes a matching of current and planned countermeasures (i.e., protection) to the threat-vulnerability pair.

When the matching is completed, risk can be estimated. In a qualitative analysis, the product of likelihood and impact produces the "level" of risk. The higher the risk level, the more immediate is the need for the organization to address the issue to protect the organization from harm.

Quantitative Risk Assessments As an organization becomes more sophisticated in its data collection and retention, and staff also becomes more experienced in conducting risk assessments, an organization may find itself moving more towards quantitative risk assessment. The hallmark of a quantitative assessment is the *numeric* nature of the analysis. Frequency, probability, impact, countermeasure effectiveness, and other aspects of the risk assessment have a discrete mathematical value in a pure quantitative analysis.

It is clear to see the benefits, and the pitfalls, of performing a purely quantitative analysis. Quantitative analysis allows the risk assessor to determine whether the cost of the risk outweighs the cost of the countermeasure, in mathematical rather than descriptive terms. Purely quantitative analysis, however, requires an enormous amount of time and must be performed by assessors with a significant amount of experience. Additionally, subjectivity is introduced because the metrics may also need to be applied to *qualitative* measures.

Methods Three steps are undertaken in a quantitative risk assessment, after the initial management approval, construction of a risk assessment team, and the review of information currently available within the organization. Single Loss Expectancy (SLE) must be calculated to provide an estimate of loss. Single loss expectancy is defined as the difference between the original value and remaining value of an asset after a single exploit. Losses can include lack of availability of data assets, due to data loss, theft, alteration, or denial of service.

Next, the organization would calculate the Annualized Rate of Occurrence (ARO). This is done to provide an accurate calculation of Annualized Loss Expectancy (ALE). ARO is an estimate of how often a threat will be successful in exploiting a vulnerability over the period of a year.

When this is completed, the organization calculates the ALE. The ALE is a product of the yearly estimate for the ARO and the loss in value of an asset after a SLE.

Given that there is now a value for SLE, it is possible to determine what the organization should spend, if anything, to apply a countermeasure for the risk in question. Remember that no countermeasure should be greater in cost than the risk it mitigates. Countermeasure cost per year is easy and straightforward to calculate. It is simply the cost of the countermeasure divided by the years of its life (i.e., use within the organization). Finally, the organization is able to compare the cost of the risk versus the cost of the countermeasure and make some objective decisions regarding its countermeasure selection.

Once risk has been determined, additional countermeasures can be recommended to minimize, transfer, or avoid the risk. When this is completed, the risk that is left over after countermeasures have been applied to the organization to protect against the risk is also estimated. This is the "residual risk," or risk left over after countermeasure application.

Selecting Tools/Techniques for Risk Assessment

It is expected that an organization will make a selection of the risk assessment methodology, tools, and resources (including people) that best fit its culture, its personnel capabilities, its budget, and its timeline. Many automated tools, including proprietary tools, exist in the field. While automation can make the data analysis, dissemination and storage of results easier, it is not a required part of risk assessment. If an organization is planning to purchase or build automated tools for this purpose, it is highly recommended that this decision be based on appropriate timeline, resource skill sets for creation, implementation, maintenance, and monitoring of the tool(s) and data stored within, long term.

Risk Assessment Steps

Identification of Vulnerabilities It is common to identify vulnerabilities as they are related to people, processes, data, technology, and facilities.

Examples of vulnerabilities could include lack of physical security within a facility, inadequate validity checking in financial transaction software, and so on.

Identification of Threats Threat sources have been identified by a number of groups, but can be compiled into a few categories:

- Human
- Natural
- Technical
- Physical/Environmental
- Operational/Functional

Each category can be expanded with specific threats, as follows in the examples:

- Human: malicious outsider, errors made by human intervention, cultural issues, such as a strike
- Natural: fire, flood, or other natural disasters

Determination of Likelihood Likelihood, along with impact, determines risk. Likelihood, as stated by the National Institute of Standards and Technology (NIST) and others can be "measured" by the capabilities of the threat and the presence or absence of countermeasures. Initially, organizations that do not have trending data available may use an ordinal scale, labeled High, Medium, and Low to score likelihood rankings. These are actually qualitative elements.

Determination of Impact Impact can be ranked much the same way as likelihood. The main difference is that the impact scale is expanded and depends upon definitions, rather than ordinal selections. Definitions of impact to an organization often include loss of life, loss of dollars, loss of prestige, loss of market share and other facets. It is highly recommended that the organization take sufficient time to define and assign impact definitions for High, Medium, Low or any other scale terms that are chosen.

Determination of "Risk" Risk is determined by the product of likelihood and impact. For example, if an exploit has a likelihood of 1 (High) and an impact of 100 (High), the risk would be 100. Using the same mapping scale as for impact, this would be the highest exploit ranking available. These scenarios (high likelihood, high impact) merit *immediate* attention from the organization.

As the risk calculations are completed, they can be prioritized for attention, as required. Note that not all risks will receive the same level of attention, based on the organization's risk tolerance and its strategy for mitigation, transfer, acceptance, or avoidance of risk.

Reporting Findings Once the findings from the assessment have been consolidated and the calculations have been completed, it is time to present a finalized report to senior management. This can be done in a written report, by presentation, or "outbrief," or by both means. Written reports should include an acknowledgment to the participants, a summary of the approach taken, findings in detail (either in tabulated or graphical form), recommendations for remediation of the findings and a summary.

Countermeasure Selection It is important for the organization to appropriately select countermeasures to apply to risks in the environment. Many aspects of the countermeasure must be considered in order to ensure it is the proper fit to the task:

- Accountability
- Auditability
- Publicly available, simple design
- Trusted source
- Independence
- Consistently applied
- Cost effective
- Reliable
- Distinct from other countermeasures
- Ease of use
- Minimum manual intervention
- Sustainable
- Secure
- Protects confidentiality, integrity and availability of assets
- Can be "backed out" in event of issue
- Creates no additional issues during operation
- Leaves no residual data from its function

While this list appears rather lengthy, it is clear that countermeasures must be above reproach when in use for protection of an organization's assets.

Implementation It is important to note that, once risk assessment is completed and there is a list of remediation activities to be undertaken, an organization must ensure that it has personnel with appropriate capabilities to implement the remediation activities, as well as to maintain and support them. This may require the organization to provide additional training opportunities to personnel involved in the design, deployment, maintenance, and support of security mechanisms within the environment.

In addition, it is crucial that appropriate policies, with detailed procedures that correspond to each policy item, be created, implemented, maintained, monitored and enforced in the environment. It is highly recommended that the organization assign accountable resources to each task and track tasks over time, reporting progress to senior management and allowing for time for appropriate approvals during this process.

Risk Management

Once the organization has performed risk assessment activities, senior management can determine how best to deal with the risk presented. This is the discipline of "risk management." Methods for dealing with risk are presented below.

Risk Avoidance

Risk avoidance can be defined as the practice of coming up with alternatives so that the risk in question is not realized (it is "avoided"). For example, if an individual wanted to avoid the risk of sports injury, he or she would not participate in sporting activities.

Risk Transfer

Risk transfer can be defined as the practice of passing on the risk in question to another entity, such as an insurance company. It is important to note that the transfer of risk may be accompanied by a cost. An example would be liability insurance for a vendor or the insurance taken out by companies to protect against hardware and software theft or destruction.

Risk Mitigation

Risk mitigation can be defined as the practice of the elimination, or the significant decrease, in the level of risk presented. For example, in order to lessen the risk of exposing personal and financial information that is highly sensitive and confidential, organizations put countermeasures in place, such as firewalls, intrusion detection/prevention systems, and other mechanisms to deter malicious outsiders from accessing this highly sensitive information.

Risk Acceptance

In some cases, it may be prudent for an organization to simply accept the risk that is presented in certain scenarios. Risk acceptance can be defined as the practice of accepting certain risk(s), typically based on a business decision that may also weigh the cost versus the benefit of dealing with the risk in another way.

The decision to accept risk should not be taken lightly, or without appropriate information to justify the decision. The cost versus benefit, the organization's willingness to monitor the risk long-term and the impact it has on the outside world's view of the organization must all be taken into account when deciding to accept risk.

Software Development Methods

The Waterfall Model

The Waterfall model (see Figure 2.5) for software development was created in the 1970s and is typically considered the oldest of the process-oriented development methods reported. It is a "phase-based" approach, meaning the completion of each heralds the commencement of the next phase; that is, development is conducted serially. Because of the serial nature of this development method, it does not scale well to large, complex projects. Another drawback of serial development is that it extends the time frame of the project, therefore usually making it an unsuitable method for projects which must developed in a short time frame (e.g., six months or less). The main advantage of using this method is that each phase is completed, including documentation, prior to the next phase commencing, therefore giving the developer a good deal of data to draw from.

An example of an organization that has used the Waterfall model is The National Aeronautics and Space Administration (NASA), for example, has used the Waterfall model its space exploration program.

The Waterfall model contains the following five stages:

- Requirements analysis and definition
- System and software design
- Implementation and "unit" testing
- System testing
- Operation and maintenance

These stages will be discussed in detail below.

Requirements Analysis and Definition

Conducting a requirements analysis allows an organization or a team to get to the heart of the problem to be solved. Requirements are determined by interactions with senior management, the business units, and the end users affected and are typically fairly high-level to start. Requirements are stated in terms of business rules, not technology. It is important to "lock down," as much as possible, requirements from a development project in advance, so that there are fewer deviations, or changes, along the way to completion of the project.

System and Software Design

Once the requirements have been gathered, documented, and finalized, a design implementing the requirements can be completed. All of the requirements documented during the requirements analysis phase must be appropriately addressed by the system design. It is important that the design be detailed enough to ensure implementation is achievable, with the minimum of difficulty, and limited to no necessity to go back to those stakeholders who assisted with requirements gathering due to lack of information.

Development

The job of writing code occurs in this phase. It is critical that the developers responsible for the project be well-versed in secure coding procedures, such as those embraced by the Open Web Application Security Project (OWASP). In addition, code should be developed to specifications (i.e., requirements analysis) and, if this is not possible, any changes must be documented, typically through a formal change control process.

Testing and Implementation

Source code must never be implemented without appropriate testing. To do so puts the organization at risk for unplanned outages, the "breaking" of

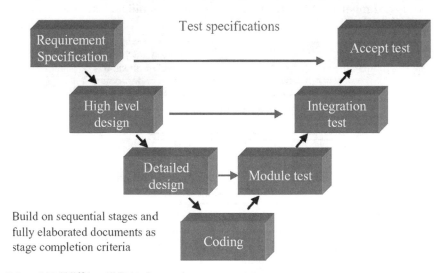

Figure 2.5 The Waterfall Model

functionality critical to the organization's operations, and other hazards. Documented test plans must be prepared by the development team and exercised by organizational staff *not* part of the development team. Test plans should include functional testing at all levels, including unit, system and user acceptance testing. When the test plans have been completed, the tester must sign the plan to indicate it has been exercised. Any errors detected during the test must also be documented on the plan, corrected and retested by personnel not responsible for the first test (and not part of the development team) prior to implementation. If it is necessary to make changes to the code for any reason, formal chance control process must be followed.

Operation and Maintenance

Operation and maintenance of the code fall into the final step of the Waterfall method.

The Iterative Development Model

The Iterative Development model (see Figure 2.6) is actually a fragmented Waterfall model. Each fragment consists of a smaller component of the foundation. While this method allows for just-in-time refinements of the development process, including requirements analysis, project design and coding, there is a danger that the project may exhibit significant scope creep as a

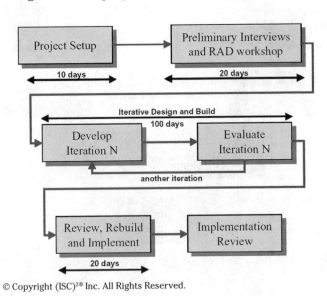

Figure 2.6 The Iterative Development Model

result, particularly if not all requirements are known up front or if there is an excessive amount of change requested during development. This type of project must be closely managed to avoid these pitfalls.

The Exploratory Model

In the Exploratory model, hypothetical requirements provide the design and implementation for the project. This can happen when requirements are not known prior to the project commencement. As requirements are discovered, a series of rapid iterations of the code are completed to incorporate the requirements. Because there is an absence of formalized requirements, verification of the design and implementation are conducted based on the resultant code base.

The Exploratory model is simple in its construction; it is composed of the following steps:

- Initial Specification Development
- System Construction/Modification
- System Testing
- System Implementation

It is difficult to determine whether the Exploratory method will yield an appropriate result. Due to the absence of specificity in the requirements and design, it is not possible to verify whether it is the most cost-effective approach for the development team. In addition, the code produced is often less than elegant, as pre-planning was not performed. This model can also only be used with languages that allow for rapid code development, such as LISP.

The Rapid Application Development (RAD) Model

RAD attempts production-ready software at highly controlled time frames, through the development of an application prototype. For projects where deadlines are very strict, this development method may prove useful. It is critical to tightly control the quality of the software produced in this method as well, given that rapid production may also lead to poor design and the resulting code from that design.

The Spiral Model

The Spiral model is a combination of both the Waterfall and Prototyping methods. Similar to prototyping, an initial version of the application is developed. However, the development of each version is carefully designed using the Waterfall model. A positive feature of this development effort is the ability to conduct a risk assessment activity during each phase of the project. The information obtained from the risk assessment is then used to update schedules, costs and so on. If at any time during the risk assessment activities it is determined that the project is in jeopardy, it can be cancelled.

The Spiral model can be identified by the presence of following steps:

- Project Objectives
- Risk Assessment
- Engineering and Production
- Planning and Management (feedback opportunity for the stakeholders)
- The Reuse Model

The hallmark of the Reuse model of software development is the "reuse" of existing coded modules to complete the task. For those who have had experience with object-oriented development, this model seems second-nature. Object-oriented programming is best suited for the Reuse model, as the objects stored within the object libraries can be exported, modified, and reused at will. Libraries of software modules are also built and maintained in the Reuse model. These libraries consist of procedural modules or database modules. Modules that do not currently exist within the libraries can be built by the developer and stored in the appropriate library for later use.

The Reuse model consists of the following steps:

- Definition of Requirements
- Definition of Objects
- Collection of Objects from Existing Code
- Creation of Customized Objects Not Currently Existing within the Module Libraries
- Prototype Assembly
- Prototype Evaluation
- Requirements Refinement
- Objects Refinement

The Computer Aided Software Engineering (CASE) Model

The CASE model was designed in the 1970s and embraced the use of computers assisting with software design, development, and maintenance activities. CASE tools have been developed to assist with both visual and object-oriented programming efforts. CASE development is most often used on significantly complex development projects, which are identified by the use of many technical components and personnel.

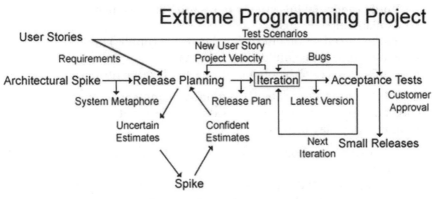

Figure 2.7 Extreme Programming Project Diagram

There are many obvious advantages to the use of CASE development methods for sizable projects. Project participants have an opportunity to work towards common goals for each program module. This sharing of knowledge and resources may result in the lowering of project costs over time. In addition, code reuse is made possible, thereby saving additional time and effort on the part of the development team. Features embedded in CASE tools include code and relational/logical database modeling simulations, object-oriented notation, and diagramming capabilities, among others.

Extreme Programming

The developer of the Extreme Programming model, Kent Beck, envisioned the use of this model to assist developers working in small groups with limited time frames, looming deadlines, and requirements that are changing rapidly (see Figure 2.7). This approach is highly disciplined and encourages developers to add functionality only as requested. This puts a functional limitation on the code itself, which enables relatively simple tracking through code improvement, testing, and implementation. In addition, this method puts significant emphasis on customer satisfaction.

Security Management Planning

For an organization to appropriately plan for managing security within its environment, it should carefully consider, at the least, the following costs to determine next steps:

- Identify the initial investment in security management
- Calculate ongoing costs
- Identify the effect on internal and external (public) perception
- Identify impact on confidential information
- Identify impact on the organization's intellectual property

In addition to the benefits of continued maintenance of security within the organization, it should also consider other potential benefits to the organization. They may include:

- Enhanced perception of the organization to internal and external stakeholders
- Potential workload reduction for personnel, particularly in Risk Management/Internal Audit, Compliance, Security, Information Systems, Human Resources, and Senior Management
- Improved business partner access
- Improved remote access
- Creation, implementation, maintenance, and monitoring of common data locations, particularly important to sensitive data

Once the costs and benefits are presented to senior management, it may be the job of the security professional to promote buy-in from the organization's business units. In order to accomplish this, the professional must:

- Understand the business of the organization
- Understand what is important to the stakeholders, both internal and external, including clients and business partners
- Be able to communicate how security can help them achieve their objectives while remaining secure

Creating the Security Statement

One of the first elements in security management planning is developing an overall general organization security statement. The statement is a high-level security "mission statement" that communicates the organization's sensitive and critical assets, as well as the most significant risks to those assets.

The organization utilizes the security statement to create operational policies and procedures. Examples of operational policies include:

- E-Mail Policies
- Telecommuting Policies
- Remote Access Policies
- Business Continuity Policies
- Fraud Policies

Security Policy Creation and Maintenance

In order to communicate management's expectations with regard to responsibilities for security within the organization, an appropriate policy foundation must be created. This foundation is comprised of "policy deliverables," which include policies, standards, procedures, guidelines and plans, in addition to working documents that provide background information for the policy deliverables.

Creation of policy deliverables occurs within a life cycle, much like technical life cycles, such as the software development life cycle. Life cycle stages include:

- Identification of the need for a policy deliverable
- Design the policy deliverable
- Create the policy deliverable based on the design
- Obtain appropriate approvals for the policy deliverable
- Perform training on the policy deliverable within the organization
- Complete implementation of the policy deliverable, including the communication of the policy deliverable to the organization

Maintenance of policy deliverables, either as a scheduled maintenance for a semiannual or annual review of the policy foundation, or as an update of policies for operational reasons, occurs in much the same fashion as detailed for creation. Steps that may be abbreviated, dependent upon the state of the existing policy deliverable, might include identification or design.

Security Policy Implementation

Policy deliverable implementation can be accomplished in a number of ways within an organization. At minimum, the following activities must occur:

- A formalized and documented implementation plan must be produced; this provides the format against which to measure effectiveness of the implementation, as well as effectiveness of the policy deliverables themselves.
- Dedicated resources must be available to implement the policies.
- Senior management must formally communicate to the environment pre-implementation that it has approved these policy deliverables and will support actions required to enforce the policy deliverables.
- Policy deliverables must be rolled out to the entire organization/those with need-to-know through more than one medium. Examples might be through a Web site and distribution by e-mail to all concerned persons.
- A timetable for implementation must be communicated to all affected persons.
- Formal, documented, mandatory training on the policies must be rolled out prior to implementation finalization. A formal signoff list of attendees must be kept for auditing purposes.

Security Procedure Development and Documentation

The development and formal documentation of security procedures is identical to the process documented above for the creation of policy deliverables (e.g., recall that policy deliverables include procedures). It is important to remember that procedures differ from policies in that they are a step-by-step tactical representation of "how" a security concern is addressed within an environment.

Organization Security Evaluation and Assistance

The Protection Profile

A Protection Profile (PP) is document detailing security requirements that are specific to certain customer needs for security. Protection Profiles are becoming more prevalent for software and database applications. These profiles are implementation-independent. Examples include Oracle's Database Management System Protection Profile, the UK Controlled Access Protection Profile, and the UK Labeled Security Protection Profile. Each Protection Profile described the target environment, security goals, functions, and assurance (confidence) requirements.

Protection Profiles must also go through a Common Criteria evaluation and those profiles that successfully navigate the evaluation are included in a central registry for use by the public. Uses will likely include prescriptions for developers with respect to best practices for security for a product or system. It is the intent of the supporting sponsors to port this information to a Web site for ease of use. This site will also help sponsors to build relevant security targets more efficiently.

Protection Profile structure is as follows:

- Description, to include the information protection issue
- Rationale, to include a justification and security policy support
- Functional requirements, such as roles and responsibilities
- Development at all phases of the assurance requirements
- Evaluation of the assurance requirements

Protection Profile development is as follows:

- Conduct a security analysis of the environment, to include threats and vulnerabilities, expected use, assumptions about the environment, and any relevant information security including documentation (policies, procedures, guidelines, standards, compliance objectives, and so on).
- Conduct requirements analysis and synthesis, including those for functional and assurance components.

Protection Profile analysis is conducted by taking into account:

- Technical soundness
- Use
- Evaluation capacity
- Uniqueness from other profiles
- Consistency with other profiles

The following represent the Common Criteria evaluation assurance classes.

- EAL-01 — Functionally Tested. This assurance class describes assessment of relevant security functionality, through the use of function and interface specifications of the target to understand the security behavior. The assessment is validated through independent testing of the security functionality.
- EAL-02 — Structurally Tested. This assurance class describes assessment of relevant security functionality, through the use of function and interface specifications, adding the high-level design of relevant subsystems from the target to understand the security behavior. Independent testing of security functionality, "black box" testing formalized documentation, and evaluation of potential vulnerabilities, as formally documented by developers conducting the search, are hallmarks for this assurance class.
- EAL-03 — Methodically Tested and Checked. Results from the assessment are supported by "gray box" testing, as well as the independent confirmation of test plan results as documented by the developer and formal substantiation that development personnel have considered appropriate potential vulnerabilities. Environmental controls and configuration management relative to the target are also required.
- EAL-04 — Methodically Designed, Tested, and Reviewed. Assessment in this assurance class evaluates the low-level design of the program modules of the target, as well as the addition of a subset of the implementation. Testing is validated through an independent search for potential vulnerabilities. Development controls include a life-cycle model, identification of tools, and automated configuration management.
- EAL-05 — Semi-formally Designed and Tested. Assessment at this assurance class includes complete review of the product/system implementation itself. Assurance objectives are supplemented by a formal model, as well as a "semiformal" presentation of the functional specification, the high-level design, and a semiformal demonstration of correspondence. The search for vulnerabilities must include formal evidence of appropriate resistance to unauthorized access or attack. Covert channel analysis and a modular design of the product/system are also required.

- EAL-06 — Semi-Formally Verified Design and Tested. Assessment of this assurance class is facilitated by a modular, layered approach to design. A structured presentation of the implementation is also required. The independent analysis of potential vulnerabilities must provide formal evidence that there is high resistance to unauthorized access or attack. The search for covert channels must be proven to be systematic. Environmental and configuration management controls are further identified, documented, and formalized.
- EAL-07 — Formally Verified Design and Tested. The formal model is supplemented by a formal presentation of the functional specification and high-level design showing correspondence. Formal verification of developer "white box" testing and complete independent confirmation of developer test results are required for this assurance class. Complexity of the design must be minimized in all ways possible.

Modes of Operation

System High Mode In system high mode, all systems and peripheral devices are classified. They are subsequently protected at the highest level of classification of data resident on the system. For example, if a system houses top secret information, but also holds information that the public can view, the system is classified as top secret.

Users who have been authorized to a system have clearance and approval to view data on that system; however, should there be information resident on the system for which the user has no "need-to-know," access would be denied.

Compartmented Mode

The following are characteristics of systems operating in compartmented ("partitioned") mode:

- Each user with access must meet the relevant security criteria for the system.
- The user has a predetermined access level for the system.
- Access is authorized by "need-to-know" *only*.
- User access may be revoked based on criticality of the data resident on the system.
- Comprehensive documentation is present that tracks the data access granted for each user.

Multilevel Secure Mode (MLS)

The following are characteristics of systems operating in MLS mode:

- Not all personnel have approval or need-to-know for all information in the system.
- Users are not allowed to access classified data at different classification levels.
- In order to combat "data leakage," processes are not allowed to interact.
- These are the only systems on which multiple levels of classified data can exist.

Operating Utilities and Software

Systems are managed by software called "operating systems." Examples are Windows and all its flavors (NT, 2000, 2003, XP, and so on), Linux, Unix, and others. Operating systems manage subsystems that are functional and resident on a system, such as:

- Software utilities
- Applications
- File systems
- Access controls for users, programs or other systems

Services provided by operating systems include:

- Program execution
- Access to I/O devices
- Controlled access to files (based on credentials)
- Access to the system itself, as well as to appropriate interconnected systems
- Error detection, potential correction and response
- Accounting functions

Operating systems also control hardware resources, such as:

- The Central Processing Unit (CPU)
- Memory
- I/O and storage devices

The Central Processing Unit

The CPU is bound by processing states. These states are the Stopped/operating state, the Wait/running state, and the Masked/interruptible state. The Stopped/Operating state is marked by a process not operating, or a computer waiting or running. The Wait state is marked by a wait, as instructions have not been executed or the system is waiting for interrupts or data. In the Running state, instructions are being executed and interrupts are being taken. In the Masked/interruptible state, if the masked bits are not set, the interrupts are disabled (masked bits are off). This is commonly called the system IRQ (Interrupt Request). CPU configurations include multitasking configurations and multiprogramming configurations. Multitasking is the performance of two or more tasks concurrently. Multiprogramming is the processor-driven interleaved execution of two or more applications.

Memory

Memory management is a critical task for systems. Requirements for memory management include:

- Relocation
- Protection
- Sharing
- Logical Organization
- Physical Organization

There are three types of memory addresses: logical, relative, and physical. Logical memory addresses require a translation to physical addresses. They are a reference to a previous data location in memory. Relative addresses are expressed as a memory location relative to a known point. Physical addresses are the actual location in memory; they are also known as the "absolute" address.

Service Level Agreement Compliance

Non-Disclosures (NDA) NDAs place restrictions on dissemination of corporate information to outside and inside interests. Non-disclosures are typically used to communicate expectations relative to the communication of sensitive information, such as information covered by regulation (e.g., health information, financials), as well as intellectual property, and so on.

Non-Competition Non-competition agreements present the signer with restrictions on work completed for competitors, the ability to contract with the company's clients or to hire away current employees of the company.

Service Level Agreements (SLA) SLAs are formalized, contractual documents that ensure that an organization receives the services for which it has contracted. For example, organizations may require external vendors, especially those responsible for network operations, business continuity/ disaster recovery, or forensics work, to sign a contract stipulating that it will ensure the organization is able to function under duress without undue downtime or loss of its assets. Internal service level agreements can include formalization of services provided to the organization from infrastructure, network, or application development units.

User Security Awareness Education

Security Awareness

Most, if not all people within an organization, have some idea about what they can do to protect themselves, the organization and its assets from harm; however, because people differ in their interpretations, opinions, outlooks and expectations, it is critical that senior management provide a single, unified message with regard to security expectations. That is, senior management must make employees, contractors, business partners, vendors, and anyone else with access to corporate assets "aware" of information security requirements. This can only be done through appropriate security awareness training.

In order to ensure a single interpretation of security requirements, *all applicable parties* must complete this mandatory awareness training. Awareness training should be conducted periodically, either online or in person, and no less than once per year. Both new hires and established personnel must complete security awareness training. Once the initial training is completed, it is advisable to present applicable parties with security "reminders." These can take the form of posters, key chains, columns in employee publications, the establishment of Security Awareness Day, and so on. Contests and awards help to motivate personnel to comply with security requirements. It is important to note that security topics should be changed often, so that new material can be presented to reflect current issues and also to ensure that personnel maintain their interest.

Security Training

Unlike general security awareness training, security training assists personnel with the development of their skills sets relative to performance of security functions within their roles. A typical security curriculum in a mature organization will include specialty classes for individuals performing specialized roles within the organization, such as those in Information Systems, Accounting, and others.

Even within these business units, specialized training will occur. For example, in the Information Systems area, it would be advisable for network staff responsible for maintenance and monitoring of the firewalls, intrusion detection/prevention systems and syslog servers to be sufficiently trained to perform these duties. Let's say senior management determined there were no funds available for training. What would be the result? Well, typically, motivated staff would perform some on-the-job learning; however, it may not be sufficient to perform the job duties adequately. As a result, the organization is breached and sensitive information is stolen. Who would be at fault in this case? The answer is that senior management is always ultimately responsible in the organization for information security objectives. Senior management failed, in this case, to adequately protect the organization by refusing to properly train staff in their respective security duties. Any legal ramifications would fall squarely upon management's shoulders.

Let's examine the previous situation in another way. Let's say that the personnel in question indicated to management that, although no paid training was available, they felt comfortable that they could perform the security functions for which they were responsible. To demonstrate, they performed the requisite functions for IT management to demonstrate capability. All is well until the organization is breached some months later and confidential information stolen. Senior management returns to Information Systems management and asks the director of Information Systems to investigate. During her investigation, she discovers that patching has not occurred for the past three months. When staff were asked about the incident, no satisfactory answer could be given. Who would be responsible for the breach in that event? The answer is: senior management is always ultimately responsible for information security within the organization; *however*, senior management held the network team accountable for failing to maintain patching levels and promptly fired them from their positions. Ensuring that a resource is properly trained can assist an organization in assigning accountability for the satisfactory completion of security tasks for which they are responsible.

The organization must also keep in mind that training should be closely aligned with security risk management activities. In doing so, the training may result in partial or complete offset of the risk within the organization.

Security Education

Security education (specifically, in this case, Information Security) revolves around the education of a potential or experienced security professional along career development lines and, as the SSCP Administrative Domain course points out, "provides decision-making and security management skills that are important for the success of an organization's security program." Security certifications versus vendor certifications, may fit into this category. Certifications such as the SSCP, CISSP®, CISA, CISM, GIAC, and others are related to the discipline of security for the practitioner. The benefits of this training have already been presented. Costs of the training, relative to benefit received by the personnel and organization, must be evaluated before training begins.

Equally important are curricula that have been introduced into the universities through the Federal government and other benefactors, implemented as Bachelor's, Master's, and PhD programs. Many of these programs present both theory and hands-on coursework to the student. Topics covered in these programs may include: policy and procedures design and development, security assessment techniques, technical and application security assessment techniques, social engineering; malicious software identification and eradication, incident response, disaster recovery, and security program development. The benefit derived from this education is self-evident; a practitioner versus a technician is created. It is important to note, however, that education of this type is typically two to six years in duration and takes significant time and resources to successfully complete. An alternative may be to train professionals on a university course-by-course basis in information security. This may be a practical alternative, given the need within the organization.

Security Awareness and Training Plan Security awareness training must be formally documented as a security requirement within an organization. This minimally requires the completion of a training plan that precedes the implementation of new or updated security controls, as well as includes provisions for periodic awareness training as required for operational and compliance reasons.

Code of Ethics

Some companies require employees to sign an Ethics (or Business Ethics) statement, which may contain overlapping information with an organization's acceptable use policy. Many ethics agreements are a synthesis of the Acceptable Use Policy, non-disclosure and non-competition agreements, among other documents.

(ISC)² Code of Ethics (ISC)² has prepared an ethics statement which must be adhered to as part of its requirement for the certification of security practitioners with CISSP or SSCP designation. A formal, signed copy of this ethics statement is required for each candidate prior to certification. A complete copy of the ethics statement can be obtained directly from (ISC)².

RFC 1087: Ethics and the Internet The policy behind this ethics statement is represented here in its entirety directly from the RFC 1987 Web site (www.rfc-archives.org).

Internet Architecture Board (IAB) Statement of Policy is as follows:

> The Internet is a national facility whose utility is largely a consequence of its wide availability and accessibility. Irresponsible use of this critical resource poses an enormous threat to its continued availability to the technical community.

> The U.S. Government sponsors of this system have a fiduciary responsibility to the public to allocate government resources wisely

and effectively. Justification for the support of this system suffers when highly disruptive abuses occur. Access to and use of the Internet is a privilege and should be treated as such by all users of this system.

The IAB strongly endorses the view of the Division Advisory Panel of the National Science Foundation Division of Network, Communications Research and Infrastructure which, in paraphrase, characterized as unethical and unacceptable any activity which purposely:

(a) seeks to gain unauthorized access to the resources of the Internet,
(b) disrupts the intended use of the Internet,
(c) wastes resources (people, capacity, computer) through such actions,
(d) destroys the integrity of computer-based information, or
(e) compromises the privacy of users.

The Internet exists in the general research milieu. Portions of it continue to be used to support research and experimentation on networking. Because experimentation on the Internet has the potential to affect all of its components and users, researchers have the responsibility to exercise great caution in the conduct of their work. Negligence in the conduct of Internet-wide experiments is both irresponsible and unacceptable.

The IAB plans to take whatever actions it can, in concert with federal agencies and other interested parties, to identify and to set up technical and procedural mechanisms to make the Internet more resistant to disruption. Such security, however, may be extremely expensive and may be counterproductive if it inhibits the free flow of information which makes the Internet so valuable. In the final analysis, the health and well-being of the Internet is the responsibility of its users who must, uniformly, guard against abuses which disrupt the system and threaten its long-term viability.

Acceptable Use Policy

An Acceptable Use Policy is the document in an organization that typically addresses the expectations an organization communicates to its employees, relative to their responsibilities with regard to information security. The Corporate Security Policy may contain the Acceptable Use Policy, but also includes additional policy documents that reflect security policies affecting people, processes, data, technology, and facilities (i.e., physical structures and their surroundings). Examples would be access control policies, after-hours entry into a building and the like.

Security Administration: Policies, Standards, and Guidelines

Security Policy Implementation

"Policies" are a communication of an expectation by an individual or group in authority. They are the "why" security is important and the "what" is expected, relative to responsibilities for information security, of employees, contractors, business partners, vendors, and others. Typically, an acknowledgement that the individual had read, and understands, the policy is required for the policy to be enforceable in the event of prosecution. This acknowledgement can take the form of a written signature on a policy document or it can also be a button that, when clicked, "accepts" the acknowledgement digitally. This type of acknowledgement is widely used for the acceptance of security and privacy policies over the Internet. Components that assist in the creation of an effective policy are:

- Definitions
- Purpose
- Authorizing individual
- Author/sponsor
- Scope of the policy
- Measurement of effectiveness
- Exception process (*only* as required; exceptions should be few and far between)
- Accountability
- Effective/expiration dates
- References (policies, procedures, other documentation)

Policies must be distributed, either electronically or manually, to all applicable parties. An acknowledgement of receipt and understanding of the policy must be signed and retained by the organization. Failure to do so opens the organization to liability in the event of a breach of policy.

"Procedures" are the detail of "how" to enact the policy. They are the nuts and bolts, step-by-step, in the trenches discussions about how security activities are to be satisfactorily completed by the organization. An example of a security procedure is the step-by-step construction of a hardened intrusion detection system (IDS).

"Standards" are governing documents that are widely used (i.e., "standard" use) by all organizations that give hard prescriptions ("requirements") relative to what is acceptable internationally for information security. An example of such a standard is the ISO 17799, the code of practice for information security, which is used as a guideline for organizations to apply best practices for information security. This guideline becomes a standard when accepted as such by the organization.

"Guidelines" are actually recommendations, and are not necessarily subject to hard and fast enforcement. Many organizations make the mistake of imposing guidelines rather than policies; this leaves the communication of expectations open to interpretation, thereby opening the organization to potential misinterpretations for which there is no redress. Guidelines are earmarked by the use of the words "should," "could," "may," and such, versus imperative language used in policies, such as the word "must." Some organizations use the work "guideline" when creating policies. This may create some confusion in the environment; however, the important thing is to clearly and unambiguously communicate expectations surrounding information security to the organization.

"Baselines" are used to communicate a current or desired state to which the organization aspires. Good examples of baselines are those provided from vulnerability scanning (e.g., the current state "baseline" of the organization's technology security involved in the scanning) and "baseline" firewall or network device configurations (e.g., to reflect either current or desired states).

While it is the security practitioner's job to ensure that security activities are completed satisfactorily, it is senior management's responsibility to ensure that expectations are formally documented and available to all applicable parties. It is also senior management's responsibility to ensure that all parties understand that information security is a corporate priority and that security requirements will be strictly enforced. Without enforcement, formalized documents are worthless and will actually become an impediment to, rather than promotion of, security within the organization.

Implementing Security Requirements Guidance

Certification and Accreditation Process Concepts

The term "certification" is best defined as the comprehensive analysis of the security features and protective measures of a system to determine how closely the measures meet security requirements. Certification considers the following in the system or product's operational environment:

- The security mode of operations
- A list of authorized users and their skill set/training
- Data sensitivity and criticality, and the applications that handle them
- Systems and facility locations and configurations
- Interconnection with other systems

Systems Accreditation

The practice of "accreditation" can best be described management's decision to accept risk and operate its certified systems. Of particular interest to accreditation is:

- Security mode in use
- Countermeasures selected for use
- Stated threat/vulnerability pairs
- Interdependence with other systems
- Stated period of time

System Certification Effort Support

British Standard (BS) 7799 As stated by Bureau Veritas, the BS7799 standard "addresses information security from the management point of view." While the BS7799 does contain technical information, the standard is not technical in nature. Management policies and procedures are counted upon to protect the organization from threats to its assets. In 1998, BS7799-2 was produced to promote requirements surrounding an "information security management system" and to promote certification against the standard. Version 2 of the standard was revised on May 15, 1999, and amended again in January 2001. In order to align the standard with ISO9001:2000 and ISO14001:1996, the standard was updated again on September 5, 2002. The BS7799-2 2002 is the current version being used for certification of an organization. This standard, as well as the ISO 17799, will be discussed in a subsequent section in this chapter.

ISO 17799 ISO 17799 is based upon the BS7799. The first version of ISO 17799 was published and adopted in December 2000. ISO 17799 is a code of practice standard for information security management that encompasses industry best practices in security through the adoption of a comprehensive set of controls. It is important to note that not all controls listed in the code of practice will be used by every organization. It also states that further guidance may be needed when aligning the organization's security practices to best practices in the field. That is why it is really a guideline until adapted and adopted by an organization as the standard.

ISO 17799 is broken into several categories for consideration:

- Scope of the recommendations for information security management within the standard
- Terms and definitions
- Security Policy
- Organizational Security
- Asset Classification and Control
- Personnel Security
- Physical and Environmental Security
- Communications and Operations Management

- Access Control
- Systems Development and Maintenance
- Business Continuity Management
- Compliance

Sections 3-12 of the standard contain significant additional information relative to controls surrounding people, process, data, technology and facilities. A full version of the standard can be obtained from the British Standards Institution (BSI; www.bsi-global.com) or from Bureau Veritas (www.bureauveritas.com).

IPSEC IPSEC is a network protocol standard. The Internet Engineering Task Force (IETF) updated this standard in 1997 and 1998. It addresses security at the Internet Protocol (IP) layer of the network model. Its key goals are authentication and encryption. Components include the IP Authentication Header (AH) and the Encapsulating Security Payload (ESP). Both provide mechanisms for access control. Key management is accomplished using ISAKMP.

TEMPEST TEMPEST is an electromagnetic shielding standard established by the U. S. Department of the Defense. It could use fiber to shield transmission lines, but that is only a small part of the shielding process. It is still in effect and utilized. More information can be obtained from governmental sources.

Security Administration: Security Control Architecture

What Is a Security Control Architecture? A security control architecture is best described as an architecture that is created, implemented, maintained, monitored, and enforced to ensure information systems are protected as stipulated in an organization's policy base. Equally important is protecting that information at the appropriate confidentiality, integrity and availability levels that meet with the functionality of the organization and the sensitivity/criticality of the data. The following are models present in the security space that assist the organization with the creation of a proper security architecture.

Bell–LaPadula Bell–LaPadula is a "confidentiality model." Bell–LaPadula applies only to confidentiality of information and identifies paths that could lead to inappropriate disclosure.

The concept of "secure state" is defined within the model. Secure state refers to the use of access modes and assignment of "subjects to objects," as such assignment meets the objectives of the organization's security policy. It also defines modes of access and provides prescriptions for the assignment of access to objects within the organization. Modes of access used in this model include read only, read/write and write only. The simple security conditions of this model surround a subject's ability to "read up." That is, a user with a set access level cannot read higher, as no access has been provided at that level. Likewise, a user is not allowed to write lower, as it might be possible to reveal "secret information" (see confidentiality) to users at that lower level. This property is called the "star property." The "strong star property" dictates that users may only read and write at their access level. Mandatory access control in TCSEC is based on the Bell–LaPadula model.

Biba Integrity Model The Biba Integrity Model was the first to address integrity in computer systems. The model is based upon a "hierarchical lattice" of integrity levels. The model's implementation is the "opposite" of the Bell–LaPadula confidentiality model.

The goal of the model is to prevent unauthorized users from making modifications to data. With that goal in mind, the model forbids reading lower (i.e., the reading of objects with "less integrity") and writing higher, which may affect the integrity of the objects at that level. So, the strict integrity policy states that a user cannot "observe" objects of lesser integrity. The star property for integrity stipulates the prohibition for writing to objects of higher integrity. An additional property in the integrity model is the "invocation property." That is, a user cannot make a logical request for service to a subject of higher integrity. This prohibition drives to the heart of preservation of accuracy.

Clark–Wilson Model Another integrity model, the Clark–Wilson model is the first to address all three integrity goals:

- Prevent unauthorized users from making modifications
- Prevent authorized users from making improper modifications
- Maintain internal and external consistency

The model does this through "well-formed" transactions; that is, it ensures internal consistency and allows users to work with data in ways that promotes this internal consistency. It does so by enforcing the "access triple." A program "middleman" ensures that a subject (the user) cannot directly access the object. This process is achieved through subject-to-program and program-to-object binding. This access triple enforces the first integrity goal as well as separation of duties. Separation of duties enforces the second integrity goal.

Non-Interference Model The non-interference model is promoted through segregation; that is, organizations create separate environments (domains) for authorized users so that they cannot interfere in each other's operations, in violation of the organization's security policy.

Access Control Matrix The access control matrix is a two dimensional matrix for a discretionary access control environment which details the approved mode of access for its users. An access control matrix is created that

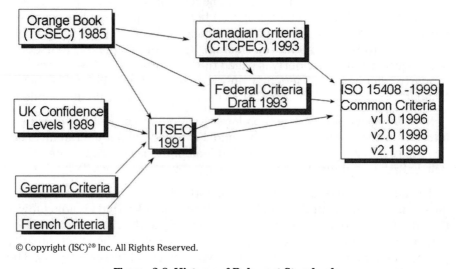

Figure 2.8 History of Relevant Standards

matches users to resources in the organization. This method has proven to be a simple way to start an investigation for covert channels within the organization.

Information Flow Model The information flow model elaborates how information can flow from one object to another. This is a variation of the access matrix model. Information flow is limited based upon the object's security properties (sensitivity). Like the access control matrix , the information flow model assists with covert channel analysis.

Evaluation Criteria

Trusted Computer System Evaluation Criteria

Developed under the auspices of the U.S. Department of Defense, the TCSEC has been used by the federal government to "rate" the security properties of a system or computer product. The current version is dated September 26, 1985 (DOD 5200.28-STD). The TCSEC is also referenced as the "Orange Book." It was developed in the early 1980s and only addressed the issue of confidentiality Additional "booklets" are available for other purposes, such as securing office automation, and are also referred to by color. The publications are collectively referred to as the "Rainbow series."

Goal of TCSEC The main goal for the creation, implementation, and maintenance of the TCSEC was to provide an organization a measurable baseline from which to declare "trust" in the security of automation within the organization. It also serves to provide guidance for vendors with regard to their provisions for security within their products.

TCSEC Classes of Trust TCSEC offers a "rating system" (classes of trust) to apply to the organization's information systems. The system is detailed below, from least protected to most protected.

- Division D — Minimal protection
- Division C — Discretionary protection
- Class C1 — Discretionary Security Protection. Minimum requirements for C1 include:
  - Documentation
  - A security user's manual, which includes privileges for use and their accompanying functions
  - Trusted Facilities manual, indicating appropriate control of facilities
  - Test plans and results
  - Design documentation, including the protection philosophy of the organization
- Class C2 — Controlled access protection. All the requirements for C1 apply, with the following in addition:
  - Object reuse protection (protection against reuse of storage objects)
  - Added protection for authorization and audit data (i.e., protected audit trail)
  - Division B: Mandatory Protection: As opposed to the discretionary access control aligned with C-level ratings, the B-level ratings impose mandatory controls
- Class B1 — Labeled security protection: All protections listed in C2 are required, along with the following additional protections:
  - Mandatory access control and access labeling of all subjects and objects (see Bell–LaPadula)
  - Data sensitivity label checking (i.e., label integrity)
  - Auditing of labeled objects
  - Mandatory access control for all operations
  - Process isolation in system architecture
  - Design specification and verification
- Class B2 — Structured Protection: All the requirements for a B1 rating are also required for B2, with the following additions:
  - Program sensitivity labels
  - Hierarchical device labels
  - Trusted path communications between the user and system (log on and authentication)
  - Separate operator and administrator functions
  - Covert channel analysis
- Class B3 — Security Domains: All the requirements for a B2 rating are also required for B3, with the following additions:

— More granularity surrounding security implementation
— Notify security after aggregation of auditable events
— Define the role of security administrator
— Recover from system or product failure without jeopardizing protection.
— Documented procedures to ensure systems and products start and achieve the secure state
— Division A: Verified protection
• Class A1 — Verified design: All the requirements for a B3 rating are also required for A1, with the following additions:
— Formalized protection and evaluation methods are required, as well as definitive proof of the integrity of TCB

The security categories delineated by the Department of Defense, above, are based upon the Trusted Computer Base (TCB). TCSEC 1983 defines the TCB as "the totality of protection mechanisms within a computer system, including hardware, firmware, and software, the combination of which is responsible for enforcing a security policy."

Information Technology Evaluation Criteria (ITSEC) ITSEC was published by The United Kingdom, the Netherlands, Germany, and France in May of 1990, based on the Orange Book and existing standards within the countries. It addressed confidentiality, integrity, and availability. Version 1.2 was published in June 1991, after vetting the completed standard to t he international community, by the Commission of the European Communities. ITSEC is used for the purpose of valuation of systems and product security. Evaluation is IT security intensive and results in holistic function and penetration testing. An agreed-upon security target serves as the baseline for assurance that a product or system meets the requisite security specification.

Security Target A Security Target is set of prescriptions that provide the baseline for evaluation of a product or system. They must be critically reviewed and determined to represent an appropriate baseline for evaluation; as such, they must be complete, accurate, and consistent. In addition to containing information on the standard against which the product or system will be assessed, it also includes a description of the security goals, as well as the potential threats, present within the organization. Prescriptions include:

• Presence of a system security policy
• Formalized, required security enforcing functions
• Optional required security mechanisms
• Claimed rating of minimum strength

Target of Evaluation (TOE) The TOE is simply the system to be evaluated. Note that in this definition, a "system" includes the people and documentation associated with it. It is also important to note that components of a system may be evaluated in lieu of a full system review. This could include evaluation of an operating system, a database, a combination of software, and the requisite hardware for its operation, and so on.

Comparison of ITSEC to TCSEC As in the TCSEC, the ITSEC classes are hierarchical; that is, each class adds additional requirements to the class prior to it. The specific functionality and mechanisms of the ITSEC are designed to correspond to the TCSEC classes of trust. The ITSEC functional classes correspond to the TCSEC classes of trust as follows:

- F-C1, E1 = C1
- F-C2, E2 = C2
- F-B1, E3 = B1
- F-B2, E4 = B2
- F-B3, E5 = B3
- F-B3, E6 = A1

Other ITSEC functionality classes exist that provide prescriptions for high integrity, high availability, high data integrity, high data confidentiality and high demand network transport confidentiality and integrity aspects.

ITSEC Assurance Classes ITSEC operates through the use of "assurance classes." Much like the TCSEC, the ITSEC assurance classes are ascending class rankings that reflect the level of confidence (i.e., assurance) that can be place in the target of evaluation's security functionality. Each class also points to the rigor with which the evaluation is conducted.

The ITSEC Assurance Classes are detailed below.

- E0 — Inadequate assurance is present (failed to meet E1).
- E1 — A security target and informal description of the target of evaluation's architectural design must be produced. Functional testing satisfies the target.
- E2 — In addition to E1 requirements, an informal description of the detailed design and test documentation must be produced. There must also be an approved distribution procedure and configuration control present.
- E3 — In addition to E2 requirements, source code or hardware drawings must be produced. Evidence of testing of security mechanisms must also be produced.
- E4 — In addition to E3 requirements, a formal model of the security policy and a semiformal specification of security enforcing functions, architecture and design must be produced.
- E5 — In addition to E4 requirements, the detailed architectural design shows close correlation to the source code and drawings.
- E6 — In addition to the E5 requirements, a formal description of the architecture and the security enforcing functions is to be produced; these must be consistent with the security policy model produced in E4.

	Consumers	Developers	Evaluators
Part 1	Use for background information and reference purposes. Guidance structure for PPs.	Use for background information and reference for the development of requirements and formulating security specifications for TOEs	Use for background information and reference purposes. Guidance structure for PPs and STs

Figure 2.9 Roadmap to the Common Criteria

Common Criteria: ISO 15408 The Common Criteria Version 2 (CC) is the culmination of the aggregation of standards from the United States (TCSEC, "Orange Book"), Canada (Canadian Trusted Computer Product Evaluation Criteria (1993)), and Europe (ITSEC), the purpose of which is to provide a unified prescription for the conducting appropriate and meaningful security product evaluation activities. The Common Criteria is composed of numerous security functional requirements that the approving bodies believe represent the current best practice for trusted products and systems. The actual security assessment considers these requirements to develop a protection profile for the target of evaluation. In addition, an appropriate security target, to be used for comparisons, can also be developed from these requirements. If the assessment is being conducted to evaluate more specialized aspects of the target system, the requirements can be combined to facilitate. Much like the ITSEC, the Common Criteria evaluation is conducted by creating comparisons against standard assurance levels, termed "Evaluation Assurance Levels (EAL0 to EAL7)." Like the TCSEC and ITSEC, the Common Criteria assurance levels are ascending class rankings that reflect the level of confidence (i.e., assurance) that can be place in the target of evaluation's security functionality. Each level also points to the rigor with which the evaluation is conducted.

A roadmap for the Common Criteria is presented Figure 2.9 (part 1), Figure 2.10 (part 2), and Figure 2.11 (part 3). The relationships among the components of the Common Criteria, and their use in evaluation, are diagrammed in Figure 2.12 and Figure 2.13.

	Consumers	Developers	Evaluators
Part 2	Use for guidance and reference when formulating statements of requirements for security functions	Use for reference when interpreting statements of functional requirements and formulating functional specifications for TOEs	Use as mandatory statement of evaluation criteria when determining whether a TOE effectively meets claimed security functions.

Figure 2.10 Roadmap to the Common Criteria (part 2)

Security Best Practices Implementation

Basic Security Mechanisms

Least Privilege The concept of least privilege dictates that personnel are only given the minimum necessary access rights and permissions to complete their required job functions. Least privilege is one of the guiding tenets of information security.

	Consumers	Developers	Evaluators
Part 3	Use for guidance when determining required level of assurance.	Use for reference when interpreting statements of assurance requirements and determining assurance approaches of TOEs	Use as mandatory statement of evaluation criteria when determining the assurance of TOEs and when evaluating PPs and STs

Figure 2.11 Roadmap to the Common Criteria (part 3)

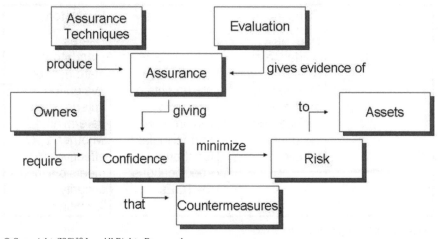

Figure 2.12 Common Criteria Evaluation Relationships

Separation of Duties Separation of duties may best be described as denying the opportunity for one individual to "hold all the keys to the kingdom." That is, separation of duties ensures that one person is not responsible for initiating and authorizing a sensitive transaction. Consider the example of initiating and authorizing a payment. If there were no separation of duties between these two functions, an individual could potentially both initiate and approve a payment to him or herself. This places an organization's assets in jeopardy for fraud. Control for this situation can be implemented by either enforcing the fact that an initiator cannot also be an authorizer of the same transaction (i.e., tied to role, which is an example of "dynamic" separation of duties) or by ensuring that initiators and not also authorizers in *any case* (i.e., an example of "static" separation of duties).

Rotation of Duties Rotation is a way to provide both cross-training for employees or contractors, and to also allow for following up or verifying the employee's or contractor's actions relative to the handling of the organization's assets. Rotation is usually based on a role, a time frame, or both. Rotation of duties can also be used to break up collusion designed to avoid the security objectives of separation of duties.

Mandatory Vacation Another mechanism that can be used by the organization to verify and validate employer or contractor activities is to ensure that all individuals within an organization be required to take a mandatory vacation of one week or longer. This allows for another employee or contractor within the organization to perform the vacationing employee's job duties and to potentially verify work performed by this individual and detect potential fraud.

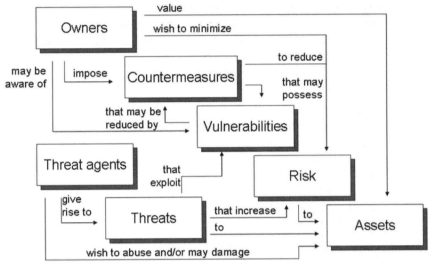

Figure 2.13 Common Criteria Evaluation Relationships (continued)

Sample Questions

1. What is "integrity?"
   a. The assurance that data stored, processed and transmitted has not been modified or destroyed in an inappropriate manner, either inadvertently or maliciously, from its original and correct state
   b. The assurance that resources can be successfully accessed by authorized users when they are needed
   c. The assurance that data is kept private, restricted only to authorized individuals
   d. None of the above

2. What is the A-I-C Triad?
   a. The security triad
   b. The risk management triad
   c. The infrastructure triad
   d. All of the above

3. What is least privilege?
   a. Access to all an organization's resources
   b. Access to sensitive resources only
   c. Access to those resources required to perform a job function
   d. All of the above
   e. A and B only
   f. B and C only

4. How can least privilege be maintained?
   a. By verifying a user's role in the organization
   b. By verifying the minimal set of data that is required for successful completion of tasks for this role
   c. By verifying the data's location
   d. All of the above

5. What is "accountability?"
   a. Evaluation of the rights minimally necessary to perform required business functions
   b. The ability to tie an activity to the individual or system that initiated it, with 100% certainty
   c. The granting of permissions, by a data owner, and the enforcement of those permissions
   d. None of the above

6. What does a risk assessment evaluate?
   a. Threats
   b. Errors
   c. Vulnerabilities
   d. A and B only
   e. B and C only
   f. A and C only
   g. All of the above

7. What are the types of risk assessment?
   a. Qualitative
   b. Quantitative
   c. Hybrid (both qualitative and quantitative)
   d. All of the above

8. How can an organization address risk?
   a. Transfer
   b. Accept
   c. Avoid
   d. Mitigate
   e. All of the above

9. Software development models include:
   a. The Waterfall Method
   b. The Scientific Method
   c. The Microsoft Method
   d. None of the above

10. Spiral Model steps include:
    a. Review and edit

    b. Risk management
    c. Engineering and production
    d. None of the above

11. ISO 17799 represents:
    a. A standard for security risk assessment
    b. A standard for information security management systems
    c. A code of practice for information security
    d. All of the above

12. Bell–LaPadula is an example of a:
    a. Security model
    b. Confidentiality model
    c. Authentication model
    d. Authorization model

13. TCSEC is also referenced as:
    a. The Yellow Book
    b. The Purple Book
    c. The Blue Book
    d. The Orange Book

14. Services provided by the operating system include:
    a. Error detection
    b. Controlled access to files
    c. Accounting functions
    d. All of the above
    e. None of the above

15. The data classification for the most sensitive of data within an organization is labeled:
    a. Confidential
    b. Internal Use Only
    c. Restricted
    d. Public
    e. None of the above

Domain 3
Analysis and Monitoring

Eric Waxvik

Analysis and monitoring play key roles in the security life cycle. Without an analysis, one can neither determine whether *policies* are correct and cover an organization's range of needs, nor whether *procedures* are correct (and if they are, are they being followed properly? Are the organization's network and authentication systems designed correctly and functioning properly? Is the incident response team properly trained and following procedures?)

This chapter explains what an analysis by audit is and why we need one, how to conduct an audit, various levels of testing, and the important aspects of monitoring.

Section 1: Security Auditing

Security Auditing Overview

This chapter addresses the issues IT security practitioners must prepare to face regarding audits of the organization's security framework (whether performed by internal or external parties). The security framework, discussed in detail in the next section, is comprised of the policies that govern organizational security as well as the tactical controls (standards, procedures, baselines, and guidelines) put in place to carry out and support the policies.

The main question answered in this section is: "What do auditors check for, and why, when performing IT security assurance services for an organization?"

By understanding these issues, the IT security practitioner can be proactive in improving and maintaining system security so as to not only pass audits, but more importantly, to safeguard the systems and data for which the IT security practitioner is responsible. IT security practitioners should aim to see past the audit itself and do the best possible day-to-day job of preparing their systems for maximum confidentiality, integrity, and availability.

At a high level, auditors check for the following:

- The existence of sound security policies appropriate for their business or activity
- The existence of controls supporting the policies
- The effective implementation and upkeep of the controls

IT security practitioners are advised to know the benchmark standard to which they will be held accountable.

What Are Security Audits? A security audit is an organized, independent technical assessment that measures how well an organization employs strategic security policies and tactical security controls for the purpose of protecting its information assets. Audits may also be part of a regulatory control by government or oversight organization or be part of a certification for a partnership program.

Activities performed by auditors seek to establish assurance that the organization has identified and managed all risks through the implementation of controls and other assurance mechanisms. Trust, or assurance, is gained when the management of an organization is confident that the controls are effective to mitigate risk to acceptable levels. This means that the systems supporting a security framework are in place and working properly. Auditing is a comprehensive process that can cover a very large or very small scope. Because it is a snapshot in time, audit studies can be used to gauge either the progress or the decline of an organization's security profile over time by comparing similar audits.

Auditors can audit the effectiveness of many technology solutions:

- High-level security policy
- Security standards effectiveness
- Processes and procedures
- Application security
- Firewalls
- Anti-virus software
- Password policies
- Intrusion detection and event monitoring systems
- System hardening policies
- Access control
- Change control processes for configuration management
- Media protection (backup tape storage)
- Cryptographic controls
- Contingency planning
- Hardware and software maintenance
- Physical security

Why Are Security Audits Performed? Audits are performed for the following reasons:

- Iterative policy improvement — an audit plays a key role in policy improvement. The process is to create a policy, implement the policy, audit effectiveness of the policy, and rework policy (audits do not make or implement policy and most auditors would be very hesitant to be too involved in this, as it would impair their independence; it would be better stated that audits may initiate policy improvements or are part of the natural policy life-cycle). That is not to say audits cannot comment on why they reported what they found, the way they found it, and give an example of something different — it is a fine line for the auditor to walk.
- Policy adherence — an audit will help to verify adherence to or variance from organizational security policies which are written to mandate organizational asset protection.
- Policy effectiveness — the fact that an organization has a security policy does not mean that it is necessarily comprehensive or effective. The effectiveness should focus on whether the control addresses the associated risk. The control is effective when it reduces the risk to an acceptable level without impeding business operations unnecessarily. Auditors must address gaps in policy because an effective policy must also address all of the issues and potential issues. An auditor should be able to highlight those gaps in policy.
- Regulation adherence — verifies adherence to mandated governmental laws and regulations that may apply to an organization's situation.
- Mitigation ranking — an audit is used to rank systems based on the seriousness of identified vulnerabilities and system criticality for the purpose of providing an overall ranking of their importance for mitigation activities. Highly ranked mitigation candidates are often a result of mission critical systems that have high vulnerabilities. Systems that have vulnerabilities that are a lower potential impact and are not as critical to mission and operation of an organization will probably be ranked lower in the mitigation system rankings.
- Corporate merger or takeover — an audit would be used to understand the status of the infrastructure, to ensure the organizations are compatible or are as described in documentation.
- After-action — an audit can also be used to find out what steps were missed and why and how to fix them.

Security policies should be pursuant to supporting the principles of due care, that is, taking prudent steps to protect the organization from anticipated events that could lead to compromise of confidentiality, integrity, and/or availability. Audits, therefore, are performed to demonstrate the following:

- Managerial due care responsibility — has management taken all of the actions and performed due diligence for the organization? Hiring one person to be the security department of a large multinational organization might not be considered due diligence.
- Corporate accountability — has the corporation or organization put in place the guidelines and standards necessary?
- Individual accountability — has each person in the structure done his job and kept up with the standards and policies required by his job description?

Defining the Audit Benchmark Auditors determine whether systems are compliant to a standard defined by the organization, as well as the adequacy of that standard. Without a standard, auditing would become too subjective, and issues deemed important to one group of auditors may be overlooked by other auditors (depending on the methodology they use to perform the audit). There will always be a need for a special review or audit so this benchmark attempts to give a more consistent baseline.

Audit methodologies might use one of the following certification guidelines (which are discussed in the next section):

- British Standard BS 7799-2:2002
- NIST SP 800-37 (still in draft form), "Guidelines for the Security Certification and Accreditation of Federal Information Technology Systems," which can be retrofitted for private industry
- Cobit (Control Objectives for Information and related Technology) TM from the Information Systems Audit and Control Association (ISACA) TM
- An amalgam of these guidelines
- Another guideline deemed appropriate – borrowed from other corporations or Web sites
- A process developed in-house

Note that ISO 17799 is not a standard against which one can certify a security framework. This is discussed more extensively in the next section.

While people may discuss the merits of one standard or another, it is more important to have a baseline for your audit that accomplishes your objectives.

Audit Participant's Role Auditors and IT security practitioners are participants in audits. Auditors ask questions and collect information. IT personnel may assist in the collection and interpretation of this information because they know their systems best. While using the IT personnel maybe helpful, they also might be the reason for the audit. It is always important for the auditor to examine why the audit is taking place. Later, the data is analyzed and compared to good practice standards.

An auditor of IT security systems has several principle responsibilities, including:

- Providing independent assurance to management that security systems are effective
- Analyzing the appropriateness of organizational security objectives
- Analyzing the appropriateness of policies, standards, baselines, procedures, and guidelines that support security objectives
- Analyzing the effectiveness of the controls that support security policies
- Stating and explaining the scope of the systems to be audited
- Limiting the audit (in some cases) if the act of the audit will affect critical applications or business

IT security practitioners are often called upon to directly interface with auditors. Security practitioners collect system information for the purpose of gauging compliance with the chosen standard, baseline, and procedures.

Auditors are not the enemy. By maintaining a professional relationship with them you can learn what is important to them and hopefully they can learn from you as well. This type of two-way professional relationship contributes to a more secure organization. Keep in mind that auditors often have access to high-level management and can help you bring previously ignored, pressing problems to the foreground. Auditors can back up the opinions of front line IT personnel so that budget funds can be allocated and action taken.

Defining the Audit Scope One way to define the scope of an audit is to break it down into seven domains of security responsibility; that is, to break up the IT systems into manageable areas upon which audits may be based.

These seven domains are:

- User Domain — the users themselves and their authentication methods
- Workstation Domain — often considered the end user systems
- System/Application Domain — applications that you run on your network, such as e-mail, database, and Web applications
- LAN Domain — equipment required to create the internal LAN
- LAN-to-WAN Domain — The transition area between your firewall and the WAN, often where your DMZ resides
- WAN Domain — usually defined as things outside of your firewall
- Remote Access Domain — how remote or traveling users access your network

The scope of the system to be audited, including the following procedures, defines how large the audit will be:

- Analyzing critical servers for vulnerabilities, including unapplied patches and unnecessary services within the LAN Domain
- Analyzing external Internet servers for vulnerabilities using vulnerability assessment testing techniques
- Analyzing firewalls for unnecessary services and misconfiguration in comparison to the security policy in the LAN-to-WAN Domain
- Reviewing the business continuity plan for one or more domains
- Comparing high-level security policy against industry good practice
- Analyzing the access controls on key business systems in the System/Application Domain
- Analyzing applications (like Web servers) in the System/Application Domain for tightness of controls
- Analyzing remote access systems for 2-factor authentication effectiveness in the Remote Access Domain

The audit scope will define a boundary to the audit, such as whether interconnected systems will be reviewed or whether this audit will be detailed and thorough or high level. The scope will be subject to change if an immediate, serious vulnerability is detected.

Defining the Audit Plan Projects require planning; otherwise, valuable time and resources are wasted. An audit plan is no different. Therefore, when approaching and planning an audit, make sure you know the steps involved.

The following list details some of these steps to consider when formulating a plan:

- Understand the scope — an auditor should know what he is being asked to audit and how long he has to perform the audit.
- Understand the intended results — an auditor needs to know the overall goal of the audit.
- Understand the personnel resources — an auditor will need to know which personnel on his own team and on the organization being audited will be involved. These people help gather and synthesize information and move the audit along.
- Review previous audits — an auditor may wish to review previous similar audit results to become familiar with past issues. Some auditors, however, may not want to be prejudiced by previous conclusions.
- Conduct a site survey — an auditor will want to understand the environment and the interconnections with other systems.
- Review documentation — an auditor will want to review system documentation and configurations.
- Review host logs — an auditor may ask to examine system logs.
- Review incident logs — an auditor may ask to review security incident logs to get a feel for problem trends.
- Review risk analysis output — an auditor will want to understand sys-

tem criticality ratings that are a product of risk analysis studies. This helps rank systems for mitigation in the reporting phase.

- Review policy — an auditor will want to understand the policies that pertain to a system.
- Review how are systems updated.
- Review the change control process.
- Review how the organization allows access.
- Review how data is classified.
- Perform hands-on analysis — an auditor may want to review the system to see first hand how it is setup. Or perform a vulnerability analysis scan on the network and/or host components with specialized software tools to gain that perspective as well.
- Gather information — one form is questionnaires — an auditor may want to construct questionnaires that query individuals in the IT organization about how they perform their jobs.

Audit Data Collection Methods Audit data collection methods include:

- Questionnaires — questionnaires provide insight into attitudes and processes performed by IT personnel.
- Interviews — interviews are a chance to initiate face-to-face dialogue with stakeholders, system owners, and system operators.
- Observation — observation of processes can provide insight into operations.
- Checklists — checklists allow for orderly and thorough collection of audit data.
- Reviewing documentation — documentation, if it exists (and is a copy off-site) provides insight as to why a system is set up the way it is. Outdated or poorly written documentation is often a sign of risk to a system.
- Reviewing configurations — configurations provide raw information about how software components are interlinked to form the system.
- Reviewing policy — reviewing policy is a way to discover how the organization deploys technology and provides a written record to which industry "good" practices can be compared. Policy must also be aligned with the strategic business mission of the organization.
- Performing security testing (vulnerability analysis) — security testing, as described later, allows for the collection of potential vulnerability information.
- Review your disaster recovery procedures for both physical and network based events.

Post Audit Activities

- Exit Interviews — After an audit is performed, an exit interview will alert personnel to glaring issues they need to be concerned about immediately. Besides these preliminary alerts, an auditor should avoid giving detailed verbal assessments, which may falsely set the expectation level of the organization with regard to security preparedness in the audited scope.

- Analyze Data — An auditor will likely perform data analysis and synthesis away from the organizational site. This stage allows the auditor to review everything learned and present her observations in a standard reporting format.
- Produce Audit Findings — An auditor will produce audit findings for presentation to the organization.
- Findings are often listed by level of compliance to the standard benchmark.
- The comparison of audit findings to stated policy or industry "good" practices produces a picture of what must be improved.
- Often findings include recommendations for mitigation or correction of documented risks or instances of noncompliance based upon system criticality.
- An audit report often begins with an executive summary followed by detailed information.
- Present audit findings — Audit findings and the audit report are often presented to management. The findings may lead to mitigation activities based on an available budget.

Security Framework

An organizational Security Framework is often based upon international and national standards and guidelines. Organizations often take these guidelines and create standards specific to their situation. A well-implemented framework forms the basis for a secure state. An organization can be said to be in a secure state when it is conforming to its stated policy.

An organization's security framework is comprised of the following:

- Organizational policies delineate the role of security in the organization. It is a formal statement by top-level management that security is important to the organization and its related activities will be supported financially and otherwise. They are often broad and will describe how a security framework will work within the organization, what individuals or groups within the organization will have responsibility for it, how the policies will be enforced, how they will be checked for compliance, and define the ramifications for noncompliance.
- The development of functional policies that succinctly describe how organizational assets are to be used and protected.
  — Functional issue-centric (acceptable use, e-mail use, remote access, extranet connection, etc.) — Functional issue-centric policies usually deal with the security of processes or activities. For example, an acceptable use policy will state that the Internet is to be used for

business during business hours and that visiting Web sites for political activism, gambling, violence, pornography, etc. is not allowed.

—Functional system-centric (anti-virus, server building procedure, firewall rules, IDS monitoring, etc.) — Functional system-centric policies usually deal with technology controls like, for example, how intrusion detection and firewalls are to be deployed, how access control is to be applied to hosts, what access controls should be placed on key network resources, how anti-virus is to be deployed and kept up to date, etc.

- The development of the supporting mechanisms to support the policies
    - Standards — Standards are compulsory component technologies (specific hardware and software products deployed in certain ways) to be used. They may define server, router, firewall, anti-virus software manufactures, and operating system versions based on what that system will be used for.
    - Baselines — Baselines define minimum required parameters to achieve a consistent security level for a system or business process. For example, a policy may define the anti-virus baseline to be, "the business unit shall update anti-virus definitions on file servers every Monday and Thursday." They may define how standard goods should be deployed and kept up to date.
    - Procedures — Procedures define actions to implement standards and baselines. They are step-by-step definitions of how to implement security technologies in the environment. For example, how the firewall is to be configured, how security desk check-in procedures should operate, how tape backups must occur.
    - Guidelines — Guidelines are recommendations for improving security; however, policy does not define them as being required, leaving implementation and interpretation up to the organization. For example, a policy may define a good anti-virus guideline to be "the business unit should check for new anti-virus definitions on a daily basis and install them if available." This implies that they are not required to do this but that it is a good idea. The baseline (see above) defines compulsory updates on Mondays and Thursdays.

Why Have a Security Framework? Organizations have a responsibility to exercise "due care" in their daily operations. When they do not exercise due care, they can be liable for negligence. There is also the potential for legal action and criminal and/or financial penalties.

Due care includes the following descriptors:

- The organization takes risk reduction seriously and takes responsibility for it.
- The organization is proactive about reducing risk to employees.

- The organization is proactive about reducing risk to organizational assets.
- The organization periodically tests its risk reduction processes through auditing.

Developing and maintaining an effective security framework reduces risk and demonstrates due care.

Security Framework Guidelines and Standards The terms "standard" and "guideline" are often used loosely and interchangeably. This is incorrect and it is important to know the difference.

Earlier we defined a security standard to be something that succinctly specifies compulsory component technologies used for security. We then defined guidelines as suggested yet nonrequired security practices. Both of these definitions are in the context of how an organization builds a security framework. Keeping that thought in mind, recognize that the terms "standard" and "guideline" are also often used in the context of practices defined to ensure compliance with a set of rules as defined by a standards body or regulatory body. For example, ISO 9001 is an international "standard" for quality from a recognized standards body (the International Organization for Standards) and some organizations engineer their internal processes to comply with this standard.

This being said, you should recognize that a security standard ("you must use brand XYZ intrusion detection system") is different from a policy development organization standard which attempts to encompass many facets of important issues. Organizations will often incorporate the security guidelines and standards published by policy development organizations (or regulatory bodies that dictate requirements) for the purpose of standardizing their security framework to harmonize with "accepted" or required practices. Good security practice from policy organizations varies widely from *general advice* on how to implement secure systems (guidelines) to *compulsory requirements* against which systems may be certified (standards).

Unlike ISO 9001, a widely accepted quality standard, there currently is no international consensus as to which security "standard" is *the* security standard. As a result, organizations use various standards as will be covered later. The standard that is used as a template is often a matter of preference. The system audit activity is performed to compare an organization's defined policy to the actual system state. It should be performed against a chosen standard to identify where systems are deficient. It is not uncommon to find organizations that modify published standards and guidelines for their own purposes and audit against that definition. Often one of the roles of an IT security practitioner is to ensure that system components adhere to the organization's chosen standard. The main idea behind meeting a standard is that your organization has demonstrated a level of assurance that its systems are secure, thus management and other organizations may take confidence in them.

Policy organizations and regulatory bodies publish a wide variety of standards and guidelines and are often criticized for making broad statements but imparting little detail about how to accomplish the requirement. Policy development organizations may issue the following to convey a best practice:

- Technical reports — often seen as suggested guidelines for secure systems and might be broadly interpreted. For example, the ISO reports (Guidelines for the Management of IT Security) are just that — reports (not standards). They are suggested guidelines.
- Technical standards — a standard includes required (compulsory) items. If you do not meet the requirements, then you do not meet the standard.

Policy Organization Guidelines Guidelines for good security practice come from several organizations and are often adapted by other organizations to form their own security frameworks. They include the following:

- International Organization for Standards
  — ISO 17799 (now 27001) — A high-level security guideline (often referred to as a standard) not meant for the certification of systems but for high-level security framework assistance. It was passed as a standard late in 2000 (based on British Standard 7799-1). It is a management standard that deals with an examination of the non-technical issues relating to installed security systems within organizations.
  — ISO GMITS — A five-part technical report guideline currently in revision that discusses many facets of security frameworks.
- Governmental Bodies
- British Standards Institute
  — BS 7799 Part 1 — A high-level checklist oriented security guideline
  — BS 7799 Part 2:2002 — A standard against which a system may be certified because it uses a lot of "the organization shall do...," words. It has fewer implementation suggestions than Part 1. An organization may be accredited as complying with the BS7799-2.
  — U.S. National Institute for Standards and Technology.
  — NIST special publications 800-12, 800-14, 800-26, 800-30, 800-37, and others provide a wealth of strategic and tactical information for developing, running, and certifying security frameworks.
- Audit Organizations
  — Information Systems Audit and Control Association (ISACA).™
  — Developers of Control Objectives for Information and Related Technology (COBIT)™ — generally applicable and accepted standards for good IT security and control practices. Their goal is to provide

a reference framework for management, users, IT auditors, and IT security practitioners.

- Professional Organizations
  - American National Standards Institute (ANSI) — U.S. liaison committees to ISO committees.
  - Technical Committee T4 participates in the standardization of generic methods for information technology security.
  - Information Systems Security Association (ISSA).
- The generally accepted information security principles (GAISP), when completed, aim to be a comprehensive hierarchy of guidance to provide a globally consistent, practical framework for information security. It is based on the ISO 17799 framework but adds specific prescriptions about how to meet the high-level objectives while not naming specific products.
- Computer Emergency Response Team (CERT) — A variety of advice on secure computing practices and incident response techniques is offered.

Guideline Summary:

- There are competing guidelines and standards for security. No one guideline or standard leads at this time.
- Oftentimes guidelines are confused for standards and vice versa. Guidelines are suggested ways to do something whereas standards are compulsory.
- If an organization modifies a standard for its own purposes, can others still take confidence in their systems? This is subjective but what is important is that the organization follows reasonable practices. You can always use a required baseline and expand on it versus modifying the required baseline thereby maintaining the integrity of the standard for trust purposes but making sure that it fits your overall needs.
- What is the importance of the guidelines that you are following and why are you following them? There are different standards and guidelines for different ways of doing business.

Security Controls

After the planning and implementation of the security framework (based upon any number of standards and guidelines), IT security practitioners are often the ones responsible for day-to-day operations. If the security framework is executed in an informed way, that is, with comprehensive policies that drive environmentally appropriate baseline security definitions implemented with effective procedures, the system should be in a reasonably secure state.

Periodically auditing the security framework is part of due care and helps ensure that the framework is maintained. Auditing helps to spot what needs to be improved to get back to a more secure state by doing the following:

- Uncovering vulnerabilities
- Uncovering deficient operations
- Uncovering insecure system changes
- Changes due to management influences
- Changes due to technology
- Changes due to business plan or model
- Changes in standards

In the next section, we will show the IT security practitioner what types of issues she may be challenged with by an auditor.

Security Controls Security controls are activities, processes, or technologies that are implemented to reduce the risk of a security event from adversely affecting the organization. Controls fall into three broad categories:

- Administrative Controls — centered on protecting the organization's overall mission and reducing the risk of asset loss. They tend to be fairly high-level ("managerial") in nature. These controls tend to be more process-, procedures-, and goal-oriented.
- Physical Controls — centered on improving operational deficiencies that could be exploited by threat sources. Physical controls are generally carried out by people using well documented procedures. These controls tend to help focus on the physical aspect — what people can touch.
- Technical Controls — centered on reducing risk by implementing specific technologies or technical processes. Technical controls are generally carried out by computers (after being deployed by people) using documented processes and procedures. Technical controls are often referred to as logical controls. These controls tend to focus more on automated systems and processes.

Security controls are the security framework items that are intended to reduce risk for the organization.

Administrative Controls Administrative controls tend to be fairly high-level ("managerial") in nature and do not deal with minute system details. The following are some security management control examples:

- Senior-level security statement, direction, support, and assignment of responsibility
- Conducting risk management activities for the reduction of risk
- Conducting periodic audits of security controls
- Security policies
- The security organization's plans for system security

- Personnel controls like separation of duties, granting and terminating user computer access, background checks, duty rotation
- Business continuity planning in case of disaster
- Incident response policies — detecting, reporting, and responding to incidents
- System documentation and maintenance thereof
- Security awareness training for organizational staff
- Data labeling to control the flow of sensitive data to unauthorized users
- Media disposal including paper and magnetically stored data
- Timely security reporting to allow for knowledge of system activities and to allow for incident response capability

Physical Controls It is important to have good physical controls because most of your IT devices are inherently weak if you have direct physical access to them. Good physical controls are also important for the safety of your personnel, property and your intellectual property. The following are some security operational control examples:

- Physical security including guards, CCTV, alarms, fences, locks
- Environmental security including fire detection, fire suppression, system cooling, emergency power
- Access security including visitor procedures, badges, biometrics, securing data centers, wiring closets
- Mobile system security including laptop locking cables, PDA security, hard drive encryption

Technical Controls Technical controls can reduce risk by implementing specific technologies or technical processes. Technical controls are generally carried out by computers but are implemented and maintained by IT security practitioners.

The following are examples of technical security control:

- Firewalls
- Host intrusion detection
- Network intrusion detection
- Anti-virus (malicious code) detection for workstations and hosts
- Access control lists
- Logging and logging analysis for event alerts
- Standard patch alerting and deployment
- Encryption standards
- Host hardening
- Remote access
- Wireless deployments
- Mobile deployments

Control Checks — Identification and Authorization An audit can provide a way to critique the effectiveness of identification and authorization systems. Sample audit questions include:

- Who approves authorized users and how is access privilege determined?
- How are users identified and authenticated?
- What is the password policy for your systems and how is it enforced?
- Are there controls in place that monitor for unauthorized access attempts?
- Do workstations use password protected screensavers?
- Do remote access systems utilize multifactor authentication in order to more succinctly identify that the person logging on is who they say they are?

Control Checks — User Access Control Access control restricts access of operating system source files, configuration files, and their directories to authorized administrators. Sample audit questions include:

- How is access privilege applied (by user, group, or other method)?
- What is the change control process for granting access? Who approves it? Who performs it? Is there separation of duty?
- Who decides who has access to what and by what method? Is it the creator of the information?
- Who implements the policy?
- Is access privilege periodically revisited by data owners?
- Are decisions for access control documented as they are modified?

Control Checks — Network Access Control (Firewalls and Filtering) Implement firewalls in accordance with organizational standards and baselines. Firewall implementation rules should support policy that defines what types of traffic are allowed and disallowed.

Implement network access control at security domain borders:

- Internet
- Business unit (i.e., marketing, sales, engineering)
- Business partner (extranet)
- Demilitarized Zone (DMZ; the place where customer facing applications are usually kept)

Policy-based network access controls (firewalls coupled with filtering routers) are generally deployed between security domains such that unnecessary services are disallowed from domain A to domain B and from domain B to domain A (inbound and outbound). Often organizations have open rules going outbound which leaves them open to attacks that originate from the inside going out. Thus, be sure to define stringent policy-based rules for outbound traffic too. Packet filtering can assist firewalls by preprocessing and dropping generally disallowed services.

Firewall and Filtering Systems sample audit questions include:

- Does the business unit implement firewalls in accordance with the organizational standard?
- Are firewalls deployed at security domain interfaces such as Internet access points, business partner network interfaces, and internal high-security segments?
- Is packet filtering by routing devices performed at security domain interfaces? Is packet filtering necessary at the routers? Are these actions to be logged? Are they being sent securely to a central processing location?
- Do the firewall rules match the intent of the security policy?
- When rule changes are necessary, what is the nature of the change control process?
- Do firewalls control traffic inbound and outbound?
- Are firewalls periodically tested for vulnerabilities and adherence to policy?
- What mechanism is in place for manufacturer notifications pertaining to patches as they become available?
- Is there a method for collecting and analyzing firewall logging event alerts?
- How are new firewall upgrades/patches tested to ensure security and continuity of operations?

Control Checks — Intrusion Detection and Intrusion Prevention Implement intrusion detection (IDS) or intrusion prevention (IPS) in accordance with organizational standards and baselines. IDS should be designed to alert on disallowed traffic and transactions that are contained within permissible traffic allowed by firewalls or network filters. IPS should be designed to alert and act on disallowed traffic and transactions. See the SSCP Analysis and Monitoring domain section (Security Monitoring) for more information.

IDS and IPS sample audit questions include:

- Is network-based IDS/IPS deployed on key network segments (server segments, segments that receive or send data traffic from one security domain to the next) so as to detect malicious code or inappropriate activity contained within permissible data channels?
- Is host-based IDS deployed on key hosts so as to detect and stop transactions that may compromise the host? Are file integrity processes deployed on key hosts (integrity checking tools)?
- Have the IDS/IPS systems been tuned appropriately for the environment?
- Do the IDS/IPS rules match the intent of the security policy?
- When IDS/IPS changes are necessary, what is the nature of the change control process?

- What mechanism is in place for manufacturer notifications pertaining to patches and signature updates as they become available?
- Is there a method for collecting and analyzing event alerts?
- Is there a method for incident alerts and responding to those incidents?
- Does the IPS fail open?

Control Checks — Host Isolation Implement host isolation in accordance with organizational standards and baselines. Isolation is meant to provide protection for internal systems from hosts that interact with untrusted networks.

Isolate publicly accessible systems sample audit questions include:

- Are publicly accessible systems such as e-mail, Web, and other hosts that service data requests isolated from the Internet as well as your internal networks?
- Do you utilize firewall demilitarized zones (DMZ) to isolate publicly accessible hosts?
- Is your firewall configured to restrict traffic down to only that which is needed for the systems to do their job?
- Do you utilize host-based and network-based IDS for isolated systems?
- Do you scan incoming data to isolated systems for viruses?
- Are unnecessary and insecure services disabled?

Examples of stringent DMZ host communication rules include:

- DMZ Web host accepts TCP port 80 (HTTP) from the Internet. No other incoming ports on TCP or any other protocol are allowed by the firewall.
- DMZ Web host cannot initiate any connections to the Internet but responses to previously initiated sessions are allowed. Web host should never need to initiate connections to the Internet but must be able to respond.
- DMZ Web host can initiate TCP port 1433 (SQL) connections to the trusted network's internal Web data host for the purpose of fetching or putting data originally requested by an Internet user via HTTP.

Additional suggested measures include:

- Implement Host IDS on the hosts — guards against internal processes performing actions that should not be allowed like the Web server process accessing data that it normally should not have access to.
- Implement Network IDS on the DMZ and the trusted network — alerts to network misuse which are attempts to use permissible data channels (in this case, HTTP and SQL) for disallowed activities.

Control Checks — Monitoring Implement monitoring in accordance with organizational standards and baselines. Monitoring should be designed to log information safely to trusted hosts for storage and analysis activities. See the SSCP Analysis and Monitoring domain section entitled "Security Monitoring" for more information.

Trusted paths are also called out-of-band management networks. Trusted paths are often dedicated to management data. For example, a network can be architected to send syslog data from hosts and devices via dedicated network segments to syslog hosts where it is stored, archived, and analyzed.

Secure storage of syslog and other monitoring data is a necessary step in preserving a chain of custody should the data ever be needed for the prosecution of criminal behavior.

Monitoring Systems sample audit questions include:

- Is device monitoring implemented from key devices and hosts via trusted paths?
- Is monitoring data parsed and analyzed for events of concern? How effective are your processes for interpreting large volumes of logging data?
- Is monitoring data securely stored in the event it is needed for forensic analysis and prosecution of offenders?
- Are sensitive log files encrypted as they are recorded?
- Do you verify that logging is still working on a regular basis?

Control Checks — System Hardening "Hardening" systems addresses the fact that many vendors, by default, have liberal or no security rules on default installations.

System hardening sample audit questions include:

- Do you deploy standard hardened configurations?
- Is there a process for hardening systems prior to deployment?
- Have you defined by policy which services are to be offered on various classes of machines with a corresponding procedure that describes how to turn off unnecessary services? Different classes of machines refer to the role that a computer might have, such as Web server, database server, user workstation, user in accounting workstation, R&D workstation.
- Do you have a procedure for tracking what systems have what software?

Control Checks — Unnecessary Services Disabling unnecessary services on firewalls and screen routers refers to closing unnecessary ports. For example, if you do not have an FTP server on an internal segment, disable FTP communications through the firewall. Disabling unnecessary services on servers and workstations refers to deploying systems such that they are not offering services they do not need to offer. For example, if a server does not need to act as a Web server, do not install Web services on it. The more services a host offers, the greater the chance that there will be a vulnerability that needs to be addressed with some sort of configuration changes or patch.

Eliminate unnecessary services sample audit questions include:

- Have unnecessary services been disabled on firewalls and screen routers?
- Have unnecessary services been disabled on servers and workstations?
- Are hosts dedicated to tasks where possible?

Control Checks — Patching System patching is the process of learning about, testing, and applying vendor-supplied "fixes" to operating systems and application software.

System Patching sample audit questions include:

- Do you have a mechanism for learning about system patches as they are released by vendors?
- Do you have a process to evaluate the applicability of patches to your environment?
- Prior to broad deployment, do you test patches on test systems when possible?
- Do you install the updates using a documented plan?
- Do you control patch deployment through a documented changed control process?
- Do you modify your standard hardened configurations to reflect newly available patches?
- After applying patches, do you create new cryptographic checksums or other integrity-checking baseline information for that computer (when this type of HIDS product is used)?

Control Checks — Anti-Virus Anti-virus software is designed to intercept malicious code before it is executed on a system.

Anti-virus controls sample audit questions include:

- Do you implement anti-virus scanning for the following (or other) systems?
- E-mail servers for inbound and outbound mail and attachment scanning
- Workstations
- Servers
- Proxy servers for applet scanning
- Internet gateways
- What is the process for keeping virus signatures up to date?
- Do you configure your anti-virus products to scan on a regular basis?
- Do you store known-good versions of anti-virus tools off line in the event they need to be used to clean infected systems?

- What are your disaster recovery procedures after a machine is suspected of being infected or found to actually be infected?
- Do you check using a second anti-virus program to reduce the chance of missing a bad file? (Overlapping protection)

Control Checks — Encryption Encryption technologies provide a means to ensure data privacy for data that travels over insecure networks or within potentially insecure devices like traveling laptops. Encryption should not be considered unbreakable. Apply encryption technologies commensurate with the value of the data being protected. This means that basic (inexpensive) encryption may be appropriate for data of a lesser value and vice versa. Economy of scale and management expenses may factor into the total cost of the software, making the more expensive software actually cheaper than two disparate solutions.

Encryption controls sample audit questions include:

- Is encryption implemented on systems for the purpose of guarding data that is of high value and sensitive nature?
- Are encryption keys managed in a secure manner?
- Do mobile laptops utilize encrypted hard drives in the event they are stolen?
- Do remote access systems utilize encryption levels effective for the protection of the business asset?

Control Checks — Logging Logs can be collected from a variety of devices. It is important to look at the logs individually for each device to see if some notable activity is happening on that device. This activity may or may not be security related. A machine that has a very high CPU utilization rate may indicate that a faster machine is needed; it might also mean that unauthorized processes are running on that machine, or the machine may be under attack. It is important to look at all the machines logs to determine the cause as well as the necessary steps to resolve the situation.

It is also important to gather the logs from all of the machines on your network and analyze them as a whole. An individual telnet attempt to one machine is not as significant as an attempt to telnet to every machine and IP address on your network. There are several tools on the market today that will help with some of the event correlation. Even vendors of firewalls and IDS solutions are opening up their log viewing tools to allow other vendors' logs to be imported and correlated into their systems. Some of these tools can be significant time savers, but the cost can also be prohibitive to smaller companies.

When gathering data, it is important to collect data from individual hosts on your network. Hosts may include end user devices like PC's and handhelds; they may also include mail, Web, and print servers. It is also important to gather data from your network devices, including routers and switches.

Not all of your network components may be capable of logging, but if they are it is probably a good thing to review. You should correlate these logs with your security appliances and devices; this will help you obtain a more complete picture of what is happening on your network and how you go about addressing it. From our initial example, we can see from the host logs that someone or something is trying to telnet to all of the machines. After looking at the firewall and IDS/IPS logs, we may be able to determine that the attack is not coming from outside your network. Looking at the router and switch logs, you may be able to trace the offending party to a specific network segment or even a port on a switch.

People often write tools or use scripts and preconfigured search filters for parsing through the data and while this is useful, it could also allow for erroneous exclusion of data. It is not meant to be implied that you should not to use the tools or filters. Those filters and tools are not all that should be used, for there is no substitution for looking at the raw data occasionally.

Your organization's policy should dictate how, and for how long, you store your records. In some cases it is critical that a copy of your logs be made and stored in an offsite facility. It is important that logs be securely managed and verified, for it is not uncommon for an attacker to attempt to edit some of the logs to remove traces of himself. He may be successful in removing some of the evidence, but a good security policy and a good variety of sources for logs will make that task far more difficult.

Getting the logs synchronized to a time standard is important; this will help you look at events as they happen across your network. If you are dealing with the fact that some devices store times in GMT and some store the logs in local time, it makes it more difficult to do log correlation by time with out recalibrating the logs first. It is important to keep in mind that there is an added step of complexity to time synchronization with organizations that span multiple time zones.

Once you have the logs, it is important to check for system anomalies such as mysterious shutdowns and restarts. Sometimes attackers will have to restart a system or part of a system to initialize their malicious code, and these restarts may be an indicator of such an attempt. Careful examination of the logs will also help with normal information management functions like disk capacity management, CPU availability, and network availability.

It is also important to look for an "escalation of privilege." This phrase describes a user who has one level of permission (e.g., an "ordinary user") and then he has elevated levels of privilege to root or administrator. This escalation may be indicative of a malicious user or the fact that an account has been compromised in some way. It is also important to look at the logs to see the user access times. A review of those logs might show a user logging in during nonbusiness hours. While this review may not be significant, if the user is working late or on weekends for a project, it might be significant if the employee badging system shows this user leaving several hours early, or if he is on vacation. This correlation is another example of the benefits of reviewing all of the data simultaneously.

Again, a careful review of the logs may show that there are some configuration changes to the system. A screening router may have an access control removed or change the rule to not log when that rule is triggered, or even an additional rule allowing connections from a specific IP or range of IP's. Another example of a system configuration that may be significant is a new service that shows up on a server or device. If remote login or telnet was not previously allowed on a device and now it is, this may show that a machine has either been compromised or is about to be compromised.

It is important to ensure you are logging and reviewing your logs according to your logging policy. Your logging policy should also be specific on the storage and review of your logs.

Information Security Guidelines, and Standards ISO Information

International Organization for Standards (ISO — ISO/IEC 17799:2000 (now 27000), Code of practice for information security management (based on BS 7799; available at www.iso.ch)...ISO GMITS are as follows:

- ISO/IEC TR 13335-1:1996, Part 1: Concepts and models for IT Security
- ISO/IEC TR 13335-2:1997, Part 2: Managing and planning IT Security
- ISO/IEC TR 13335-3:1998, Part 3: Techniques for the management of IT Security
- ISO/IEC TR 13335-4:2000, Part 4: Selection of safeguards
- ISO/IEC TR 13335-5:2001, Part 5: Management guidance on network security

British Standard Information is available from the British Standards Institute (http://www.bsi-global.com/).

National Institute for Standards and Technology (NIST; http://www.csrc. nist.gov) information includes:

- SP 800-12 An Introduction to Computer Security: The NIST Handbook, October 1995
- SP 800-14 Generally Accepted Principles and Practices for Securing Information Technology Systems, September 1996
- *Security Self-Assessment Guide for Information Technology Systems*, November 2001 (SP 800-26)
- *Risk Management Guide for Information Technology Systems*, January 2002 (SP 800-30)
- *Guidelines for the Security Certification and Accreditation of Federal In-*

formation Technology Systems, October 2002 (SP 800-37; based on BS 7799-1)

- *Minimum Security Controls for Federal Information Technology Systems* (SP 800-53)
- *Techniques and Procedures for the Verification of Security Controls in Federal Information Technology Systems* (SP 800-53A)

American National Standards Institute (ANSI) — International Committee for Information Technology Standards (http://www.incits.org/tc_home/t4.htm). Technical Committee T4 participates in the standardization of generic methods for information technology security. This includes development of: security techniques and mechanisms, security guidelines security evaluation criteria, and identification of generic requirements for information technology system security services. This technical committee is the U.S. TAG to ISO/IEC JTC 1 SC27 and provides recommendations on U.S. positions to the ISO JTC 1 TAG.

ISSA Information Information Systems Security Association (ISSA; http://www.issa.org) — the generally accepted information security principles (GAISP), when completed, aim to be a comprehensive hierarchy of guidance to provide a globally consistent, practical framework for information security. These principles provide specific prescriptions about how to meet the high-level objectives in other guidelines while not naming specific products. The final body of the GAISP will provide three levels of guiding principles to address security professionals at all levels of technical and managerial responsibility.

- Pervasive Principles — Targeting governance and executive-level management, the Pervasive Principles outline high-level guidance to help organizations solidify an effective information security strategy.
- Broad Functional Principles — Broad Functional Principles are the building blocks of the Pervasive Principles and more precisely define recommended tactics from a management perspective.
- Detailed Principles — Written for information security professionals, the Detailed Principles provide specific, comprehensive guidance for consideration in day-to-day information risk management activity.

ISO 17799 Information

An interesting Web site that addresses BS 7799-2:2002 and ISO 17799 is available at http://www.gammassl.co.uk/bs7799/works.html.

- ISO/IEC 17799:2000, Code of Practice of Info Security Management. It was passed as a standard late in 2000 (based on British Standard 7799-1 of the same name). It is a management standard that deals with an examination of the nontechnical issues relating to installed security systems within organizations.

- This standard provides loose guidance on suggested principles to keep in mind when developing a security framework or ISMS (Information Security Management Systems). It is *not* a standard against which security systems can be certified and was not developed to be.
- Its stated objective is to provide a common basis for developing organizational security standards and security management practices.
- It is very high level. It does not give enough guidance to provide an in-depth information security review. It does not support a certification program since the results of a study using it cannot really be quantified with any metrics.
- This ISO standard could potentially be used (informally) in conjunction with BS 7799-2 (a national standard in Britain and many other parts of the world) but a system analyzed with these standards cannot be deemed as an ISO-certified information security infrastructure.
- It does not provide any "how-to's," but addresses things in terms of good practice; a self-described "starting point."
- Major topics:
  — Establishing organizational security policy
  — Organizational security infrastructure
  — Asset classification and control
  — Personnel security
  — Physical and environmental security
  — Communications and ops management
  — Access control
  — Systems development and maintenance
  — Business continuity planning
  — Compliance
- BS 7799 is a two-part standard. Part 1 is what the ISO 17799:2000 is based upon. BS 7799-1 is self-described as not being a specification for an organizational information security program, referred to as an ISMS (Information Security Management System). BS 7799-1 cannot be used to certify.
- To reiterate, both BS 7799-1 and ISO 17799 cannot be used to certify anyone to a level of information security preparedness.
- BS 7799-2 (part 2) is a specification for an ISMS and has supporting checklists of controls and can be used for certification.
- There is no lineal relationship between BS 7799-2 and ISO 17799:2000 — there is a definite relationship; one is just a lot tougher than the other
- There is no close relation between ISO 17799 and ISO 15408, the Common Criteria, which is a way to technically evaluate security products.

Section 2: Security Testing

Now that we have the general ideas and principles as to *what* an audit is and *why* we should conduct one, we'll explore the details of *how* to conduct an audit. We'll start by looking at an overview of the security testing process, then discuss some of the reconnaissance and mapping techniques that are used by auditors, and finally we'll dig deeper into vulnerability and penetration testing techniques.

Security Testing Overview

This section presents the terminology, processes, and common tools used to evaluate technology systems for vulnerabilities (physical security control testing is not covered). Keep in mind that security testing is an ever-evolving subject and can become very deep and specific depending on the system being tested. This text should be used as a starting point for research related to constructing cogent and effective testing procedures.

Security testing is a security management activity that provides insight to the tester about the vulnerabilities a system might have for the purpose of reducing risk to the system through mitigation activities.

What do we mean by "security management"? Security management in this context refers to managing or controlling the level of security inherent in a system. Is the system really vulnerable or on the other end of the spectrum, is it really secure?

What do we mean by "system"? A system is a series of interrelated components that accomplish some goal. A system can be many things, including the physical security system that protects a building, network security controls that protect an Internet connection, network security controls that protect key internal servers from internal or external adversaries, application security controls, or any other *systemized* components.

What do we mean by "mitigation activities"? Mitigation, in the context of computer security, is defined as an activity that makes a system less vulnerable. If an organization has determined that a particular aspect of a system creates some sort of vulnerability for them, mitigation of the vulnerability reduces the risk borne by that vulnerability. Mitigation examples include the following:

- After learning of a newly discovered exposure in AcmeDNS (fictitious), applying an operating system patch on a server offering AcmeDNS services to mitigate (fix) exposure to the known vulnerability
- Programming a Web-based application to protect against buffer overflows
- Adding new firewalls rules that not only filter incoming data traffic but also filter outgoing traffic.

In general, computing risks are centered on one or more of the following unauthorized or inappropriate activities:

- Compromise of a system
- System and data access
- System and data possession
- System and data disclosure
- System and data modification
- System and data destruction or denial of service

Excessive vulnerabilities introduce unacceptable operational risk. Security testing uncovers vulnerabilities in order to mitigate them, which maintains a computing environment with an acceptable level of risk. Responsible organizations implement standards and define procedures for reducing the risk to systems. This is the duty of senior management and the day-to-day responsibility of IT staff charged with security and risk reduction.

In the real world, it often costs more to fix all known vulnerabilities than budgets allow. Security testing in combination with knowing the value a system holds for an organization gives the IT management and staff a road map indicating which systems should be fixed first. The goal may not be to remove vulnerabilities from systems at *any* cost, but to reduce overall risk to an acceptable level as defined by the organization. The risk reduction is almost always done within the confines of a specified budget. For example, if security testing exposes vulnerabilities that will cost $15,000 in new software and labor to mitigate, but the budget allows for only $10,000, then the organization must make a judgment call:

1. Fix the most mission critical/valuable systems first and put off fixing the other systems. In this case the organization must accept the residual risk for the systems they could not afford to fix, or
2. Secure more funding for mitigation activities.

These things being said, security testing is the activity of defining the vulnerabilities that exist so that you can do something about them.

Security testing often begins with reconnaissance, and then proceeds to network-based techniques that test the services available on a network of hosts; this exposes possible vulnerabilities that exist within those services. As you will see, security testing may stop at exposing vulnerabilities or it may go further by attempting to exploit them just like an attacker would. In the security testing area, confusion abounds as to which term means what. Terms are often used interchangeably, but succinct definitions are important to understand. Security testing is comprised of the following activities:

1. Reconnaissance — this activity centers on learning about the system you want to test by using public information sources and other low-tech methods like the telephone or persons working for an organization.

2. Network mapping — this activity centers on using software tools that scan for services that are up and running on systems.
3. Vulnerability testing — this activity centers on using software tools to ascertain which services may be vulnerable to attack.
4. Penetration testing — this activity centers on carrying out an attack by exploiting one or more vulnerabilities.

Mitigation may occur at any of these steps. Based on the results of any of these tests, the following tests may be tailored differently. As an ethical tester you *must* have permission to perform any of these activities.

These activities can be done independently or they may be done to build one upon the other. This is defined by the testing plan agreed upon by the tester and the organization that owns the systems to be tested. Doing one or all allows for a picture of what you should be concerned about and what you should move to resolve. As stated previously, when performing mitigation activities, systems that are more valuable to an organization should be ranked for mitigation before less valuable ones.

Security testing is also known as:

- Vulnerability assessment testing
- Vulnerability auditing
- Security testing and evaluation (ST&E)
- Pen testing (Penetration testing)
- Attack and penetration (A&P)
- Ethical hacking

One of the educational goals of this section is to help you differentiate among the various security testing activities.

Why Is Security Testing Performed? There is no such thing as a static system. Consider the following:

- Hosts change. New functions, software, and services are often added but not tested or cross-referenced for vulnerability. A seemingly innocuous system change may create a hole in your system. New system patches are released all of the time. Some of these patches may unintentionally increase risks to your system.
- Networks change. Changes to the rules that govern firewalls and routers will open and close the services available from one security domain to the other. What if you open a new application service to an untrusted security domain (like the Internet) but the host servicing the application has inherent known (and unpatched) flaws?
- Even when changes are not made, new vulnerabilities are constantly exposed within operating systems and the services they host (like DNS, FTP, Web, etc.). When system weaknesses are not patched or fixed vulnerabilities wait to be exploited.

Security testing can help with following:

- It exposes unauthorized hosts or back doors into the network. *War dialing*, which is discussed later, spots unauthorized modems connected to devices. Wireless access point studies aim to find unauthorized wireless bridges. Both backdoors can give an outsider direct access to the internal network regardless of other effectively implemented network security controls.
- It exposes unauthorized or weakly implemented conduits into the network (i.e., a business partner's peer-to-peer connections, the Internet connection, the user network to server farm connection). Networks can be segmented into security domains. These are the choke points through which services flow. If two networks are connected in a haphazard way, the chokepoint allows too much unnecessary flow from one domain to the other, which in turn allows the security weaknesses of one domain to be introduced to the other.
- It exposes unauthorized services running on hosts. If FTP is specifically disallowed by policy but a security test shows a host offering this service, the service must be terminated or the policy modified to accommodate it.
- It identifies available services and applications running on hosts and whether or not they might be vulnerable. If they are, it can suggest ways to mitigate the vulnerability. For example, if a departmental administrator adds Web services to her server but neglects to reapply operating system patches that mitigate vulnerabilities in that application, this server is vulnerable and something should be done to fix the weakness that was introduced.
- It provides information to test for variances from security policy in general for the purpose of bringing a system back to compliance.

When Is Security Testing Performed? The security policy of the organization should dictate when testing should be performed. Doing otherwise increases the possibility that it will not be done at all, or if it is done, it will be done in an inconsistent manner.

Security testing can be performed at several system life-cycle junctions. These are some suggested times:

- During the security certification phase — This is the time prior to a system being officially deployed. The goal here is to see if the system meets the security criteria defined by policy.
- After major system changes — Security changes can spot vulnerabilities that were introduced by the changes.
- During system audits — Security testing is a necessary part of system auditing and uncovers vulnerabilities and gaps between stated security policy and the actual system state.
- Periodically depending on the nature of the system.

- Systems with sensitive or critical organizational data may be, for example, tested every month.
- Systems exposed to the Internet may be, for example, tested weekly.
- Systems of a less critical nature may be tested less frequently.

It is often best to choose test times when the liability from failure or disruption is smallest, although some organizations wish to test the impact of how their detection systems will work during an increased or live traffic time (will their systems be able to discern the attack in the "noise" of day to day activity?).

Who Should Perform Security Testing? Security testing is performed either by internal IT staff, their appointees (usually outside contractors), internal audit staff, or external auditors.

IT staff or their contractors will often perform the testing in between official independent audits to ensure their implementations follow security policy. There are times when an interim security test is necessary. The point of interim testing is for the IT staff to learn of vulnerabilities their systems may be susceptible to as time goes on.

For example, assume that the IT staff has created a new Web site for the research and development group, the data owners of that system. A Web server standard exists that dictates a particular security baseline. Procedures exist that explain the actions to be taken to implement the standard and baseline. The baseline defines the types of system software and their parameters in order to achieve a consistent level of security among like systems. Prior to making the system live, a security test is prescribed to certify the system for operation. The test is aimed at identifying vulnerabilities brought on by the baseline configuration being improperly implemented. The test may also uncover an out-of-date baseline definition in the case where the system was built according to specification but vulnerabilities were still noted. This new information can be fed back into the process to create a new baseline definition that takes into account new vulnerabilities.

Periodically, internal staff auditors or external auditors hired by the organization will be tasked with evaluating systems for the purpose of gauging how well the stated security policy is being followed by the IT staff. Security testing processes are an important part of the audit function. Auditing is covered more extensively in the SSCP Analysis and Monitoring Domains, Security Auditing section.

To continue the example above, the auditor's role would be to ensure that the system security of the Web server is being maintained over time.

Security testers take one of two roles:

- Covert Tester — These testers generally perform unannounced tests that even the security and/or IT staff may not know about. Sometimes these tests are ordered by senior managers to test their staff and the systems for which the staff are responsible. Other times the IT staff will hire covert testers under the agreement that the testers can and will test at any given time, such as four times per year. The object is generally to see what they can see and get into whatever they can get into — without causing harm, of course. Qualities include:

— Play the role of hostile attacker.
— Perform testing without warning.
— Receive little to no guidance from the organization being tested.
— Pros — You will get a better overall view of your network without someone "being prepared" for the testing.
— Cons — The staff may take the findings personally and show disdain to the testing team and management.
— Overt Tester — These testers perform tests with the knowledge of the security and/or IT staff. They are given physical access to the network and sometimes even a normal username and password. Qualities include:
— Full cooperation of organization
— Planned test times
— Network diagrams and systems configurations are supplied.
— Pros — You should get good reaction and support from your team being tested and fixes can occur more rapidly. It is also good to use as a dry run for your incident response procedures.
— Cons — You may get an inaccurate picture of your network response capabilities because they are prepared for the "attack."

Security Testing Goals Without defined goals, security testing can be a meaningless and costly exercise. The following are examples of some high-level goals for security testing, thereby providing value and meaning for the organization:

• Anyone directly or indirectly sanctioned by the organization's management to perform testing should be doing so for the purpose of identifying vulnerabilities so that they be quantified and placed in a ranking for subsequent mitigation.
• Since a security test is merely the evaluation of security on a system at a point in time, the results should be documented and compared to the results at other points in time. Analysis that compares results across time periods paints a picture of how well or poorly the systems are being protected across those periods (otherwise known as base-lining).
• Security testing can be a form of self audit by the IT staff to prepare them for the "real" audits performed by internal and external auditors.
• In the case of covert testing, testers aim to actually compromise security, penetrate systems, and determine if the IT staff notices the intrusion and an acceptable response has occurred.

Security Test Software Tools Software tools exist to assist in the testing of systems from many angles. Tools help you to interpret how a system functions for the purpose of evaluating its security. This section presents some tools available on the commercial market and in the open source space as a means to the testing end. Do not interpret the listing of a tool as a recommendation for its use. Likewise, just because a tool is not listed does not mean it is not worth considering. Choosing a tool to test a particular aspect is a personal or organizational choice.

Some points to consider regarding the use of software tools in the security testing process:

- Do not let tools drive the security testing. Make a strategy and pick the right tool mix for discovery and testing based upon your overall testing plan.
- Use tools specific to the testing environment. For example, if your aim is to test the application of operating system patches on a particular platform, analyze the available ways you might accomplish this process by seeing what the vendor offers and compare this against third-party tools. Pick tools that offer the best performance tempered with your budget constraints.
- Tool functions often overlap. The features found on one tool may be better than those on another.
- Security testing tools can make mistakes, especially network-based types that rely on circumstantial evidence of vulnerability. Further investigation is often necessary to determine if the tool interpreted an alleged vulnerability correctly.
- Network tools sometimes negatively affect uptime; therefore, these tests should often be scheduled for off-hours execution.
- By increasing network traffic load.
- By affecting unstable platforms which react poorly to unusual inputs.
- Network scanners are affected by network infrastructure.
- Placement of probes is critical.
- When possible, place them on the same segment you are testing so that filtering devices and intrusion detection systems do not alter the results (unless you plan to test how your intrusion detection systems react).
- Be aware that the models for detection of vulnerabilities are inconsistent among different toolsets; therefore, results should be studied and made reasonably consistent among different tools.

Analyzing Testing Results It is often easier to understand the testing results by creating a graphical depiction in a simple matrix of vulnerabilities, ratings for each, and an overall vulnerability index derived as the product of vulnerability and system criticality. More complicated matrices may include details describing each vulnerability and sometimes ways to mitigate it or ways to confirm the vulnerability.

Tests should conclude with a report and matrices detailing the following:

- Information derived publicly
- Information derived through social engineering or other covert ways
- Hosts tested and their addresses
- Services found
- Possible vulnerabilities
- Vulnerability ratings for each
- System criticality
- Overall vulnerability rating
- Vulnerabilities confirmation
- Mitigation suggestions

Testers often present findings matrices that list each system and the vulnerabilities found for each with a "high, medium, low" ranking. The intent is to provide the recipient a list of what should be fixed first. The problem with this method is that it does not take into account the criticality of the system in question. You need a way to differentiate among the urgency for fixing "high" vulnerabilities across systems. Therefore, reports should rank true vulnerabilities by seriousness, taking into account how the organization views the asset's value. Systems of high value may have their medium and low vulnerabilities fixed before a system of medium value has any of it vulnerabilities fixed. This criticality is determined by the organization and the reports and matrices should help reflect a suggested path to rectifying the situation. For example, the organization has received a testing report listing the same two high vulnerabilities for a print server and an accounting database server. The database server is certainly more critical to the organization; therefore, its problems should be mitigated prior to those of the print server.

As another example, assume the organization has assigned a high value to the database server that houses data for the Web server. The Web server itself has no data but is considered medium value. In contrast, the FTP server is merely for convenience and is assigned a low value. A security testing matrix may show several high vulnerabilities for the low value FTP server. It may also list high vulnerabilities for both the database server and the Web server. The organization will likely be interested in fixing the high vulnerabilities first on the database server, then the Web server, and then the FTP server. This level of triage is further complicated by trust and access between systems. If the Web server gets the new pages and content from the FTP server, this may increase the priority of the FTP server issues over that of the usually low-value FTP server issues.

Results should provide a basis for how mitigation is progressing over time as subsequent tests are performed.

Reconnaissance and Network Mapping Techniques

- Basic security testing activities include reconnaissance and network mapping.
- Reconnaissance — collecting information about the organization from publicly available sources, social engineering, and low-tech methods. This information forms the test attack basis by providing useful information to the tester.
- Network mapping — collecting information about the organization's Internet connectivity and available hosts by (usually) using automated mapping software tools. In the case of internal studies, the internal network architecture of available systems is mapped. This information further solidifies the test attack basis by providing even more information to the tester about the services running on the network and is often the step prior to vulnerability testing which is covered in the next section.

Note: Security testing is an art. This means that different IT security practitioners have different methods for testing. This chapter attempts to note the highlights to help you differentiate among the various types and provides information on tools that assist in the endeavor. Security testing is an ethical responsibility and the techniques should never be used for malice. This information is presented for the purpose of helping you spot weaknesses in your systems or the systems you are authorized to test so that they may be improved.

Reconnaissance Defined Often reconnaissance is needed by a covert penetration tester who has *not* been granted regular access to perform a cooperative test. These testers are challenged with having little to no knowledge of the system and must collect it from other sources to form the basis of the test attack.

Reconnaissance is necessary for these testers because they likely have no idea what they will be testing at the commencement of the test. Their orders are usually "see what you can find and get into but do not damage anything."

Once you think you know what should be tested based on the information you have collected, always check with the persons who have hired you for the test to ensure that the systems you intend to penetrate are actually owned by the organization. Doing otherwise may put delicate systems in harms way or the tester may test something not owned by the organization ordering the test (leading to possible legal repercussions). These parameters should be defined prior to the test.

Social Engineering and Low-Tech Reconnaissance Social engineering is an activity that involves the manipulation of persons or physical reconnaissance to get information for use in exploitation or testing activities. Low-tech reconnaissance uses simple technical means to obtain information.

Before attackers or testers make an attempt on your systems, they can learn about the target using low technology techniques such as:

- Directly visit a target's Web server and search through it for information.
- View a Web page's source for information about what tools might have been used to construct or run it.
- Employee contact information
- Corporate culture information to pick up internally used "lingo" and product names
- Business partners
- "Googling" a target
- "Googling" a target refers to the reconnaissance activity whereby an attacker uses search engines that have previously indexed a target site. The attacker can search for files of a particular type that may contain information they can use for further attacks. Google and other search engines can be very powerful tools to a cracker because of the volume of data they are able to organize. Example: Search a particular Web site for spreadsheet files containing the word "employee" or "address" or "accounting."
- Make sure that Web servers are configured correctly and require authentication in order to access private information.
- Dumpster Diving — retrieving improperly discarded computer media and paper records for gleaning private information about an organization.
- Documentation located in trash bins and dumpsters, never meant for continued consumption, but stolen for content.
- Computer hard drives and removable media (floppies, CDs, etc.) thrown away or sold without properly degaussing to remove all private information.
- Equipment (routers, switches, specialized data processing devices) discarded without configuration data removed without a trace.
- Shoulder surfing — furtively collecting information (e.g., someone else's password).
- Social Engineering Using the Telephone — Attackers often pose as an official technical support person or fellow employee and attempt to build a rapport with a user through small talk. The attacker may ask for the user's assistance with (false) troubleshooting "tests" aimed at helping the attacker collect information about the system. If the attacker finds a particularly "helpful" user, he might be bold enough to ask for their username and password because "we've been having trouble with the router gateway products interfacing with the LDAP directories

where your username and password are stored and we think it is getting corrupted as it passes over the network, so if you could just tell me what it is that would be great," or some such nonsense aimed at gaining the user's confidence. Other scenarios include:

— New employee requiring information — (attacker says to an employee) "Hi, I'm Jill. I'm new here and can't get on the system because IT hasn't given me an account. Can I use your computer while you're at lunch so I can get a few things done?"

— Angry manager needing new password — (attacker says to IT support with urgency) "I've got to get this report out for the senior vice president. I can't log onto the system and I don't have time for you to come up here to reset my password. I want a new password now and I don't want to have to tell the VP that you were the cause of my lateness. What is the new password?"

— System administrator calling employee to fix account requiring password — (attacker says to employee) "Hi, Joe here with IT support. We've been having some virus problems and I need to access your PC from where I am so I'll need you to tell me what your username and password are...otherwise I'll need to come and get your PC and we'll have to keep it for a day."

— Field employee needs remote connection info — (attacker says to IT support) "I had to setup my system again. What is the password to the remote access server?"

— Usenet Searches

— Usenet postings can give away information about a company's internal system design and problems that exist within systems. For example: "I need advice on my firewall. It is an XYZ brand system and I have it configured to do this, that, and the other thing. Can anyone help me? — signed joe@big_company_everyone_knows.com"

— Posters should never use their company e-mail address when posting. Attackers can identify all postings of that individual allowing him to learn the target's hobbies, skills, problems, and internal system details if the poster is naïve enough to expose such details.

Mid-Tech Reconnaissance — Whois Information Mid-tech reconnaissance includes several ways to get information that can be used for testing.

Whois is a system that records Internet registration information, including the company that owns the domain, administrative contacts, technical contacts, when the record of domain ownership expires, and DNS servers authoritative for maintaining host IP addresses and their associated friendly names for the domains you are testing. With this information you can use other online tools to "dig" for information about the servers visible on the Internet without ever sending a single probing packet at the Internet connection. The contact information provided by Whois can also be used for social engineering and war dialing.

The following are example attacks:

- Using Whois, collect information about DNS servers authoritative for maintaining host IP addresses for a particular domain. Use the tools like those found at http://www.samspade.org to dig for information about hosts and IP addresses associated with the domain. Use network mapping software (discussed in the next section) to map those IP addresses.
- Using Whois, identify the administrative contact and his telephone number. Use social engineering on that person or security-unaware staff at the main telephone number to get unauthorized information.
- Using Whois, identify the technical contact and her area code and exchange (telephone number). Using *war dialing* software (discussed later), you attempt to make an unauthorized connection with a modem in the block of numbers used by the organization for the purposes of gaining backdoor entry to the system.

There are many sources for Whois information and tools, including:

- http://www.internic.net
- http://www.networksolutions.com
- http://www.samspade.org (includes other tools as well)

Mid-Tech Reconnaissance — DNS Zone Transfers In an effort to discover the names and types of servers operating inside or outside a network, attackers may attempt zone transfers from DNS servers. A zone transfer is a special type of query directed at a DNS server that asks the server for the entire contents of its zone (the domain which it serves). Information that is derived is only useful if the DNS server is authoritative for that domain. To find a DNS server authoritative for a domain, whois search results often provide this information. Internet DNS servers will often restrict which servers are allowed to perform transfers but internal DNS servers usually do not have these restrictions.

Secure systems lock down DNS. Testers should see how the target does this by keeping the following in mind:

- Attackers will attempt zone transfers; therefore, configure DNS's to restrict zone transfers to only approved hosts.
- Attackers will look for host names that may give out additional information — accountingserver.bigfinancialcompany.com.
- Avoid using Host Information Records (HINFO) when possible. HINFO is the Host Information Record of a DNS entry. It is strictly informational in nature but serves no function. It is often used to declare the computer type and operating system of a host.
- Use a split DNS model with internal DNS and external DNS servers. Combining internal and external function on one server is potentially

dangerous. Internal DNS will serve the internal network and can relay externally bound queries to the external DNS servers that will do the lookup work by proxy. Incoming Internet-based queries will only reveal external hosts because the external hosts only know these addresses.

- There are a variety of free programs available that will resolve DNS names, attempt zone transfers, and perform a reverse lookup of a specified range of IPs. Major operating systems also include the "nslookup" program, which can also perform these operations.

Network Mapping Defined Network mapping is a process that "paints the picture" of which hosts are up and running externally or internally and what services are available on the system. Commonly, you may see mapping in the context of external host testing and enumeration in the context of internal host testing, but this is not necessarily ironclad, and mapping and enumeration often seem to be used interchangeably. They essentially accomplish similar goals and the terms can be used in similar ways.

When performing mapping of any kind, the tester should limit the mapping to the scope of the project. Testers may be given a range of IP addresses to map, so the testers should limit themselves to that range. Overt and covert testing usually includes network mapping, which is the activity that involves techniques to discover the following:

- Which hosts are up and running or "alive"?
- What is the general topology of the network (how are things interconnected)?
- What ports are open and serviceable on those hosts?
- What applications are servicing those ports?
- What operating system is the host running?

Mapping is the precursor to vulnerability testing and usually defines what will be tested more deeply at that next stage. For example, consider a scenario where you discover that a host is listening on TCP port 143. This probably indicates the host is running application services for the IMAP mail service. Many IMAP implementations have vulnerabilities. During the network mapping phase, you learn that host 10.1.2.8 is listening on this port but you tend not to learn which IMAP implementation it is. IMAP vendor X may have an ironclad implementation whereas IMAP vendor Z's system may be full of bugs and vulnerabilities. Network mapping may provide insight about the operating system the host is running which may in turn narrow the possible IMAP applications. For example, it is unlikely that the Microsoft Exchange 2000 IMAP process will be running on a Solaris computer; therefore, if network mapping shows a host with telltale Solaris "fingerprints" as well as indications that the host is listening on TCP port 143, the IMAP server is probably not MS Exchange. As such, when you are later exploring vulnerabilities, you can likely eliminate Exchange IMAP vulnerabilities for this host.

Mapping results can be compared to security policy to discover rogue or unauthorized services that appear to be running. For example, an organization may periodically run mapping routines to match results with what should be expected. If more services are running than one would expect to be running, the systems may have been accidentally misconfigured (therefore opening up a service not approved in the security policy) or the host(s) may have been compromised with, for example, a Trojan horse program that makes connections to an unauthorized outside system.

Network Host and Port Mapping Techniques As discussed earlier, network mapping software can help map the address ranges you discovered in the reconnaissance step. Network mapping will help you understand which hosts are alive and servicing applications. Specialized tools that perform these functions can be used internally and externally. The common term for software that includes these functions is "port scanner." Port scanners may or may not include vulnerability (of the ports) assessment components.

When performing mapping, make sure you are performing the mapping on a host range owned by the organization. For example, suppose an nslookup DNS domain transfer for bobs-italianbookstore.com showed a mail server at 10.2.3.70 and a Web server at 10.19.40.2. Assuming you do not work for bobs-italianbookstore.com and do not have intimate knowledge of their systems, you might assume that they have two Internet connections. In a cooperative test, the best course of action is to check with their administrative staff for clarification. They may tell you that the mail is hosted by another company and that it is outside of the scope of the test. However, the Web server is a host to be tested. You should ask which part of the 10.0.0.0 bobsbookstore.com controls. Let's assume they control the class-C 10.19.40.0. Therefore, network mapping of 10.19.40.1 through 10.19.40.254 is appropriate and will not interfere with any one else's operations. Even though only one host is listed in the DNS, there may be other hosts up and running.

Depending on the level of stealth required (that is to avoid detection by IDS systems or other systems that will "notice" suspected activity if a threshold for certain types of communication is exceeded), network mapping may be performed very slowly over long periods of time. Stealth may be required for covert penetration tests.

Network mapping can involve a variety of techniques for probing hosts and ports. Several common techniques are listed below:

- ICMP echo requests (ping) — If you ping a host and it replies, it is alive, i.e., up and running. This test does not show what individual services are running. Be aware that many networks block incoming echo requests. If the requests are blocked and you ping a host and it does not reply, you have no way of knowing if it is actually running or not because the request is blocked before it gets to the destination.

- TCP Connect scan — A connect scan can be used to discover TCP services running on a host even if ICMP is blocked. This type of scan is considered "noisy" (noticeable to logging and intrusion detection systems) because it goes all the way through the connection process. This basic service discovery scan goes all the way through a TCP session setup by sending a SYN packet to a target, receiving the SYN/ACK from the target when the port is listening, then sending a final ACK back to the target to establish the connection. At this point, the test host is "connected" to the target. Eventually the connection is torn down because the tester's goal is not to communicate with the port, but only to discover whether it is available.

- TCP SYN scan — SYN scanning can be used to discover TCP services running on a host even if ICMP is blocked. SYN scanning is considered less noisy than connect scans. It is referred to as "half-open" scanning because unlike a connect scan (above) you do not open a full TCP connection. Your test host directs a TCP SYN packet on a particular port as if it were going to open a real TCP connection to the target host. A SYN/ACK from the target indicates the host is listening on that port. A RST from the target indicates that it is not listening on that port. If a SYN/ACK is received, the test host immediately sends an RST to tear down the connection in order to conserve resources on both the test and target host sides. Firewalls often detect and block these scan attempts.

- TCP FIN scan — FIN scanning can be used to discover TCP services running on a host even if ICMP is blocked. FIN scanning is considered a stealthy way to discover if a service is running. The test host sends a TCP packet with the FIN bit on to a port on the target host. If the target responds with a RST packet, you may assume that the target host is not using the port. If the host does not respond, it may be using the port that was probed. Caveats to this technique are Microsoft, Cisco, BSDI, HP/UX, MVS, and IRIX-based hosts that implement their TCP/IP software stacks in ways not defined by the standard. These hosts may not respond with a RST when probed by a FIN. However, if you follow up a nonreply to one of these systems with, for example, a SYN scan to that port and the host replies, you have determined that the host is listening on the port being tested and a few possible operating systems (see OS fingerprinting).

- TCP XMAS scan — XMAS scans are similar to a FIN scan (and similarly stealthy) but they additionally turn on the URG and PSH flags.

- TCP NULL scan — NULL scans are similar to a FIN scan (also stealthy) but they turn off all flags.

- UDP scans — A UDP scan determines which UDP service ports are opened on a host. The test machine sends a UDP packet on a port to the target. If the target sends back an ICMP port unreachable message, the target does not use that port. A potential problem with this methodology is the case where a router or firewall at the target network does not allow ICMP port unreachable messages to leave the network, making the target network appear as if all UDP ports are open (because no ICMP messages are getting back to the test host). Another problem is that many systems limit the number of ICMP messages allowed per second, which can make for a very slow scanning rate.

Available mapping tools include:

- Nmap — http://www.insecure.org — this is perhaps the best known open source port scanner. It does not offer vulnerability analysis but does tell you which ports are open using a wide variety of techniques.
- Solarwinds — http://www.solarwinds.net
- Superscan — http://www.foundstone.com

Another technique for mapping a network is commonly known as "firewalking," which uses traceroute techniques to discover which services a filtering device like a router or firewall will allow through. These tools generally function by transmitting TCP and/or UDP packets on a particular port with a time to live (TTL) equal to at least one greater than the targeted router or firewall. If the target allows the traffic, it will forward the packets to the next hop. At that point, the traffic will expire as it reaches the next hop and an ICMP_TIME_EXCEEDED message will be generated and sent back out of the gateway to the test host. If the target router or firewall does not allow the traffic, it will drop the packets and the test host will not see a response.

Available firewalking tools include:

- Hping — http://www.hping.org/
- Firewalk — http://www.packetfactory.net/projects/firewalk/

By all means, do not forget about the use of basic built-in operating system commands for discovering hosts and routes. Basic built-in and other tools include:

- Traceroute (Windows calls this tracert) — uses ICMP or TCP depending on the implementation of a path to a host or network.
- Ping (personal inter network groper) — see if a host is alive using ICMP echo request messages.
- Telnet — telnetting to a particular port is a quick way to find out if the host is servicing that port in some way.
- Whois — command line whois can provide similar information to the Web-based whois methods previously discussed.

System Fingerprinting System fingerprinting refers to testing techniques used by port scanners and vulnerability analysis software that attempt to identify the operating system in use on a network device and the versions of services running on the host. Why is it important to identify a system? By doing so, you know what you are dealing with and later on, what vulnerabilities are likely for that system. As mentioned previously, Microsoft-centric vulnerabilities are (usually) not going to show up on Sun systems and vice versa.

For example, fingerprinting may try to ferret out information such as:

- Windows NT 4.0 running Internet Information Server 4.0
- Cisco IOS 12.1
- Red Hat Linux 6.1 running BIND (DNS)

This fingerprinting can be determined by using a portmapper such as:

- 10.5.5.5 looks like Windows NT based on the way its TCP/IP communications are structured
- 10.5.5.6 looks like Windows 2000 because it did not respond with a RST when I sent a FIN and it runs IIS 5 according to the http banner
- 10.5.5.7 looks like Linux because it did send back a RST in response to my FIN and its TCP/IP communications behave like Linux

Fingerprinting tools are generally looking for the following types of information to carry out the fingerprinting process:

- Banner information — banners can reveal much information about the services running on a system and help you understand if this version is vulnerable.

test-host>telnet ftp.bobs-italianbookstore.com 21

Trying 10.99.55.3...

Connected to ftp.bobs-italianbookstore.com.

Escape character is '^]'.

220 ftp29 FTP server (UNIX(r) System V Release 4.0) ready.

SYST

215 UNIX Type: L8 Version: SUNOS

TCP/IP Protocol Stack Variations — Even though TCP/IP is a standard, different vendors implement it in different ways. Furthermore, these variations are sometimes implemented differently among versions of a vendor's TCP/IP network protocol stacks; that is, they might be done differently in version 1 of a product when compared to version 2. These variations can be an indicator of the system you are testing. Refer back to TCP FIN scan techniques as one example of how some operating systems react differently to packets with FIN flags turned on when no previous TCP session existed.

Vulnerability and Penetration Testing Techniques

This section presents some more advanced security testing activities grouped together as vulnerability and penetration testing.

Vulnerability Testing — probing systems for possible vulnerabilities and reporting on them. This information can form the penetration attack basis or the basis for a vulnerability mitigation plan for the organization.

Penetration Testing — acting upon possible vulnerabilities by using custom tools, scripts, and techniques for the purpose of subverting, controlling, and "owning" systems.

Vulnerability Testing Defined The next sophistication level in security testing is vulnerability testing, which is an activity that takes the results of reconnaissance and network mapping and adds testing techniques to probe systems to gauge their susceptibility to exploitation and attack. Vulnerability studies are overt tests, which means that the testers have the full cooperation of the organization receiving the test. Testers usually receive network diagrams, systems configurations, logon credentials, and other information necessary to make a complete system evaluation. The point is to not make the testers work (like an attacker) at getting administrative access, then probing systems. The goal is to study the security level of the systems, identify problems, offer mitigation techniques, and assist in prioritizing improvements.

Goals of vulnerability tests include:

- Study the security posture of the organization.
- Identify and prioritize mitigation activities for security improvement based on business need and system criticality.

The scope of vulnerability testing can include the following:

- Internal or external testing
- An analysis of known vulnerabilities within systems
- Host
- Network device
- Application

The benefits of vulnerability testing include:

- It identifies system vulnerabilities.
- It allows for the prioritization of mitigation tasks based upon system criticality and risk.
- It is considered a useful tool for comparing security posture over time especially when done consistently each period.

The disadvantages of vulnerability testing include:

- It may not effectively focus efforts if the test is not designed appropriately. Sometimes testers "bite off more than they can chew."
- It has the potential to crash the network or host being tested if dangerous tests are chosen. (Innocent and noninvasive tests have also been known to cause system crashes.)

Note that vulnerability testing software is often placed into two broad categories as follows:

- General vulnerability
- Application-specific vulnerability

General vulnerability software probes hosts and operating systems for known flaws. It also probes common applications for flaws. Application-specific vulnerability tools are designed specifically to analyze certain types of application software. For example, database scanners optimized to understand the deep issues/weaknesses of Oracle databases, Microsoft SQL Server, etc. and can uncover implementation problems therein. Scanners optimized for Web servers look deeply into issues surrounding those systems.

Vulnerability testing software, in general, is often referred to as V/A (vulnerability assessment) software, and sometimes combines a port mapping function to identify which hosts are where and the applications they offer with further analysis that pegs vulnerabilities to those applications. Good vulnerability software will offer mitigation techniques or links to manufacturer Web sites for further research. This stage of security testing is often an automated software process. Results are best examined with close scrutiny to determine their accuracy. It is also beneficial to use multiple tools and cross reference the results of those tools for a more accurate picture.

Vulnerability testing usually employs software specific to the activity and tends to have the following qualities:

- OS fingerprinting — This technique is used to establish the operating system in use on a target (note that OS fingerprinting was also covered previously in the network mapping section; it is mentioned again here for thoroughness). This function is sometimes built into mapping software and sometimes into vulnerability software.
- Stimulus and response algorithms — These are techniques to identify application software versions, then referencing these versions with known vulnerabilities. Stimulus involves sending one or more packets at the target. Depending on the response, the tester can infer information about the target's applications. For example, to determine the version of the HTTP server, the vulnerability testing software might send an HTTP GET request to a Web server, just like a browser would

(the stimulus), and read the reply information it receives back (the response) for information that details the fact that it is Apache version X, IIS version Y, etc.

- Privileged logon ability — The ability to automatically log onto a host or group of hosts with user credentials (administrator-level or other level) for a deeper "authorized" look at systems is desirable.
- Cross referencing — OS and applications/services (discovered during the port mapping phase) should be cross referenced to more succinctly identify possible vulnerabilities. For example, if OS fingerprinting reveals that the host runs Red Hat Linux 8.0 and that portmapper is one of the listening programs, any pre-8.0 portmapper vulnerabilities can likely be ruled out. Keep in mind that old vulnerabilities have resurfaced in later versions of code even though they were patched at one time. While these instances may occur, the filtering based on OS and application fingerprinting will help you better target systems and use your time more effectively.
- Update capability — Scanners must be kept up-to-date with the latest vulnerability signatures; otherwise, they will not be able to detect newer problems and vulnerabilities. Commercial tools that do not have quality personnel dedicated to updating their product are of reduced effectiveness because your scanner will not have the ability to detect all it could. Likewise, open source scanners should have a following in order to keep them up-to-date.
- Reporting capability — Without the ability to report, a scanner does not serve much purpose. Good scanners provide the ability to export scan data in a variety of formats, including viewing in HTML or PDF format or to third party reporting software and configurable enough to give the ability to filter reports into high-, mid-, and low-level detail depending on the intended audience for the report. Reports are used as basis for determining mitigation activities at a later time.

Problems that may arise when using vulnerability analysis tools include:

- False positives — When scanners use generalized tests or if the scanner does not have the ability to somehow look deeply at the application, it might not be able to determine whether or not the application *actually* has vulnerability. It might result in information that says the application *might* have vulnerability. If it sees that the server is running a remote control application, the test software may indicate that you have a "High" vulnerability. But if you have taken care to implement the remote control application to a high standard, your vulnerability is not as high.
- Crash exposure — V/A software has some inherent dangers because much of the vulnerability testing software includes denial of service test scripts (as well as other scripts) which, if used carelessly, can crash hosts. Ensure that hosts being tested have proper backups and

that you test during times that will have the lowest impact to business operations.

- Temporal Information — Scans are temporal in nature, which means that the scan results you have today become stale as time moves on and new vulnerabilities are discovered. Therefore, scans must be performed periodically with scanners that are up to date with the latest vulnerability signatures.

Vulnerability testing is the first attempt to begin looking for holes that can later be exploited. Remember that the point of security testing is to learn what is vulnerable and what needs to be fixed.

The high-level intent during scanning is to determine the following:

- Verify the service ports available on the hosts.
- Associate vulnerabilities to these service ports.
- Gather information about vulnerability mitigation.

What is the purpose of doing this?

- To discover vulnerabilities about which you were previously unaware
- To gauge your general security posture
- To gauge the effectiveness of security controls
- To gauge your adherence to your own security policies
- To fix issues and limit your organization's exposures to problems

Vulnerability scan caveats:

- Scanning provides a starting point for learning about service vulnerabilities, especially if your scanner is up-to-date!
- Scanning requires post scan investigation for completeness and accuracy.
- Results should be verified.

Scanner tools:

- Nessus open source scanner — http;//www.nessus.org
- Internet Security Systems' (ISS) Internet Scanner — http://www.iss.net
- eEye Digital Security's Retina — http://www.eeye.com
- SARA — http://www.arc.com
- SATAN — http://www.fish.com
- SAINT — http://www.wwdsi.com

Weeding Out False Positives Even if a scanner reports a service as vulnerable, or missing a patch that leads to vulnerability, the system is not necessarily vulnerable. Accuracy is a function of the scanner's quality; that is, how complete and concise the testing mechanisms are built (better tests equal better results), how up-to-date the testing scripts are (fresher scripts are more likely to spot a fuller range of known problems), and how well it performs OS fingerprinting (knowing which OS the host runs helps the scanner pinpoint issues for applications that run on that OS). Double check the scanner's work. Verify that a claimed vulnerability is an actual vulnerability. Good scanners will reference documents to help you learn more about the issue.

The following scenario illustrates verification of vulnerability results: A host running Red Hat Linux 7.0 is scanned over a network connection with an open source vulnerability scanner. Port enumeration techniques show that the host is listening on TCP port 123 (NTP — network time protocol). A vulnerability scanner may reference an NTP daemon (service) vulnerability that exists in *some* NTP implementations. Keep in mind that scanners should know about this common NTP issue, though not all scanners know about this vulnerability (note comments about scanner quality mentioned earlier).

The point here is to verify whether the tool correctly pinpointed this potential problem as a true problem. In other words, is this a true positive or a false positive?

Issues that affect the scanner's accuracy include:

- Is the detected listening port, in this case TCP port 123, really running the service commonly seen on that port? Or was some other service redefined to run on port 123? Scanners often use test techniques like banner grabbing to ensure that the service that generally is listening on a particular port is indeed that service.
- Was the scanner able to correctly fingerprint the OS? If no NTP vulnerability exists in Red Hat Linux 9, for example, then there should be nothing to report. Making this claim depends heavily on the scanner's confidence that Red Hat 9 is in use.
- Was the scanner able to ascertain through some test whether the NTP service has been upgraded to a fixed version? Scanners can derive more information from a system if it has logon credentials to that system. If it has no algorithm to determine whether the NTP service is the default (vulnerable) one or an upgraded one, the reports may show that the NTP service *may* be vulnerable, not that it *is* vulnerable.

Common Vulnerabilities and Exposures (CVE) references are definitions of vulnerabilities that try to note which vendor products and application versions are potentially vulnerable. Note that the CVE references Red Hat Linux advisory RHSA-2001.045-05 for more vendor specific information. Many other vendors had the same problems and their sites are referenced as well.

Red Hat Linux advisory RHSA-2001.045-05 notes that two of its software distributions, versions 6.2 and 7.0, contained NTP services vulnerable to exploitation and that patched versions exist for download and subsequent upgrade. The tool correctly identified the OS and the problem with the NTP service. Mitigation measures were linked in the reporting output.

You should come away from this with the idea that all scanner reports should be treated with skepticism until the results are verified.

Other examples include:

- "Patch 008-132 is missing." Verify that this is actually the case using the operating system's patch management systems or some other third party tool engineered specifically for patch management.
- "Sendmail may be vulnerable." Reference the vendor's Web site to see if there are known issues with your OS and sendmail versions.
- "Windows remote registry connection is possible." Look at the host's appropriate registry key to see if this is true.

Host Testing Organizations serious about security create hardened host configuration procedures and use policy to mandate host deployment and change. There are many ingredients to creating a secure host but you should always remember that what is secure today may not be secure tomorrow, as conditions are ever-changing. There are several areas to consider when securing a host or when evaluating its security:

- Disable unneeded services — Services that are not critical to the role the host serves should be disabled or removed as appropriate for that platform. For the services the host does offer, make sure it is using server programs considered secure, make sure you fully understand them, and tighten the configuration files to the highest degree possible. Unneeded services are often installed and left at their defaults but since they are not needed, administrators ignore or forget about them. This may draw unwanted data traffic to the host from other hosts attempting connections and it will leave the host vulnerable to weaknesses in the services. If a host does not need a particular host process for its operation, do not install it. If software is installed but not used or intended for use on the machine, it may not be remembered or documented that software is on the machine and therefore will likely not get patched. Likewise, when evaluating a host's security you should ask critical questions like:
  — "Is this Web process really needed on this server performing DNS?"
  — "Does this workstation host really need the miniature version of SQL server that was installed along with this office productivity application?"
  — "Are these RPC programs really needed for this server's administration?"

Port mapping programs use many techniques to discover services available on a host. These results should be compared with the policy that defines this host and its role. One must continually ask the critical questions, for the less a host offers as a service to the world while still maintaining its job, the better for its security (because there is less chance of subverting extraneous applications).

- Disable insecure services — Certain programs used on systems are known to be insecure, cannot be made secure, and are easily exploitable; therefore, only use secure alternatives. These applications were developed for private, secure LAN environments, but as connectivity proliferated worldwide, their use has been taken to insecure communication channels. Their weakness falls into three categories:
- They usually send authentication information unencrypted. For example, FTP and Telnet send username and passwords in the clear.
- They usually send data unencrypted. For example, HTTP sends data from client to server and back again entirely in the clear. For many applications this is acceptable; however, for some it is not. SMTP also sends mail data in the clear unless it is secured by the application (e.g., the use of pretty good privacy [PGP] within Outlook).
- Common services are studied carefully for weaknesses by people motivated to attack your systems.

The following is a list of common services known to be insecure. This is a *partial* list. You should research all protocols and applications in use:

- Telnet
- FTP
- NFS, NIS
- Finger
- Rlogin, rsh, rwhod
- Chargen
- Portmap
- Smb
- Sendmail

Therefore to protect hosts one must understand the implications of using these and other services that are commonly "hacked." Eliminate them when necessary or substitute them for more secure versions. For example:

- To ensure privacy of login information as well as the contents of client to server transactions, use SSH (secure shell) to login to hosts remotely instead of Telnet.
- Use SSH as a secure way to send insecure data communications between hosts by redirecting the insecure data into an SSH wrapper. The details for doing this are different from system to system.
- Use SCP (Secure Copy) instead of FTP.
- Remove or turn off chargen (character generator) since it is of little or no use to most people.
- Ensure least privilege file system permissions — Least privilege is the concept that describes the minimum number of permissions required to perform a particular task. This applies to services/daemon processes as well as user permissions. Often systems installed out of the box are at minimum security levels. Make an effort to understand how se-

cure newly installed configurations are, and take steps to lock down settings using vendor recommendations.

— Make sure file system permissions are as tight as possible.

— For UNIX-based systems, remove all unnecessary SUID and SGID programs that embed the ability for a program running in one user context to access another program. This ability becomes even more dangerous in the context of a program running with root user permissions as a part of its normal operation.

— For NT-based systems, use the Microsoft Management Center (MMC) "security configuration and analysis" and "security templates" snap-ins to analyze and secure multiple features of the operation system including audit and policy settings and the registry.

- Employ a patching policy — Patches are pieces of software code meant to fix a vulnerability or problem that has been identified in a portion of an operating system or in an application that runs on a host. Keep the following in mind regarding patching:

— You need a way to learn about patches when they become available. Subscribe to vendor mailing lists for patch alerts.

— Not all patches must be applied. Evaluate their appropriateness in your environment, depending on what they aim to fix, and explore other compensating controls that exist to mitigate the vulnerability.

— Patches should be tested for functionality, stability, and security. You need a way to test whether new patches will break a system or an application running on a system. When patching highly critical systems, it is advised to deploy the patch in a test environment that mimics the real environment. If you do not have this luxury, only deploy patches at noncritical times, have a back-out plan, and apply patches in steps (meaning one-by-one) to ensure that each one was successful and the system is still operating.

— Use patch reporting systems that evaluate whether systems have patches installed completely and correctly and which patches are missing. Many vulnerability analysis tools have this function built into them, but be sure to understand how often your V/A tool vendor updates this list versus another vendor who specializes in patch analysis systems. You will probably find that some vendors have better updating systems than others.

— Optimally, tools should test to see if a patch has been applied to remove a vulnerability, that the vulnerability does not exist. Patch application sometimes includes a manual remediation component like a registry change or removing a user and if the IT person applied the patch, but did not perform the manual remediation component, the vulnerability may still exist.

— Tools for evaluating patches installed include:

- Sun PatchPro

- Microsoft Baseline Security Analyzer
- Hfnetchk products from http://www.shavlik.com for Microsoft systems
- Red Hat Satellite Server/Red Hat Network

- Examine applications for weakness — In a perfect world, applications are built from the ground up with security in mind. Applications should prevent privilege escalation and buffer overflows and myriad other threatening problems. However, this is not always the case, and applications need to be evaluated for their ability not to compromise a host. Insecure services and daemons that run on hardened hosts may by nature weaken the host. Applications should come from trusted sources. Similarly, it is inadvisable to download executables from Web sites you know nothing about. Application testing is an area in its infancy because of its huge range of possibilities. Some programs can help evaluate a host's applications for problems. In particular, these focus on Web-based systems and database systems:
  - Nikto from http://www.cirt.net evaluates Web CGI systems for common and uncommon vulnerabilities in implementation.
  - Web Inspect from http://www.purehacking.com.au is an automated Web server scanning tool.
  - AppDetective from http://www.appsecinc.com evaluates applications, especially various types of databases, from vulnerability.
  - ISS Database Scanner from http://www.iss.net evaluates databases for security.
- Use anti-virus — Anti-virus is a must-have component for systems. Keep the following in mind when choosing anti-virus solutions:
  - What is the host's role? Workstations have different scanning requirements than e-mail gateways. Workstations need to scan files on access, floppies, and files via application access (like e-mail clients). E-mail gateways must scan incoming and outgoing e-mail messages and their attachments for viruses. Choose a product that meets the objective.
  - An anti-virus e-mail proxy might be necessary to offload the task of scanning incoming mail. Some mail servers are processor intensive and adding the scanning engine to the mail server may cripple its functionality. The mail proxy can still be set up to scan all internal or external messages so there is no security compromise.
- Use products that encourages easy management and updates of signatures; otherwise, the systems may fail to be updated, rendering them ineffective to new exploits.
- Use products that centralize reporting of problems in order to spot problem areas and trends.
- Use system integrity checking — Products like TripWire (as discussed in the SSCP Analysis and Monitoring domain Security Monitoring sec-

tion) can ensure that key system files have not been modified and if they *have* been, provide a path to restoration.

- Use system logging — Logging methods (as discussed in the SSCP Analysis and Monitoring domain Security Monitoring section) are advisable to ensure that system events are noted and securely stored, in the event they are needed at a later time.
- Subscribe to vendor information — Vendors often publish information regularly, not only to keep their name in front of you but also to inform you of security updates and best practices for configuring their systems. Other organizations like http://www.securityfocus.com and http://www.cert.org publish news of vulnerabilities.

Firewall and Router Testing Firewalls are designed to be points of data restriction (choke points) between security domains. They operate on a set of rules driven by a security policy to determine what types of data are allowed from one side to the other (point A to point B) and back again (point B to point A). Similarly, routers can also serve some of these functions when configured with access control lists (ACLs). Organizations deploy these devices to not only connect network segments together, but also to restrict access to only those data flows that are required. This can help protect organizational data assets. Routers with ACLs, if used, are usually placed in front of the firewalls to reduce the noise and volume of traffic that the firewall has to see. This allows for the firewall to be more thorough in its analysis and handling of traffic. This strategy is also known as layering or Defense in Depth.

Changes to devices should be governed by change control processes that specify what types of changes can occur and when they can occur. This prevents haphazard and dangerous changes to devices that are designed to protect internal systems from other potentially hostile networks, such as the Internet or an extranet to which your internal network connects. Change control processes should include security testing to ensure the changes were implemented correctly and as expected.

Configuration of these devices should be reflected in security procedures and the rules of the access control lists should be engendered by organizational policy. The point of testing is to ensure that what exists matches approved policy.

Sample policy for the Internet perimeter systems:

- Edge routers will have the following qualities:
- For management — Telnet disabled; SSH enabled
- An authentication system that verifies that the person logging onto the router (for managing it) is who they say they are. Accomplished with one time password system
- An authorization system that verifies that the logged on administrator

has the privileges to perform the management routines they are attempting to invoke

— An accounting system that tracks the commands that were invoked. This forms the audit trail.
— Basic intrusion detection signature recognition functionality
— Syslog event reporting to an internal host
— Blocking of RFC1918 (nonroutable addresses) and packets sourced from 0.0.0.0 inbound and outbound
— Blocking of inbound MS networking, MS SQL communication, TFTP, Oracle SQL*Net, DHCP, all type of ICMP packets except for path MTU and echo replies

- Firewalls will have the following qualities:
  — For management — Telnet disabled; SSH or SSL enabled
  — An authentication system that verifies that the person logging onto the firewall (for managing it) is who they say they are. Accomplished with one time password system
  — An authorization system that verifies that the logged on administrator has the privileges to perform the management routines they are attempting to invoke
  — An accounting system that tracks the commands that were invoked (this forms the audit trail)
  — Event report logging to an internal host
  — Network address translation functionality, if required, is working properly
  — Enabling inbound transmissions from anywhere to the organizational Web server, FTP server, SMTP mail server, and e-commerce server (for example)
  — Enabling inbound transmissions back to internal users that originally established the connections
  — Enabling outbound HTTP, HTTPS, FTP, DNS from anyone on the inside (if approved in the policy)
  — Enabling outbound SMTP from the mail server to any other mail server
  — Blocking all other outbound access

With this *sample* policy in mind, port scanners and vulnerability scanners can be leveraged to test the choke point's ability to filter as specified. If internal (trusted) systems are reachable from the external (untrusted) side in ways not specified by policy, a mismatch has occurred and should be investigated. Likewise, internal to external testing should conclude that only the allowed outbound traffic can occur. The test should compare devices logs with the tests dispatched from the test host.

Advanced firewall testing will test a device's ability to perform the following (this is a partial list and is a function of your firewall's capabilities):

- Limit TCP port scanning reconnaissance techniques (explained earlier in this chapter) including SYN, FIN, XMAS, NULL via the firewall
- Limit ICMP and UDP port scanning reconnaissance techniques
- Limit overlapping packet fragments
- Limit half-open connections to trusted side devices. Attacks like these are called SYN attacks, when the attacker begins the process of opening many connections but never completes any of them, eventually exhausting the target host's memory resources.

Advanced firewall testing can leverage a vulnerability or port scanner's ability to dispatch denial of service and reconnaissance tests. A scanner can be configured to direct, for example, massive amounts of SYN packets at an internal host. If the firewall is operating properly and effectively, it will limit the number of these half-open attempts by intercepting them so that the internal host is not adversely affected. These tests must be used with care since there is always a chance that the firewall will not do what is expected and the internal hosts might be affected.

Security Monitoring Testing IDS and other monitoring technologies including host logging (syslog) are discussed in detail in the SSCP Audit and Monitoring section entitled "Security Monitoring." IDS systems are technical security controls designed to monitor for and alert on the presence of suspicious or disallowed system activity within host processes and across networks. Device logging is used for recording many types of events that occur within hosts and network devices. Logs, whether generated by IDS or hosts, are used as audit trails and permanent records of what happened and when. Organizations have a responsibility to ensure that their monitoring systems are functioning correctly and alerting on the broad range of communications commonly in use. Likewise you can use testing to confirm that IDS detects traffic patterns as claimed by the vendor.

With regard to IDS testing, methods should include the ability to provide a stimulus (i.e., send data that simulates an exploitation of a particular vulnerability) and observe the appropriate response by the IDS. Testing can also uncover an IDS's inability to detect purposeful evasion techniques which might be used by attackers. Under controlled conditions, stimulus can be crafted and sent from vulnerability scanners. Response can be observed in log files generated by the IDS or any other monitoring system used in conjunction with the IDS. If the appropriate response is not generated, investigation of the causes can be undertaken.

With regard to host logging tests, methods should also include the ability to provide a stimulus (i.e., send data that simulates a "log-able" event) and observe the appropriate response by the monitoring system. Under controlled conditions, stimulus can be crafted in many ways depending upon your test. For example, if a host is configured to log an alert every time an administrator or equivalent logs on, you can simply log on as the "root" user to your UNIX system. In this example, response can be observed in the system's log files. If the appropriate log entry is not generated, investigation of the causes can be undertaken.

The overall goal is to make sure the monitoring is configured to your organization's specifications and that it has all of the features needed.

The following traffic types and conditions are those you should consider testing for in an IDS environment, as vulnerability exploits can be contained within any of them. If the monitoring systems you use do not cover all of them, your systems are open to exploitation:

- Data patterns that are contained within single packets — this is considered a minimum functionality since the IDS need only search through a single packet for an exploit.
- Data patterns contained within multiple packets — this is considered a desirable function since there is often more than one packet in a data stream between two hosts. This function, stateful pattern matching, requires the IDS to "remember" packets it saw in the past in order to reassemble them, as well as perform analysis to determine if exploits are contained within the aggregate payload.
- Obfuscated data — this refers to data that is converted from ASCII to Hexadecimal or Unicode characters and then sent in one or more packets. The IDS must be able to convert the code among all of these formats. If a signature that describes an exploit is written in ASCII but the exploit arrives at your system in Unicode, the IDS must convert it back to ASCII in order to recognize it as an exploit.
- Fragmented data —IP data can be fragmented across many small packets which are then reassembled by the receiving host. Fragmentation occasionally happens in normal communications. In contrast, overlapping fragments is a situation where portions of IP datagrams overwrite and supercede one another as they are reassembled on the receiving system (a teardrop attack). This can wreak havoc on a computer, which can become confused and overloaded during the reassembly process. IDS must understand how to reassemble fragmented data and overlapping fragmented data so it can analyze the resulting data. These techniques are employed by attackers to subvert systems and to evade detection.
- Protocol embedded attacks — IDS should be able to decode (i.e., break apart, understand, and process) commonly used applications (DNS, HTTP, FTP, SQL, etc.) just like a host would, to determine whether an attacker has manipulated code that might crash the application or host on which it runs. Therefore, testing should employ exploits embedded within application data.
- Flooding detection — An IDS should be able to detect conditions indicative of a denial of service flood, when too many packets originate from one or more sources to one or more destinations. Thresholds are

determined within the configuration. For example, an IDS should be able to detect if more than ten half-open (embryonic) connections are opened within 2 seconds to any one host on your network.

Monitoring Test Tools:

- Nessus open source scanner — http://www.nessus.org. This tool includes a list of interesting evasion techniques that craft packets in special ways in an attempt to trick IDS systems.
- Nikto — http://www.cirt.net/code/nikto.shtml. This is a tool primarily used to test CGI functions on Web servers and includes IDS evasion techniques made famous by Rain Forest Puppy's Whisker code. Whisker was retired by RFP in mid-2003.

Intrusion Protection Systems (IPS) are discussed in detail in the SSCP Analysis and Monitoring section — Security Monitoring. IPSs are technical security controls designed to monitor and alert for the presence of suspicious or disallowed system activity within host processes and across networks, and then take action on suspicious activities. Likewise, you can use testing to confirm that IPS detects traffic patterns and reacts as claimed by the vendor. When auditing an IPS, its position in the architecture is slightly different than that of an IDS; an IPS needs to be positioned inline of the traffic flow so the appropriate action can be taken. Some of the other key differences are: the IPS acts on issues and handles the problems, while an IDS only reports on the traffic and requires some other party to react to the situation. The negative consequence of the IPS is that it is possible to reject good traffic and there will only be the logs of the IPS to show why the good traffic is getting rejected. Many times the networking staff may not have access to those logs and may make network troubleshooting more difficult.

Security Gateway Testing Some organizations use security gateways to intercept certain communications and examine them for validity. Gateways perform their analysis on these communications based on a set of rules supplied by the organization — rules driven by policy — and pass them along if they are deemed appropriate and exploitation-free, or block them if they are not. Security gateway types include the following:

- Anti-virus gateways — these systems monitor for viruses contained within communications of major application types like Web traffic, e-mail, and FTP.
- Java/ActiveX filters — these systems screen communications for these components and block or limit their transmission.
- Web traffic screening — these systems block Web traffic to and from specific sites or sites of a specific type (gambling, pornography, games, travel and leisure, etc.).

Security testing should encompass these gateway devices to ensure their proper operation. Questions to ask during testing include:

- Is the anti-virus gateway system catching viruses? Is the gateway up-to-date with its virus signature definitions?
- Is the Web traffic proxy system scanning and blocking Java and ActiveX applications?
- Is the Web traffic proxy system allowing Web traffic to sites that are specifically disallowed by policy (gambling, etc.)?

Wireless Networking Testing With the proliferation of wireless access devices comes the common situation where they are not configured for even minimal authentication and encryption because the people deploying them generally have no knowledge of the ramifications. Therefore, periodic wireless testing to spot unofficial access points is needed. See the SSCP Networks and Telecommunications section for details on wireless setup and related security issues.

Adding 802.11-based wireless access points (AP) to networks increases overall convenience for users, mostly because of the new mobility that is possible. Whether using handheld wireless PDA devices, laptop computers, or the newly emerging wireless voice over IP telephones, users are now able to flexibly collaborate outside of the office confines — ordinarily within the building and within range of an AP — while still remaining connected to network-based resources. To enable wireless access, an inexpensive wireless access point can be procured and plugged into the network. Devices that need to connect require some sort of 802.11b, 802.11a, or 802.11g (the various types of wireless systems) network interface card that is compatible with the AP. Communication takes place from the unwired device to the AP. The AP serves (usually) as a bridge to the wired network.

The problem with this from a security perspective is that allowing the addition of one or more AP units onto the network infrastructure will likely open a large security hole. Therefore, no matter how secure your wired network is, when you add even one AP with no configured security, basic security, or even what seems to be high security, this is similar to adding a network connection in your parking lot allowing anyone with the right tools and motivation access to your internal network. The implication here is that most APs as originally implemented in the 802.11b standard have security that is easily breakable. Security testers should have methods to detect rogue APs that have been added by employees or unauthorized persons. By doing so, these wireless security holes can be eliminated. Organizations are beginning to add provisions to their security policies that specifically name APs as unauthorized devices and employees that add them to the network, no matter what the reason, are subject to stiff penalties including job loss.

The following wireless networking high points discuss some of the issues surrounding security of these systems:

- Wireless-enabled devices (e.g., laptop) can associate with wireless access points or other wireless devices to form a bridged connection to the wired network.

- If wireless equivalent privacy (WEP encryption) is not enabled on the AP, anyone within signal range of an AP can associate with it and get onto the network. This can be done from inside or outside a building. The attacker only needs to be within the signal range of the AP, which is generally 50 to 150 feet and is a function of the transmission power of the AP, obstructions that impede radio waves, interference, and the type of signaling used (802.11b, a, and g). To join the network, the attacker only needs to detect the SSID (service set identifier) which is usually broadcast from an AP, and plug that information into their setup. Even if SSID information is not broadcast, it can be snooped out of radio frequency transmission; note then, that disabling SSID broadcast is a security protection fallacy.

- Wireless networks can use MAC address (OSI Layer 2 address) filters so that only approved MAC addresses can access the network AP. This security approach is also suspect because MAC addresses can easily be "sniffed" out of normal wireless communications and be reused (spoofed) by an attacker.

- If wireless equivalent privacy (WEP encryption) is enabled, weaknesses in the WEP algorithm can be exploited to derive the key that is used to both authenticate a device to the network and provide data privacy (encryption). On a busy network, enough data can be passively collected in about 15 minutes to derive the key using easily obtainable special software. The key can then be used for unauthorized access. Furthermore, those weaknesses in WEP can be exploited using active attacks like bit flipping and key replay to derive the WEP key for the same purpose.

- WEP in its basic and most common form has no provisions for managing and rotating keys; therefore, single, nonchanging keys are hardcoded into software. If a laptop is stolen, for example, the key has been compromised and can be used for network access. To mitigate this particular problem, the keys must be changed on all APs and devices that access those APs. If you manage ten devices this is easy; if you manage over 100 devices, the issue becomes more complicated.

- 802.1x is an authentication standard that can be used for key management in an 802.11x (where x = b, a, or g wireless) environment. When possible, deploy systems that utilize this to ensure more advanced authentication schemes and key rotation.

- Wireless protected access (WPA) and 802.11i are advanced wireless security specifications that employ 802.1x for superior authentication and encryption at OSI Layer 2.

- Risks can be lessened by using a network design in which all of the wireless access points are considered an extranet and all of the devices connecting through those access points must connect and authenticate via a VPN. If a user does not connect via a VPN, his connection into the network will not be accepted, his action will be logged, and appropriate security measures and reactions will be taken. This design also limits the amount of data that an outsider can snoop.

With this information, a security tester can test for the effectiveness of wireless security in the environment using specialized tools and techniques as presented here.

- To search for rogue (unauthorized) access points, you can use some of the following techniques:
  - Use a network vulnerability scanner with signatures that specifically scan for MAC addresses (of the wired port) of vendors that produce AP units, then attempt to connect to that interface on an HTTP port. If the unit responds, analyze the Web code to determine if it is a Web page related to the management of the AP device. This requires periodic scanning and will leave you vulnerable until the time you have the opportunity to scan again.
  - Use a laptop or handheld unit loaded with software that analyzes 802.11x radio frequency (RF) transmissions for SSIDs and WA wired side MAC addresses that do not belong to the company or are not authorized. Make sure discovery tools pick up all bands and 802.11x types; that is, if you only test for 802.11b, you may miss rogue 802.11a units. This requires periodic scanning by physically walking through the organization's grounds and will leave you vulnerable until the time you have the opportunity to scan again.
  - Up and coming solutions allow for authorized APs and wireless clients to detect unauthorized RF transmissions and "squeal" on the rogue access point. This information can be used to automatically disable an infrastructure switch port to which a rogue has connected.
- To lock down the enterprise from the possibility of rogue APs, you can do the following:
  - Enable MAC address filtering on your infrastructure switches. This technique matches each port to a known MAC address. If someone plugs in an unapproved MAC to a switch port expecting another MAC address, the AP will never be able to join the network from the wired side.
- To gauge security effectiveness of authorized APs:
  - Discover authorized APs using the tools described herein and ensure they require encryption (if this is your security policy).
  - Ensure discovered APs meet other policy requirements such as the type of authentication (802.1x or other), SSID naming structure, and MAC address filtering.
  - Ensure APs have appropriate Layer 2 ethertype filters, Layer 3 protocol filters, and Layer 4 port filters (to match your configuration

procedures) so that untrusted wireless traffic coming into the AP is limited to only that which is needed and required.

Wireless Tools:

- Netstumbler — http://www.netstumbler.com — Windows software that detects 802.11b information through RF detection including SSID, whether communication is encrypted, and signal strength.
- Kismet — http://www.kismetwireless.net — Linux software that detects 802.11b and 802.11a information through RF detection including SSID, whether communication is encrypted, and signal strength. It features the ability to rewrite MAC address on select wireless cards.
- Wellenreiter — http://www.remote-exploit.org — Linux software that detects wireless networks. It runs on Linux-based handheld PDA computers.
- Nessus — http://www.nessus.org — Linux software for vulnerability assessment that includes thirty plus signatures to detect WAP units.
- Airsnort — http://airsnort.shmoo.com — Linux software that passively collects wireless frames and exploiting WEP weakness, derives the WEP key.

War Dialing War dialing attempts to locate unauthorized (a.k.a. rogue) modems connected to computers that are connected to networks. Attackers use tools to sequentially and automatically dial large blocks of numbers used by the organization in the hopes that rogue modems will answer and allow them to make a remote asynchronous connection to it. With weak or nonexistent authentication, these rogue modems may serve as a back door into the heart of a network, especially when connected to computers that host remote control applications with lax security.

Security testers can use war dialing techniques as a preventative measure and attempt to discover these modems for subsequent elimination.

War Dialing Tools:

- Toneloc — http://www.securityfocus.com/tools/48 — Short for tone locator. Automatically dials numbers and records results in a log
- THC-Scan — http://www.thc.org
- Phone Sweep — http://www.sandstorm.net/products/phonesweep

Password Testing Password length, character mix (the use of upper case, lower case, numerals, and special characters), and rotation schedule should be governed by policy. Password testing is an activity to test the implementation of policy. It examines the password policy implementation by examining password strength and validity as defined by policy. Furthermore, password testing shows whether systems are using weak or ineffective cryptographic algorithms.

Password testing software does its work in one of three ways:

- Sequential interactive login attempts using a dictionary of possible words
- Sniffing password interactions on a network and deriving them
- Dictionary and brute-force cracking of hashes contained within a password file

Sequential interactive login is performed from special software that mimics client software such as HTTP, POP3, IMAP, FTP, Telnet, SMB (Windows). The software, for example, looks like an FTP client and tries username and password combinations over and over until it gets it right. Target systems that specify account lockout on a certain number of failed attempts guard against this vulnerability; however, certain key accounts, like a Microsoft administrator account do not by default have lockout, therefore, it is vulnerable.

Sniffing passwords off of the wire involves observing data packets, placing related ones into a related session, and using the session information to reverse engineer a password.

Brute force cracking can be used if you have obtained the system files that contain cryptographic password hashes, perhaps through the use of penetration techniques. A cooperative tester will obtain the hashes in an acceptable, nondeceptive way and use software tools to evaluate the hashes and thus the policy that drives them.

Password hash files are stored on systems in different ways:

- Windows NT-based systems — for systems that have had at least one emergency repair disk created, they are stored in the \{main NT installation directory}\repair\sam._. If this directory does not exist, use a tool like pwdump3 to obtain the hashes from active memory processes.
- UNIX systems usually store password hashes in /etc/shadow or /etc/passwd.
- UNIX systems that have the ability to connect to Windows NT systems via SMB communications store passwords for those NT systems in /etc/smbpasswd.

Obtain the password hash files and use one or more of the following techniques to "crack" them:

- Use brute-force password cycling software
- Perform dictionary-based guessing

Once the hashes are cracked you can evaluate how well passwords are constructed and whether they meet policy specifications. Take care to guard password hash files and resulting cracked hashes as this information is of the utmost sensitivity.

Interactive Password evaluation tools:

- Brutus — http://www.hoobie.net/brutus/
- NAT — http://www.nardware.co.uk/Security/NetBIOS/NetBIOSscan3.htm

Sniffing password evaluation tools:

- Cain & Abel — http://www.oxid.it/cain.html

Brute force password evaluation tools:

- John the Ripper — http://www.openwall.com/john/
- L0phtCrack — http://www.securityfocus.com/tools/1005

Penetration Testing Defined The highest level of sophistication in security testing is penetration testing, an activity that takes the results of reconnaissance, network mapping, and vulnerability testing and adds techniques to carry out an attack by exercising one or more vulnerabilities. Penetration testing uses custom tools and procedures to circumvent in-place security controls to expose weaknesses that might be exploited. This step often tries to perform the exploit without doing permanent damage. It can expose deficient or nonexistent security controls. It is often considered the most radical of approaches and has been used to gain the attention of senior managers who do not take security as seriously as they should.

This phase of testing revolves around gauging the risk of (possible) vulnerabilities identified in the previous step and prioritizing them by likelihood of success. A tester's goal is to verify that the vulnerabilities are valid not just by examining them more closely — as is done with a vulnerability analysis follow-up — but by trying to exploit them. For example, assume that you have determined that a particular host running Web services is vulnerable to a directory traversal exploit. Penetration testing would employ techniques to attempt an actual traversal across networks, gain control of files normally off limits, and escalate privilege, which would lead to taking further system control. Penetration testing not only *identifies* vulnerability but also *attempts* to perform the exploitation.

Penetration testing techniques are as numerous as vulnerabilities are and testing varies considerably. Unlike vulnerability testers, penetration testers usually do not receive network diagrams, systems configurations, logon credentials, and other information necessary to make a complete system evaluation. Penetration testing is often conducted by persons who have little to no knowledge of your systems; therefore, tests are usually covert in nature and IT personnel and system owners often have no idea they are taking place. To gain access, testers must hunt for information the same way an attacker would in order to get a foothold into your network — which means that the reconnaissance stage discussed earlier is important to a penetration tester. Depending on the budget for the project, the penetration test can look something like the following:

- Zero knowledge — Testers have no knowledge of the systems they are testing. This type of test will likely require a larger budget because more time will be spent ferreting out weaknesses.
- Some knowledge — Testers have an idea of which hosts they are to test and which hosts they are not to test. This arrangement would require fewer funds because testers are directed to the systems that need testing.
- Step-by-step — Testing where what is found is relayed to the trusted insider before proceeding. This type of testing allows for the test to be stopped if any glaring flaws are found or discoveries are made.

Goals of penetration tests include:

- Attempt to compromise security and gain privileged user access
- NT domain administrator level access
- Novell administrator equivalent
- UNIX root
- Penetrate systems and gain access to critical data
- Demonstrate tester could deny service
- Determine if the IT organization can detect the intrusion

The scope of penetration testing can include the following:

- Location of testing
  - Internal testing of internal systems
  - External testing of external systems
  - External testing of internal systems
- A technical attack to subvert software
  - Host
  - Network device
  - Application
- Social engineering
  - Coaxing humans to give up information they should not give up to help in system penetration
  - Deriving or finding remnant information that should have been destroyed but was not

The benefits of penetration testing include:

- Can help prove that inadequate security may cause significant loss
- Allows you to fully test system and network patches
- Allows you to fully test response procedures
- Help highlight weaknesses not shown in a vulnerability test (exploitation of trusts)

The disadvantages of penetration testing include:

- Considered by many practitioners as being least useful in most situations for improving security because it only identifies a narrow slice of security issues

- Proves only that the system can be compromised
- Does not identify all vulnerabilities
- Potential to crash the network or host being tested

Most of these disadvantages can be mitigated by using a step-by-step approach and by combining the results of the penetration test with those of the vulnerability testing. This combination may verify the results found in vulnerability testing or may even find some weaknesses that the other testing was unable to uncover.

It is also good practice to back up all devices on a network prior to conducting a penetration test. In case the testing does cause some issues, the back-ups can easily be restored and the network can return to its past state.

Penetration testing requires skilled personnel because:

- The potential risk for system damage is high, as testers may be performing unorthodox system manipulation leading to unpredictable results.
- It may also cause disruption on production systems if dangerous tests are performed.
- The tester needs to be able to determine that a machine being tested has already been compromised and understand the necessary actions they need to take once that determination has been made.

Penetration Testing — General Examples Warning: Think twice before attempting to exploit a possible vulnerability that may harm the system. For instance, if the system might be susceptible to a buffer overflow attack, do not necessarily perform the attack. Weigh the benefits of succinctly identifying vulnerabilities against crashing the system.

Here are some samples:

- Vulnerability testing shows that a Web server may be vulnerable to crashing if it is issued a very long request with dots (i.e., ../../../../ ../../../../ 1000 times). You can either try to actually crash the server using the technique (although this may have productivity loss consequences) or alternatively and perhaps for the better you can note it for further investigation, perhaps on a test server. Make sure you have permission prior to attempting this type of actual exploitation.
- Vulnerability testing shows that a UNIX host has a root account with the password set to root. You can easily test this find to determine whether this is a false positive.
- Vulnerability testing shows that a router may be susceptible to an SSH attack. You can either try the attack with permission or note it for further investigation.

Penetration Testing High-Level Steps

The following outline provides a high-level view of the steps that could be taken to exploit systems during a penetration test. It is similar in nature to a vulnerability test but goes further to perform an exploit.

1. Obtain a network address (usually center on internal testing when you are physically onsite) — With the advent DHCP on the network, a tester can often plug in and get an IP address right away. DHCP assigned addresses usually come with gateway and name server addresses. If the tester does not get a DHCP address, the system may be setup for static addresses. You can sniff the network for communications that detail the segment you are on and guess at an unused address.
2. Reconnaissance — Gather target information
   - DNS information obtained via DHCP
   - DNS zone transfer when allowed by the server
   - Whois
   - Browsing an internal domain
   - Using Windows utilities to enumerate servers
3. Network mapping and discovery
   - Pings sweeps
   - Traceroute
   - Port scans (TCP connect, SYN scans, etc.)
   - OS fingerprinting
   - Banner grabbing
   - Unix RPC discovery
4. Target selection based upon:
   - Likelihood of success with hosts that look like they run many services
   - Key hosts like domain controllers or other key systems with many services running
5. Target vulnerability analysis and enumeration
   - Using techniques that are less likely to be logged or reported in an IDS system (that is less "noisy" techniques) evaluate the vulnerability of ports on a target
   - For NT systems, gather user, group, and system information with null sessions (NT), "net" commands, nltest utility
   - For UNIX systems, gather RPC information
6. Exploitation — Identify and exploit the vulnerabilities
   - Buffer overflows
   - Brute force
   - Password cracking
   - Vulnerability chaining
   - Data access

Penetration Testing — NT Host Enumeration Example

- Gain access to the network.
- Enumerate NT operating system details.
- Identify domain controllers for the purpose of attempting password file access.
- Attempt NULL connections to servers to enumerate vital information.
- Attempt administrator access based on the user list obtained.
- If administrator access is obtained, use utilities to obtain the password file.
- Crack the password file.
- Explore other trusted domains using password derived from the crack.

This example shows an overview of a Microsoft Windows penetration test. The premise is that security consultants have been hired by the CIO to perform a penetration test to discern whether reasonable security controls are in place. The IT staff is not aware that this covert test is scheduled. Their goal is to attempt access on the NT domain system. They are not supposed to use penetration techniques likely to damage data or systems. The following steps show how the testers might go about their task. Keep in mind that this is an example and that conditions might be different in your situation.

1. The testers arrive at the organization's headquarters and sign in with physical security. They make small talk and claim they are from an office in another city. The testers are granted access and make themselves at home in a conference room.
2. They plug into the LAN ports. One of two ports is live. The PC on the live port receives a DHCP IP address along with domain name information, gateway, WINS, and DNS server addresses.
3. Using built-in Windows commands and NT Resource Kit commands, the tester begins to gather useful network information and identify potential targets. By design, Windows systems offer up rich content about the details of systems on the network. This detail, while used for normal operation, can also be used against the servers. Since many of the net commands found on Windows systems do not require authenticated access, information can be obtained from any NT workstation on the network. The tester identifies NT domains (this also came as part of the DHCP address details but this command shows *all* the domains in the domain browser list) using the built-in net command:

   ```
   C:\sectools>net view /domain
   Domain
   ```

   ```
   HQ
   HQ-ACCOUNTING
   WORKGROUP
   The command completed successfully.
   ```

The tester now identifies computers belonging to the HQ domain specifically:

C:\sectools>net view /domain:HQ
Server Name   Remark

Server Name	Remark
\\CAD	Administrators remarks
\\OFFICESERV	Application server
\\RND	Research Server
\\IT	Server
\\IT2	Server

The command completed successfully

Identify HQ domain controllers with the Windows resource kit "nltest" utility. Note that nltest includes the means to obtain a huge array of domain information:

C:\sectools>nltest /dclist:HQ
Get list of DCs in domain 'HQ' from '\\OFFICESERV '.
  officeserv.hq.com [PDC] [DS] Site: Default-First-Site-Name

The command completed successfully

Once the available systems in the domain are identified, the tester will select potential targets usually based on their name and whether they are domain controllers. The tester can generally determine the IP address or name of the target server using the following ping technique if a name server (DNS or WINS) was specified as part of the DHCP address information:

C:\sectools>ping officeserv

Pinging officeserv.hq.com [10.90.50.5] with 32 bytes of data:

Reply from 10.90.50.5: bytes=32 time<1ms TTL=128
Reply from 10.90.50.5: bytes=32 time<1ms TTL=128
Reply from 10.90.50.5: bytes=32 time<1ms TTL=128
Reply from 10.90.50.5: bytes=32 time<1ms TTL=128

Ping statistics for 10.90.50.5:
  Packets: Sent = 4, Received = 4, Lost = 0 (0% loss),
Approximate round trip times in milli-seconds:
  Minimum = 0ms, Maximum = 0ms, Average = 0ms

The tester can enumerate the role of server in the domain using the "netdom" tool found in the Windows resource kit. In this example the tester queries for the role of member server RND and its relationship to its domain controller OFFICESERV:

C:\sectools>netdom query \\rnd
NetDom 1.8 @1997-98.

Querying domain information on computer \\RND...
Computer \\RND is a member of HQ.
Searching PDC for domain HQ...
Found PDC \\OFFICESERV
Connecting to \\OFFICESERV...
Verifying secure channel on \\RND...

Secure channel established successfully with \\officeserv.hq.com for domain HQ.

The tester decides to target the domain controller because it maintains the password file (also known as the SAM file) for the entire domain. In order to get detailed information from the target server, the tester has to, at a minimum, establish a "null session" to the server. A null session is an anonymous, nonauthenticated connection to a Windows host. Once the connection is established, detailed information about the system can be obtained. Note that support for null sessions can be disabled which makes the job of exploiting the host more difficult.

C:\sectools>net use \\officeserv\ipc$"/user:"
The command completed successfully.

With an established null session, the tester can use a tool like SomarSoft's DumpSec to derive vital domain controller information, including domain user names, password policy information, permissions, and trusted domains. DumpSec allows for the retrieval of information using an anonymous connection to a computer including the following:

- "Dumping" of user names to identify administrators, accounts used for application services, and other user accounts
- Detailed user information including last logon, password last changed times, account status, RAS permissions, SID, etc.
- Group information including which ones exist and which users are contained within them
- File permissions including user and group permissions and file level auditing
- Registry permissions including user and group permissions and key level auditing
- Share permissions including user and group permissions for existing shares

DumpSec allows for the retrieval of information using an administrator connection to a computer including the following:

- Policies including account policy, trusts, audit policy, replication, and null sessions
- Rights including detailed rights assigned to groups and individuals
- Services including which services are installed and running on the host

Once all user information is enumerated via DumpSec (remember that at this point the tester only has an anonymous connection to the target), the tester terminates the null session.

C:\sectools>net use \\officeserv\ipc$ /delete

The tester now attempts to logon as administrator (or some other username they learned from DumpSec) and manually guesses passwords for the account on the target domain controller using the "net use" command. If the tester were to target a member server (i.e., a nondomain controller), he would be attempting access on the local user database (SAM) file. Domain-wide SAM files are only resident on domain controllers.

C:\sectools>net use \\officeserv\ipc$ * /user:HQ\administrator
Type the password for \\officeserv\ipc$:{password guess 1}
Logon failure: unknown user name or bad password
C:\sectools>net use \\officeserv\ipc$ * /user:HQ\administrator
Type the password for \\officeserv\ipc$:{password guess 2}
Logon failure: unknown user name or bad password

C:\sectools>net use \\officeserv\ipc$ * /user:HQ\administrator
Type the password for \\officeserv\ipc$:{password guess 3}
Logon failure: unknown user name or bad password

C:\sectools>net use \\officeserv\ipc$ * /user:HQ\administrator
Type the password for \\officeserv\ipc$:{password guess 4}
Logon failure: unknown user name or bad password

Administrator accounts do not normally have a lockout feature that deactivates the account if too many bad logon attempts are made. However, the "passprop" utility adds this function and forces administrators to go to the host's console to unlock the administrator account. The tester, who does not have physical server access, checks to see if the passprop utility is being used to lock the administrator account remotely if excessive bad logon attempts are made. Using DumpSec via another anonymous IPC$ connection, she determines whether the administrator account has been locked after two to six attempts. If it is not, she again deletes the IPC$ connection to the server and begins using automated password guessing tools.

Using Secure Networks Inc.'s NAT (NetBIOS Auditing Tool — there are others like this including Brutus and SMBGrind), the tester attempts to guess passwords in an automated fashion by specifying one or more administrator accounts learned from DumpSec. Assuming that at least one of those accounts has a weak password, the tester will learn the password and get privileged access. The section in this chapter — Password Testing explains this activity more fully.

C:\sectools>nat –o <output_file> –u <user_list> –p <password_list> <ip_address>

Next the tester uses the "pwdump3" utility to make an administrative level connection to the host with the administrator credentials learned from cracking activities and extracts the SAM file out of the server's running memory (the SAM file itself is locked during operation because it is always in use). Pwdump3 logs onto the host, installs itself as a service, turns itself on, grabs the information from memory, copies it back to the tester's host, stops itself from running in host memory, and uninstalls itself.

C:\sectools\pwdump3v2>pwdump3 officeserv sam-hashes.txt administrator

pwdump3 (rev 2) by Phil Staubs, e-business technology, 23 Feb 2001 Copyright 2001 e-business technology, Inc.

This program is free software based on pwpump2 by Todd Sabin under the GNU General Public License Version 2 (GNU GPL), you can redistribute it and/or modify it under the terms of the GNU GPL, as published by the Free Software Foundation. NO WARRANTY, EXPRESSED OR IMPLIED, IS GRANTED WITH THIS PROGRAM. Please see the COPYING file included with this program (also available at www. ebiz-tech.com/pwdump3) and the GNU GPL for further details.

Please enter the password >*********

Completed.

Now that the tester has the domain controller's SAM file, he can use a password cracking utility like John the Ripper or L0phtcrack to crack the passwords for many of the users. The following is the contents of the hash file obtained by pwdump3:

Administrator:500:CFB4021690DA871A944E2DF489A880E4:179BE7 084BBB5FFA2D96AB59F6AA6D96:::

bill:1002:E52CAC67419A9A22F96F275E1115B16F:E22E04519AA757 D12F1219C4F31252F4:::

Guest:501:NO   PASSWORD*******************:NO   PASSWORD*******************:::

IUSR_HQ:1004:E0C510199CC66ABDAAD3B435B51404EE:352DFE55 1D62459B20349B78A21A2F37:::

mary:1001:FB169B026D5B9DE72CFBD46F2C07EC6B:6AD16A97C21 9C6DB8AAAAC8236F769E0:::

roger:1003:62B4F4E39B2EF8637F8E43D4EB012C81:A4D9F51558777 8C30F31ACD76844AE56:::

While the password cracker is running, the test team can access this host and other hosts with trust relationships and look around for "interesting" data. Within a few hours, 40–90 percent of the passwords in the SAM file are likely to be cracked providing access from host to host in any allowable user context. Perhaps one of the most damaging exploitation activities is accessing an organizational leader's e-mail with their user credentials learned from the SAM file cracking activity.

Penetration Testing Example Closing Notes Penetration testers will often use the information learned to perform further host and domain exploitation. Often when one administrator or equivalent account falls, it is only a matter of time before they all fall. Furthermore, any trusting domain of the compromised domain can in turn be compromised. Access at this level allows a penetration tester access to potentially sensitive system files and data files. It allows for the installation of backdoor programs like NetCat and VNC (among others) for continued easy access into hosts thought to be secure.

As stated in other sections of this courseware, to protect NT hosts from this type of exploitation, use some of the following countermeasures:

- Disable unnecessary system services.
- Disable anonymous registry access.
- Use Passprop.exe for remote lock out of administrator accounts when a specified threshold of failed login attempts is reached.
- Implement complex password policies.
- Test system patches for effectiveness and stability and patch systems as fixes become available.
- Tighten file and registry permissions on production systems using tools like the security policy editor.
- Enable auditing of system events and review log files regularly.

Section 3: Security Monitoring

In the previous sections we discussed the features of the audit. Now we will address the monitoring of systems. We will explore the overall concept of monitoring and look at methods and technologies of monitoring from an IDS/IPS viewpoint. We will then take a look at the logs of this monitoring and see how they are gathered, stored, and analyzed. From an auditor's or attacker's point of view, we will also examine a way to evade monitoring, and we will discuss the implementation issues that arise in monitoring.

This section demonstrates how the IT security practitioner evaluates the effectiveness of deploying one or more methodologies in order to support organizational security policies.

Security Monitoring Concepts — Why Are Systems Attacked?

It would be naïve to believe that any system is completely safe, no matter how extreme the measures that are employed to ensure protection of its confidentiality, integrity, and availability. You should assume that all systems are susceptible to attack. This mindset helps an IT security practitioner prepare for inevitable system compromises. Comprehensive policies and procedures and their effective use are excellent mitigation techniques for stemming the effectiveness of attacks. Security monitoring is a mitigation activity used to protect systems and encompasses several techniques as discussed in this SSCP section.

Attackers are those persons who perform overt and covert intrusions or attacks on systems. They are often motivated by one of the following:

- Notoriety/ego/sport — exemplifies the attacker's "power" to his or her audience, whether to just a few people or to the world. To the attacker, the inherent challenge is "I want to see if I can do it and I want everyone to know about it."
- Greed/profit — the attacker is attempting personal financial gain or financial gain of a client; that is, an attacker might have been hired by a business to furtively damage a competitor's system or gain unauthorized access to the competitor's data. An attacker may use or resell information found on systems, such as credit card numbers.
- Political agenda — attacking a political nemesis physically or electronically is seen as a way to further one's own agenda or ideals or call attention to a cause.
- Revenge — the overriding motivation behind revenge in the attacker's eyes is, "I've been wronged and I am going to get you back." Revenge is often exacted by former employees or those who were at one point in time trusted by the organization that is now being attacked.

What Is an Intrusion? Intrusions are acts by persons, organizations, or systems that are unwanted by the recipient. They are considered attacks but are not just limited to computing systems. If something is classified as an intrusion, it will fall into one of following two categories:

- Intrusions can be overt and are generally noticeable immediately.
- Intrusions can be covert and not always noticeable right away, if at all.

Examples of overt intrusion include the following:

- Someone breaking into your automobile
- Two people robbing a bank
- An airline hijacker
- Flooding an E-commerce site with too much data from too many sources, thereby rendering the site useless for legitimate customers
- Attackers defacing a Web site

Covert intrusions may be harder to discover because the attacker may be after, for example, sensitive research and development plans but he does not want the victim to know they were intruded upon.

Examples of covert intrusions include the following:

- A waiter stealing your credit card number after you have paid your bill and using it on the Web that evening
- An accounting department employee manipulating financial accounts for illegal and unauthorized personal financial gain
- A computer criminal collecting information about your systems by using slow and measured reconnaissance techniques to map your network for vulnerable systems
- An authorized user that improperly obtains system administrator logon credentials in order to access private company records to which they are not authorized
- An attacker who poses as an authorized computer support representative to gain the trust of an unknowing user, in order to obtain information for use in a computer attack.

A variety of controls will stop these attacks. For example:

- Integrity monitoring may have alerted administrators that the main Web site page had changed by comparing the "known good" main page to the one that replaced it.
- Network IDS may have detected in real-time that the exploitation technique used for system access that enabled them to change the page was, in fact, happening.
- Host IDS may have detected in real-time that a process that normally does not alter pages was altering the main page.
- System and application logs can show suspicious activities taking place over time.

When an attacker is out to prove to themselves (and the world) that they are superior in some way and they deface a Web page, customer confidence suffers. The intrusions produce consumer doubt that can destroy commerce.

Determining What Is Acceptable Organizations may create their standards from policy guidelines produced by standards bodies. Acceptable and unacceptable transactions should be defined by policy. How do we determine what is acceptable? Acceptable system activity is defined as communications within acceptable bounds and of acceptable type and are stated in a policy document. Examples include:

- We find data traffic of types X, Y, and Z to be acceptable as they flow between Segment 1 and Segment 2.

- If the system detects less than ten connection attempts per minute from one machine, this is acceptable. Anything above this is suspect and may represent a denial of service attack.
- There shall be no administrative logons between 10 p.m. and 6 a.m. unless approved by the manager of information technology or his superior. Logons at off hours may be a sign of suspicious activity.
- Web traffic is acceptable as long as it contains no embedded exploits as defined by the network intrusion detection system database of signatures and the host intrusion detection system anomalous activity software engine.
- Between the hours of 9 a.m. and 6 p.m. Monday through Friday, employees may access any external Web site as long as it assists them with their work. For all other times, employees may access business and nonbusiness Web sites for educational purposes as long as the sites are not prohibited (gambling, pornography, political, etc.) by the Web content filter systems.

How do we determine what is unacceptable? Unacceptable system activity is defined as communications specifically disallowed in a security policy or something that may potentially cause damage to a system's integrity, reveal confidential information, or make it unavailable even if it is not specifically stated by policy. Unacceptable system activity may be everything that is not considered acceptable. Examples include:

- Since data traffic of types X, Y, and Z is allowed between Segment 1 and Segment 2, all other traffic shall be deemed unacceptable until explicitly added to the acceptable traffic list.
- Users within the Marketing organization are prohibited from accessing any host owned by the Research and Development organization.
- Any inbound communications from the Internet shall be inspected by the firewall and if the communication is not allowed by the communication rules detailed in the firewall configuration, the communication shall be dropped and the event logged.
- Using a known buffer overflow and attempting to exploit an operating system vulnerability is unacceptable.
- If a system detects that an unauthorized process is attempting to access the data used by the Web process, this attempt is unacceptable.
- If the system detects that incoming packets are irregularly formed (or malformed), that is, they do not adhere to RFC standards, this malformation shall be disallowed.
- A user attempting to access a device or information that they have not been authorized to do so is unacceptable.

With regard to our personal lives, an obvious unwanted attack would be someone breaking the window in your car and stealing a box from the back seat. Regarding computing systems, some acts are obviously unwanted, such as the technical attack of a DNS server or a virus running wild throughout the Internet that has the potential to infect our systems.

In the professional world, acceptable transactions should be defined by policy so it is clear what actions are acceptable and what actions are unacceptable. This makes your organization's reactions to unacceptable activities defensible. As you will see in the SSCP Analysis and Monitoring Domain's Auditing section, companies create their organizational standards from policy guidelines produced by standards bodies like the ISO, governmental bodies like NIST, and professional organizations like ISSA. Organizational policy should address what types of communications are acceptable. This can be defined through an acceptable use policy or another policy that defines how communications are to flow.

Security Monitoring for Everyday Life Everyday life intrusion monitoring control examples include the following:

- We do not want our vehicles or homes broken into; therefore, some people purchase and install burglar alarms as a deterrent to this unacceptable behavior by thieves.
- We do not want our places of business to suffer losses; therefore, these organizations employ an array of physical security measures such as vaults, guards, alarms, and cameras to act as a deterrent to intrusions by thieves.
- We do not want our credit card numbers stolen but unfortunately this sometimes happens. To limit our exposure to fraudulent purchases, credit card companies have systems in place that aim to notice anomalous purchasing patterns, thereby reducing this type of financial intrusion. These systems can automatically halt the validity of a card if atypical purchase patterns are detected.
- We do not want our airports and airline travel to be unsafe; therefore, multiple layers of physical security comprised of inspectors and officers trained in intrusion monitoring are present to thwart those persons who might try to smuggle weapons or unsafe goods (e.g., baggage x-ray machines and metal detectors).

Security Monitoring for Computing Systems The monitoring of computers and systems is the process of identifying and terminating overt or covert intrusive acts using a variety of technical controls. The monitoring of computer systems has many parallel or equivalent methods in the physical world.

Examples of computing security monitoring that likely applies to most organizations:

- We do not want our Web site defaced by replacing the picture of the CEO with a picture of Elvis; therefore, we can monitor for the unauthorized access techniques that attackers employ.

- We do not want an attacker perpetrating a denial of service attack (an attempt to slow down or bring a system to a halt) against our e-mail server; therefore, we can monitor to spot network behavior indicating this event.
- We do not want an attacker performing reconnaissance studies against our systems in an effort to discover open services that may have vulnerabilities leading to exploitation; therefore, we can use IDS to alert us about unusual data traffic.
- We do want to have an ongoing record of important system events stored in a manner resistant to repudiation.

Monitoring systems for hosts and key network infrastructure devices, which are discussed in more detail later, can be broken down into two classes:

- Real-time monitoring — provides a means for immediately identifying and sometimes stopping (depending on the type of system used) overt and covert behavior that is defined as unacceptable. They include network and host intrusion detection systems. These systems keep watch on systems and (can) alert administrators as disallowed activity is happening. They can also log events for subsequent analysis if needed. IDS technology for computers is like the burglar alarm for your home. When someone breaks in, it sounds the alarm.
- Non-real-time monitoring — provides a means for saving important information about system events and monitoring the integrity of system configurations in a nonimmediate fashion. These technologies include application logging, system logging, and integrity monitoring. Logging and integrity systems might tell you that a burglar was at your home, but he is likely gone by the time you find out. This does not mean that non-real-time systems are not as good as real-time systems. Each fulfills a different niche in monitoring. These system logs would be more like the footprints or fingerprints a burglar would leave behind.

Logging provides a means for recording activities by sending log data to a repository for forensic analysis at a later time.

Integrity systems, which are a form of IDS, have knowledge of what a non-corrupted/noncompromised system profile looks like so that the "known good" profile can be compared to the current profile. Any differences can be investigated.

Why Is Monitoring Necessary? Data produced by monitoring systems can be used for a variety of purposes. Consider the following:

- Audit trail — logs can uncover the steps a user or system process took to modify components of a system. This, of course, depends on the level of logging detail.
- Events — event logs can uncover system events that took place in the past.

- Forensics — untainted logs can help examiners piece together what happened prior to system exploitation. These may also be required for legal purposes.
- Variance from security policy — actions uncovered in logs can show variance from security policy.

Monitoring Issues With the size of networks and the number of access points within them, the data gathered can be staggering. This is further complicated by the following:

- Quality of Data — how complete is the logging data sent to logging systems and are the logging systems working as designed?
- Volume of traffic — how much data volume is being stored and is it possible to effectively analyze it?
- Spatial distribution — where is the data coming from within the organization?
- More sophisticated attacks — do data analysis systems have the capability to detect sophisticated attacks embedded within the data we have collected?
- Complexity of the networks — how complex is our network and does its complexity outstrip our ability or the ability of our analysis systems to comprehend the attacks taking place on it?
- Encryption — is encryption being used against us?
- Protection of reported network event data.
- Identifying attacks on an encrypted network.
- Attacks concealed within encrypted data.
- Switched Networks — are the advantages of our switch networks keeping us from being able to see the data that might represent an attack?
- Decreased network event visibility.
- Complexity of a network IDS increases.
- Packet loss for a network IDS increases with bandwidth.

Other Monitoring Notes Monitoring is one type of security control, specifically a technical control. Monitoring should be designed to positively identify actual attacks (true positive) but not identify regular communications as a threat (false positive), or do everything possible to increase the identification of actual attacks and decrease the false positive notifications.

Monitoring event information can provide considerable insight about the attacks being perpetrated within your network. This information can help organizations make necessary modifications to security policies and the supporting safeguards and countermeasures for improved protection.

Usually monitoring technology needs to be "tuned," which is the process of customizing the default configuration to the unique needs of your systems. In order to tune out alarms that are harmless (false positives), you must know what types of data traffic are considered acceptable.

Deploying monitoring systems is one part of a multilayer security strategy comprised of several types of security controls. This being said, monitoring should never be the sole means of system security. Monitoring should typically be deployed alongside the following partial list of security controls:

- Implement firewalls and routers with data traffic access controls. These network devices serve as choke points between security domains.
- Implement host security hardening to eliminate or at least reduce vulnerabilities by periodically applying patches and disabling unnecessary and insecure services.
- Implement user authentication and access controls to keep unauthorized users away from confidential data.
- Implement anti-virus systems.

For a listing of system vulnerabilities visit the CERT Web site at http://www.cert.org/advisories/. Monitoring vendors often design updates to coincide with vulnerabilities.

Terminology Monitoring terminology can seem arcane and confusing. The purpose of this list is to define by example and reinforce terminology commonly used when discussing monitoring technology.

- Safeguard — a security control implemented to provide protection against threats
- Countermeasure — another word for safeguard
- Vulnerability — a system weakness
- Exploit — a particular attack. It is named this way because these attacks exploit system vulnerabilities.
- Signature — a string of characters or activities found within processes or data communications that describes a known system attack. Some monitoring systems identify attacks by means of a signature.
- Event — a single instance of some observed action that may (or may not) be cause for concern. An event might be a logged instance of the UNIX "root" user logging onto the system. Whether this is cause for concern is unknown because the action may be legitimate.
- Triggering an event — providing notice that the monitoring system "thinks" that an event is cause for concern. For example, the monitoring system may define that UNIX "root" logon outside of normal business hours and scheduled maintenance windows is cause for concern. Therefore, a root logon at 2 a.m. may trigger an event.
- Firing an alarm — same as triggering an event
- Firing a signature — same as triggering an event for signature-based monitoring systems
- False positive — monitoring triggered an event but nothing was actually wrong and in doing so the monitoring has incorrectly identified benign communications as a danger.

- False negative — the monitoring system missed reporting an exploit event by not firing an alarm. This is bad.
- True positive — the monitoring system recognized an exploit event correctly.
- True negative — the monitoring system has not recognized benign traffic as cause for concern. In other words, it does nothing when nothing needs to be done. This is good.
- Tuning — customizing a monitoring system to your environment.
- Promiscuous interface — a network interface that collects and processes all of the packets sent to it regardless of the destination MAC address.

IDS Monitoring Technologies and Methods

Monitoring Technologies Overview Monitoring technology varies widely depending on the manufacturer and philosophy. Also, new approaches to IDS are continually evolving. This SSCP domain strives to present the high points of the major types.

Monitoring technology is one of two varieties:

- Network-based
  - NIDS monitoring — A network-based IDS (NIDS) generally connects to one or more network segments via a network interface card. It monitors and interprets the signals on the wire and using various techniques, as you will see later, determines which data on the network represents system misuse or system anomalies. NIDS strives to discover when data communications are unacceptable by looking deep into portions of a datagram.
- Host-based
  - HIDS monitoring — A host-based IDS (HIDS) usually resides as a software agent and strives to discover when processes occurring within a host computer are unacceptable or when key system files or parameters have changed. They can be categorized as follows:
  - System call/application proxy — A software process residing on one or more key computers that intercepts system calls and examines them for validity. This HIDS type attempts to uncover and stop application misuse.
  - Log scrubber — A software process that examines application and system logs for evidence of systems misuse.
  - Target monitor — A software process that takes a snapshot of a known clean file system and regularly compares the snap shot to the current system state to ensure certain files have not been altered without authorization. These systems are generally referred to as file integrity checkers.

- Log monitoring — Traditional hosts (servers, workstations, etc.) and network infrastructure equipment (routers, switches, firewalls, etc.) can save their event information locally (when possible) or to a logging host via a network.

NIDS NIDS systems are devices that monitor network traffic for security events. They often have the following qualities:

- A network interface in promiscuous mode. Promiscuous mode is a state of operation whereby the interface "hears" all packets it sees on the network. The interface dissects and interprets all the data traffic conversations on the port to which it is connected. The interpretation is the intrusion detection activity.
- A network interface for control which operates like any other host interface. The control interface allows you to interact and manage the IDS unit.
- NIDS sensing interfaces connect to OSI Layer 2 devices (hubs and switches) so they can collect data.

Since switches are in reality multi-port bridges, the IDS port must be configured to aggregate all traffic from the other ports or segments in the switch in which you are interested. Otherwise, the NIDS will not be able to hear all of the data conversations occurring on the switch. Each manufacturer has specific ways to aggregate data from multiple ports into a single port.

As the NIDS collects data off of the network, it processes it to spot attacks. NIDS usually focuses on attacks that occur in the following areas of network communications:

- The structure and contents of the IP header of the IP datagram
- The structure and contents of the TCP, UDP, or ICMP packet headers found within the IP datagrams
- The contents of TCP, UDP, and ICMP payloads found within layer 4 packets

Network IDS vendors take on the task of identifying the security problems within IP datagram communications. Not all NIDS systems perform all types of analysis. A Systems Administrator must check with his vendor to understand the capabilities of their system. NIDS systems might look at communications in one or more ways as follows:

- Do the IP headers exhibit characteristics that are illegal or unlikely?
- Do the TCP, UDP, or ICMP headers exhibit characteristics that are illegal or unlikely?
- Does the payload of a single packet contain a pattern of bits associated with a known attack?
- Do the payloads of multiple packets related to one host-to-host conver-

sation session add up to a pattern of behavior known to be defined as an attack?

- When the payload data is decoded by the IDS just like a host would, does the behavior of the data conform to RFC specifications?
- Do communications go outside an accepted normal baseline?

To accomplish this, IDS systems analyze OSI layers 3 through 7, and many can keep track of what they have observed in the past and compare this to what they are seeing in the present. One can then decide whether the aggregate data flow adds up to something suspect.

HIDS HIDS technology adds to your entire system's protection by keeping watch on sensitive processes inside a host. HIDS generally have the following qualities:

- HIDS systems are usually software daemons or services that are designed to run on hosts.
- They intercept and examine system calls or specific processes (e.g., database and Web servers) for patterns or behaviors that should not normally be allowed.
- HIDS daemon can take a predefined action like stopping or reporting the infraction.

In general, HIDS asks, "Should this internal transaction be allowed?" If the answer is yes, the transaction succeeds, otherwise it is blocked.

IDS as a Firewall Complement IDS technology on the network and on hosts complements firewall technology. Firewalls with stringent rules serve as choke points between domains of control and act as a filter to unwanted and unneeded communications. IDS can then study the remaining communications that were allowed by the firewall for embedded attacks. The newer firewall technologies can incorporate signature based detection. As packets are inspected to be allowed through the firewall, they are matched against attack signatures also. This will reduce the errant traffic that gets through the firewall.

For example, Web traffic is allowed in from untrusted sources through ABC Company's firewall. The firewall's role is to keep all data traffic out of the internal network except for packets destined for TCP port 80. The firewall performs this function well but has no knowledge of any attacks that may be embedded with the TCP port 80 packets. Therefore, if an attack is launched through the firewall via this permissible data channel and the receiving internal host is vulnerable to the attack, the host will likely be exploited. IDS technology can alert to this condition and help stop it.

With the newer technology, the firewall knows there is an attack embedded within the packet being inspected and takes appropriate action; in this case, the packet gets dropped and logged. This new technology joins the IDS/IPS and the firewall into one package.

IDS Detection Methods Overview Recall that a security event is an instance of some observed action that may (or may not) be cause for concern.

NIDS and HIDS event detection are generally classified in three ways as follows:

- Misuse detection (also known as signature detection or pattern detection) is the most common detection method. It relies on a database of known attacks and matches them with data the IDS is observing. Some IDS take misuse detection to a higher level by identifying events that resemble known patterns even though they do not necessarily match 100 percent.
- Anomaly detection is less common than misuse detection. It does not rely on strict pattern definitions (like misuse detection) but instead uses a definition of normal operational behaviors as its benchmark. Events outside of "normal" behavior are considered anomalies and thus events.
- Target Monitoring Detection is used as a HIDS attack detection method.

Some IDS systems combine these detection methods.

A match of a known exploit signifies an event. Misuse detectors are not always this rigid and can often spot events that are similar to known exploits even when they are not exactly the same (see the heuristics section that follows).

A ping is an action. If you do not want a particular host pinged and you detect a ping, this can be considered an event. Whether it is cause for concern is something you must determine.

Misuse Detection — Simple and Stateful Pattern Matching NIDS devices and HIDS software analyze the data to which they are exposed for suspect bit patterns. NIDS pattern matching capabilities look inside each IP datagram for bit patterns (signatures) that match known exploits. These patterns may exist in any part of one or more datagrams because different exploits manifest themselves in different ways. HIDS pattern matching capabilities look at software code to be executed for similar bit patterns indicating system misuse. Misuse detection is generally broken down into several subcategories:

- Single transaction simple pattern matching is the most elementary form of intrusion detection. This approach is often called packet or code grepping because the IDS will search through one or more packets (NIDS) or internal host communications codes (HIDS) looking for an exact string of bits that has been associated with a known attack.

- Multiple transaction stateful pattern matching keeps track of many back and forth communications between a client and server to create a picture of what is happening. Analysis of the entire flow is grepped for matches.

Single transaction simple pattern matching example for payload contents: the word "bomb" in a TCP port 80 (HTTP) packet.

Multiple transaction stateful pattern matching example: a Telnet session to a host shows that the remote user is attempting access to "/etc/shadow" on a UNIX host. Telnet usually transmits one character per packet. By keeping state on the session, the IDS is able to know that the sum of each character indicates an attack of some sort.

Single transaction simple pattern matching example for TCP header contents: A TCP packet is destined for port 12345, which is a known Trojan port for the Netbus attack. The IDS matches on the destination port number.

Stateful signatures match against data patterns appearing in more than one packet. Data communications commonly require more than one packet to accomplish a task. Similarly, attackers may divide their exploit into two or more packets. This attack methodology requires the IDS to "remember" which packets it has seen in the past and compare them with packets it is "seeing" now. When it puts them all together, the aggregate activities may indicate system misuse.

Misuse Detection — Protocol Analysis Protocol Analysis adds intelligence to the way IDS analyze protocol transactions. Also known as protocol decode analysis, decode detection is designed to break apart the packets in exactly the same manner as a target host. For example, most advanced IDS technology can interpret packet flows associated with Web, SMTP, and DNS servers the same way the actual servers will. The IDS then compares how the protocol is supposed to be structured to the way the observed packet is actually structured or what it contains. If there are variations to the structure that are not defined by the RFC definition or common practice, then that flow may be considered an attack.

Protocol analysis examples:

- Decode analysis can be used to identify buffer overflow conditions in Telnet data sent to (certain) Unix systems. This signature will fire when excessive environment variables are exchanged during a Telnet session. Detecting this requires decode analysis because the sensor must break down the packets in the flow (like a host would) and identify that too many environment variables are being received.
- A call to RPC program number 100202 procedure 2 with a UDP packet length > 1024 bytes is defined as illegal in normal working circumstances.

Decode analysis is most effective for protocols that are well defined by standards, as the inherent flow behaviors will be more predictable. If the standards allow for broad interpretation, it may be harder to ascertain what conditions constitute an exploit.

Misuse Detection — Heuristical Analysis Heuristics implies that a certain amount of learning and inference about the network traffic the IDS is seeing will take place in order for it to determine if system misuse is occurring. Heuristical analysis uses logic, intelligence, and statistics. These NIDS signatures are often related to ferreting out reconnaissance attacks like port sweeps perpetrated against your network, or with HIDS systems, too many login attempts in a specified time period.

Heuristics examples:

- A network reconnaissance FIN scan taking place within 20 seconds with the following qualities:
  — Five or more TCP packets with the FIN flag turned on
  — Destined for any port
  — Going to two or more of your hosts
  — Coming from one source host
- Someone logging in as root to a UNIX host repeatedly over short time span

Anomaly Detection Anomaly detection starts with a baseline definition of network traffic trends or system operations that are considered normal. Anomalies are activities that are outside a normal baseline. In contrast to signature-based IDS, anomaly detection does not necessarily have strict definitions for data bits it seeks, but instead uses statistics for identifying events outside the norm.

Anomaly examples:
- An SMTP server has become infected with an e-mail worm, causing a large increase in the amount of outbound e-mail traffic. The traffic volume exceeds normal operational patterns, thus triggering an alarm from a NIDS.
- A Web server process that does not normally need to access Web server data causes the installed HIDS agent to trigger an alarm when that process accesses the data, as this activity is outside the normal baseline of system operations.

Warning: When installing a system that uses Anomaly and Heuristic analysis, be careful to ensure that your network is not currently under attack. If a system is learning a network while it is under attack, the system may think that the network "normal" or baseline is "under attack" and, therefore, these attacks are normal and may not alert when you face this attack or future attacks.

Target Monitoring Detection Target monitoring is a detection method concerned with the integrity of systems and is generally associated with HIDS products. It compares attributes of known good file systems and data files on a host to the current state of those files during ongoing operations. When the values of the known good do not match the current value, the system may have been compromised. Administrators can then investigate further to decide if the unauthorized change must be reversed in order to maintain integrity.

A target monitoring system often employs the use of cryptographic hash values of known good files and compares them to the current files. If the values match, confidence is high that the file has not been changed.

Logging, Log Storage, and Analysis

Most systems (hosts and other devices) generate event information as a part of normal processing. Systems logging is a system function whereby these events are sent to a destination for storage and subsequent analysis. Organizations should plan for and implement effective logging, as this information can aid in understanding what events transpired in the past and can become a permanent record for the organization. As such, logging should be part of a security policy that describes a monitoring plan because it helps IT security practitioners track important events. The following lists several reasons why an organization will want to enable logging on their key systems:

- Provides storage of system-generated events for analysis — suspicious events can be noted and investigated
- Provides a record of what happened (forensics) — an attacker's activities that caused the event can be reconstructed
- Provides system recovery information — logs can help you back out the changes that were made by telling you what the changes were since the last known good snapshot
- Provides a permanent record — forensic evidence can be used in legal proceedings as long as a reasonable chain of custody is used

Logging provides the hard data to be used as the basis for determining the following:

- Are atypical events occurring above a particular baseline of normal activity?
- Are system attacks happening and if so are they successful?

Detailed resources for building logging infrastructure include:
http://www.counterpane.com/log-analysis.html
http://www.cert.org/security-improvement/practices/p091.html
http://www.cert.org/security-improvement/practices/p092.html

Types of Log Information The word "system" in this context is used to describe either a device or a software component that runs on a device. Various system components can generate log information. Keep in mind that several component processes on one physical device can simultaneously produce their own logging data. A single machine can be the host for four separate components producing logging information which is being directed to one or more logging hosts. System components that can produce logging information include:

- A host IDS agent
- A network IDS device
- A network router
- A network switch
- A firewall
- An operating system running on a host
- A Web server process
- A database process

The data derived from logs varies widely and is determined by how the system was developed and programmed. It is also determined by how much logging information you specify the system to send. Often the default logging level does not match the needs of the security policy, as there may be too much or too little of one type of information or the other being sent.

The following categories are indicators of the type of security-centric logs entries you might see:

- Low-Level Host Information Logs
- System hardware and software errors
- System restart, shutdown, and startup notifications
- Peripheral operational activities and new device detection for modems, printers, and other devices
- Network interface errors
- Higher-Level Host Information Logs
- Changes to system policy
- Password change confirmation (note that the passwords themselves should not be logged)
- Process (services and daemons) start time and files/arguments used for execution
- Process (services and daemons) exit time and termination status
- Identification of the user executing a process
- Successful and failed logons for normal and privileged users to hosts, domains, remote access systems, or other systems that require authentication
- Changes in user role, privileges, or identity that indicate rights escalation
- Notification of failed attempts to access information not authorized for the user or process

- File open, create, modify, execute accesses
- Changes to file sizes, locations, and protections
- Changes to access control lists
- File and directory adds and deletes
- Device Logs
- Security gateway (firewall, remote access server, etc.) connection attempts (including port and protocol), confirmation, session duration
- Security device resource depletion messages
- Intrusion detection signature events
- Interface up/down state
- Configuration modification
- Application/Service Specific Logs
- FTP — files GET and PUT, general connection statistics
- Web — general statistics, page hit statistics, authentication and connection statistics
- Mail — server queue statistics, encoding errors
- DNS — errors, zone transfers
- Database — transactions, rollback information
- General file server — see list above

Choosing a Logging Priority Logging data should be analyzed periodically; otherwise, there is little benefit to doing it. For example, if all systems log to a central repository but no person or process "combs" through the logs looking for suspect indications, then the logging activity has little value. Since system logging can produce vast amounts of data, the organization must decide which systems will be enabled for logging and which log information from those systems will be captured. Note that often systems do not provide flexibility in deciding what will be logged; therefore, all events must be logged (or an entire class of logs like "all" security events or "all" system events) and subsequently filtered at the repository.

You should weigh the number of systems you wish to log against the resources available to perform the analysis on the logs. Consider the following when making the decision from which systems or parts of systems you will capture logs:

- System priority — Highly mission critical systems should be ranked before less critical systems. Critical systems should log events and those events should be analyzed.
- System role — Is the system a database server, a general purpose server, a firewall, a Web server, or some other kind of system? This will drive which parts of the system are configured to log.
- Analysis capacity — Can the organization effectively monitor the logs for all of the systems performing logging?
- Data Utility — Logging should be performed if the derived data will be useful in some fashion; that is, if the data provides a concrete benefit and the resources are available to deal with it, then it should probably be done.

Enabling Secure Logging After determining which systems or system components will log data, you must decide how and where the data will be stored. Key issues for logging include:

- Turn logging on and be selective about what is logged:
  - — Identify the logging mechanisms available on the platform. Logging mechanisms include the following:
    - Direct logging to a file on a local hard disk.
    - Network logging from the source host to a destination log host using UDP port 514, the most common network logging mechanism.
    - Network logging from the source host to a destination log host using another mechanism. For example, Cisco Systems has a network intrusion detection device that logs data from the network sensor to a log host using a proprietary format called PostOffice protocol that runs on UDP port 45000.
    - Protecting network logging by inserting inherently insecure data streams (like UDP 514) into secure data streams (like SSH or a VPN) for transmission to a log host.
    - Logging from the source host to a printer or another device via a serial cable.
  - — As previously mentioned, when possible log only the events or classes of events that will need to be analyzed.
- Choose a storage repository location — Choosing a storage location is a function of the security you need for your logs.
  - — Local storage is convenient and fast but is potentially exposed if an attacker gains control of the host. For example, if the attacker has gained host control through some means of exploitation, she can easily alter the local logs to cover her tracks.
  - — Remote storage on another host does require a network connection and will produce network overhead but is potentially more secure than local storage, because an attacker may have difficulty altering log information sent to the host. Of course, this benefit is nullified if the attacker compromises the log host.
  - — Remote storage has the benefit of centralizing logs onto one or a few hosts as opposed to many hosts.
  - — Logging to a printer generates a permanent record that is difficult to alter but harder to analyze.
- Protection from access and modification by unauthorized persons (also referred to as anti-alteration).
  - — Ensure that only authorized parties can access the system components used to configure logging (i.e., administrators).
  - — If appropriate, log information to a write-once and read-many device to prevent subsequent changes.
  - — If supported by the platform, set log file permissions such that the file can only be appended but that data already in the file cannot be changed.

- — Consider encrypting log files for data privacy (encryption in storage).
- — Consider digitally signing log files to detect alteration.
- Transit Security
  - — Consider the risk of sending logging messages in the clear across untrusted networks. Syslog messages can be sniffed and interpreted, which may be counter to your security policy. If an attacker gets control of these messages, they can be used by the attacker to determine whether his efforts have tripped any sensors or been discovered in any way. If logging to a remote host, place the log host on a separate network segment from the log sources and separate the two segments with a restrictive firewall.
  - — Consider using a secure means of transport from the source to the log host. Many implementations support streaming logging by tunneling syslog on UDP 514 through SSH (secure shell) from the source to the destination. Other implementations use an IPsec connection from the source to the destination and the data is contained within the VPN connection. Some systems allow for the storage of logs locally with a periodic SCP (secure copy) from the source to the destination.
- Storage capacity of the repository
  - — Ensure that the storage repository has the capacity to store the volume of data expected. Consider storing log files on a separate partition from the host's operating system so that if the disk fills, it does not impact host operations. You should also compress log files when possible to save on storage space.
- Log rotation
  - — Periodically transition from one log file to a new log file so that the old file may be archived. This also makes log files smaller and more manageable. It is also a good idea to rename old log files appropriately based on their contents.
- Storage format (flat file versus database)
  - — It is wise to choose a storage method based upon the log sources and log host capability. Choose a storage method based upon the analysis tools you wish to use. Flat file analysis will be different than database analysis.

Event Alerting and Interpretation The purpose of logging is to save event messages of particular interest so they can be analyzed. The analysis is the activity that uncovers unauthorized activities or system problems that you may not otherwise know about. System logging without corresponding analysis is futile; therefore, only employ logging if the data will be used.

Event interpretation falls into two categories:

- Real-time — real-time monitoring systems evaluate the output of hosts and devices on a continuous basis. These systems examine the logging information continuously by parsing and processing it, looking for events defined as "interesting" to the organization. Alerts can be generated for select, interesting events. Real-time monitoring implies that the attacker is attempting to break in at that moment.

- Periodic — periodic monitoring systems evaluate the output of hosts and devices at defined intervals. These systems, like real-time systems, examine the logging information and parse and process it looking for events deemed "interesting" to the organization but they do not do it continuously. Alerts can be generated for select interesting events. Periodic monitoring implies that analysis occurs after an attack has been carried out and usually involves inspecting various system and network log files and performing data and system integrity tests.

With the distinction made between real-time and periodic analysis, the tools that are deployed to perform the jobs must be commensurate with the requirements set down by the security policy. Tools appropriate to the task should be used.

Another issue is whether to use commercial or "home grown" scripts to perform the task. This is a matter of preference, budget, and reliability. Commercial products may have more features and may be easier to use. They also generally have a support structure and are maintained by a company. However, they do cost more and like free products are not guaranteed to be bug-free.

It is important to determine which events should produce an alert — too many alerts over time will result in administrators ignoring most, if not all, alerts. Events requiring immediate administrator analysis should be designated as urgent alerts. Alerts can take the form of the following:

- An e-mail to the administrator.
- A page to an administrator.
- A voice mail or phone call to an administrator (often synthesized voice generation).
- An alert on a security information management (SIM) console — a SIM is a new type of product that (often) takes input from many security device types, stores the input in a database, and provides event analysis and correlation.
- A custom console (i.e., software specifically mated to a monitoring system) visual alert. For example, if an event is serious, a visual device schematic might turn red. Similar to a SIM but might only support data input from one type of device.
- An alert on a network management console — many organizations have these systems in place and have engineered solutions to take security information sourced from security devices and send them to the NMC.

Links to tools that allow for periodic and real-time analysis can be found at the following Web sites:

- http://www.counterpane.com/log-analysis.html#app_parsing
- http://www.cert.org/security-improvement/implementations/i042.07.html
- http://www.securityfocus.com/infocus/1613
- http://www.info-secure.org/

Techniques Used to Evade Monitoring

Monitoring-evasion is the practice of exercising stealthy system attack techniques for the purpose of not being detected by the system. It is an attacker's attempt to "fly below the radar." No attacker wishes to be caught; therefore, his tools and techniques often leverage evasion technology.

The purpose of presenting this information to the security practitioner is to make you aware of the common evasion techniques, so you can compare them to the capabilities of your systems and determine to what evasion techniques you are potentially vulnerable.

Facts:

- System attackers have varying skill levels from "script kiddie" (novice) to true cracker (experienced).
- True crackers will generally understand the issues surrounding not being "noticed" by an IDS.
- Common software attack tools have evasion technology built into them, bringing advanced, script-based techniques to novices.

With this in mind, do not take the likelihood of evasion lightly!

The following Web sites have information about evasion:

- Whisker anti-IDS tactics software and techniques can be found at www.wiretrip.net/rfp/.
- Nmap network mapping software can be found at www.insecure.org/nmap.
- Nessus vulnerability testing software can be found at www.nessus.org.

Packet Floods An attacker sends massive amounts of communication at target systems at one site, raising many alarms. However, the attacker is really after only one of those systems. IDS must be able to keep up with packet floods and provide useful alerts to rank and prioritize action. The flood causes many red herrings and the security staff often does not know which alert to deal with first, or that the attacker is really after just one system. Attacks may originate from many source IP addresses, causing greater confusion. If the IDS cannot keep up with the flood and provide organized and structured alerting, confusion will reign.

Mitigation techniques include the following:

- Monitoring systems that can handle packets or transactions at wire speed. In other words, use systems that can cope with the maximum volume of data possible.
- Monitoring systems that group together like alarms and provide information about the number of alarms of type A, number of alarms of type B, and so on. This is in contrast to a reporting system that sends each alarm, even if they are identical, to the reporting console in a sequential fashion, thus overwhelming the operator.
- Monitoring systems that rank alarms by likelihood of success. For example, if Windows-based attacks are being used against UNIX hosts, the likelihood of success is nil. If a Windows IIS Web server attack is attempted on a Windows-based host without a Web server process, the likelihood of success is also nil. Therefore, a likelihood ranking helps practitioners focus their attention on exploit attempts likely to succeed, whether the attacker means them to be red herrings or not.

Packet Fragmentation An attacker sends purposely fragmented IP datagrams to disguise attacks or disable systems that cannot handle these crafted packets. Taken individually, the datagrams may not be a threat but when recombined, the entire datagram may represent a known attack. To be effective, IDS must be able to track and reassemble fragmented datagrams, then perform protocol analysis and signature matching against the fragmented session.

Another form of packet fragmentation that should normally not be seen is overlapping packet fragmentation. These are crafted attacks where packets are fragmented as discussed above but parts of one fragment overlap parts of another fragment as they are reassembled in the host's memory. This has the unfortunate side effect of crashing some types of hosts.

Mitigation techniques include the following:

- Use firewall devices that will reject packet fragments that overlap.
- Use NIDS devices that can reassemble fragmented packets.
- Use NIDS devices that can alert on the observation of overlapped fragments.

Obfuscation Obfuscation is defined as an attacker's attempt to hide his true intent. Instead of using ASCII characters, hexadecimal, or Unicode characters are used in the attack. Basic IDS systems can be fooled in this way because they do not convert the hex or Unicode back to ASCII (which the signature is based upon). Obfuscation is commonly used in HTTP attacks because servers can interpret all three forms of code.

For example, assume a signature is written so that the ASCII character string "cmd.exe" within a URL is considered an attack. If the IDS does not perform de-obfuscation and cmd.exe appears in its HEX form as:

%63%6D%64%2E%65%78%65

or in its Unicode form as

cmd.ex&#101,

this IDS will not recognize the attack because it does not know how to convert those characters to ASCII. When signatures are looking specifically for certain ASCII characters that represent an attack and there is no facility to convert HEX or Unicode back to the original ASCII, the attacker will be able to evade detection by the IDS.

Mitigation techniques include the following:

- Use IDS that has the ability to convert among the types of encoding.

- Use IDS that can maintain stateful inspection of packets and also be able to de-obfuscate them.

Encryption Today's IDS/IPS systems cannot perform analysis on communication streams that are encrypted; thus, if an attacker has a means of communicating with an internal system via an encrypted stream, the IDS/IPS analyzing the encrypted stream has no way of knowing that any sort of system exploitation is occurring. This evasion technique generally assumes that the attacker has some sort of previous access to systems allowing for the establishment of an encrypted stream.

For example, assume that an employee, through social engineering, unknowingly provided an attacker with authentication credentials to a VPN concentrator. The attacker can then make a connection to the network to perform unauthorized activities. The data stream from the attacker to the VPN concentrator cannot be analyzed because of encryption.

Trojan programs, for example, can be planted on systems that enable an attacker to gain trusted access to that system. The attacker could then install software that enables encrypted communication via the communication channel from the host to the attacker. IDS/IPS might not be able to interpret data flowing through the covert communication channel.

Mitigation techniques include the following:

- Use IDS/IPS systems that can analyze the decrypted stream prior to it entering the network. This can be done by connecting a VPN endpoint's trusted interface to a firewall. The firewall can then analyze and let through permissible data and the IDS can analyze it.
- Configure IDS/IPS systems to alert on types of data traffic not allowed to flow from trusted hosts. That is, if the Trojan program tries to communicate out to the attacker, the IDS should be able to weed out this disallowed traffic and alert administrators.

Slow Scans If attackers take a very slow and methodical approach to systems reconnaissance, IDS systems may not notice, as the discovery takes place over a long period of time. This is in contrast to script-based scans that are often "noisy" and noticeable to IDS. Slow scans can be very difficult to detect due to the volume of data produced by monitoring systems and the correlation necessary to bring together the clues that show a slow scan is in progress.

For example, an attacker might only scan one TCP port on one host IP address once per day with one packet to determine if the host is listening on that port. The IDS may not raise an alarm because only one request was issued.

Mitigation techniques include the following:

- Log correlation systems that have the ability to pick out small pieces of data found in logs over extended time periods and identify them as related.

Log Alteration Skilled attackers may attempt to cover up the systems changes they performed by using the privileged access they gained using a privilege escalation technique by altering the system log files. System log files can contain information such as what was done, by whom, at what time, and from what address. The attacker may modify the logs to completely wipe out the fact that a change was made or they might alter the logs to make it appear as if another (innocent) party was responsible for the changes.

Mitigation techniques include the following:

- Redirect log output from the source host to another host that is secured and independent from the source.
- Use logging techniques that allow logs to be written but not subsequently changed.
- Encrypt log files.

Implementation Issues for Monitoring

You should remember the security tenets *confidentiality, integrity,* and *availability.* IDS can alert to these conditions by matching known conditions (signatures) with unknown but suspect conditions (anomalies).

- Confidentiality — unauthorized access may breach confidentiality
- Integrity — corruption due to an attack destabilizes integrity
- Availability — denial of service keeps data from being available

The security organization must make decisions concerning the deployment of monitoring systems. What types to deploy and where to deploy are functions of budget and system criticality. Implementation of monitoring should be supported by policy and justified by the risk assessment. The actual deployment of the sensors will depend upon the value of the assets.

Monitoring control deployment considerations include:

- System criticality drives deployment.
- Choose one or more monitoring technique types — HIDS/NIDS/Logging.
- Choose an analysis paradigm — Statistical anomaly/Signature.
- Choose a system that meets timeliness objectives — Real-time/Scheduled (non-real-time).
- Choose a reporting mechanism for incident response — Push or pull; that is, does a management system query the monitoring devices for data or does the device push the data to a repository where it is stored or analyzed.
- Make the update mechanisms part of policy with well-defined procedures, especially for signature-based devices.
- Tune monitoring systems to reflect the environment they support.
- Choose automatic response mechanisms wisely.

Criticality-Based Deployment For most organizations, budgetary constraints generally do not make it possible to monitor every host and every network segment; therefore, choose carefully when deciding what to monitor. Generally you will want to use monitoring security controls to guard segments and hosts with the highest data value and corresponding greatest organizational impact should they be subverted. A complete risk analysis, as discussed in the SSCP Risk, Response, and Recovery section, should be performed to determine component criticality.

Ask yourself the following:

- Which are my most valued network segments?
- The segment outside your Internet router will likely be noisy with attacks from many places, but these attacks are not necessarily getting through the firewall. NIDS placed here will alert to general attacks. Some people decide that placing a NIDS outside their firewall is ineffective, since the firewall will block most of the traffic, and because of the cost considerations, they'll be more interested in placing a NIDS inside only. While this second design will tell you what gets through your firewall, it might be too late. Placing a NIDS outside your firewall can alert you to the level of intention of an attacker. An analogy would be someone trying to get into a door with a large ring of keys. While you would definitely want to know if someone got into the door, you also might want to see the person trying repeatedly. In this case, you should be able to check your security posture and policy before they find the right "key."
- The segment just inside a stateful firewall with stringent rules should generally only show incoming exploits capable of being operated over the ports allowed through the firewall. Incoming attacks seen here are getting through the firewall because they are contained within ports al-

lowed by your security policy, and correspondingly configure through the firewall configuration procedure.

- Segments with hosts of high value (key organizational data for R&D, payroll and accounting, etc.) should be considered good candidates for NIDS monitoring.
- Which are my most valued hosts?
- The hosts with key data are good candidates for HIDS monitoring of OS processes, Web processes, database processes, and/or other specialized processes supported by your HIDS vendor.
- Hosts that are exposed to the public Internet in some way directly or indirectly, such as a Web server or a back end database server that hands data to a public Web server, should employ HIDS.
- Hosts and network devices should log operation data to dedicated secure logging hosts.

Maintenance and Tuning For the long-term use and effectiveness of the monitoring controls, systems should be cared for like any other mission critical component:

- Keep IDS signatures (if applicable) current — Signature-based IDS must be kept up to date as previously unknown vulnerabilities are revealed. Take, for example, the ineffectiveness of a host anti-virus system with virus signatures that are a year old. Since several new viruses emerge each week, a system with old signatures may be effective for the old exploits but the system is defenseless for new viruses. IDS systems operate on the same principle. IDS vendors often have notification systems to alert you about new signature definitions or the capability for automatic update.
- Keep IDS subsystems current — As new revisions of IDS subsystems (the operating systems and software engines that drive the system) become available, consider testing, then deploying these if they add to your ability to detect exploits but do not introduce instability.
- Tune IDS based on the types of traffic you expect to see on systems — NIDS systems have limitations on how much processing they can handle; therefore, limit what the NIDS must monitor based on your environment. For example, if you do not have any Windows-based hosts, consider disabling monitoring for Windows-based exploits. Conversely, if you have a UNIX environment and UNIX-based signatures are not enabled, you will likely miss these events.
- As system changes are made, the security systems that protect them should be considered. During the change control process, new changes should factor in how the security systems will handle them. Some sample questions are as follows:
  - Will the host configuration change require a reconfiguration of the HIDS component?

— Will the addition of a database application of a host require the HIDS agent to be configured to screen database transactions for validity?

— Will the network change require alterations to the way the NIDS collects data?

— Will the new services offered on a host require the NIDS to be tuned to have the appropriate active and / or passive responses to exploits that target those new services?

— Will the DMZ to management network firewall rules need to be changed to accommodate the logging stream from the new Web server placed on the DMZ?

Collecting Data for Incident Response Organizations must have a policy and plan for dealing with events as they occur and the corresponding forensics of incidents.

Ask yourself the following:

- How do I plan to collect event and forensic information from the IDS/IPS? — Organizations cannot expect IDS/IPS to be a "set it and forget it" technology. Human interaction is required to interpret events and high level responses. IDS can organize events by priority and can even be set to react in a certain way to an observed event but humans will periodically need to decide if the IDS is doing its job properly.
- How will I have the IDS/IPS respond to events? — Depending on your IDS/IPS capabilities, you will need to decide how you want it to react to an observed event. The next section discusses active vs. passive IDS response.
- How will I respond to incidents? — What investigative actions will the security staff take based on singular or repeated incidents involving one or more observed events? This is a function of your security policy.

When organizations suffer attacks, logging information, whether generated by a host, network device, IDS/IPS, or other device may be at some point considered evidence by law enforcement personnel. Preserving a chain of custody for law enforcement is important so as not to taint the evidence for use in criminal proceedings. See the SSCP Risk, Response, and Recovery section for a discussion of these rules in detail.

Monitoring Response Techniques If unauthorized activity is detected, IDS/IPS systems can take one or both of the following actions:

- Passive response — notes the event at various levels but does not take any type of evasive action. The response is by definition passive because the event is merely noted.
- Active response — notes the event and performs a reaction so as to protect systems from further exploitation.

The following are examples of Passive IDS/IPS response:

- Logging the event to a log file
- Displaying an alert on the console of an event viewer or security information management system
- Logging the details of a packet flow that was identified to be associated with an unauthorized event for a specified period of time, for the purpose of subsequent forensic analysis
- Sending an alert page to an administrator

The following are examples of Active IDS/IPS response:

- In the case of an unauthorized TCP data flow on a network, initiate a NIDS reset the connection (with a TCP reset) between an attacker and the host being attacked. This only works with TCP-based attacks because they are connection oriented.
- In the case of any IP dataflow (TCP, UDP, ICMP), initiate a NIDS instruct a filtering device like a firewall or router to dynamically alter its access control list to preclude further communications with the attacker, either indefinitely or for a specified period.
- In the case of a disallowed system call or application specific behavior, initiate the HIDS agent to block the transaction.

With TCP resets, often the IDS will send a TCP packet with the FIN flag set in the TCP header to both the attacker and the attacked host in order to gracefully reset the connection from both host's perspective. By resetting the attacker, this discourages future attacks (if they keep getting resets). By resetting the attacked host, this frees up system resources that may have been allocated as a result of the attack.

With system calls, if a process that does not normally need to access the Web server's data tries to access the data, the HIDS agent can disallow this access.

Response Pitfalls Active IDS response pitfalls include:

- Cutting off legitimate traffic due to false positives
- Self-induced denial of service
- Breaking the law

Many monitoring systems provide the means to specify some sort of response if a particular signature fires, although doing so may have unintended consequences.

Entertain the notion that a signature has been written that is too generic in nature. This means that it sometimes fires as a result of exploit traffic and is a true positive but sometimes fires as a result of innocent traffic and is a false positive. If the signature is configured to send TCP resets to an offending address and does so in a false positive situation, the IDS may be cutting off legitimate traffic.

Self-induced denial of service can also be a problem with active response systems. If an attacker decided to spoof the IP address of your business partner and sends attacks with the partner's IP address and your IDS reacted by dynamically modifying the edge router configuration, you would cut off communications with the business partner.

Take note that active response mechanisms should be used carefully and be limited to the types of actions listed above. Some organizations take it upon themselves to implement systems that actively counter attack systems they believe have attacked them as a response. This is highly discouraged and may result in legal issues for the organization. It is irresponsible to counter attack any system for any reason.

Sample Questions

1. A security audit is best defined as:
   a. A covert series of tests designed to test network authentication, hosts, and perimeter security
   b. A technical assessment that measures how well an organization uses strategic security policies and tactical security controls for protecting its information assets
   c. Employing Intrusion Detection Systems to monitor anomalous traffic on a network segment and logging attempted break-ins
   d. Hardening systems before deploying them on the corporate network

2. Why is it important for organizations to have a security framework?
   a. To show that the organization has exercised "due care"
   b. So they can adhere to regulations developed by an institutional or governmental body
   c. To avoid possible legal action or financial penalties
   d. All of the above

3. Creating Incident Response policies for an organization would be an example of:
   a. Administrative control
   b. Technical control
   c. Physical control
   d. Logical control

4. Which of the following would be a good example of a host isolation security control?
   a. Encrypting syslog activity on the network
   b. Applying the most recent patches to a system
   c. Installing anti-virus on a local machine
   d. Setting up a DMZ between the public and private network

5. What is the most important reason to analyze event logs from multiple sources?
   a. They will help you obtain a more complete picture of what is happening on your network and how you go about addressing the problem.
   b. The log server could have been compromised.
   c. Because you cannot trust automated scripts to capture everything.
   d. In order to prosecute the attacker once he can be traced.

6. Security testing does not include which of the following activities?
   a. Performing a port scan to check for up and running services.
   b. Gathering publicly available information.
   c. Counter-attacking systems determined to be hostile.
   d. Posing as technical support to gain unauthorized information.

7. Why is system fingerprinting part of the security testing process?
   a. Because it is one of the easiest things to determine when performing a security test.
   b. It shows what vulnerabilities the system may be subject to.
   c. It shows the auditor whether a system has been hardened.
   d. It tells an attacker than a system is automatically insecure.

8. What is the difference between vulnerability and penetration testing?
   a. Vulnerability testing attempts to exploit a weakness found from penetration testing.
   b. Penetration testing attempts to exploit a weakness found in Vulnerability testing.
   c. Vulnerability testing uses scripts to find weaknesses while penetration testing uses a GUI-based program.
   d. Penetration testing is used to uncover vulnerabilities without harming the system.

9. The following are benefits to performing vulnerability testing except:
   a. They allow an organization to study the security posture of the organization.
   b. They identify and prioritize mitigation activities.
   c. They can compare security postures over a period of time when done consistently.
   d. It has the potential to crash the network or host.

10. What is the primary purpose of testing an Intrusion Detection System?
    a. To observe that the IDS is observing and logging an appropriate response to a suspicious activity.
    b. To determine if the IDS is capable of discarding suspect packets.

    c. To analyze processor utilization to verify whether hardware up-grades are necessary.

    d. To test whether the IDS can log every possible event on the net-work.

11. Which of the following is true regarding computer intrusions?

    a. Covert attacks such as a Distributed Denial of Service (DDOS) at-tack harm public opinion of an organization.

    b. Overt attacks are easier to defend against since they can be read-ily identified.

    c. Network Intrusion Detection Systems (NIDS) help mitigate com-puter intrusions by notifying personnel in real-time.

    d. Covert attacks are less effective since they take more time to ac-complish.

12. The main difference in real-time vs. non-real-time monitoring is:

    a. Non-real-time monitoring is not as effective as real-time monitoring.

    b. Real-time monitoring provides a way to immediately identify dis-allowed behavior, while non-real-time monitoring can be used to trace an attacker's activity.

    c. Non-real-time monitoring is more effective in catching overt activ-ity.

    d. Real-time monitoring is more effective in catching covert activity.

13. Why is security monitoring necessary?

    a. Because logging activity can show the steps an attacker used to modify or gain access to a system.

    b. Log files can be correlated to form a timeline of events to be used in a forensic investigation.

    c. Log files can show deviance from a security policy.

    d. All of the above.

14. NIDS and HIDS generally employ the following techniques except:

    a. Using a database of known attack signatures and comparing that to current traffic flow.

    b. Analyzing traffic flow to determine unusual activity.

    c. Monitoring for specific file changes by referencing known good file sets.

    d. Counter-attacking a system to cut-off communication and prevent possible damage.

15. Why are secure methods of logging system or device data impor-tant?

    a. The hosts storing the log files are often easily compromised.

    b. Common transport methods of log files are insecure and can be easily sniffed.

    c. Unencrypted and unprotected log files are easily altered.

    d. Both B & C.

Domain 4
Risk, Response, and Recovery

Eric Waxvik

Section 1: Risk Management

Elements of Risk Management

In order to perform the activities required for Risk Management, one must understand risk and the fundamental elements of which it is composed. Risk is defined as the probability of an unwanted occurrence or the realization of a threat. Basic Elements of Risk are:

Asset — An item or entity of quantitative or qualitative value to an organization. This can include products, processes, electronically stored information, and physical as well as intellectual property resources, or information pertinent to relationships with partners.

Threat — Any agent or circumstance that could potentially cause harm to an asset. In IT these may be categorized as occurrences that affect the confidentiality, availability, or integrity of information assets in terms of destruction, disclosure, modification or corruption of data, or denial of service.

Vulnerability — A weakness or functionality that may be exploited and thereby enable a threat to harm an asset. A specific vulnerability may manifest as anything from a weakness in system design to the implementation of an operational procedure or may be inherent in the system. Vulnerabilities may be eliminated or reduced by the correct implementation of safeguards and countermeasures.

Risk Management Definitions

Countermeasures or Safeguards — Controls that mitigate potential risks. Examples include policy and procedures put in place for accountability or security devices like cameras or firewalls.

Exposure — An instance of an asset being susceptible to losses from a threat.

Exposure Factor — The exposure is calculated by determining the percentage of loss to a specific asset due to a specific threat.

Risk Management — The process of reducing risk to identified assets by identifying and minimizing vulnerabilities through the application of countermeasures or redesign.

Risk Analysis — The process of identifying the severity of potential risks, identifying vulnerabilities, and assigning a priority to each. This may be done in preparation for the implementation of selected countermeasures designed to mitigate specific high-priority risks. The analysis is the basis upon which management makes its decision and implements the countermeasures and safeguards.

Risk Management Overview

This is the process of controlling the interactions between the elements of risk from a risk reduction view that encompasses the entire enterprise. Risk management includes the components of risk analysis, the selection of countermeasures evaluated by specific criteria, and the implementation of preventative, detective and corrective controls chosen to mitigate specific high-priority threats. It also includes the elements of acceptable risk — those threats for which senior management has chosen not to implement countermeasures due to the low likelihood or impact to the organization if the threat is realized. While it is common to follow "best practices," it is necessary to ensure your risk management decisions are based upon your organization's specific threats and risks.

Risk Analysis This describes the process of determining the objective and subjective value of assets, the identification of specific threats to them, and the loss that will occur to the assets if the threat is realized. It is then calculated using either a qualitative or quantitative methodology. The result will be a report to management identifying the elements of risk as they exist within the organization, with specific recommendations as to how to handle them.

Asset Valuation The first priority for risk management is to identify corporate assets, and to prioritize them by their value to the organization. The process for determining an asset's value or asset valuation is important for many reasons; it can help you determine your recovery priorities. In the event of a disaster, there is little time to waste in bringing up your most critical functions in the order they may best help the organization. As you will see later, these priorities are not just based on value but also on the cost to recover these assets.

The process is also important in determining the selection of the safeguards. While your company image is important, the justification for having more firewalls and security measures in place to protect your company's Web site may outweigh the need for uniformed security officers standing by your organization's road signage.

The asset valuation is also important for insurance and legal reasons. Organizations must often show "due care" (i.e., take the appropriate precautions to protect resources of a certain value). When an insurance claim is filed, you must often show that you took reasonable and necessary precautions to protect that resource. It is probably more difficult to get an insurance company to reimburse you for losing your car if you had left your windows down, keys in the ignition, with the car is running while you went into the store for two hours versus if you had rolled up the windows, locked the doors, and activated the alarm. In the latter, you showed that you had practiced due care.

Another reason that asset valuations are important is that they serve as a basis for cost benefit analysis. Without knowing the value of an asset it is difficult to know what the appropriate countermeasures and safeguards should be to protect it. More money might be spent to protect a biological engineering laboratory than its break room.

Asset valuation should be approached both quantitatively and qualitatively, depending on the type of risk analysis you're doing. A quantitative risk analysis process identifies objective numeric values for each asset, countermeasure, and estimated loss. The quantitative value of an asset will include the monetary expenditures required for purchasing and maintenance of the asset. This may also include such costs as licensing or development and deployments costs, user training, documentation and upgrades.

A qualitative valuation is a subjective determination of an asset's value to the organization. The qualitative value of an asset will include considerations of regulatory compliance such as how mission-critical the asset is to the organization's viability and its estimated proprietary or intellectual property value. This value may be considered as the market value of the asset to the organization's competition. Qualitative research tends to be more inductive.

A quantitative valuation more so involves assigning direct numbers and values. A quantitative value will include the direct cost of an asset and the man-hours associated with purchasing and replacing that asset. The value may also include the cost to develop and deploy an asset. Quantitative research tends to be more deductive.

The value and criticality of the IT infrastructure and information resources must be determined by individuals that understand how it supports the business mission. The dependencies of different business functions on IT resources must be documented. Infrastructure components such as hardware, storage devices and communications infrastructure should be the subjects of both quantitative and qualitative risk analysis within the department. Information Systems Audit and Control Association (ISACA; http: www.isaca.org).

The results of these analyses should be presented to senior management in order to facilitate the overall risk analysis of the organization and provide an accurate IT asset valuation.

Threat Identification It is important that at this stage, all threats be considered and listed. Threats may be categorized in many ways; the best categorization is one that readily fits the needs of your organization. For example, the threats to a sod farm may not be the same threats that impact an automotive manufacturer. While both may have some threats in common (tornado, fire, earthquake), there will be unique threats to both organizations. These threats can be: external or internal, natural or man made, intentional or accidental. These are just general example categories; within these categories will be more specific threats. Information concerning these may be available from users, auditors, system administrators with trust relationships and informational sites such as CERT/CC (http://www.cert.org).

After the threats have been identified, they must be ranked in order of the magnitude of impact if they are realized, as well as the likelihood that they will be realized. Since there are so many threats in the IT environment, this ranking may be facilitated by associating the threats that are relevant to vulnerabilities in your particular IT assets. Known vulnerabilities in your software are examples of this.

When the assets have been assigned appropriate value and the relevant threats identified and ranked, the next step is to determine whether the risk analysis will use a *qualitative* or *quantitative* approach. Most analyses will be a combination of the two.

Examples of specific threat to your systems may include items such as:

- Electrical outage
- Unauthorized access information resources
- Unauthorized modems within the network
- Circumstances dangerous to personnel
- Object reuse
- DDOS
- Network intrusion
- Specific application vulnerability
- Water damage
- IP operations/procedures

Quantitative Risk Analysis Because completion of a purely quantitative risk analysis requires a great deal of time and personnel resources, automated tools have been developed to help with the process. These tools allow the user to run "what if?" scenarios, and quickly perform calculations, such as estimated losses. An important thing to remember is that the preparation and data gathering required to use one of these tools can be substantial.

Steps for Quantitative Risk Analysis:

- Define the Asset Value for each asset
- Identify threats to the asset
- Determine the Exposure Factor for each asset in relation to the threat
- Calculate the Single Loss Expectancy
- Calculate the Annualized Rate of Occurrence
- Calculate the Annualized Loss Expectancy

Remember these formulas:

- Single Loss Expectancy (SLE) — this is a dollar figure that represents organizational loss from a single loss event. The formula for figuring the SLE is:
  — Asset Value ($) × Exposure Factor (EF) = SLE
- Annualized Rate of Occurrence (ARO) — this is and estimation of the number of times a threat is likely to occur during the year.
- Annualized Loss Expectancy (ALE) — this is a dollar value representing the expected loss in the course of the year. The formula for figuring the ALE is:
  — SLE × ARO = ALE

Examples of automated tools include but are not limited to: RiskWatch, Buddy System, and ACEIT (Automated Cost Estimating Integrated Tools).

QUALITATIVE RISK ANALYSIS   Qualitative risk assessments are reasoned estimates concerning credible threats made by people with experience and expertise in the business operations. They may address such issues as "what if our programming capability was lost due to malicious code?"

A qualitative risk analysis is scenario-based, with one scenario for each major threat. This analysis would result in a ranked list of triples. The triple includes the asset, the threat, and the exposure, or level of loss that would occur if the threat were realized.

Although there may be several dozen (or more) short written scenarios created during this process, it may be necessary to use only a few for testing purposes. Testing of the scenarios is accomplished by a walk-through of the scenario and evaluation of the current countermeasures. This will identify vulnerabilities and the participants can make recommendations on possible controls. This type of exercise helps individuals gain a sense of ownership over the analysis process as well as reinforcing awareness of organizational interdependencies and mission critical functions.

Final Results The final results of a risk analysis should include quantitative/qualitative valuations of critical assets, as well as detailed listing of significant threats and vulnerabilities associated with each. It will also address the annualized loss expectancy for each threat.

The risk analysis should also contain a recommendations section. This section will outline the recommended strategies for handling risk. These strategies will fall into one of three categories:

- Reduction — Implementation of countermeasures or control safeguards to reduce risk to an asset. This might include alteration to the physical IT environment, such as revised access controls, change in documentation or backup procedures and the implementation of preventative and detective controls, such as a firewall or IDS.
- Acceptance — A management decision to accept or absorb the loss that will occur if a specific threat is realized.
- Transference — Transferring the potential impact of a loss to a third party such as an insurance company.

The recommendations section may also include suggestions concerning the implementation of specific countermeasures.

Countermeasure Selection Criteria If risk reduction by the implementation of countermeasures is a recommendation, there are several criteria by which one can evaluate various options. Most important are the auditing features of the countermeasure. These allow tracking of access and may be vital in the event of an incident or investigation.

The countermeasure should be implemented in such a way that accountability of those responsible for it is ensured. Those persons responsible for administering the countermeasure should not also be constrained by it. This preserves the concepts of separation of duties, and of independence of the controller and the subject.

When recommending countermeasures, considerations should include:

- Accountability — both for the device and those using it.
- Independence from other controls — it should not rely on another control.
- Noncommon mechanism — this provides another layer of defense, in case one mechanism is compromised.
- Fail secure — in case of a failure, the device will fail in such a way as to ensure the confidentiality and integrity of the data (this point will be one of the ones most debated with upper management because it is sometimes stated that "the show must go on").
- Vendor-specific elements such as security, ease of use, useable logging, past performance and product support should also be considered.

As part of a defense in-depth architecture, the countermeasure should be independent from other controls and it is recommended they fail-secure in the event of a disruption. This applies not only to confidentiality controls, but also to integrity controls such as transaction commit/rollback features for databases. The actions that occur are often business driven.

A hypothetical example: If your online ordering Web site is connected to a mail server and the mail server becomes compromised, the decision must be made whether to continue processing customer order confirmation through the compromised box, knowing that mail may or may not be processed. If you do not have a mail system in place, your order processing software will not function. (It requires a device to accept hello packets on Port 25.) If no orders are taken, the company cannot afford to operate. In this case, a business decision should be made to decide the proper course of action. (Failing closed or secure might not be the best choice.)

Cost-Benefit Analysis Since cost, along with regulatory requirements and industry standards, will be a major factor in the selection and approval of recommended countermeasures, it is important that the list of recommended options includes a cost-benefit analysis for each, which will identify all of the costs associated with purchase, deployment, required resources and maintenance of the countermeasure.

The first step is to examine the projected operational and maintenance costs for the life of the countermeasure. The second step is to examine the projected benefits. In this case, it may be addressed as a reduction of loss or risk due to the implementation of the countermeasure. The costs and benefits will then be compared to determine if the tangible benefits justify the costs for operation and maintenance.

The value of a countermeasure to an organization can be determined by the following formula:

- ALE (before safeguard) — ALE (after safeguard) — safeguard
- (Annualized cost) compared to
- Safeguard (purchase and deployment costs)

It is important to remember that even after appropriate countermeasures have been implemented, there may still be a level of risk that has not been addressed. This is called residual risk, and may be due to budget constraints, low likelihood of a threat occurring, a low expected impact on the organization's operations, or other circumstances. Although some people consider acceptable risk and residual risk equivalent, in reality they may not be the same. When a risk analysis is performed, resources such as budget and time required for the countermeasures needed to reduce the probability of high priority risks may not extend to all the probable threats that have been identified. Therefore, some risks will receive "countermeasures as priorities and resources," while some will be left as acceptable risk. Those remaining are what are referred to as residual risks.

When the comparison shows little difference between the cost before implementing a safeguard and the cost after implementing a safeguard, a Return on Investment (ROI) analysis should be considered.

Return on Investment (ROI) Analysis   The way ROI is applied will change depending upon the company, the type of project and the expected type of return. The type of return can be either tangible, increased market share, or intangible, such as the improved productivity and morale within the organization, or increased customer satisfaction outside the organization.

The generally accepted definition of a ROI analysis is: a measure of the net income that an organization is able to earn by employing its total assets. The ROI is calculated by dividing net profits after taxes by total assets. Metrics used for this analysis include:

- Payback Period — The amount of time required for the benefits to pay back the cost of the project
- Net Present Value (NPV) — The value of future benefits restated in terms of today's money
- Internal Rate of Return (IRR) — The benefits restated as an interest rate

For example, consider a simple ROI as a cost savings for a project that will result in an intangible 10 percent improvement in productivity for a group of workers. A formula that could be used here would be:

Tangibles + Intangibles = (Increased business productivity) / (IT costs, training, support) = Return on business investment

When calculating the ROI, do not forget to take into account such things as software licensing and maintenance.

Roles and Responsibilities   Although successful risk management and risk analysis processes must be supported by senior management, it is frequently those individuals who are on the "front lines" of the organization who first recognize the need for the process. For those in IT, where technology has created a culture of change, the need for ongoing asset valuation, threat identification and countermeasure evaluation is obvious. The IT department is then an excellent vehicle for this ongoing process to be brought to the attention of senior management at the appropriate times.

Frequency of Risk Analysis

A Risk Analysis should be reviewed on a periodic, usually annual basis, or reinitiated in response to any significant changes in the environment, including:

- New hardware technologies
- New software applications
- Changes in corporate strategy, focus or structure
- Changes in information protection requirements
- Business plans and goals

Controls

Whether performing audits, security assessments, or risk analysis, controls are key items for evaluation. These are the mechanisms by which security policy is implemented and an acceptable level of risk is achieved. They are the polices, procedures, technical and physical mechanisms, practices and organizational structures that have been designed to provide assurance that business objectives will be accomplished and that threats will be mitigated and undesirable event impacts will be detected and corrected in order to minimize loss.

Controls are usually divided into three broad classes based upon function. These three — preventative, detective, and corrective — are further broken into categories according to the method used to implement the control.

Control Objectives Any information system should have controls for each of its major functions included as part of its natural structure. The function of the controls will be defined by the "control objective," which is a measurement of the control function as it relates to legal, regulatory, internal policy requirements and assurances of integrity, confidentiality, availability, nonrepudiation, and accountability.

A control objective is rarely achieved by one control mechanism or procedure. Strong and weak controls may compensate for each other. Take, for example, a situation where there were no locks on the data center door; however, there was a guard at the door requiring employees to show their badges and sign an access log. The lack of a lock is a weakness; however, the guard and access log are compensating for this weakness and are called compensating controls.

Compensating controls frequently use a different implementation. For example, the lock was a physical implementation of an access control, whereas the access log is an administrative implementation.

Examples of control objectives specific to individual information systems include:

- All changes to transaction processing software are approved and tested before implementation.
- All data files are adequately backed-up to allow for proper recovery (can be in terms of Maximum Allowable Downtime [MAD]).

Table 4.1.

Class	Function	Implementation	•
Preventive	• To predict problems before they occur • Control operations • Control data inputs • Prevent errors • Prevent unauthorized actions	• Technical • Physical • Administrative	Technical • Software access control • Constrained user interfaces • Anti-virus applications • Encryption • Secure communication protocol Physical • Fences • Guards • CPTED (Crime Prevention Through Environmental Design) • Data Center door locks • HVACR and environmental controls • Magnetic badges access systems Administrative • Transaction authorization procedures • Well-designed, sequentially numbered documents • Background checks • Segregation of duties • Training and awareness
Detective	• Detect errors and omissions • Detect unauthorized access • Detect unauthorized resource usage • Detect policy violations • Monitor compliance with procedures • Detect security violations • Report detection of possible violations, errors, omissions, access, or usage	• Technical • Physical • Administrative	Technical • Hash totals • Network Echo (PING) • Error messages • Automatic logging features • IDS • Sniffers Physical • Facility Intrusion Alarm Systems • CCTV • Motion detectors • Trip lighting Administrative • Check points in batch or production processes • Variance reporting • Internal audit • Enforcement of vacation • Logging access to sensitive information • Inventory controls • Employee background check updates • Control testing

Class	Function	Implementation	•
Corrective	• Minimize the impact of a realized threat • Identify a vulnerability • Identify a threat agent • Error correction • System modifications • Implementation/ strengthening of safeguards • Process/operational modifications • Error correcting code	• Technical • Administrative • Physical	Technical • Mirroring • Redundant systems • Hot swappable components • Backups • System recovery Administrative • Incorporation of "lessons learned" into policies and procedures • Training and awareness • Contingency planning Physical • Additional physical controls

- All rejected or duplicate transactions are reported.
- Information is stored securely on the network.
- Information is current.
- All events/transactions/processes requiring authorization, received it only one time.

Control Objectives   These controls are outlined by the IT Governance Institute and the ISACA in a set of good practices called Control Objectives for Information and Related Technology (CobiT). There are 34 high-level objectives, and over 318 detailed objectives divided into four domains — Planning and Organization, Acquisition and Implementation, Delivery and Support, and Monitor — which ensure that the effective implementation of the controls will result in an adequate control system for the IT environment. When controls for information are implemented in the form of processes or procedures rather than mechanisms, they may fall into one of the following categories:

- Access to data/applications/programs/network resources
- Support of organizational policy
- System development
- Data gathering/information processing
- Technical support
- Information processing quality assurance

Controls internal to the system may be grouped into internal accounting controls, operational controls, or administrative controls. The first is focused upon the reliability of records, especially those of a financial nature, and the safeguarding of corporate assets. The second group deals with the daily operational practices that support the mission critical functions and business objectives. The final group is concerned with operational efficiency within functional areas and compliance with organizational policies.

A thorough plan to test the system controls would include the following steps:

- Review the system to identify controls.
- Perform compliance testing to determine whether controls are functioning as expected.
- Determine the relationship between controls and any basis for reliance upon those controls.
- Determine if the controls still satisfy the requirements.
- Identify the nature, scope, and timing of substantive tests.
- Perform substantive test against the validity of the data.
- Test balances and transactions.
- Test analytical review procedures.

Control Implementation   Examples of the related processes and entities affected by these controls include but are not limited to:

- Network management and operations
- Authorization of data input
- Transaction and referential integrity
- Backup procedures
- Incident response
- Validation and verification of user requirements
- Reliability of processing activities
- Information classification procedures and enforcement
- Business continuity and cisaster recovery plans
- Security, accuracy, and completeness of system output
- Application and data integrity

Control Testing   Controls must be tested to determine whether they have achieved the control objective. There are two complimentary testing approaches, which together provide a thorough evaluation of the controls in an IT environment; these are referred to as *compliance* and *substantive* tests.

Compliance testing is performed to test control procedures and see if controls are working as expected and are being applied in accordance with management policies. Compliance testing requires that the tester be evaluating a specific objective. This type of testing includes examination of documentary evidence.

Substantive tests evaluate the integrity of data, individual transactions, information and actual processing. This is to ensure the validity and accuracy of the balances of financial statements as well as the transactions supporting them.

Results of the testing may be shown in a matrix. This may have the relevant known types of errors on the top, and the known controls on the other axis. Using a ranking method such as high, medium, or low, the relationship between the errors and the controls may be shown. The completed matrix will highlight areas where controls are weak or lacking, or where compensating controls have been identified.

Documentation   Although most of us do not enjoy creating documentation, it is often found that there is never enough useful and accurate documentation. This is especially true within the IT environment where changes can happen easily and quickly. Because of this, IT documentation of control mechanisms and practices will be carefully reviewed during risk analyses and audits.

It is important that you have all of your documentation organized, completed, and accurate. IT should also be gathered together in one place; this will not only make your job much easier on a daily basis, it will make a big difference for the risk analysis process as well as when IT audits take place. Documentation that will be helpful in these situations includes, but is not limited to:

- Change management procedures
- System configuration
- Information Systems (IS) development procedures
- System deployment processes
- System maintenance processes and logs
- IS policies, standards, baselines
- Staffing practices
- Staff training
- Security architecture
- Roles and responsibilities
- Management of third-party services
- Procedures for acquisition, installation, and maintenance of system hardware devices
- Procedures for acquisition, deployment, and maintenance of software and utilities
- Procedures for acquisition installation and maintenance of communications infrastructure components
- Help desk standard operations
- User support functions
- System performance logs
- System monitoring processes, tools, and techniques
- The design deployment and monitoring of logical access controls
- Network infrastructure security
- Acceptable use policies and procedures

- The design, implementation, and monitoring of environmental controls including heating, ventilation, air conditioning, refrigeration (HVACR)
- The design, implementation, and monitoring of physical access to the network or network operations center (NOC)
- Backup procedures
- Recovery procedures
- IT and organizational Business Continuity Plans
- Database management documentation
- Programming and application development documents
- Organizational best practices
- Relevant benchmarking
- The design and implementation of logical and manual controls
- Document compliance with risk management procedures
- Document compliance with organizational policies
- Interdependencies, both network and operational
- Trusted network relationships
- Internal process controls
- System accreditation and/or certification documents
- Identification of mission critical IT support for business functions
- Accurate network diagrams
- Information infrastructure inventory
- Software licenses
- User documentation for hardware and software
- Incident response procedures

Section 2: Response

This section addresses two main topics: Business Continuity Planning (BCP) and Disaster Recovery Planning. When completed, these plans will guide upper management and you through the necessary steps to plan and execute your response to an event or disaster.

Business Continuity Planning

BCP is defined as preparation that facilitates the rapid recovery of mission-critical business operations, the reduction of the impact of a disaster, and the continuation of critical business functions.

Disaster Recovery Planning is a subset of BCP that emphasizes the procedures for emergency response relating to the information infrastructure of the organization. This includes extended backup operations and post-disaster recovery for data center, network and computer resources.

A BCP is the tool that results from the planning and is the basis for continued life-cycle development.

Gartner Research has found that:

- Forty percent of all downtime is due to application errors including performance issues and bugs and utilities failure — power, communications.
- Forty percent is due to operator error.
- Twenty percent is due to system or environmental issues; nearly 60 percent of this category is composed of hardware failures.
- Less than 5 percent of downtime can be attributed to disasters.

Some of these areas are within our control, and can be fixed or improved to reduce the potential downtime. Other factors are outside of our control; we must do our best to find ways to reduce or mitigate the potential down time.

The Importance of Business Continuity Planning   Gartner estimates that two out of five enterprises that experience a disaster will be out of business within two years, but further states that enterprises can improve those odds, but only if they take the necessary measures before and after the disaster. In some cases, the disruption of normal business operations causes customers to lose confidence in the viability of the enterprise. In other cases, the cost of recovery may simply be too great, and sometimes the failure is caused not by the disaster but by the loss of key personnel and/or the corporate knowledge of the personnel.

Purpose of the BCP   The BCP plans the support and activities required to sustain mission-critical activities/functions of the organization. The creation of, and ability to offer, services and products are the lifeblood of an organization. These are the mission-critical activities of an enterprise. The dependencies between different business units that support these activities are vital and must be identified. It is upon these activities that the BCP must be focused. Remember that these functions may be dependent upon other functions or activities, and these dependencies may be internal or external.

A key factor to consider is whether the mission-critical activity has a single point of failure. This can be operational, technical, physical or administrative. If this is the case, there is no alternative unless plans are made to remedy the situation.

Before the BCP is put into action, a disaster must be declared by senior management with the responsibility and authority to do so. Guidelines for making the decision concerning whether to declare a disaster should be included within the BCP. A disaster may be declared for reasons ranging from the routine to the extraordinary, but the key element for declaring a disaster is the impact of the expected duration of the outage to the mission critical functions of the organization.

Categories of disasters include:

- Manmade/natural

- Internal/external
- Intentional/accidental

Examples of disasters include:

- Extreme weather — hurricane, tornado damage
- Criminal activity — theft of credit card numbers from CDNOW at E-commerce sites
- Civil unrest/terrorist acts
- Operational —Microsoft Web down three days in 2001
- Capacity — Victoria's Secret — spikes in business volume due to fashion shows
- Application failure — London Stock Exchange down one day in April 2000
- Loss of physical structures — Los Alamos National Lab buildings lost and damaged due to wild fires

IT Support of the Mission-Critical Functions during a Disaster Each component or department of the organization should be evaluated to identify the mission-critical functions. These will vary according to internal priorities and the actual business of the organization. The evaluations should include representatives from each department, external partners, and management representatives who are able to see the overall structure and business priorities within the organization.

Representatives of the BCP development team include, but are not limited to:

- Senior management, chief financial officer, and the like
- Legal staff
- Business unit/functions
- Support systems
- Recovery team leaders
- Information security department
- Data and voice communications department

This is just a sample of possible members. Each organization will also identify their key personnel and the BCP planner/coordinator, who serves as the focal point during all phases of the BCP process. Each department should send representatives who are knowledgeable about the organization.

Understanding the IT environment for the mission critical activities requires:

- An understanding of how the systems support the mission critical activities
- Identification of all internal and external mission critical functions that are dependent in any way upon the systems

- Identification of all single points of failure to the mission critical activities
- External influences that may impact the system

Identification of mission-critical activities is determined from the Business Impact Analysis (BIA). Identification of the dependencies and single points of failure are the results of the risk assessment and analysis processes. IT must have a copy of the BIA and a ranking of the mission critical activities, processes, functions and areas. From this the IT department can determine the proper support for the mission critical activities as well as the appropriate countermeasures.

Mission Critical   The term "mission critical" is defined as a system, function, or process that is critical to the functioning of an organization and the accomplishment of its mission. Mission critical activities are usually processes that include many elements within the organization:
- Human resources
- Stakeholders/customer or clients/suppliers
- Facilities/support systems/HVACR
- Functions/processes
- Material
- Technology
- Telecommunications/infrastructure
- Data in all formats

Since each organization is different from any other organization, it is imperative you consider what is necessary to keep your business alive and make sure it is included as "what is mission-critical" in your BCP.

Phases of the BCP   The BCP is composed of five separate phases:

- Project management
- Business impact analysis
- Recovery strategies
- BCP development
- Testing, verification, validations, and maintenance

Project Management Phase Tasks   The project management phase includes tasks such as:

- Performance of a risk analysis, which will serve as one of the basic requirements for development of the BCP. This will also contribute to the business impact analysis in a later step and will show the potential risk and loss to the organization in case of a disaster.
- Identification of the scope and objectives of the BCP. This project may be done for a sector, business unit, or the entire organization.
- Identification of internal and external resources that would be required in the event of a disaster:

- — Equipment
- — Personnel
- — Emergency services
- — Logistical support
- — BC policy & steering committee
- Establishment of the BCP team and the identification of:
- — Roles and responsibilities
- — Project plan
- — Project management procedures
- — Supporting resources
- — Authority

Business Impact Analysis   A BIA is similar to a risk analysis. It identifies the impacts of the loss of business functions on the organization over specific periods of time. This helps to identify the critical business area or processes, the priorities of the business functions, the Recovery Time Objective (RTO) and the Maximum Tolerable Downtime (MTD), also known as MAD, as well as to identify the interdependencies between functions and processes that may not otherwise be obvious. These elements are critical in the recovery or continuation of the business functions during and after a disaster.

Unlike the risk analysis, the BIA is not concerned with specific events, but with the consequences of any event upon the business viability of the organization.

CRITICAL SUCCESS FACTORS   The critical success factors for a BIA include, but may not be limited to, the following, due to the organization and specific circumstances:

- Support of senior management
- Assignment of financial value to business processes, data, and functions
- Definition of the scope of the analysis
- Accurate identification of the MTD
- Determination of the resource requirements needed to support the mission critical business functions during the incident and to meet the MTD

Other factors that you should consider:

- Metrics — How will you know when, and to what degree, you have succeeded?
- Amount and type of dedicated resources for completion of the project.

IT ASSETS   The identification and quantification of the Information Systems (IS) assets must be done by someone who understands the importance of the IS infrastructure. Things that must be identified and measured include:

- Inventory of IS resources
- The degree of use of IS resources by various business functions/processes
- The amount of reliance of mission critical business functions/processes upon the IS infrastructure
- The IS resources that are required to support the mission critical business functions/processes
- The replacement cost/current value of the devices and elements that comprise the IS infrastructure

Remember that replacement costs for equipment will not be the same as original purchase costs. When these are calculated, do not take into account any insurance coverage. You will need to have funds set aside for immediate purchase. Insurance may take months to pay and if you rely solely on that you may not have the ability to purchase what you need.

Other vital elements that may fall within the area of responsibility of IT may include:

- Creation of up-to-date documentation of all operating procedures that can be used by a knowledgeable person to restore or recover network devices
- Step-by-step procedures for performing a system restore from backup media such as tape
- Detailed configuration documentation
- Detailed network diagrams
- Ensuring that all documentation is up to date
- Ensuring that all procedures and documentation, including software documentation, is kept together, and that this documentation is mirrored at the alternate site
- Creating a life-cycle process so all of the information and plans keep up to date with current business processes

Conducting a **BIA** There are several accurate and useful approaches to conducting a BIA, all of which include the same essential elements, with the difference being the way activities are organized.

BIA Models

This section will use a model that has six major phases:

- Project planning
- Data collection
- Vulnerability analysis
- Data analysis
- Presentation of findings
- Reanalysis

For reference, we have included one of the other most recognized approaches, which uses the following eight steps:

1. Select the interviewees
2. Determine the information-gathering techniques
3. Customize the questionnaire to gather economic and operational impact information — using both quantitative and qualitative questions
4. Analyze the information
5. Determine the time-critical business systems
6. Determine the MTD
7. Prioritize critical business systems based on MTDs
8. Document findings and report recommendations

PROJECT PLANNING   In a fashion similar to the BCP, the BIA is most easily managed as an independent project. This area requires accurate and detailed planning and is vital to the BIA process.

Important tasks during this phase include:

- Defining the scope of the analysis
- Identification of all team members including support staff and other participants
- Identification of data collection methodology
- Identification of critical success factors and metrics
- Obtaining management support
- Identifying the resources required for the project

DATA COLLECTION   Since the purpose of the BIA is to identify the mission-critical business functions, it is important to examine all parts of the organization. It is not unheard of for intuitive estimates that are not based on valid data to result in the use of recovery resources for low-priority processes instead of higher priority, more critical processes.

Information may be gathered using a variety of methods, from review of charts and documentation to interviews with senior departmental staff.

Information to be gathered for each business function/process includes:

- Criticality of the business function for the organization.
- Processes of the business function.
- Interdependencies between this business function and others.
- What other processes rely on this one for input or support?
- What financial and operational impacts would there be on the organization if this business function were lost for a specified period of time (minutes, hours, days, weeks)?
- Would this impact change over time, or be different at different times of the year?

- What lead time is required to have these support resources or critical support structure in place?
- What contractual, regulatory or financial obligations are related to this function?
- Is this function key to the organization's competitive position?
- If everything were lost in a disaster, how long would it take to reconstruct the data and information required to support this function?
- What internal and external relationships or resources are required to support this function?

VULNERABILITY ANALYSIS   The Vulnerability Analysis involves dividing data collected in the previous step into two distinct parts — quantitative and qualitative.

Examples of the quantitative items are those that have specified monetary value such as:

- Loss of revenue
- Cost of resources required to maintain and or recover this function
- Loss from failure to meet regulatory requirements due to the disaster

Examples of qualitative items include:

- Loss of public confidence
- Damage to corporate reputation with suppliers and business partners

Once you have this information divided, you will have to understand the data and see where it is most susceptible. You must look at all aspects of the organization. This includes the data, how the data is handled, how the data is stored, how the data transits your network, how the network components are protected on an electronic layer, how the network components are protected on a physical layer, how the employees are protected on a physical level, and how the facilities are protected. You must look at the data from creation to the final product. You must look at your organization from a customer's point of view, a competitor's point of view, an employee's point of view, and a partner's point of view. You must look at the employee life-cycle, how they are hired, their background check, the day-to-day operations of the employees, and the termination of employees.

Just looking at the example list, you can see the range of material that must be covered for the analysis. This list will also vary from organization to organization and compiling it will be time-consuming and tedious. Mitigating the results that are found as a result of this analysis will be very worth your time.

DETERMINATION OF MAXIMUM TOLERABLE DOWNTIME   The MTD is defined as the longest period of time that a critical business function can remain down before the business can no longer recover.

The discrete tasks involved in this phase include:

- Quantitative analysis of functions and recovery
- Qualitative analysis of functions and recovery

The business units and senior management make the decisions concerning the importance of business functions. They will rank them according to business priorities.

In this process the quantitative losses are tallied and the qualitative losses are ranked, usually in a matrix depicting the seriousness of the impact for each of the listed vulnerabilities.

Table 4.2 presents an MTD qualitative scale that may be used to rank the various functions of an E-business.

Due to the differences between fields and even between organizations in the same field, each organization must develop its own methodology, according to its specific requirements.

For example, financial institutions must meet regulatory requirements that do not apply to other types of businesses. Best practices exist for most types of businesses.

The MTD will be used at a later point of this process but it is very important to determine these measurements. As you will see, it will help determine the priority for restoring a system.

ANALYSIS   This phase entails the examination of the vulnerability analysis results in order to determine which functions of the organization are mission critical as well as the degree of time criticality, and the MTD for each business function. The mission-critical functions are prioritized in order of importance, so those identified as the most critical functions (with the least amount of allowable downtime) will be the first recovered, and will receive the most resources during a recovery effort.

Remember that the prioritization of critical business functions may change depending upon circumstances, such as seasonal or contractual priorities or other considerations. For example, company XYZ may produce

Table 4.2

Recovery Ranking	Maximum Tolerable Downtime
Mission Critical	Minutes to ½ hour
Urgent	8 hours
Important	12 hours
Routine	3 days
Optional	5+ days

several products. The product that generates the most income may also be the one that has the highest recovery cost. Due to this, a management decision may be to recover a different product first because it has a lower recovery cost and generates an adequate amount of revenue.

Another important consideration is that the loss figures be determined without deducting insurance coverage of the loss. This is because of the amount of time that may elapse between a disaster, the actual filing of the insurance paperwork and reimbursement of the insurance monies resources may vary greatly depending upon the circumstances, and may extend beyond the company's recovery timeframe. Therefore, if a company is depending upon the reimbursement of insurance funds in order to recover the mission-critical functions of the organization, any delay in the process may prove catastrophic.

At this point, all of the functions, dependencies, and processes within the organization should be documented. The results of this analysis should be reviewed with senior management to verify the data and maintain critical management support.

Discrete tasks included in this phase are:

- Determination of mission critical functions
- Determination of MTD for each function
- Prioritization of functions for recovery based upon mission and time criticality
- Documentation of processes, dependencies, and functions

PRESENTATION OF FINDINGS   After the determination of the MTD, this may be the most important step of the BIA. A successful presentation to senior management may result in an endorsement for the project as well as financial support throughout the BCP project life-cycle. You should ensure that all of your figures are accurate, supported by facts, and not misleading. Relationships, dependencies and financial data may be more easily represented graphically. The overuse of statistics or long explanations may be counterproductive, depending upon your audience. You should also ensure that all points of your presentation are relevant to the managerial interests of the audience. Remember that this is an excellent time to demonstrate the value of the IT infrastructure to the mission critical functions of the organization.

REANALYSIS   This phase of the BIA is essential to ensure its lasting viability and usefulness to the organization. Reanalysis entails the continuing integration of system and process update information as well as the reevaluation of strategies as business goals change. Because of this, it may be helpful to consider updating it in concert with change management procedures. The BIA should be reviewed annually to determine whether it still reflects an accurate picture of business functions and priorities.

The BIA should also be reviewed when there are changes in:
- Business functions
- Market focus
- Senior management
- Stakeholders

Or there are:

- Acquisitions
- Mergers
- Reorganizations

Recovery Planning

This section outlines recovery strategies, which are firmly based upon the findings in the BIA. This is why the BIA is such an important element of the BCP. Remember that the goal of the BCP is to restore critical business functions within a predetermined acceptable time frame, so the recovery strategies must address a solution that will fall within the MTD identified in the BIA. This section will consider the recovery categories and associated IT responsibilities.

Recovery planning phase tasks include:

1. Document all costs with each alternative solution for continuity of the mission-critical functions and activities.
2. Obtain cost estimates for all outside services or resources.
3. Negotiate written agreements with providers or vendors for such services and resources.
4. Evaluate resumption strategies based on a full loss of the facility so that sufficient budget and planning are included.
5. Document all recovery strategies and associated costs and prepare a presentation for management. This should address the issue from a management perspective. Ask for both comments and approval.

Recovery Categories

- Business recovery of mission-critical functions — the resources identified in the BIA that are required to support the mission critical functions
- Data and information
- Facility and supply
- Network/communications
- User

Responsibilities for Business Recovery The IT department may find that it has significant responsibility for supporting and ensuring continuity of mission critical functions. These responsibilities may encompass not only the networking communications infrastructure, but also the data and information required for business operations as well as the processing facility. Always plan for the worst-case scenario to ensure that financial estimates are sufficient and that recovery plans are of adequate scope. It may be helpful to evaluate the use of a standard BCP Software package for organizational use. Although initially they require the same intensive data gathering that one would have with the manual process, they save time afterwards, and make plan maintenance much easier.

Some of the many examples of well-known BCP software packages are:

LDRPS by Strohl Systems
Precovery by SunGuard Planning Solutions
Recovery PACII by CCSI Professional Services Inc.

IT Responsibilities for Data and Information   The IT department must ensure that all information required during a disaster has been backed up, stored off-site, and kept up-to-date. This information spans the organization, and is vital for the continuity of operations.

Some recommended information to take to the backup site includes:
• System documentation
• Application manuals and documentation
• Technical material
• Network diagrams
• Log files
• System configuration files
• Backups
• Operating procedures

Having this information will enable you to better prepare your disaster recovery site and transition to that site once a disaster occurs. If a disaster were to occur, it is best not to have to recreate things from memory; it is much easier to restart a business function if you are reading from a checklist. You should ensure that the confidentiality and integrity of data and information are preserved even in the case of a massive systems or business failure.

Other information to consider includes:

• Contact lists for employees, vendors, service, and resource providers, local emergency response services
• Contingency plans, BCP, disaster recovery plans, incident response procedures
• Vital record storage (i.e., medical, personnel, HR)
• Essential forms for mission-critical processes

It is important to remember that in this effort you may be creating the office-working environment completely from the ground up. For example, common, everyday items like employee badges need to be functioning at the Disaster Recovery Site, as well as more complex issues need to be addressed.

IT Responsibilities for Facility and Supply Restoration During plan development, it is important to ensure that the recovery strategies will include sufficient computing capabilities or arrangements for acquiring them. Plans for supporting equipment, such HVACR must also be evaluated. During this planning phase it is very important to work with senior management to secure a facility that will maintain at least minimum continuity of operations.

The focus of facility and supply restoration and recovery should include:

- Facility
  - Main building
  - Remote facilities
- Inventory
  - Supplies
  - Equipment
  - Forms
  - Paper
- Supply and equipment logistics
- Support equipment
  - HVACR
- Site security
- Site operations

IT Responsibilities for Network and Communications Restoration There are many tasks that must be completed in order to get network connectivity up and running in the new location in a manner similar to that of the main site. In today's organizations, most of the day-to-day activities are conducted over the network communications channel. For that reason, it is imperative that the restoration be as smooth and efficient as possible.

What needs to be restored can be further broken down. For example:

- Data/voice communications
  - PBX
  - Voice over IP equipment
- Necessary configuration documentation and files
  - Product licensing
  - Network diagram
  - Security rules
- Hardware
  - Mainframes/servers/workstations
  - LANs, WANs
  - Peripherals

- — Routers
- — Switches
- — Gateways
- — Firewalls, IDSs, VPNs
- Software
  - — Backups
  - — Applications and documentation
  - — Usage parameters
  - — Gateways
- Supporting equipment
- Power
- Safety
- Security
  - — Uninterruptible Power Supply (UPS)/ Back-up power supply

IT Responsibilities for User Restoration Because the IT department has already identified strategies for protecting important documentation and the controls for the processing facility, the remaining responsibilities for user restoration fall under the category of preparing user workspace and equipment.

Some factors to consider in user restoration are:

- Manual procedures for critical functions
  - — Making sure that critical equipment or data stores are carried to the new site
  - — Notify employees of transition to alternate site and remind them of the procedures
- Critical documentation and forms
  - — Your plans and programs
  - — Mission-critical call list
- Employee logistics
  - — Transportation
  - — Family support
  - — User workspace and equipment
- Alternate site procedures
  - — Access control
  - — Safety/site security

BCP Development At this point the planning and data gathering is complete and the actual BCP is written. This plan should be a workable roadmap for recovery of operations. The organizational BCP should be a structure within which individual departmental plans are included without conflict. Those individual departmental plans are subordinate to the organizational plan and are designed to support the overall organizational goals and plans. The departmental plans will outline specific procedures and processes for the salvage, maintenance and restoration of departmental DRP resources.

It is imperative that the finished plans have senior management approval and support; without them the plan will not succeed. The BCP should also include procedures for keeping the information up-to-date.

IT Responsibilities for Plan Development   During the plan development phase, the information technology department plays a vital role in providing accurate information and ensuring that the recovery strategies within the BCP address all required control categories.

Information that should be provided includes:

- Identification of internal and external information dependencies
- Determining adequate data backup procedures and reliable restoration processes
- Ensuring that off-site media storage is kept current and accessible
- Identification of the required physical, logical, and administrative controls to protect hardware, software, and data resources and ensure sufficient authentication and authorization controls for critical information and data
- Identification of resources and procedures that ensure adequate hardware, software, media, and media storage

IT BCP   The IT department should have plans to cover the salvage and immediate replacement of equipment to support the overall BCP. There should also be plans that address the implementation of all departmental plans at a variety of alternate processing sites and in a variety of situations. These departmental plans should be detailed enough that a reasonably knowledgeable individual can execute them. Having the detailed plans is important because the person who is supposed to implement the plans could be on vacation, have left the organization, or have succumbed to the disaster. It is not wise to "count" on people just knowing what to do or filling in the blanks. During times of crisis, it is much better to read from a checklist than to try and think clearly and remember all of the things that should be done.

Ensure that personnel in key positions have access to copies of the departmental BCP. The plan should first address the continuation of critical functions, and secondly the recovery of noncritical functions. It should also include procedures for return to the primary site and deactivation of the emergency or alternate site. If the disaster is severe enough, a new primary site may be designated, or the backup site may be converted to the primary site.

When returning to the primary site, ensure that all systems have been tested, and start noncritical processes first. This way, if there are still problems with the systems at the primary site, they will be discovered without risking vital functions. After all noncritical functions are backed up at the primary site, start to transfer the mission critical functions.

Testing, Verification, Validation, Maintenance   The BCP must be tested to see how workable it is and to find and remedy weaknesses in the planning, to enable participants to practice the recovery process and to ensure that all goals are achieved.

Verification of the plan means that all the processes and procedures actually work the way they are documented within the plan.

Validation of the plan is making sure that it accurately meets the requirements of the organization. These may change over time. There should be processes included in the plan that specify the maintenance procedures.

BCP Testing   There are several ways to test the BCP, ranging from nondisruptive and requiring few resources, to the other end of the spectrum where they disrupt the business and require many dedicated resources. The methods may vary according to the organization.

Disaster Recovery

Disaster recovery is a subset of BCP that deals specifically with the recovery and restoration of the information processing capabilities. Although similar to the BCP, here the critical areas that were the focus in the BCP have already been identified and the focus is on the implementation of recovery procedures.

After discussing the various recovery categories and associated IT responsibilities, it is helpful to place those categories within the context of various strategies that may be used for business continuity.

Goal of Disaster Recovery   The goal of Disaster Recovery Planning is to ensure that in the case of a disruption to business operations, rapid recovery procedures will be executed that will ensure the smooth implementation of the information system capabilities of critical processing and support of mission critical business functions. This implementation may be at an alternate site, and then returned to a primary site at the appropriate time, with the absolute minimum loss of time and money.

Online resources include:

http://www.disaster-recovery-plan.com/
http://www.binomial.com/
http://www.disasterplan.com/
http://www.disaster-recovery-guide.com/
http://www4.gartner.com/5_about/news/disaster_recovery.html
http://palimpsest.stanford.edu/bytopic/disasters/

Objectives   The MTD that was identified during the BIA is of vital importance here, as the strategies for alternative processing must fit within its predefined timeframe.

Although these may vary according to the organization and business, objectives that contribute to the overall success of the main goal include:

- Prevention of information systems disruptions
- Minimization of risk resulting from processing delays
- Ensuring reliable alternatives for processing
- Minimizing the decisions to be made during a disaster
- Ensuring there is no breach of information confidentiality due to a disruption
- Ensuring there is no question about information integrity due to a disruption
- Minimizing the impact of unavailable resources
- Ensuring there will be no opportunity for unauthorized systems activities

Strategies   These are the most commonly accepted strategies for alternate processing in case of an emergency:

- Subscription Service
- Service Bureaus
- Reciprocal agreements
- In-house sites
- In-house resource redundancy

We will cover each of these below in more detail.

Subscription Service Alternatives

Hot Site   This alternative includes a facility with clean electrical power, HVACR, fully configured hardware, installed software, and possibly current data. Ideally, the organization is using mirroring or remote transaction journaling to keep the data current. A hot site is usually operated by a third party that leases the systems to several organizations in the expectation that not all subscribers will experience disasters at the same time. The third party operates the hot site, maintains and updates the equipment, and provides opportunity for the subscribers to test their disaster recovery plans at the site several times per year.

Cold Site   A cold site is a facility with HVACR and utilities. In the event of a disaster, all servers, workstations, and hardware will need to be delivered, set up and configured, and all software applications installed. When this is complete, data must be restored from backup. Although this alternative does not require continuous maintenance, it requires an enormous expenditure of resources and loss of time to prepare it for use.

Mobile Site   Some vendors offer backup services that are moved by truck. In the event of substantial, but not total, damage to a primary facility, a mobile site may be moved to a convenient location such as the parking lot at the primary site. The servers and other equipment in the truck are then wired to the organization's network.

Warm Site   The readiness of the warm site will depend upon the agreement between the organization and the subscription service. Usually, it will have power, HVACR, and hardware. However, applications may have to be installed and data restored from backup. When using a warm site, the IT department must be aware of other resources required by the agreement. Setting up the site may require use of the equipment that had been stored at the primary site, or that may be delivered according to prearranged agreements from vendors.

Regardless of which strategy is chosen by the organization, it is the responsibility of the IT department to ensure that all equipment that has been identified as necessary is in place at the alternate site. This includes the necessary files, documentation, and other items that were identified in the recovery categories.

Service Bureaus   A service bureau is an organization that provides support or processing services. This type of arrangement allows quick response to any disruption; however, it can be expensive and in the case of a regional disruption, there may be difficulties providing resources for a large number of organizations. In the event of a disruption, many organizations use service bureaus to handle such tasks as customer contact, call centers, and payroll, so the organization can focus its resources on other core operations.

Another advantage to service bureaus is that it is possible to test their response capability and use them on occasion where workload demands exceed the normal processing capability of the organization, though the cost of this option may be prohibitive to some organizations.

Reciprocal Agreements   Reciprocal Agreements, also known as Mutual Aid Agreements, are arrangements between organizations that agree to support each other in case of a disruption. This type of agreement is usually between organizations that have similar processing needs. In the case of a large disruption, both organizations may need the processing resources and contention may arise. The joint use of equipment may also cause security concerns; however, it does cut costs for an alternate site. In this instance it is important for IT to verify that the other organization had the required hardware, software, and telecommunications capabilities. Other issues to consider include access control and security of the site as well as costs and required resources. Reciprocal agreements can be especially useful in cases involving special or very expensive hardware not normally available at a subscription service.

DRP Testing   Testing should not unnecessarily disrupt essential work operations. The tests will run more effectively if planned in advance and if written test plans are used. The results of the testing should be well documented and reported to management, especially such areas as weaknesses, mistakes, problems and lessons learned.

In order from least to most disruptive, test types include:

- Checklist — the plan is reviewed independently by all stakeholders to validate the plan requirements and strategies.
- Structured walk-through — This walk-through needs to be conducted with all personnel with plan responsibility. The plans and procedures are reviewed in a step-by-step process to ensure they will operate effectively in a real crisis situation.
- Parallel — Run a fully operational test at the alternate site but with the primary site capabilities still functioning. In this test, only the operational staff is included.
- Simulation — This practice should be performed by all recovery participants according to a written scenario. This may be as disruptive as a mock test affecting large parts of the organization. Participants come from all areas of the organization and also include various stakeholders such as business partners, emergency service, or vendors.
- Full interruption — Normal operations at the primary site are shut down and the alternate processing plans are executed or restored at the alternate site. This is normally not recommended for large organizations because of the possibility of precipitating an actual disaster when restoring processing at the primary site.

It is important that lessons learned be incorporated into the plan and, as the plan is updated and changed, each responsible individual has the current version.

The focus thus far has been on Business Continuity and Disaster Recovery. These are planned and managed responses to major business disruptions that could threaten the continuation of business. However, not all disruptive forces will act on the business as severely as a disaster. There are many smaller and less serious situations that may still have significant impact on the business or its processing capability. These are dealt with in this next section on Incident Response.

Incident Response

Definitions vary from CERT to CERT and from organization to organization. These are some examples and what we will be using for reference:

- Incident — Any adverse event resulting in computer systems, networks, or data being accessed, viewed, manipulated, destroyed, damaged, modified, or made unavailable by an unauthorized person or authorized person operating beyond their authorized privileges or the use of an information system in an unauthorized or unlawful manner;

or where the system is used in the commission of a crime or contains evidence of a crime.

- Event — An observable occurrence, or an aspect of an occurrence that can be documented, verified, and analyzed. This may be part of an investigation, or related to an incident.
- Response — Action(s) or measure(s) taken to recognize, respond to, or mitigate the impact of an incident.

The Need for Incident Response   Why incident response? Survey results from 503 companies in 2002 show that many attacks are occurring and the trend of these attacks is increasing every year:

- Ninety percent had detected computer security breaches within the last 12 months.
- Eighty-five percent detected computer viruses.
- Eighty percent acknowledged having financial losses due to computer breaches.
- Seventy-four percent said the Internet connection was a frequent point of attack.
- Forty percent detected system penetrations from the outside.
- Forty percent detected denial of service attacks.
- Thirty-four percent reported the intrusions to law enforcement.
- Thirty-three percent cited their internal systems as a frequent point of attack.
- Seventy-eight percent detected employee misuse of Internet access privileges.

(These figures were taken from the "Highlights of the '2002 Computer Crime and Security Survey'" document, which can be found at: http://www.gocsi.com.)

There are many different types of computer crime that the security practitioner should be aware of:

- Unauthorized access to computer or system resources by unauthorized individuals
- Hacker/cracker/phreaker
- Misuse by authorized user
- Theft of hardware/software/data/information
- Piracy/counterfeiting/unlicensed use
- Computer or system used for planning/conducting a crime

Computer Incident Response Issues   There are a number of indicators, including those listed below, that may be evidence of some type of incident, ranging from the obvious, such as discovery of a rootkit, to the subtle, such as increased disk space by an employee on vacation.

- System crashes or anomalies
- Attempts to change system files

- Suspicious or increased probes
- Attempted penetration
- Intrusion detection alarm
- Account lockout
- Incorrect access controls
- Buffer overflow
- Denial of service
- Loss or decrease of system storage
- Accounting discrepancies
- Unexplained files/file or data manipulation
- Malicious code
- Suspicious entries
- New user accounts
- New or unfamiliar file names or modified file names or types
- Modifications to file lengths, dates, or extensions
- Unexplained deletion of data
- Poor or degraded system performance
- Detection of a sniffer device to capture network traffic
- Reported social engineering attempts
- Unusual usage patterns or times
- Conflicts in reported last accessed times compared to actual last accessed times
- User complaints or questions to the helpdesk

Threats   The security practitioner should be aware of common threats and attacks. Some of the classic ones are:

- Sniffing — A program to capture data across a computer network. It is a software tool that audits and identifies network traffic packets. It is most often used legitimately by network operations and maintenance personnel to troubleshoot network problems, although this tool is one of the favorites that are misused by hackers to capture user ID names and passwords.
- Spoofing — Pretending to be someone or something else. The deliberate inducement of a user or a resource to take an incorrect action. Attempt to gain access to an Automated Information System by pretending to be an authorized user. Impersonating, masquerading, and mimicking are forms of spoofing.
- Fragmentation Attacks — The creating and sending of bogus fragmented packets that when reassembled are reassembled in an illegal way. This causes the operating system to shut down, as it does not know how to handle the combination.
- Penetration — The penetration attack works when firewalls filter only the first fragment to avoid slowdown of incoming traffic through a firewall. This allows fragments to be overlapped causing an illegal packet to be passed through the firewall. This is known as a penetration attack.

- Denial of Service — The overlapping or gapping of fragments may cause a kernel crash on an OS that is incapable of dealing with the illegal fragment reassembly.
- Broadcast Storms/Smurfing — A denial of service attack in which an attacker spoofs the source address of an echo-request ICMP (ping) packet to the broadcast address for a network, causing the machines in the network to respond en masse to the victim thereby clogging its network.
- ICMP (Internet Control Message Protocol) provides a communication service at the data link layer, which provides for error messaging, such as "DESTINATION UNREACHABLE." ICMP also provides an alternative method for router discovery for use on multicast links eliminating the need for manual address configuration (RFC 1256).
- When ICMP router discovery messaging is implemented on a router, there are certain default values specified. This extension of ICMP poses some security problems. It is possible for any system attached to this link to masquerade as a default router for other hosts attached to the same link.
- Traffic sent to the masquerader is subject to eavesdropping, denial of service, and packet alteration to include packet insertion and packet deletion.
- Routing Attacks — Taking advantage of routing by slowing down, re-routing, or misrouting packets on a network.
- Source routing is a network layer option that permits the owner of a packet to deliberately specify the route that a packet will take to a host, and what route the return packet or packets will take. It is legitimately used for network diagnostic purposes (RFC 791).
- ARP attacks — Because ARP is stateless, ARP replied messages can be forged. For example, an attacker could send a message to a victim stating that the legitimate resource has a fictitious MAC (Modified, Access, and Created) address. This would cause a denial of service of the resource. False ARP entries could be sent to routers, switches and hosts. This is known as ARP poisoning. The result could be sniffing, spoofing, DOS, interception, hijacking, modification of the data flow, and decrypting (man in the middle attack). These attacks are all possible by manipulating ARP entries on the network.
- Session Hijacking — Where an attacker uses a program to watch traffic as it flows back and forth between two hosts and then predicts the next sequence number in the stream and takes control of one of the host's session. In most, but not all cases, sequence number generation does follow some form of a pattern. As operating systems become more sophisticated and powerful they are gradually starting to create truly random sequence numbers. These numbers are extremely difficult to predict. After viewing the traffic flowing from host to host a program can predict, then insert, a packet with the proper sequence number

and effectively take over the connection. The connection takeover may be accepted by the host as long as it has a valid IP address and the sequence number is valid. Once a socket is established it will accept a segment if:
— The IP address is valid.
— The sequence number is valid.

- SYN Floods — sending many SYN packets to open multiple sessions in a port until the port is overwhelmed trying to respond.
- UDP Floods — sending many UDP packets to open multiple sessions in a port until the port is overwhelmed trying to respond.
- Connection Killing — steps are:
  — Put NIC into promiscuous mode.
- Listen for three-way handshake (initial SYN):
  — Forge a packet with RST flag to client requesting the connection.
- The results:
  — Prevents TCP connections from being established.
  — Eliminates all TCP traffic on an Ethernet segment.
- Requires:
  — IP address of destination host.
  — TCP port of listening process.
  — Client's initial sequence number (ISN).
- Connection hijacking steps:
  — May be applied to Telnet sessions and other unencrypted sessions.
  — Allows take-over after initial authentication (S/Key, plaintext).
  — Find/guess the sequence number and insert data into the stream.

Incident Response Process   Although each incident will vary, and with it the actual details and procedures required to address it, this process can be used as a framework for decision-making and implementation of the actual procedures that will be performed in a given situation. In order to use this effectively, the options and possible procedures used during each of the phases should be documented to minimize the number of decisions to be made during an actual incident. This not only helps guide the process and reduce stress, it provides a comprehensive and consistent approach that will be helpful should legal action be required.

The following is a high-level example of the Incident Response Process. More detailed information concerning the steps to the process is presented later in the chapter.

- Preparation and Planning — The process should start with preparation and planning for the event.
- Detection — Once an event is detected and determined to be an incident, the level of containment should be determined and implemented.
- Notification — Management should be notified as per the incident re-

sponse policy. All others affected should also be notified. This notification includes those responsible for logging and security measures to prep them for gathering evidence. Other business units that may be affected might also be notified.

- Investigation — From this point, the evidence should be gathered and processed.
- Recovery — Once the investigation is complete or sufficiently underway that no more evidence can be gathered, the next step is to begin recovery. It is at this point that servers might be reconstructed and data attempted to be recovered. Also, during this phase in of the process, a new server might be installed to replace the compromised system. All lessons learned from the investigation should be implemented to prevent a subsequent incident. All passwords should also be changed.
- Response — In this phase, actions such as prosecution and tightening up security through installation of patches, changes to network architecture, or implementation of additional security measures would be implemented.
- Follow-up — Final notification to participants should be completed and all evidence required for prosecution should be handed over to the appropriate law enforcement agencies. Lessons learned should be documented and implemented into the new policies. Other actions or processes learned from this incident would be incorporated into day to day running of the organization.

The life-cycle then resets to the planning and preparation phase. In this phase, new developments to the processes and procedures should be implemented to prevent any new incidents.

Preparation and Planning   The foundation, authorization, restrictions, and permission for any incident response activities must be expressly detailed in the corporate policies. All departmental policies and procedures are subordinate to these.

Corporate policies provide approval for:

- Resources
- Personnel
- Equipment
- Procedures
- Training

It is important to have all of the policies in place before an event occurs. If you do not have the right equipment or training, the results of the investigation may not be admissible in court.

Computer Incident Response Policy Issues   There are many layers of security policy within each organization, starting with the overarching corporate statements to functional policies regarding:

- Contingency operations
- Acceptable use
- Privacy
- Partner security
- Law enforcement notification and response
- Publicity and media

It is important to have these statements formally documented; when employees violate them, it allows for easier justification for conducting an investigation. The statements can also be incorporated into Service Level Agreements with partners. Having these policies defined prior to an investigation simplifies the steps and smoothes the process, allowing your organization to more quickly return to normal operations.

Policy Attributes   To be effective, policies must be:

- Supported by senior management
- Easy to understand and to the point
- Comprehensive
- Acknowledged by users and management
- Fairly and consistently implemented
- In accordance with the law
- Enforceable

Policy Issues   Senior management support of security policy demonstrates due care. It is important that the policies also:

- Meet business needs.
- Support the legal position of the organization.
- Include implementation and reporting processes as well as consequences for violation.

Policy Implementation   When policies are developed, approved, and acknowledged, the information concerning them should go to all employees. When new employees are hired, part of their in- processing should be the receipt and understanding of these policies. The information systems should have warning banners that explain user policies before the user is allowed to log on to the system.

Other implementation issues include:

- Resources needed for implementation and maintenance
- Development of processes and procedures based on the policies
- Testing of all processes and procedures
- Procedures for updating and disseminating versions

Incident Response Policies   Incident response policies should include reporting procedures and a decision-making "chain of command." These policies should also include definitions of incident types and should categorize them for ease of response. This process will facilitate rapid and appropriate response measures. Although these categories will differ from organization to organization, an example would be:

- Level 1 — Single machine
- Level 2 — Multiple machines
- Level 3 — Business unit
- Level 4 — Single site
- Level 5 — Organizationwide

Incident Response Categories Each incident category should have a series of predetermined procedures that are used to respond to given incident types. For example, there will be different procedures for a malicious code attack from the outside than there will be for internal computer misuse or compromise of the corporate firewall.

Categorization of incidents facilitates appropriate and measured responses. For instance, the policy may state that level 1 and 2 incidents can be handled by the IT department and the security team, whereas level 4 and above should be handled exclusively by a trained incident response team.

Table 4.3 is an example of a matrix that will reduce decision-making and facilitate active and effective response during an incident. Notice that each step is dated and approved by an individual with proper corporate authority. The individual or role that has this responsibility should be specified within the corporate policies.

The Incident Response Team (IRT) IRT responsibilities include:

- Developing appropriate response procedures
- Acquisition of required resources
- Investigating computer incidents
- Determining the cause of the incident
- Managing evidence from the incident, including hardware and software
- Recommending countermeasures and control to management

IRT It is essential that you have all the people you need on your team from various specialty areas. Not all organizations will have all of the areas, but it is best to have people who are responsible for various aspects of the corporation. You do not want to start your investigations without having the staff that knows how to do their job, and how to do an investigation properly. There are two components to the IRT — the response group and the support group. Suggested members of the response group include representatives from:

- IS auditing
- Information security
- Physical security

Table 4.3 Incident Process Matrix

Level	Description	Date	Approval
Detail	The specifics of this incident		
Approved Response Options	Which options/procedures are pre-approved for addressing this?		
Other	Are the pre-approved options adequate?		
Required Personnel	What skills sets and knowledge are required?		
	Are these available internally?		
	If not, where are they available externally?		
	Are agreements in place to provide required services, skills from external sources?		
IT Support	Required hardware, software		
	If not available in-house are arrangements in place to get it from vendors?		
Logistics	Transportation of equipment, personnel, food, human services, lodging, supplies, work areas, etc.		
Approved Budget	What has been pre-approved for this level incident?		
Estimated Time	How rapid can the initial response be?		
	What is the estimated timeframe for completion of the response?		
Escalation	Process and required approval for escalation if there is no resolution, what procedures and approvals are required to hand this to another entity unresolved (i.e., law enforcement)?		
Follow-up	What steps must be taken after incident resolution? Procedures for returning to normal operations		
Report	Who is responsible for creation and presentation of report?		
	What were the lessons learned?		
	How should they be incorporated into current procedures and policies?		

- Corporate legal
- IT/Network engineering
- IRT manager
- External specialty areas (digital forensics)

The support group should include representatives from:

- Human resources
- Corporate communications
- Senior management
- Administration
- Logistics

MISSION   An example of the IRT mission is to:

Identify:
- The problem
- The target
- The damage
- Investigate
- Collect evidence
- Contain damage
- Prevention
- Recovery

The IRT has a wide range of responsibilities. The basic mission is to conduct a measured and appropriate response to an incident. This mission varies from company to company, and is determined by corporate policy.

OBJECTIVES   Some of the objectives of the IRT procedures include:

- Determine how the system was accessed
- Explain why the victim was chosen
- Identify the objective of the incident
- Preserve the scene, gather the evidence and establish a chain of custody
- Help to determine suspects
- Document damage
- Determine need for law enforcement
- Recovery
- Prevention

These are fundamental; however, there are specific objectives for each phase of the IR process and may vary depending upon the situation and the goal of the response. If the goal is to determine how the exploit was accomplished, contain the damage and recommend countermeasures, the objective of preserving the scene and managing the evidence may be of low priority. However, if the goal is prosecution, the collection and management of evidence would be paramount.

Sometimes the goal will be to continue operations. This decision is one that needs to be cleared and signed off by upper management. If continued operations are paramount, then some of the logging, data handling, and chain of custody can be disregarded. Although continuing operations is the goal, you should try to contain the incident or prevent its recurrence if possible. If left unchecked and uncontained, the incident may make continued operations impossible and the recovery quite unlikely.

PRIORITIES Priorities will vary depending upon the organization and the situation. The following are among those that may vary according to the circumstances:

- Protection of property
- Protection of sensitive data
- Notification of partners or others affected
- Minimization of disruption to systems and business functions
- Protection of information
- Incident containment
- Data recovery
- Systems recovery

The only constant is that the safety of personnel should be paramount.

Liaisons These should be developed well in advance of an incident:

- Law enforcement
- IRT's in partner organizations
- Vendors of required software and hardware
- Emergency Services
  — Fire
  — Medical
- IR organizations
- Specialists/consultants

Knowing your contacts and their requirements, and understanding how they work, will help you reduce the time of your investigations. It may also help your case go forward. An example of this is turning over evidence to law enforcement for prosecution. The collection and handling of evidence may vary from locale to locale. If you do not collect and handle the evidence according to how the local law enforcement collects and handles the evidence, you may have a tougher time in the prosecution of your case.

Each liaison should include a specific point of contact and clearly defined procedures to follow, and should be supported by policy and senior management.

Based upon the recommendations of the security practitioner, senior management is responsible for making the decision to contact outside organizations as well as placing parameters upon the information to be shared with them.

Detection Detection of incident indicators can come from many places besides the network administrators. Users are common sources of information and frequently see indicators first. The process of gathering those indicators can be facilitated by:

- Providing a list of indicators
- Creating a reporting structure that provides for anonymity
- Ombudsman — to investigate, report findings and help to achieve equitable settlements
- Developing simple and convenient notification procedures

At this phase, it is vital that the security practitioner first determine whether this is an incident or if it was a simple mistake or false report. This determination will make a difference in the procedures used. For example, if it is a mistake, the next step should be recovery, but if it is an actual incident, the security practitioner must preserve the scene, assess damage, begin the chain of custody for the evidence and notify the appropriate individuals.

To establish the chain of custody the practitioner should:

- Identify each piece of evidence.
- Photograph the evidence if applicable.
- Permanently mark each piece of evidence in a place that will not cause damage to it or obscure the data.
- Log each piece of evidence.
- Note the physical condition.
- Note the exact location where it was found.
- Note its relation/connection to other pieces of evidence (connectors, cabling, etc.).
- Seal each piece in a numbered individual envelope or container.
  — Sign it.
  — Date it.
- Have each recipient sign and date the log.
  — Record the condition of the evidence upon receipt.
  — Keep evidence in the control of a custodian.
  — Store it in a secure location with restricted access.

When trying to detect an incident occurring within your organization, it is important to look at network traffic. In order to determine whether traffic on the network is legitimate, it is important to be familiar with it. Network monitoring is one way to achieve this. When there is not enough time to perform this regularly, an alternative is to capture the traffic and view it later:

- Capture of network data and attack signatures
  — Tcpdump
- Viewing and analysis of network data and attack signatures
  — Ethereal

VIEWING TRAFFIC   When used with specific options and Ethereal, another tool, the system administrator can do an in-depth analysis of the traffic.

Tcpdump
-c specifies the number of packets to collect

-s increases the packet size from the default
-w will write data to a named file
-i will monitor a specific interface
-host will monitor all traffic going to or from a specific IP address
-port will monitor all traffic going to or from a specific port

Ethereal is a sniffer that breaks down the information and will read the output from either tcpdum*p* or ipgrab.

Snort   Another option for viewing network traffic is Snort. Snort is an Open Source network intrusion detection tool that has flexible filtering rules and a good logging capability.

An example of some of the rule syntax:

- Action (alert, log, pass)
- Source/destination
  — <protocol> <source-addr/net> <source-port> -> <dest-addr/net> <dest-port>
  — tcp any any -> 192.168.1.0/24 80:100
  — udp 192.168.1.245/32 53 -> any any
  — icmp any any -> any any
- Content filter
  — (msg:"<text-alert>";content:"<packet- content>"; flags: <TCP flags>; TTL: <n>; itype: <n>)

Snort will enable you to monitor traffic in real time, allow you to capture the data and use it to correlate issues. The results from Snort can be combined with multi-source data to verify network-based attacks.

RESPONSE TYPES   When an intrusion takes place, the security practitioner should already have procedures in place and know how to respond. The options are:

- Passive versus active
- Automatic versus manual

You can have combinations of these responses as well. Logging may be both passive and automatic in some instances, and in other instances you might have to turn on special logging, so that would fall under the "manual" category.

Logging and documenting are sound choices. Attacking back is never a recommended response.

Real-time IDSs must be implemented to take full advantage of the technical infrastructure. The placement of sensors should be carefully considered. A carefully developed architecture should already have detection capabilities in place.

Many IDS implementations have a requirement for secure transmission of data from a remote capturing device to a local database server. The live network event data that is transmitted for analysis must also be protected from exploitation. To keep this event data private, some organizations use a private network so none of the IDS traffic is sent over the live network. Once *crackers* have initial access to a system on a network, they will launch a nonthreatening attack that they know most IDS sensors will pick up. Organizations that do not have the private or back channel communications set up will tip their hand to the attacker. The attacker would then see the IDS register the traffic and send the report to the management station. Often times "low" level alerts don't get the attention afforded "higher" level alerts. If the attacker has a sniffer on the network, he too will see the notification sent to the management station. A sophisticated or knowledgeable attacker will then be able to determine the type of IDS, the position of your IDS and management station. An attacker can then determine if he wants to avoid the IDS, try to kill all of the traffic between the IDS and the management station, or flood the management station with useless traffic making the log analysis extremely difficult.

Correlation Issues   Correlation issues are a concern for successful IDS implementation in distributed systems. Problems include:

- Sensors being in different time zones
- Unsynchronized system clocks
- Different vendor implementations
- Roles of the IDS versus the IPS and how the corporate policy comes into play

Whether to implement an IDS or an IPS depends on your corporate policy. It is often set up so that your IDS is more of a passive device and the IPS as more of an active device. You will have to decide if you want to have a device take action on your behalf — or not.

IDS Implementation   Freeware versus COTS (commercial off-the-shelf) — There are any number of options for ready-to-go products. The limits are set by resources, time, money, and personnel.

Single versus Multiple Vendors — Depending upon how the IDS is integrated into the network, a single vendor solution might keep the implementation simple.

If not carefully researched and implemented, multiple IDS products in a network environment may present conflicts in reporting policies and procedures on how to handle network events.

More information about the IDS and IPS can be found in the Data Communications portion of this book.

Issues As IDS technology continues to evolve and become more sophisticated, so do the attacks against it. The growth of distributed systems has further complicated the issue:

- Global network environment
- Continually changing
- Heterogeneous
- Interdependent
- Multiple avenues of approach and entry

With the size of networks and the number of access points within them, the data gathered can be staggering. This is further complicated by:

- Quality of Data
  - Volatile
  - Incomplete
- Volume of traffic
- Spatial distribution
- More sophisticated attacks
- Complexity of the networks
- Aggregation and correlation
- Encryption
  - Protection of reported network event data
  - Identifying attacks on an encrypted network
  - Attacks concealed within encrypted data
- Switched Networks
  - Decreased network event visibility
  - Complexity of a network IDS increases
  - Packet loss for a network IDS increases with bandwidth

Containment Phase Containment is the process of limiting the scope and damage of an incident. It is important to contain the incident as quickly as possible and to quietly take control of the incident area. Remember that data may change or be lost if not immediately captured. The systems and/or scene must be kept in pristine condition. *Do not alter the scene or the system* if you plan to gather any evidence. It is important that an image copy of the systems be made before there are any alterations. This will be covered in detail in the section on forensics.

Remember — there is only one chance to gather evidence. If it is not done correctly and completely the first time, there is no remedy. Identify and avoid code that may have been altered or compromised. Change passwords to prevent a recurrence.

Computer Incident Response Issues If the security practitioner must deal with a crime scene, do not touch anything until pictures and video have been taken. Ensure that the pictures include such things as the original position of evidence and the connections, cabling, etc. of the system. The scene should also be sketched and measured. When the scene has been captured intact, each connection should be labeled so the scene can be reconstructed later (sometimes years later). Each action should be precisely logged and described in detail.

Considerations for intrusion incidents:

- The perpetrator may be looking for signs of detection, so do not use obvious methods to find or contact him or her (ping, nslookup, finger, telnet, etc.).
- If you intend to monitor the intruder the next time he enters the system, and you have permission to do this, do not change your system profile.
- Be suspicious of potentially compromised systems. Do not log onto root or administrator accounts and try to run commands.
- Evaluate potentially compromised code.
- Preserve and evaluate all relevant systems logs.

Considerations if the threat may be internal:

- Isolate subnet at router level.
- Review logs and signatures from other connected subnets and systems.

Notification Phase The reporting system needs to be outlined in policy and maintained throughout an incident. A break in communications may flaw the response.

Ensure that appropriate individuals are notified and kept informed of events:

- IRT members
- Management
- Other effected sites
- Connecting networks
- IR Organizations
- Law enforcement

Depending upon the organization, there may be other appropriate individuals or groups to notify. It is always important to ensure that shared information falls within the parameters of written policy.

Investigation Phase Investigations are not straightforward. There are any number of legal issues and implications. First ensure that you are acting with the permission and within the bounds of a legal corporate policy. Act within the advice of corporate legal counsel and understand the rules of evidence:

- Hearsay
- Best evidence
- Probative value
- Exclusionary rules

COMPUTER EVIDENCE ISSUES   Electronic records may be considered hearsay, not direct evidence. This is because the records show only the state of the computer at the time the record was captured, not necessarily at the time of the incident.

Hearsay is defined as:

> A rule of evidence which makes out of court statements used to prove the truth of the matter stated inadmissible. Hearsay evidence comes not from the personal knowledge of the witness, but from the repetition of what he has heard others say. (http://www.thelawyerpages.com/legalterms/H)

Best evidence is defined as:

> Primary as opposed to secondary evidence, e.g., a written contract is the 'best evidence' of an agreement. (http://www.thelawyerpages.com/legalterms/B)

Probative value is defined as:

> Evidence that is sufficiently useful to prove something important in a trial. However, probative value of proposed evidence must be weighed by the trial judge against prejudicing in the minds of jurors toward the opposing party or criminal defendant. A typical dispute arises when the prosecutor wishes to introduce the previous conduct of a defendant (particularly a criminal conviction) to show a tendency toward committing the crime charged, balanced against the right of the accused to be tried on the facts in the particular case and not prejudice him or her in the minds of the jury based on prior actions. (http://dictionary.law.com/definition2.asp?selected=1623&bold=%7C%7C%7C%7C)

In order for the records to be accepted as evidence, they must be:

- Produced in the normal course of business
- Relevant
  - Provide proof that a crime occurred
  - Proof of means, opportunity or motive (MOM)
  - Demonstrate a sequence of events
  - Identify timing of events
  - Identification of methods used for committing a crime

Also:

- Author(s) or custodian of electronic records must be identified.
- Author(s) or custodian must authenticate the records.
- Author must testify as to the accuracy and use of records.
- Describe:
  — Normal business use of the records.
  — Why the records were created?
  — Any precautions or error checking done that would ensure or affect the integrity of the data.

Exclusionary rules:

- Evidence can be excluded from consideration if:
  — It was obtained illegally.
  — If it is tainted, corrupted or otherwise changed from its original state.
  — If the chain of custody is not intact.

Steps of the investigations include:

- Evidence collection
- Ensure that you have preserved and secured all relevant records
- Follow the appropriate procedures for the type of incident. For example, investigation of a network intrusion will be different from that of an actual crime scene where a computer is seized.
- The constants
  — Preserve the initial scene.
  — Gather all relevant evidence.
  — Establish a chain of custody.
  — Follow the written investigation procedures as closely as possible, checklists are a good idea.
  — Determine when to terminate the investigation.

Investigative Issues At this phase of the IR process, it must be assumed that the easily identifiable physical and/or electronic evidence has already been gathered, as that should be done first. The investigation phase deals with bringing all that evidence together, finding out evidence that was not initially obvious and determining the relationships, if any, between them. A vital element is being able to recognize what constitutes the evidence. It is often better to gather more material than less. You can always return material that is not evidence to the case but once you leave the scene, evidence you leave there and are forced to return to retrieve is much more difficult to defend. It is also important to have an open mind when looking at the scene. Evidence and information may not be evident early in the investigation.

There are a number of ways to discover evidence:

- Search and seizure

- Network monitoring
- Reviewing system logs
- Interviewing

RECOGNITION OF EVIDENCE It is important to understand what is and can be evidence. This list will provide you with just a few examples; it is by no means all-inclusive.

- Hardware
  - Peripherals — anything with memory
    - External drives
    - PDAs
    - Digital cameras
    - Scanners
  - In the case of a RAID system:
    - Hardware
    - Must get the RAID controller
- Software
  - Utilities
  - Applications
- Media
- Floppy diskettes
  - CD, DVD
  - FireWire drives
  - USB Thumb drives
  - Keychain drives
- Documents
  - Documentation
  - User
  - Hardware
  - Software
  - Media
- Log files
- User created information on or near the computer area
- Contact address and telephone lists
  - Notes
  - Passwords
  - Phone numbers
  - Relevant documents (even in trash bin or shred bin)

SEARCH AND SEIZURE If the IRT must perform a computer search and seizure:

- Ensure that you are acting within the parameters of legal organizational policy.
- Ensure that you work within the guidelines of corporate legal counsel.
- Have specific roles and responsibilities for each member of the team.

- Follow accepted guidelines, such as the DOJ Search and Seizure Guidelines.
- Follow accepted forensic procedures, such as those from (International Association of Computer Investigative Specialists (IASCIS) and outlined in the forensic section of this section.
- Document, document, document.

NETWORK MONITORING Reasons for network monitoring include:

- Verification of suspicions concerning an incident
- Determination of the scope of an incident
- Identification of involved individuals
- Determination of the skill level of the attacker
- Gaining additional information and evidence

Ensure that your goals are clear when you start, as that will determine which procedures to use:

- Monitoring traffic to or from a specific machine/network
- Looking for attack signatures
- Verifying an internal/external attempt to misuse the system

Monitoring may allow the collecting of evidence that resides on the victim's network but not necessarily on a specific machine on that network. When a network is set up with appropriate logging and monitoring, most traffic leaves some sort of trail. Places to look for it include:

- Routers
- Firewalls
- Servers
- Intrusion Detection Systems (IDS)

It should be noted that you should always have this network monitoring in place. If you try to install it after the first signs of an incident, you might have missed most of the valuable information. When choosing tools for network monitoring, consider the following:

- Active operating system
- Data file format (most tools have proprietary logging formats)
- Skills and/or training required to use the tool
- Network traffic volume
- Remote administration capability
- Selected protocol
- Resources required
  — Cost
  — Time
- Location of the monitor
- Type of monitor and or adaptor
  — Silent

Some examples of the many excellent tools that may be helpful for monitoring network and Web traffic include, but are not limited to:

- Tcpdump
- Etherreal
- Snort
- Airsnort
- Sun Solaris Snoop
- Iptrace
- NetTL
- Sniffer Pro
- Etherpeek
- Air Peek
- Netcat
- LinkFerret
- Netnanny
- Cybersitter
- URLSnarf
- Webspy

The main steps to network monitoring after an intrusion include:

- Identify the relevant traffic.
- Capture the relevant traffic (some might defend capturing all of the traffic since further investigation reveals more of what might have been relevant).
- Reconstruct the incident using all possible facts.
- Perform trace back to suspected source (be careful how you go about tracing back to the original source. Do not "hack back" since that would ruin any chances of prosecuting the original offender. Work with the appropriate CERT and law enforcement communities.)
- Analyze the source.
- Determine the reasons the target was chosen.
- Identify any intermediaries.
- Hypothesize the way the attack occurred.
- Interpret what happened.

CONSIDERATIONS   Before deployment, gaining additional information may be helpful:

- Type of computer system
- What hardware, software, cabling, packaging, etc., will be needed
- Determine what computer equipment to expect
- Determine what assistance, if any, may be required

Reviewing System Logs

Ensure that all systems logs from the time of the incident have been thoroughly reviewed to find any relevant information. What to look for will change depending upon the type of incident. It may be vital to contact the ISP and have them keep the logs for the time of the incident. Note: Remember that for your legal protection, all actions must be in accordance with your organization's policies, and taken only with permission of management.

Examine syslog, firewall, router, and security files for unusual activity. (It is helpful if you log to append-only media, and ensure that system files are not world-writable).

If you have received no warnings of indicators from users, but are looking for signs of a UNIX system compromise, you may consider looking for:

- Connections from unusual locations
- setuid and setgid files
  - The UNIX find program will search the whole system
  - find / -user root -perm -4000 -print
  - find / -group kmem -perm -2000 -print
- To avoid searching everything, you can use the-xdev" option:
- find / -user root -perm -4000 -print -xdev
- Or use the ncheck on each disk partition /dev/rsd0g:
- ncheck –s/dev/rsd0g
- Check system binaries against known good copies:
  - /etc/inetd.conf
  - login
  - su
  - find
  - netstat
  - libc
  - sync
  - ifconfig
  - ls
  - du
  - df
- Nonmatching hashes or checksums to check for Trojan Horse programs
- Sniffer use
- Backdoors in files run or referenced by:
  - cron
  - at
- Unauthorized services
- /etc/inetd.conf (also check this one for Trojans)
- Unauthorized shell entries /bin/sh or /bin/csh
- Unused legitimate services that should be turned off
- Changes to the /etc/passwd file
- Unauthorized new accounts
- Accounts with no passwords

- UID changes to existing accounts
- System and network configuration files
  — +
- non-local host names
  — /etc/hosts.equiv
  — /etc/hosts.lpd
  — .rhosts
  — root
  — uucp
  — ftp
- Files that:
  — Start with periods or spaces
  — Are hidden
  — Look unusual

If one host has been compromised, there is a good chance that others have been compromised as well.

Interviewing Interviewing is an excellent way to elicit additional information and determine the fact pattern. Interviewing should take place as soon after the event as possible in order to capture accurate recollections. Interviewing tips include:

- Develop all questions (or as many as possible) in advance.
- Ensure that questions cover all relevant points.
- Add open ended questions.
- Never conduct interviews alone.
- Always record interview with video and audiotape, and receive permission from the interviewee to do so.

It is a good idea to prioritize your interview (i.e., speak with the key witnesses first and the actual suspects last). In this way you may be able to elicit information that will allow you to communicate more effectively with the suspect.

Always consider:

- Means — how it was done
- Opportunity — the access that allowed it to happen
- Motive — why it was done

Terminating the Investigation At some point the investigation must be terminated, regardless of the outcome. If there has been no resolution, the decision to terminate the investigation will belong to senior management. The security practitioner is responsible for providing senior management with a full and accurate accounting of the state of the investigation at that time, and for making recommendations concerning whether it should be terminated or referred to another agency or organization such as law enforcement.

The considerations that help determine this end point are:

- Impact on normal operations
- Inability to resolve the issue
- Resources
- Cost
- Time
- Personnel
- Political considerations
- Transfer of authority (i.e., case goes to law enforcement)

Recovery Phase The recovery phase of the incident response process is concerned with returning the business operations to the normal state.

- Secure the system
  — The systems should have been secured during the containment phase of the process.
- Determine the cause(s)
  — To recover the system, the security practitioner must determine what caused the problem(s) so that it can be fixed.
  — If the discrete cause cannot be isolated, determine the ones that are most likely and rank them in order of probability.
- Determine the exploited vulnerability.
- Perform a vulnerability analysis on the systems and the network to search for vulnerabilities related to the one that was exploited.
- Remove cause of incident.
- Examples include:
  — Identification of malware
  — Quarantine
  — Eradication
- Removal of protocol analyzers.
- Elimination of backdoors and unauthorized accounts.
- Closing of ports.
- Change of default values on network devices.
- Change in access controls.
- In the case of a root level compromise, the security practitioner may also consider:
  — Sanitizing the media (overwrite)
  — Reinstalling operating system and applications
- Restore clean backup.
- It is important that the backup used be tested to ensure that it works.
- Ensure the backup is clean of compromised code.
- Validate the system.
- Test the system according to the established test plans.

- Monitor the system and ensure it is working properly. It may take a while for remaining problems to be detected.
- Securely change passwords across the network.

Response Phase With the recovery of the system completed, it is vital that an active response phase be implemented. At this point in the investigation, when vulnerabilities have been identified and there is no question about the priorities, it is an excellent time to improve countermeasures, add layers of defense and implement compensating controls.

Tasks for this phase include:

- Continue monitoring for the system looking for indicators of other problems.
- Determine if there is other work that should be done at this time.
- Decide the best time to bring the system back up.

You must continue monitoring the systems until you are sure there are no residual effects from the incident and you should also improve your defenses because malicious intruders may share information about your system.

You may consider new or different:

- Controls
- Technologies
- Implementations
- Security architectures
- Network architectures

Before the system goes live consider what work must be done:

- Patches
- Upgrades
- Installation of countermeasures
- Testing
- New network topology to ensure better use of security, monitoring, and countermeasures.

Follow-Up Phase Ensure follow-up with all organizations or individuals that have been contacted or involved in the process. The IRT should meet and be debriefed by management and legal concerning the incident. At this point there should be a concerted effort to ensure that all records are complete, accurate, and securely preserved. If this incident or anything related to it goes to court, these records may be needed later. The last action of this phase is to develop a follow-up report detailing what has been done.

RECORD KEEPING There are many elements that should be captured for complete documentation:

- System name
- IP addresses of hosts

- Times
- Dates
- Observations
- Indicators
- Names of respondents
- Logs of actions taken during incident
- System logs
- Evidence logs
- Input from corporate legal
- Applicable corporate policies
- IRT procedures
- Authority and mission statement
- All of these should be:
- Signed by appropriate individuals
- Dated
- Securely stored

LESSONS LEARNED The lessons learned may have as much value to the organization as the containment and eradication of the incident, but the effects may be more lasting. Lessons learned will provide experience and wisdom that will identify:

- Prime vulnerabilities
- Most effective procedures
- Most effective countermeasures
- New testing procedures for vulnerabilities
- Ways to prevent recurrence of the same type of incident
- New solutions
- Ways to improve your incident handling policy and procedures

However, they are only helpful if the lessons are integrated into the existing procedures, policies and security.

All lessons learned must be documented. Details that should be included are:

- Indicators
- Effective countermeasures
- Prevention

The lessons learned must be incorporated into the institutional knowledge, and the appropriate modifications implemented and tested. Updated documentation should be identified and available.

FINAL REPORT The last step of the follow-up final report is the creation and presentation of the final report to senior management. The report should include:

- Executive summary

- Conclusions
- Ranked alternative explanations
- Lessons learned
- Recommendations as to how lessons learned should be, or have been, incorporated into the organizational procedures
- Recommendation for prosecution

This should also have a series of appendices that include:

- List of all IR processes followed
- List of all investigative processes followed
- Copies of all documentation
- Copies of all interviews
- List of evidence
- Explanation of disposition of evidence
- IRT members and responsibilities
- Involvement of other agencies and points of contact

Computer Incident Response Issues

In today's high tech world we hear almost daily reports of computer crime occurring somewhere in the world. Moreover, since the headlines include the word *computer* most observers assume that the crime being committed is something new. In reality, the vast majority of computer crimes are simply the same schemes that have been perpetrated for hundreds (or even thousands) of years. The new aspect in computer crime is the instrument, victim or witness — a computer or other electronic device. Just as the difference between robbery and armed robbery is the instrument (a gun, knife, or other weapon), the difference between crime and computer crime is also the instrument (a computer). An additional complication in computer crime is that unlike traditional crimes where tools, victims and witnesses all have different roles, in computer crime the computer may be the instrument of the crime, victim of the crime, witness to the crime, or play a combination of roles. The point here is that very little of the actual investigative process differs between crime and computer crime. The computer crime investigator is different in that he must not only have training in the investigative process for the crime (murder, fraud, espionage, etc.), he must also be formally schooled in the capability and function of computers.

Electronic Forensics The word "forensic" comes from the Latin word for public. It means something that is characteristic of or suitable for a court, public debate or formal argument. In other words, it is the making public of facts related to an incident in such a way that they are acceptable in court. Many people associate the term forensics with the pathological forensics made popular by television. In this context, it applies to the post-mortem gathering of evidence to explain a crime, both at the crime scene and during the formal autopsy.

Electronic forensics is also a post-mortem gathering of evidence to reveal and explain the facts relating to either a computer crime or an incident that is associated with, or recorded on, some form of electronic media or information system.

There are two main branches of electronic forensics:

- Media analysis
- Intrusion

Electronic forensics should always be performed by a trained individual, for there is only one chance to gather evidence correctly. Due to the range of responsibilities for keeping the networks up and for the initial response to incidents, system or network administrators may be called upon to perform some forensic tasks. Therefore, it is vital that the procedures are thoroughly understood and that they are performed properly. Training is very helpful for all levels of Administrators, and certifications on the use of forensic products are also helpful if the case does go to court.

In the same way that an autopsy is not to be performed upon a living individual, forensic investigation happens after the initial incident. Even in the case of intrusions where there may be real time monitoring of an intruder, this happens after the initial incident — after the intruder has first entered the system. Everything done prior to the incident/investigation is properly categorized as security.

Security and Recovery versus Electronic Forensics   Procedures such as network and process logging, implementation of firewalls and intrusion detection, network and workstation imaging, and even data recovery are not considered forensics. These are normal security, business continuity and recovery actions. However, when procedures such as imaging, data recovery and log analysis are used *in response to an incident* they become forensic processes and must be conducted by trained electronic forensics personnel.

Media Analysis Procedures   Since electronic forensics is still an emerging field, there are many approaches and few standards or guidelines to be found. Because procedures must be competent, consistent and structured to be proven effective in court, it is important that there be some industry-accepted framework for analysis procedures. To achieve these characteristics and provide a truly useful set of procedures, this section will follow those established by the International Association of Computer Investigative Specialists (IACIS). These procedures were established to ensure that IACIS members would always perform competent and professional forensic examinations, and are among the most respected and accepted standards in the field.

Although each investigation and each analysis will have its own characteristics, it is acknowledged that almost all forensic examinations of electronic media are different and that every examination cannot be conducted
in the exact same manner. However, there are three essential requirements
of a competent forensic examination.

- Forensically sterile examination media must be used.
- The examination must maintain the integrity of the original media.
- Printouts, copies of data and exhibits resulting from the examination
  must be properly marked, controlled and transmitted.

Media Analysis   The seventeen steps that will be explained in this section
are those recommended by IACIS for conducting a complete examination
of a hard disk drive. While there are other approved methods, this one will
give you a firm baseline and general understanding of what is required during an investigation.

Hard Disk Examination: Step 1 — Sterile Media   When beginning an
examination, it is imperative that the media used by the examiner to make
an image of the suspected hard drive is forensically sterile. This means that
the media has been overwritten so that there is no retrievable data remaining. This can be done using a forensically sound and tested utility that overwrites the entire accessible area of the hard drive. Common system utilities
such as FDISK and Format are not acceptable, as they do not overwrite ambient data. The drive should be written with a character that is easily dis-
tinguishable from the data that will be restored to it. When there are many
examiners working in the same environment, it is often helpful to have each
examiner use a different character so that it is immediately evident who was
working with the media.

This overwriting prevents the allegation that the recovered information
was actually something that was on the image media (an artifact) as opposed to evidence recovered from the suspect drive.

Although a forensically overwritten hard drive should not contain any
data other than the data string used for the overwriting process, it is recommended that a virus scan be performed. Performing the scan will do two
things: first, it will prevent any viruses that might be on the examination
media from infecting the suspect drive. Second, should there actually be
malicious code on the suspect drive, it will prevent the allegations or legal
arguments that the malicious code on that drive came from the examination
media or was present prior to the restoration of the seized data to the target
media. Then verify that the media has been both overwritten and scanned
for viruses. Ensure that you then mark the media to prevent confusion.

Hard Disk Examination: Step 2 — Legal Software   In this section the
term "examiner" will be used to refer to whomever is tasked with the media
examination. This may be a first responder, network or system administra-

tor, or an individual responsible for conducting forensic procedures within the organization, law enforcement, or a trained individual from an outside organization.

It is imperative that the software used in the examination be licensed to, authorized for use by, or belong to the examiner or to the company for which the examiner works. This is also applicable to the imaging software used by the first responder or network/system administrator for the initial copy.

The evidence gathered from this examination may go to court. When testifying in court, the professional credibility of the examiner and other responsible individuals is as important as the actual procedures used for the examination. One of the ways to support that credibility is to use licensed and legal software. It is difficult to convince a judge or jury to convict an individual for what is often seen as a "technical" violation of law when the examiner giving evidence is also in violation of the law by using unlicensed or unauthorized software.

Hard Disk Examination: Step 3 — Physical Examination of the Evidence   The original computer is physically examined. A specific description of the hardware is made and noted. Comments are made indicating anything unusual found during the physical examination of the computer. It is important to specifically note all removable media devices such as CD and DVD readers or writers, Zip or JAZ drives, etc. Unusual configurations such as multiple CD or DVD writers should also be noted. During the examination, the examiner should always inspect removable media devices for the presence of removable media. In many cases, a drive contains removable media of investigative value that may not have been noticed by the person seizing the equipment.

The sterilized media that belongs to the examiner is used as a place to copy an image of the suspect drive. This may be referred to as the examination, analysis, target or image drive.

In this section, the seized hard drive will be referred to as the evidence drive or the suspect drive.

It is not always evident which incidents will go to court, or what evidence may be relevant or important at a later date. The first responders to an incident are therefore responsible for ensuring that all evidentiary items are handled correctly and that all actions taken are logged.

This step is important for the chain of custody and records the condition of each evidentiary item. The condition of the hardware may provide clues to the examiner. These could include things such as pry marks on the case or obvious damage.

When evidence is seized it is logged and may be returned to the owner when the case has been settled. It is important that the examiner be able to demonstrate that the equipment is in the same condition upon return as when it was seized. It is possible for an examiner or organization to be held liable for any damage to the seized equipment.

Hard Disk Examination: Step 4 — Avoid Altering the Evidence   A key aspect of any electronic forensic investigation is the ability to show that the original evidence was not altered during the forensic process. One standard precaution is the use of write-blocking devices during any procedure involving access to the original evidence or a forensic (exact) copy of the original evidence. This is very important; as it ensures that the examiner does not accidentally overwrite any of the evidence on the suspect drive or contaminate the evidence with artifacts. This mistake is difficult or impossible to recover from, depending upon the information on the drive. These devices fall into two basic categories: software write-blockers (also known as a write blocker utility) and hardware write-blockers.

Common software write-blockers include PD Block from Digital Intelligence (http://www.digitalintel.com) and mounting the media in read-only mode using the Linux operating system.

Hardware write-blockers are actual physical devices that are connected between the media and the imaging/examining computer to physically prevent writes to the drive being examined. Two very useful such devices are FireBlock and SCSIBlock, also from Digital Intelligence. FastBloc from Guidance Software (http://www.guidancesoftware.com) is another well-tested physical write-blocker.

Hard Disk Examination: Step 5 — Capture CMOS (RTC/NVRAM) and Date/Time Information   The original IBM AT systems used a real-time clock (RTC) and CMOS RAM chip. The clock used 10 bytes of RAM. The additional 54 bytes were used to store the system configuration. Today these functions are incorporated into the South Bridge of the motherboard chipset or Super I/O chip or use a special battery and nonvolatile RAM (NVRAM) chip. However, we frequently still refer to the information contained in these areas as CMOS data although CMOS is actually a technology and not a storage area.

The time and date of the internal clock is frequently very important in establishing file modified, accessed, and created (MAC) times.

The correctness or the variation between the internal clock and the external time is important as it may change the relevance of the evidence. If a case rests upon a very accurate chain of events tied to a specific time, the entire foundation of the case may change due to variations in the internal clock.

Other information that my be contained in these areas are boot sequence, hard disk type, floppy disk type, advanced Basic Input/Output System (BIOS) setup options, and power-on password (normally encrypted).

Hard Disk Examination: Step 6 — Create an Exact Image In an electronic forensic examination, the original media is not normally used for the examination; a bitstream copy or other image of the original media is made and used for the actual examination. A bitstream copy is an actual bit-by-bit physical image of a hard drive or item of removable media. This is important because it will replicate each sector or block of the data to include information from deleted files and slack space. This is different from a logical image, which will show only the active files on the system, excluding those that have been deleted (unless they are currently in the "Recycle Bin," which is an active file).

Forensic bitstream images must be made using approved and tested forensic imaging software such as SafeBack or Copy QM from New Technologies Incorporated (http://www.forensics-intl.com), EnCase from Guidance Software or Linux dd with the proper command-line switches.

The ideal for analysis is to make two bitstream copies of the suspect media. The integrity and accuracy of the images should be verified by running a hash or CRC against them. The original evidence drive is preserved and not touched again. One of the images will be used as a working copy, and the other will be preserved as a library copy.

In this way, the examiner can work with an image without fear of tainting it. For example, when files are "undeleted" there are changes to the system. An examiner can undelete the files, make careful notes of the findings, and then go back to the library copy to get a clean image. The integrity of this clean image will of course be verified by a CRC or hash value.

There are several ways to make the images; both hardware and software solutions are available. The important thing is to ensure that the application you choose actually makes a physical bit-level copy that can be verified against the original suspect media, and the appropriate forensic tools can readily examine the image.

Bitstream copies are sometimes also referred to as 'evidence grade' backups and they differ substantially from traditional computer file backups and network server backups.

Hard Disk Examination: Step 7 — Logically Examine the Image The copy or image of the original HDD is logically examined and a description of what was found is noted. Remember that a logical examination only deals with the files that are currently active on the system. However, depending upon the situation, this may be all that is needed to find the relevant facts.

Using a negative hashing procedure to eliminate factory standard files that have not been modified by the user can significantly reduce the number of logical files an examiner must review. This technique compares the standards hashs from a factory installation to those of the hard drive being investigated. If the hashs match, then it is highly improbable that the file has been modified and the investigator can eliminate having to thoroughly examine that file. The result is a reduced work load and allows for a more effective use of the examiners time on the files that truly need to be examined.

A logical examination of the image entails going through the active files captured from the suspect drive, including the system files, and in the case of a Windows OS, the Registry.

The logical exam may provide clues beyond the actual facts of the case. The desktop layout, themes, graphics, etc., may help an experienced examiner determine where to look, or reveal the technical sophistication of the user.

Hard Disk Examination: Step 8 — Examine the Boot Record Data and User-Defined Files The boot record data and user-defined system configuration and operation command files (such as, the CONFIG.SYS file and the AUTOEXEC.BAT files in a Microsoft system) are examined and findings are noted. Examining the boot record will disclose such information as the operating system being used, the number of logical volumes on a drive, and whether there are any drive management programs or "overlays" in use. Useful utilities for examining the boot record are Norton Disk Editor from Symantec and Partinfo from Powerquest.

The sophistication of the user may be partially determined by any changes to the user- defined systems files. These changes may be as simple as changing the file extension, or marking sectors holding information "bad" (FAT systems), to changing system calls and "trusted" binaries.

The examiner should have tools appropriate to the file system used by the organization, or those that may be encountered in the case of an incident. There are a great many tool choices available.

Common partition types:

- FAT 12, partition smaller than 32 MB and ends below 8 GB: Type "01"
- FAT 16, partition smaller than 504 MB and ends below 8 GB: Type "04"
- FAT 16, partition smaller than 2 MB and ends below 8 GB: Type "06
- FAT 16, partition smaller than 2 GB and ends below 8 GB: Type "0E"
- FAT 32, ends below 8 GB: Type "0B"
- FAT 32, ends above 8 GB: Type "0C"
- NTFS, begins below cylinder 1024: Type "07"
- ext2fs, begins below cylinder 1024: Type "83"
- Linux Swap Partition: Type "82"
- Partition larger than 8 GB or above 8 GB: Type "0F"

- Netware 286: Type "64"
- Netware 3.11: Type "65"

Hard Disk Examination: Step 9 — Recover and Examine All Deleted Files All recoverable deleted files are restored. When the examiner recovers a file on a Windows-based system, he should change the first character of the restored file from a lower case sigma (HEX E5) to a consistent character of his choice to aid in identifying files that have been "undeleted." Files should be undeleted to sterile media and not undeleted "in-place" on the drive being examined, as such an action would overwrite unallocated space and has the potential to destroy evidence.

The examiner should never try to guess the first letter of a recovered file for the purpose of restoring the file, as such actions could have legal ramifications. In systems that support long file names, the full original name may be recovered in a forensically sound manner and used as evidence in a court of law.

Recovery of deleted information on a corporate server, especially one using UNIX or UNIX-based systems such as Linux, is problematic due to the rapidity with which space on the server may be overwritten.

Remember that when a file is deleted, the actual information that was in the file does not go away. The pointer that allows the system to find a file is removed from the system files or from the File Allocation Table.

In the case of a system using a Recycle Bin, the actual file is called the INFO2 file. When the Bin is emptied, the file is reduced to a small size and the system information or "pointers" (that allow users to "undelete" their files) have been removed. The information that resided within the deleted files may then be recoverable using a tool that will search unallocated space.

Hard Disk Examination: Step 10 — Create a Listing of All Files A listing of all the files contained on the examined media, whether they contain potential evidence or not, is normally made at this time. There are many utilities that will perform this function for the examiner. However, the results should always be verified, either by the examiner or by another tool.

This step is done more to show that a comprehensive examination was performed than to simply show how many files were on the computer. It is possible that the file listing may provide clues when considered in context.

Hard Disk Examination: Step 11 — Examine Unallocated Space for Lost or Hidden Data Depending upon the operating system, unallocated space may contain fragments of deleted files that were not detected by recovery tools, system swap files, artifacts of system operation and information that no longer has a logical structure due to the elimination of a file allocation table or drive partition. Examination of this information is vital in constructing a complete forensic review of the media.

Swap space, the operating system's "scratch pad," may contain any amount of useful information, including e-mail addresses, Internet information, file fragments, and other forensically useful information.

In some cases, a carve tool may be needed to examine unallocated space. A carve tool functions by examining the unallocated space and looking for file signatures known as file headers. Once a header is located, the carve tool extracts a set portion of data surrounding the header for the examiner to evaluate.

When files are erased or deleted in DOS, Windows, Windows 95, Windows 98, Windows NT, Windows 2000, Windows XP, and Windows 2003, the content of the file is not actually erased; only the file system pointer is deleted. The actual data from the "erased file" remains behind. Since the space where the data was stored is no longer marked by a pointer, the system considers the space to be available for allocation to other files. It is therefore known as unallocated space.

Unallocated file space is an important source of leads and information for the computer forensics investigator. It may contain intact files, remnants of files and subdirectories as well as the many temporary files, which are constantly created and deleted by computer applications and the operating system without user intervention.

Hard Disk Examination: Step 12 — Examine File Slack   The Windows operating system allocates secondary storage in units known as clusters. A cluster is a collection of smaller units called sectors. When the data being written to secondary storage does not fill the entire cluster, space known as slack is created. There are two types of slack: drive or disk slack and RAM slack.

Disk or drive slack is simply the information already present on the disk (unallocated space) that resides between the last sector occupied by the file (and RAM slack) and the end of the newly allocated cluster.

Files in DOS and Windows systems are stored in fixed-size sectors that are allocated by the system in groups called clusters. It is very rare that a file size exactly matches the size of one or more clusters.

The data storage space between the end of the file and the end of the last cluster assigned to the file is called "file slack." Systems with large cluster sizes contain larger amounts of file slack than those with smaller clusters. When the file is not long enough to fill this slack space, it contains information that was previously on the storage device, such as information from deleted files. This is called drive slack.

The system uses different padding to fill the space between the end of the files and the end of the 512-byte sector. This is another type of slack that is referred to as RAM slack. It contains dynamic information from the RAM buffers. RAM slack fills the space from the end of the file being written to the end of the last sector used by that file. The data used to fill RAM slack is normally (at least in older operating systems) taken from the system's RAM (information resident in dynamic memory).

RAM slack potentially contains whatever information has been stored in RAM since that computer session began, including files that have been created, viewed, modified, downloaded or copied as well as login IDs or passwords. For example, the file is FILE and is stored in a two-sector cluster. The RAM slack between the end of the files and the end of the sector is denoted by X, while the Drive Slack that fills the remaining area to the end of the cluster or allocation unit is denoted by 0. The EOF marker is the end of file designation used by the FAT file system.

FILEFILEFILEFILEXXXXXXXX00000000000000000000000000000000EOF

Hard Disk Examination: Step 13 — Examine All User Created Files Examination of all user-created or modified files may be done manually using a file reader such as Quick View Plus by Jasc Software (http://www.jasc.com/products/qvp), the application used to create the file, or a disk editor. Text searching programs (also called string searching programs) may also be used to search text within user-created or modified files. Graphics files may be quickly reviewed using a graphics-viewing program such as Thumbs Plus by Cerious Software (http://www.thumbsplus.com).

It is important to note that this step may take a while. While viewing user files make sure that you keep detailed notes about the files you viewed.

Hard Disk Examination: Step 14 — Unlock and Examine Password-Protected Files Examining files that are password-protected can involve significant resources and take a considerable amount of time. One source of password-cracking software is Access Data (http://www.accessdata.com). Manual password attacks can also be used on files produced by some applications such as Microsoft Money 2.0 or Quicken 3.0.

Hard Disk Examination: Step 15 — Create Printouts of All of the Apparent Evidence In today's world of 200GB hard drives, this step is a bit outdated. A better solution is for an examiner to copy items of evidence to removable media such as a CD or DVD and hot-link the information to relevant portions of the media analysis report. New drives contain such capacity that it would be like trying to print out the contents of a library.

Hard Disk Examination: Step 16 — Examine Executable Files and Run Applications Executable programs of specific interest should be examined. User data files that could not be accessed by other means are examined at this time using the native application. This is also the step where the examiner may choose to boot the examination copy of the hard drive (assuming it is a bootable drive with an operating system) and observe the boot process and application functions in an operational environment.

Since running applications causes information to be written to the hard drive, this step will destroy the forensic integrity of the media. Once an examiner has performed this step, a fresh forensic image must be created if it becomes necessary to return to any previous step of the examination process.

Hard Disk Examination: Step 17 — Write the Forensic Analysis Report   The examiner must produce a report that gives a full accounting of the procedures followed and investigative findings. A full copy of the examiner's notes taken during the examination process should accompany the examination report. The report must be quite detailed, as it may be used in court at a much later time. If this is the case, the examiner must be able to accurately remember each step and process in the case from the report.

There are may formats for organizing this report. Most media analysis labs or law enforcement agencies have specific report templates. There are also examples of the report and other documentation available on the Internet. A CD or DVD that contains a soft copy of the report with links to specific findings may accompany the report.

Floppy Diskette Examinations   Floppy disks or similar media may also require examination as part of an investigation. The procedures are similar to the previous 17 steps, so they will not be discussed in the same detail here. Floppies use the FAT 12 file system.

One of the issues in examining floppy disks is they're soft-sectored, which means that by using special utilities they can be formatted in such a way as to appear blank or hide data. A normal 3.5-inch HD floppy disk has 80 data tracks and 2880 sectors of 512 bytes each (1.44MB). However, using special software, the disk can be reformatted to an odd formant (such as 40 data tracks), which will make the disk appear blank and unformatted while it actually contains 720 KB of data. Additional "invisible" data tracks may also be added using special software.

There are specific forensic utilities available for floppy disk analysis, such as Anadisk from New Technologies Incorporated, which will allow the examiner to identify and access customer formats and hidden data on floppy disks.

Floppy Disk Examinations

IACIS® Procedures

1. Forensically sterile conditions are established. All media utilized during the examination process is freshly prepared, completely wiped of nonessential data, scanned for viruses and verified before use.
2. All forensic software utilized is licensed to, or authorized for use by, the examiner or agency/company.

3. The media is physically examined. A specific description of the media is made and noted. The media is marked for identification.

4. Hardware/software precautions are taken during any copying process or access to the original media and examination to prevent the transference of viruses, destructive programs, or other inadvertent writes to or from the original FD or to or from the examination equipment.

5. The write–protect capability of the floppy disk drive (FDD) on the examining machine is tested.

6. A duplicate image of the original write-protected FD is made to another FD. The duplicate image is used for the actual examination. A detailed description of the process is noted.

7. The copy of the examined FD is logically examined and a description of what was found is indicated. Anything unusual is noted.

8. The boot record data, and user defined system configuration and operation command files (if present) are examined and findings are noted.

9. All recoverable deleted files are restored. When practical or possible, the first character of restored files is changed from a HEX E5 to "-", or other unique character, for identification purposes.

10. The unallocated space is examined for lost or hidden data.

11. The "slack" area of each file is examined for lost or hidden data.

12. The contents of each user data file in the root directory and each subdirectory (if present) are examined.

13. Password-protected files are unlocked and examined.

14. If the FD holds apparent evidentiary data that is to be utilized, a listing of all the files contained on the FD, whether they contain apparent evidentiary data or not, is made. The listing will indicate which files were printed, copied, or otherwise recovered.

15. A printout or copy is made of all apparent evidentiary data. The file or location where any apparent evidentiary data was obtained is noted on each printout. All exhibits are marked, sequentially numbered and properly secured and transmitted.

16. Executable programs of specific interest should be examined. User data files that could not be accessed by other means are examined at this time using the native applications.

17. Comments and findings are properly documented.

Limited Examinations

In some instances, a complete examination of all the data on media may not be authorized, possible, necessary or conducted for various reasons. In these instances, the examiner should document the reason for not conducting a complete examination. Some examples of limited examinations cited by IACIS® include, but are not limited to:

- The scope of examination is limited by the search warrant or the courts.
- The equipment *must* be examined on premises. If the examiner does not have portable equipment (a luggable forensic system), this may require examination of the original media. Extreme caution must be used during this type of examination and it is recommended that this not be done, but rather some other arrangements for equipment be made.
- The *media size* is so vast that a complete examination is not possible. This is possible in many new storage systems. Also, if the suspect system is a RAID, it is important that the examiner have the hardware AND software of the system. This is especially applicable to the specific RAID controller.
- The *weight of the evidence* already found is so overwhelming that a further search is not necessary for the presentation of the case.
- It is just *not possible* to conduct a complete examination because of hardware, operating systems or other conditions beyond the examiner's control.

This is a sample of some Incident Response Procedures for Windows. While they may differ slightly for other operating systems the basic principles will remain the same.

Incident Response Procedures (Specific to Windows NT/2000)

Introduction

Several methodologies have been developed over time for incident handling. One of the oldest methods, created by a workshop at Carnegie Mellon Software Engineering Institute in July of 1989, has a six-step methodology in handling incidents with the acronym PDCERF (preparation, detection, containment, eradication, recovery, and follow-up). The steps have taken different meanings over time, and the following procedures have modified them while maintaining the same goals of the methodology.

Preparation

Prior planning is perhaps the most important part of incident response. The preparation stage includes organizing efforts to respond to an incident before one even occurs. Incident response is closely linked to policy, procedures, and business continuity planning, with a goal minimizing impact. Preparing the "fly-away" kit is an essential part of responding to an information security incident. An arsenal of hardware and software should be packed in sturdy travel cases and be ready to be deployed at any time.

Hardware should include powerful systems that would yield for analysis and forensic duplication of evidence if needed. The kit should anticipate all types of hardware and not assume that a standard PC with an IDE hard drive will be dealt with; this is a common mistake made by incident response teams. Be prepared to deal with SCSI, IDE, PDAs, removable media devices, and obsolete technology. Drive-copying devices have become more popular as their technology advances, to ensure forensically sound duplication at a fast rate with the convenience of not using a computer to create a forensic image. Software in the kit must be trusted. Trusted software uses known binaries and applications known to be pure and free of malicious code. This will be discussed in further detail in the hands-on portion of the methodology.

Part of the preparation and fly-away kit includes the personnel that will be responding. Making sure each team member understands his or her role and is properly trained prior to the incident is crucial. Every incident has an element of urgency, and the team must have a variety of skill sets to cover the need.

Administrative items are also commonly forgotten when fly-away kits are prepared; not just paper, pens, and evidence tags are needed, but contacts lists are important. One list would include all current Internet service providers with points of contact and the ability to cease and desist malicious activity. Law enforcement and legal contacts should be readily available if an incident elevates to a higher level of severity. Among the most important items in the kit are the actual written procedures and worksheets, with copies for every team member. For an internal team, points of contact within a company should be included in the kit. A typical mistake made here is to include only phone numbers and pagers of information technology employees. A public relations contact, for example, would be needed to help with potential media exposure and negative publicity. Another list to consider would be a reference of common Trojans or back doors and their default ports. These can be found on the Internet.

Detection

The second step is detection. Incidents occur all the time without being detected, and a team can never respond if they never know an attack exists. One way an incident is detected is by an Intrusion-Detection System (IDS). Host-based and network-based IDSs are generally effective in detective attacks; however, they can be defeated. Anti-virus and anti-Trojan applications are very effective as long as the virus definitions are maintained and up-to-date. Simply installing virus software is not good enough, and even when definitions are up-to-date, new malicious code can go undetected. Thankfully, commercial anti-virus software developers are very timely in adding new virus definitions and making them available to the public immediately.

You must ensure that logging is enabled. Many nonseasoned administrators are unaware that system logging is *not* the default in Windows NT environments; the logs must be enabled before analysis can ever occur.

Another element of detection is the human element. A user may report unexplained events on his system, a system administrator may notice the presence of hacker utilities, or even an extortion e-mail may be received by a senior company official. Educating personnel on how to report an incident is critical to detection.

Strategy

Once the incident has been reported, a strategy must be formulated before deployment can occur. Gathering intelligence about the incident should be carefully documented. Several questions must be answered and can be incorporated into a worksheet made as part of the fly-away kit: What type of situation has occurred? Has malicious code been deployed or has a natural disaster caused physical damage? Did the attack result in the intruder gaining administrator privileges? The date and time of when the incident was detected needs to be documented as well as recording how it was detected. Information about the systems themselves is needed, including operating systems, IP address, any recent changes in applications, who are you supporting, and what their business interests are.

Containment

The next phase is the reaction stage, when personnel have deployed to manage and contain an incident. Often a covert response may be coordinated to minimize the knowledge that an incident has been detected. It is more likely than not that an insider is responsible for an incident. Upon arrival, the scene must be physically secured. Only those directly involved need to be present. Ask the system administrator or point of contact for any IDS logs, and firewall/router logs to correlate with later findings.

Notification

It is important that the chain of command be carefully observed during the notification process so there will be no confusion. The written policies and procedures will state who should be notified.

Investigation

Finally, the initial response has begun. Before making a single keystroke on the system, document and if possible, photograph the current display on the system monitor. Volatile data must be obtained before any decisions regarding containment or system shut down. Data needed includes: system date and time, a list of the currently running processes, all the users who are currently logged on, all of the open sockets, evidence of alternate data streams, and a list of computers currently or recently connected to the system.

A bootable floppy with known good applications should be prepared ahead of time and included in the fly-away kit. The first step in collecting the volatile data is to establish a trusted shell. This is done to safeguard against activating tripwires placed by attackers. Insert the bootable floppy into the system. Do this by clicking "start" and then "run," and type a:\cmd. exe (assuming a: is the drive letter assigned to the floppy drive you are using). Now that a trusted shell has been established, record the system date and time by typing "date /t" and "time /t" from the command line. The /t type switch displays the date and time without giving the option to make accidental changes.

The next pieces of volatile data can be gathered by using tools from various vendors and developers, and it is suggested these applications, at a minimum, are included on your bootable floppy.

To determine who is currently logged into the system, the "loggedon" utility by Sysinternals (http://www.sysinternals.com/) displays all users connected locally and remotely. Not only will this display a potential perpetrator, but you will also see who you will be disrupting if the system indeed needs to be taken down.

Additional utilities by Sysinternals include "pslist," used to list all of the running processes on the system, and "listdlls," which lists the loaded DLLs on the system. This data must be obtained prior to shutting the system down or it will be lost forever.

Next run the "netstat" command to record all open ports on the system. This is native to Windows. Common switches used are *netstat –a* to display all connections and listening ports, and *netstat –n*, which displays addresses and port numbers in numerical form. Refer to the list of common backdoors in your "fly-away" kit to determine if any unknown activity is potentially malicious.

A utility, "fport.exe," developed by Foundstone (http://www.foundstone. com), will map the processes to the open ports. This is an easy way to determine exactly which application is listening on each port.

To list recently connected systems use the netbios name cache. The nbstat –c command will list the IP addresses and names of the systems.

Once the above initial volatile information has been gathered, run the date and time command again to record when the incident response was completed. Then run the "doskey/history" command to record a history of the typed commands during the incident response, and store the information retrieved to the floppy.

At this stage, a decision should be made if a forensic duplication of the system will be obtained. When unsure, always duplicate. However, some business or mission critical systems cannot be shut down and more in-depth analysis will have to continue on the running system.

If forensic duplication is not possible, more intrusive processes will have to be utilized. The use of a forensic workstation remotely connected using netcat may be necessary to transfer needed data from the incident system. There are several utilities needed for the live system analysis and is suggested that this only be performed by seasoned incident handlers, as the process can be intrusive.

The first step in this phase of the incident response is to obtain all of the MAC times of the entire logical file system. Depending on the size of the data, a floppy diskette may not be able to store all of the collected data. Rather, the data must be transferred to other media or to a remotely connected forensic workstation. The following commands can be executed to gather the MAC times in three separate steps:

dir /t:a /a /s /o:d c: > x:

The above command provides a directory listing of all files and their respective **access** times on the hard drive where:

dir /t:a switch is for the access time
/a is for all files
/s is for all sub-directories
/o:d if for order by date
c: is the drive letter assignment for the source drive
> x: maps the output to target drive letter assigned x
dir /t:w /a /s /o:d c:

The above command provides a directory listing of all files and their respective *modified* times on the hard drive where:

dir/t:w is for the modified time

The above command provides a directory listing of all files and their respective *created* times on the hard drive where:

dir /t:c is for the modified time

Once the MAC times have been recorded, the rest of the pertinent information can be collected. Event logs, registry files, and other relevant files can now be obtained. Several tools found in the Windows NT Resource Kit (NTRK) are very useful for this process. "Dumpel" is used to dump the event logs.

dumpel –l security –t is used to dump the security log
dumpel –l application –t is used to dump the application log
dumpel –l system –t is used to dump the system log

To dump the registry as a text file use the "regdump" tool, and to determine the audit policy of the system use the "auditpol" tool, both found in the NT Resource Kit.

Another useful tool, "DumpACL," created by Somarsoft (http://www.somarsoft.com), will dump the permissions, and audit settings for the file system, registry, and printers.

With NTFS, files consist of several data streams that contain different pieces of information, such as access rights and the actual data. The very nature of the file system allows for files to be hidden within the NTFS file system. A tool, "lads.exe," developed by Frank Heyne (http://www.heysoft.de), is a utility that detects these hidden files within the alternate data streams (ADSs).

Additional logs to be gathered for correlation with the event log are the IIS logs. The default location is \WINNT\system32\LogFiles. Use the type command to obtain these files and direct the output to the forensic workstation.

J.D. Glaser of Foundstone (http://www.foundstone.com) created a tool, "ntlast," that displays successful and failed login attempts. This tool will only be useful if the system had logging enabled for logons and logoffs.

The above list should by no means be considered all-inclusive; it merely provides a few examples of what to include as part of an incident response fly-away deployment kit.

Forensic Duplication

If it is possible to shut the system down (by simply removing the power), then a bit-for-bit copy of the original media should be acquired for forensic media analysis. Simply copying the logical files will not satisfy law enforcement and proper forensic procedures. Critical data, such as deleted files and file slack would not be available if logical copy was performed. Specialized forensic software that is generally accepted by the computer forensic community should be used. SafeBack, by New Technologies Inc. (http://www.forensics-intl.com), was specifically designed for forensics purposes and makes exact copies of the evidence drive. *Linux DD* also creates an exact data dump of the media that meets the criteria for forensic use. EnCase (http://www.guidancesoftware.com) is an integrated imaging and analysis tool that also creates forensically sound duplicate images.

Steps in Acquisition

1. All target media should be wiped of all data prior to image acquisition.
2. All forensic software should be licensed or authorized for use by the examiner.
3. A physical inventory of the original system must be documented.
4. All software used must be trusted and free of malicious code.
5. The CMOS information, such as the system date and time, should be recorded.

6. Remove the drive from the original system and place in forensic workstation.
7. Boot the forensic workstation to a controlled boot disk (floppy or CD).
8. Run a software hard drive lock utility, if available.
9. Run fdisk/status to obtain the volume and partition information.
10. Run imaging application to create forensic duplication and verify the integrity.
11. Use proper chain of custody and evidence collection techniques to withstand legal critique.
12. Properly document in a detailed manner and report findings in a timely manner.

Forensic analysis can now be performed on the forensic copy of the hard drive. Findings from the system media should be correlated with the initial incident report and any available IDS, firewall, and router logs.

Recovery, Response, and Follow-up

Once the volatile data has been gathered and forensic duplications made, the system must be returned to an operational state; however, the cause of the incident itself may still be a problem that must be rectified. If an intrusion occurred, how was the system exploited to gain access? During the response phase, system controls and defenses are strengthened and countermeasures are deployed.

The follow-up phase reviews lessons learned and implements security measures. Maybe a patch needs to be installed to fix a known vulnerability, or maybe virus definitions need to be updated to detect malicious code. This is also a time when security policies and response policies should be reviewed and updated as necessary.

Video Forensics

The security practitioner may also be called upon to work with CCTV systems. This may include selection, installation, maintenance, and/or examination of the images if there has been a security incident. The video camera can provide illustrative evidence or be considered a silent witness to a crime. However, the capabilities and limitations of video systems are largely misunderstood.

Video forensics is defined as:

- Examination of images and sound captured by a video camera
- Can be recorded to video tape or digital media
- Consists of photographic comparisons made between known entities and those captured by the video camera. These entities include:

- People
- Property
- Clothing

Corporate Application of CCTV   Examples include:

- Applications and Systems development
  — Artificial Intelligence (AI)
  — Robotics
  — High tech engineering
- Security management
  — Policy
  — Employee monitoring
  — Privacy
  — Investigations
  — Surveillance
    - Lobbies
    - Retail areas
    - Cash rooms
    - Tills
    - Vandalism and theft
    - Traffic control and monitoring
  — Secure facilities
  — Historic sites
  — Public areas
- Hospitals
  - Airports
  - Safety
  - Recreation areas
  - Loading areas
  — Fire detection (IR)
- Relevance
- In case of a serious incident, the captured images should be examined by a forensic video specialist
- The results of an examination can be influenced by the deployment of the system

Deployment   In order for the system to be deployed and used effectively, the security practitioner must understand:

- CCTV functional basics
- Capabilities/limitations
- What you are trying to monitor
- What results can be reasonably expected
- Legal issues

If a system is not implemented correctly, the resulting images may prove to be valueless to the organization.

- Determine the goal of the system
  — Deterrence
  — Prosecution
  — Safety
- Use this to evaluate the implementation

Analog Tapes   When looking at tape selections you have several choices of machines and tapes on which these machines record.

- Formats (how the image is transferred to the tape)
  — Composite
  — S-Video
  — Component
- Types of videotape (how the images are stored on the tape)
  — Multiplex
  — Time lapse
- Standards (formatting of the tape in relation to playback)
  — NTSC
  — PAL

Frames versus Fields   Video is recorded in frames at the rate of approximately 30 frames per second (29.97). A frame is a complete picture drawn onto the screen. A field is one of the two half-frames in interlaced video. These fields are:

- Odd (composed of the odd numbered scan lines)
- Even (composed of he even numbered scan lines)
- Captured in about 1/60th of a second

Each field may be a different image, and some of the dominant fields may hide the images of nondominant fields. When viewed later, it may be required that the fields be separated and a new frame created for each. Most multiples systems are designed to record different images on each field. Each has 243 lines of visual information (NTSC).

Color versus Monochrome   If the environment has a small, known population, color may aid in identification of individuals; however, if the population is large and unknown, the monochrome image will more clearly provide the small details that are used for identification.

Digital CCTV   There are currently many issues associated with digital CCTV:

- It was not developed for security, but for the entertainment industry.
- Compression of over 2:1 for transmission and storage causes loss of detail to the image.

- Identification of details is what makes digital forensics useful to security.

Due to the ease of alteration, digital images are not widely accepted in court, though there are systems currently being developed to overcome these issues. Digital format eliminates the aspect ratio issues associated with transfer from an analog to a digital environment. Digital CCTV uses a Charge Coupled Device (CCD) for image capture. This device converts light intensity into numeric values (from 0 to 65,535) for each image pixel. The values are stored, and the image reconstructed using the metrics representing luminance (light) and chrominance (color values). Of course, the higher the resolution or greater the number of pixels, the more useful the digital image is in the security environment, because it will be capturing more details.

Aspect Ratio   When images are taken from an analog format and converted into digital, the aspect ratio must be preserved or the image will be distorted. Resolving this dilemma simply entails preserving the proportions of an image during the conversion from one media type to another. For example, when moving an image from analog, where the pixels are rectangles, taller than they are wide, to digital where the pixels are square, it is evident that the image will be shorter (because the pixels are shorter) but remain the same width. This causes the image to appear shorter and wider than in the analog version.

Other issues:

- Analog:
  — Tape reuse
  — Maintenance
  — Storage
  — Stretching
- Digital:
  — Resolution
  — Compression
  — Modification
  — Storage
  — Bandwidth
  — Admissibility

Results   In order to understand what can be expected from the system, realize:

- All factors combine to determine results
- An understanding of the functions, capabilities and limitations of CCTV technology will set reasonable expectations for examination results
- Limitations:
- Show on the camera view

- No hidden objects
- Detail:
- Time duration of the image
- Multiplexed/switched cameras with different views

Capabilities It helps to remember that images obtained from video evidence can be reasonably clarified, resized, highlighted, lighted, and stabilized. These actions can be done while maintaining your data integrity but allow the presentation to be more easily perceived and made clear to the viewer.

One thing to keep in mind when dealing with various degrees of camera sophistication is that some may record in the near-infrared. The result of this in a monochrome image is a reversal of the dark and light values, causing an object to appear white when it is black, for example. This may not affect the admissibility of the tape, as long as it is proven by example what happened. For example, use the camera to view an object real-time. The audience will see the object and the reversed light value on the camera simultaneously.

Thermal infrared will increase the capability of detecting or tracking an intruder whose image may not have been captured on tape due to switching. The thermal infrared will record the lingering traces of body heat from the individual. This may show as glowing foot prints or hand marks where the individual touched something that may have been overlooked by the initial investigators.

Legal Issues Ensure that you consult corporate legal counsel and follow company policy and legal advice regarding all relevant legal concerns. Also coordinate with your legal department on what type of evidence you are planning to obtain from the video surveillance, and how this video will be admissible in court. Will the video have any relevance? Is the type of system used considered reliable? How will the integrity of the data gathered from the system be insured? Other legal concerns may include federal and state laws that require the posting of signage about video monitoring.

Issues to Consider

- Posting the use of cameras
- Deterrent
- Privacy issues
- Posting whether the camera is monitored

Admissibility Videotape is commonly admitted as evidence in court. Videotape that is used as evidence in a criminal proceeding may be either illustrative or staged. There are also different perspectives concerning the use of videotape admissibility. Is it used for pictorial communication or as a silent witness?

Characteristics of admissible evidence:

- Relevance
- Reliability
- Ensure
  - — Integrity
  - — Continuity
- Prejudicial effect

Relevance

- This is established by comparison with the testimony permitted by an eyewitness.
- If an imaginary eyewitness would be allowed to describe to the court the content of the videotape, then it is relevant to the case.

Reliability

- Proves that the videotape has not been altered
- Elements that must be proven include:
- Location
- Date
- Time

Integrity and continuity

- Essential to prove validity of evidence
- Examiner must work with original tape (unlike computer forensics!)
- Prove true copy if a copy is used in court
- Evidence is available for review

Prejudicial effect

Although relevant, evidence may be excluded if its probative value is substantially outweighed by the danger of unfair prejudice, confusion of the issues, or misleading to the jury, or by considerations of undue delay, waste of time, or needless presentation of cumulative evidence (Federal Rule of Evidence 403).

Section 3: Recovery

Recovery Time

The most successful Disaster Recovery Strategy is one that will never be implemented; therefore, risk avoidance is a critical element in the disaster recovery process (B. C. Martin).

Sample statistics from "midrange data centers" include:

- 15 percent could recover more than 30 percent of their applications in any time frame
- 3.8 percent could recover their applications within the same day
- 2.5 percent could recover within four hours

During development of the BIA, organizations identify the MTD, which specifies the length of time a company can survive before recovery becomes impossible. Everything in this section must depend upon that MTD value. By definition, any recovery efforts that extend beyond that timeframe may not serve to save the business and may prove to be a resource drain.

Ensure that all employees know their responsibilities for recovery efforts.

Recovery Objectives

Recovery Point Objective (RPO) — A measurement of how old the data is when the systems are recovered. The processing and information gap between the RPO and the most current data must be either accepted and the data lost or the information must be reconstructed. Either alternative has points for and against. The goal is have as small a gap as possible between the RPO and the most current data.

Recovery Time Objective (RTO) — The actual time required for recovery operations.

Processing and Information Gap   The security practitioner should use all available resources to ensure that the data used for recovery is as current as possible. This gap will be determined by the back-up policies and procedures used by the organization.

For example a company that does only a full back-up once a week will save time and resources doing backups, but if a recovery must be performed, the recovery data could be up to a week old, and more current data must be reconstructed or may be lost. This could greatly extend the time required for recovery operations as well as making the company lose even more business and information during the reconstruction process.

If a company does full back-ups weekly and incremental ones daily, there could be up to six generations of backups to restore.

If the company does remote journaling to an alternate site, there will be little to no gap between the RPO and the current data.

Recovery Time Objective

Although this initially sounds much like the MTD, there are significant differences. MTD includes the RTO and the lead time that is required to set things into action. For example:

- Assume the MTD for a data center at four hours.
- Assume the RPO to be about one hour (data one hour old).
- Assume the RTO (time required to actually restore the tape backups) at two hours.
- Assume the lead time — the time required to get the back up tapes from storage, to ensure that the proper personnel are on-site to restore the tapes, etc. at about one hour.

This timetable allows the business to recover, and meet the RPO objective within the MTD.

Recovery Resources

- Emergency Operation Coordinator
- Damage Assessment Team
- Salvage Team
- Recovery Teams
- Business Recovery of Mission Critical Functions
- Data and Information
- Facility and Supply
- Network and Communications
- User

Personnel Resources   The emergency operations coordinator will be the central authority for recovery operations.

The damage assessment team goes into action as soon as there is a disruptive event. The job of this team is to assess the situation and make recommendations to senior management, through the emergency operations coordinator, as to whether a disaster should be declared and the BCP activated.

In the event a disaster is declared (e.g., a tornado or a flood) and business operations are moved to an alternate site, the salvage team will go to the primary business site and determine what resources can be salvaged. The salvage team would return to the damaged primary site to search for recoverable assets.

The recovery teams go into action when the decision is made to declare a disaster. Their primary job is to go to the alternate site and ensure that all of the requirements within their area of responsibility have been fulfilled, and needed resources are available.

Recovery Phase   Recovery activities should be conducted using a phased approach. The emphasis will be on following the BCP and recovering mission critical functions as effectively and efficiently as possible.

There are seven phases to the recovery process:

1. Begin implementation.
2. Recover critical functions.
3. Recover remaining functions according to priority.
4. Salvage assets from primary site.
5. Repair primary site.
6. Return to primary site.
7. Deactivate alternate site.

We will cover each of these areas in a little more detail.

Phase 1 Beginning implementation includes such items as:

- Contacting vendors for required hardware or software
- Retrieving known good backups for restoration
- Contacting and gathering teams
- Migrating people and resources to the alternate site
- Setting up the emergency operations control center
- Verifying readiness of alternate site systems and connectivity
- Restoring backups
- Verifying resources and requirements in all recovery categories

Phase 2 This is the recovery of critical functions, all of which were identified in the BIA. The functions should be restored in order of priority, with the most critical being restored first. Do not forget to notify critical personnel of the schedule, security procedures, contact information, and location of the alternate site.

Phase 3 It may be decided that due to resources, some functions will not be restored until after return to the primary site. This decision should be made in advance by senior management and based upon the recommendations of the business continuity team, with representation from the user community and the security practitioner.

Phase 4 The salvage team should have guidelines concerning salvage priorities. If there is any requirement for assistance from consultants or outside specialists, the request should go through the Emergency Operations Coordinator. An example would be data recovery from the hard drives of damaged computers.

Review the insurance paperwork and ensure that the cooperation of the insurance adjustors is obtained to document the damage and see what may be covered.

Phase 5 This deals with the restoration and repair of the primary business site. Remember that personnel safety is always the top priority and care should be taken to ensure that the primary facility is properly repaired and secured. All repairs and changes to the facility should be inspected and verified by management before business operations are returned to the primary site.

Phase 6   This phase involves the return of business operations to the primary business location.

Other concerns:

- Verification that all support systems for mission critical functions at the primary site are functioning correctly
- Transfer of mission critical functions, one at a time, from the alternate site back to the primary site, moving the least critical functions first
- Testing and verification of the functioning of mission critical business functions and systems once the move is completed

Phase 7   The seventh and final phase of recovery is deactivation of the alternate site. It is important to always leave the alternate site in such a condition that immediate and rapid return is possible if required. This may be especially important if the disruption was caused by a natural disaster such as an earthquake.

All assets should be recovered or protected as appropriate.

Success Criteria   These criteria, if met, describe a successful recovery effort.

- Mission-critical systems have been restored within the predetermined time frame
- Data has been restored to the most current available versions

It is important to remember that even with practice, processing speeds may not match those of normal operations.

During practice drills, mistakes can provide important information concerning weaknesses in the plan or its implementation. Careful notes should be taken so that this information can be integrated into the plan.

A Successful Recovery   The eight R's of a successful recovery plan and implementation are:

- Reason for planning
- Recognition
- Reaction
- Recovery
- Restoration
- Return to normal
- Rest and relax
- Re-evaluate and re-document

A successful recovery is predicated upon a comprehensive and detailed DRP.

The personnel should understand the importance of the recovery, recognize the need for it, and be able to respond rapidly and effectively.

Detailed written recovery processes should include procedures for:

- Malicious code attacks
- Hardware failures
- Data corruption
- Network intrusions
- Physical facility damage
- Loss of key personnel
- Restoration of a single workstation/multiple workstations
- Restoration of the server

Recovery and restoration procedures should be detailed enough that any knowledgeable person can perform them. The term "knowledgeable person" should also be something that is considered by management. Does *knowledgeable* mean someone who knows the inner workings of your organization or does it mean someone who is familiar with the types of operating systems and network architecture you deploy? In your planning for disaster are your employees also set up to be redundant? If an earthquake or tornado destroys your data center with your key IT inside, what level of "knowledgeable" personnel does your disaster recovery plan call for at the back-up data center to implement your procedures?

Recovery and restoration procedures should encompass three key areas:

- Identify arrangements and agreements that must be performed in advance.
- Ensure that necessary resources are available when needed.
- Ensure that critical business functions, such as client support, can be resumed with the minimal amount of disruption.

Identification and integration of the lessons learned from disasters, practice or test situations or experiences of other organizations may be the most important products of the experience.

Related Processes

A major issue during a recovery effort is the disbursement of funds. The Emergency Operations Coordinator should have an available budget for operations. Once this is exhausted, there should be a detailed but expedient process by which this budget can be augmented as required, as well as a process of approval to act as a security check.

Security at all business locations is important, especially if the business disruption was caused by civil uprisings or by a natural disaster affecting a large area.

Information security must also be addressed. The systems at the primary site should be designed to fail safe, and the systems at the alternate site should offer the required levels of confidentiality, integrity and availability.

In all cases, personnel safety is the primary concern. When this has been addressed, employee support measures must be considered. For instance, there may be a need for support for families, logistics, accommodations, communications, stipends, and travel. Key personnel will not be available to support the organization if they are first needed to support their families. When an organization helps with this, employees are much more likely to put their full effort into the business recovery effort.

It is important that policy identifies the individual(s) who will represent the corporation to outside entities such as community groups, business partners, associations, emergency services, and of course, the media. These people should be trained in how to deal with media as well as briefed as to the appropriate amount and detail of information to provide. No other individuals should speak on behalf of the corporation.

IT Management Role during Recovery

IT management responsibilities during recovery include:

- Delegate data and system recovery roles
- Manage and monitor the recovery effort
- Clearly communicate responsibilities and expectations
- Continuously:
  — Prioritize and monitor resource allocation according to the BIA
  — Reassess original recovery plans
  — Assess alternate site stability
  — Assess adequacy of information security
  — Assess adequacy of system security
  — Monitor timeframes

Recovery can be stressful and complicated. Because of this, IT management should also:

- Monitor personnel
- Productivity versus burnout
- Morale
- Ensure communication capability and capacity
- Track asset losses
- Track recovery costs
- Prepare for possible disruptions or errors that may occur during the recovery
- Document, document, document

IT Management Role after Recovery

When the disaster is over, it is time to stop, relax, breathe, and reassess everything. This is an excellent time to perform a risk analysis and get funding for recommended countermeasures, update policies, and evaluate employee skills and required training.

Then the time has come to reassess and rewrite all of the step-by-step procedures in the department. They should be:

- Easy to perform
- Easy to understand
- Effective
- Efficient
- Relevant
- Important
- Supported by policy
- Reviewed
- Tested

Verify and Update Procedures

Identify the most probable scenarios for server recovery, and write step-by-step procedures to address them. Examples of procedures that may be useful in a Windows 2000 environment include:

- Recovery using an emergency repair disk
- Restoring System State Data
- Restoring the Registry
- Restoring Active Directory
- Restoration when the hardware is damaged
- Moving a Windows installation to another computer
- Restoring a domain controller
- Restoring a tape backup to a different computer
- Malicious code recovery

Windows NT

Windows NT server recovery procedures to consider include:
- Using the startup floppy diskette and/or the emergency repair disk
- Verification of system files
- Replacing the Master Boot Record and/or the Partition Boot Sector
- Restoring the Registry
- Repairing the Partition Table
- Restoring a tape backup to different computer
- Malicious code recovery

References

Anonymous. (1998). *Maximum Security: A Hacker's Guide to Protecting Your Internet Site and Network.* Indianapolis: Sams Publishing.

Austin, G. R. (Ed.). (2002). *2002 CISA Review Manual* (12th ed.). Rolling Meadows, IL: Information Systems Audit and Control Association.

Bosworth, S., and Kabay, M. E. (2002). *Computer Security Handbook.* New York: John Wiley.

Broder, J. F. (2000). *Risk Analysis and the Security Survey.* Boston: Butterworth-Heinemann.

Brunetto, T. (2001). *Protecting Your Most Valuable Asset.* Paper presented at the ASIS School Security Threats and Strategies Conference, New Orleans.

Business Continuity Institute 2002, Version BCI DJS 1.0 01/11.02.

Cain, A., Gross, J., and Purvis, K. (1996). "Broadband ISDN Communications," retrieved March 10, 1999, from http://www.geocities.com/SiliconValley/1047/bisdn.html.

Carter, E. (2002). *CISCO: Secure Intrusion Detection System.* Indianapolis, IN: CISCO Press.

Casad, J. N. D. (1997). *MCSE Training Guide: Networking Essentials.* Indianapolis, IN: New Riders Publishing.

CERT Intrusion Detection Checklist http://www.cert.org/tech_tips/intruder_detection_checklist.html

CERT Coordination Center. (1999)." Intrusion Detection Checklist," retrieved February 25, 2003.

Chapman Jr., D. W., and Fox, A. (eds.). (2002). *CISCO Secure PIX Firewalls.* Indianapolis, IN: CISCO Press.

Christianson, J. (2003). *Incident Response Procedures: For Windows NT/2000* (White Paper No. 1): High Tech Forensics, Inc.

COBiT, S. C. (Ed.). (2000). *Cobit: Governance, Control and Audit for Information and Related Technology.* Rolling Meadows, IL: IT Governance Institute.

Cole, E. (2002). *Hackers Beware: Defending Your Network from the Wiley Hacker.* Indianapolis, IN: New Riders Publishing.

Department of Justice Computer Search and Seizure Guidelines: http://www.cybercrime.gov/s&smanual2002.htm

Dulaney, E., Sherwood, L., Scrimger, R., Tilke, A., White, J., Williams, R., et al. (1998). *MCSE Training Guide to TCP/IP.* Indianapolis, IN: New Riders Press.

Eoghan, C. (2000). *Electronic Evidence and Computer Crime.* New York: Academic Press.

Evans, N. D. (2002). "High Risk, High Rewards," Retrieved March 1, 2002.

Foundstone R&D Lab Tools http://www.foundstone.com/rdlabs/tools.php?category=Forensic

Frisch, A. (1998). *Essential Windows NT System Administration.* Cambridge: O'Reilly.

Gartner Inc. 2001 — KEYNOTESPOTLIGHT 1002

Hamilton, A., & Votteler, T. (Eds.). (1999). *Managing an NT Network: Notes from the Field.* Redmond, WA: Microsoft Press.

Hancock, G. (Ed.). (2002). *CCSA: Next Generation Check Point Certified Security Administrator.* Berkley, CA: McGraw-Hill Osborne.

Held, G. (1998). *Ethernet Networks* (3rd ed.). New York: John Wiley.

ISACA (Ed.). (2001). CISA Review *Questions, Answers, and Explanations 2002 Supplement.* Rolling Meadows, IL: Information Systems Audit and Control Association.

Jackie Davis(ed.). (2003). *Disaster Prevention and Recovery for Windows Servers.* Virginia Beach, VA.

Jones, J. G., & Landes, C. (2001). *A+ Exam Cram.* Scottsdale, AZ: Coriolis.

Jumes, J. G., Cooper, N. F., Chamoun, P., & Feinman, T. M. (1999). *Microsoft Windows NT 4.0 Security, Audit, and Control: In-depth Techniques to Ensure System Security.* Redmond, WA: Microsoft Press.

Lammle, T., Porter, D., & Chellis, J. (1999). *CCNA Cisco Certified Network Associate Study Guide.* Alameda, CA: Sybex Inc.

Lang, D. T. (2004). *Introduction to Computer Forensics.* Boca Raton, FL: CRC Press

Mandia, K., and Prosise, C. (2003). *Incident Response and Computer Forensics, Second Edition* Emeryville, CA: Osborne/McGraw-Hill.

Martin, B. C. (2002). "Disaster Recovery Plan Strategies and Processes," retrieved January 15, 2003.

Nothcutt, S. (2000). *Network Intrusion Detection: An Analyst's Handbook.* Indianapolis, IN: New Riders Publishing.

Purpura, P. P. (1998). *Security and Loss Prevention.* Boston: Butterworth-Heinemann.

"Quick Reference Guide to Ethernet." (1995). Retrieved March 5, 1999, from http://wwwhost. ots.utexas.edu/ethernet/100quickref/ch11qr_1.html.

Rapagnani, L. (1998). "Catalyst 5000 Switching Platform Anchors Extensive Fast Ethernet Network," retrieved March 15, 1999, from http://www.cisoc.com/warp/public/752/profiles/ undam_cp.htm.

Schultz, E., & Shumway, R. (2002). *Incident Response: A Strategic Guide to Handling System and Network Security Breaches.* Indianapolis, IN: New Riders Publishing.

Sennewald, C. A. (1998). *Effective Security Management.* Boston: Butterworth-Heinemann.

Shelly, G. B., Cashman, T. J., & Rosenblatt, H. J. (1998). *Systems Analysis and Design.* Cambridge: Course Technology.

Skoudis, E. (2002). *Counter Hack: A Step-by-Step Guide to Computer Attacks and Effective Defenses.* Upper Saddle River, NJ: Prentice-Hall.

Tipton, H. F., & Krause, M. (2000). *Information Security Management Handbook* (4th ed.) Washington D.C.: Auerbach/CRC Press.

"UNC Network Assessment Minimum Network Specifications." (1998). Retrieved February 10, 1999, from http://www.ga.unc.edu/its.netstudy/netspec.html.

Useful Web Sites

AnaDisk and CopyQM from NTI are examples of the many good floppy disk tools available from many different manufacturers.

http://www.althes.fr/ressources/avis/smartspoofing.htm

CERT: http://www.cert.org

http://www.cert.org/tech_tips/intruder_detection_checklist.html#A

CIAC: http://ciac.llnl.gov

http://www.sans.org/rr/recovery/resumption.php

http://www.computeruser.com/resources/dictionary/definition.html?lookup=7278.

http://www.cops.org/

http://www.crime-research.org/eng/

http://www.cybercrime.org/

http://www.disasterrecoveryworld.com/

http://www.drj.com/

http://www.drj.com/special/wtc/

http://www.drj.com/special/wtc/kpmg-checklist.pdf

FedCIRC: http://www.fedcirc.gov/otherir.html

FIRST: http://www.first.org

http://www.forensics-intl.com

http://www.hightechcrimecops.org/

IBM ERS: http://www.brs.ibm/services/brs/ers/brspwers.nsf/home

Internet Storm Center: http://isc.incidents.org/

http://htcia.org/

http://www.medasys.com/company/fr/mis/securite/avisoct02.htm

New Technologies, Inc.: http://www.forensics-intl.com.

http://www.ncmec.org/

http://www.nsa.gov/isso/

NIST http://csrc.nist.gov/topics/inchand.html

Security Organizations: http://www.securitypointer.com/organizations.htm

http://www.utoronto.ca/security/drp.htm

Sample Questions

1. What is a key objective of risk analysis?
   a. Identify high priority risks
   b. Select countermeasures and safeguards
   c. Optimize insurance coverage
   d. Identify high priority assets

2. Which is not a threat to IT systems?
   a. Weakness in an application
   b. Power or HVAC outage
   c. Civil unrest
   d. Intruder

Use the following information for questions 3 and 4.

Historical records indicate a fire twice in 30 years of operation, destroying 30 percent of the data center. The data center is currently valued at $1M. A fire protection and safety engineer recommends an additional sensor and suppression system to limit loss to 5 percent and lower incidence estimate to once in twenty years. The proposed system would cost $50,000, and it can be annualized over 10 years.

3. What is the current annual loss expectancy?
   a. $300,000
   b. $30,000
   c. $200,000
   d. $20,000

4. What is the value of the proposed system?
   a. $12,500
   b. $17,500
   c. $2,500
   d. $5,000

5. An example of a detective technical control is:
   a. Error correcting code
   b. Hot swappable disk
   c. Error message
   d. Process checkpoints

6. Qualitative risk analysis methods include, all except:
   a. Scenarios
   b. Rankings
   c. Ratings
   d. Annual loss expectancy

7. Mission critical processes or applications are:
   a. Integral to operations

    b. Strategic to the company

    c. Support regulatory compliance

    d. Employ the most people

8. A weak business impact analysis may lead to:

    a. Unsatisfactory recovery objective

    b. Regulatory non-compliance

    c. Lost revenue stream

    d. Unemployment

9. All the following should be considered when determining IT resources necessary at the recovery site, except:

    a. Staffing

    b. Process interdependencies

    c. Critical supply requirements

    d. Insurance

10. Data recovery point objective and recovery time objective can be improved the most with:

    a. Daily archives

    b. Remote journaling

    c. Database shadowing

    d. Electronic tape vaults

11. Which is the prudent order for disaster recovery plan testing:

    a. Parallel, simulation, interruption and walk-through

    b. Walk-through, parallel, simulation, interruption

    c. Walk-through, simulation, parallel, interruption

    d. Simulation, walk-through, parallel, interruption

12. Disaster recovery plans should:

    a. Be reviewed every six months

    b. Provide details

    c. Expect staff to report to duty

    d. Assume sufficient supplies, materials and data are available

13. A business impact analysis indicates a maximum tolerable downtime of six hours. What is a reasonable alternative?

    a. Hot site

    b. Warm site

    c. Mutual processing site

    d. Mirror site

14. Numerous environments complicate intrusion detection analysis except:

    a. Synchronized clocks

    b. Multiple entry points

    c. Switched networks

    d. Load balancers

15. During an investigation, who should be kept informed:
    a. Users
    b. Law enforcement
    c. Shareholders
    d. Management

16. Many judicial systems consider computer records:
    a. Best evidence
    b. Hearsay
    c. Conclusive
    d. Demonstrative

17. Computer evidence may have a higher burden of proof. Typical challenges include, all except:
    a. Relevancy
    b. Authenticity
    c. Accuracy
    d. Confidentiality

18. A critical element for investigators is to:
    a. Gather all evidence forensically
    b. Follow investigative procedures
    c. Preserve evidence under chain of custody
    d. Thoroughly analyze logs and user reports

19. Media that is the target of an investigation should be copied on to:
    a. New media
    b. Forensically sterile media
    c. Reformatted and portioned media
    d. Controlled and protected media

20. An investigator should prevent changes to target media with:
    a. Integrity verification controls
    b. Write blocker
    c. Configuration management
    d. Basic input and output system (BIOS) controls

21. In addition to searching files and logs on media, an investigator should search all but:
    a. Unallocated space
    b. Disk slack
    c. RAM slack
    d. System slack

Domain 5
Cryptography
Doug Andre, CISSP

According to Webster's *Revised Unabridged Dictionary*, cryptography "is the act or art of writing in secret characters; also, secret characters, or cipher."

The Cryptography Wikiportal[1] expands this definition further, defining cryptography as:

> The study of means of converting information from its normal, comprehensible form into an incomprehensible format, rendering it unreadable without secret knowledge — the art of *encryption*. In the past, cryptography helped ensure secrecy in important communications, such as those of spies, military leaders, and diplomats. In recent decades, the field of cryptography has expanded its remit in two ways. Firstly, it provides mechanisms for more than just keeping secrets: schemes like digital signatures and digital cash, for example. Secondly, cryptography has come to be in widespread use by many civilians who do not have extraordinary needs for secrecy, although typically it is transparently built into the infrastructure for computing and telecommunications, and users are not aware of it.

Essentially, cryptography pertains to the process of concealing information from others. This has wide application in business and government, as well as personal transactions. Cryptography is not the only mechanism available to provide information security; rather, it provides a set of tools for the IT security practitioner.

In cryptography there are two basic types of ciphers: transposition and substitution. A transposition cipher (also known as a permutation cipher) rearranges characters or bits of information. A substitution cipher replaces bits, characters, or blocks of information with other bits, characters, or blocks of information.

Substitution ciphers either operate on a continuous basis, steadily encrypting information, or operate on multiple bits at a time (a block of information). Any type of cipher that combines a continuous stream of keying values (known as a keystream) with plaintext is called a stream cipher. Most

---

1. http://en.wikipedia.org/wiki/Portal:Cryptography

stream ciphers operate bit-by-bit. A cipher that operates on larger elements of plaintext (usually 8-bit bytes) is known as block cipher. Modern substitution ciphers use either stream or block ciphers, and are implemented in hardware or software.

Business and Security Requirements for Cryptography

The basic goal of cryptography is to make the cost or the time required to decrypt a message without the key, exceed the value of the information being protected. Thus, information that is worth no more than $100 could be effectively protected with a cipher (an algorithm used for cryptographic purposes is known as a cipher) that costs $1,000 to break each time. This is an important concept, as it provides one of the basic rationale for selecting cryptographic tools and ciphers. The number of possible keys to a cipher is known as a key space. Without any knowledge of the key, an opponent with access to an encrypted message and the decryption cipher could try every possible key to decode the message. This is known as a "brute force" attack. By making the key space sufficiently large, it is possible to make the cost of a brute force attack infeasible. Assuming there are no mathematical weaknesses in the cipher, a larger key space usually implies greater security.

Ciphers can be either known to the public (open source) or hidden from the public (closed source or proprietary). Experts can subject those that are open source to extensive analysis. As a result, flaws and weaknesses are identified that could restrict the safety of the cipher. Although one cannot necessarily "prove" that a cipher is completely secure, a single exception can prove that a cipher is not completely secure. Thus, the more a cipher withstands public scrutiny without any major flaws being identified, the more likely it is to be secure. The Digital Encryption Standard, or DES, published January 15, 1977 as Federal Information Processing Standard (FIPS) 46, is probably the most scrutinized cipher in history.

By using cryptographic tools in a number of ways, the IT security practitioner can develop solutions to business problems that enforce the security goals of integrity, confidentiality, authentication and on-repudiation.

Integrity

The concept of integrity is the protection against unauthorized modification or destruction of information. Data integrity ensures that no party has altered or deleted information after origination. For example, payroll information requires data integrity to ensure that amounts are not modified after being sent to the check printer. Data integrity can be achieved with either asymmetric or symmetric ciphers; both can provide a level of assurance that information has not been tampered with.

Confidentiality

Confidentiality is keeping information secret from all except those who are authorized to see it. This can be done with a number of techniques, including locking safes, posting armed guards, and whispering in someone's ear in a remote field. However, this is often cited as the primary benefit of using cryptography. Cryptography provides confidentiality by rendering information unintelligible to anyone other than those who know the encryption cipher and the proper key. This knowledge may be as a result of being an authorized user, or as a result of effective cryptanalysis (or theft of cryptographic material). The value of confidentiality is straightforward — certain communications contain information that could either prove detrimental to the correspondents if disclosed, or could prove useful to an opponent. Confidentiality can be achieved by either asymmetric or symmetric ciphers; both have the capability to encode information and hide it from prying eyes.

Authentication

Authentication corroborates the identity of an entity, whether the sender, the sender's computer, some device, or some information. As humans, we instinctively authenticate each other based on physiological characteristics such as facial appearance, voice, skin texture, and so forth. A traditional military authentication mechanism is a password — if you know it, the sentry lets you pass. If you don't know it, you're in trouble. In the digital realm, cryptography provides a mechanism to authenticate entities. Entity authentication or identification can be achieved with either asymmetric or symmetric ciphers. The most straightforward form of digital authentication is a UserID and password. Note that this is not considered to be strong authentication, as anyone else who gains access to this fixed information can provide the same information (e.g., UserID = "Aladdin"; Password = "Open Sesame") to the recipient to be acknowledged as a legitimate user. Symmetric cryptography, in general, has this problem. If an opponent can listen in on all conversations, including the initial setup where sender and receiver agree on cipher and key, that opponent can masquerade as a legitimate user. Thus, to maintain an ability to authenticate in a symmetric cryptography world, parties must first distribute keys among themselves securely. This is often expensive and time-consuming for large numbers of users, but the value of authenticating all parties is sufficiently important in environments (e.g., the military) that this protection is worth the cost. In an asymmetric environment, authentication is dependent upon a secure public key storage directory. Knowing what secret key was used to encrypt information can provide a means of identification. Asymmetric cryptography offers a more straightforward means of providing authentication, and in fact, it, along with confidentiality, is the cornerstone to electronic commerce on the Internet.

Non-Repudiation (Digital Signatures)

Non-repudiation provides a means of preventing a party from denying a previous statement or action. For example, an investor may send an e-mail to her broker that states "buy 1,000 shares of XYZ at 50." Shortly after the order is executed, XYZ stock drops to 20. The investor then tries to deny that she said "buy"; she states that she really said "sell." How does one resolve this he-said-she-said dilemma? The security principle non-repudiation can be satisfied with an asymmetric digital signature, but not a symmetric digital signature. If both the sender and the recipient possess the same secret key, one cannot prove to a third party that a message exchanged originated with one party rather than the other. Therefore, the prerequisites for substantiating non-repudiation are as follows:

- An effective asymmetric key algorithm
- A strong hash function
- A means to apply the private encryption key to the hash value to produce a digital signature
- A tamper-proof or trusted third-party timing device (if desired)
- An agreed-upon protocol for validating digital signatures
- A secure key management and distribution system
- A public key repository that has an assured level of integrity
- Key escrow, to be able to produce keys from parties in case of legal dispute
- Procedures to handle disputes

Through the use of asymmetric cryptography, one can prove mathematically, usually to the satisfaction of a judge or a jury, that a particular party did indeed originate a specific message at a specific time.

Principles of Certificates and Key Management

In the most fundamental sense, cryptography deals with two types of information: not encrypted (i.e., in "understandable" form), and encrypted (i.e., in "scrambled" form). Information that is not encrypted is known as plaintext (or sometimes cleartext). Information that has been encrypted is known as ciphertext. The act of scrambling plaintext into ciphertext is known as encryption. The act of unscrambling ciphertext into plaintext is known as decryption. Encryption uses a known mathematical process for performing its function, known as an algorithm. An algorithm used for cryptographic purposes is known as a cipher. An algorithm is a repeatable process that will, given the same inputs, produce the same result. This repeatability is important to ensure that information, once encrypted, can be decrypted. Note that the algorithm used to encrypt may or may not be the same algorithm that is used for decryption. For example, a simple algorithm that adds X to each value to encrypt would have to subtract X from each value to decrypt. Additionally, there are encryption algorithms for which there is no associated decryption algorithm available. These are known as one way algorithms. The output of a one-way algorithm is known as a hash.

In addition to a cipher and plaintext to be encrypted, encryption involves a third component: a key (also known as a crypto variable). The encryption cipher uses the cryptographic key to vary its output so that two correspondents can protect their information from anyone else with access to the same cipher. By changing the key, one changes the output of the cryptographic function, even if the plaintext remains the same.

Encryption ciphers fall into two general categories. Those that use the same key to encrypt and decrypt are called symmetric or private key. Those that use different keys to encrypt and decrypt are called asymmetric or public key. Because the terms "public key" and "private key" are often used to refer to the two different keys in asymmetric ciphers (which together are known as a key pair), to avoid confusion, we will use the "symmetric" and "asymmetric" naming convention for ciphers.

Digital signatures require asymmetric cryptography and are not digitized signatures (i.e., electronic images of handwritten signatures). Digital signatures bind the identity of an entity to a particular message or piece of information. Thus, digital signatures do not provide privacy or secrecy, but they perform an important function of ensuring data integrity and verifying authorship of a particular message. A digital signature is made with a private key from an asymmetric key pair, and includes a hash of the message being signed. This combination provides dual assurance — that a message originated from a particular entity, and that the contents have not been tampered with. Anyone with access to a signer's public key can verify the digital signature. However, only the holder of the private key can create the digital signature. The most common digital signature algorithms used are Rivest-Shamir-Adelman (RSA) and the Digital Signature Algorithm (DSA). The patent on RSA expired in September 2000, and it is now public domain. The DSA signs the Secure Hash Algorithm (SHA) hash of the message. Although most commercial systems use RSA, the Digital Signature Standard (DSS), DSA, and SHA are established as U.S. Government standards, and are more likely to appear in government products.

Given a message, the sender wishes to append a digital signature. First, the sender computes a hash or message digest of the entire message. This produces a result of a known length. Next, the sender will encrypt this one-way hash with a private key, and append the results to the message. Usually, messages that have digital signatures will have a prefix as well that indicates the start of the message. Both the message and the digital signature are sent to the recipient. The recipient, upon receiving the message, can verify the integrity of the message (and the identity of the sender) by decrypting the digital signature with the sender's public key (usually available in a trusted directory). This produces the hash or message digest, along with sender-specific information such as time and date. The recipient then uses the same algorithm to recompute the one-way hash or message digest for the original message. The recipient then compares the results of these two operations. If the values match, then it is deemed a "good" signature, and the message is considered valid. If the values do not match, this is deemed a "bad" signature, and the recipient should request a retransmission of the message from the sender. A bad signature could be a result of the use of different one-way functions by sender and recipient, data corruption of the message or signature in transit, tampering with the message or signature, or use of the incorrect key in the trusted directory. Thus, a bad signature does not necessarily indicate tampering, although it is a possibility.

A public key certificate (or identity certificate) is a certificate that uses a digital signature to bind together a public key with an identity — information such as the name of a person or an organization, their address, and so forth. The certificate can be used to verify that a public key belongs to an individual.[2] A trusted third party digitally signs the certificate attesting that the identity information and the public key belong together.

Issuing and Validating

Today, all business cryptography is done with computers, and algorithms of choice have been scrutinized, sometimes for decades, by some of the best minds on the planet. Therefore, it is reasonably safe to assume that an opponent will not defeat your cryptography by breaking the mathematics behind it. Rather, human behavior, and most importantly, human error, has much to do with compromise of crypto systems. A major problem of public (asymmetric) key encryption is the distribution and use of public keys. Improper key management is one of the most likely candidates for cryptographic compromise, particularly in symmetric key encryption.

Implementing Keys A key is a value that is an input to a cryptosystem that causes the message being transformed to be done so in a particular manner. The importance of a key is that a well-designed cryptosystem will produce different outputs of the same message for each key that is used. Another way to think about keys is that a cipher performs a particular task, and a key provides the specific directions for how to do the task. Physical keys are similar, but not exactly the same as cryptographic keys. Many popular door locks have five tumblers, and each has ten possible positions. Thus, there are $10**5 = 100,000$ possible cuts for house keys. This provides a reasonable assurance that a person trying a random key in your front door won't get in. The set of all possible keys is called a key space. The larger the key space, usually (but not necessarily), the more secure the algorithm.

2. http://en.wikipedia.org/wiki/Digital_certificate

Diffie and Hellman point out, "The cost and delay imposed by this key distribution problem is a major barrier to the transfer of business communications to large teleprocessing networks." In their paper, they introduce the concept of public key cryptography. (Note: this is often referred to as asymmetric cryptography.) Public key cryptography is a system whereby correspondents can communicate solely over a public channel using publicly known techniques, and establish a secure connection. One does not need to wait until an out-of-band letter arrives with a key in the envelope, or issue and manage millions of key pairs just in case they wish to communicate securely with a new correspondent. The impact of this discovery is profound, and has far-reaching effects on cryptography.

There are four properties of asymmetric key ciphers:

1. The existence of two associated algorithms that are inverses of each other.
2. Each of these two algorithms is easy to compute.
3. Knowing the first algorithm, it is computationally infeasible to derive the second algorithm. (Note: If you have the private key, you can derive the public key, but not the reverse.)
4. Given some random input, one can generate associated key pairs that are mathematically related to each other.

The first property means that this solution involves two components that are different, but associated with each other. This implies that what is used to encrypt is different than what is used to decrypt. Because asymmetric systems use different keys to encrypt and to decrypt, this means something fundamentally different than the differences between the encrypt and decrypt functions of a symmetric key cipher. In the case of symmetric key ciphers, the same key is used for both functions. It's just that in some cases, the algorithm needs to be run "backward." In asymmetric key ciphers, there are two separate keys that are related to each other. One will encrypt a message using the encryption algorithm, and one will decrypt a message using the decryption algorithm. Although intuitively, it would seem that the decryption function is the encryption function run backward, this is not the case in asymmetric key cryptography. Rather, the nature of the mathematics used accomplishes this inverse function.

The second property means that this approach can be implemented in computer software without significant difficulty. As a result, it becomes a practical approach for secure digital communications. "Easy to compute" means that a large number of tries to guess the right solution are not required. Rather, if one has special knowledge (the second key), this acts like a trap door to quickly decrypt the message. (Note: This paragraph is confusing because the trapdoor is contained in the private key and that enables derivation of the public key, however, the trapdoor is not used to decrypt — the opposite key is.)

The third property means that one key can be posted widely for anyone to use without compromising the contents of its associated key. These are sometimes referred to as a public key and its associated private key, or a public-private key pair. Since public key cryptosystems have private keys, you can see why we've stuck to the asymmetric key naming convention.

The fourth property means that any party can generate public-private key pairs, keep one private, and post the other in a directory for any other correspondent to use. Because the private key is kept secret and never transmitted, an eavesdropper cannot learn this value.

One of the closest equivalents in the everyday business world to asymmetric key ciphers is the night deposit box at a bank. A merchant takes his receipts to the bank, opens the slot with his key, and drops the money down the chute. The envelope slides down and into the safe. If he turned around and a robber held him up at gunpoint and demanded his key, the merchant can safely surrender the key and run away while the robber attempted to recover the money. Since the envelope has dropped out of reach, the robber would be unable to recover it. The next morning, the bank officer would use her key to open the safe, remove the money, and deposit it into the merchant's account. Each party has a different key, but they are associated with each other. Make this process reversible (where the bank officer could leave messages for the merchant), and you have the equivalent of an asymmetric or public key cryptosystem.

Keys for asymmetric ciphers are generated in pairs. Although they are related to each other mathematically, they are used independently. One key, the private key, is kept secret by the owner and never shared with anyone else. It is used to encrypt messages that can only be decrypted with the public key, or to decrypt messages that were encrypted by the public key. The other key, the public key, is usually posted in a public key directory. Anyone can access this key. It can be used to encrypt messages that only the private key will decrypt. Note also that it can decrypt messages encrypted with the private key. If anyone can access this public key, why would anyone want to encrypt with the private key? Because that key can serve as proof that the holder of the private key originated the message.

In a secure asymmetric key cryptographic transaction, the originator looks up the public key of the recipient, and encrypts the message with that key, and sends it through the Internet. Only the recipient's private key will decrypt the message; although an eavesdropper could intercept the message, and even read all of the keys in the public key directory, the message will remain unintelligible.

Note that the originator could authenticate the message by also encrypting with his private key. With this as an "inner" wrapper, surrounded by the recipient's public key "outer wrapper," the message can be read only by the recipient, who can then download the public key of the sender and verify that only the sender could have originated the message. This provides a message that is both secure and signed. The signing provides non-repudiation — the sender can't deny sending the message.

Implementing IVs   The term "initialization vector" (IV) refers to a pseudo-random value that is often used to begin encrypting information. The exact value of the IV is not particularly important. Its primary value is ensuring that the same message encrypted with the same key does not result in the same ciphertext. Otherwise, a third party intercepting encrypted messages could determine if the same message has been resent, or if the same initial text is present in different messages. This latter property is important to camouflage the format of the message.

IVs are implemented differently in block ciphers and in stream ciphers. In straight-forward operation of block ciphers, called Electronic Code Book (ECB) mode, encryption of the same plain text with the same key results in the same ciphertext which is a considerable threat to security. Use of an initialization vector linearly added to (i.e., XORd with) the first block of plaintext or included in front of the plaintext prior to encryption in one of the streaming modes of operation resolves this problem. XOR acts the same way as the logical either/or (i.e., the output is 1 if the inputs are different and 0 if the inputs are the same).

Electronic codebook (ECB) uses the same, fixed key to encrypt each block of plaintext. No block of ciphertext is dependent upon the other, and if you know the key, you can decrypt any block independently of any other block. This is the most straightforward, and cryptographically the weakest, mode of operation. This is because each time the same block of information is enciphered, the same ciphertext block is produced. In the extreme case of each block representing a single character, this is nothing more than a simple substitution cipher.

Cipher block chaining (CBC) takes the ciphertext of the previous block, XORs it with the next plaintext block, and then feeds that into the encryption algorithm. It is important to start this process with an initialization vector so that encrypting the same message with the same key does not result in the same ciphertext. An interesting property of CBC is that if the ciphertext is garbled in transit, the error will only propagate one more block before the message starts to decrypt correctly again. This property is known as self-synchronization.

Cipher feedback mode (CFB) takes the ciphertext of the previous block (which can be considered to be a pseudorandom bit string) and XORs it with the current plaintext block to create both the ciphertext of the current block as well as the input to DES to start the next block. This mode, too, requires an IV to ensure that the ciphertext is not the same for identical messages. Unlike CBC, an error in transmission will propagate for a while until all of the errors have shifted out of the input block.

Output feedback mode (OFB) is really a stream cipher where an IV is used to produce an ongoing string of pseudorandom bits that are XORd to the plaintext. The plaintext is not run through the encryption algorithm, only the output from the previous round of encryption. This is a type of Vernam cipher, and has the property that if any bit of the ciphertext is garbled, only one bit of the decrypted plaintext will be garbled. This is because no "downstream" blocks depend on any previous plaintext. Note that this mode is not self-synchronizing. If the encryption and decryption process get "out of synch," the system must be reinitialized. However, if the reinitialization process does not randomize the IV, then the same plaintext will produce the same ciphertext as before.

Standards

X.509 v3 —The public key for a user (or device) and a name for the user (or device), together with some other information, rendered unforgeable by the digital signature of the certification authority that issued the certificate, encoded in the format defined in the ISO/ITU-T X.509 standard. All X.509 certificates have the following data in addition to the signature as described in RFC 3280:

- tbsCertificate — The tbsCertificate contains information associated with the subject of the certificate and the CA (Certificate Authority) who issued it. Every tbsCertificate contains the names of the subject and issuer, a public key associated with the subject, a validity period, a version number, and a serial number; some may contain optional unique identifier fields.
- Version — This identifies which version of the X.509 standard applies to this certificate, which affects what information can be specified in it. When extensions are used, as expected in this profile, use X.509 version 3 (value is 2). If no extensions are present, but a UniqueIdentifier is present, use version 2 (value is 1). If only basic fields are present, use version 1 (the value is omitted from the certificate as the default value).
- Serial Number — The entity that created the certificate is responsible for assigning it a serial number to distinguish it from other certificates it issues. This information is used in numerous ways, for example when a certificate is revoked its serial number is placed in a Certificate Revocation List (CRL).
- Signature — This identifies the algorithm used by the CA to sign the Certificate.
- Issuer — Identifies the entity that signed and issued the certificate. This is normally a CA.

- Validity — Each certificate is valid only for a limited amount of time. The certificate validity period is the time interval during which the CA warrants that it will maintain information about the status of the certificate. The field is represented as a Sequence of two dates: the date on which the certificate validity period begins (not Before) and the date on which the certificate validity period ends.
- Subject — The name of the entity whose public key the certificate identifies. It is intended to be unique across the Internet.
- Subject Public Key Information — This is the public key of the entity being named, together with an algorithm identifier that specifies which public key crypto system this key belongs to and any associated key parameters.
- IssuerUniqueID and subjectUniqueID — These fields may only appear if the version is 2 or 3. The subject and issuer unique identifiers are present in the certificate to handle the possibility of reuse of subject or issuer names over time.
- Extensions — This field may only appear if the version is 3. The extensions defined for X.509 v3 certificates provide methods for associating additional attributes with users or public keys and for managing the certification hierarchy.

PKCS — PKCS refers to a group of Public Key Cryptography Standards devised and published by RSA laboratories in California. RSA Data Security Inc. was assigned the licensing rights for the patent on the RSA asymmetric key algorithm and acquired the licensing rights to several other key patents as well (e.g., the Schnorr patent).

As such, RSA Security, and its research division, RSA Labs, were interested in promoting and facilitating the use of public key techniques. To that end, they developed the PKCS standards. They retained control over them, announcing that they would make changes/improvements as they deemed necessary, and so the PKCS standards were not, in a significant sense, actual industry standards despite the name. Some, but not all, have in recent years begun to move into "standards track" processes with one or more of the standards organizations (and notably the IETF PKIX working group).[3] Table 5.1 describes the Public Key Cryptography Standards as shown by Wikipedia:

DER — Distinguished Encoding Rules is a method for encoding a data object (e.g., an X.509 certificate) to be digitally signed or to have its signature verified.

The Distinguished Encoding Rules of ASN.1 is an international standard drawn from the constraints placed on BER encodings by X.509. DER encodings are valid BER encodings. DER is the same thing as BER with all but one sender's options removed. For example, in BER a boolean value of true can

---

3. http://en.wikipedia.org/wiki/PKCS

Table 5.1. Public Key Cryptography Standards

	Version	Name	Comments
PKCS#1	2.1	RSA Cryptography Standard	See RFC 3447. Defines the format of RSA encryption.
PKCS#2	—	Withdrawn	No longer active. Covered RSA encryption of message digests, but was merged into PKCS#1.
PKCS#3	1.4	Diffie-Hellman Key Agreement Standard	
PKCS#4	—	Withdrawn	No longer active. Covered RSA key syntax, but was merged into PKCS#1.
PKCS#5	2.0	Password-Based Encryption Standard	See RFC 2898 and PBKDF2.
PKCS#6	1.5	Extended-Certificate Syntax Standard	Defines extensions to the old v1 X.509 certificate specification. Obsoleted by v3 of the same.
PKCS#7	1.5	Cryptographic Message Syntax Standard	See RFC 2315. Used to sign or encrypt messages under a PKI. Used also for certificate dissemination (for instance as a response to a PKCS#10 message). Formed the basis for S/MIME, which is now based on RFC 3852, an updated Cryptographic Message Standard (CMS).
PKCS#8	1.2	Private-Key Information Syntax Standard	
PKCS#9	2.0	Selected Attribute Types	
PKCS#10	1.7	Certification Request Standard	See RFC 2986. Format of messages sent to a Certification Authority to request certification of a public key.
PKCS#11	2.20	Cryptographic Token Interface (cryptoki)	An API defining a generic interface to cryptographic tokens
PKCS#12	1.0	Personal Information Exchange Syntax Standard	Defines a file format commonly used to store private keys with accompanying Public key certificates protected with a password-based symmetric key.
PKCS#13	—	Elliptic Curve Cryptography Standard	(Under development)
PKCS#14	—	Pseudo-Random Number Generation	(Under development)
PKCS#15	1.1	Cryptographic Token Information Format Standard	Defines a standard allowing users of cryptographic tokens to identify themselves to applications, independent of the application's cryptoki implementation (PKCS #11) or other API. RSA has relinquished IC card related parts of this standard to ISO/IEC 7816-15.

be encoded in 255 ways, while in DER there is only one way to encode a boolean value of true.[4]

BER — Basic encoding rules (BER) are ASN.1 encoding rules for producing self-identifying and self-delimiting transfer syntax for data structures described in ASN.1 notations.

BER is a self-identifying and self-delimiting encoding scheme, which means that each data value can be identified, extracted, and decoded individually.

You view it as a kind of "binary" XML. Currently, effort is being made to join these two technologies, such as the XML Encoding Rules (an alternative to BER), ASN.1 Schema (an alternative to XML Schema), ASN.1 SOAP (to exchange XML with PER on Web services).[5]

AES — (Advanced Encryption Standard), also known as Rijndael (rain'-doll), is a block cipher, designed by Vincent Rijmen and Joan Daemen, and issued as FIPS PUB 197. The AES algorithm is capable of using cryptographic keys of 128, 192, and 256 bits to encrypt and decrypt data in blocks of 128 bits, although the cipher can operate on variable block lengths. It is both strong and fast.

RC2 — is a variable key-size block cipher designed by Ronald Rivest (RC stands for Rivest Cipher or Ron's Code). It was designed as a "drop in" replacement for DES, and operates on 64-bit blocks. It uses a salt (salt is used to modify a password hash by using a random string of data to prohibit password hash matching types of attacks) as part of its encryption routine to make cryptanalysis more difficult. It is owned by RSA Security.

RC4 — is a variable key-size stream cipher with byte-oriented operations produced by RSA Security. RC4 is used frequently in Internet browsers to provide a secure sockets layer (SSL) connection.

Wired Equivalent Privacy (WEP) — is a wireless encryption standard for 802.11b that is based on RC4, but implemented incorrectly.

ANSI X9.17 — This industry standard was established and adopted by the financial industry to define key management procedures. It defines a symmetric key exchange protocol this is widely implemented in hardware encryption devices. Although asymmetric key exchange offers some advantages, the high cost of investment in X9.17 compliant equipment means it will be in use for some time. According to FIPS Pub 171, X9.17 specifies the minimum standards for:

- Control of the keying material during its lifetime to prevent unauthorized disclosure, modification, or substitution;

---

4. http://en.wikipedia.org/wiki/DER
5. http://en.wikipedia.org/wiki/Basic_Encoding_Rules

- Distribution of the keying material in order to permit interoperability between cryptographic equipment or facilities;
- Ensuring the integrity of keying material during all phases of its life, including its generation, distribution, storage, entry, use, and destruction;
- Recovery in the event of a failure of the key management process or when the integrity of the keying material is questioned.

Distribution

Key distribution, involves issuing keys to all valid users of a cryptosystem to enable them to communicate with each other. The classic solution to key distribution was to utilize out-of-band communications using a trusted channel to distribute keying material in advance. This could be by registered mail, by courier, or even by telephone, if it were certain the phones were not being tapped. The primary disadvantages of this strategy are that it is expensive and slow. Nonetheless, organizations with the resources and the ability to plan in advance implemented special infrastructures to manage this function.

In an asymmetric key distribution system, there is no need for couriers, back channels, or expensive storage and inventory procedures. The primary reason one can dispense with these elements is that in an asymmetric key distribution system, there is no requirement for each party to first share a secret key. This solves the chicken–egg problem of first needing a secure channel before one can establish a secure channel.

Key distribution can be done with either type of cipher, and key distribution techniques typically fall into one of three forms: paper, digital media, and hardware. Paper distribution requires no technology to implement. However, it does require a person to perform some action to install the key, and this can introduce errors or provide a disgruntled person an opportunity to compromise a system.

Digital distribution can be in the form of CDs, disks, or even e-mail. However, the keys must be protected in transit, so some form of secure transmission is used. For physical media, tamper-proof cases and registered mail provide a certain level of assurance. For electronic distribution, some other higher-level key, known as a key-encrypting key, must protect the keys in transit and storage. This, of course, requires that the key encrypting key is first distributed by some alternate secure mechanism. Key encrypting keys, if used, should only be used to encrypt other keys, and not information. Excessive usage of any key could lead to possible compromise.

Hardware distribution can be in the form of a PCMCIA card, a smart card, or a plug-in module. The advantage of this format is that the keys are transferred directly from the key transport mechanism into the crypto device without anyone viewing them, or any copies existing outside of these components.

To protect against a key being intercepted in transit, keys can be split. Splitting the key into two equal sized pieces is not a very good idea; if one piece is intercepted, the difficulty factor of brute-forcing the other half of the key is made much easier. Therefore one strategy to split a key K is to generate another random key J, which becomes the key-encrypting key. Combining K and J results in an encrypted key, which is sent by one channel, and the key-encrypting key is sent by another channel. If one of the two messages is intercepted, the attacker does not learn the underlying key.

$$\text{Channel 1:} \quad J$$
$$\text{Channel 2:} \ K \oplus J$$

$$\text{Recombine:} \ J \oplus K \oplus J = K$$

This scheme requires a new key-encrypting key for every key. (Note: In more recent times, asymmetric cryptography is often used to distribute symmetric keys as a more secure way of distributing the shared keys. This is usually done at the start of a session.)

Key revocation can be a problem in both environments. Key revocation occurs when an entity is no longer trusted or authorized to use a crypto-system. In a symmetric key system, where everyone shares the same secret, compromising one copy of the key comprises all copies. This is analogous to all employees having the same office key. If a disgruntled employee is dismissed and refuses to return the key, the lock must (should) be re-keyed, and new keys are issued to all employees. After a few dismissals, one can see that this approach can become both expensive and cumbersome to manage.

In an asymmetric key environment, the key directory is a trusted repository of all entities' public keys. If a particular entity is no longer trusted, the manager of the directory can remove that public key from the directory. Anyone attempting to initiate communications with the disenrolled party would be unable to locate a key with which to send. Although the disenrolled party could still initiate encrypted communications to other parties by using their posted public key, if protocol requires all messages to be digitally signed, the recipient would not find a valid key to check the signature, and should reject the message.

Ad hoc secure communications are the exclusive domain of asymmetric key systems and are the foundation of Internet e-commerce. Typically, asymmetric key technology is used to exchange a symmetric key, which is then used as a session key. Again, this is because asymmetric crypto is orders of magnitude slower than symmetric crypto. Once each party securely shares a secret key, communications can begin in earnest.

Digital signatures can be done with symmetric or asymmetric keys. However, a symmetric key digital signature can be duplicated by anyone who holds that key. This is typically used in situations where only a closed group of individuals share information, and want to ensure that it came from someone within the group. Checking the public key and verifying that the hash correctly decrypts can validate an asymmetric digital signature. Non-repudiation, or proving that a party originated a message, typically uses asymmetric key crypto. However, if a trusted key escrow system is used, then symmetric keys can perform this function. The traditional means of non-repudiation is a hand-written signature. By applying a digital signature to a document and by having a business arrangement that supports this implementation, one can also provide non-repudiation.

Concepts (e.g., Types, Formats)

PKI is the abbreviation for public key infrastructure. Public key (or asymmetric key) systems require some sort of infrastructure for issuing, distributing, storing, managing, and revoking keys. A number of vendors have developed products to provide this functionality.

It's important to understand that PKI is an infrastructure, not an application. Thus, it is not a "plug 'n' play" tool that is effortless. PKI requires time, money, and effort to be successful. Ideally, it should be transparent to a user base. If it takes all of that investment, why bother with PKI? The reason is that PKI integrates trust into the infrastructure.

There are a number of components involved in building a public key infrastructure. At the server level, one requires:

- A certificate authority (CA) is a trusted third party that generates public key certificates and can vouch for their authenticity
- A certificate repository that publishes certificates and CRLs
- A card issuing system for issuing certificates, usually embedding them in a smartcard or other device
- A key recovery and escrow authority that can securely store a copy of keys in the event they are lost or stolen
- A time-stamping authority to provide a secure source of time information
- There are a number of administration components to PKI, including:
  - Registration authorities (RA), authorizes local registration authorities, and issues lists of revoked certificates (called a certificate revocation list or CRL)
  - Local registration authorities (LRA) are usually located near a user base to provide the customer service function of registering users
  - Notarization authority (NA) vouches for the validity of public key signatures

And, of course, there needs to be a client component of PKI, with a certificate that is stored in a token, which can be hardware or software. All of this requires one more component to work effectively, and that is a PKI policy.

Essentially, PKI is all about trust. The concept of trust has some interesting characteristics:

- Trust is hierarchical (we each may trust our own Cas, but don't have to trust each other's).
- Trust is not transitive (if Alice trusts Bob and Bob trusts Eve, Alice doesn't necessarily trust Eve) (Note: Except in the PGP Web of Trust concept.).
- Trust is not distributive (if you change allegiances, the trust I gave to you may not remain with you).
- Trust goes to the device, not the person (we actually issue trust to the token, not the human using the token).

PKI may have potential risks. Ellison and Schneier[6] point out the ten risks of PKI:

- Who do we trust, and for what?
- Who is using my key?
- How secure is the verifying computer?
- Which John Robinson is he?
- Is the CA an authority?
- Is the user part of the security design?
- Was it one CA or a CA plus a Registration Authority?
- How did the CA identify the certificate holder?
- How secure are the certificate practices?
- Why are we using the CA process, anyway?

This list is not to discourage your perspective on PKI, but rather to stimulate your thinking as to how PKI can be implemented correctly.

Hash Function and Data Integrity

Hash functions help to detect forgeries. Hash functions compute a checksum of a message, and then combine it with some cryptographic function so that the result is tamper-proof. Hashes are usually of a known, fixed size based on the algorithm used.

If you recall, a checksum is a one-way calculation that yields a result that can be easily verified by re-running the data through the checksum function. For example, given a series of decimal numbers such as:

---

6. Ellison C., and Schneier, Bruce, "Ten Risks of PKI: What You're Not Being Told About Public Key Infrastructure," *Computer Security Journal*, v16 n1, 2000, pp. 1–7.

71 77 61 114 107 75 61 114 100 121

A simple checksum could be the two rightmost digits of the sum of these numbers. In this case, we add them together to get 901, drop the 9, and our checksum is 01. Now, if you were to transmit this sequence of ten numbers to someone over a noisy communications channel, it's possible that some of the information may be garbled. By also sending the checksum, the recipient can recalculate to see if the numbers "add up." If not, he knows to request a retransmission.

Is it possible for the numbers to become garbled and still have the checksum come out correctly? Yes. It's also possible for someone to deliberately modify the numbers, but tweak them so that the checksum still matches. This illustrates the point that checksums are not designed for security, but for ensuring reliability.

A hash is like a checksum, but it is designed so that a message cannot be forged that will result in the same hash as a legitimate message. Hashes are usually a fixed size, and the result is known as a hash value. Hashes act as a "fingerprint" of the data — they can be published as a reference so that recipients can see if the information has changed. Software publishers often provide hash values so that customers can verify the integrity of the software they receive. To be effective, hashes usually have to be sufficiently long so that it would take an inordinate amount of time to generate an alternate message that matched the correct hash value.

The MD5 message digest algorithm was developed by Professor Ronald Rivest of MIT (he's the R in RSA). RFC 1321 contains the specifications for the algorithm. It takes an input of any arbitrary length, and generates a 128-bit message digest that is computationally infeasible to match by finding another input. This message digest can be considered to be uniquely associated with its source. As a result, information such as compiled source code can be published with, and compared to, an MD5 hash to verify it has not been modified by a virus or some other means.

The Secure Hash Algorithm (SHA-1) is defined by the Federal Information Processing Standard Publication 180-2 (FIPS 180-2). SHA-1 produces a 160-bit hash from a message of any arbitrary length. Like MD5, it creates a unique "fingerprint" of a file.

Four more variants have since been issued with increased output ranges and a slightly different design: SHA-224, SHA-256, SHA-384, and SHA-512 — sometimes collectively referred to as SHA-2. Attacks have been found for both SHA-0 and SHA-1. No attacks have yet been reported on the SHA-2 variants, but since they are similar to SHA-1, researchers are worried, and are developing candidates for a new, better hashing standard.[7]

---

7. http://en.wikipedia.org/wiki/SHA-1

Secure Protocols

SSH

Definition   In computing, Secure Shell or SSH is a set of standards and an associated network protocol that allows establishing a secure channel between a local and a remote computer. It uses public-key cryptography to authenticate the remote computer and (optionally) to allow the remote computer to authenticate the user. SSH provides confidentiality and integrity of data exchanged between the two computers using encryption and message authentication codes. SSH is typically used to login to a remote machine and execute commands, but it also supports tunneling, forwarding arbitrary TCP ports and X11 connections; it can transfer files using the associated SFTP or SCP protocols. An SSH server, by default, listens on the standard TCP port 22.[8]

Capabilities   The bulleted items below describe the most common uses and capabilities of SSH:[9]

- In combination with SFTP, as a secure alternative to FTP which can be set up more easily on a small scale without a public key infrastructure and X.509 certificates;
- In combination with rsync to backup, copy, and mirror files efficiently and securely;
- In combination with SCP, as a secure alternative for rcp file transfers — more often used in environments involving Unix;
- For port forwarding or tunneling, frequently as an alternative to a full-fledged VPN. In this type of use, a (non-secure) TCP/IP connection of an external application is redirected to the SSH program (client or server), which forwards it to the other SSH party (server or client), which in turn forwards the connection to the desired destination host. The forwarded connection is cryptographically encrypted and protected on the path between the SSH client and server only. Uses of SSH port forwarding include accessing database servers, e-mail servers, securing X11, Windows Remote Desktop and VNC connections or even forwarding Windows file shares.
- With an SSH client that supports dynamic port forwarding (presenting to other programs a SOCKS or HTTP "CONNECT" proxy interface), SSH can even be used for generally browsing the Web through an encrypted proxy connection, using the SSH server as a proxy; with an SSH client that supports terminal protocols, for remote administration of the SSH server computer via terminal (character-mode) console;
- With an SSH client that supports SSH exec requests (frequently embed-

---

8.   http://en.wikipedia.org/wiki/Secure_Shell
9.   same as 8.

ded in other software, e.g. a network monitoring program), for automated remote monitoring and management of servers.

- Using just a normal SSH login on a server, the SSH File system can securely mount a directory on the server as a file system on the local computer.

Implementation The SSH-2 protocol has a clean internal architecture (defined in RFC 4251) with well-separated layers:[10]

- The transport layer (RFC 4253). This layer handles initial key exchange and server authentication and sets up encryption, compression and integrity verification. It exposes to the upper layer an interface for sending and receiving plaintext packets of up to 32,768 bytes each (more can be allowed by the implementation). The transport layer also arranges for key re-exchange, usually after 1 GB of data have been transferred or after 1 hour has passed, whichever is sooner.
- The user authentication layer (RFC 4252). This layer handles client authentication and provides a number of authentication methods. Authentication is client-driven, a fact commonly misunderstood by users; when one is prompted for a password, it is the SSH client prompting, not the server. The server merely responds to client's authentication requests. Widely used user authentication methods include the following:
  — "Password": a method for straightforward password authentication, including a facility allowing a password to be changed. This method is not implemented by all programs.
  — "Public key": a method for public key-based authentication, usually supporting at least DSA or RSA keypairs, with other implementations also supporting X.509 certificates.
  — "Keyboard-interactive" (RFC 4256): a versatile method where the server sends one or more prompts to enter information and the client displays them and sends back responses keyed-in by the user. Used to provide one-time password authentication such as S/Key or SecurID. Used by some OpenSSH configurations when PAM is the underlying host authentication provider to effectively provide password authentication, sometimes leading to inability to log in with a client that supports just the plain "password" authentication method.
  — GSSAPI authentication methods which provide an extensible scheme to perform SSH authentication using external mechanisms such as Kerberos 5 or NTLM, providing single sign on capability to SSH sessions. These methods are usually implemented by commercial SSH implementations for use in organizations.
- The connection layer (RFC 4254). This layer defines the concept of channels, channel requests and global requests using which SSH ser-

---

10. http://en.wikipedia.org/wiki/Ssh

vices are provided. A single SSH connection can host multiple channels simultaneously, each transferring data in both directions. Channel requests are used to relay out-of-band channel specific data, such as the changed size of a terminal window or the exit code of a server-side process. The SSH client requests a server-side port to be forwarded using a global request. Standard channel types include:

— "shell" for terminal shells, SFTP, and exec requests (including SCP transfers)
— "direct-tcpip" for client-to-server forwarded connections
— "forwarded-tcpip" for server-to-client forwarded connections

This open architecture provides considerable flexibility, allowing SSH to be used for a variety of purposes beyond secure shell. The functionality of the transport layer alone is comparable to TLS; the user authentication layer is highly extensible with custom authentication methods; and the connection layer provides the ability to multiplex many secondary sessions into a single SSH connection, a feature comparable to BEEP and not available in TLS.

SSL/TLS

Definition Secure Sockets Layer (SSL) and Transport Layer Security (TLS), its successor, are cryptographic protocols which provide secure communications on the Internet. There are slight differences between SSL 3.0 and TLS 1.0, but the protocol remains substantially the same. The term "SSL" as used here applies to both protocols unless clarified by context. SSL provides endpoint authentication and communications privacy over the Internet using cryptography. In typical use, only the server is authenticated (i.e., its identity is ensured) while the client remains unauthenticated; mutual authentication requires public key infrastructure (PKI) deployment to clients. The protocols allow client/server applications to communicate in a way designed to prevent eavesdropping, tampering, and message forgery.[11]

Capabilities Most Web sites that exchange confidential user information with browsers protect sessions using secure sockets layer (SSL) encryption. By convention, Web pages that use SSL encryption begin with https:// instead of http://. This is also known as the https protocol. SSL uses a private key to transmit information over an SSL connection that is initially negotiated using asymmetric key exchange between the Web server and the user's browser software. All major Web browser software supports SSL. The SSL handshake establishes the initial secure communications session between a client and a server. This process is described nicely on the RSA Web site.[12]

11. http://en.wikipedia.org/wiki/Secure_Sockets_Layer
12. http://www.rsasecurity.com

Implementation   The SSL Handshake Protocol consists of two phases: server authentication and an optional client authentication. In the first phase, the server, in response to a client's request, sends its certificate and its cipher preferences. The client then generates a master key, which it encrypts with the server's public key, and transmits the encrypted master key to the server. The server recovers the master key and authenticates itself to the client by returning a message authenticated with the master key. Subsequent data is encrypted and authenticated with keys derived from this master key. In the optional second phase, the server sends a challenge to the client. The client authenticates itself to the server by returning the client's digital signature on the challenge, as well as its public-key certificate.

Essentially, what SSL does is to utilize asymmetric cryptography to establish a secure session between a Web server and a client. First implemented in Netscape, all current leading browser software has this capability built in. A Web site owner obtains a certificate from a recognized secure source (e.g., VeriSign), and loads it into the server-side portion of the SSL software. When a client connects to the Web site, the client-server key exchange sets up a secure communications session.

The sequence of information exchange for SSL is as follows:

1. The client sends the server the client's SSL version number, cipher settings, randomly generated data, and other information the server needs to communicate with the client using SSL.
2. The server sends the client the server's SSL version number, cipher settings, randomly generated data, and other information the client needs to communicate with the server over SSL. The server also sends its own certificate and, if the client is requesting a server resource that requires client authentication, requests the client's certificate.
3. The client uses some of the information sent by the server to authenticate the server (see Server Authentication for details). If the server cannot be authenticated, the user is warned of the problem and informed that an encrypted and authenticated connection cannot be established. If the server can be successfully authenticated, the client goes on to Step 4.
4. Using all data generated in the handshake so far, the client (with the cooperation of the server, depending on the cipher being used) creates the premaster secret for the session, encrypts it with the server's public key (obtained from the server's certificate, sent in Step 2), and sends the encrypted premaster secret to the server.
5. If the server has requested client authentication (an optional step in the handshake), the client also signs another piece of data that is unique to this handshake and known by both the client and server. In

this case the client sends both the signed data and the client's own certificate to the server along with the encrypted premaster secret.

6. If the server has requested client authentication, the server attempts to authenticate the client (see Client Authentication for details). If the client cannot be authenticated, the session is terminated. If the client can be successfully authenticated, the server uses its private key to decrypt the premaster secret, then performs a series of steps (which the client also performs, starting from the same premaster secret) to generate the master secret.

7. Both the client and the server use the master secret to generate the session keys, which are symmetric keys used to encrypt and decrypt information exchanged during the SSL session and to verify its integrity—that is, to detect any changes in the data between the time it was sent and the time it is received over the SSL connection.

8. The client sends a message to the server informing it that future messages from the client will be encrypted with the session key. It then sends a separate (encrypted) message indicating that the client portion of the handshake is finished.

9. The server sends a message to the client informing it that future messages from the server will be encrypted with the session key. It then sends a separate (encrypted) message indicating that the server portion of the handshake is finished.

10. The SSL handshake is now complete, and the SSL session has begun. The client and the server use the session keys to encrypt and decrypt the data they send to each other and to validate its integrity.

SHTTP

Definition   HTTPS or SHTTP is a URL scheme which is syntactically identical to the http: scheme normally used for accessing resources using HTTP. Using an https: URL indicates that HTTP is to be used, but with a different default port and an additional encryption/authentication layer between HTTP and TCP. This system was invented by Netscape Communications Corporation to provide authentication and encrypted communication and is widely used on the Web for security-sensitive communication, such as payment transactions.[13]

Capabilities   Secure HTTP or SHTTP protocol can be used for secure data exchange however, unlike SSL, which creates a secure connection that can be used to exchange a large amount of data; S-HTTP securely exchanges individual messages. Thus, these two protocols are not different names for the same process, but represent different applications of asymmetric key cryptography. S-HTTP is outlined in RFC 2660.

---

13. http://en.wikipedia.org/wiki/HTTPS

Implementation   In order for a Web server to accept https connection, a public key certificate must be created. First implemented in Netscape, all current leading browser software has this capability built in. A Web site owner obtains a certificate from a recognized secure source (e.g., VeriSign), and loads it into the server-side portion of the SSL software. When a client connects to the Web site, the client-server key exchange sets up a secure communications session. RFC 2660 lists implementation recommendations and requirements, these are:[14]

- All S-HTTP agents must support the MD5 message digest and MAC authentication. As of S-HTTP/1.4, all agents must also support the RSA-MD5-HMAC construction.
- All S-HTTP agents must support Outband, Inband, and DH key exchange.
- All agents must support encryption using DES-CBC.
- Agents must support signature generation and verification using NIST-DSS.

IPSEC

Definition   IPsec is a set of cryptographic protocols for (1) securing packet flows and (2) key exchange. Of the former, there are two: Encapsulating Security Payload (ESP) provides authentication, data confidentiality and message integrity; Authentication Header (AH) provides authentication and message integrity, but does not offer confidentiality. Originally AH was only used for integrity and ESP was used only for encryption; authentication functionality was added subsequently to ESP. Currently only one key exchange protocol is defined, the IKE (Internet Key Exchange) protocol.[15]

Capabilities   IPsec was intended to provide either (1) tunnel mode: portal to portal communications security in which security of packet traffic is provided to several machines by a single node, or (2) transport mode: end to end security of packet traffic in which the end point computers do the security processing.[16] IPsec protects IP packets from disclosure or modification. The protocol provides privacy and/or data integrity. Each header contains a security parameter index (SPI) that references a particular encryption key. Additionally, the header may contain up to two security headers — the authentication header (AH), which provides integrity-checking, and the encapsulating security payload (ESP), which encrypts the packet to provide confidentiality.

---

14. http://www.rfc-archive.org/getrfc.php?rfc=2660
15. http://en.wikipedia.org/wiki/IPSEC
16. same as 15.

Implementation   Hosts using IPsec establish a security association with each other, which involves agreement on crypto methods to be used, keys to be used, and the host associated with the SPI. Key management is accomplished with ISAKMP/IKE. The Internet Security Association and Key Management Protocol (ISAKMP) is a key management strategy that has become increasingly prevalent. Pronounced ice-a-camp, it is defined in RFC 2408 as a set of procedures for authenticating a communicating peer, creation and management of Security Associations, key generation techniques, and threat mitigation (e.g., denial of service and replay attacks). All of these are necessary to establish and maintain secure communications (via IP Security Service or any other security protocol) in an Internet environment.

The basic element of ISAKMP key management is the security association (SA). An SA contains all of the information necessary to execute a variety of network security services. ISAKMP acts as a common framework for agreeing to the format of SA attributes, and for negotiating, modifying, and deleting SAs. It uses Diffie–Hellman key exchange signed with RSA.

Sample Questions

1. Digital Signatures provide?
    a. Non-repudiation
    b. Encryption
    c. Privacy
    d. Key escrow

2. Encryption of the same plain text with the same key resulting in the same ciphertext can be prevented by using?
    a. Digital signature
    b. Initialization vector
    c. Cipher feedback
    d. Public key certificate

3. What is a trusted third party that generates public key certificates?
    a. Local Registration Authority
    b. Notarization Authority
    c. Certification Authority
    d. Timestamping Authority

4. Which of the following is currently used in conjunction with most Internet-based certificates to provide continuous authentication?
    a. Secure Multipurpose Internet Mail Extension (S/MIME)
    b. Secure Sockets Layer (SSL)
    c. Secure Shell (SSH)
    d. Secure Electronic Transaction (SET)

5. Encryption ciphers that use the same key to encrypt and decrypt are called?
   a. Asymmetric encryption
   b. Symmetric encryption
   c. Public key encryption
   d. Digital signature encryption

6. A Digital Signature is made with?
   a. A private key from an asymmetric key pair, and includes a hash of the message being signed
   b. A public key from an asymmetric key pair, and includes a hash of the message being signed
   c. A private key from a symmetric key pair, and includes a hash of the message being signed
   d. A public key from a symmetric key pair, and includes a hash of the message being signed

7. What protocol is typically used to login to a remote machine and execute commands?
   a. Secure Sockets Layer (SSL)
   b. Secure Electronic Transaction (SET)
   c. Secure Shell (SSH)
   d. Secure Multipurpose Internet Mail Extension (S/MIME)

8. Rendering information unintelligible to anyone other than those who know the encryption cipher and the proper key is the concept of?
   a. Confidentiality
   b. Integrity
   c. Authentication
   d. Non-repudiation

9. By changing what crypto variable, can one change the output of the cryptographic function, even if the plaintext remains the same.
   a. Hash
   b. Algorithm
   c. Ciphertext
   d. Key

10. What uses a digital signature to bind together a public key with an identity?
    a. Message digest
    b. Identity certificate
    c. Secure Hash Algorithm (SHA)
    d. Digital Signature Standard (DSS)

11. What type of digital signature can be duplicated by anyone who holds that key?
    a. Public key
    b. Asymmetric key
    c. Symmetric key
    d. Ad-hoc key

12. Non-repudiation, or proving that a party originated a message, typically uses what type of key cryptography?
    a. Asymmetric
    b. Symmetric
    c. Private
    d. Password

13. What helps detect forgeries?
    a. Notarization
    b. Initialization vector
    c. Checksum
    d. Hash function

14. Without any knowledge of the key, an opponent with access to an encrypted message and the decryption cipher could try every possible key to decode the message. This is known as?
    a. Cipher block chaining attack
    b. Man in the middle attack
    c. Brute force attack
    d. Birthday attack

15. In IPSEC, what protocol provides authentication and message integrity, but does not offer confidentiality?
    a. Authentication Header (AH)
    b. Encapsulating Security Payload (ESP)
    c. Security Parameter Index (SPI)
    d. Internet Security Association and Key Management Protocol (ISAKMP)

Domain 6
Networks and Telecommunications
Eric Waxvik

Aspects of networks and telecommunications have a large impact on the development of security policy, the audit plan and procedures, how access controls and encryption are implemented, and how to best mitigate the risks of malicious code. How your organization's networks and telecommunications are configured will also affect how you minimize the risks to your network, respond to negative events, and recover from those events.

This chapter provides a brief introduction to networking and data communications and how an IT Security Practitioner can minimize their inherent security risks. The risks may be found in the LAN or WAN environment, in the remote access to the LAN and WAN environment, or in the components that make up these environments.

Introduction to Networks and Telecommunications

This chapter is not intended to be a basic introduction in data communications; rather, we will be looking at all of the elements of a data network to see what security is, or is not, inherently provided (versus just another review of networking basics).

It is important to note that many organizations are pursuing a redundancy scenario for constant communications. More and more, an organization's livelihood rests on these networks and telecommunications, so it is important to know how that redundancy can affect the organization's security posture.

In the past, some of the people who needed their communication lines open all of the time would rather have their firewalls fail *open* and allow all traffic, good and bad, to pass, rather than fail *closed* and not pass any traffic. This decision was based on the companies' risk acceptance policies. In today's communication arena, there are capabilities that are available in which firewalls can fail over from one firewall to another with times ranging from minutes to fractions of a second. There are also load balancing technologies available that spread the load across many firewalls.

High availability and redundancy are not just limited to firewalls; internal and external network connections can also be set up in a redundant capacity. Another important redundancy option is having a completely redundant remote site, so in case of an emergency all of your network functionality and security are already in place. This capacity should be an integral part of your disaster recovery plans.

In this section, we will take a look at the following elements of a data communication network:

- OSI Model
- Network Topology
- Network Devices
- Network Access Methods

The Basic OSI Model: Its Security Strengths and Weaknesses

The International Organization for Standards (ISO) set out to simplify communications by creating standards for networking protocol/hardware and software. The model they created — the Open System Interconnect (OSI) model — is actually a framework from which protocols can be created. Security was not built into the base model, although security recommendations were made for each of the layers. The OSI model defines how communication will work across the network with the intention of ensuring its success.

In reality this model is used mainly as a reference model. While some OSI networks were created, most of today's common protocols are actually built against a different model such as the DOD TCP/IP model or the B-ISDN model. We will look at the TCP/IP model later.

Let us take a quick look at each of the layers of the OSI model. While looking at each layer of the model, be sure to consider its basic job and the security that is inherent at that layer or what can be added to enhance the security of your network.

The layers of the OSI model are:

Application
Presentation
Session
Transport
Network
Data Link
Physical

The OSI model is intended as a representation for how we build and use a network and its resources.

Application Layer

Basic Job: Manages program requests as needed to access a remote system.

Inherent Security: None

Added Security Features: Encryption, Digital Signature, Access Control, Authentication exchange, Traffic Padding, Routing control are all features that the ISO intended as possible add-ons for this layer.

Protocols: FTAM, X.400, Telnet, FTP, SMTP

FTAM — File Transfer and Access Management

FTP — File Transfer Protocol

SMTP — Simple Mail Transfer Protocol

Presentation Layer

Basic Job: Translates data from one format to another if necessary for a system to understand the received text, e.g., ASCII to EBCDIC.

Inherent Security: None

Added Security Features: Encryption and routing control can be added.

Protocols: ASN.1, SSL, and TLS

ASN.1 — Abstract Syntax Notation One

SSL — Secure Socket Layer

TLS — Transport Layer Security

Session Layer

Basic Job: Establishes and maintains connection between the local and remote systems. This layer utilizes TCP/IP ports to coordinate communications between cooperating application processes.

Inherent Security: None

Added Security Features: Logins and passwords can be added at the layer.

Protocols: RADIUS, TACACS

Transport Layer

Basic Job: Provides reliable, transparent data transfers between session entities. Assures end-to-end reliability and integrity through packet sequencing, detecting and correcting errors and by regulating the data flow.

Inherent Security: Data Integrity

Added Security Features: Encryption, digital signature, authentication exchange, access control are all security features that can be added.

Protocols: TCP, UDP

TCP — Transmission Control Protocol

UDP — User Datagram Protocol

Network Layer

Basic Job: Defines network address and segmentation schemes.

Inherent Security: None

Added Security Features: The address provided at this layer can be utilized by routers, switches, etc., to create inclusion or exclusion rules. Encryption, routing control, digital signature, access control, authentication exchange, and traffic padding are all security features that can be added at this layer.

Protocols: X.25, CLNP, IP, ICMP, IGMP

CLNP — Connectionless Network Service

IP — Internet Protocol

ICMP — Internet Control Message Protocol

IGMP — Internet Group Management Protocol

Data Link Layer

Basic Job: Transmits frames across the network links. Utilizes hardware or link layer addresses. This layer can also check data integrity through the use of frame checksums.

Inherent Security: None

Added Security Features: The address provided at this layer can be used by bridges, switches, and the like to create inclusion and exclusion rules. **Encryption and routing control can be added at this layer as well.**

Protocols: Frame Relay, 802.3, 802.2, FDDI, PPP, SMDS, HDLC, SLIP, ARP

FDDI — Fiber Distributed Data Interface

PPP — Point to Point Protocol

SMDS — Switched Multi-megabit Data Service

HDLC —High-level Data Link Control

SLIP — Serial Line Interface Protocol

ARP — Address Resolution Protocol

Physical Layer

Basic Job: Defines physical and electrical specifications for transmissions, e.g., connector, pin-outs, impedance, resistance, and the like.

Inherent Security: None

Added Security Features: Encryption, data integrity, routing control, traffic padding are all security features that can be added at this layer.

Protocols: ATM, SONET, T1, V.35

ATM —Asynchronous Transfer Mode

SONET — Synchronous Optical Network

DOD TCP/IP Model

The DOD TCP/IP protocol model is the basis of most of our LAN technologies today. This protocol stack was created for the Department of Defense, although it has been carried around the world. This model is identical to the ISO OSI model in the lower four layers; the difference is in that layers five through seven (Application, Presentation, and Session) of the OSI model are combined into the application layer (layer 5) in the DOD model.

The layers of the DOD TCP/IP Model are:
Application
Transport
Network
Data Link
Physical

Network Topologies and Their Security Issues

There are a few commonly implemented network topology schemes. Each scheme has its own native security level and security issues. We will take a look at the following network topologies:
- Star
- Bus
- Ring
- Point-to-point

Star Topology   A star topology, also known as a hub and spoke topology, has a device in the center and PCs, servers, and such branch out from there. The center device will have a great deal to do with the transmission characteristics of the star topology. The progression of devices that have been used in center of the star topology has gone from hub and bridges to switches and routers.

A weakness of the standard star topology is that it is a single point of failure. If the device at the center of the star fails, then all communication in the star stops. In a modified star configuration, the device in the center of the star has been set up in a redundant configuration. This redundancy can be load balancing, failover, or hot-swapping the device. The last redundancy option requires human intervention to switch the device from the failed device to the backup device.

The fact that there is one device to protect may be either a potential strength or potential weakness of the star topology. If an intruder can get physical access to this device, they can monitor all communications on your network — an obvious weakness. Monitoring all of the communications does not require physical access to the device at the center of the star if the device is a simple hub. The nature of hubs is to rebroadcast all of the information they receive out to all ports. If an attacker has a device off of one of these ports, all of the information passing through the hub will be sent to him as well. This ability to monitor communications at one central point also benefits the security practitioner. It allows for a single point to monitor activity on the network or a single point to place an Intrusion Detection System (IDS) or an Intrusion Prevention System (IPS).

The modified star or the modified hub and spoke are the more common types of network topologies. In this modification the points of various hubs are interconnected. If all points of all of the hubs are interconnected, this redundant configuration is called *fully meshed*. The fully meshed topology is probably the goal of most network architects. It is the most redundant of all the configurations.

To protect data transmissions from unauthorized viewers, encryption would be a valuable addition to this topology, although it is often considered impractical in most situations today.

Bus Topology Bus topologies have given way to star topologies over the years. The bus topology has the major disadvantage of passing all information down the wire to all connected users. This means that all transmitted traffic by all users is visible to all other users. Cable providers have used this type of bus architecture for their transmission of television signals for years; the result is the use of the same physical infrastructure for their Internet access as well. If you place a packet sniffer on a cable modem connection, you will see all of this data on this shared transmission media. Encryption would be a valuable addition to this topology for that reason, especially when connecting to a head office from a remote office.

Ring Topology A ring topology is similar in nature to the bus topology in that the distribution of information is sent to all users connected to the ring. Two of the most common types of ring topologies are Synchronous Optical Network (SONET) and Token Ring. There have been some developments in this type of architecture with high speed SONET rings. Some types of SONET rings can be self-healing and have some great redundancy features. While Token Ring topology is an older technology, it is still in use today. Some ring topologies have the security disadvantage of not secluding a conversation to the two involved parties. Anyone connected to the ring can view all traffic on the ring. A security benefit can be gained using encryption. Adding encryption would protect the data transmissions from unauthorized viewers but this is often considered impractical in most situations today. In a simple ring configuration, a single break in the link shuts down communication completely. Redundancy can be added by have a second ring.

Point-to-Point Topology A point-to-point connection is the most secure of the aforementioned topologies. Only the sender and receiver are connected to the line. Although this method is still susceptible to eavesdropping, it is harder to listen in on than the shared media methods. While it may be more secure, it is not always fiscally practical to implement this type of topology to multiple remote sites. Again it is also possible to increase the security with the use of encryption and firewalls.

If your overall network security is dependent on this point-to-point connection, you introduce several single points of failure. A backup connection that would failover in case of a disaster would solve this issue. A higher level of redundancy could be achieved by using a link through another provider whose initial connection goes through a different Point of Presence (POP) and runs over a completely different backbone. This higher level solution is often cost prohibitive since most service providers will give you their backup link at a reduced cost. The backup link from the same service provider is also a good solution but not quite as redundant.

WAN Access and Its Security Issues

Access to the outside world always carries security risks. The challenge is to have enough security to guard your network assets and still be able to maintain full functionality. The balance between security and functionality must be outlined by your risk analysis policy.

We will look at the physical access methods that can be used from the home or the remote office to gain access to the corporate network structure. With all of the connections you should have a personal firewall and current anti-virus on all computers that connect to the network directly. For higher speed network access that may support multiple computers, a SOHO-sized firewall may be a better fit. Many of the SOHO-sized firewalls have extra options available, such as high availability, anti-virus scanning capability, wireless access points, or network print servers. While the last two may come with some of the home-based routing solutions, companies that use broadband access may be more concerned with the first two options and with a solution that will serve as a VPN (Virtual Private Network) back to their headquarters.

When dealing with computers that interact in a collision domain, there must be a way for the computers to communicate. A collision domain is like a large courtroom and the people in the courtroom are the computers. In order to understand someone you must take your turn to speak. If two people start talking at the same time, neither one can be understood, and they will have to start again. Usually people wait for some period of time and start talking again if the other person has not started talking already. The same type of collision happens in the world of computers on a network. There are a couple of ways to deal with those conflicts to enable computers to communicate better in a collision domain, such as the Carrier Sense Multiple Access methods described below.

Carrier Sense Multiple Access (CSMA) CSMA is a Media Access protocol that simply makes sure that no one else is transmitting (talking in our example) before sending data. This approach is very basic and therefore prone to problems. If two devices try to broadcast and collide, they will often just try again and again with no intelligent way of solving the problem.

Carrier Sense Multiple Access with Collision Avoidance (CSMA/CA) CSMA/CA is a Media Access Control (MAC) protocol that is designed to make sure no other devices are transmitting on the wire at the same time by transmitting a notification of intent to send and then sending the data. If two intents are transmitted at the same time, the result is the same as CSMA. This has an increased degree of complexity and sophistication that will limit the number of collisions and retransmissions.

Carrier Sense Multiple Access with Collision Detection (CSMA/CD) CSMA/CD is another MAC protocol that is designed to detect the collision and stop the transmission for a random period of time before trying again. One hopes that if the wait times are random, then the likelihood of collision is reduced because transmission will probably not happen at the same time. This protocol is a little more complex and does require more sophisticated hardware to operate than the previous protocols. This protocol is commonly used today.

Carrier Sense Multiple Access with Bitwise Arbitration (CSMA/BA) CSMA/BA is an even more complex protocol in which priorities or identification values are provided. When a collision occurs the device transmitting with the higher priority will be allowed to transmit first. This method is different that CSMA/CD because one can assign higher priorities to critical traffic nodes, without relying on randomness.

Dial-Up Access/Narrowband Access Dial-up access allows a home- or small-office user with a PC and a modem to access the network. The modem bank could be maintained by the Internet Service Provider (ISP) or by the corporate office itself. While this was once seen as an economical, albeit slow, means of connection from the home, newer technologies can be more cost effective.

Anyone who gains access to the corporate phone number computer can call in and connect. If they do not have your phone number, a simple war dialer will eventually find these phone banks. Crackers then post the numbers they have found on Web sites and you will not remain hidden for long. Passwords and encryption can help to control these unwanted connections, and dial-back connections can also add a layer of security. The problem with these dial-back connections is that they are often preset, so users who are traveling may not be able to connect.

Broadband Access   There are several additional WAN access protocols that are commonly found in the Small Office/Home Office (SOHO). These access methods include the most popular xDSL (where x represents the various forms of DSL, to include Asynchronous (ADSL), Synchronous (DSL), etc.), Cable access, ISDN (Integrated Service Digital Network), and PPPoE.

DSL Access   Digital Subscriber Line (DSL) has been a welcome addition to the access family for Internet use. It, along with Cable, has increased overall performance for thousands of home users and small businesses.

DSL access is more secure than Cable access. It has security issues similar to that of a T1 used for a larger corporation in that it is a dedicated connection to the DSL service provider. All data will flow over a Permanent Virtual Circuit (PVC) that is created from the user's home or small office to the Internet. A PVC is a circuit that is always up and available for your use. It is still recommended that you have a firewall to protect all computers connected to the DSL network and a VPN if connecting to a corporate network.

xDSL is a popular method of Internet access from the SOHO. The dedicated/always-on connection provides speeds up to 28 times faster than a 56 kbps modem. The most common xDSL method in use today is ADSL, with some SDSL in use. DSL is a physical layer technology that utilizes existing copper lines and is actually analog, not digital in nature.

Cable Internet Access   Cable access utilizes the co-ax connection provided by the television cable company to access the Internet. As more and more homes are wired for cable TV, Internet access via cable access has surged over the past few years. The speed of Internet access combined with reasonable cost has made this a very attractive connection method. The unfortunate side to this access is that this is a shared media. As more users on your block connect simultaneously, your access speed will decrease.

The other major disadvantage: it is possible for your neighbors to "listen in" on your network connection as all traffic passes by. This is the limitation of the bus topology used in the end user portion of cable networks.

A firewall solution along with a VPN should be used to access any critical resources such as the corporate network or banking information.

ISDN Integrated Service Digital Network (ISDN) was designed by the phone companies to create a method of bringing digital connections all the way down the last mile. The phone network was, for the most part, upgraded to digital a long time ago, but the last mile is still predominately analog.

ISDN does not have any built-in encryption or authentication. This protocol is similar to SLIP in that its job is to send traffic across the interface. There is no security inherent in the ISDN protocol; any desired security would have to be added by some other means.

PPPoE Access When Point-to-Point Protocol over Ethernet (PPPoE) is added to a connection such as DSL, a level of security has been added through the authentication of the user. The user's PC or router must be configured with the correct user name and password to gain access to the Internet. This makes it a little more difficult for someone to steal your access line from you or spoof your connection. This access method is growing as more and more communities are adding "Fiber to the Home" wiring.

VPN Access A VPN creates an authenticated and encrypted channel across a network. The authentication and encryption adds some security to an otherwise insecure network, such as the Internet. There is also some sense of data integrity when using a VPN. If the data cannot be decrypted you know that it is possible that someone attempted to intercept the data and tried to change it. It is very difficult, although not impossible, to hijack a VPN session and take over the session with encryption. This hijacking attempt's greatest chance of success is with a very weak encryption scheme. It is still possible for the connection to be compromised through the end user's computer. If someone gains access to that computer, he will have access to the corporate network. This compromise can be eliminated by not allowing split tunneling on your VPN client (split tunneling is allowing connection to the secure or trusted network at the same time as allowing a connection to a nonsecure or untrusted network). For example, if an individual uses his work laptop from an unsecured home network, a compromise of the laptop in this unprotected home network would be an on-ramp for attackers to connect to the individual's corporate network. This type of attack is a growing trend for crackers because it is easier to find unprotected home computers with little or no monitoring, or other defensive measures in place, than to attack a heavily monitored and defended corporate target. A nontechnical (and also unrealistic) example is as follows: someone wanting to get into a heavily defended fort could try attacking the fort — very difficult if not impossible — or he could attack the armored cars en route that carry all the supplies and daily needs for the fort (also very difficult), or he could go to the public library, get into the truck while it is unprotected, and ride it into the heavily protected fort. In this example, the heavily protected fort is the corporate network, the armored cars are the VPN, and the library represents the unprotected home network. The attacker would choose the easiest way into the network: walking into the armored van.

Network Protocols and Security Characteristics

Network Protocols Introduction

In this section, we will take a look at some of the network layer protocols currently in use, primarily Transport Control Protocol/Internet Protocol (TCP/IP).

A protocol is a standard system used for the transmission of data across a network. A network protocol governs how various pieces of networking equipment interact with one other to deliver data across the network. For example, these protocols are used to manage the transfer of data from a server to a personal computer, from the beginning of the data transfer to the end. The protocol stack is made up of several layers that work together to accomplish the transmission of data.

TCP/IP Overview   TCP/IP is the primary networking protocol in use at this time. TCP/IP is actually a suite of protocols that was developed for the Defense Advanced Research Project Agency (DARPA) to provide a highly available and fault-tolerant network infrastructure. The concentration was on making the network highly reliable, not on making it a secure network.

IP Addressing   One of the primary functions of the network layer protocols is to provide an addressing scheme. The addressing scheme in TCP/IP is found at the Network layer. IP addressing is a four-byte address, whose goal is to uniquely identify every device on the network.

Depending on the manner in which the addressing is implemented or protected, there may be security concerns. If an attacker knows your location and your address, it is much easier for him to break through your security barriers.

Some features to add to your network to protect your IP addressing scheme are NAT (Network Address Translation) and PAT (Port Address Translation). The level of added security is relatively minor and is often considered "security" by obscurity. A better solution would be to implement a firewall solution.

There are two ways addresses are assigned to devices on a network: static assigned addresses and Dynamic Host Configuration Protocol (DHCP). The first method is often used for core pieces of a network infrastructure such as routers, switches, mail servers, and firewalls. DHCP is commonly used within a network to simplify the network configuration of each user's computer. This allows the computer to dynamically get its configuration information from a network device rather than the network administrator, who has to manually enter the configuration information into the computer. DHCP has simplified the configuration job of many network administrators.

DHCP has its own security issues. The DHCP server gives out IP addresses, default gateways, and DNS information freely to anyone who asks. With this information, it is possible for someone to physically connect a device to your network, receive a network configuration, and gain access to your LAN, which could leave computers, servers, and network devices vulnerable. An application for the DHCP address information can be requested through a connection such as a virtual private network (VPN), wireless or direct physical access within your building. A request through the VPN authentication process does add an extra level of security to the process because the user would have to be authenticated before the DHCP request would be forwarded. There are also some available products that require a user to authenticate before any information is pushed down to the user. These devices also record the IP address and at what time it was given. Having users authenticate before assigning addresses also assists in any future forensics investigation or violation of "proper usage policy."

NAT/PAT   Network Address Translation (NAT) and Port Address Translation (PAT) were not designed for security, but their addition to a network can add a small measure of security that would otherwise not exist.

NAT was designed to contend with the ever-shrinking number of available IP addresses. It allows a set of computers to be represented on a public or private network, such as the Internet, as only one IP address. NAT will translate from a hidden internal address to the known external address.

When the network layer address translation of NAT is combined with TCP port number translation, you arrive at PAT. Due to the method of translation that is found with PAT, the added security is greater.

Other technologies that can be employed by network devices for security purposes are:

- NAT
- PAT
- Packet Filtering and Access Control Lists

As mentioned above, while NAT was implemented initially to compensate for our growing limitation of IP addresses, today it also provides security by hiding the true IP address of a device. A computer will send a request bound for outside the network, and the device used for NATing the connection will translate the IP address from the internal/real address to another IP address, usually that of the external interface of the device used for NATing. The device can also assign an address from an external pool of addresses, to which the device will respond when the Address Resolution Protocol (ARP) request is issued. The device then logs the location from which the connection is coming and where it is going. When the return packet is sent back, the device compares the new source to its table, then redirects the packet to the real internal address. The security features provided by NAT are usually considered security by obscurity, but they will significantly reduce your threat from less skilled crackers.

Port Address Translation (PAT) increases the security by also monitoring the port numbers used.

ICMP Internet Control Message Protocol (ICMP) is a management and control protocol for IP. ICMP has the responsibility of delivering messages between hosts regarding the health of the network.

ICMP messages carry information regarding the accessibility of hosts in addition to routing information and updates. PING and Traceroute utilize ICMP messages to carry their information.

ICMP can be an open door for some would-be attackers, and you should consider how you use ICMP, the roles it plays in your network management schema, and how it traverses your network. Controlling how ICMP flows in and out of your network will reduce the amount of information that can be used against you.

ICMP can be used to create a Denial of Service attack against a network. One example of this type of attack is known as a Smurf attack. The attack works by sending spoofed ICMP echo requests to a broadcast address on a network, hoping that the hosts on that network will all respond. If enough replies are sent, it is possible to bring down a T1 from an attack that was launched from a dial-up connection.

SMTP Simple Mail Transfer Protocol (SMTP) is used to send and receive e-mail. SMTP is used to control how two mail servers interact and the type of controls they use to transfer mail.

E-mail is one of the most commonly used services on the Internet today, and as a result, SMTP servers have been the largest target of crackers. Most sites may not have a Web server but they usually have a mail server. Because the protocol and the mail handling software have been so heavily scrutinized, many programming bugs and security vulnerabilities have been found. The following security risks may leave your organization vulnerable to several different types of attacks:

- The mail server's underlying operating system is vulnerable to "buffer overflows" and similar types of attacks. The most severe effects of these attacks will leave the cracker with the highest level permissions and in complete control of the mail server. With that control the attacker could read all of the mail that is stored or passing through the mail server. The attacker could also use the mail server as a launching point to assail the rest of your network.

- For convenience, roaming users forward confidential business e-mail to public mail servers like Hotmail or Yahoo.
- Common viruses are propagated as e-mail attachments.
- Hackers can send executable Trojans disguised as legitimate e-mail attachments, e.g., "Nimda."
- E-mail travels in the clear, unless encryption is used, which may result in organizational sensitive information being exposed.
- The network administrator fails to install important security patches. This can easily happen due to the large number of patches and difficulty of installation, especially if multiple servers are involved.
- Hackers can target your server with SYN floods or other network level attacks.
- Hackers can flood your mail server with huge messages to exhaust resources.
- Default installation of some mail handling software results in an insecure installation.
- It is easy to spoof (pretend to be someone else) e-mail due to the open architecture and origins.

One security recommendation is to put your Mail Transfer Agent (MTA) in a DMZ. If the MTA is compromised, then the attacker will only have access to the DMZ, not your entire internal network. There are hardened security appliances that will act as an MTA, severely limiting the likelihood of a compromise. Some of these appliances will also block unauthorized e-mail content, spam, viruses and other malicious code.

TFTP   Trivial File Transfer Protocol (TFTP) is a simplified File Transfer Protocol (FTP). TFTP does not have any authentication or encryption capabilities. This lack of authentication and encryption leaves TFTP as a very insecure protocol.

A network administrator commonly uses TFTP inside a network to allow easy configuration of the network devices, and as a result, TFTP can be an open door into your network devices.

TFTP is used by network users to transfer files to and from a common, shared file server. TFTP servers are set up with anonymous logins, allowing anyone to connect and view the stored files. Depending on the server's mission and the files stored on the server, serious security concerns may arise from the use of a TFTP server on a corporate network. TFTP capabilities should be turned off on all networking devices unless it is necessary to have them enabled.

Syslog   The syslog of a router/firewall can provide valuable information as to how your network is working, as well as who is accessing the network, when, and how. If the syslog is maintained on the router itself, there may be space constraints. Redirecting the syslog to display on another device in the network can alleviate this problem.

One of the most critical elements of having a syslog is the periodic review of the information it contains. This may not be the most exciting part of a system administrator's job, but it is nonetheless an important one.

Syslog's protocol has been known to have its own security problems, as when its messages are unauthenticated and there is no mechanism to provide verified delivery and message integrity. If your security device is sending the syslog messages, this also presents a problem: since syslog messages are sent clear text, an attacker or anyone else on the network can see the content of the logs. Therefore, what your security system does or does not capture should not be sent in the clear.

Network Level Security

Now that we have taken a look at some of the networking protocols that are responsible for delivery or maintenance of information across the network, let us take a look at the security capabilities of this level.

As a general rule of thumb, there is not much security to be found at the network layer. One element that has been added to alleviate this problem is encryption. Encryption has traditionally been done at the Presentation layer, but in the interest of system compatibility and speed, several network layer encryption methods have been invented. The most predominate network layer method at this time is IPSec.

IPSec IPSec provides the following security services: data origin authentication, replay protection, data confidentiality, limited traffic flow confidentiality, and key negotiation and management.

IPSec has two methods for security: Authentication Header (AH) and Encapsulated Security Payload (ESP). AH integrity authenticates only the payload, whereas ESP confidentiality authenticates and encrypts the payload. Therefore, ESP is considered a more secure option.

AH protocol uses a key-hashed function to ensure the integrity of a packet and provide data origin authentication. This is done by passing a portion of the packet through a hashing algorithm, which generates a message authentication code value and can be checked by the receiving device.

ESP works in a similar fashion to AH but it also adds on the encryption of the packet.

IPSec also has two functional modes: tunnel and transport. Transport mode only protects the data payload, whereas tunnel mode protects the headers as well as the payload.

One of the drawbacks to IPSec is that it could be incompatible with NAT. Many of the devices that NAT allow for IPSEC traffic to pass through them. The feature of allowing the IPSEC packet to be transmitted through the device is called IPSEC pass-through.

PPP/SLIP Point-to-Point Protocol (PPP) and Serial Line Internet Protocol (SLIP) are two protocols that are used over a serial line such as DSL, dedicated circuit, or a serial line between two routers. Both PPP and SLIP are considered data link layer protocols. SLIP will only carry a single protocol (i.e., TCP/IP), whereas PPP can carry multiple protocols at the same time on the same connection (i.e., TCP/IP, Appletalk, IPX).

SLIP is the older of the two and is used to encapsulate data for transmission across the line. This unfortunately is about the extent of this protocol: it follows along with the link layer's basic job. SLIP delivers data across the link.

PPP is the more commonly used protocol of the two. It takes the basic function of SLIP and adds:

- Header and data compression for efficiency and better use of bandwidth
- Error detection and correction
- Support of different authentication methods
- Encapsulation of protocols other than IP

PAP Password Authentication Protocol (PAP) is an authentication protocol used to identify a remote user before allowing access to a network. The method of authentication requires a user to enter a username and password for authentication purposes.

The unfortunate side to PAP is that the username and password are sent as clear text across the network, rendering this a very insecure method of authentication. The username and password are also static, allowing replay attacks or spoofing to occur.

CHAP Challenge Handshake Authentication Protocol (CHAP) is a little more secure than PAP as an authentication method. CHAP uses a challenge/response mechanism to authenticate users. This replaces the sending of a password over the network.

CHAP uses a random value challenge, which is encrypted for transfer across the network. The predefined password at the user's station is used as the encryption key and is then able to reply to the challenge.

CHAP is not as susceptible to man-in-the-middle or replay attacks because the challenge or response process is repeated several times over the life of the connection.

Some things to watch out for in your configuration of CHAP authentication: some systems will fail back to PAP in the event of a CHAP authentication failure and the passwords must be stored in clear text on the machines. In a Microsoft environment, you can use MS-CHAP. MS-CHAP is an extension to the current RFC in which the passwords are not required to be stored clear text.

EAP Extensible Authentication Protocol is a recently standardized protocol from the IETF (RFC 2284). Because it is so new, its use is still limited. Unlike PAP and CHAP, it provides the facilities to create a more flexible, general purpose authentication protocol, and it can be extended as new authentication methods become available. For example, EAP is the first PPP authentication protocol to provide a standard way to support digital certificates.

The following steps are part of the authentication process using EAP:

1. Client connects to the Network Access Server and sets up a PPP link.
2. The server asks for the userid.
3. The server sends one or more challenges, including a nonce.
4. The client sends the userid in reply to the request in step 2.
5. The client sends a response to each of the challenges, using whichever authentication type the NAS requested. If using simple passwords, the challenge is for an MD5 hash of the password and the nonce, much like CHAP.
6. The server checks the credentials and either allows the connection or indicates failure.

There is replay protection because of the nonce.

Wide Area Network Protocols

Whenever you connect your network to networks other than your own, you open the possibility that someone will take advantage of that connection. Most often, organizations have their networks connected to the Internet to conduct day-to-day operations. These operations may include a Web site/"public presence" or opportunity to exchange e-mail with customers and partners. Organizations can also take advantage of what the Internet offers, namely, the opportunity to connect to remote sites without paying for the long-haul costs. The caveat is that any access to the outside world can open your doors to an intruder. We are going to take a look at a few of the protocols used for these connections to see what level of security they add to the connection on their own.

Integrated Services Digital Network (ISDN) Integrated Services Digital Network is a type of circuit switched telephone system that provides multiple types of data over a single circuit. (i.e., voice, data, video). This system and the protocols involved are designed to use the same copper wires that were previously used in the Plain Old Telephone System (POTS) to transmit the traffic digitally instead of via the old analog method. Transmitting digitally usually results in increased throughput and quality.

Digital Subscriber Lines (DSL)   DSL is technology that provides for increased data over the normal telephone copper wires. The speed of the data is based on the technology, the gauge of the wire and the distance the wire is run from the Central Office, taps loops and other interference. Data throughput rates are usually higher than with ISDN. There are many types of DSL, including:

> Asymmetrical DSL (ADSL) — Traffic is downloaded faster than it is uploaded (used more for personal connections).
> Symmetrical DSL (SDSL) — Traffic is the same speed in both directions (used more for businesses).
> High data rate DSL (HDSL) — Capable of handling higher speeds of traffic but uses multiple phone lines instead of just one.
> Symmetric High bit rate DSL (SHDSL) — Symmetric traffic handling using only one set of twisted pair.

T-Carriers (T1, T3)   T-Carriers are signaling schemes that were originally designed by Bell Labs. A T1 can also be called a Digital Signal 1 (DS1), as the terms are often used interchangeably. The T1 actually refers to the physical piece and the DS1 actually refers to the data riding over that physical connection. A T1 circuit consists of 24 8bit channels that can handle 1.544 Mbits per second. A T3 is a circuit that consists of 28 T1s or 642 channels to create a connection that can handle 44.5 Mbits per second. In Europe the coding is slightly different and their circuits are labeled using the E designation; an E1 has 32 channels and an ability to handle 2.048 Mbits per second, and an E3 has 512 channels with the ability to handle 34.268 Mbits per second of traffic.

Optical Carriers (OC-x)   Optical Carriers are usually used to describe the levels or categories of bandwidth on a Synchronous Optical Network (SONET) network. As a general rule, to calculate the bandwidth an OC carrier can handle, one can use the x from the OC-x and multiply it by 51.8 Mbits per second. An OC-1 would therefore be capable of handling 51.8 Mbits per second. An OC-3 would be approximately three times as fast.

SDLC/HDLC   Synchronous Data-Link Control (SDLC) and High-level Data-Link Control (HDLC) are two more data link layer protocols that are used to send data across a serial link. IBM designed SDLC. HDLC was the International Organization for Standards' (ISO) revision and standardization of the SDLC protocol. SDLC is used primarily in a mainframe environment or a point-to-point WAN connection with IBM equipment. HDLC is more commonly used than SDLC.

There is no authentication or encryption with HDLC. In fact, HDLC does not even include information regarding the type of network layer traffic it is carrying.

Frame Relay   Frame Relay is one of the most predominate WAN protocols in use today. Frame Relay is a link layer protocol that delivers traffic from one link to the next, spanning the entire Frame Relay network. Frame Relay was developed to replace the old X.25 network standard.

X.25 had the disadvantage of being designed for low-quality network connections, so it spent a lot of time checking and rechecking the user's traffic for errors. In the process of building a replacement for the slow X.25, the decision was made to remove all unnecessary functions from Frame Relay, essentially leaving them to the upper layer protocols.

Frame Relay does not include any authentication or encryption. The one advantage of Frame Relay is its use of Permanent Virtual Circuits (PVC). PVCs make it very difficult for someone to "connect" to your system through the Frame Relay network. Mistakes have happened at service providers' routers and nothing is guaranteed 100 percent, so it is always safer to have firewalls protect the network segment and VPNs encrypt any data running across them.

ATM   Asynchronous Transfer Mode (ATM) was designed to replace Frame Relay. ATM is being used in the LAN for desktop connectivity. Again, in the design, ATM was scaled down to make it an even faster data transfer protocol. For this reason there are no authentication or encryption methods included in ATM.

At this time, most connections and networks are designed for Permanent Virtual Circuits (PVC), although ATM can and does support Switched Virtual Circuits (SVC). A PVC requires configuration on all routers and switches that the connection traverses. An SVC is created dynamically when an edge device such as a router places a call across the ATM network. In order to place a call, the edge device must know the address of the destination that it is trying to reach. The addressing system that is used in ATM is called the ATM End Station Address (AESA). The AESA was created based on the Network Service Access Point (NSAP) address system from OSI. Due to the static and manual configuration of a PVC, it is a more secure type of connection on an ATM network.

Transport Layer Security Protocols

Out of concern for our financial information, several secure protocols have been created to transmit banking and financial information across a network. These protocols can be used to secure any information being sent but are most commonly used for online banking and online purchases today.

SSL The Secure Socket Layer (SSL) is another option for providing security that is often associated with HTTP browsers, although SSL can be used for telnet, FTP, or anything else. SSL operates at the Session layer, just above the Transport layer. SSL was originally published by Netscape to allow applications to have authenticated, encrypted communications across a nontrusted network.

SSL encrypts all data to be transported using one of a variety of encryption algorithms. SSL uses digital certificates to authenticate systems and distribute encryption keys. SSL provides RSA encryption using public/private key encryption. System authentication can be done in a one-way format, to verify you have reached the correct destination, or as mutual authentication (which is rare).

If a user logs onto a Web site using SSL, say for online banking, the following steps are needed to be followed to create a secure session:

1. The client establishes communication with a server.
2. The server sends the client a certificate to authenticate itself.
3. The client checks the trustworthiness of the server's certificate.
4. The client uses the certificate authority's public key to verify the server's digital signature.
5. The client computes a message digest of the certificate to compare to the message digest of the certificate to verify integrity.
6. The client checks validity dates and the URL in the certificate.
7. The client extracts the server's public key.
8. The client creates a session key.
9. The session key is encrypted with the server's public key and is then sent to the server.
10. The server decrypts the session key.
11. Secure communication has been established between the client and the server.

The Internet Engineering Task Force (IETF) has taken SSL and created Transport Layer Security (TLS). TLS is backward-compatible with SSL.

SET Secure Electronic Transmission (SET) was created as a form of protection against fraud. SET was created by Visa and MasterCard as a method of securing credit card transactions by using a public key infrastructure.

SET has not yet gained a lot of acceptance. Both the users and the companies they are communicating with must load special software for SET communications. This is complicated more by the financial institutions' need to buy more hardware and coordinate the effort with their customers.

SET takes a customer's entered credit card information and sends it in encrypted format to a merchant's Web server. The merchant's Web server forwards the encrypted information to a payment gateway with their own digital signature attached. The payment gateway sends this information on to the merchant's bank. The merchant's bank then checks with the issuer of the credit card to see if the necessary funds are in that account and available for this purchase. Once confirmed, the message goes back to the merchant, and the transaction is complete. Using this technology both the customer and the merchant are authenticated and there is no repudiation about the payment. This technology could reduce the amount of fraud and theft for electronic transactions over the Internet although newer technology like 3-D Secure from VISA will probably replace it.

Application Layer Security

Application Layer security such as Secure Multipurpose Internet Mail Extensions (S/MIME), Privacy-Enhanced Mail (PEM), Public Key Infrastructure (PKI), Pretty Good Privacy (PGP), and Message Security Protocol (MSP) were designed to add security to the application itself rather than relying on some lower layer protocol to secure network transmissions. Since e-mail is so widely used to transmit all kinds of traffic across the Internet, these protocols were developed to protect our traffic from attackers.

The basic steps that the sender must take with these protocols are:

1. Calculate message digest on the e-mail message.
2. Use the session key to encrypt the e-mail message.
3. Use a private key (digital signature) to encrypt the message digest.
4. Use the receiver's public key to encrypt the session key.

The basic steps for the receiver are:

1. Use the receiver's private key to decrypt the session key.
2. Use the sender's public key to decrypt the message digest.
3. Use the session key to decrypt the message.
4. Recalculate the message digest and compare the senders for authentication.

S/MIME   Secure/Multipurpose Internet Mail Extensions (S/MIME) is a specification for secure e-mail transmission. MIME was created to allow e-mail users to attach binary messages to their e-mails in a standardized method. S/MIME is the security extension to MIME.

Cryptographic Security services were added to MIME to create S/MIME. The standardization provides interoperability for e-mail clients from a variety of vendors.

The following are components used within the S/MIME standard to ensure authentication, non-repudiation, message integrity, and confidentiality:

- DES, 3DES, or RC4 for content encryption

- MD5 or SHA-1 for data integrity
- DSA or RSA for digital signatures
- Diffie–Hillman or RSA for symmetric key encryption
- X.509 for public key certificates

PEM   Privacy-Enhanced Mail (PEM) is defined in RFC 1421, 1422, 1423 and 1424. PEM is rarely used because of its use of a proprietary form of RSA encryption. PEM is designed to provide authentication, message integrity, encryption and key management. PEM operates in a hierarchical trust model, meaning all users and resources trust one entity. Through association everyone is able to trust each other.

The following are components used within the PEM to ensure authentication, non-repudiation, message integrity, and confidentiality:

- 3DES-CBC for content encryption
- MD2/5 for data integrity
- RSA for sender authenticity, key management, and non-repudiation

Pretty Good Privacy (PGP), written by Phil Zimmerman, is an example of a public key/private key algorithm. While originally freeware, PGP has also branched off into a commercial product.

Message Security Protocol (MSP) is the military's version of PEM and was developed by NASA.

Data Communications and Network Infrastructure Components and Security Characteristics

Introduction

We are now going to take a look at data communications and network infrastructure components and their security characteristics. In order to secure your corporate resources from an attacker, it is necessary to first look at the network, its components, their functions, configurations, and their security limitations and capabilities.

We will discover in this section that there may be much vulnerability in a network environment. The inherent security of our data communications and network infrastructure is only the first step in the process of securing our corporate resources. In order to complete this process, we must know where our network is vulnerable and take the steps necessary to prepare our defense against attacks.

Physical Transmission Medias

Infrastructure is defined as the "underlying foundation or basic framework" in the Merriam–Webster dictionary. The key to network infrastructure is the wiring and cabling plant. There are several different types of cables, wires, and wireless network connections that are used in networks today. The type of cabling used in any given section of the network depends on the environmental requirements.

Local area networks (LANs) typically use one of three types of cabling: co-ax, unshielded twisted pair (UTP), or fiber. Recently, there has been the addition of wireless to the LAN connectivity options.

Different Transmission Medias

The Security Limitations of Physical Media We seldom look at our physical media as lending itself to being a cause of insecurity of our networks, but it may be. Each of the physical media types that we use has its own level of security or insecurity. For example, digital communication has a very predictable method of transmission. Certain combinations of pulses represent certain transmitted characters. One could take advantage of the predictability of digital communication, depending on the type of physical media selected for your network.

It is recommended that you protect your network cable. This includes the cable itself as well as unused connectors. Any intruder who can gain access to your network cables or a network port can cause a great deal of damage by either gaining access to your network or by disabling the network by cutting cables. Something to consider in this decision is how easy is it for someone to walk into your building, or do damage if already inside.

For a high-security site, you may need to seal the cable conduits.

Coaxial Cable Thin-net or 10Base-2 networks use co-ax cabling with T-connectors to interconnect networking devices. Thick-net or 10Base-5 networks use co-ax cable with vampire tape and AUI transceivers to interconnect networking devices. Co-ax networks are connected in a bus configuration. A resister (terminator) is placed at each end of the bus to stop the signal once it has passed the entire length of the connected cables. Due to the bus configuration, a single point of failure anywhere along the length of the cable will stop all communication on the network. The difficulty of locating and repairing a single point of failure renders this type network difficult to manage and troubleshoot.

When using an electrical circuit running over media such as CAT5 or coax, the electrical pulses used to transmit characters exposes your network to a potential security problem: electromagnetic interference (EMI).

Sophisticated monitoring devices can detect the EMI radiation from electrical circuits. This radiation can be converted into the actual transmitted characters by these monitoring devices. It is also very easy to tap into a co-ax cable undetected.

UTP   Unshielded twisted pair (UTP) is the most common cabling type in use for today's networks. UTP is used for 10Base-T and 100Base-TX networks. The cabling specification for UTP is Category 3, 4, 5, 5E, 6, and 7. The category of wire is determined by the number of wires, the number of twists in the wires, and the signal quality capability of the cable. The most widely used cable is Category 5. Because UTP is not shielded, as the name states, it is very susceptible to outside electromagnetic interference such as florescent lights. UTP is configured in a star topology, resulting in a much easier- to-diagnose network.

Fiber Optic   Fiber Optic cable is predominately used for backbone and network device interconnectivity. It consists of three layers: the inside core fiber, the surrounding cladding, and the outside buffer. The core fiber is used for light transmission, while the cladding reflects the light back in that tries to leave the core. The outside buffer or coating is usually made of PVC or plenum and is either in direct contact with the cladding or is separated with a layer of gel. Single Mode Fiber Optic cable is made of a cylindrical glass thread center core wrapped in cladding that protects the central core. This is encapsulated in a jacket of tough KEVLAR®, and then the entire cable is sheathed in PVC or Plenum.

Multimode fiber optic cable is made of a plastic core wrapped in cladding. This is encapsulated in a jacket of tough KEVLAR and then the entire cable is sheathed in PVC or Plenum. Fiber optic cable transmits light rather than electricity. Due to the light transmission, there is no EMI radiation with fiber-optics and no susceptibility to the same kind of monitoring as electrical circuits. Single mode fiber uses laser as the light source, whereas multimode fiber uses LED as a light source. Fiber optic cable is more delicate than UTP or co-ax and is more expensive, although the cost has dropped significantly over the last several years. The maximum transmission capability of fiber has not been reached at this time, but is at least well into the terabits per second.

Wireless   Wireless networks are quickly becoming a common way to connect network devices. This is especially true in homes and small offices (SOHO). Most commonly, wireless networks use radio transmissions for data transfer. There are several standards available at this time with more to come (e.g., 802.11a, 802.11b, 802.11g, and Bluetooth). With wireless networks, one of the most critical considerations at this time is to be certain that all equipment you buy is compatible.

Wireless transmissions are not constrained by any formal boundaries so the atmospheric medium is referred to as an unbound medium. Unbound transmissions are more susceptible to interception and monitoring. Different wireless transmissions include:

- Light transmissions

- Radio waves
  — Fixed frequency signals
  — Spread spectrum signals

Inherent Security Vulnerabilities   There are inherent security vulnerabilities with all types of cabling. As we compare the different technologies, we'll see that the severity of the risk is significantly different depending on the technology.

Coaxial cable is the least-used of the media in a LAN environment. Thin-net and Thick-net have given way to UTP, fiber-optic, and now wireless. Possibly the most susceptible part of co-ax would be a denial of service attack. It is so easy to cause a link failure on a co-ax network, resulting in a downed network that can take tremendous effort to troubleshoot.

UTP is now the most commonly used cable, though it is susceptible to eavesdropping. There are devices available that allow an attacker to listen in on the traffic being transmitted across the line. Another problem with UTP is a physical security issue — any person with a laptop and a cable can easily gain access to the network.

Fiber optic is the most secure of the transmission methods. First, fiber optic cable is not as easily susceptible to eavesdropping because the light does not escape the cladding or the outside buffer. Second, just about all attempts to cut through the cladding or buffer will result in too much bleed off of the light, and the link signal will fail. Third, a splitter could be inserted at one end of the fiber so a listening device could be attached, but to insert the splitter's require the fiber to be unplugged from one of the networking devices, and this will cause a link failure. In a point-to-point, ring, or self-healing ring environment, the connected devices may be affected by the link failure but the attachment of the splitter would be a quick process, and the link will be back up. Such a short break in the availability of a link will not usually result in a physical inspection of the circuit. Unless the circuit is examined physically, the insertion of the splitter and listening device would probably never be discovered. If the networking devices are under lock and key, this is an even more difficult, but possible, attack to achieve. There are other devices coming about today that make it possible to intercept the traffic over a fiber cable without splicing or causing bleed off.

Wireless transmission is the least secure of the transmission methods. It is very difficult to control the direction and distance that the wireless signal will travel. This makes it very difficult to keep the signal away from any area that an attacker may enter. A safeguard to implement would be to secure the transmission using encryption, but the IEEE standard for encryption is susceptible to cracking. The use of a private encryption method and VPNs can create a more secure wireless signal.

Wiring and Communication Closets and Data Centers Physical security may be the most critical element of the security plan when the communication closets, data centers, and wiring are considered. As discussed on the previous page, the wiring used in our networks today is susceptible only when an attacker gains access to the wires themselves or comes within the signal range of a wireless network.

Communication closets have a similar physical security risk. If an attacker gains access to the closet, the potential damage to a corporate network or the corporate resources is enormous. One often-forgotten element to a wiring closet is that lone modem-connected router used by the IT professional for connection and management purposes. An attacker doing war dialing may encounter this modem and possibly use this unprotected or poorly protected access to gain entry to the rest of the corporate network and its resources.

Data Centers are the same — if an attacker is able to walk around inside of the data center, all corporate resources are at risk.

The Enterprise Network Environment and Its Vulnerabilities

There is a common network scenario that exists within most enterprise environments. The types of equipment that are normally used are hubs, switches, and routers. These devices are usually connected in a star configuration utilizing the Ethernet protocol. When connecting computers together, whether it is two or two hundred, those connected computers are called a Local Area Network (LAN). The local area network (LAN) is essential to our corporate environment as well as our homes at this point. The equipment and its topological configuration, as well as the protocols we place on top of them, have a great impact on the vulnerability of our network. LANs can spread across a wide area of a campus environment and are not generally limited to certain-size geographic space. When a network grows to encompass a city, it is usually called a Metropolitan Area Network (MAN). A network that encompasses many LANs in different cities and countries is called a Wide Area Network (WAN).

Local Area Networking Earlier, we took a look at some of the protocols and topologies in use on the network. Now let us take a look at the equipment we use in the LAN.

Hubs

Basic Job: A hub is the center device in a star configuration. It is used to join media connections. Once the hub is connected, it will essentially act as a repeater to take in traffic from one port and forward it out all other ports.

Inherent Security: None

Added Security Features: None

Security Risks: Anyone who can connect to one of the attached cables will be able to see all of the traffic on that segment of the network. Also anyone can plug in to any one of the empty ports on a hub and see all of the traffic that passes through that hub.

Bridges

Basic Job: A bridge will connect multiple network segments. The bridge will then listen to all network traffic that passes through it and build its bridging table based on the port through which the traffic arrived. The bridge table will contain the MAC addresses of all attached devices that are active. Bridges are mostly a waning technology, being replaced by switches.

Inherent Security: A bridge selectively forwards traffic to the correct destination.

Added Security Features: None

Security Risks: Broadcast traffic is still forwarded to all attached devices.

Switches

There are two layers at which switches can operate: Layer 2 and Layer 3.

Layer 2 Switch

Layer 2 switches are a wonderful way to increase the transmission speed of a LAN. The networking device used to connect PCs, servers, and printers is changed from a hub or bridge to a Layer 2 switch. Instead of processing the transmitted frame completely, the switch will read the least amount of information necessary to be able to send the frame on to its destination. Since a switch has a much higher throughput than a bridge, implementing switches throughout our network can increase the transmission speed of frames across the LAN.

Layer 3 Switch

The Layer 3 switch is used to increase the transmission speeds between network segments. The Layer 3 switch will act as a router by reading the network layer address information and then sending the frame on to the correct destination. In fact, the Layer 3 switch is often incorporated into a router, which increases the throughput capabilities of the router by reducing the amount of processing required per frame. A Layer 3 switch also has the capability of falling back to Layer 2 switch mode when necessary.

Basic Job: The switch will monitor each of the network interfaces and thereby learn the MAC addresses of all attached devices. The traffic that is destined for a device attached to that interface will be sent out that interface only.

Inherent Security: Traffic is only sent to the intended destination.

Added Security Features: Some "smart" or managed switches have the ability to shut off nonused ports.

Security Risks: A switch port can be configured as a monitoring port and hear all traffic that passes through the switch. It is also possible to cause the switch to dump its MAC address table and fail to an open configuration, similar to a hub.

Access Points

Basic Job: An Access Point acts as a bridge for a wireless network between the wireless connected computer and the other devices whether they are wired or wireless.

Inherent Security: Most access points have little to no security, but some have firewalls integrated into the device.

Added Security Features: Station Set IDs (SSID), Wired Equivalency Privacy (WEP). While these methods are weak, they do provide some protection.

Security Risks: This uses an unbound medium so it is possible for anyone in the area to listen in on the traffic.

Routers

Basic Job: A Router handles traffic in from multiple ports and then forwards the traffic out based on the network layer protocol and address. A port on a router could be dedicated to a single device, shared through the use of a switch or hub or connected to another router.

Inherent Security: Broadcast traffic can be blocked.

Added Security Features: Packet filtering, stateful firewall features, Network Address Translation (NAT), Virtual Private Network (VPN) support

Security Risks: Dynamic Routing

Firewalls

Basic Job: Enforce an access control policy at the access points of a network.

Inherent Security: Stateful Firewalling, static packet filtering, dynamic packet filtering, proxy, dynamic content inspection

Added Security Features: Some of the new firewalls can serve as Intrusion Detection Systems (IDS), Intrusion Prevention Systems (IPS), and anti-virus.

Security Risks: Improper installation or misconfiguration

VPN Termination Points   Virtual Private Networks (VPNs) are a good way to increase the security of data that is transmitted across the public data network. Using a VPN for remote network access provides a cost-effective security solution, especially compared to the cost of a dedicated connection between the same two sites. Using a VPN over an already-in-place broadband connection could also provide substantial savings when compared to the cost of a modem bank and the dial-up, long distance, or toll free charges. Many hotels and airport hotspots have connection points that could be used for a VPN.

The security added by the VPN can vary, depending on the configuration of the tunnel and the encryption level that is used. It is also important to have a strong authentication mechanism in place to make sure that the appropriate people are using the network.

One major disadvantage with a VPN is that it requires the use of your gateway equipment processing cycles to handle the encryption algorithms. This increased utilization can be off-loaded to another device through the use of another VPN endpoint rather than terminating the VPN on your router or firewall. The increased utilization may not be a factor if the firewall is designed to be a VPN as well and this capability is built into the product. Consult the manufacturers for more specifications on their products.

One other security consideration is the level of security on an end user's PC. Many security companies allow you to package their VPN software for remote users so they will not be able to have split tunneling available while connected over the VPN. Split tunneling — connecting to the outside world while also connected to another network (most commonly the Internet) — is a practice that should be avoided if your firewall/VPN software is not set up to handle the risks properly. The risks of not properly handling split tunneling include allowing a Trojan horse that is installed on the end user's computer to act as an ingress point into your network once your VPN has been established. A prior action, such as a previously installed Trojan horse, is not the only worry for split tunneling; a cracker could compromise your end users' computers while they are connected to the corporate network and take advantage of that tunnel.

Compromising a network is also possible via split tunneling when a computer that is connected to a LAN or a broadband connection is dialed up to the corporate network. Having a host-based firewall or a network-based firewall and a current anti-virus solution would greatly minimize the risks of this potential vulnerability, especially when your network-based firewall acts as the VPN termination point.

Routers and Routing Protocols   Static routing, dynamic routing, and most commonly a combination of both routing methods are used in routers.

Static routing requires a network administrator to have the knowledge of the other IP networks, how to reach them and the backup means of reaching them to correctly configure the router. Dynamic routing allows for the routers to update the path on which traffic flows. These updates could redirect traffic around bottlenecks or link outages, allowing for the data to flow seamlessly.

If your router is not carefully controlled, all of your routing information could be sent back to an attacker or false routing information could be sent from the attacker to a corporate router. Getting the information from your routers would help the attacker map your network and enable him to better target segments for future compromise. False routing information that is injected into a router could create a black hole. A black hole is a way for routers to exclude/drop information that the administrator has deemed it should not forward. This exclusion could be to prevent routing loops, or to prevent other networks from using your network as a cheaper shortcut. If the router were misconfigured or intentionally changed by an attacker, the router could black hole all traffic that is passed to it, causing a denial of service (DOS) attack.

Another means of causing a denial of service can be through false route injection. This DOS can also be caused through a carefully crafted update of a dynamic protocol. The false update would be used to send traffic away from the intended recipient and possibly flood some other network. The routing protocol used should also be carefully considered. Some routing protocols have the ability to use route authentication, which requires a secret password to be configured on a router. These routing protocols include RIPv2, OSPF, EIGRP, and BGP. It should be noted that RIPv1 and IGRP do not support route authentication.

Care should be taken to control dynamic routing updates on each router link. Access Control Lists (ACL) can also be used as a security defense. For example, an ACL can configure a router interface with the range of allowed or disallowed IP routing information.

Router Placement   The placement of a router within the network architecture is critical since there are two basic locations of a router: as a border router and as an internal router.

A border router is directly subject to attack from an outside source. In planning the configuration of the router, it should be determined if the router is the lone defense or acts in conjunction with another device such as a firewall. The lone defense router can protect internal resources but is subject to attack itself. It is not normally recommended that you have a router as a lone defense, but instead use a defense in-depth technique where some of the harmful traffic can be dropped by the router and a finer in-depth look at the packets can be handled by a firewall. If an organization can only afford one device, then serious consideration should be given to a firewall appliance that has built-in routing functionality.

The internal router might be configured to allow all traffic to pass or it might be configured to protect some internal resources. Internally, more and more companies are using firewalls to segment off or protect in-depth their internal network. This technique is on the rise because it has been reported that a large percentage of the attacks occur from inside and because more companies are adopting a "need-to-know" posture. For example, this "need-to-know" posture would be used to keep the workings of Human Resources and Finance away from unauthorized viewers, much as it would protect a new project that is vital to the corporate future from industrial espionage or disgruntled employees.

Packet filtering is something that routers can do well. Packet filters can be configured for Access Control Lists (ACLs), and may be used to increase the security of a router's defense, but if done poorly, only add to the security vulnerabilities. Some of the access control lists can be difficult to configure and can give you a false sense of security.

Remote Access   With the growth of telecommuting and greater employee travel, remote access has become a common part of many corporate networks. There are many companies today that have employees who never or rarely come into the corporate office. In the United States, some states provide tax breaks for companies that have their employees telecommute two to three days a week. Federal programs are also in place that mandate that a certain percentage of federal employees telecommute.

Although these users are at home or on the road, they still need access to corporate resources. This means providing access to more corporate resources via the Internet, thus increasing potential security risks. The job of the security practitioner is to allow the necessary access that these traveling employees need, while reducing the exposure of all internal systems to outside compromise.

Clientless VPNs   As the workplace becomes more mobile and decision-making time decreases, there is a greater need for mobile access. Employees no longer have the luxury of leaving the office for long periods of time, like a week-long training class or a conference, without checking their e-mail. Also, as more and more workers check their mail or need access to corporate resources from a home machine or Internet kiosk, the need to access these corporate resources securely also increases. Because most users do not have control over the computers at an Internet kiosk or at a large conference, and Information Technology departments don't want to maintain an end user's home machine, the ability for them to use an IPSEC solution decreases in these scenarios. Instead, many companies are opting to use a clientless VPN for these situations.

There are many benefits:

- There is no user end configuration necessary and no additional software to install.
- A clientless VPN usually uses the SSL/TLS-capable Internet browser that is already included in most systems.
- The clientless VPNs use the standard ports that people would use to surf the Net or conduct secure transactions, like ordering something from a Web site or checking their banking records.
- Clientless VPNs are mainly used for Web-based applications but many of them have the ability to allow non-Web-based applications (such as telnet, ftp, or file sharing) to ride over the encrypted tunnel via port forwarding.
- Clientless VPNs are also a benefit to some end users whose service providers block UDP port 500 to prevent them from using VPNs without paying for the "business" class of service. No service provider would dare block port 80 (HTTP) or port 443 (SSL), since even checking your Web-based mail requires these ports.

There are security risks:

- Using a public nontrusted machine to connect to your internal network could be risky.
- The machine may have viruses, Trojan horse applications, keystroke monitoring tools, or other common attack tools running in the background.
- Some of the clientless VPNs on the market today allow you to change the level of access or deny access to the corporate network based on the results of a scan of the machine being used to try and access the network.

Some of the machines provide redundancy via high availability and session persistence. High availability comes in several forms, including having a second device on the same network segment that will share the load with the other clientless VPN termination point or pick up connections when the first clientless VPN termination point goes off line. High availability can also be a distributed design. The distributed design fails over everything to hot or cold sites when a major catastrophe or impact happens to the main site.

Session persistence is a great security tool for the administrator and end user. If an end user walks away from the connection for a customizable set of time, the connection requires that the user re-authenticate. Upon re-authentication, the end user resumes his previous activity, such a typing a mail message, losing none of his work. These redundancies strengthen your network security architecture and provide continuity of operation.

Remote Access Servers   Microsoft's Terminal Server and Citrix's server solutions are very common in corporate networks. Both solutions are considered thin clients and allow remote users to log onto a server and operate as if they were sitting in the office. This gives them access to the corporate network, printers, and data. This would be no different than if they were using their computers within the corporate building. The risk is that if an attacker gains access to the Terminal or Citrix server, he may also have access to other corporate resources.

Identification and Authentication for Remote Users

RADIUS, TACACS, LDAP, SecureID, and other two-factor authentication servers are common methods of authenticating remote users. These methods of authentication allow centralized management of user logins and passwords. When a client attempts to connect to the network, they are prompted for a user name and password combination that the server verifies. Digital Certificates are also a very useful means of authenticating the user.

Firewalls   Firewalls are a critical element of our networking security today, but they are just that, an element. Firewalls will not solve all of our security problems, but they do play a large part in our efforts to secure our networks.

Firewalls are designed to control the flow of traffic by preventing unauthorized traffic from entering or leaving a particular portion of the network. They can be used between a corporate network and the outside world, or within the corporate network, to allow only authorized access to corporate assets.

Firewalls can be configured in a locally high-availability scenario or a distributed high availability scenario. Within these scenarios the firewalls can be configured in load balancing or load sharing, failover, or a less desirable stand-alone solution. The load balancing and load sharing are very similar, with the difference being that the first method more evenly distributes the load across the firewalls. The latter may share the load between the firewalls but it could be severely unbalanced. Failover is not quite as effective as load balancing, and may occur in seconds or as much as minutes. The stand-alone solution may leave you with a single point of failure on your network. Any single point of failure could be a liability to your operations. If that point failed, it could cause your data transmission to cease. You will have to compare the requirements of your risk analysis plan against your solution. These redundant configurations are critical to maintaining an organization's ability to conduct business across the Internet or other transmission medium.

Different Types of Firewalls   There are six basic types of firewalls:

- Stateful Inspection — Stateful inspection firewalls monitor the state of all connections that pass through them. In other words, if a user were to send a request to a Web site, the firewall would allow the return information to pass because it knows that the user's connection is waiting for a response. The firewall is also aware of the established connection and upon inspection of the packet to make sure that it is in fact part of the previously established connection, will allow the traffic to pass. Stateful inspection firewalls are the most popular type of firewall today.

- Packet Filtering — Packet filtering firewalls are very similar in nature to a router. They compare received packets against a set of rules that define which packet is permitted to pass through the firewall.

- Dynamic Packet Filtering — Dynamic packet filtering firewalls function by queuing all of the connectionless packets that have crossed the firewall and, based on that, will allow responses to pass back through.

- Application Proxy — Application proxy firewalls read the entire packet up through the Application layer before making a decision as to whether the data is allowed to pass. The client is really communicating with an application proxy that in turn communicates with the destination service. This allows the application proxy to examine packets in order to protect against known application and data stream attacks. As a result these firewalls are slower but more effective than packet filtering firewalls.

- Kernel Proxy — Kernel proxy firewalls are specialized firewalls that are designed to function in the kernel mode of the OS. This firewall technology is much older and is currently used in very few firewalls. Any new service that is introduced, such as Voice over IP (VoIP) or NetMeeting, would require changes to the kernel. These firewalls are often much slower.

- Circuit Level Gateway — Circuit level firewalls relay TCP connections by reading and tracking header information such as source and destination addresses and ports. The caller connects to a TCP port on the firewall, which connects to some destination on the other side. During the call, the firewall's relay program copies the bytes back and forth, in essence acting as a wire. A circuit level gateway just checks the source and destination addresses before allowing connectivity. Once the connectivity is established no further checking is done. This type of firewall is rarely used today. This firewall is one step more secure than a packet filter as it checks the actual connections before passing the traffic and traffic appears to be handled by the gateway. A disadvantage is it checks the initial connection but none of the subsequent packets.

Firewall Configuration Alternatives There are two main examples of security configuration architectures:

- Packet-Filtering Routers — Packet-filtering routers are designed to sit between an internal trusted network and an external nontrusted network. Security is maintained through an ACL which may be time consuming to manage. These firewalls also lack authentication and usually have weak auditing capabilities.

- Dual or Multi-Homed Host Firewall — Dual or multi-homed host firewall systems have the gateway connected to the internal network on one interface and the external network on another. (In the multi-homed configuration, another network interface could be connected to a DMZ, partner network, extranet, or many other possibilities.) The security is maintained through the firewall rule set. This type of firewall is the most commonly used type of firewall today. The benefits of this type of firewall are that it can be less expensive because you can deploy only one firewall and protect many network segments and it simplifies your network configuration. A disadvantage of this type of firewall is that one incorrect or erroneous rule or filter may allow traffic in to your network without a secondary security check. This potential is the reason to choose a firewall with an easy to understand and implement configuration tool or GUI.

A clarification of terms:

- Filters — A list of rules that allow or block traffic. These rules could be based on source, destination, service, time of day, port, day of the week, user, authentication type, combination of any or all of these, and more.
- Gateway — A machine or a set of machines that enforce the policy or filters.
- DMZ — A network attached to a firewall or between two firewalls, which usually has limited permissions for some type of public traffic but often not as limited a set of permissions as traffic intended for the internal segment. In the past, the DMZ was placed between two routers with different ACLs, with more stringent controls on the internal router. With today's modern technology, the DMZ is usually just another interface off of the firewall with a rule set governing the access to and from the external network, to and from the internal network, and in some instances, to and from another DMZ or extranet.
- Bastion host — This terminology is outdated and the roles of the bastion host are now incorporated into a gateway. It provided a single entry/exit point or gateway to your network.
- Proxy Server — Used as an intermediary device between a client and a server, which acts on behalf of the client to access the resources on the server.

Intrusion Detection Systems Intrusion detection is critical to a corporate network defense because you can be sure that your systems will come under attack. When you come under attack, you will want to be alerted as soon as possible and have as much information as possible for the investigation. An IDS should alert you and log the critical information about the attack. It is estimated that any new system on the Internet will be attacked within three days. There are enough attackers out there, attacking for various reasons, to guarantee that the first attack will not be the last. The IDS has the ability to monitor incoming and outgoing traffic to determine if the passing traffic is a threat to your network.

A passive attack could be just simple eavesdropping. In this attack the attacker is just waiting for login and password information to pass or an e-mail with an attached financial file to be passed across the network. This type of attack requires that they have physical access to your network or have already compromised a device on your network.

An active attack could be one of many such as brute-force, denial-of-service, spoofing, or exploitation of a vulnerability. What must be remembered is that there is always a way into a system; it may take longer to breach a well-protected system, but there is always a way in.

Intrusion detection systems will not notify you of a passive attack since it generates little to no noise on the network. IDSs are mostly used to detect an active attack.

Auditing and Monitoring Auditing and monitoring are a critical part of intrusion detection. "Prevention is ideal, but detection is a must" is a key motto in security. As long as your network is connected to an external network, your system is subject to attack at any time. A well-setup system will be able to prevent most attacks from getting through, but will not prevent 100 percent of the attacks. Therefore, you must monitor your network systems to detect, and learn from any attack that is launched at your system.

Different Types of IDS Solutions There are two basic types of IDS solutions: host-based and network-based.

A host-based IDS requires loading software on the host machine. The IDS software then listens to traffic coming into and exiting the host machine. To be truly effective, host-based IDS software should be loaded onto every host in the network. This software can also take advantage of information in the computer's logs and monitor the integrity of the file system for a broader picture of changes and attempted changes that might mean an intrusion attempt is or has happened. If it is cost-prohibitive to place software on all machines on the network, then serious consideration should be given to monitoring devices deemed critical to your mission.

Network-based IDS devices monitor the traffic on the network. These devices can add some other helpful features such as network monitoring, traffic analysis, and statistical collection. Unlike routers or firewalls, the IDSs only monitor the traffic.

Ideally, the network-based IDSs should be placed outside of your firewall, on your DMZ link, just inside your firewall, and on internal network segments or at least on any critical network segment or any network device (switch or hub) providing connectivity for that segment. The IDS outside your firewall will alert you to the types of attacks that intruders are trying to use against your system. Knowing what types of attacks an intruder is trying to use would help you make sure that you are patched and prepared for those types of attacks.

Having an IDS on your DMZ would enable you to see what types of attacks are allowed through your firewall rule set into your DMZ. Usually company Web servers and mail servers are kept in the DMZ. A compromise of one of these devices may allow for a follow-on attack to the internal part of your network or public embarrassment.

The IDS on the network segment inside the firewall may alert you to a misconfigured firewall policy or for the potential that an attack is coming from inside your network.

An IDS on the internal network segments could alert you to the possibility that a disgruntled employee, a saboteur, or spy (industrial or governmental) has gotten onto your network.

All IDS solutions should provide alerting, logging, and reporting capabilities.

Techniques for IDS Monitoring IDS solutions have two basic methods of intrusion detection available to them — signature matching and anomaly detection.

Signature matching is also called pattern matching. These IDS systems maintain a database of known attack signatures. The first obvious problem to this type of monitoring is that any unknown methods of attack will not be detected. The IDS database works in a similar fashion to that of virus detection software. You must continually update the signature database with the latest known methods of attack. The IDS then monitors traffic to see if it conforms to any known attack methods. The problem with this type of IDS is the amount of time between when an attack is released into the wild and the vendor has a pattern match or signature for that type of attack. Your system will not recognize and not flag that type of attack.

Anomaly detection is done by first determining the normal network traffic patterns and then watching for traffic that does not fall within the normal patterns. The advantage to this is both new and known methods of attack can be detected. The difficulty with this method of IDS is that what is normal can change over time for any given company or if where the device is located is under a heavy attack or already compromised while taking the baseline.

IDS audit logs can be very useful in computer forensics. The logs can show what systems were attacked and how the systems were attacked, as well as the possible source of the attack. With attacks that are spoofed, you most likely will not see the actual source.

Wide Area Networking   The wide area network (WAN) is a critical element to every corporate network today. A corporation must be able to connect between their offices, their remote users, their customers, and perhaps to their competition on occasion. The WAN allows access to the corporate resources from almost anywhere in the world. There are several different types of WAN protocols and configurations in use today. Each configuration has its advantages and disadvantages like all other aspects of networking.

Circuit Switched versus Packet Switched WANs   The first thing to consider is the different manner in which the WAN can operate. Public networks operate in either a circuit-switched or a packet-switched manner.

Circuit switched networks include the telephone network (POTS; modem access) and ISDN.

Packet switched networks include X.25, Frame Relay, SMDS, and ATM .

A circuit-switched network operates in a time division manner by allocating timeslots (DS0s) to each user's connection. The connection is established between two end points or between two corporate offices. This connection could be dynamically (SVC) created as in a telephone call or statically (PVC) created to permanently connect two locations/devices.

A packet-switched network operates in a similar fashion to the circuit-switched network in that it establishes either dynamic (SVC) or static (PVC) connections between two end points on the network. The difference is in the bandwidth that is allocated to the connection. The packet-switched connection works on a first-come, first-served basis, allowing users to share all of the available bandwidth.

In either scenario, there is a security risk with dynamically created connections. These connections are created by one end location dialing the address of the requested destination. The network then places the call across the network. The network is not designed to limit or filter connections for the users. Once the connection is established across the network, it is up to the receiving device to accept or decline the connection attempt.

Common WAN Infrastructures Used in Enterprise Networks   The most common WAN infrastructure used at this time in Enterprise networks is a PVC-based Frame Relay network. X.25 has given way to Frame Relay, and ATM is still a growing network.

The Permanent Virtual Circuit (PVC) used in Frame Relay adds to the security of the network. Frame Relay networks do not support Switched Virtual Circuits (SVC) at this time even though the standard does exist. A PVC is manually configured by the IT department for the corporation, utilizing the

Frame Relay network at the router and the carrier at the network switches. This manually-intensive process makes it harder for an attacker to create an illegal connection to a corporate router.

As with all configurations, there is a possible way in for an attacker. If an attacker were to gain access to one of the networks in a corporate office, then the Frame Relay PVC will not protect corporate resources. Remember, the modem connected to the router in the wiring closet or the unprotected wireless network will let an attacker right in. There is also a remote possibility that an attacker could gain access to the carrier's switches and reconfigure the PVC.

Wireless Local Area Networking

Wireless Introduction

Wireless networks have become very popular for connecting devices within the home, small office or even large office buildings. They are used to connect laptops, desktops, PDAs, and so much more. Wireless has added a true feeling of mobility to laptops and freedom with a PDA in hand.

Configuring a wireless network has proved to be fairly easy with a wide variety of products on the market and interoperability at work. The question then becomes: What does wireless do to the security of my network? If it is so easy for an employee to connect to the network, does that mean that others can connect as well?

Some of the biggest blunders with wireless networks so far are:

- Encryption not enabled
- Forgetting that a wireless network can extend outside the perimeter of the building
- Broadcasting your wireless networks presence (SSID)
- Treating the wireless network as an integral part of the wired network, rather than a perimeter to the wired network

Setting up a secure wireless network (at least as secure as any of our wired networks) is possible, but it must be done with careful planning, execution, and testing.

IEEE 802.11 Standard   The IEEE committee for Local and Metropolitan Area Network Standards began the 802.11-working group in 1990. The first wireless standard was complete in 1997. 802.11 standards define the interface between wireless clients and their network access points; this includes both the physical and the MAC layers of the OSI model. These standards also define how roaming between access points and the WEP security mechanism works.

There are three transmission types that are defined within the 802.11 standard: diffuse infrared, DSSS radio, and FHSS radio.

The MAC layer has two main standards of operation: a distributed mode (CSMA/CD) and a coordinated mode.

IEEE 802.11a Specification The 802.11a specification was begun before 802.11b as the letter A suggests, although it was completed afterward. 802.11a uses the 5 GHz band and is designed to pump through 54 Mbps worth of information using the new modulation scheme known as Orthogonal Frequency Division Multiplexing (OFDM).

Due to the different band used than 802.11b, these two standards are not compatible, although vendors are making equipment that supports both standards. Using the 5 GHz range should provide cleaner transmissions. Other wireless devices such as cordless phones, microwave ovens, baby monitors, and Bluetooth devices use the 2.4 GHz band. This standard is also referred to as WiFi5.

IEEE 802.11b Specification 802.11b is the most widely recognized standard currently in use. This standard was approved in September 1999 allowing for transmission rates of up to 11 Mbps using the 2.4 GHz radio band. Due to Media Access Control (MAC) overhead, errors, and collision, the actual data transfer rate is about 6 Mbps.

802.11b uses Complimentary Code Keying (CCK) and direct sequence spread spectrum (DSSS) which allows it to be fully backward compatible with DSSS implementations of 802.11. This standard is also referred to as WiFi.

IEEE 802.11g 802.11g was approved by IEEE on June 12, 2003, although. vendors began shipping products well before this date. This is another high-speed extension of the standard that is similar to 802.11b. 802.11g uses DSSS (like 802.11b). The changes that exist in this version of the 802.11 standard allow for transmission rates up to 54 Mbps.

802.11g is being designed to have backwards compatibility and interoperability with 802.11b DSSS-based products.

One of the drawbacks with 802.11g is that it uses the same radio frequency as other devices such as wireless phones, microwaves, and Bluetooth devices, which could cause some interference with the transmission.

IEEE 802.11i 802.11i, also known as WPA2, is an amendment to the original 802.11 standard to include security mechanisms for wireless networks. This amendment was the result of the security features lacking in Wired Equivalent Privacy and the original Wi-Fi Protected Access (WPA). There were two main developments: WPA security improvements and Robust Security Networks (RSN). The WPA uses the Temporal Key Integrity Protocol (TKIP) to exchange keys. This protocol strengthens and changes the way keys are created and changed. It also adds a message-integrity-check function to prevent forged packet playbacks from occurring. RSN takes advantage of Extensible Authentication Protocol (EAP) and Advanced Encryption Standard (AES). RSN allows for dynamic negotiation of authentication and encryption protocols. This flexibility allows the protocol to adapt to the new threats and new advancements in the encryption schemes. RSN will likely not run very well on legacy hardware since the encryption and security computations require more processing power. Until devices, both the mobile device and the wireless access point, are given more processing power or specific hardware accelerators to handle this processing, RSN will likely have a slow acceptance.

IEEE 802.11 Wireless LAN Equipment and Components   To install a wireless LAN there are a few pieces of equipment that are required. First, the computer/laptop/etc. must have a wireless network interface card (NIC) installed. The wireless NICs can be built in to the computer or the NIC can be connected through a PCI slot, a USB port, or PCMCIA slot. Second, there must be a wireless access point for the NIC to communicate with or an additional NIC that can accept connections. Optionally, there can also be additional antennas for added distance.

IEEE 802.15   The IEEE 802.15 is broken down into four task groups: The first task group is targeted toward Wireless Personal Area Networks (WPANs). This technology focuses around Bluetooth. It has derived the Media Access controls and physical layer stipulations from Bluetooth 1.1. The second task group is focused on the interaction between WPANs and 802.11 standards. The third task group is broken into two subgroups dealing with WPAN high rate and WPAN alternate higher rate. Both of these groups deal with a WPAN with data connection speeds in excess of 20Mbits per second. The fourth task group deals with a very low rate WPAN but with an extremely long battery life.

IEEE 802.16   IEEE 802.16 is also known as WiMAX. WiMAX is derived from the Worldwide Interoperability for Microwave Access. It was targeted to set the standards for Broadband Wireless Access to Metropolitan Area Networks (MANs). This standard varies from the traditional WiFi MAC. In the standard WiFi MAC, every device wishing to talk with the Access Point interrupts the access point while contacting it. Higher priority services like Voice over IP and video may get dropped or severely interrupted in this type of environment. In the WiMAX environment, devices compete for the initial entry into the network and from then on the device is allocated a time slot from the base station or access point. This allows for more efficient use of bandwidth and does not suffer under a heavy load or possible oversubscription.

Wireless Access Points   Wireless Access Points (AP) are the connection points between the wired and wireless networks. As a result, if they are not secured properly they can provide easy entry into your wired network. There are several recommended actions that you take to begin securing the APs.

One of the first recommended actions is to change the Station Set Identifier (SSID) from the factory default. The SSID identifies the AP by name on your network. If the name is known or discoverable, then an attacker is one step closer to gaining access to the network. Therefore, the second action is to disable the broadcasting of the SSID from the AP.

The third recommended security practice for your AP is to enable MAC address filtering. When MAC address filtering is enabled only the MAC addresses that were previously specified to the AP will be allowed to connect. While it is possible to spoof a MAC address, you are increasing the level of difficulty for the attacker to compromise your network. The fourth recommended security practice is to set up logging on the AP. This will allow you to monitor the activity of your AP.

The fifth recommended security practice is to disable all unnecessary services such as SNMP. If you neglect to disable unused services you may be inadvertently providing an open door to your wired network through the AP.

The sixth recommended security practice is to limit the power output of your AP if possible. You might find that the coverage area of your AP as configured from the factory extends beyond your building limits.

The seventh recommended security practice is to enable Wired Equivalent Privacy (WEP) encryption. WEP has known vulnerabilities at this time and there are tools available to exploit these vulnerabilities, but nevertheless you should enable WEP encryption. The longer your WEP key is and the less traffic you send on your wireless network, the more security WEP provides. If your AP supports WPA or WPA2, that should be configured instead of WEP.

The final recommendation would be design your architecture so that behind your wireless access point you would have a Firewall/VPN that would prohibit any traffic that is not encrypted and authenticated. The firewall should be set to drop and log all other traffic. Placing an IDS solution between the Firewall/VPN and the access point is also another good idea. While it may not tell you who is passively listening on your network, it may alert you to attacks or probes against your network.

Antennae   When creating a wireless network for the purpose of a point-to-point connection between two buildings, antennas must be considered. There are two basic types of antennas: omni-directional and directional.

Omni-directional antennas are more of a security concern due to the nature of the horizontal beam width covering a full 360 degrees. If you are using omni-directional antennas consider terrain masking, or blocking the transmission of the signal in the unwanted direction with a "backstop" such as a roof, stairwell, or a heavily constructed wall.

Directional antennas contain the beam within a limited spread and allow for finer control of the area that they cover.

Antenna Configuration and Placement Once you choose either an omni-directional or directional antenna, the real work begins. Obstructions and signal attenuation are two concerns to be addressed when placing and configuring your antenna.

The following are considerations when planning your antenna placement:

- Trees
- Buildings
- Weather
- Curvature of the earth (with connections with distances greater than seven miles)

These items can work with you or against you. Consider how they will affect the intended wireless users as well as the attackers.

When using a site to site wireless connection, there is no reason not to use a VPN to add an extra layer of security for the data. The VPN termination points can also be set up to disregard all traffic not being sent via the other termination point, therefore limiting the external access for an intruder.

Wireless Network Interface Cards and Adapters The wireless NIC or adapter for your mobile device needs little configuration. The first configuration might be the SSID that you want this device to attach to. If you have disabled the SSID broadcast capability in your AP, then you must configure the SSID in the NIC. Also, if there are multiple APs available you may wish to configure the NIC for the SSID that you want it to connect to.

The second configuration is for WEP. When you have enabled WEP, the key usually needs to be entered into the NIC configuration as well as the AP configuration.

If you have increased security on your wireless network, you may also have to change or set up your WPA setting. Another setting that you may have to change is how you will authenticate to the network.

Inherent Security Vulnerabilities with IEEE 802.11x There are many inherent security vulnerabilities with IEEE 802.11x. The nature of a wireless network alone can leave a WLAN subject to attacks. Wireless is not bound by the same physical principles as a wired network and is accessible from any location within the antenna's signal beam.

The security included with 802.11x has been discovered to be vulnerable to attacks. The first common problem with wireless networks is that by default security mechanisms are disabled and are often not enabled by network administrators. This leaves a wireless network susceptible to both passive and active attacks, which includes everything from simple eavesdropping to WLAN jacking.

Over the next several pages, we will take a look at these vulnerabilities and attack techniques.

802.11 Authentication and Its Weaknesses   The authentication options with 802.11 are few. 802.11b includes an option called "open authentication." Open authentication is basically no authentication at all. This authentication is not appropriate for corporate environments but might be suitable for public access points such as libraries or coffee shops.

If a company is relying on 802.11b authentication for security, they have missed the boat. The way that authentication is accomplished is with the SSID in the following way:

1.   The user's station will send out a probe frame (active scanning) with the desired Station Set ID (SSID).
2.   The AP with that SSID will send back a probe response frame.
3.   The user's station will accept the SSID, Timing Sync Function (TSF), timer value, and physical setup values from the AP frame.

Since the SSID is often broadcasted from the AP, there is little security in this approach.

WEP Encryption and Its Weaknesses   WEP allows for a standards-based form of encryption on a wireless network. WEP relies on the RC4 encryption algorithm created by RSA. WEP can be used in either a 64-bit or 128-bit form. Some vendors will advertise a 40-bit or 104-bit WEP encryption method. The 40-bit and 64-bit formats are identical to each other it is just a matter of linguistics. WEP 64-bit uses 40 bits for the private key and 24 bits for the Initialization Vector (IV).

There are a couple of inherent weaknesses with WEP encryption. The first is the authentication is not mutual. The client never has the opportunity to authenticate the AP so it is subject to man in the middle attacks.

The second weakness with WEP is that the key can be recovered if the attacker gathers enough of the transmission. There are tools available on the Internet that allow an attacker to listen to your wireless transmission, gather the data, and then recover your WEP key within a few hours of beginning. The WEP key will only slow an attacker down, it will not stop the attack. Relying on WEP alone for security would be a mistake.

Passive Network Attacks   Passive network attacks are relatively easy to implement and are very difficult to detect. The most common problem with wireless technology is that any anonymous attacker could be listening in. Anyone could set up a laptop with relatively little extra time and equipment, and start listening in to wireless communications. These attacks could be simple eavesdropping or Man in the Middle (MITM) attacks.

The equipment needed to listen in on a wireless connection is a computer (laptop, PDA, etc.), a wireless card, and some downloadable software to detect and then eavesdrop on any unsecured wireless network. A WLAN with security enabled could take a little more work, but is still vulnerable to attacks. The MITM attacks require a little more work because the attacker will intercept the user's transmission and then forward it on to the actual network device. The goals of MITM attacks include injecting data, modifying communications, or simply eavesdropping on a network or its clients.

Active Network Attacks   Active network attacks can take the form of:

- Rogue Client
- Rogue Network Access Point
- Client-to-Client Attacks
- Infrastructure Equipment Attacks
- Denial of Service (DOS) Attacks
  — Client Jamming
  — Base Station Jamming

There are many actions that an attacker can do to gain access to a WLAN. First, an attacker can mimic the identity of a known WLAN client. The attacker could steal an access point or setup a rogue access point to impersonate a valid network resource. They can attack another unprotected client on the WLAN to gain authentication information for some other part of the network. The attacker could gain access to your APs through a default login and password or a guessed password such as your company name. It is also possible to attack a switch by using a MAC or ARP table flood causing the switch to fail open.

War Driving   The term "War Driving" derives from the term "War Dialing," and refers to the practice of dialing different phone numbers to locate an open and available modem to connect to. This can also be used to dial numbers looking for an open PBX that will allow the attacker to place long distance or international calls. The War Driving attacker drives around in a car equipped with everything that they need to connect to your WLAN — a laptop or PDA with a wireless card, a network discovery tool such as NetStumbler (free downloadable software), and a homemade antenna. As an addition to their configuration, they can add a GPS to record the location of the networks that they discover.

WLAN Jacking   Once a network has been discovered, the attacker can exploit it. Many attackers are only looking for a way to connect to the Internet, although some are looking for information or resources on your network that they can exploit. Caution needs to be taken in setting up a wireless network (or any network for that matter) to avoid potential fines or lawsuits in the event that your network is used for malicious intent.

WLAN jacking is easy for an attacker if there is no security turned on at the AP. All the attacker needs is a laptop or PDA, a wireless card, a network discovery tool such as NetStumbler, and optionally a GPS and an antenna to boost the signal of the target network. Once the network is discovered, he attacker can connect. Once connected to your network, he has access to your network resources and your Internet access.

The current legal argument is that looking for unsecured WLANs is not a crime, however a crime is committed if the perpetrator then uses the network for illegal activity.

There is also an argument that if there is no security turned on at the AP, then how does the attacker know that this is not just a public access network, like you can find at coffee houses and such, and, therefore, is not breaking the law by using your network.

If there is any form of security turned on at the AP, then it may take the attacker a little more work to crack through the WEP or to try guessing your SSID or intercepting a transmission from a user and 'stealing' their connection. There are enough tools available on the Internet to exploit WLANs to make this all possible.

Securing 802.11 Wireless LANs   It is possible to secure your wireless network (relatively speaking) from outside attack. You should not rely on one method alone to secure your wireless network though. Actions to consider implementing include:

- MAC address filtering
- Authentication
- Authentication Servers
- WEP Keys
- VPN
- Firewalls

MAC Address Filtering   Media Access Control (MAC) address filtering can be enabled on most APs today. MAC filtering allows you to control which MAC addresses are allowed to connect to your AP. For a small network, this is relatively easy to manage. As your network reaches 100 wireless users and beyond, this becomes a little more difficult to manage. In a large network, the wireless user would be restricted to the AP that her or his MAC address has been programmed into. This may or may not be considered a limitation for your network.

There is still a way around this security mechanism though. With the network discovery tools and listening capabilities that are on the market, an attacker with the right wireless NIC could discover an active MAC on your network and then change their NIC to use a valid MAC.

The second way around this security mechanism is our weak password habits. An AP with default or easy-to-guess passwords is easy prey for attackers. The attacker can gain access to your AP and then add their MAC to the list.

Authentication   As stated earlier in this chapter, the authentication that comes with 802.11b might as well be considered no authentication at all. There are other authentication methods that can be added to your wireless network to increase the security. The authentication methods include EAP-TLS, EAP-TTLS, or proprietary methods such as Cisco's LEAP. It is necessary for a Security Practitioner to be constantly vigilant. Recent announcements have identified the security vulnerabilities in LEAP and the vendor announced that no fixes would be readily available. This announcement could dramatically impact your organization's strategy, policy and procedures.

Extensible Authentication Protocol (EAP) provides an authentication method that allows an administrator to centrally manage access to the wireless network and is, therefore, more robust than the authentication found with 802.11b. This method allows the administrator to enable per-user, per-session keys (EAP-TLS). This requires the user to enter a username and password to gain access to the wireless network.

As an example, a username and password are authenticated by a RADIUS server. Once authentication is completed, the RADIUS server sends the session key to the client. This process greatly improves the security of the wireless connection over static WEP keys and open authentication. The TLS portion of the authentication continues the process of authenticating between the client and the RADIUS server.

It is also recommended to use either WPA or WPA2 instead of simple WEP.

Authentication Servers   Adding a Remote Authentication Dial-In User Service (RADIUS), SecureID, or other two factor authentication Server, or Digital Certificates to your WLAN has many advantages:
- Reduction or elimination of WEP vulnerabilities
- Centralized MAC address management
- Centralized user management
- Domain/directory authentication
- Accounting reports
- Interoperability

There are many other types of authentication server that could be used. We have listed a few for example purposes. The most important idea is that you should have a strong method of authentication before you allow anyone on your network, especially through a wireless LAN connection.

WEP Keys   Due to the weaknesses with WEP keys if used alone, your network is susceptible to attack, as discussed earlier in this chapter. There are many additions and changes that are being made to the standard to enhance the effectiveness of this element of security. They include:

- Temporal Key Integrity Protocol (TKIP) implements key hashing to prevent attacks on the WEP key.
- Message Integrity Control (MIC) appends a unique identifier to each packet to enable verification in both transmission directions to prevent MITM attacks.
- Extensible Authentication Protocol (EAP), as previously discussed, adds a per-user, per-session key to enhance security.
- IEEE 802.1X standard is a refinement of the current authentication mechanism for WEP.

IEEE 802.1x Standard   802.1x was approved in June 2001 as an authentication method that can be used on wireless and wired networks. This standard uses existing protocols for user authentication, such as EAP and RADIUS. Windows XP as well as some wireless equipment already has the capability of 802.1x built-in.

The basic purpose of 802.1x is to authenticate users, although it can be used to optionally establish encryption keys. The authentication can be performed by any means the vendor chooses, such as RADIUS or KERBEROS. Until authentication is complete, traffic is not allowed to pass onto the network. The 802.1x standard includes the mandatory use of 128-bit keys for RC4 data encryption and encryption key rotation.

With 802.1x, the user device is referred to as the Supplicant. For wireless purposes, the Access point is referred to as the Authenticator System. The RADIUS server is referred to as the Authentication Server.

VPN in a Wireless Network   A Virtual Private Network (VPN) is a valuable addition to a wireless LAN. A useful point of view to take about your WLAN is that it is an external part of your network and VPNs and firewalls are good measures to add to protect this entry into your network. A common trap with WLANs is to consider them an internal part of the network. Since they are so hard to secure, if an attacker compromises your WLAN, your entire network is potentially compromised.

A WLAN secured with a VPN has the following benefits:

- The VPN increases the security of the WLAN well beyond the capabilities of WEP.
- Security tools such as RSA SecureID increases the strength of the authentication used.

Wireless LAN Policy, Standard, and Procedures   A network security policy must be amended to include wireless networking and devices. This should be the case even if a network does not include a wireless segment. It is possible for a user to add wireless capability to their network-connected desktop for the purpose of file sharing from their laptop. Their desktop could and probably does allow access to the wired network. If an attacker were to discover this unprotected wireless AP, then the network would be compromised.

The network policy should include a policy prohibiting a user to add wireless equipment unless they have the express permission of the IT department. PDAs and handheld computers should also be included in the network security policy. If these devices offer either Bluetooth or 802.11 connections, they may be subject to attack.

Need for Security Policies, Standards, and Procedures for the IT Infrastructure

The need for security policies, standards, and procedures becomes readily apparent when one recognizes that an IT infrastructure is only as secure as the weakest link in the chain of security responsibility. For example, one could secure data resources and maintain the confidentiality by storing it in an encrypted database stored on a server positioned on a LAN behind a firewall. However, if that same server is not installed in a data center or hosting center with proper physical security measures where access is limited to authorized personnel, is that IT resource secure? It is safe to say no, and, unfortunately, it has been shown to be a frequent scenario.

Securing the IT Infrastructure

The roles and responsibilities for maintaining confidentiality, integrity, and availability of a company's information technology infrastructure require defining. Until people are held responsible for each and every aspect of the IT infrastructure, there is sure to be a weakness that can be exploited by an attacker.

To secure your network and assets requires thought and planning. The following ten tips for creating a network security policy are from http://www.windowsecurity.com:

1. Identify and locate your assets.
2. Perform a threat risk assessment.
3. Adopt a "need-to-know" philosophy.
4. Perform an informal site survey of your organization.
5. Institute a standard for classifying all information.
6. Ascertain who needs access to external resources.
7. Create a disaster recovery plan.

8. Appoint someone to be responsible for security policy enforcement.
9. Review the impact of any intended procedural changes on your employees.
10. Understand that the implementation of any security policy needs regular validation.

Domains of IT Security Responsibility

When identifying and locating your corporate assets, the entire IT infrastructure must be examined. For a logical breakdown of your assets, the IT infrastructure can be broken down into seven domains:

- User domain
- Workstation domain
- LAN domain
- Remote Access domain
- LAN-to-WAN domain
- WAN domain
- System/Application domain

User Domain The user domain defines the roles, responsibilities, and accountability for employees and nonemployees that will be accessing corporate owned resources and systems. The policies and standards that apply to the user domain must be reviewed, signed, and executed by all users, employee or not, before they have access to the network and its resources. This policy should include the Acceptable Use Policy (AUP) for Internet access, e-mail access, and system access.

An audit is necessary to verify that the end user is indeed who they claim to be; this should be done for both employees and nonemployees that will be accessing the corporate systems and resources.

Workstation Domain The workstation domain defines the roles and responsibilities for the workstation device (thin client, Windows workstation, UNIX workstation, etc.) that resides on the user's desktop. This domain pertains to maintaining and updating the user workstations and devices (e.g., hardware, software, firmware, operating systems, memory, etc.) that are authorized and approved for access and connectivity to company owned resources and systems.

This domain includes the following hardware:

- Desktop computers
- Laptop computers
- Printers/scanners
- Handheld computers
- Wireless equipment (access points)
- Modems

This domain's specifications for the workstation operating systems, anti-virus software updates, and other workstation configuration standards must be kept current and validated in order to maintain the integrity of the workstation domain. Workstation client software used for remote access and security is also part of this domain. An audit is necessary to verify that the workstation has the appropriate "hardening" completed. This would include appropriate and up to date anti-virus protection software.

LAN Domain   The LAN domain defines the roles and responsibilities for the local area network physical connection (e.g., LAN hub/switch setup and configuration) as well as the logical connection to corporate file servers from the workstation devices on the user's desktop.

The physical connection for the LAN includes infrastructure elements, wiring, switches, and the physical connection to the departmental or building local area network systems. The logical connection from the desktop includes the authorized logon UserIDs and passwords for access to the LAN server.

An audit and assessment would need to check and verify that the local area network server, OS, and access control methods are implemented as per the appropriate data classification level. A review and "hardening" of the LAN components both physically and logically is typical for the LAN domain. This would include an assessment of the location of the server (e.g., LAN server hosted in a data center with secured access, UPS electric power, behind VPN termination point on server farm, behind firewall when WAN connectivity is required, etc.).

In addition, more stringent back-up procedures are required for a server and an audit and assessment of the CD-ROM or disk storage devices and procedures are necessary. Logical "hardening" will typically occur on the OS of the server and the client. This "hardening" may include more stringent system administration and access control procedures, stricter user login and password changing requirements, or system audit entries that are triggered when access to certain folders, applications, or data is needed.

LAN-to-WAN Domain   The LAN-to-WAN domain defines the roles and responsibilities for the End Site Router and Firewall providing interconnectivity between the LAN and the WAN domain.

Router configuration, firewall configuration, system monitoring, intrusion detection monitoring, and on-going system administration for the router, firewall, and intrusion detection system are part of this domain.

An audit is necessary to verify that the LAN-WAN domain is configured to permit only authorized access between these two domains. This domain is also where session monitoring and intrusion detection monitoring systems are best utilized when access to data of a sensitive nature is required.

WAN Domain   The WAN domain defines the roles and responsibilities for the WAN that provides end-to-end connectivity for all company end site locations.

This domain is comprised of backbone circuits, POP switches, routers, firewalls, intrusion detection systems, and end site devices (e.g., routers, CSU/DSUs, codecs) that will be installed at identified end site locations.

An audit is necessary to verify that the WAN domain is properly configured to permit traffic flows between it and the end user workstation and LAN. This is especially important if tunnels or VPNs are utilized between end points.

Remote Access Domain   The remote access domain defines the roles and responsibilities of authorized users who access corporate resources remotely (e.g., secured and authenticated remote access).

This domain applies to both company-owned and user-owned systems that provide remote access (e.g., authorized users from home or other remote location) to corporate owned resources and systems through the public Internet (e.g., dial-up, DSL, or cable modem Internet access) or a dedicated connection to outside entities or value added services. In addition, this domain pertains to the logical workstation-to-network connection via an authorized logon UserID and password for access to company owned resources and systems. Remote workstations that require client software for VPN or thin client support or intrusion detection monitoring are also part of this domain.

An audit is necessary to verify that any remote access to data conforms to the level of data classification assigned. This is important because remote access to sensitive data or applications typically requires VPN technology between client and server or an additional level of authentication as part of the access control procedures.

System/Application Domain   The system/application domain defines the roles and responsibilities of the systems and applications that are to be accessed by the Users from their desktop workstation device (e.g., mainframe, departmental LAN servers, application servers, Web servers).

This domain includes the configuration and "hardening" of the operating systems software as well as application security implementations and data base security measures. This domain encompasses all server platforms (Mainframe, UNIX, and Windows).

An audit is necessary to verify that the systems and applications include embedded security elements for access control, data storage, data encryption, and such. This includes systems and applications that reside on mainframes, departmental LAN servers, application servers, or Web servers, and the like.

Defining Standard and Enhanced Security Requirements

Defining standard and enhanced security requirements would include the following categories:
- Data sensitivity to attack
- Insertion of malicious code
- Loss of critical business functions
- Disaster recovery planning
- Confidentiality of sensitive information
- Physical security
- Security policies
- Response of personnel to security policies

Implementing Standard and Enhanced Security Solutions

There are many security counter measures that can be implemented and deployed throughout a LAN and WAN network environment. Some of the tools, requirements, and items to incorporate into a security counter measure strategy are:

- Internet-facing systems should run the vendor's most stable and secure operating systems and have any necessary patches applied.
- Network-based intrusion detection systems (IDS) should monitor the outside perimeter segment to provide details on outside system attacks taking place prior to their entry into the firewall. These IDS should report activity back to the security information management system.
- As budgets allow, key network devices should be deployed in pairs with automatic fail over capability to increase overall network availability.
- VPN clients with built-in software firewalls should be used to prevent tunneling attacks. Incoming remote access data streams should be decrypted outside of or at the corporate firewall, optionally analyzed by an IDS system, run through the firewall rulebase, and analyzed by an IDS system once inside the system.
- Key network devices should employ the use of out of band management channels that only allow a minimum of management communication from a dedicated management segment to the devices. Devices that are remotely located and cannot be connected to the management segment should employ VPN tunnels for their management. Other out of band management techniques (e.g., asynchronous terminal servers) should be considered.
- The organization's servers and workstations should employ the use of centrally managed and updated anti-virus systems.
- Network-based IDS should monitor key segments for post-firewall data traffic intrusions and internal intrusions. These IDS should report activity back to the security information management system.

- Host-based IDS should be utilized on key hosts, if not all hosts, and be configured to report back to the security information management system.
- Internal WAN data traffic should be encrypted over private links if the data's value is sufficiently high and risk of exposure exists.
- Make sure that your remote VPN connections and internal network users are authenticated using one or more types of authentication servers.

References and Useful Web Sites

A a wireless scanner may be purchased at http://www.airmagnet.com/products.htm.

A freeware network discovery tool is available at http://www.netstumbler.com.

A list of over 90 intrusion detection systems is available at http://www-rnks.informatik.tu-cottbus.de/sobirey/ids.html.

A list and short explanation of many wireless security tools can be found at http://www.networkintrusion.co.uk/wireless.htm.

A network utility used to sniff passwords, read e-mail, monitor Web traffic, and perform active sniffing known as dsniff is available at http://monkey.org/~dugsong/dsniff.

A warning about BOOTP and TFTP: http://etherboot.sourceforge.net/doc/html/security-8.html.

A Web site with information on how to exploit the firewall when it is not blocked from sending ICMP messages through is: http://www.opennet.ru/base/sec/p49-06.txt.html.

Another look at 802.11g is available at http://www.oreillynet.com/pub/a/wireless/2003/01/23/80211g.html.

ATM Theory and Applications, Signature Edition by David McDysan and Darren Spohn, ISBN: 0-07-045346-2

AT&T Labs and Rice University's attempt at a WEP attack, how they performed the attack, and the results: http://www.cs.rice.edu/~astubble/wep/wep_attack.html.

Computer Security Basics by Deborah Russell and G.T. Gangemi Sr.

For additional information see "Formulating a Security Policy: Relevant Issues, Considerations, and Implications" at http://www.giac.org/practical/David_Quay_GSEC.doc.

For information on building a homemade wireless antenna see http://www.turnpoint.net/wireless/has.html.

For more info on OFDM see http://www.ofdm-forum.com.

Frame Relay Principles and Applications by Philip Smith, ISBN: 0-201-62400-1

"HP Small and Medium Business How To Guide for Security Policies" is available at http://www.hp.com/sbso/productivity/howto/security/.

IEEE 802.11 working group is available at http://grouper.ieee.org/groups/802/11/.

IETF S/MIME working group at http://www.ietf.org/html.charters/smime-charter.html .

IETF syslog security group: http://www.ietf.org/html.charters/syslog-charter.html.

IETF TLS protocol: http://www.ietf.org/internet-drafts/draft-ietf-tls-rfc2246-bis-03.txt

Information security policy information is available at http://www.metasecuritygroup.com/policy.html.

Internet mail consortium on S/MIME and PGP at http://www.imc.org/smime-pgpmime.html.

ISDN and SS7 Architectures for Digital Signaling Networks by Uyless Black ISBN: 0-13-259193-6

IPSec working group: http://www.ietf.org/html.charters/ipsec-charter.html

IPSec white papers: http://www.bitpipe.com/data/rlist?t=soft_10_100_66_4&sort_by=status&src=over

Kismet is an 802.11 wireless network sniffer. This is a UNIX-based application that also has the capabilities of detecting networks that do not advertise their SSID: http://www.kismetwirelss.net.

NCSA, PEM, and PGP are available at http://hoohoo.ncsa.uiuc.edu/docs/PEMPGP.html.

NIST computer security division: http://csrc.nist.gov/

PPP and L2TP Remote Access Communications by Uyless Black - ISBN 0-13-022462-6.

Sample policy from Rutgers University is available at http://rucs.rutgers.edu/wireless-policy.html.

The "Site Securities Policies Procedure Handbook" is available at http://www.ietf.org/rfc/rfc2196.txt?Number=2196.

Security policy Web sites include:

    http://www.securityfocus.com/data/library/Why_Security_Policies_Fail.pdf

    http://www.security.kirion.net/securitypolicy/

    http://www.network-and-it-security-policies.com/

    http://www.brown.edu/Research/Unix_Admin/cuisp/

    http://iatservices.missouri.edu/security/

    http://www.utoronto.ca/security/policies.html

    http://irm.cit.nih.gov/security/sec_policy.html

    http://w3.arizona.edu/~security/pandp.htm

    http://secinf.net/policy_and_standards/

    http://www.ruskwig.com/security_policies.htm

    http://razor.bindview.com/publish/presentations/InfoCarePart2.html

    http://www.cisco.com/warp/public/126/secpol.html

Some interesting information on war driving is available at http://www.wardriving.com/.

The wireless working groups can be found at www.ieee802.org/11/.

Understanding Fiber Optics Second Edition by Jeff Hecht ISBN: 0-672-30350-7

WEP cracking tool for Linux: http://sourceforge.net/projects/wepcrack.

WLAN supported RADIUS servers can be found at http://www.funk.com, http://www.freeradius.org, and http://www.radius.cistron.nl.

WLAN/VPN integrated equipment can be found at http://www.colubris.com/en/ and http://www.fortresstech.com.

Sample Questions

1.   Match the topology with the appropriate description and vulnerabilities.

    1. Star
    2. Bus
    3. Ring
    4. Point to point

    a. In its most basic setup, the traffic flows in one direction. A break in the link and all traffic flow is severely limited.

    b. One of the more secure topologies due to the limited opportunities to intercept the traffic.

    c. The type of topology used in older networks or by cable companies. It is easy to listen to all of the traffic being broadcast on the wire.

    d. If the center point fails or is compromised, the traffic can be completely stopped.

2.   Match the following protocols with their descriptions.

    1. SMTP
    2. ICMP

      3. TFTP

      4. DHCP

      a. This protocol is used as an unauthenticated protocol to transfer data.

      b. This protocol is used between two mail servers to determine how they will communicate.

      c. This protocol is used to transmit the health and status of a network.

      d. This protocol is used in assigning IP addresses, default gateways, and DNS information.

3. True or False – It is not important to look at the syslog files because they are being backed up and can be reviewed at any time.

4. Choose the best description for the following protocols:

      1. SSL

      2. IPSEC AH

      3. IPSEC ESP

      4. NAT

      a. Message confidentiality is provided by encrypting the payload.

      b. Originally designed to compensate for a decreased number of IP addresses; has been used for security purpose of hiding IP addresses.

      c. Message integrity is performed by authenticating the payload and the origin of the information.

      d. Operates at the session layer and is often used with Digital Certificates.

5. Which of these protocols is not normally used to help make E-Mail more Secure:

      1. PGP

      2. S/MIME

      3. PEM

      4. MSP

      5. SNMP

6. Match the network equipment with its most common PRIMARY function:

      1. Firewall

      2. Router

      3. Switches

      4. VPN Termination Points

      a. Will pass traffic from one network to another network based on IP address.

    b. Will pass traffic to the appropriate network segment based on the MAC address.

    c. Enforced access control policy at given points of the network.

    d. Terminates encrypted communications and forwards them to the internal network.

7. Choose the descriptions and benefits or risks that best match the following Remote Access Solutions:

    1. RAS

    2. VPN

    3. Clientless VPN

    a. Allows the user to access the network without necessarily having to have his own device with him. Using a third party device might increase the network vulnerability by the use of hidden Trojans or keystroke monitoring tools.

    b. Does not require Internet access and can be secured by other means like two-factor authentication, is not easily sniffed. Usually requires a large phone bank to receive calls, can be expensive for long distance bills, subject to discovery by War dialing.

    c. Allows for the user to have a strong means of authentication and verification. Often requires the IT department to touch and maintain every device, and the device is required to connect to the network.

8. Choose which of the following actions will help secure a wireless access point.

    1. Choosing WPA2 over WEP

    2. Hiding the SSID

    3. Activate MAC address filtering

    4. Having an access control technology with authentication capability built into the device or having this access control product immediately behind the access point.

    5. All of the above

Domain 7
Malicious Code
Diana-Lynn Contesti, CISSP

Introduction

The malicious code domain addresses computer software/code that can be described as being malicious or destructive to the computing environment. This includes the virus, worm, logic bomb, Trojan horse, and other related code that exhibits deviant behavior.

Information Protection Requirements

The A-I-C Triad This chapter discusses techniques that can be used to help address issues associated with Availability as they relate to the A-I-C triad (see below). The goal is to ensure that information and computer systems are available for use when required. Malicious code (in any form) can make either a system unusable, data unavailable, or both. Viruses can contain a payload that is able to compromise both the confidentiality and integrity of files on an infected computer system.

Availability

Integrity   Confidentiality

A History of Computer Viruses

The history of computer viruses shows that since the late 1980s the number of computer viruses has grown exponentially and that their behaviors have changed over time. Figure 7.1, shows the growth in numbers of computer viruses. At the end of 2003, it was estimated that 1,200 viruses were being created each month.

In 1949, John von Neumann wrote a paper titled "Theory and Organization of Complicated Automata" for the Institute for Advanced Study in Princeton, New Jersey. In the paper, he theorized that it was possible for a computer

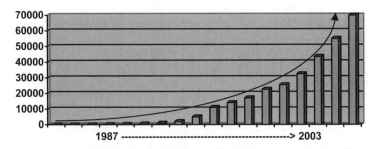

Figure 7.1 The exponential growth of viruses

program to replicate. Included in the paper was a model for what we call a computer virus.

Early in the 1950s, Bell Laboratories (McIlroy, Vysottsky, and Morris), developed a game that would test von Neumann's theory. The intent of game was to create programs which would attack, erase, and propagate on an opponent's system.

Author John Brunner published *The Shockwave Rider* in 1975. This book is often referred to as the cyberpunk novel as Brunner envisioned computer worms as they autonomously move from host to host, rather than attaching their code to other programs in the manner of viruses. This work documented the basic concept of computer programs that could self-replicate. It was not until 1984, that Dr. Fred Cohen's "Computer Viruses—Theory and Experiments" defined the computer virus and described experiments he and others performed to prove the viability of viral code.

The first computer virus to pass (or replicate) from PC to PC was Brain, although viruses had been passing between other platforms (VAXs and Apple IIs for some time). Brain was a boot sector virus that would stealthily leave contact information for Brain Computer Services (making it the only known virus to contain the creators' real names, addresses, and phone numbers). Stealth is a technology that enables a virus to actively hide itself from anti-virus software by either masking the size of the file that it hides in or temporarily removing itself from the infected file and placing a copy of itself in another location on the drive, replacing the infected file with an uninfected one that it has stored on the hard drive. The owners of Brain Computer Services, Basit and Amjaad (software vendors in Pakistan) claimed that they wrote the code to prevent their software from being pirated in Pakistan. The virus would just put a copyright in the directory of the program. Also, this virus could not affect hard disks; it could only affect floppy disks. However, Brain leaked through the Pakistani borders and infected computers worldwide

The only mainframe worm was the Christmas tree worm and it was a combination of a Trojan and a chain letter. It successfully managed to paralyze the IBM network on Christmas day, 1987.

Written in a language called Exec, it asked the user to type the word "Christmas" on the screen. Then it drew a Christmas tree and sent itself to all the names of people stored in the user files "Names" and "Netlog" and in this way propagating itself.

In the late 1980s, the Internet was a network that primarily connected university computers to each other. This network was vulnerable to programs, which could propagate using existing communications protocols. A university student named Robert Morris, who unleashed a major malware[1] incident, the Morris Worm, in November 1988, demonstrated this. This UNIX-based worm overwhelmed approximately 10 percent of all DEC computers on the Internet, causing a lot of media interest and many headlines.

Through the 1990s viruses began to change in their form and behaviors. Virus writers began to encrypt viruses and cause them to change their form as they spread to avoid detection (a trait that would later be coined as polymorphic). The decrypted version was stored at the beginning of the virus. This made it more difficult to determine if something was a virus as the virus signature was moved or changed. To detect a virus, it was necessary to write an algorithm that applied logical tests to the file, and decide whether the bytes it was looking at were one of the possible decryptors. The advent of polymorphic viruses brought about an increased false alarm rate as many innocent files were marked as being infected.

The most significant event of the 1990s was probably the Michelangelo virus. The virus was first discovered in 1991, and upon examination it was determined that it would erase PC hard disks on March 6 —birthday of Renaissance painter Michelangelo. Until 500 PCs were accidentally shipped with the virus in January of 1992, Michelangelo remained a limited threat. Coincidentally, another manufacturer immediately announced its decision to include anti-virus software with every computer.

To compound the growing number of virus problems, virus hoaxes were becoming popular in the 1990s. Electronic mail (e-mail) hoaxes were being sent out to see how far the e-mail would go and how fast it would travel. Similar to chain letters, their purposes included harassment, pyramid schemes, or defamation of someone's (or an organization's) reputation. Spotting hoaxes and how to handle them will be covered later in this chapter.

By the end of the decade, most companies were relying on local area networks for communications (particularly e-mail and data file transfer) and use of the Internet had become widespread. Traditional viruses (Boot Sector and File Infector) began to diminish in frequency as Macro (document) viruses arrived on the scene. Another contributing factor may have been

---

1. Malware is short for malicious software. Software designed specifically to damage or disrupt a system, such as a virus or a Trojan horse or a worm.

the change in how software programs were distributed with the introduction of CD-ROM technology.

The first computer virus that would affect computer hardware arose in 1999. The CIH/Chernobyl virus would infect executable files and spread once that file was executed. This virus had the ability to spread quickly as many files are executed during normal use of a computer. Once active, CIH would attempt to erase the entire hard drive and then overwrite the system BIOS causing some machines to need a new BIOS chip to recover the computer.

As e-mail grew in popularity, it provided people with a new venue to create malicious code that could be used to spread new computer viruses. This new form of computer virus had the ability to disguise itself as an innocent looking file attachment and then would generate and send numerous infected e-mail messages to addresses found in the personal contact list. These early e-mail-based viruses required a user to open the attachment to be successful. Some of the newer forms (or worms) do not require user intervention, instead they exploit security weaknesses in the operating systems. Code Red, for instance, was designed to exploit vulnerabilities in Microsoft® Web servers (IIS) and had exceptional replication speed.

In addition, new programming languages designed for portability and functionality presented new opportunities to develop additional forms of malicious code. StrangeBrew (while harmless and actually more a proof of concept virus) was the first virus to infect Java files.The virus modifies Java "CLASS" files to contain a copy of itself within the middle of the file's legitimate code. When the "infected" class file is executed, the virus gets control and then passes control to the original code in the file. Being Java based, StrangeBrew is capable of executing in almost any platform that has Java runtime environment installed. While StrangeBrew did not do anything except spread, the virus is capable of executing on Windows and Linux platforms and in PDA devices that have Java runtime installed.

Nimda is a complex virus with a mass-mailing worm component that utilizes multiple methods to spread itself. The W32/Nimda worm, taking advantage of back doors left behind by the Code Red II worm, will propagate itself via several methods (multipartite), including e-mail, network shares, and an infected Web site. The worm spreads between clients and Web server by using the client to scan for vulnerable servers. It then uses a Unicode exploit to infect the Web server, and subsequently "uses" the Web server to propagate itself to other clients browsing the site. The e-mail variant transmits an attachment, which might be executed automatically on the recipient machine.

Klez is an e-mail virus that infects executables by creating a hidden copy of the original host file and then overwriting the original file with itself. There are numerous variants of this hybrid that exhibit characteristics of different forms of malicious code, including classic worms, polymorphic viruses, and file infector viruses. Klez variants all follow the same basic form. Polymorphic is a virus that changes its virus signature (i.e., its binary pattern) every time it replicates and infects a new file in order to keep from being detected by an antivirus program. In some variants, it searches and disables anti-virus and integrity checker software (retro virus), and even attacks other virus forms (such as Nimda, SirCam, and Code Red). In many variations, it acts as a worm (generates e-mail messages to propagate itself to other systems) but also "drops" a file infector virus called Elkern (Win32. Klez.b), which then survives independently of Klez.

The replication speed of Internet worms, using today's high-speed computers, as well as constant probing for vulnerabilities by hostile individuals and groups, mandate continuous awareness, improvement, monitoring, and testing of IT security by organizations and user communities. As personal and corporate Internet connectivity has continued to increase over the past several years, authors of popular browser technologies have added numerous companion tools, or plug-ins, using specialized scripting codes that can automate common functions. These tools comprise a generation of active content code that exposes additional opportunities to attackers. Table 7.1 pressents a brief overview of the chronological progression of computer viruses.

Macro   Typically affecting Microsoft Office Products (e.g., Melissa, Concept), macro viruses are currently portable between platforms making them an extremely popular virus attack format.

Most macro viruses known to be in the wild infect MS Word files, but they can infect Excel files (although this is less common than Word macro infectors). Word macro viruses replicate into other documents by first copying themselves into the Word global template (normal.dot). Once the Normal. dot (this is the default template for all Word documents) is infected, any document opened will be infected.

Excel macro viruses show a less distinctive pattern, when compared to Word viruses. From the few that exist, they all replicate by creating their own workbook, containing an auto startup macro (auto_open), and place that workbook in the Excel startup directory — normally ...\Excel\XLStart.

Macro viruses infect other programming codes within a document by inserting or creating additional macro commands. When the infected document is transmitted and opened within the application, the infection spreads to the application components and then may re-propagate to other similar documents as they are accessed.

File Infector   Typically attached to .COM or .EXE files (e.g., Monkey, AntiEXE), file infectors attack executable program files, typically those with a

Table 7.1 A Chronological Progression of Computer Viruses

1949	von Neumann suggests computer programs could reproduce
1950s	Bell Labs creates a game that attacks other computers
1975	Brunner imagines a computer worm
1984	Fred Cohen introduces the term "computer virus"
1986	First virus created (BRAIN)
1987	Christmas tree Worm cripples IBM
1988	Internet worm spreads through DARPA
1990	First polymorphic virus (1260) — Mark Washburn
1992	Michelangelo spreads and so does the panic
1994	First virus HOAX hits (Good Times)
1995	First MACRO virus hits (Concept)
1995	First virus specifically for Windows 95
1998	First virus to affect computer hardware (CIH/Chernobyl)
1999	First e-mail virus — Melissa forwards itself
1999	First virus infects computer when e-mail is read (Bubbleboy)
2000	Love Bug becomes the most successful e-mail virus
2000	First virus for the Palm operating system
2001	An estimated $2 billion in damages caused by Code Red Worm
2003	Attackers change their method of operation by combining viruses/worms with hacking techniques causing new concerns that are more difficult to fight against
2004	83% of all computer viruses are transmitted via electronic mail (e-mail) Approximately 20 billion e-mails are sent each day

COM or EXE extension. Sometimes files having an executable structure are targeted by viruses, regardless of their extension name. File infectors may corrupt non-executable files as well but they cannot spread this way.

File infectors can be memory resident (TSR). Once an infected file is executed, the virus will remain resident in the computer's memory until the computer is powered off. While in memory, the virus will continue to infect other programs. This activity could eventually interfere with normal operations. Once the PC is turned off, the virus will lie dormant in infected files until those programs are executed.

These viruses exhibit the classic "replicate and attach" behavior. Because of the wide acceptance and popularity of MS-DOS and Windows-based platforms, most of the well-know file infectors target those systems. They attack (typically) DOS program files with "COM" or "EXE" file extensions. Newer 32-bit virus strains are designed to work as well with "SYS" and many other file types.

Many of these viruses are written and compiled in C++ and other higher level languages, unlike Boot Record infectors which are often written in Assembly. While the coding of file infector viruses can be quite complex, the architecture of PC DOS .COM and .EXE applications is relatively straightforward.

The objective of this virus type is to attach itself to the original program file in such a manner as to control the execution of that file until it can replicate and infect other files, and possibly deliver a payload.

One derivative file infector, called a *Companion Virus*, is really a separate program file that does not require attachment to the original host program. Instead, a new (companion) program with a matching file name but a higher precedent extension is created that will be executed first in the same directory path as the real program. DOS will always execute COM files before EXE files, so issuing the Run command (or clicking the program icon) causes the virus to be directly executed instead of the intended legitimate program (e.g., Format.com and Format.exe). Once virus activity is completed, the illicit program simply executes the command to start the original program.

Boot Sector Infectors These typically affect boot sectors of hard disks and floppies (e.g., Form, Michelangelo). Figure 7.2 depicts how boot infectors work.

All disks (hard and floppy, bootable and non-bootable) contain a boot sector. The boot sector contains specific information relating to the formatting of the disk, the data stored there and also contains a small program called the boot program (which loads the DOS system files). You can be

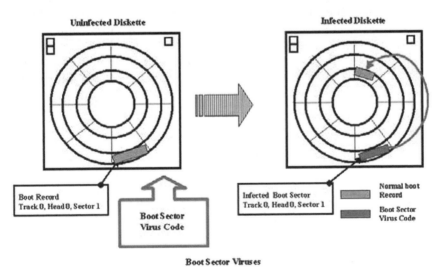

Figure 7.2 Multipartite viruses (boot and file infectors; e.g.,Tequila)

infected with a boot sector virus by using a diskette with a virus in a floppy drive and rebooting the machine. Once the boot sector program is read and executed, the virus becomes memory resident and will infect the boot sector on your hard drive.

System Infectors include a family of viruses targeting key hardware and system software components in a computing platform. The infected components are usually associated with system startup processes, allowing the virus to take control and execute before most software protective measures can be implemented. The most prevalent types of system infectors include Floppy Boot Record Infectors and Hard Drive Master Boot Record Infectors. These viruses are transmitted predominantly through the exchange of media (typically floppy disks) or are "dropped" as a special payload from a file infector virus.

Multipartite viruses infect both executable files and boot-partition sectors, sometimes the boot sector on floppies. Some multipartite viruses become infectious only after rebooting the computer from the infected MBR (Master Boot Record), like Tequila, others can be equally infectious if loaded from a file or through the boot process.

A Master Boot Record Infector moves or destroys the original Master Boot Record and replaces it with viral code. It can then gain control from the Bootstrap program and perform its hostile mission. Typical Master Boot Record infectors perform most of their tasks and then return control to the legitimate master boot record or the active partition boot record in order to mask their existence.

Both types of Boot Record Infectors typically load a viral proxy for the ROM-based system service provider process, thereby intercepting all normal application and operating system hardware requests. These requests include functions like opening and closing files and file directory services, thus creating an opportunity for the virus to execute other types of malicious code routines and also cover its tracks.

Virus Characteristics

Virus Structure   All computer viruses typically, only an infection has to be present to be called a virus, have a Trigger, a Payload, and an Infection. The trigger is typically defined as the mechanism that defines whether a payload will be delivered or not. The payload is defined as what the virus does (beside the replication). The infection is defined as the way or ways that the virus spreads.

The payload of some computer viruses while sometimes harmless to an individual, can be used to clog e-mail systems and in some cases cause them to crash.

Table 7.2. Payloads Delivered by Computer Viruses

Payload	Action
Access denied	Files have been password protected, owner cannot read own files
Data corruption	Changes are made to the original data
Data deletion	Hard disks are overwritten
Data theft	E-mails information about the user or a machine to the author
Display messages	Messages can be displayed on a user's screen
Hardware disabled	The BIOS is overwritten, making the machine unusable
Pranks	Like displaying messages, it may play a game or a tune on the PC

Other viruses have a destructive payload that might change or corrupt files or post strange/obscene messages on the screen. The effect of these payloads can be immediate or in some cases, the virus may lay dormant until a specific date or time. See Table 7.2 for some of the payloads that can be delivered by computer viruses/worms.

Polymorphic Viruses While duplicating the main body of the virus, polymorphic viruses include a separate encryption engine which stores the virus body in encrypted format. Only the decryption routine itself is exposed for detection. The control portion of the virus is embedded in this decryption routine, which seizes control of the target system and decrypts the main body of the virus so that it can execute.

True polymorphic viruses use an additional mutation engine to vary the decryption process for each iteration, making even this portion of the code more difficult to identify.

Bugbear.B is a very complex polymorphic virus that spreads through both e-mail and network shares. The worm sends e-mails with various contents. It uses a known vulnerability to execute the attachment automatically when the e-mail is opened.

Stealth Viruses Stealth viruses use a number of techniques to conceal themselves from the user or detection software. By installing a low-level system service function, they can intercept any system request and alter the service output to conceal their presence. Stealth viruses are further classified as having size stealth, read stealth, or both.

Size stealthing is typically used by file infector viruses to mask the increase in file size by intercepting system requests for file information and subtracting its size from the reply before passing it back to the requesting process.

Read stealthing is typically used by boot viruses, again by intercepting any read/write requests for the normal boot sector (which has been relocated and replaced by the viral code). The request is essentially redirected to the new hidden location as necessary to satisfy the request, thus masking the presence of viral code.

Slow Viruses These viruses were conceived to counter the ability of anti-virus programs to detect changes in files that become infected. This class of virus is memory-resident (where anti-virus software cannot detect it) and is programmed to wait until certain tasks are requested, like copying or moving files. As the file is read into memory, the virus alters it before writing to the output file, making it much harder to detect.

Retro Viruses Some viruses (one term is Retro viruses) are designed specifically to attack or defeat countermeasures, such as anti-virus signature files or integrity databases. The virus, once active, searches for these data files and deletes or alters them, thereby crippling the AV software's ability to fully function. Other viruses, especially boot viruses (which gain control of the target system at startup) modify Windows Registry keys and other key files to disable AV, firewall, and IDS software if found. "Cpw" is a retro-virus that will delete SCAN.EXE if it's attempted to run (http://www.europe.f-secure.com/v-descs/cpw.shtml).

Zarma is a memory resident encrypted COM and EXE infector (stealth). It was found in France during May, 1995. Zarma is a stealth virus that intercepts interrupt functions to mask its presence on an infected system. The virus hooks int 3 to its own decryption routine. This routine decrypts a second decryptor on the stack. Zarma is also a retro-virus and is able to deactivate VSAFE, VDEFEND and VWATCH.

Klez, a more recent virus (or worm) example, also exhibits counterattack technology by searching for a variety of specific (AVP related) text strings in running processes. If it recognizes any of those Strings, it terminates that process. It can also remove or alter Registry keys of anti-virus software so that it is disabled when Windows starts. The virus strain W32/Elkern-C, which is dropped by Klez-H, contains routines to disable the on-access component of popular virus scanners.

Why Care?

Global competition has led many businesses to rely on their computing infrastructure. Technologies like the Internet, while a key business enabler, have also opened vulnerabilities in some organizations. The more connected computers become the faster computer viruses (or malicious code) can spread.

In August of 2003 virus developers demonstrated new techniques for the delivery of computer viruses. In one week, the names Welchi, Lovsan/Blaster, and Sobig became household names. Computer users worldwide began experiencing network problems, such as slow response or in some cases lost e-mails. Sobig at its height was able to send over 100 million e-mails from the computers it had successfully infected.

As previously stated, these new blended threats (hacker techniques combined with virus like behaviors) can spread faster, farther, and can cause more damage than before.

Annually, the FBI and the Computer Security Institute (http://www.gocsi.com) gather statistics for a "Computer Crime and Security Survey." These surveys confirm that the threat from computer crime and other information security breaches continues unabated, and that the financial toll is mounting. The survey states that financial loss due malicious code attacks or computer breaches continues to increase with the most serious financial losses occurring through theft of proprietary information.

Worms and Trojan Horses As we have already seen, computer worms have been around, or at least thought about, as long as computer viruses. A computer worm is a computer program that self-replicates, similar to a computer virus. The main difference between the two is that a virus attaches itself to, and becomes part of, another executable program, while a worm is self-contained; it does not need to be part of another program to propagate itself.

On November 2, 1988, Robert Tappan Morris (then 23) unleashes a worm that invades ARPANET computers. The small program disables roughly 6,000 computers on the network by flooding their memory banks with copies of itself. Morris later confessed that he created the worm out of boredom. His fine was $10,000 and three years' probation (he was convicted under the US Computer Crime and Abuse Act). Some of the notable computer worms were MELISSA and the CODE RED worm; the latter gained notoriety because it targeted the White House Web site.

Worms remained relatively simple until the early 2000s, when Klez sparked speculation that such worms could employ genetic algorithms.[2] Klez uses electronic mail to propagate, infecting Microsoft Windows systems (typically Outlook mail clients). Klez had both a text portion and attachment(s). The first attachment contained the worm. Ironically, the internals of this worm would vary slightly. The text portion would either contain a HTML[3] internal frame tag, which could be mistakenly executed by clients that were not properly patched or simply a few lines of code that claimed to be a fix for the Klez worm.

January of 2003 brought about a new form of the computer worm known as the SQL Slammer. This worm caused widespread problems on the Internet, as it created a denial of service attack, which caused general traffic on

---

2. A *genetic algorithm* is used to find approximate solutions to difficult-to-solve problems.
3. HTML — HyperText Markup Language — is a markup language designed for the creation of Web pages, that will be presented on the World Wide Web

the Internet to slow down. This worm spread to 75,000 host computers in less than ten minutes. SQL Slammer did not actually use SQL to deliver its payload but instead, it exploited two buffer overflow bugs in Microsoft's SQL Server. A buffer overflow is a type of computer bug. When the length limitation of a space reserved for data — a buffer — is not properly enforced, a buffer overflow may occur. Input data is written to the buffer and, if the input data is longer than the buffer size, the space beyond the end of the buffer is overwritten. If this space then contains executable code, it may execute in privileged mode.

Both Sobig and Blaster worms were released in August of 2003, resulting in the highest clean-up costs and largest downtime related to computer worms. These latest worms sparked many people to call for government intervention to prevent further damages.

Sobig is a computer worm in the sense that it replicates by itself, but is also a Trojan horse as it masquerades as something different than a virus. The Sobig "viruses" infect a host computer by way of attachments. However, when the attachment is run, the worm begins to replicate by using its own SMTP agent engine. This particular worm harvests e-mail addresses and stores the gathered information in files on the host computer. One of the variants (Sobig.F) was programmed to contact 20 IP addresses using UDP port 8998 and begin installing programs or simply updating itself. The Sobig worm was written using the Microsoft Visual C++ compiler, and was subsequently compressed using a data compression program.

In January, 2004, MyDoom became the fastest spreading worm and quickly exceeded all records set by previous worms.

Trojan Horses A Trojan horse is a computer program with an apparent or actual useful function that contains additional, malicious hidden functions[4] (sometimes a method of placing logic bombs, salami attacks, viruses, and such onto a system). The name comes from ancient Greek history. In this story, a giant wooden horse was offered as a gift to the citizens of Troy. To the dismay of the citizens, they quickly learned that this wondrous gift housed an army of their enemies. The name is usually shortened to Trojans.

Differing from a virus that is a stand-alone program, the Trojan does not attach itself to other programs. While a worm moves from computer to computer on its own, a Trojan does not as it requires human interventions, such as an e-mail.

One of the earliest known forms of a Trojan was in 1975, when the ANIMAL program, a game to identify an animal, also spread itself to other users on UNIVAC Exec 8 computers.

---

4. Tipton and Ruthberg, *Handbook of Information Security Management* (Boca Raton, FL: Auerbach, 1993), 757.

A Trojan can be easily hidden in the code of common business applications, which can be composed of hundreds of thousands of lines of code. The Trojan waits for the execution of the target program. Once executed, the Trojan can insert the new malicious instructions, execute them and then remove all traces in only a few milliseconds.

If a Trojan is suspected, a comparison of the operational program to the master or backup copy can be done to determine if there are any unauthorized changes. Additionally, examining system logs or audit logs may provide information on suspicious programs.

Typically, Trojans do not infect other programs and are quite simple to delete.

Double File Extensions   Viruses, worms, and Trojan horses all make use of the double file extension. The Windows operating systems allows the creation of files names with a number of spaces in it. This trick is intended to fool users into believing that the file they are viewing cannot be executed. as in this example:

PLAIN.TXT.EXE

The .EXE at the end of the spaces, makes the program executable. Unfortunately in e-mail, users will only see the .TXT and potentially believe that the file is simply a Text file. This is why much has been done to educate users on not running e-mail attachments.

As a number of file extensions can be used to deliver or contain malicious code, it is recommended that the administrators block specific File Extensions at the Firewall. Table 7.3 is a partial list of suggested file extensions that should be blocked.

It is difficult for end users to understand all the file extensions that can be used and those that may be considered dangerous or Executable. Therefore, it is a good idea to develop a list of extensions that will be blocked at the Firewall by default. Every organization is unique and the list that is correct for one organization may not be correct for another. It is a good idea to educate users on some of the basic file extensions that you may not be able to block (i.e., .EXE, .PIF, .SCR, .COM).

A complete list of file extensions and their meanings is available at http://filext.com; also view http://whatis.techtarget.com/fileFormatA/ 0,289933,sid9,00.html.

Other Attacks   There are many other forms of attacks that can affect the operation of a computer system. These attacks include (but are not limited to):

- Denial of service
- Flooding

Table 7.3 A Partial List of File Extensions That Should Be Blocked

File Extension	Descriptions
.API	Acrobat Plug-in Used to view Adobe Acrobat files
.BAT	Batch processing file Used to execute a series of commands in a sequential order
.BPL	Borland package libraries Used in programs developed with the Delphi software language
.CHM	Compiled HTML Help file Could include a link that would download and execute malicious code
.COM	Command File Contains scripts and executables for DOS or windows
.DLL	Dynamic Link Library Executable code that is shared by other programs on the system
.DRV	Device Driver Used to extend the hardware support of a Windows machine
.EXE	Windows binary executable program
.OCX	Object linking and embedding (OLE) control Used to orchestrate the interaction of several programs on a windows machine
.PIF	Program Information File Used to tell windows how to run non-windows applications
.SCR	Screen saver programs Includes binary executable code
.SYS	System configuration file Used to establish system settings
.VB*	Visual Basic® files (VBE and VBS) Used to script in visual basic which is built into many Windows-based machines
.WSH	Windows Script Host Settings File Used to configure the script interpreter program on Windows machines

- Brute force
- Dictionary attacks
- Spoofing
- Spamming
- Logic bombs

Denial of Service Attacks

TCP SYN Flood Attacks When a system ("the client") attempts to establish a TCP connection to a system providing a service ("the server"), the client and server exchange a set sequence of messages. This connection technique applies to all TCP connections — Telnet, Web, e-mail, and so forth.

The client system begins by sending a SYN message to the server. The server then acknowledges the SYN message by sending SYN-ACK message to the client. The client then finishes establishing the connection by responding with an ACK message. The connection between the client and the server is then open, and the service-specific data can be exchanged between the client and the server.

The potential for abuse arises at the point where the server system has sent an acknowledgment (SYN-ACK) back to client but has not yet received the ACK message. This is what is meant by a half-open connection. The server has built in its system memory a data structure describing all pending connections. This data structure is of finite size, and it can be made to overflow by intentionally creating too many partially open connections.

Creating half-open connections is easily accomplished with IP spoofing. The attacking system sends SYN messages to the victim server system; these appear to be legitimate but in fact reference a client system that is unable to respond to the SYN-ACK messages. This means that the final ACK message will never be sent to the victim server system.

The half-open connections data structure on the victim server system will eventually fill, then the system will be unable to accept any new incoming connections until the table is emptied out. Normally there is a timeout associated with a pending connection, so the half-open connections will eventually expire and the victim server system will recover. However, the attacking system can simply continue sending IP-spoofed packets requesting new connections faster than the victim system can expire the pending connections.

In most cases, the victim of such an attack will have difficulty in accepting any new incoming network connection. In these cases, the attack does not affect existing incoming connections or the ability to originate outgoing network connections. However, in some cases, the system may exhaust memory, crash, or be rendered otherwise inoperative.

The location of the attacking system is obscured because the source addresses in the SYN packets are often implausible. When the packet arrives at the victim server system, there is no way to determine its true source. Since the network forwards packets based on destination address, the only way to validate the source of a packet is to use input source filtering.

Systems providing TCP-based services to the Internet community may be unable to provide those services while under attack and for some time after the attack ceases. The service itself is not harmed by the attack; usually only the ability to provide the service is impaired. In some cases, the system may exhaust memory, crash, or be rendered otherwise inoperative.

SYN Denial of Service attack begins with (1) spoofed TCP SYN request to standard port, with spoofed source address. Server responds to spoofed

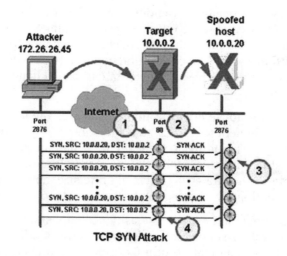

Figure 7.3 TCP SYN attack

address with SYN-ACK (2) and opens a connection state (see Figure 7.3). Since spoofed host did not originate SYN, it ignores the message (3), and the half-open sessions accumulate on the server (4), filling up buffer space and preventing legitimate new requests from being serviced.

Smurf Attacks In the "smurf" attack (see Figure 7.4), attackers are using ICMP echo request packets directed to IP broadcast addresses from remote locations to generate denial-of-service attacks. The two main components to the smurf denial-of-service attack are the use of forged ICMP echo request packets and the direction of packets to IP broadcast addresses.

There are three parties in these attacks: the attacker, the intermediary, and the victim (note that the intermediary can also be a victim). The intermediaries receive an ICMP echo request packet directed to the IP broadcast address of their network. If the intermediary does not filter ICMP traffic directed to IP broadcast addresses, many of the machines on the network will receive this ICMP echo request packet and send an ICMP echo reply packet back. When (potentially) all the machines on a network respond to this ICMP echo request, the result can be severe network congestion or outages.

The ICMP message is sent as a directed broadcast to all hosts in a network with a spoofed source address which appears to be from the target system. All hosts respond with a reply to the target, overloading it with traffic.

Distributed Denial of Service (DDoS) Attacks (DDoS) (see Figure 7.5) also uses intermediaries (unsuspecting) hosts to conduct an attack. These intermediaries are compromised systems on which Trojan handler pro-

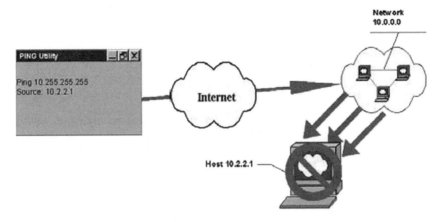

Table 7. 4 Smurf attack

grams are installed. These Trojan programs then act as agents to execute a coordinated attack on a target system or network. The attacker(s) control one or more "master" handler servers, each of which can control many agents or "daemons." The agents are all instructed to coordinate a packet-based attack against one or more victim systems.

There are three parties in these attacks: the attacker, the intermediaries

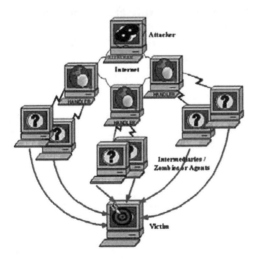

Figure 7.5 DDos attack

Table 7.4 Tools Used for Flooding or Attacking

Tools	Flooding or Attack Methods
Trin00	UDP
Tribe Flood Network	UDP, ICMP, SYN, Smurf
Stacheldracht	UDP, ICMP, SYN, Smurf
TFN 2K	UDP, ICMP, SYN, Smurf
Shaft	UDP, ICMP, SYN, combo
Mstream	Stream (ACK)
Trinity, Trinity V3	UDP, SYN, Random Flag, ACK, Fragment

(handlers and agents), and the victim(s). Even though the intermediary is not the intended "victim," the intermediary can also be victimized by suffering the same types of problem that the "victim" does in these attacks.

Attackers have developed automated DDoS tools (see Table 7. 4) that enable them to send these attacks to multiple intermediaries at the same time, causing all of the intermediaries to direct their responses to the same victim. Attackers have also developed tools to look for network routers that do not filter broadcast traffic and networks where multiple hosts respond. These networks can then subsequently be used as intermediaries in attacks.

Additional information on these exploits can be researched at CERT (http://www.cert.org) or by searching on the exploit.

IP Fragmentation and RPC Null Fragment Attacks IP fragmentation exploits involve generating TCP or ICMP packets using tools or command extensions which permit arbitrary modification of the packet flag fields. This takes advantage of the protocol's ability to break large messages into fragments for transmission across firewalls to meet transmission size constraints (Maximum Transmission Units or MTU).

Under normal circumstances, destination hosts must wait until all fragments have arrived before processing the message. If the message appears to contain additional fragments, the destination service must wait. The exploit arbitrarily generates multiple messages which indicate more fragments are to follow.

Mail Bombing and Spamming E-mail bombing is characterized by abusers repeatedly sending an e-mail message to a particular address at a specific victim site. In many instances, the messages will be large and constructed from meaningless data in an effort to consume additional system and network resources. Multiple accounts at the target site may be abused, increasing the denial of service impact.

E-mail spamming is a variant of bombing; it refers to sending e-mail to hundreds or thousands of users (or to lists that expand to that many users). E-mail spamming can be made worse if recipients reply to the e-mail, causing all the original addressees to receive the reply. It may also occur innocently, as a result of sending a message to mailing lists and not realizing that the list expands to thousands of users or as a result of an auto-responder message that is setup incorrectly.

E-mail bombing/spamming may be combined with e-mail spoofing or through the use of bulk "re-mailers" (which alter the identity of the account(s) sending the e-mail), making it more difficult to determine who actually sent the e-mail. Re-mailer services are becoming popular for individuals wanting to privatize their personal e-mail, but they can be used as an agent to distribute spam as well. When large amounts of e-mail are directed to or through a single site, the site may suffer a denial of service through loss of network connectivity, system crashes, or failure of a service because of:

- Overloading network connections
- Using all available system resources
- Filling the disk as a result of multiple postings and resulting in syslog entries

(Note: There is an increasing amount of pending legislation designed to place controls and restrictions on anonymous bulk mailing due to the serious business impact of spam and other unsolicited high volume traffic.)

Pestware and Pranks   A Pest can refer to undesired processes or code that might be found on your PC or your network after installing freeware applications that are downloaded from an Internet site.

Pests are generally nuisances but might include more dangerous Trojans, spyware, remote administration tools, hacker tool kits, and more. Pestware may threaten confidentiality and privacy, and, due to the increasing incidence of this, there is an administrative impact on productivity.

Pestware in the form of tracking cookies, is sometimes employed by commercial Web sites as a means of tracking a user's Internet browsing habits or as pop-up or pop-under Web pages to push unsolicited offers to a user who visits a competitive Web site.

Pranks, on the other hand, are often the work of adventurous "script kiddies" or other internal or external users, and can be malicious as well as a nuisance.

ANSI Bombs   These were quite possibly the original e-mail "virus," although they were not viruses at all. ANSI Bombs are simply modified TEXT or ANSI files that, when TYPED (with the DOS command) would re-map the target host keyboard. ANSI Bombs use the ANSI Escape sequence (with the reserved command "P") that was designed to perform a relatively simple

Macro task when you typed certain keys and relied on two very critical factors that were generally present under DOS:

- The ANSI driver (ANSI.SYS) was loaded in CONFIG.SYS
- The software displayed information via the system BIOS

The attacker would disguise the ANSI bomb as a downloadable DOS program (game, etc.) application on BBS sites or transmit the file via diskette. Once executed, the program could re-map keyboard keys (e.g., the space bar) to perform some malicious task such as formatting drives or erasing critical files.

These threats generally diminished when Microsoft Windows became the dominating operating system on PCs. Windows applications do not utilize the system BIOS to process and display information, thus the character sequence is never routed through the ANSI driver.

Again, they were not viruses — they were simple commands, designed to be loaded into the ANSI driver and modify the behavior of your display and/or keyboard.

Adware, Web Site Tracking Cookies (Trackware)   Many adware applications install Trojan advertising components on your system, that run — downloading ads and wasting system resources — even if you are not using the software that installed them. Often, these components operate in stealth mode and remain installed and continue to perform after the associated app has been uninstalled. These advertising Trojans make clandestine connections to adservers behind your back, consume precious network bandwidth and may compromise the security of your data. These include the TimeSink/Conducent TSADBOT and the Aureate/Radiate advertising Trojans.

A "cookie" is a token that stores information about a browser session. The server side of a user connection to a Web server can place certain information in the cookie, then give that cookie to the user's browser. On some other page, that server can ask the browser for the cookie, and retrieve the information previously stored. This becomes useful in any intelligent interaction between browser and Web site, because the connection between a browser and server is not persistent.

Cross-site tracking cookies (sometimes referred to incorrectly as spyware) are simply those cookies that are not used only by a single site for its private interactions with its users, but are shared across sites. Some cookies are persistent and are stored on your hard drive indefinitely without your permission. They can reveal and share private information collected among multiple sites, as they are visited.

Cookie Poisoning   While cookies are intended to store personal information and only forward that information back to the server, this information can be modified by an attacker. As an example, if one is able to modify the total value of an online order, they could pay less than originally intended when the data is returned to the server.

Homepage Hijacking   The goal of these attacks is to change your browser's homepage to point to their site. There are two forms of hijacking:

- Exploiting an IE vulnerability to automatically reset the homepage.
- Covert installation of a Browser Helper Object (BHO) Trojan program, which contains the hijacking code.

Once a BHO Trojan gets executed, it changes (or forces) the browser's homepage back to the hijacker's desired site. Typically, hijacker programs put a reference to themselves into the Windows StartUp folder or Registry Run key, so that the hijacker runs every time the computer is started. If the user tries to change any of these settings, the hijacker repeatedly changes them back until the hijacking software can be found and removed.

Web Page Defacements   The terms "Web defacement" or "Web graffiti" refer to an incident when someone gains unauthorized access to a Web server and alters the index page of that particular violated site. Usually the attacker exploits known vulnerabilities in the target server and gains administrative access. Once in control, html pages are replaced with altered versions.

Typically, the defacement represents graffiti; however, while most security practitioners consider this attack a nuisance, the potential for embedding more malicious active content code (such as viruses or Trojans) into the Web site exists. Code Red, for instance, included payload that installed a backdoor Trojan. This Trojan allows remote access to an infected IIS server which can be used to deface the front page of the Web server.

Ensuring that current software versions and security patches are installed and active monitoring of Web sites will minimize the risks.

Brute Force Attacks   Brute force attacks utilize exhaustive trial and error methods to obtain the information about passwords or cryptographic keys.

If a brute force attack was launched against a password containing five (5) numbers, there would be 10*10*10*10*10 or 100,000 possible combinations that the system would test. Adding the complexity of numbers (0–9), characters (upper and lower case A–Z) and special characters (! @ # $) increases the number of possible combinations making a brute force attack less attractive and more difficult as it would require more processing power. Brute force can eliminate a large number of possible combinations.

Trying to crack a 56 bit DES[5] key using a brute force attack with today's processing power could take hundreds of years with one PC. However, with

---

5.   DES — Data Encryption Standard

the growth of the Internet and the ability to link computers on the Internet, the time to perform this exhaustive task has been drastically reduced. As this is the case, you will find that DES is obsolete and AES or triple DES are now the standard.

Dictionary Attacks Using a dictionary attack, an attacker will take a specific list of words (typically a dictionary listing) and compare those words against passwords stored in the access control listing. Once the attacker has obtained the password file, tools can be used to try to obtain the password. Most passwords can be guessed using a brute force attack but utilizing one of these tools drastically cuts the attacker's time as words in the list are compared.

In order to gain access to the password files, one must either be internal to an organization or be able to break through the corporation's defenses. Once this is accomplished, tools are available that will allow the dump (or make a copy of) the password file to an alternate location, allowing the attacker ample time to extract the passwords.

The reader is reminded that the English dictionary is not the only one that can be used. All foreign language dictionaries as well as dictionaries such as Lord of the Rings, Star Trek, Star Wars, and so forth have been written and can be used with these tools.

Hashed Password or Password-Verifier Passwords stored in a database should be stored in a one-way hashed form, to prevent casual retrieval of the information. Since passwords are often vulnerable to a dictionary attack, preventing unauthorized access to this data thus remains a high priority. In general, the requirement for secure host storage is characteristic of all mutual authentication cryptographic systems. Alternative public-key methods are especially sensitive to the theft of a stored private key. Since the hashing algorithm to "encrypt" the password file can be discovered easily, it is not difficult to use that to hash the dictionary words and compare the hashed versions to the downloaded password file to find a match that leads to the password in the dictionary. That is why reusable passwords are considered to be virtually useless today.

Online versus Offline Attack An online attack requires the active participation of a legitimate user or host. The important things are to minimize the information revealed in each attack, and to ensure that the legitimate party is aware that an attack or failure has occurred. A user naturally becomes suspicious and reports trouble when a large number of failures occur, and the system should encourage this. A host typically counts bad or suspicious attempts, and takes remedial action when a limit is exceeded.

Offline password attacks have historically been harder to prevent. We must assume that an attacker has a large amount of CPU power, has technical expertise, and can monitor or probe the network to gather password protocol messages. This is true for anyone who has a Pentium, Web access, and can click to download and run a cracker's tool. Strong password protocols ensure that gathered messages cannot be used offline to computationally determine the password.

Salt "Salt" is a value incorporated into the calculation of the hashed-password. The salt is typically chosen randomly at the time of password selection, and stored along with the hashed-password. Another choice is to calculate salt from the user's name. Using salt, two users with the same password will have different hashed values, which makes it harder to create a pre-built dictionary of likely hashes. This technique decreases the efficiency of broad-based dictionary attack against a readable password database for many users.

The UNIX /etc/passwd mechanism used a random two-character salt for each user. Modern protocols use a larger salt, which makes broad-based attack impossible — each hashed-password must be attacked individually.

Salt plays the same role in a hashed-password database for network authentication, to reduce the threat if the database is revealed. The salt is typically sent from the host to the client as a prelude to password verification. But regardless of whether salt is used, protection of the password database remains a higher priority.

Logic Bombs A logic bomb is code added to the software of an application or operating system, which will lie dormant until an event occurs. The event can be a date or a specific condition on the system. This event will trigger the code to take some actions. Typically, logic bombs are malicious in their nature. The ultimate motive of a logic bomb is usually to delete, alter or corrupt data that the program has access to.

Ping of Death Ping is a "utility" program used to determine if a specific IP address is accessible and is primarily used to troubleshoot network or Internet connections. Ping sends packets to the specified address and waits for a reply.

Typically, IP packets are 65,535 bytes in length (as per RFC-791), including the header length (generally 20 bytes if no IP options are specified). Packets that are bigger than the maximum size the underlying layer can handle (the MTU) are fragmented into smaller packets, which are then reassembled by the receiver. For ethernet devices, the MTU is typically 1500.

An ICMP ECHO request "lives" inside the IP packet, consisting of eight octets of ICMP header information (RFC-792) followed by the number of data bytes in the "ping" request. Hence, the maximum allowable size of the data area is 65535 - 20 - 8 = 65507 octets.

Most computers do not process packets until all the fragments have been reassembled. A Ping of Death would occur when an illegal echo packet with grater than 65507 bytes is sent due to the way the fragmentation is performed. Fragmentation relies on the offset value in each fragment to determine where the packet goes on reassembly. Thus, when the packets are reassembled, there is the chance for system buffers to overflow causing the system to crash, reboot, hang protocols, or the like.

Spoofing Attacks

IP Spoofing Spoofing is a technique used to attain unauthorized access to computers or in a sense, masking the true identity or source.

IP Spoofing allows an attacker to attain unauthorized access to a network or computer making it look like the message (malicious or not) is coming from a trusted source. This is accomplished by forging the IP address of the trusted source.

Through the years there have been many forms of IP spoofing attacks, some of which are still pertinent to security today.

Non-Blind Spoofing To perform this type of spoof, the attacker is usually on the same subnet as the victim.

In this attack, a sniffer is used to gather information on the sequence and acknowledgement numbers eliminating the potential difficulty of calculating them accurately. Once gathered, the largest threat is typically session hijacking. An established connection is interrupted (or corrupted) and a new session connected using the sequence and acknowledgement numbers that were collected using the sniffer. This can effectively bypass any authentication measures built into the process.

ARP Spoofing An ARP spoof forges the packet source hardware address (MAC address) to the address that the attacker wishes to use.

Man in the Middle Attack In a Man in the Middle attack (sometimes referred to as TCP hijacking), the attacker intercepts communications between trusted parties. Once the communication is intercepted, the attacker has control of the communications and can modify or delete the information that is being sent between the victims. This attack is useful in attaining confidential information.

Denial of Service Attack (DoS) In this attack, the attacker attempts to flood the victim with as many packets as possible in a relatively short space of time. A DoS attack is difficult to defend against as the cracker will use multiple spoofed IP addresses to perform the attack making it almost impossible to trace or stop.

Active Content Vulnerabilities The term "active content" includes ActiveX™, Java, JavaScript/JScript, VBscript, macros, browser plug-ins, scrap files, Windows scripting host files, and Postscript™. This code runs in the context of the user signed on to a PC and can do everything that the user can do. Another term that seems to be gaining in usage, "vandal," is defined as any malicious auto-executable application, which includes the above-mentioned active content.

These active content threats, including ActiveX, Java, and JavaScript code in HTTP data streams, are often referred to as "mobile code" since these programs are written to run on a wide variety of computer platforms. Key points to consider regarding active code:

- Java applets are considered to be untrusted code.
- They are run within a *virtual machine* that uses a *sandbox* approach to theoretically restrict what they can do, preventing inappropriate actions on the user's computers.
- It is possible for Java code to trigger (or spawn) execution of OS functions that do not have this restriction (although this is more of an issue of loopholes prevalent in Microsoft Internet Explorer implementations).
- ActiveX is widely considered to be the greater threat because it is essentially an outgrowth of *OLE*, which permits direct access to native Windows calls and links them to system functions.
- ActiveX has no built-in language restrictions controlling code behavior.
- ActiveX controls can be built utilizing many different programming languages.

Many Internet Web sites now rely on Java applets and ActiveX controls to create their look and feel. For these schemes to operate properly, these bits of mobile code are downloaded to the user's PC, where they gain access to the local host and can then spawn malicious activity (viral infections, worm behavior, or Trojan functions).

Types of Mobile Code Attacks   While mobile code attacks can take many forms, there are four primary types of assaults:

- **Launch Point** — The malicious mobile code can use the targeted computer as a launch point to infect and target other computers.
- **Distributed Denial of Service (DDoS)** — In a DDoS attack, zombie agents automatically generate hundreds of authentication requests to the server simultaneously, which can quickly overwhelm targeted Web sites. Since all the requests have false return addresses, the server is unable to find the user when it tries to send the authentication approval. The server waits, sometimes more than a minute, before closing the connection. When it does close the connection, the zombie agent sends a new batch of forged requests, and the process begins again, tying up the service indefinitely.
  —This attack will impact Availability of computers, networks, and servers.

- **Data Modification** — The mobile code is instructed to access a file on a local or network drive, and modifies, deletes, or overwrites it with new data. Sometimes this type of mobile code is used to modify system settings or browser security settings. Data modification can impact the Integrity of data.
- **Data Export** — Malicious mobile code can steal information from your computer and forward it over the Internet or e-mail to an attacker. For instance, many Trojan horses will forward your user name and password to an anonymous e-mail address on the Web. A third party can then use the password to access protected resources. Exporting data could impact the Confidentiality of the data.

Attacks and Exploits Using Malformed Data

Server applications, in general, operate within some defined set of protocols or program specifications. These define the normal or expected parameters of operation of the related service. Exploitation of the sometimes inflexible boundaries of these parameters has been a popular target for years. Common exploits include:

- Overwhelming the predefined capacity of these services to handle new requests (denial of service types of exploits).
- Sending information in specially crafted packets that contain erroneous information (such as size information or commands that contain special characters), which causes program buffer overflows. This error condition may freeze or crash the server, or may open error handling services which can be exploited to gain control and execute additional (malicious) code.
- Sending specific strings of characters to well know services (IIS for instance), which contain nested or imbedded command syntax that is arbitrarily executed by the server.

As an example, there are two major Unicode vulnerabilities: the IIS/PWS Extended Unicode Directory Traversal Vulnerability and the IIS/PWS Escaped Character Decoding Command Execution Vulnerability. Many current worms have used these two Unicode vulnerabilities in IIS to good effect

Worms having being using buffer overflow conditions to gain service control of a target platform since 1988.

These vulnerabilities can allow attackers to run arbitrary code on the target servers, possibly uploading further compromises (as Nimda does using TFTP).

IT security practitioners can protect themselves from these specific vulnerabilities by installing the recent service packs and security updates from Microsoft. Other recommendations include:

- Do not use default directory/share names or locations. Customize them for your site.
- Carefully set permissions on shares.
- Turn off all unneeded functions or disable unused extensions in IIS.

How Active Content Operates

Active content comes in many types these days from application macros, to applets to background scripts. Postscript, Java, JavaScript, and Visual Basic Script, ActiveX, Macros, and browser plug-ins are all capable of being exploited through well-defined and documented active content features. All of these have potential weaknesses that can be exploited.

ActiveX is part of the Microsoft® Component Object Model, COM for short, that provides reusable code segments for application programs. These compact code modules help control many aspects of Wintel applications and hardware and allow for the automation of many background tasks.

The security model for ActiveX relies heavily on user interaction in order to ensure that unsigned controls are not downloaded or executed on a host system. Other than this trust model, ActiveX controls have little restrictions on what they can do once they are given permission to proceed. Once active, ActiveX assumes all of the rights of any local program on the host, and as such, can arbitrarily execute any damaging routines that other malicious code can.

ActiveX controls can be registered and digitally signed by commercial certificate authorities like Verisign (and also by local/private CAs). These signed applets, like any legitimate application program, become known as "Authenticode" and carry a digital signature to verify their integrity and source.

Of the 1,000 or so registered controls, only 50 to 100 have the marked designation as safe for scripting. Privately signed controls (possibly custom controls) authenticated by CAs which do not maintain Certificate Revocation Lists (CRLs) present an additional concern, since the security model is based on all or nothing permissions. If the control appears safe, and is executed (accepted), then it will assume full permissions and capability.

One problem with unsigned ActiveX controls is they are vulnerable to exploits launched by text (scripts) imbedded within HTML documents. Accessing an infected HTML file may cause a malicious script in the HTML file to run automatically if your browser security settings allow it.

In viruses carried by this method, infected script might search for all *.HTM and *.HTML files in the current directory and all directories above it and infect them as well. The infection basically prepends the virus to the

HTML file which can then be propagated to other hosts accessing that Web page or e-mail.

JavaScript and Visual Basic Script

Both of these languages belong to a class of scripting tools whose code can be embedded into Web pages for creating highly interactive documents. The theory of their operation dictates that they cannot directly access a client file system and communications are restricted to the host from which the content originates. There are numerous design and implementation bugs in both of these products.

The biggest flaw is that they work within the context of the browser and, in theory, are limited or bounded by whatever is legal within the browser. Unfortunately, modern browsers are bound tightly to other applications, such as e-mail and have various plug-ins and ActiveX controls that can be accessed. Additionally, these scripts will assume whatever your privileges are on the systems you are logged into at the time of their execution. If you hit a malicious script while logged in as an administrator, then the script will run with administrative privileges which could be devastating to security.

Java Active Code

Java is the universal code that is similar in nature to ActiveX in stated purpose only. It is the reusable code set that can be written once and run on many different types of hardware platforms if there is an interpreter called the Java Virtual Machine (JVM) on the target host.

The resulting byte code created from Java is conveyed by an HTML Web page as an applet. Java, unlike ActiveX, tried to address the security shortcomings of other modular programming languages by addressing security from the onset. It provides a security architecture known as a *sandbox.*

According to the National Institute of Standards and Technology (NIST), the sandbox is a bounded area that "restricts the access of the applet code to computational resources based on its permissions." That is to say, unless the applet is trusted, it can only use resources within the bounded area (it does not acquire permissions to execute external code). The problem with permissions is that they are defined again as trusted resources (e.g., where it comes from and who wrote the applet).

While the sandbox is supposed to prevent the applet from accessing files or even changing them and prevent accessing the network, there have been many successful exploits that circumvent the sandbox security construct.

These exploits are primarily related to implementation flaws in developing applets.

Structure and Focus of Malicious Code Attacks

Uncoordinated (or unstructured) attacks against network resources are generally perpetrated by moderately skilled persons such as script kiddies and cyberpunks. Often, the initial intent is personal gratification (or the thrill of the challenge) of achieving illegal access to a network or target system without any real purpose in mind. Any level of success may in fact lead to further exploration and more malicious activity such as defacements or crashing systems. All such activity is of concern to IT security practitioners as it represents a compromise of defensive measures.

Occasionally, such an uncoordinated attack exposes an unintended vulnerability and the attacker may then change his or her activities to a more methodical approach. When an attacker finds additional or unplanned targets to pursue during or after an attack this is is sometimes called "rat dancing," "shaking doors," or "rattling locks."

Coordinated, pre-planned attacks are usually conducted by adversaries who are highly motivated and technically skilled crackers, using complex tools and focused efforts. These attackers may act alone or in groups, and they understand, develop, and use sophisticated hacking techniques to locate, identify, penetrate, probe, and then carry out malicious activities. Such an attacker's motives may include money, anger, destruction, or political objectives.

Regardless of the motivations, these attackers can and do inflict serious business damage to networks. Structured attacks are usually conducted in phases, once an overall goal is established. It may be aimed at a specific organization or a specific technology (such as an OS version).

Directed Attacks against specific targets (specific organizations) or target classes (i.e., networks that are using certain hardware, operating system versions, or services) are often conducted as interactive sessions using predefined exploits. An example might be an IIS Unicode attack against specific Web servers in an organization.

These exploits may be uncoordinated or unstructured, as when a script kiddie uses well-known hacker tools to discover vulnerable sites, and then conducts random exploits to rat dance around the compromised network through trial and error.

They may also be conducted as coordinated or pre-planned attacks, by individual crackers or by coordinated cyber-terrorist groups, and advance methodically through phases to achieve their desired goals.

Indirect Attacks occur as a natural result of preprogrammed hostile code exploits, such as Internet worms or viruses. These attacks are unleashed indiscriminately and are designed to propagate rapidly and widely. While the worm or virus itself may be written to exploit a specific system or application vulnerability, the replication and transmission components of the code are designed to propagate indiscriminately.

It is very likely that one of the goals of a directed attack against a specific target might be to establish a starting point for a more indirect attack against a more widely disbursed population. The compromise of a single Web server to install an e-mail worm as a denial of service exploit might be the intended goal.

Phases of an Attack

Reconnaissance and Probing

Once the overall goal or objective of an attack is clear, an attacker must then probe a target network and identify points of possible entry (the vulnerabilities). This phase generally involves the use of common tools that are readily available on the Internet, are part of the underlying protocol suite, or a custom developed to exploit specific or potential targets. These can include:

- Use of DNS and ICMP tools within the TCP/IP protocol suite
- Use of standard and customized SNMP tools
- Using port scanners and mappers to locate potential target services
- Dissemination of spyware Trojan programs to collect reconnaissance data

These tools might be used independently or as a coordinated suite of activities designed to provide a complete understanding of a targeted network (what protocols and operating system is used, what server platforms exist, what services/ports are open, what actual or probable network addressing and naming is being used, etc.).

The Internet and other public sources can provide additional information necessary to profile targets, including locations of facilities, key personnel, and likely business partners. This last piece of information may seem trivial, but an indirect assault committed through a trading partner having serious security breaches is very possible.

DNS Commands and Tools

The Domain Name System (DNS) is a hierarchy of servers that provide an Internet-wide symbolic name to IP address mapping for hosts connected to the Internet. Publicly available information on registered addresses is obtainable through a number of searchable Web sites. In addition, discovery tools that are built into TCP/IP, such as whois and finger, can be used to gather preliminary information in profiling a target site.

Reverse DNS lookup or nslookup are additional utility commands that will also interrogate DNS information and provide cross-referencing. These services are often provided free on the Internet and can be located simply by searching on the command name itself.

The example above is from http://ww1.arin.net/whois/ which can be used to locate the IP address of a potential target network. Arin's whois will *not* locate any domain-related information, or any information relating to military networks. Many operating systems provide a whois utility. To conduct a query from the command line, the format generally is:

Whois-h hostname identifier (e.g., whois-h whois.arin.net<query string>).

ICMP and Related TCP/IP Tools

The Internet Control Management Protocol (ICMP) PING command and several closely related tools are readily available on most computer operating systems and would be a key profiling tool to verify that target systems are reachable. The PING command can be used with a number of extension flags to test direct reach ability between hosts or as part of the actual attack plan (see Ping of Death attacks).

Once a target network has been located, many attackers then perform a Ping Sweep of all, or a range of, IP addresses within the major network or subnet to identify other potential hosts that may be accessible. This information alone sometimes exposes the likely network size and topology, and, because many networks use a structured numbering scheme, may also point to likely server and network device locations.

If gaining access is one of the objectives, a simple telnet login attempt might be performed initially to test the softness of perimeter controls. Rpcinfo might also be used to determine if this service is active for remote command execution.

Remote SNMP Agent Discovery utilities let you discover responsive SNMP agents running on network devices. This example reflects, for instance, a server ("APOLLO"), located at 212.30.73.70, which is responding to SNMP queries, and might now be probed or scanned for other open service ports.

Using SNMP Tools

The Simple Network Management Protocol (SNMP) is an application layer protocol that facilitates the exchange of management information between network devices. It is part of the Transmission Control Protocol/Internet Protocol (TCP/IP) protocol suite. SNMP enables network administrators to manage network performance, find and solve network problems, and plan for network growth.

Many of the more popular Network Management software suites, like HP OpenView, SunNet Manager, and AIX NetView, are SNMP compliant and offer full support for managed devices, agents, and network-management systems. In addition, there are many utility programs which can be used to gather network device information, including platform, operating system version, and capabilities. Poorly configured network management facilities would allow moderately skilled attackers to gather significant attack profile information.

Port Scanning and Port Mapping

Once a target network has been initially identified, the attacker might proceed to explore what systems and services are accessible for further investigation. There are several popular port scanning applications an attacker might use. One of the most popular, shown above, is nMap (available for UNIX and Windows). MingSweeper is another network reconnaissance tool for Windows NT/2000, designed to facilitate large address space, high-speed node discovery and identification.

These tools permit an attacker to discover and identify hosts by performing ping sweeps, probe for open TCP and UDP service ports, and identify operating systems and vulnerable applications that might be running.

The utility program (CHKSATAN) represents a countermeasure often used to detect the presence of SATAN (Security Administrator Tool for Analyzing Networks) performing a ping sweep and remote procedure call probe. If detection is made, the routine creates a temporary access control filter blocking further access for the specified period (ten minutes).

Security Probes

SATAN is a tool designed to help systems security administrators evaluate a number of vulnerabilities. It recognizes several common networking-related security problems and reports the problems without actually exploiting them. SATAN collects information that is available to anyone with

410

access to the network. With a properly configured firewall in place that should be near-zero information for outsiders.

For each type or problem found, SATAN offers a tutorial that explains the problem and what its impact could be. The tutorial also explains what can be done about the problem: correct an error in a configuration file, install a bugfix from the vendor, and use other means to restrict access, or simply disable service.

On networks with more than a few dozen systems, SATAN will inevitably find problems, such as:

- NFS file systems exported to arbitrary hosts or to unprivileged programs via portmapper
- NIS password file access from arbitrary hosts
- Arbitrary files accessible via TFTP
- Remote shell access from arbitrary hosts
- Writable anonymous FTP home directory

These are well-known problems. They have been subject of CERT, CIAC, or other advisories, or are described extensively in practical security handbooks. The problems have been exploited by the intruder community for a long time.

SATAN is a two-edged sword, however; like many tools, it can be used for good and for evil purposes. It is a good idea to include scanning for evidence of SATAN reconnaissance of your network.

Use of Spyware and Backdoor Trojans

Spyware is a term for Trojan software that employs a user's Internet connection in the background (the so-called "back-channel") without his or her knowledge or explicit permission. Spyware exists as an independent, executable program on your system, and has the capability to monitor keystrokes, arbitrarily scan files on your hard drive, snoop other applications such as word-processors and chat programs, read your cookies, change your default homepage, interface with your default Web browser to determine what Web sites you are visiting, and monitor other user behavior, and transmitting this information back to the author.

War Dialing A war dialer is a computer program used to identify the phone numbers that can successfully make a connection with a computer modem. The program automatically dials a defined range of phone numbers and logs and enters in a database those numbers that successfully connect to the modem. Some programs can also identify the particular operating system running in the computer and may also conduct automated penetration testing. In such cases, the war dialer runs through a predetermined list of common user names and passwords in an attempt to gain access to the system.

A war dialer, usually obtained as freeware, is typically used by a hacker to identify potential targets. If the program does not provide automated penetration testing, the intruder attempts to hack a modem with unprotected log-ins or easily cracked passwords. Commercial war dialers, also known as modem scanners, are also used by system administrators to identify unauthorized modems on an enterprise network. Such modems can provide easy access to a company's intranet.

Access and Privilege Escalation

Once a potential target network has been profiled and probed for potential vulnerabilities, an attacker must succeed in accessing the target system(s). The primary goal of access is to establish the initial connection to a target host (typically a server platform). In order to conduct additional reconnaissance activities, such as covert installation of hacking tool kits, the attacker must then gain administrative rights to the system.

The method of access depends upon the connection technology necessary to reach the target network. As many organizations evolve to Web-centric business models, they often maintain legacy dial-up access infrastructures, either as secondary remote gateways or due to oversight. In some instances, organizations may not even be aware of modem facilities left connected to outside phone lines or PBXs or may not consider the security risks of leaving unattended modem connections, which often compromise existing network perimeter defenses.

A more recent problem issue is wireless networks which are inadequately configured to restrict access. A very common vulnerability relates to reliance on default settings (SSIDs) and passwords on new installations.

Password Capturing and Cracking

A password logger may be installed as a backdoor Trojan on a target machine and monitor specific protocol and program activity associated with remote login processes. Or, if login strings are captured remotely, a program such as LophtCrack (http://www.atstake.com/research/lc/download.html) might be used to decrypt and compromise administrator and user passwords very quickly.

Malformed Data Attack   Crafting commands or scripts containing illegal or unrecognized commands, or incorrectly coded parameters, is a method of attacking a target system once it has been identified. One of the more popular exploits to gain access to Microsoft Web servers, for example, is the IIS Unicode attack, discovered in Microsoft Internet Information Server 4.0/5.0 (as well as the Microsoft Personal Web Server shipped on client systems). Remote users (attackers) can write URLs that allow them to access and run files anywhere on the Web server. Then the attacker can run the "CMD.EXE" file, which allows him to execute any command and have full run of the system.

For example, if an attacker sent the UR: www.victim123.com/scripts/ ..%c1%1c../winnt/system32/cmd.exe?/c+dir

to a vulnerable server, he would open a command shell and execute the "dir" command. More nefarious commands could be substituted, allowing an attacker to upload a rootkit to deface a site or hijack the site for other attacks.

The string "/..%c1%1c../" translates as "/../ /../," which causes the Web server to go up to the root directory when looking for a file. IIS is smart enough to recognize and block the attack if an attacker tried this in the clear.

However, since the string is obfuscated in Unicode, the server doesn't recognize the attack and readily executes the code. Microsoft issued a patch to fix this, but many older servers exist which are still vulnerable.

Eavesdropping, Data Collection, and Theft

Covert Channel Communication   Covert channels refers to hiding malicious code (or simply sending command strings) within normal appearing traffic in such a manner that it is not normally inspected by firewalls, intrusion detection, or other screening countermeasures. As an example, ICMP_ECHO traffic can be used to construct covert communications channels through networks.

The normal PING protocol involves the originating host sending an ICMP_ECHO REQUEST packet to a target destination Host. That destination host then sends an ICMP_ECHO REPLY back. These ICMP_ECHO packets have an option to include additional data about timing information to determine round-trip packet times.

Firewalls and filtering routers only forward or filter these packets based on the protocol itself, but do not inspect the data content, so it is possible to transmit malicious information inside this packet. Because there is no inspection of the content, it is possible to masquerade (hide) Trojan packets inside valid ICMP_ECHO packets. This would be a covert channel attack.

A Remote Administration Tool, or RAT, is a Trojan that, when executed, provides an attacker with the capability of remotely controlling a machine via:

- A "client" in the attacker's machine, and
- A "server" in the victim's machine.

The server in the victim "serves" incoming connections to the victim and runs invisibly with no user interface. The client is a GUI front-end that the attacker uses to connect to victim servers and "manage" those machines. Examples include Back Orifice, NetBus, SubSeven, and Hack'a'tack. What happens when a server is installed in a victim's machine depends on the capabilities of the Trojan, the interests of the attacker, and whether or not control of the server is ever gained by another attacker.

Infections by remote administration Trojans on Windows machines are becoming as frequent as viruses. One common source is through File and Print Sharing. Another common method of installation is for the attacker to simply e-mail the Trojan to the user along with a social engineering hack (compelling message) that convinces the user to run it against his or her better judgment.

Backdoor programs are typically more dangerous than computer viruses as they can be used by an intruder to take control of a PC and potentially gain network access. Until now, the most widely distributed backdoors have been Netbus and the first version of Back Orifice. These programs are also commonly referred to as Trojan horses due to the fact that they pretend to do something other than they actually do.

Backdoor programs are typically sent as attachments to e-mails with innocent looking file names. Back Orifice also has a plug-in architecture that enables it to be disguised upon installation.

Authors of these programs often make the claim that they have not written them as intrusion tools, but rather as remote-control tools or (sometimes) to demonstrate the weaknesses in operating systems. Their real purpose however, as seen by past activity, is to gain access to computers for unauthorized use.

Hackers, Crackers, and Other Perpetrators

What's in a Name?

There are a number of popular descriptive terms used to refer to individuals and groups engaging in exploiting software and system vulnerabilities, although these are by no means standardized. The IT security practitioner should understand the differences. By understanding their motives and methods, you can better protect your systems against malicious code threats from each of these groups:

- Hackers
- Crackers

- Phreakers
- Organized cyber-terrorists and cyber-criminals

Hackers The term "hacker" was initially used by computer programmers to recognize someone who was a computer enthusiast. However, the definition has changed over time to refer to someone who uses computers to commit computer crimes. This change has come about due to the media who have used the term to refer to anyone who gains unauthorized access to computer systems. Hackers maintain the true name for these people is crackers.

To distinguish benevolent from malicious intent, several derivatives have emerged to classify individuals who engage in compromising IT protective measures of third-party organizations:

- Ethical Hackers (sometimes referred to as White Hats)
- Black Hat (corrupt) Hackers
- Wannabes, Grey Hats, or Whackers

White Hat (or Ethical) Hackers are generally described as information security or network professionals using various penetration test tools to uncover and fix vulnerabilities. They are typically hired by concerned organizations to perform their activities with explicit permission of the "victim" in order to identify vulnerabilities and stress test protective measures. Many of these individuals may have actually evolved from less benevolent backgrounds, but have become recognized specialists at discovering and exploiting weaknesses in security systems.

Black Hat Hackers might be described as esoteric hackers who engage in compromising IT security for the mere challenge, to prove vulnerabilities or technical prowess, usually without regard to observing the ethics of who owns which networks. They probe and penetrate target organizations on an ad hoc basis without permission, and their goals often are malicious. Because they most often publicize their exploits to emphasize weaknesses found, it can be argued that these groups contribute something to overall improvements in information security.

Wannabes (also Wnnabes) often refers to "would-be-hackers" capable of becoming black hat, who investigate and study the IT security field and perform general reconnaissance of systems and networks as a prelude to possibly more devious undertakings.

There is another popular term for this type of hacker — Grey Hats. These people may ultimately become either criminals or security consultants.

The term "whacker" has also recently been recirculated to refer to an emerging group of hackers focusing on attacking wireless networks.

The "Cracker," who is primarily defined by hostile intent and sophisticated skills, may have any one of dozens of motivations, not the least of which is financial gain.

System Crackers are the individuals and groups (whether organized or not) who pose the greatest threat to networks and information resources and who are actively engaged in developing and propagating viruses, worms, and Trojans. They may also engage in interactive (real-time) probing and reconnaissance activities by exploiting common security flaws in network operating systems and protocols. Once they discover a security weakness, they often script the exploit and create automated tool-kits for others to reuse and improve upon. They frequent popular news groups and Web sites to "share" exploits and tools. As their success and notoriety increase, their exploits usually escalate to more sophisticated and damaging activities.

Program crackers are technically skilled individuals who take commercial application software programs and "crack" their protections, usually by altering the programs or by reverse engineering them to see how they work and then creating bogus registration keys. They generally limit themselves to stealing popular software, perhaps distributing it to others as black market products or simply giving it away free of charge. These "cracked" programs may actually contain poorly modified (even viral or Trojan) code and thus pose a serious concern for IT Security Practitioners. Beyond the significant legal implications of using pirated software, users should be educated to avoid these "WAREZ," which may also contain malicious code.

Script Kiddies is the name given to less sophisticated, often younger crackers, who generally rely on automated tools ("scripts") written by the more skilled system crackers. They show no bias and scan all systems, regardless of location and value. Their methodology is a simple one, scan the Internet for a specific weakness, and when you find it, exploit it. Since most of the tools they use are automated, requiring little interaction, once they gain access to a network, they will launch the tool(s), then return later to get the results. Their exploits are much less successful if organizations disable unnecessary services and ensure that security patches are up to date.

Click Kiddies is a newer term coined to reflect the enhancements due to GUI-based point and click software.

Phreakers are persons who break into telecommunications networks (telephone and cellular) to exploit and illegally use the provider's services. This includes physical theft and reprogramming of equipment, as well as compromising codes and other mechanisms to gain unauthorized use of facilities.

Cyberpunks, Cyber-Criminals, and Cyber-Terrorists may represent composites of all of the above descriptions and may be engaged in coordinated, potentially state-sponsored acts of defacement, denial of service, personal identity and financial theft, or worse, compromise of government or industrial secrets.

There are a number of known, organized, hostile groups engaged in ongoing exploitation of the Internet on a global basis. There is mounting evidence that malicious cyber-activity by various terrorist organizations is also on the rise. As these groups have become more organized and sophisticated, government, law enforcement, and intelligence agencies in the United States and many other countries have increased coordination and collaboration efforts to monitor and respond to these threats.

These types of activities have been limited mostly to individuals claiming to represent groups. However, the overall global security environment is becoming much more problematic for IT security practitioners as these activities require constant vigilance.

Where Do Threats Come From?

Employees While the more popular security threats are initiated from outside a corporate network, a number of significant vulnerabilities still exist inside a trusted network and require the IT security practitioner's attention.

Probably the most common vulnerabilities are exploitable due to unsafe computing practices by employees such as:

* Exchange of untrusted disk media and files among host systems
* Installation of unauthorized, unregistered software (application and OS)
* Unmonitored downloading of files from the Internet
* Uncontrolled dissemination of e-mail attachments, which may release malicious code
* Other unrestricted and unsafe use of network resources

In addition to unsafe practices, traditional security breaches, both reported and unreported, have originated from within the victim organization, perpetrated by current and former employees and are often undetected due to weak personnel and security policies or ineffective countermeasures, or unreported by the organization involved. These include:

* Unauthorized access to system and network resources
* Privilege escalation
* Theft, destruction, and unauthorized dissemination of data
* Use of corporate network to initiate hostile code attacks against outside target

Social Engineering

Exploits from the Internet

While the more popular security threats relate to intentional hostile attacks or unsafe security practices, another growing concern is the unscrupulous practices engaged in by both legitimate and illicit marketing activities.

This includes "spam" (high-volume, bulk unsolicited e-mail), exploitation of active-code browser plug-in features such as "pop-up" ads and home page hijacking, and the more insidious proliferation of spyware (Trojan-like) applications propagated to monitor and track Internet use.

While specific malicious intent may not be the primary motivation, the negative organizational impact on network productivity and service availability is becoming a key business issue among those companies heavily committed to Internet-based commerce.

One of the current phenomena is personal identity theft and financial destabilization by organized groups hacking into banking and other financial networks and stealing account and other personal information for use in financing criminal and terrorist activities. Propagation of Trojan password sniffers and other keystroke monitoring software through e-mail, instant messaging software, and other pervasive personal computing applications has increased over the past few years.

Spyware and Adware   Any unsolicited background process that is installed on a user's computer when he or she visits a Web site for the purpose of collecting information about the user's browsing habits and activities is considered spyware. These programs are generally installed when users download freeware programs and they impact privacy and confidentiality. Adware programs, which trigger such nuisances as pop-up ad pages and banners when users visit certain Web sites, impact productivity, and may also be combined with techniques like home-page hijacking code and other active background activities.

Spam   According to Ferris Research (http://www.ferris.com), spam will cost U.S. organizations over $10 billion in 2003. For U.S.-based ISPs, 30 percent of inbound e-mail is spam, while at U.S.-based corporate organizations, spam accounts for 15–20 percent of inbound e-mail. Despite the increasing deployment of anti-spam services and technology, the number of spam messages, and their size, is continuing to increase rapidly. Some more recent research in this area indicates even higher percentages of unwanted e-mail traffic.

While not specifically malicious code, spam represents the following threats to organizations:

- Spam consumes computing resources (bandwidth and CPU time).
- Spam diverts IT personnel's attention from more critical network security efforts.
- Spam e-mail is a potential carrier of malicious code attachments.

Spammers have developed techniques to compromise intermediate systems to facilitate "re-mailing" services, masking the real source addresses and constituting a denial of service for victimized systems. Opt-out (unsubscribe) features in spam messages can represent a new form of reconnaissance attack to acquire legitimate target addresses.

How Can I Protect against These Attacks

Defense in Depth is the practice of "layering" defenses into defensive zones to increase overall the protection level and provide more reaction time to respond to incidents. It should be designed such that a failure in one safeguard is covered by another. This combines the capabilities of people, operations, and security technologies to establish multiple layers of protection, eliminating single lines of defense and effectively raising the cost of an attack. By treating individual countermeasures as part of an integrated suite of protective measures, the IT security practitioner is able to ensure that all vulnerabilities have been addressed. Managers must strengthen these defenses at critical locations and then be able to monitor attacks and react to them quickly. With respect to malicious code threats, these layers of protection extend to specific critical defensive zones (see Figure 7.6):

- Application defenses
- Operating system defenses
- Network infrastructure defenses

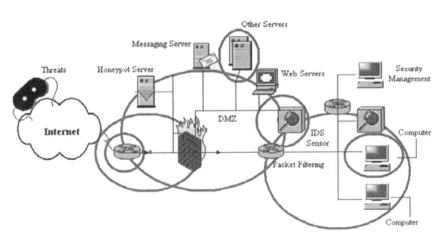

Figure 7.6 Critical defensive zones

While "defense in depth" represents a much broader issue than just protecting against forms of malicious code, this approach means:

- Creating multiple layers of security and detection capability, even on single systems (AVP, IDS, restrictive settings in applications, etc.)
- Implementing acceptable use policies and monitoring for compliance
- Limiting methods of acquiring data and program code (media restrictions)
- Using the other defense in depth measures depicted in the graphic to add robustness of the overall system of safeguards

This graphic depicts a number of countermeasures that might be deployed to create multiple zones of defense. They include techniques like screening routers, firewalls, intrusion detection, anti-virus protection, honeypot techniques, and other measures used to add layers of protection.

Application countermeasures (see Figure 7.7) include things such as hardening of applications, anti-virus and IDS protection on hosts and servers, host-based intrusion detection, and network security monitors.

Application Defenses

- Educate users on malware in general and implement acceptable use policies.
- Implement regular anti-virus screening on all host systems and network servers and ensure that virus definition files are kept up to date.

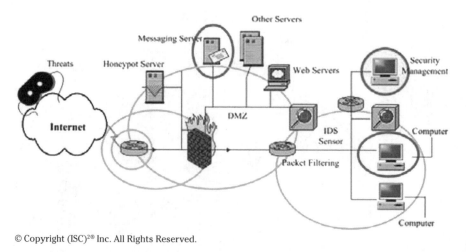

Figure 7.7 Application countermeasures

- Require scanning of all removable media and e-mail (especially attachments.
- Consider installation of personal firewall and IDS software on hosts as an additional security layer.
- Deploy change detection/integrity checking software and maintain logs.
- Implement e-mail usage controls and ensure that e-mail attachments are scanned.
- Deploy specialized anti-malware software and e-mail filters to detect and block unwanted traffic (anti-spam filters, etc.).
- Establish a clear policy regarding new software development/engineering practices, installations and upgrades.
- Ensure only trusted sources are used when obtaining, installing, and upgrading software, through digital signatures (e.g., authenticode and other validations).

Operating system countermeasures (see Figure 7.8) such as hardening of operating systems include all devices involved in network communications, including routers and switches, servers, as well as hosts. The practitioner should regularly check to ensure that the latest security patches are deployed.

Operating System Defenses (Hardening the OS)

- Deploy change detection software and integrity checking software and maintain logs.

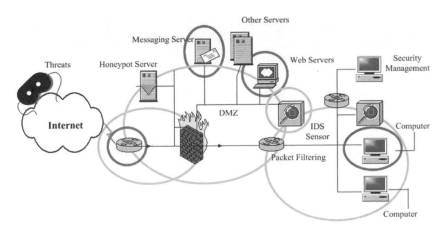

Figure 7.8 Operating system countermeasures

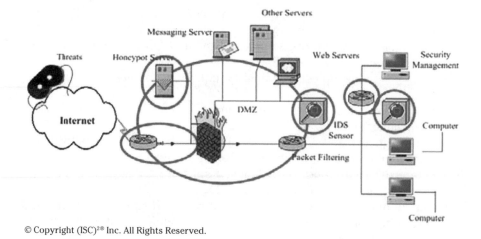

Figure 7.9 Network infrastructure defenses

- Deploy or enable change detection and integrity checking software on all servers.
- Ensure that all operating systems are consistent and have been patched with the latest updates from vendors.
- Ensure only trusted sources are used when installing and upgrading OS code.
- Disable any unnecessary OS services and processes which may pose a security vulnerability.

Network infrastructure defenses (see Figure 7.9) involve identifying where the traffic patterns are and where to deploy various countermeasures. The red circles indicate some of these locations, and the devices which might provide elements of protection.

Network Infrastructure Defenses

- Create choke points in the network.
- Use Proxy services and Bastion hosts to protect critical services.
- Use content filtering at chokepoints to screen traffic.
- Ensure only trusted sources are used when installing and upgrading OS code.
- Disable any unnecessary network services and processes that could pose a security vulnerability.
- Maintain up-to-date IDS signature databases.
- Apply security patches to network devices to ensure protection against new threats and to reduce vulnerabilities.

Incident Detection Tools and Techniques

Intrusion Detection Systems

Intrusion detection tools are an integral component of Defense in Depth and should be deployed in critical areas of the network as an early warning system. There are a variety of implementations and each has features that provide unique capabilities to protect networks and hosts from malicious activity.

Intrusion detection is designed to quickly recognize a security event (malicious code attack, denial of service attack, network reconnaissance attack, and the like) so that immediate countermeasures can be executed to isolate and react to the event.

Intrusion detection can be deployed on separate appliances called sensors that are managed by a security server, or they can be deployed as software on the hosts within the network. Each type has advantages and disadvantages.

Network-Based Intrusion Detection is typically deployed on dedicated appliances and is independent of the operating systems being run on network hosts and servers. This tool is available in a range of price-performance classes for small to enterprise networks.

To minimize the risk of compromise, network-based intrusion detection platforms use hardware sensors that are ideally connected at key choke points in the network infrastructure. The physical connections to the monitored network are passive (promiscuous) and often nonaddressable (to avoid attack and compromise).

Each sensor has a second connection to a special command-and-control network that hosts the IDS management server. When a network attack profile is detected, sensors alert the management server and begin logging the suspected traffic.

Some configurations permit active attack responses, such as IP traceback, transmitting TCP session resets to terminate the activity, or reconfiguring firewall or router access lists dynamically (shunning).

One of the weaknesses of network-based sensors is that they cannot normally analyze encrypted host traffic or easily recognize attack profiles in fragmented packets.

Host-Based Intrusion Detection is typically implemented in software on individual hosts in the network. These programs might be installed as a component of an overall personal computer anti-virus/firewall/IDS package, or as a client/agent component of a security server suite.

An advantage to host-based detection is that it can detect and log the success or failure of an attack against the host. However, these systems are limited in perspective to the host and may not detect general attacks against other network resources.

They are also OS dependent and, to be effective, must be deployed on all network hosts.

Signature-Based IDS profiling involves code pattern matching against a database of known attack profiles. This requires the IDS signature database to be continuously updated for new signatures.

The advantages of signature-based detection are a lower incidence of False Positive detections (misdiagnosing a benign event as something malicious). False Positives can result in a high volume of unnecessary alarms being triggered, which tend to encourage administrators to lower triggering thresholds to compensate.

One disadvantage due to the increasing number of new virus strains and those that utilize stealth or polymorphic features, is the potential for False Negatives, that is, incorrectly missing a new form of malicious code that is not recognized by the sensor. In addition, these types of detection algorithms require regular updating to ensure that the latest threats are recognized.

Anomaly Detection is based on developing a network baseline profile of normal or acceptable activity (such as services or traffic patterns), then measuring actual network traffic against this baseline.

This technique might be useful for detecting attacks such as denial of service or continuous login attempts, but it requires a learning or preconfiguration period.

An advantage to anomaly based detection is that events that are unusual or out of the ordinary tend to prompt administrators to focus on the network and attempt to understand traffic patterns and normal behavior, and exception events may receive quicker attention. Another advantage is that new forms of malicious code, and new attack methodologies may be recognized quicker.

The main disadvantage of anomaly-based detection is the higher incident of False Positives. New application deployments or changes in traffic flow may trigger alarms which require attention. The tendency of administrators to lower sensitivity levels (alarm thresholds) to reduce this overhead can lower the overall effectiveness of the countermeasure. Baselining what is normal is usually a cumbersome task as well.

A layered defense in depth approach (see Figure 7.10) would suggest deploying both network-based and host-based intrusion detection and products that permit both signature-based and anomaly-based detection schemes.

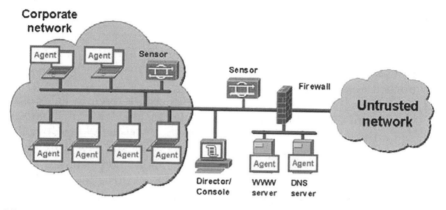

Figure 7.10 Layered defense in depth

Anti-Virus Scanning Software   Most PC users today use some form of virus protection to detect and prevent infection. Just as intrusion detection can be layered at the host and network levels, anti-virus protection should be deployed on all devices that support the programs. The key vulnerabilities to host-based anti-virus software are:

- The continuing requirement to keep every host system updated to the most current virus definition files, and
- Potential compromise of the protection through unsafe user practices (such as installing unlicensed or unauthorized software or indiscriminately exchanging infected e-mail or document files).

Network-based anti-virus software is an option that permits screening of files and e-mail traffic at the servers and providing remote scanning and inoculation of clients on a consistent basis.

Many organizations employ both network and host-based protection; some deploy multiple products in order to maximize detection capabilities. It is imperative, however, that virus definition files be kept up-to-date. Most vendors now offer automatic updating of software as soon as new definitions are added.

Types of Anti-Virus (Anti-Malware) Software

There are a variety of anti-virus software packages that operate in many different ways, depending on how the vendor chose to implement their software. What they have in common, though, is that they all look for patterns in the files or memory of your computer that indicate the possible presence

425

of a known virus. Antivirus packages know what to look for through the use of virus profiles (sometimes called "signatures") provided by the vendor.

- New viruses are discovered daily. The effectiveness of antivirus software is dependent on having the latest virus profiles installed on your computer so that it can look for recently discovered viruses. It is important to keep these profiles up to date.
- First generation anti-virus scanners used brute force to analyze every byte of data in boot records and files looking for known patterns and strings associated with virus activity. This method is obviously time consuming and, with the number of known and new virus strains around, this became obsolete, in favor of more intelligent algorithms that searched specific portions of files where virus code typically resides. Although these scanning approaches are still used today, other more efficient techniques (like algorithmic code entry point scanning) are used to combat newer forms of viral code such as polymorphic strains.
- Generic Decryption (GD) is a newer technique designed to use a virtual machine (isolated and controlled) environment to trick a polymorphic virus into decrypting itself and exposing recognizable viral code components. As long as there is at least a small portion of the malicious code in machine language that can be executed in a virtual environment, and the code successfully decrypts and transfers control to the resulting virus instructions, this type of AVP can usually detect it. Most new viral code, even polymorphic varieties, generally are iterations of previous generation code.

Heuristic scanners operate by looking for telltale signs or patterns of behavior consistent with known virus activity, and then logging this and alerting the user to its presence (allowing the user to make a final decision on eradication). This is how many Anti-Spyware products work as well. There are also schemes called behavior blocking that monitor system calls and other signs of activity which might indicate the presence of viral code. Many of these will isolate the offending code and prompt the user to make a decision or link to additional descriptive information on the vendor's Web site.

Data integrity tools are also important tools for discovering whether any files have been modified on a system. This is useful for protecting systems against computer viruses because integrity checkers do not require updating signature files to detect computer viruses. When an integrity checker is installed it creates a database of checksums for a set of files.

The integrity checker can then tell if files have been modified by comparing the current checksum to the checksum it took when installed. If the checksums do not match, then the file has been modified in some manner. Some integrity checkers may be able to identify the virus that modified a file, but others may just be able to alert you to the changes. Integrity checkers are not only useful for detecting a possible infection, but also useful for helping to detect intruders.

Network Monitors and Analyzers   In order to ensure that security practices remain effective, IT security practitioners should consider regular use of network monitoring software or appliances, as well as periodic analysis of network traffic.

Periodically run a security scanning tool such as the Internet Scanner, Nessus, Satan, Trinux, or some combination of all of them, depending upon the operating systems in use. Keep in mind that these same tools can also be used by attackers.

In addition, on a regular basis, the network should be scanned for unnecessary open service ports, as upgrades to software often reset default settings.

Content/Context Filtering and Logging Software   Privacy and security must be balanced when implementing countermeasures that are designed to screen content; however, when combined with a clear corporate policy on acceptable use, these become additional layers of defense against malicious code. One of the more popular countermeasures in this category today is Content Filtering, which allows management to control Internet use.

Plug-ins to screen e-mail attachments and content- and context-based filtering (access control lists) on network routers also permits an additional layer of security protection.

Content-based filtering includes analyzing network traffic for active code (Java, Active-X) components and administrative disabling of script processing on Web browser software. Context-based filtering involves comparing patterns of activity to baseline standards, so that unusual changes in network behavior can be evaluated for possible malicious activity.

Other Techniques to Actively Detect and Analyze Hostile Activity   Honeypots are sacrificial hosts and services deployed at the edges of a network to act as bait for potential hacking attacks. Typically, the systems are configured to appear real and may be part of a suite of servers placed in a separate network (honeynet), isolated from the real network. The purpose of the honeypot is to provide a controlled environment for attacks to occur so they can be easily detected and analyzed to test the strength of the network. Host-based intrusion detection and monitoring software is installed to log activity.

A honeypot is a tool intended to be compromised. All traffic to and from the honeypot is suspicious because there are no production applications on this system. Few logs should be produced on the honeypot unless the honeypot is under heavy attack. Logs should be easy to read and understand. Once a production honeypot is probed or attacked, an administrator can place preventive controls on his "real" production network.

Honeypots should contain at least the following elements:

- Looks and behaves like a real host
- Does not disclose its existence at any point
- Has a dedicated firewall that prevents all outbound traffic, in case the honeypot is compromised
- Lives in a network DMZ, untouched by normal traffic
- Sounds silent alarms when any traffic goes to or from it
- Begins logging all intruder activity when it first senses an intrusion

Classes of Honeypots

- Low involvement
- High involvement
- Honeynet

A *low involvement* **honeypot** provides a number of fake services such as HTTP (Hyper Text Transfer Protocol) or SMTP (Simple Mail Transfer Protocol). Low involvement honeypots allow hackers to connect to services, but do nothing else. With this type of honeypot a hacker usually cannot gain operating system access and, therefore, poses no threat.

A *high involvement* **honeypot** produces genuine services and vulnerabilities by providing a real operating system for the attacker to interact with. This class of honeypot is designed to be compromised so that realistic data can be collected. The difficulty in high involvement honeypots is they must be tightly controlled. A compromised system can become a host to begin an attack on another system.

Honeynets are a group of honeypots made to simulate a real live network. There is added value in honeynets as they provide more data and are more attractive to hackers. However, the set-up and maintenance of honeynets are a little more advanced. A honeynet may include many servers, a router, and a firewall. A honeynet may be identical to the production network or it may be a research lab. Nonetheless, honeynets allow for a more real environment for a hacker to attack.

Attack Prevention Tools and Techniques

One of the simplest prevention techniques is to disable unnecessary network services, especially certain TCP and UDP listening ports. This will defeat any attack that is aimed at exploiting those services. This may not be efficient if those services are required for legitimate users, however. The optimum solution is to ensure availability of services to legitimate users while minimizing vulnerabilities.

By creating perimeter zones of defense, techniques can be deployed which are preventative, detective, or deterrent. Through the use of honeypots or "faux" resource environments, attacks can also be deflected to controlled and monitored zones where they can be analyzed and used to strengthen controls.

As countermeasures are deployed, each countermeasure depends upon the effectiveness of the layer outside it. Ideally, the defensive zone starts outside the network at the entry points. Simple packet filtering reduces the amount of traffic which then needs to be inspected by the firewall. The firewall, through selective and stateful filtering, then limits the number of packets that an intrusion detection sensor needs to analyze, and so on. Finally, host-based preventative software (ant-virus protection, etc.) is one of the last layers protecting network hosts.

There are a wide variety of countermeasures (see Figure 7.11) and practices that can assist in preventing and detecting malicious code attacks, including:

- Employing filtering software that blocks traffic to and from network segments or specific services that will prevent those resources from being accessed and exploited
- Employing active sensors (intrusion detection, anti-virus detection) that react quickly enough to prevent or mitigate damage

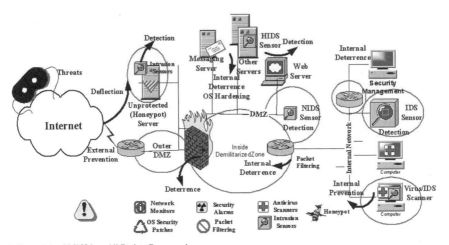

Figure 7.11 Countermeasure techniques

- Employing chokepoints in the network to force traffic to flow through zones of protection, allowing sensors and filters to inspect traffic before allowing it to be passed into the protected network
- Setting security properties within browsers to prohibit or prompt before processing scripts and active code
- Eliminating unnecessary remote connections to networks and employing effective access control measures to protect those connections required to remain open or available
- Avoid circumventing any existing control systems and countermeasures

Safe Recovery Techniques and Practices

Once an event has occurred, it is often difficult or impossible to restore the network resources to their original condition, unless steps are taken beforehand to facilitate quick recovery capability. File backups allow you to restore the availability and integrity of data. Some of the steps that should be taken are:

- Consider storing OS and data file backup images on CD-ROM to prevent possible virus infection.
- Backup all critical configuration files on network devices and servers
- Ensure that new and replacement media is scanned for viruses before re-installation of software.
- Disable network access to systems being restored or upgraded until protection software or services have been re-enabled or installed.

The following is taken from CERT regarding backups (http://www.cert. org/security-improvement/practices/p071.html):

Develop a File Backup and Restoration Plan   All system and user files should be backed up on a regular basis. If you have regularly created cryptographic checksums for all files and have securely stored these checksums, you can plan to restore files from trusted backups against which such checksums have been calculated.

Then you must reinstall site-specific modifications, relevant patches, and bug-fixes. You need to ensure that these modifications do not introduce additional defects or vulnerabilities.

Exercise caution when restoring user files from untrusted backups and instruct all users to check for any unexpected changes to their restored files.

For workstations, files are backed up locally at each workstation, often by the user(s) of that workstation and then centrally administered.

For network servers that provide information services backups of the entire information content, OS and application suite; should be backed up on a separate and secure machine. Data is then backed up on a regular basis.

Determine the appropriate medium to contain your backup files based on your requirements for speed (for both reading and writing), reliability, and storage duration. Media you should consider include magnetic tape, optical disk, and CD-ROM.

The plan should specify that

- Source data is encrypted before being transmitted over a network or to the storage medium.
- Data remains encrypted on the backup storage media.
- Storage media are kept in a physically secure facility that is protected from manmade and natural disasters.

The plan should be designed to ensure that backups are performed in a secure manner and that the contents of the backups remain secure.

Install File Backup Tools

- Select file backup tools to allow you to implement your backup plan. You may need to use third-party software, although the backup capabilities of some operating systems are likely to be sufficient. You may also need to install storage devices, either centrally or on each workstation and server, to store the backup copies.
- The tools used to recover backed-up files should be kept offline, rather than on individual workstations and servers. If a computer has been compromised and you need to recover a file, you cannot trust the integrity of any of the tools on that computer.

Configure the Backup Tools and Initiate the Scheduled Backups

- Tool configurations need to reflect your backup and restoration plan. Configure the tools to save access control settings along with file contents, if that feature is available.
- Do the first full backup just before deploying the computer, and then confirm that you can perform a full restoration from that backup.

Confirm that the Scheduled Backups Are Being Performed Successfully

- In many organizations, file backups are completely automated, so system administrators tend to forget that they are happening. Therefore, confirm that the backup procedures for a newly deployed workstation are actually working.

Test the Ability to Recover from Fackups

- For many system administrators, recovering a file from a backup is an uncommon activity. This step assures that if you need to recover a file, the tools and procedures will work.

- Performing this test periodically will help you to discover problems with the backup procedures so you can correct them before losing data.
- Some backup restoration software does not accurately recover the correct file protection and file ownership controls. Check these attributes of restored files to ensure they are being set correctly.
- Periodically test to ensure that you can perform a full system recovery from your backups.

Policy Considerations

Your organization's security policy for networked systems should:

- Require the creation of a file backup and recovery plan.
- Inform users of their responsibilities (if any) for file backup and recovery.

Implementing Effective Software Engineering Best Practices

The organization should adopt an Acceptable Use Policy for network services and resources. This would include prohibitions on certain network activities and PC user habits regarding software licensing and installation and procedures for transmitting files and media. Adopt standardized software so that patches and upgrades can be controlled to ensure vulnerabilities are addressed.

Consider implementing an ISO 17799 compliant security policy. ISO 17799 is one of the most widely recognized security guidelines. Adoption of ISO/IEC 17799 (or indeed any detailed security practice) as an internal standard, can be a far from trivial undertaking, even for the most security conscious of organizations. Security practitioners should evaluate those practices which make business sense to the organization, and keep in mind that policies need senior management commitment to be effective.

Sample Questions

1. Which of the following is a reason to use a Firewall?
   a. To evaluate intrusions as they happen
   b. To watch for internal attacks
   c. To prevent or stop potential intrusions
   d. To signal an alarm on a suspected intrusion

2. Which of the following is an attribute of polymorphic code?
   a. It mutates while keeping the original algorithm intact
   b. It uses encryption for all the code

c. It operates based on specific conditions

d. It is written to self replicate altering the computer configuration

3. Flooding network ports is an example of which type of attack?
   a. Man-in-the-Middle
   b. Brute force
   c. Denial of service
   d. Birthday

4. Which of the following is typically a characteristic exhibited by Script Kiddies?
   a. They are very talented.
   b. They leave no trace of what they are doing.
   c. They are concerned with the quality of the attack.
   d. They see the number of attacks being something to be proud of.

5. Which of the following virus types typically affects the normal.dot file?
   a. Macro virus
   b. Multipartite
   c. Boot sector
   d. MacIntosh

6. Which of the following represents the "SALT" value in a password?
   a. The value is a constant chosen by the system.
   b. The value is chosen randomly.
   c. The value is time based.
   d. The value is a constant chosen by the user.

7. Which of the following techniques BEST defines "Spam"?
   a. Filling a field with false information
   b. Expressing a strong criticism of something
   c. Inducing a resource to take incorrect actions
   d. Posting information repeatedly to overburden the network

8. Which of the following defines a Man-in-the-Middle attack?
   a. Searching through databases for specific information
   b. Bypassing the user authentication system
   c. Manipulation of packets being sent over a network
   d. Overwriting the system buffers with data

9. Which of the following features of the Internet Protocol is used by the Ping of Death to execute?
   a. Its ability to fragment packets
   b. Its capability to encrypt data
   c. Its ability to do site routing
   d. Its capability to parse log files

10. Which of the following defines a Trojan Horse?
    a. It has the ability to gain access to a computer system by circumventing the usual security checks.
    b. It has the ability to self-propagate from one computer to another on the network.
    c. It has the ability to replicate itself between files on the system.
    d. It has the ability to convince the user that is has one function whilst hiding another function.

11. All of the following EXCEPT are forms of Symmetric Block Cipher Attacks?
    a. Linear cryptanalysis
    b. Weak keys
    c. Key streams
    d. Algebraic attacks

12. Which of the following is NOT a phase of a Social Engineering attack?
    a. Intelligence gathering
    b. Eavesdropping
    c. Target selection
    d. The attack

13. Which of the following can be susceptible to a Birthday attack?
    a. Digital signatures
    b. Asymmetric algorithms
    c. Password hashs
    d. Private keys

14. Which of the following defines session hijacking?
    a. Compromising the session between two machines is taken over
    b. Exploitation of the trust relationship in the Internet Protocol
    c. Creation of random addresses for each network packet
    d. Making compute resources unavailable

15. Which of the following is NOT a characteristic of Computer Virus Hoax?
    a. Asks that you send it to everyone to warn them
    b. Makes reference to a false authority
    c. Contains technical sounding nonsense
    d. Usually has a hidden function that executes unknown to the user

Appendix A
Answers to Sample Questions

Domain 1: Access Controls

1. What are the three principle components of access control systems?
   a. Access control objects
   b. Biometrics
   c. Access control subjects
   d. Access control systems

Answer: **a, c, d** are the three principle components of an access control system. While biometrics are devices used in some access control systems to confirm an individual's identity, they are not considered to be one of the three principle components of an access control system.

2. Which of the following are behavioral traits in a biometric device?
   a. Voice Pattern
   b. Signature Dynamics
   c. Keystroke Dynamics
   d. All of the above

Answer: **d.** Voice Pattern, Signature Dynamics, and Keystroke Dynamics all are behavioral traits in biometric devices.

3. In the measurement of biometric accuracy which of the following is commonly referred to as a "type two error"?
   a. Rate of false acceptance — False Acceptance Rate (FAR)
   b. Rate of false rejection — False Rejection Rate (FRR)
   c. Cross over error rate (CER)
   d. All of the above

Answer: **a.** FRR is a type one error, FAR is a type two error and CER is the intersection when FRR equals FAR.

4. The three functional areas of TACACS known as AAA (triple A) are?
   a. Authentication
   b. Authorization
   c. Availability
   d. Accounting

Answer: **a, b, c.** Authentication, Authorization, and Accounting are the three functional areas of AAA.

5. Which of the following is an International Telecommunications Union — Telecommunications Standardization Sector (ITU-T) recommendation originally issued in 1998 for indirect authentication services using public keys?
    a. Radius
    b. X.509
    c. Kerberos
    d. SESAME

Answer: **b.** X.509 is the International Telecommunications Union — Telecommunications Standardization Sector (ITU-T) recommendation originally issued in 1998 for indirect authentication services using public keys.

6. Which of the following is NOT one of the three primary rules in a Biba formal model?
    a. An access control subject cannot access an access control object that has a higher integrity level.
    b. An access control subject cannot access an access control object that has a lower integrity level.
    c. An access control subject cannot modify an access control object that has a higher integrity level.
    d. An access control subject cannot request services from an access control object that has a higher integrity level.

Answer: **a.** An access control subject cannot access an access control object that has a "higher" integrity level is not one of the three primary rules in the Biba formal model.

7. Which of the following is an example of a firewall that does not use Context Based Access Control?
    a. Application proxy
    b. Static packet filter
    c. Stateful inspection
    d. Circuit gateway

Answer: **b.** Context Based Access control also considers the "state" of the connection and in a static packet filter, no consideration is given to the connection state. Each and every packet is compared to the rule base regardless of whether it had previously been allowed or denied.

8. In consideration of the three basic types of authentication which of the following is incorrect:
    a. Knowledge based = password
    b. Token based = smartcard
    c. Characteristic based = biometric
    d. None of the above

Answer: **d.** Knowledge based is something that you know such as a Password or Passphrase. Token based is something that you have such as a Token or Smartcard. Characteristic based is something that you are such as Biometric or Behavioral.

9. In the authorization provided to the access control subject by an access control system, which of the following is not a consideration for an Access Control Subject?
   a. Temporal — time of day, day of request
   b. Password or token utilized
   c. False Rejection Rate
   d. Locale from where the access control subject authenticated

Answer: **c.** The False Rejection Rate is a component in the measurement of biometric accuracy and is not a consideration for the Access Control Object nor the Access Control Subject.

10. Password selection is typically based on which of the following criteria?
    a. Minimum password length
    b. Authorizations, rights, and permissions
    c. Required usage of letters, case, numbers, and symbols in the makeup of the password
    d. All of the above

Answer: **a, c.** Minimum password length and the required usage of letters, case, numbers, and symbols in the makeup of the password are typical criteria for password selection. Authorizations, rights, and permissions are associated with account creation not password selection criteria.

11. Which of the following should be considered in the routine monitoring of an access control system?
    a. The regular monitoring of changes to accounts can help to mitigate the risk of misuse or unauthorized access.
    b. All changes to accounts within the access control system should be logged and reviewed on a regular basis.
    c. Particular attention should focus on any newly created accounts as well as any escalation of the privileges for an existing account to make certain that the new account or the increased privileges are authorized.
    d. All of the above

Answer: **d.** All of the above tasks should be considered in the routine monitoring of an access control system.

12. Which of the following is not true in the consideration of Object Groups?
    a. It is a common practice to assign the appropriate permissions to

437

   a directory, and each object within the directory inherits the respective parent directory permissions.

b. Although configuring individual objects affords maximum control, this granularity can quickly become a administration burden.

c. By incorporating multiple objects with similar permissions or restrictions within a group or directory, the granularity is thereby coarsened and the administration of the access control system is simplified.

d. Configuring individual objects affords maximum control, this granularity can reduce administration burden.

Answer: **c**. Although configuring individual objects affords maximum control, this granularity can quickly become a administration burden.

13. In the three basic types of authentication, which of the following are related to "something you have"?
   a. Synchronous or asynchronous token
   b. Biometric
   c. Smartcard
   d. All of the above

Answer: **a, c**. Synchronous or asynchronous token and a Smartcard are something you have while a Biometric is something you are.

14. Which of the following is an asynchronous device?
   a. Time-based token
   b. Event-based token
   c. All of the above

Answer: **b**. Event-based tokens are asynchronous as the password is changed with every use and is not based on time. Time-based tokens change their password based on a time interval and are therefore synchronous.

15. Which of the following are characteristics in biometric behavioral-keystroke dynamics?
   a. The length of time each key is held down
   b. Tendencies to switch between a numeric keypad and keyboard numbers
   c. Acceleration, rhythm, pressure, and flow
   d. All of the above

Answer: **a, b**. The length of time each key is held down and tendencies to switch between a numeric keypad and keyboard numbers are characteristics of biometric behavioral-keystroke dynamics. Acceleration, rhythm, pressure, and flow are characteristics of signature analysis.

Domain 2: Security Operations and Administration

1. What is "integrity?"
   a. The assurance that data stored, processed and transmitted has not been modified or destroyed in an inappropriate manner, either inadvertently or maliciously, from its original and correct state
   b. The assurance that resources can be successfully accessed by authorized users when they are needed
   c. The assurance that data is kept private, restricted only to authorized individuals
   d. None of the above

Answer: **a**

2. What is the A-I-C Triad?
   a. The security triad
   b. The risk management triad
   c. The infrastructure triad
   d. All of the above

Answer: **a**

3. What is least privilege?
   a. Access to all an organization's resources
   b. Access to sensitive resources only
   c. Access to those resources required to perform a job function
   d. All of the above
   e. A and B only
   f. B and C only

Answer: **c**

4. How can least privilege be maintained?
   a. By verifying a user's role in the organization
   b. By verifying the minimal set of data that is required for successful completion of tasks for this role
   c. By verifying the data's location
   d. All of the above

Answer: **d**

5. What is "accountability?"
   a. Evaluation of the rights minimally necessary to perform required business functions
   b. The ability to tie an activity to the individual or system that initiated it with 100 percent certainty
   c. The granting of permissions by a data owner and the enforcement of those permissions
   d. None of the above

Answer: **b**

6. What does a risk assessment evaluate?
   a. Threats
   b. Errors
   c. Vulnerabilities
   d. A and B only
   e. B and C only
   f. A and C only
   g. All of the above

Answer: **f**

7. What are the types of risk assessment?
   a. Qualitative
   b. Quantitative
   c. Hybrid (both qualitative and quantitative)
   d. All of the above

Answer: **d**

8. How can an organization address risk?
   a. Transfer
   b. Accept
   c. Avoid
   d. Mitigate
   e. All of the above

Answer: **e**

9. Software development models include:
   a. The Waterfall Method
   b. The Scientific Method
   c. The Microsoft Method
   d. None of the above

Answer: **a**

10. Spiral Model steps include:
    a. Review and edit
    b. Risk management
    c. Engineering and production
    d. None of the above

Answer: **c**

11. ISO 17799 represents:
    a. A standard for security risk assessment
    b. A standard for information security management systems
    c. A code of practice for information security
    d. All of the above

Answer: **c**

12. Bell–LaPadula is an example of a:
    a. Security model
    b. Confidentiality model
    c. Authentication model
    d. Authorization model

Answer: **b**

13. TCSEC is also referenced as:
    a. The Yellow Book
    b. The Purple Book
    c. The Blue Book
    d. The Orange Book

Answer: **d**

14. Services provided by the operating system include:
    a. Error detection
    b. Controlled access to files
    c. Accounting functions
    d. All of the above
    e. None of the above

Answer: **d**

15. The data classification for the most sensitive of data within an organization is labeled:
    a. Confidential
    b. Internal Use Only
    c. Restricted
    d. Public
    e. None of the above

Answer: **c**

Domain 3: Analysis and Monitoring

1. A security audit is best defined as:
   a. A covert series of tests designed to test network authentication, hosts, and perimeter security. This is a good example of a type of security audit, but does not answer the question of what a security audit is.
   b. A technical assessment that measures how well an organization uses strategic security policies and tactical security controls for protecting its information assets. This is the correct answer.
   c. Employing Intrusion Detection Systems to monitor anomalous traffic on a network segment and logging attempted break-ins. This is an example of how systems are monitored.

    d. Hardening systems before deploying them on the corporate network. This is a security control check used to harden a host against vulnerabilities.

Answer: **b**

2. Why is it important for organizations to have a security framework?
    a. To show that the organization has exercised "due care." — Having a security framework shows that the organization has exercised "due care," and cares about mitigating security risks.
    b. So they can adhere to regulations developed by an institutional or governmental body. — "Organizations will often incorporate the security guidelines and standards published by policy development organizations (or regulatory bodies which dictate requirements) for the purpose of standardizing their security framework to harmonize with "accepted" or required practices."
    c. To avoid possible legal action or financial penalties. — This is a part of answer A.
    d. All of the above.

Answer: **d**

3. Creating Incident Response policies for an organization would be an example of an:
    a. Administrative Control — Administrative Controls are "managerial" and are a part of corporate security policy.
    b. Technical Control — Technical controls implement specific technologies. A policy would not constitute a specific technological process.
    c. Physical Control — Physical controls constitute elements such as Closed Caption Television (CCTV), padlocks, or any other physical barrier or device to bar access.
    d. Logical Control — This is a fictitious term and not found in the text.

Answer: **a**

4. Which of the following would be a good example of a host isolation security control?
    a. Encrypting syslog activity on the network — This would be an example of a monitoring control check.
    b. Applying the most recent patches to a system — This is an example of a patching or system hardening check.
    c. Installing anti-virus on a local machine — This deals with mitigating against threats such as worms or viruses.
    d. Setting up a DMZ between the public and private network. — This would provide protection for internal hosts when communicating with untrusted networks.

Answer: **d**

5. What is the most important reason to analyze event logs from multiple sources?
   a. They will help you obtain a more complete picture of what is happening on your network and how you go about addressing the problem. — By analyzing various logs sources it is possible to piece together a timeline of events and user activity.
   b. The log server could have been compromised. — This is partially correct, but not the most fitting answer. This is only a small picture of what the attacker could have done.
   c. Because you cannot trust automated scripts to capture everything. — This may be true, but again is not the most important reason. This answer is meant to distract.
   d. In order to prosecute the attacker once he can be traced. — This may apply in some cases, but this is not the primary goal of correlating event logs.

Answer: **a**

6. Security testing does not include which of the following activities?
   a. Performing a port scan to check for up and running services. — This is part of security testing. Using a network mapping technique such as nmap will reveal security holes.
   b. Gathering publicly available information. — This technique can involve "googling" an organization to determine information for future attacks.
   c. Counter-Attacking systems determined to be hostile. — This is never something an organization wants to do, and does not constitute security testing.
   d. Posing as technical support to gain unauthorized information. — This is an example of social engineering and part of an organizations security.

Answer: **c**

7. Why is system fingerprinting part of the security testing process?
   a. Because it is one of the easiest things to determine when performing a security test. This may or may not be true depending on the system, and is not a reason to determine the O/S or other system details.
   b. It shows what vulnerabilities the system may be subject to. — Some versions of an O/S or software may be vulnerable, and this information is useful to an attacker. Found on page 83.
   c. It shows the auditor whether a system has been hardened. — This is true, but it does not answer why system fingerprinting is part of the security testing process.
   d. It tells an attacker than a system is automatically insecure. — This is not true. Just because a machine is running a particular O/S for

example does not mean it has not been updated and patched to prevent certain vulnerabilities.

Answer: **b**

8. What is the difference between vulnerability and penetration testing?
   a. Vulnerability testing attempts to exploit a weakness found from penetration testing. — This is incorrect. It should be the other way around.
   b. Penetration testing attempts to exploit a weakness found in Vulnerability testing.
   c. Vulnerability testing uses scripts to find weaknesses while penetration testing uses a GUI-based program. —This is untrue as both can use either scripts or a graphical tool.
   d. Penetration testing is used to uncover vulnerabilities without harming the system. — This is not the situation in all cases. In some cases testers want to gain the attention of management by showing the possible harm a security breach can cause.

Answer: **b**

9. The following are benefits to performing vulnerability testing except:
   a. They allow an organization to study the security posture of the organization. — This is true as vulnerability testing will give a picture of how secure the network is at a point in time.
   b. They identify and prioritize mitigation activities. — This is true as systems can be ranked according to how vulnerable they are.
   c. They can compare security postures over a period of time when done consistently. — This is true because a vulnerability test is a snapshot in time. Many snapshots over a period of time will give a good overall picture of security postures.
   d. It has the potential to crash the network or host. — Sometimes innocent tests have the ability to crash a system and thus, this answer would be a disadvantage.

Answer: **d**

10. What is the primary purpose of testing an Intrusion Detection System?
    a. To observe that the IDS is observing and logging an appropriate response to a suspicious activity. — The primary purpose of an IDS is to detect known attacks or anomalous activity.
    b. To determine if the IDS is capable of discarding suspect packets. — This would fall more along the line of an Intrusion Prevention System or a firewall.
    c. To analyze processor utilization to verify whether hardware up-

grades are necessary. — CPU utilization is not the primary concern of an IDS, but rather load balancing or bandwidth limiting.
  d. To test whether the IDS can log every possible event on the network. — This is an unrealistic and storage consuming goal unrelated to the primary purpose of an IDS.

Answer: **a**

11. Which of the following is true regarding computer intrusions?
  a. Covert attacks such as a Distributed Denial of Service (DDOS) attack harm public opinion of an organization. — A DDOS attack is an example of an overt attack.
  b. Overt attacks are easier to defend against because they can be readily identified. — This is not true, as overt attacks can be just as complex and hard to defend against as covert attacks.
  c. Network Intrusion Detection Systems (NIDS) help mitigate computer intrusions by notifying personnel in real-time. — NIDS can monitor data in real-time and notify appropriate personnel.
  d. Covert attacks are less effective because they take more time to accomplish. — This is certainly not true. A waiter can steal a credit card number just as fast as any overt method.

Answer: **c**

12. The main difference in real-time vs. non-real-time monitoring is:
  a. Non-real-time monitoring is not as effective as real-time monitoring. — Both are effective in capturing network or system data.
  b. Real-time monitoring provides a way to immediately identify disallowed behavior, while non-real-time monitoring can be used to trace an attacker's activity. — Real-time is concerned more with immediate discovery while non-real-time is more concerned with data preservation.
  c. Non-real-time monitoring is more effective in catching overt activity. — Neither are better than the other at catching overt or covert activity.
  d. Real-time monitoring is more effective in catching covert activity. — Neither are better than the other at catching overt or covert activity.

Answer: **b**

13. Why is security monitoring necessary?
  a. Because logging activity can show the steps an attacker used to modify or gain access to a system. — This is true. Logs can show what files or systems an attacker used in the process of "escalating privilege" or compromising a system.
  b. Log files can be correlated to form a timeline of events to be used in a forensic investigation. — Log times can be pieced together to form a timeline that will help investigators.

   c. Log files can show deviance from a security policy. — If security policy or access rights are changed a log file can show evidence of this.

   d. All of the above. — All of the above are reasons to maintain system logs and monitor activity.

Answer: **d**

14. NIDS and HIDS generally employ the following techniques except:

   a. Using a database of known attack signatures and comparing that to current traffic flow. — This is widely used by NIDS and HIDS, known as misuse detection.

   b. Analyzing traffic flow to determine unusual activity. — This is the technique of anomaly detection used by some NIDS and HIDS.

   c. Monitoring for specific file changes by referencing known good file sets. — This is referred to as target monitoring, mostly used by NIDS.

   d. Counter-attacking a system to cut-off communication and prevent possible damage. — This is the correct answer. Counter-attacking is not the goal of any NIDS or HIDS.

Answer: **d**

15. Why are secure methods of logging system or device data important?

   a. The hosts storing the log files are often easily compromised. — The system storing the data has nothing to do with security holes. The system may quite likely be hardened.

   b. Common transport methods of log files are insecure and can be easily sniffed. — Syslog is a common device logger that sends over data over an insecure UDP protocol.

   c. Unencrypted and unprotected log files are easily altered. — Attackers can easily alter data if the log file is unencrypted or file permissions are set improperly.

   d. Both B & C. — Both B & C show how insecure data can be used by an attacker.

Answer: **d**

Domain 4: Risk, Response, and Recovery

1. What is a key objective of risk analysis?

   a. Identify high priority risks.

   b. Select countermeasures and safeguards.

   c. Optimize insurance coverage.

   d. Identify high priority assets.

Answer **a**. The outcome of both quantitative or qualitative risk analysis is to prioritize risks. Both answers b & c are part of the controls selection phase of risk management. Answer d is a sub-step of risk analysis.

2. Which is not a threat to IT systems?
   a. Weakness in an application
   b. Power or HVAC outage
   c. Civil unrest
   d. Intruder

Answer **c**. All listed items are threats to organizations. However, the question focuses on IT systems. Of the answer group, answer c is not a direct threat to IT systems.

Use the following information for questions 3 and 4.

Historical records indicate a fire twice in 30 years of operation, destroying 30 percent of the data center. The data center is currently valued at $1M. A fire protection and safety engineer recommends an additional sensor and suppression system to limit loss to 5 percent and lower incidence estimate to once in twenty years. The proposed system would cost $50,000, and it can be annualized over 10 years.

3. What is the current annual loss expectancy?
   a. $300,000
   b. $30,000
   c. $200,000
   d. $20,000

Answer **d**. The formula to be used is: Asset Value * Exposure Factor & Annual Rate of Occurrence = Annual Loss Expectancy.

4. What is the value of the proposed system?
   a. $12,500
   b. $17,500
   c. $2,500
   d. $5,000

Answer **a**. Take the ALE before the proposed control, subtract the ALE using the proposed control, and then subtract the annualized cost of the proposed control.

5. An example of a detective technical control is:
   a. Error correcting code
   b. Hot swappable disk
   c. Error message
   d. Process checkpoints

Answer **c** is a detective technical control. Both a and b are corrective technical controls. Answer d is a detective administrative control.

6. Qualitative risk analysis methods include, all except:
    a. Scenarios
    b. Rankings
    c. Ratings
    d. Annual loss expectancy

Answer **d** is a quantitative risk analysis method. The other choices are qualitative approaches.

7. Mission critical processes or applications are:
    a. Integral to operations
    b. Strategic to the company
    c. Support regulatory compliance
    d. Employ the most people

Answer **b**. Numerous characteristics may be used to identify critical processes, including a, c, and even d.

8. A weak business impact analysis may lead to:
    a. Unsatisfactory recovery objective
    b. Regulatory non-compliance
    c. Lost revenue stream
    d. Unemployment

Answer **a** is the best choice because an organization determines its recovery objective. The other choices are too specific.

9. All the following should be considered when determining IT resources necessary at the recovery site, except:
    a. Staffing
    b. Process interdependencies
    c. Critical supply requirements
    d. Insurance

Answer **d**. Insurance factors into financial support for business interruption and restoration.

10. Data recovery point objective and recovery time objective can be improved the most with:
    a. Daily archives
    b. Remote journaling
    c. Database shadowing
    d. Electronic tape vaults

Answer **c** ensures remote data is recorded and durable with the last committed transaction and minimizes the time to ready the recovery site.

11. Which is the prudent order for disaster recovery plan testing:
    a. Parallel, simulation, interruption and walk-through
    b. Walk-through, parallel, simulation, interruption
    c. Walk-through, simulation, parallel, interruption

    d. Simulation, walk-through, parallel, interruption

Answer **c** minimizes cost and impact for the early plan testing.

12. Disaster recovery plans should:
    a. Be reviewed every six months.
    b. Provide details.
    c. Expect staff to report to duty.
    d. Assume sufficient supplies, materials and data are available.

Answer **b**. The DRP should be specific to direct the activation of the recovery team along with recovery procedures. Every plan should be reviewed and maintained, typically annually or upon change requirement. Choices c and d may be faulty assumptions.

13. A business impact analysis indicates a maximum tolerable downtime of six hours. What is a reasonable alternative?
    a. Hot site
    b. Warm site
    c. Mutual processing site
    d. Mirror site

Answer **a**, a hot site could be readied within that timeframe. Warm site takes longer and a mutual processing site has unique terms and conditions. A mirror site would definitely be ready, however, this is a more costly approach.

14. Numerous environments complicate intrusion detection analysis, except:
    a. Synchronized clocks
    b. Multiple entry points
    c. Switched networks
    d. Load balancers

Answer **a**, unsynchronized, mistimed or various source time zones would complicate intrusion detection analysis. Setting clocks to a standard time source and time zone, such as Greenwich Mean Time benefits intrusion detection analysis.

15. During an investigation, who should be kept informed:
    a. Users
    b. Law enforcement
    c. Shareholders
    d. Management

Answer **d**. Management should be kept informed throughout to make decisions based on containment and recovery recommendations.

16. Many judicial systems consider computer records:
    a. Best evidence
    b. Hearsay
    c. Conclusive

d. Demonstrative

Answer **b**, computer evidence is hearsay. Computer records show only the state of the computer at the time the record was captured, not necessarily at the time of the incident. Computer evidence is not from the personal knowledge of a direct witness. Best evidence is the original document, object or substance. Conclusive is evidence that can't be refuted. Demonstrative includes illustrations, diagrams or animations.

17. Computer evidence may have a higher burden of proof. Typical challenges include, all except:
    a. Relevancy
    b. Authenticity
    c. Accuracy
    d. Confidentiality

Answer **d** confidentiality is the correct choice. The other choices are challenges to all evidence, including computer evidence. However proving that computer evidence is genuine and not been deliberately or accidentally modified is more difficult than non-electronic evidence.

18. A critical element for investigators is to:
    a. Gather all evidence forensically.
    b. Follow investigative procedures.
    c. Preserve evidence under chain of custody.
    d. Thoroughly analyze logs and user reports.

Answer **b**, follow investigative procedures is correct. Personnel who are trained on well written procedures, encompasses the other answer choices.

19. Media that is the target of an investigation should be copied on to:
    a. New media
    b. Forensically sterile media
    c. Reformatted and portioned media
    d. Controlled and protected media

Answer **b** is the legally accepted standard. Answer a may contain factory files. Answers c and d may have remnant files from prior processing.

20. An investigator should prevent changes to target media with:
    a. Integrity verification controls
    b. Write blocker
    c. Configuration management
    d. Basic input and output system (BIOS) controls

Answer **b**, a write blocker functions to prevent modification to target media. Furthermore, write blockers can be proven to be effective through independent evaluation testing.

21. In addition to searching files and logs on media, an investigator should search all but:
    a. Unallocated space
    b. Disk slack
    c. RAM slack
    d. System slack

Answer **d**, system slack is a distracter. Unallocated space, answer a may include fragmented or deleted files. Disk slack, answer b is space between sector and end of cluster, and it may hold information like deleted files. RAM slack, answer c is space between file and end of sector, and it may contain information from RAM.

Domain 5: Cryptography

1. Digital signatures provide?
   a. Non-repudiation
   b. Encryption
   c. Privacy
   d. Key escrow

Answer: **a**. A prerequisite for substantiating non-repudiation is a Digital Certificate. A digital signature is made with a private key from an asymmetric key pair, and includes a hash of the message being signed. This combination provides dual assurance — that a message originated from a particular entity, and that the contents have not been tampered with.

2. Encryption of the same plain text with the same key resulting in the same ciphertext can be prevented by using?
   a. Digital signature
   b. Initialization vector
   c. Cipher feedback
   d. Public key certificate

Answer: **b**. Use of an initialization vector linearly added to the first block of plaintext or included in front of the plaintext prior to encryption in one of the streaming modes of operation resolves this problem.

3. What is a trusted third party that generates public key certificates?
   a. Local Registration Authority
   b. Notarization Authority
   c. Certification Authority
   d. Timestamping Authority

Answer: **c**. A Certificate Authority (CA) is a trusted third party that generates public key certificates, and can vouch for their authenticity.

4. Which of the following is currently used in conjunction with most Internet-based certificates to provide continuous authentication?
   a. Secure Multipurpose Internet Mail Extension (S/MIME)
   b. Secure Sockets Layer (SSL)
   c. Secure Shell (SSH)
   d. Secure Electronic Transaction (SET)

Answer: **b.** Most websites that exchange confidential user information with browsers protect sessions using secure sockets layer (SSL) encryption.

5. Encryption ciphers that use the same key to encrypt and decrypt are called?
   a. Asymmetric encryption
   b. Symmetric encryption
   c. Public key encryption
   d. Digital signature encryption

Answer: **b.** Encryption ciphers that use the same key to encrypt and decrypt are called symmetric or private key.

6. A digital signature is made with?
   a. A private key from an asymmetric key pair, and includes a hash of the message being signed
   b. A public key from an asymmetric key pair, and includes a hash of the message being signed
   c. A private key from a symmetric key pair, and includes a hash of the message being signed
   d. A public key from a symmetric key pair, and includes a hash of the message being signed

Answer: **a.** A digital signature is made with a private key from an asymmetric key pair, and includes a hash of the message being signed.

7. What protocol is typically used to login to a remote machine and execute commands?
   a. Secure Sockets Layer (SSL)
   b. Secure Electronic Transaction (SET)
   c. Secure Shell (SSH)
   d. Secure Multipurpose Internet Mail Extension (S/MIME)

Answer: **c.** SSH is typically used to login to a remote machine and execute commands, but it also supports tunneling, forwarding arbitrary TCP ports and X11 connections; it can transfer files using the associated SFTP or SCP protocols.

8. Rendering information unintelligible to anyone other than those who know the encryption cipher and the proper key is the concept of?
   a. Confidentiality
   b. Integrity

    c. Authentication

    d. Non-repudiation

Answer: **a**. Cryptography provides confidentiality by rendering information unintelligible to anyone other than those who know the encryption cipher and the proper key.

9. By changing what crypto variable, can one change the output of the cryptographic function, even if the plaintext remains the same.

    a. Hash

    b. Algorithm

    c. Ciphertext

    d. Key

Answer: **d**. The encryption cipher uses the cryptographic key to vary its output so that two correspondents can protect their information from anyone else with access to the same cipher. By changing the key, one changes the output of the cryptographic function, even if the plaintext remains the same.

10. What uses a digital signature to bind together a public key with an identity?

    a. Message Digest

    b. Identity certificate

    c. Secure Hash Algorithm (SHA)

    d. Digital Signature Standard (DSS)

Answer: **b**. A public key certificate (or identity certificate) is a certificate which uses a digital signature to bind together a public key with an identity — information such as the name of a person or an organization, their address, and so forth. The certificate can be used to verify that a public key belongs to an individual. A trusted third party digitally signs the certificate attesting that the identity information and the public key belong together.

11. What type of digital signature can be duplicated by anyone who holds that key?

    a. Public key

    b. Asymmetric key

    c. Symmetric key

    d. Ad-hoc key

Answer: **c**. Digital signatures can be done with symmetric or asymmetric keys. However, a symmetric key digital signature can be duplicated by anyone who holds that key. This is typically used in situations where only a closed group of individuals share information, and want to ensure that it came from someone within the group.

12. Non-repudiation, or proving that a party originated a message, typically uses what type of key cryptography?

    a. Asymmetric

     b. Symmetric
     c. Private
     d. Password

Answer: **a**. Non-repudiation typically uses asymmetric key crypto. However, if a trusted key escrow system is used, then symmetric keys can perform this function.

13.   What helps detect forgeries?
     a. Notarization
     b. Initialization vector
     c. Checksum
     d. Hash function

Answer: **d**. A hash is like a checksum, but is designed so that a message cannot be forged that will result in the same hash as a legitimate message.

14.   Without any knowledge of the key, an opponent with access to an encrypted message and the decryption cipher could try every possible key to decode the message. This is known as?
     a. Cipher block chaining attack
     b. Man in the middle attack
     c. Brute force attack
     d. Birthday attack

Answer: **c**. This is known as a brute force attack.

15.   In IPSEC, what protocol provides authentication and message integrity, but does not offer confidentiality?
     a. Authentication Header (AH)
     b. Encapsulating Security Payload (ESP)
     c. Security Parameter Index (SPI)
     d. Internet Security Association and Key Management Protocol (ISAKMP)

Answer: **a**. Authentication Header (AH) provides authentication and message integrity, but does not offer confidentiality. Originally AH was only used for integrity and ESP was used only for encryption.

Domain 6: Networks and Telecommunications

1.   Match the topology with the appropriate description and vulnerabilities.
     1. Star
     2. Bus
     3. Ring
     4. Point to point
     a. In its most basic setup, the traffic flows in one direction. A break in the link and all traffic flow is severely limited.

b. One of the more secure topologies due to the limited opportunities to intercept the traffic.

c. The type of topology used in older networks or by cable companies. It is easy to listen to all of the traffic being broadcast on the wire.

d. If the center point fails or is compromised, the traffic can be completely stopped.

Answer: 1-**d**. 2-**c**, 3-**a**, 4-**b**

2. Match the following protocols with their descriptions.
   1. SMTP
   2. ICMP
   3. TFTP
   4. DHCP
   a. This protocol is used as an unauthenticated protocol to transfer data.
   b. This protocol is used between two mail servers to determine how they will communicate.
   c. This protocol is used to transmit the health and status of a network.
   d. This protocol is used in assigning IP addresses, default gateways, and DNS information.

Answer: 1-**b**, 2-**c**, 3-**a**, 4-**d**

3. True or False – It is not important to look at the syslog files because they are being backed up and can be reviewed at any time.

Answer: False – It is very important to look at all of your log files. These files are the keys for how you understand what is happening to your network.

4. Choose the best description for the following protocols:
   1. SSL
   2. IPSEC AH
   3. IPSEC ESP
   4. NAT
   a. Message confidentiality is provided by encrypting the payload.
   b. Originally designed to compensate for a decreased number of IP addresses; has been used for security purpose of hiding IP addresses.
   c. Message integrity is performed by authenticating the payload and the origin of the information.
   d. Operates at the session layer and is often used with Digital Certificates.

Answer: 1-**d**, 2-**c**, 3-**a**, 4-**b**

5. Which of these protocols is not normally used to help make E-Mail more Secure:
   a. PGP
   b. S/MIME
   c. PEM
   d. MSP
   e. SNMP

Answer: **e.** Simple Network Management Protocol is used for network monitoring and management while the other protocols are often used to help make e-mail more secure.

6. Match the network equipment with its most common PRIMARY function:
   1. Firewall
   2. Router
   3. Switches
   4. VPN Termination Points
   a. Will pass traffic from one network to another network based on IP address.
   b. Will pass traffic to the appropriate network segment based on the MAC address.
   c. Enforced access control policy at given points of the network.
   d. Terminates encrypted communications and forwards them to the internal network.

Answer: 1-**c**, 2-**a**, 3-**b**, 4-**d.** There can be some reference made that some switches can route traffic based on IP address, some routers and firewalls can terminate VPN connections, and firewalls, routers, and VPNs can often pass traffic to host on the directly connected network via their MAC address. The idea was to understand and define the PRIMARY functionality of these devices.

7. Choose the descriptions and benefits/risks that best match the following Remote Access Solutions:
   1. RAS
   2. VPN
   3. Clientless VPN
   a. Allows the user to access the network without necessarily having to have his own device with him. Using a third party device might increase the network vulnerability by the use of hidden Trojans or keystroke monitoring tools.
   b. Does not require Internet access and can be secured by other means like two-factor authentication, is not easily sniffed. Usually requires a large phone bank to receive calls, can be expensive for long distance bills, subject to discovery by War dialing.
   c. Allows for the user to have a strong means of authentication and verification. Often requires the IT department to touch and main-

tain every device, and the device is required to connect to the network.

Answer: 1-**b**, 2-**c**, 3-**a**

8. Choose which of the following actions will help secure a wireless access point.
    a. Choosing WPA2 over WEP
    b. Hiding the SSID
    c. Activate MAC address filtering
    d. Having an access control technology with authentication capability built into the device or having this access control product immediately behind the access point
    e. All of the above

Answer: **e**.

Domain 7: Malicious Code

1. Which of the following is a reason to use a Firewall?
    a. To evaluate intrusions as they happen
    b. To watch for internal attacks
    c. To prevent or stop potential intrusions
    d. To signal an alarm on a suspected intrusion

Answer: **c**. Firewalls are strategically placed to detect and stop intrusions gaining access to the inside of the protected network. All other items relate to an Intrusion Detection System (IDS).

2. Which of the following is an attribute of polymorphic code?
    a. It mutates while keeping the original algorithm intact
    b. It uses encryption for all the code
    c. It operates based on specific conditions
    d. It is written to self replicate altering the computer configuration

Answer: **a**. This tactic allows a computer virus to remain undetected and to hide their presence; b. All the code is not encrypted, a small portion is left unencrypted to allow execution; c. This is a characteristic of a logic bomb; d. This is an attribute of all computer virii.

3. Flooding network ports is an example of which type of attack?
    a. Man-in-the-Middle
    b. Brute force
    c. Denial of service
    d. Birthday

Answer: **c**. This is one example of a DoS; a. Typically reads messages between two computers; b. Consists of running through all possible combinations to achieve a result; d. Another form of a brute force attack.

4. Which of the following is typically a characteristic exhibited by Script Kiddies?
   a. They are very talented.
   b. They leave no trace of what they are doing.
   c. They are concerned with the quality of the attack.
   d. They see the number of attacks being something to be proud of.

Answer: **d**. The only correct key here is d. They are not concerned with much except the number of attacks they can release as this implies notoriety to them.

5. Which of the following virus types typically affects the normal.dot file?
   a. Macro virus
   b. Multipartite
   c. Boot sector
   d. MacIntosh

Answer: **a**. This it the only virus list that affects this file. These virii are focused directly on Microsoft applications and specifically copy themselves directly to this file thus infecting anything that is opened subsequently.

6. Which of the following represents the "SALT" value in a password?
   a. The value is a constant chosen by the system.
   b. The value is chosen randomly.
   c. The value is time based.
   d. The value is a constant chosen by the user.

Answer: **b**. The value is chosen randomly at the time the password is created and is stored with the hashed password.

7. Which of the following techniques BEST defines "Spam"?
   a. Filling a field with false information
   b. Expressing a strong criticism of something
   c. Inducing a resource to take incorrect actions
   d. Posting information repeatedly to overburden the network

Answer: **d**. SPAM is the act of posting information repeatedly to many places in an attempt to overburden a network.

8. Which of the following defines a Man-in-the-Middle attack?
   a. Searching through databases for specific information
   b. Bypassing the user authentication system
   c. Manipulation of packets being sent over a network
   d. Overwriting the system buffers with data

Answer: **c**. a. is an example of Targeted Data mining; b. is an example of a Trap Door; d. is an example of a buffer overflow

9. Which of the following features of the Internet Protocol is used by the Ping of Death to execute?
   a. Its ability to fragment packets
   b. Its capability to encrypt data
   c. Its ability to do site routing
   d. Its capability to parse log files

Answer: **a**. The problem occurs due to manner in which packets fragmentation occurs on most systems. Usually systems do not attempt to process a packet until all fragments are received. Once all fragments are received, a packet is formed and this packet can be malformed and caused the system to crash due to buffer overflows.

10. Which of the following defines a Trojan Horse?
    a. It has the ability to gain access to a computer system by circumventing the usual security checks.
    b. It has the ability to self-propagate from one computer to another on the network.
    c. It has the ability to replicate itself between files on the system.
    d. It has the ability to convince the user that is has one function while hiding another function.

Answer: **d**. a. is backdoor; b. is computer worm; c. is a computer virus.

11. All of the following EXCEPT are forms of Symmetric Block Cipher Attacks?
    a. Linear cryptanalysis
    b. Weak keys
    c. Key streams
    d. Algebraic attacks

Answer: **c**. Key Streams is a Stream Cipher attack.

12. Which of the following is NOT a phase of a Social Engineering attack?
    a. Intelligence gathering
    b. Eavesdropping
    c. Target selection
    d. The attack

Answer: **b**. Eavesdropping may happen as part of the intelligence gathering but it is not the entire phase and an attack would most likely fail based on just this form of data.

13. Which of the following can be susceptible to a Birthday attack?
    a. Digital signatures
    b. Asymmetric algorithms
    c. Password hashs
    d. Private keys

Answer: **a**. Birthday attacks leverage the vulnerability of popular hashes such as MD and SHA to be estimated, thereby making digital signatures susceptible to attack.

14. Which of the following defines session hijacking?
    a. Compromising the session between two machines is taken over
    b. Exploitation of the trust relationship in the Internet Protocol
    c. Creation of random addresses for each network packet
    d. Making compute resources unavailable.

Answer: **a**. Session hijacking is the compromise of the session between two computers (similar to a man in the middle attack)

15. Which of the following is NOT a characteristic of Computer Virus Hoax?
    a. Asks that you send it to everyone to warn them
    b. Makes reference to a false authority
    c. Contains technical sounding nonsense
    d. Usually has a hidden function that executes unknown to the user

Answer: **d**. a, b and c are some of the characteristics.

Appendix B
Systems Security Certified Practitioner (SSCP®) Candidate Information Bulletin

This Candidate Information Bulletin provides the following:

- Exam blueprint to a limited level of detail that outlines major topics and subtopics within the domains that are listed in alphabetical order
- Suggested reference list
- Description of the format of the items on the exam
- Basic registration/administration policies

Applicants must have a minimum of one year of direct full-time security work experience in one or more of the seven domains of the (ISC)² SSCP® CBK®.

SSCP practitioner's experience includes:

- Work requiring special education or intellectual attainment, usually including a technical school, liberal education, or college degree
- Work requiring habitual memory of a body of knowledge shared with others doing similar work
- Management of projects and/or other employees
- Supervision of the work of others while working with a minimum of supervision of one's self
- Work requiring the exercise of judgment, management decision-making, and discretion
- Work requiring the exercise of ethical judgment (as opposed to ethical behavior)
- Creative writing and oral communication
- Teaching, instructing, training, and the mentoring of others
- Research and development
- The specification and selection of controls and mechanisms (i.e., identification and authentication technology) (does not include the mere operation of these controls)

1 — Access Controls

Overview

Access controls permit management to specify what users can do, which resources they can access, and what operations they can perform on a system.

Access controls provides system managers with the ability to limit and monitor who has access to a system and to restrain or influence the user's behavior on that system. Access control systems define what level of access that individual has to the information contained within a system based upon predefined conditions such as authority level or group membership. Access control systems are based upon varying technologies including passwords, hardware tokens, biometrics, and certificates, to name just a few.

Each access control system offers different levels of confidentiality, integrity and availability to the user, system and stored information.

The candidate is expected to demonstrate knowledge in how different access control systems operate and are implemented to protect the system and its stored data. In addition, they must demonstrate knowledge in account management, access control concepts, and attack methods that are used to defeat access control systems.

Key Areas of Knowledge

- Understand logical access controls in terms of subjects
- Understand logical access controls in terms of objects
- Implement authentication techniques
- Understand access control concepts

2 — Security Operations and Administration

Overview

Security operations and administration entails the identification of an organization's information assets and the documentation required for the implementations of policies, standards, procedures and guidelines that ensure confidentiality, integrity and availability. Working with management, information owners, custodians and users, the appropriate data classification scheme is defined for proper handling of both hardcopy and electronic information.

The candidate is expected to demonstrate knowledge in privacy issues, data classification, data integrity, audit, organization roles and responsibilities, policies, standards, guidelines, procedures, security awareness and configuration controls, and the application of accepted industry practices.

Key Areas of Knowledge

- Understand Security Administration
- Understand Change Management Concepts
- Participate in System Development Life Cycle (SDLC)
- Provide Security Evaluation and Assistance to The Organization
- Educate Users in Security Awareness
- Adhere to Code of Ethics
- Evaluate the Security Infrastructure using available tools
- Perform Security Policy Administration
- Understand the Concepts of the Certification and Accreditation Process
- Implement, Recommend, and Promote Security Best Practices

3 — Analysis and Monitoring

Overview

Monitoring is an activity that collects information and provides a method of identifying security events, assigning a priority to those events, taking the appropriate action to maintain the security of the system, and report the pertinent information to the appropriate individual, group, or process. The analysis function provides the security manager with the ability to determine if the system is being operated in accordance with accepted industry practices, and in compliance with any specific organization policies and procedures.

Understanding the analysis components prepares the candidate to work with either internal or external auditors during a formal audit review. The candidate is expected to demonstrate knowledge in the various methods of data collection, including data logging, sampling and reporting, in addition to analysis and audit review, and compliance check techniques. An understanding of the legal requirements for monitoring and audit activities is essential.

Key Areas of Knowledge

- Understand principles, practices, and mechanisms
- Perform audits
- Maintain effective monitoring systems
- Conduct analysis of exploits

4 — Risk, Response, and Recovery

Overview

Risk management is the identification, measurement and control of loss associated with adverse events. It includes overall security review, risk analysis; selection and evaluation of safeguards, cost benefit analysis, management decisions, safeguard implementation, and effectiveness review.

The candidate is expected to demonstrate knowledge in risk management including risk analysis, threats and vulnerabilities, asset identification, and risk management tools and techniques.

Incident handling provides the ability to react quickly and put highly trained people at the forefront of any incident, and allows for a consistently applied approach to resolving the incident. Investigations include data collection and integrity preservation; seizure of hardware and software; evidence collection, handling, and storage; and reporting.

The candidate is expected to demonstrate knowledge in event identification, damage recovery, data integrity and preservation, evidence collection and handling, reporting, and prevention.

Business Continuity Planning is planning that facilitates the rapid recovery of business operations to reduce the overall impact of the disaster, through ensuring continuity of the critical business functions. Disaster Recovery Planning includes procedures for emergency response, extended backup operations and post-disaster recovery when the computer installation suffers loss of computer resources and physical facilities.

The candidate is expected to demonstrate knowledge in how to prepare business continuity or disaster recovery plan, techniques and concepts, identification of critical data and systems, and finally the recovery of the lost data.

Key Areas of Knowledge

- Participate in Risk Management Process
- Participate in Security Assessments
- Participate in Incident Handling Analysis
- Understand and Differentiate between a Business Continuity Plan (BCP) and a Disaster Recovery Plan (DRP)
- Participate in Disaster Recovery Plan
- Participate in the Business Continuity Plan (BCP)

5 — Cryptography

Overview

The ability of any organization to protect its information from unauthorized access or modification has become a major concern in recent years. The application of cryptography for the storage and transmission of information attempts to address these concerns.

Cryptography is concerned with the protection of information by modifying the information to ensure its integrity, confidentiality authenticity and non-repudiation. Cryptanalysis is the opposite of cryptography, concerned with defeating the cryptosystem and violating the confidentiality or integrity of the protected data.

The candidate will be expected to know basic concepts in cryptography; public and private key algorithms, key distribution and management, methods of attack; and the application, construction and use of digital signatures, and the principles of public key infrastructure and certification.

Key Areas of Knowledge

- Understand business and security requirements for cryptography
- Understand principles of certificates and key management
- Understand secure protocols

6 — Networks and Telecommunications

Overview

In today's global marketplace, the ability to communicate securely with others is a mandatory requirement. The networks and telecommunications domain encompasses the network structure, transmission methods, transport formats and security measures used to maintain the integrity, availability, authentication and confidentiality of the transmitted information over both private and public communication networks.

The candidate is expected to demonstrate an understanding of communications and network security as it relates to data and telecommunications in local area and wide area networks; remote access; internet/intranet/extranet configurations, use of firewalls, network equipment and protocols (such as TCP/IP), VPN's, and techniques for preventing and detecting network based attacks.

Key Areas of Knowledge

- Understand business and security requirements

- Understand remote access architecture
- Understand firewalls
- Understand networks
- Understand wireless

7 — Malicious Code

Overview

The number and types of attacks using malicious code is increasing. The requirement for an individual or an organization to protect themselves from these attacks is extremely important. The malicious code domain addresses computer code that can be described as being harmful or destructive to the computing environment. This includes viruses, worms, logic bombs, the Trojan horse, and other technical and non-technical attacks.

While there are a variety of methods available to build a virus, many viruses are still targeted a specific computing platform. With the availability of platform independent languages such as Perl, Active-X and Java, it is becoming easier to write malicious code that can be run across different platforms. The candidate is expected to demonstrate knowledge in the concepts of malicious and mobile code, types of malicious code threats, how malicious code is introduced into the environment, and various protection and recovery methods.

Key Areas of Knowledge

- Differentiate between viruses, Trojan Horse, and worms
- Identify virus activity
- Differentiate between trap doors and back doors
- Understand implications of virus hoaxes and myths
- Recognize and identify characteristics of malicious code
- Identify and implement appropriate security measures

References

(ISC)² does not intend that candidates purchase and read all of the books and articles listed in this reference list. Since most of the information tested in the examination pertains to a common body of knowledge, this additional information serves only as a supplement to one's understanding of basic knowledge. A reference list is not intended to be inclusive but is provided to allow flexibility. The candidate is encouraged to supplement his or her education and experience by reviewing other resources and finding information in areas which he or she may consider himself or herself not as skilled or experienced. (ISC)² does not endorse any particular text or author. Although the list may include more than one reference that covers a content area, one such reference may be enough. The candidate may also have resources available that are not on the list but which will adequately cover the content area. The list does not represent the only body of information to be used as study material.

Questions in the examination are also developed from information gained through practical experience. This reference list is not intended to be all-inclusive, but rather, a useful list of references used to support the test question development process. Use of the references does not guarantee successful completion of the test.

Below is the suggested reference list:

A Handbook Of Computer Security	Heanden Keith
Actually Useful Internet Security Techniques	Larry J. Hughes, Jr
Building A Security Computer System	Morrie Gasser
Commonsense Computer Security	Martin Smith
Computer Fraud And Countermeasures	Leonard I. Krauss and Aileen Macgahan.
Computer Security Basics	Russell and Gangemi
Computer Security Handbook	Hutt Bosworth & Hoyt
Computer Security Risk Management	I. C. Palmer and G. A. Potter
Computer Viruses	Robert Slade
Computers Business & Security	James A. Schweizer
Defending Your Digital Assets	Nichols Ryan
Designing Information Systems Security	Baskerville, Richard
Designing Network Security	Merike Kaeo
Effect Physical Security	Lawrence Fennelly
E-Mail Security	Schneier
Firewalls And Internet Security	Repelling, Wiley, Hakiv, Choswick, and Bellovia
Fundamentals Of Computer Security Technology	Edward Amoroso
Guide To Computer Viruses	Robert Slade
Hacker Proof	Lars Klander
Hacking Exposed: Network Security and Solutions	Stuart McClure, Joel Scambray, and George Kurtz
Handbook Of Information Security Management	Krause-Tipton
Handbook Of Information Security Management	Ruthberg/Tipton
Information Management: Strategies, Systems and Technologies, Risk, and the Need for Disaster Recovery Planning	Denise Johnson McManus and Houston H. Carr
Information Protection and Other Unnatural Acts	Harry B. DeMaio
Information Systems Security: A Practitioner's Reference	Fites and Kratz

Information Systems Security Officer's Guide	Dr. Gerald Kovacich
Internet Cryptography	Richard Smith
Internet Security Professional Reference	Derek Atkins, Paul Buis, Chris Hare, Robert Kelley, Carey Nachenberg, Anthony B. Nelson, Paul Phillips, Tim Ritchey, & William Steen
Intrusion Detection	Escamilla
Mastering Network Security	Chris Brneton
Network Security	Fred Simonds
Network Security Data And Voice	Simonds
Practical Unix & Internet Security	S. Garfinkel & G. Spafford
Secure Computing	Rita C. Summers
Secure Electronic Commerce	Warwick Ford, Micheal S. Baum
Security ID Systems And Locks	Konecek and Little
Security in Computing	C.P.Pfleeger
Time Based Security	Winn Schwartau
Understanding and Deploying LDAP Directory Services	Timothy Howes, Mark C. Smith, Gordon S. Good
Virtual Private Networks	Charlie Scott, Paul Wolfe & Mike Erwin
Web Security & Commerce	Garfinkel & Spafford

Sample Questions

1. When properly installed, which type of card or badge reader is **MOST** tamper resistant?
   a. Card swipe device
   b. Optical reader
   c. Proximity reader
   d. Card insertion device

Answer: **c.**

2. Which one of the following describes how a polymorphic virus attempts to hide from anti-virus software?
   a. By repeatedly changing the boot record of the host disk
   b. By changing the routines that encrypt the body of the virus
   c. By directly attacking the anti-virus software
   d. By directly attaching itself to an e-mail

Answer: **b.**

3. Which one of the following is the technique used to prevent inference violations by allowing different versions of the same information item to exist at different classification levels?
   a. Appropriate labeling

b. Query restriction
c. Auditing
c. Polyinstantiation

Answer: **d.**

General Examination Information

1. **General Information**. The doors to all examination rooms will open at 8:00 a.m. Examination instructions will begin promptly at 8:30 a.m. All examinations will begin at approximately 9:00 a.m.

   The CISSP® exam will end at approximately 3:00 p.m. All other exams will end at approximately 12:00 noon. Please note there will be no lunch break during the testing period of 9:00 a.m. to 3:00 p.m. However, you are permitted to bring a snack with you. You may, at your option, take a break and eat your snack at the back of the examination room. No additional time will be allotted for breaks.

2. **Examination Admittance**. Please arrive at 8:00 a.m. when the doors open. Please bring your admission letter to the examination. In order to be admitted, a photo identification is also required. **You will not be admitted without proper identification.** The only acceptable forms of identification are a driver's license, government-issued identification card, or passport. No other written forms of identification will be accepted.

3. **Examination Security**. Failure to follow oral and written instructions will result in your application being voided and forfeiture of your application fee. Conduct that results in a violation of security or disrupts the administration of the examination could result in the confiscation of your test and dismissal from the examination. In addition, your examination will be considered void and will not be scored. Examples of misconduct include, but are not limited to, the following: writing on anything other than designated examination materials, writing after time is called, looking at another candidate's examination materials, talking with other candidates at any time during the examination period, failing to turn in all examination materials before leaving the testing room.

   You must not discuss or share reference materials or any other examination information with any candidate during the entire examination period. You are particularly cautioned not to do so after you have completed the exam and checked out of the test room, as other candidates in the area might be taking a break and still not have completed the examination. You may not attend the examination only to review or audit test materials. You may not copy any portion of the examination for any reason. No examination materials may leave the test room under any circumstances and all examination materials must be turned in and accounted for before leaving the testing room. No unauthorized persons will be admitted into the testing area.

Please be further advised that all examination content is strictly confidential. You may only communicate about the test, or questions on the test, using the appropriate comment forms provided by the examination staff at the test site. At no other time, before, during or after the examination, may you communicate orally, electronically or in writing with any person or entity about the content of the examination or individual examination questions.

4. **Reference Material**. Candidates writing on anything other than examination materials distributed by the proctors will be in violation of the security policies above. Reference materials are not allowed in the testing room. Candidates are asked to bring as few personal and other items as possible to the testing area.

   Hard copy language translation dictionaries are permitted for the examination, should you choose to bring one to assist you with language conversions. Electronic dictionaries will not be permitted under any circumstances. The Examination Supervisor will fully inspect your dictionary at check-in. Your dictionary may not contain any writing or extraneous materials of any kind. If the dictionary contains writing or other materials or papers, it will not be permitted in the examination room. Additionally, you are not permitted to write in your dictionary at any time during the examination, and it will be inspected a second time prior to dismissal from the examination. Finally, (ISC)² takes no responsibility for the content of such dictionaries or interpretations of the contents by a candidate.

5. **Examination Protocol.** While the site climate is controlled to the extent possible, be prepared for either warm or cool temperatures at the testing center. Cellular phones and beepers are prohibited in the testing area. The use of headphones inside the testing area is prohibited. Electrical outlets will not be available for any reason. Earplugs for sound suppression are allowed. No smoking or use of tobacco will be allowed inside the testing area. Food and drinks are only allowed in the snack area located at the rear of the examination room. You must vacate the testing area after you have completed the examination. If you require special assistance, you must contact SMT at least one week in advance of the examination date and appropriate arrangements will be made. Due to limited parking facilities at some sites, please allow ample time to park and reach the testing area.

6. **Admission Problems**. A problem table for those candidates who did not receive an admission notice or need other assistance will be available 30 minutes prior to the opening of the doors.

7. **Examination Format and Scoring**.
   - The CISSP examination consists of 250 multiple choice questions with four (4) choices each.
   - The SSCP exam contains 125 multiple choice questions with four (4) choices each.
   - The ISSAP®, ISSEP®, and ISSMP® exams contain 125, 150, 125 multiple choice questions respectively with four (4) choices each.
   - The Certification and Accreditation Professional (CAP) exam contains 125 multiple choice questions with four (4) choices each.

   There may be scenario-based items which may have more than one multiple choice question associated with it. These items will be specifically identified in the test booklet.

   Each of these exams contains 25 questions which are included for research purposes only. The research questions are not identified; therefore, answer all questions to the best of your ability. Examination results will be based only on the scored questions on the examination. There are several versions of the examination. It is important that each candidate have an equal opportunity to pass the examination, no matter which version is administered. Expert certified information security professionals have provided input as to the difficulty level of all questions used in the examinations. That information is used to develop examination forms that have comparable difficulty levels. When there are differences in the examination difficulty, a mathematical procedure is used to make the scores equal. Because the number of questions required to pass the examination may be different for each version, the scores are converted onto a reporting scale to ensure a common standard. The passing grade required is a scale score of 700 out of a possible 1000 points on the grading scale.

8. **Examination Results**. Examination results will normally be released, via U.S. first class mail, within four to six weeks of the examination date. A comprehensive statistical and psychometric analysis of the score data is conducted for each spring and fall testing cycle prior to the release of scores. A minimum number of candidates must have taken the examination for the analysis to be conducted. Accordingly, depending upon the schedule of test dates for a given cycle, there may be occasions when scores are delayed beyond the four to six week time frame in order to complete this critical process. Results WILL NOT be released over the phone. In order to receive your results, your address must be current and any address change must be submitted to SMT in writing.

9. **Exam Response Information**. Your answer sheet MUST be completed with your name and other information as required. The answer

sheet must be used to record all answers to the multiple choice questions. Upon completion, you are to wait for the proctor to collect your examination materials. Answers marked in the test booklet will not be counted or graded, and additional time will not be allowed in order to transfer answers to the answer sheet. All marks on the answer sheet must be made with a No. 2 pencil. You must blacken the appropriate circles completely and completely erase any incorrect marks. Only your responses marked on the answer sheet will be considered. An unanswered question will be scored as incorrect. Dress is "business casual" (neat... but certainly comfortable).

Any questions should be directed to:

(ISC)²
c/o Schroeder Measurement Technologies, Inc.
2494 Bayshore Blvd., Suite 201
Dunedin, FL 34698
(888) 333-4458 (U.S. only) (727) 738-8657

Appendix C
Glossary

802.11: Family of IEEE standards for wireless LANS first introduced in 1997. The first standard to be implemented, 802.11b, specifies from 1 to 11 Mbps in the unlicensed band using DSSS direct sequence spread spectrum technology. The Wireless Ethernet Compatibility Association (WECA) brands it as Wireless Fidelity (Wi-Fi).

802.1X: An IEEE standard for port based layer two authentications in 802 standard networks. Wireless LANS often use 802.1X for authentication of a user before the user has the ability to access the network.

Abend: An acronym for the abnormal end of a task. The abnormal termination of a computer application or job because of a nonsystem condition or failure that causes a program to halt. It generally means a software crash.

Abstraction: The process of identifying the characteristics that distinguish a collection of similar objects; the result of the process of abstraction is a type.

Acceptable Use Policy: A policy that a user must agree to follow to gain access to a network or to the Internet.

Acceptance Testing: The formal testing conducted to determine whether a software system satisfies its acceptance criteria, enabling the customer to determine whether to accept the system.

Access: The ability of a subject to view, change, or communicate with an object. Typically, access involves a flow of information between the subject and the object.

Access Control: The process of allowing only authorized users, programs, or other computer system (i.e., networks) to access the resources of a computer system. A mechanism for limiting use of some resource (system) to authorized users.

Access Control Certificate: ADI in the form of a security certificate.

Access Control Decision Function (ADF): A specialized function that makes access control decisions by applying access control policy rules to a requested action, ACI (of initiators, targets, actions, or

473

that retained from prior actions), and the context in which the request is made.

Access Control Decision Information (ADI):   The portion (possibly all) of the ACI made available to the ADF in making a particular access control decision.

Access Control Enforcement Function (AEF):   A specialized function that is part of the access path between an initiator and a target on each access that enforces the decisions made by the ADF.

Access Control Information (ACI):   Any information used for access control purposes, including contextual information.

Access Control List (ACL):   An Access Control List is the usual means by which access to, and denial of, service is controlled. It is simply a list of the services available, each with a list of the hosts permitted to use the services. Most network security systems operate by allowing selective use of services.

Access Control Mechanisms: Hardware, software, or firmware features and operating and management procedures in various combinations designed to detect and prevent unauthorized access and to permit authorized access to a computer system.

Access Control Policy: The set of rules that define the conditions under which an access may take place.

Access Controls: The management of permission for logging on to a computer or network.

Access Path: The logical route that an end user takes to access computerized information. Typically, it includes a route through the operating system, telecommunications software, selected application software and the access control system.

Access Period: A segment of time, generally expressed on a daily or weekly basis, during which access rights prevail.

Access Rights: Also called permissions or privileges, these are the rights granted to users by the administrator or supervisor. These permissions can be read, write, execute, create, delete, and so forth.

Access Type: The nature of access granted to a particular device, program, or file (e.g., read, write, execute, append, modify, delete, or create).

Accountability: (1) A security principle stating that individuals must be able to be identified. With accountability, violations or attempted violations can be traced to individuals who can be held responsible for their actions. (2) The ability to map a given activity or event back to the responsible party; the property that ensures that the actions of an entity may be traced to that entity.

Accreditation: A program whereby a laboratory demonstrates that something is operating under accepted standards to ensure quality assurance.

ACI: Access control information.

Acknowledgment (ACK): A type of message sent to indicate that a block of data arrived at its destination without error. A negative acknowledgment is called a "NAK."

ACL: *See Access control list.*

Action: The operations and operands that form part of an attempted access.

Action ADI: Action decision information associated with the action.

Active Object: An object that has its own process; the process must be ongoing while the active object exists.

Active Threat: The threat of a deliberate unauthorized change to the state of the system.

Active Wiretapping: The attachment of an unauthorized device (e.g., a computer terminal) to a communications circuit to gain access to data by generating false messages or control signals or by altering the communications of legitimate users.

ActiveX: Microsoft's Windows-specific non-Java technique for writing applets. ActiveX applets take considerably longer to download than the equivalent Java applets; however, they more fully exploit the features of Windows. ActiveX is sometimes said to be a "superset of Java."

Ada: A programming language that allows use of structured techniques for program design; concise but powerful language designed to fill government requirements for real-time applications.

Add-On Security: The retrofitting of protection mechanisms, implemented by hardware, firmware, or software, on a computer system that has become operational.

Address: (1) A sequence of bits or characters that identifies the destination and sometimes the source of a transmission. (2) An identification (e.g., number, name, or label) for a location in which data is stored.

Address Mapping: The process by which an alphabetic Internet address is converted into a numeric IP address, and vice versa.

Address Mask: A bit mask used to identify which bits in an IP address correspond to the network address and subnet portions of the address. This mask is often referred to as the subnet mask because the network portion of the address can be determined by the class inherent in an IP address. The address mask has ones in positions corresponding to the network and subnet numbers and zeros in the host number positions.

Address Resolution: A means for mapping network layer addresses onto media-specific addresses.

Address Resolution Protocol (ARP): The Internet protocol used to dynamically map Internet addresses to physical (hardware) addresses on the local area network. Limited to networks that support hardware broadcast.

Administrative Controls: The actions or controls dealing with operational effectiveness, efficiency, and adherence to regulations and management policies.

Administrative Security: The management constraints, operational procedures, accountability procedures, and supplemental controls established to provide an acceptable level of protection for sensitive data.

Administrative Security Information: Persistent information associated with entities; it is conceptually stored in the Security Management Information Base. Examples are: security attributes associated with users and set up on user account installation, which is used to configure the user's identity and privileges within the system information configuring a secure interaction policy between one entity and another entity, which is used as the basis for the establishment of operational associations between those two entities.

AEF: Access control enforcement function.

Agent: In the client/server model, the part of the system that performs information preparation and exchange on behalf of a client or server application.

Aggregation: A relation, such as consists of or contains between types that defines the composition of a type from other types.

Aging: The identification, by date, of unprocessed or retained items in a file. This is usually done by date of transaction, classifying items according to ranges of data.

Alarm Collector Function: A function that collects the security alarm messages, translates them into security alarm records, and writes them to the security alarm log.

Alarm Examiner Function: A function that interfaces with a security alarm administrator.

Algorithm: A computing procedure designed to perform a task such as encryption, compressing, or hashing.

Aliases: Used to reroute browser requests from one URL to another.

American National Standards Institute (ANSI): The agency that recommends standards for computer hardware, software, and firmware design and use.

American Registry for Internet Numbers (ARIN): A nonprofit organization established for the purpose of administration and registration of Internet Protocol (IP) numbers to the geographical areas currently managed by Network Solutions (InterNIC). Those areas include, but are not limited to North America, South America, South Africa, and the Caribbean.

American Standard Code for Information Interchange (ASCII): A byte-oriented coding system based on an 8-bit code and used primarily to format information for transfer in a data communications environment.

Amplitude Modulation (AM): The technique of varying the amplitude or wavelength of a carrier wave in direct proportion to the strength of the input signal while maintaining a constant frequency and phase.

Analog: A voice transmission mode that is not digital in which information is transmitted in its original form by converting it to a continuously variable electrical signal.

Analysis and Design Phase: The phase of the systems development life cycle in which an existing system is studied in detail and its functional specifications are generated.

Annual Loss Expectancy (ALE): In risk assessment, the average monetary value of losses per year.

Anonymity: The state in which something is unknown or unacknowledged.

Anonymous File Transfer Protocol (FTP): (1) A method for downloading public files using the File Transfer Protocol. Anonymous FTP is called anonymous because users do not provide credentials before accessing files from a particular server. In general, users enter the word anonymous when the host prompts for a username; anything can be entered for the password, such as the user's email address or simply the word guest. In many cases, an anonymous FTP site will not even prompt for a name and password. (2) A type of FTP that allows a user to log on to a remote host, which the user would otherwise not have access to, to download files.

ANSI: *See American National Standards Institute.*

Anti-virus Software: Applications that detect prevent and possibly remove all known viruses from files located in a microcomputer hard drive.

API: Application Programming Interface. The interface between the application software and the application platform, across which all services are provided. The application programming interface is primarily in support of application portability, but system and application interoperability are also supported by a communication API. *See also Application Program Interface (API).*

Applet: A small Java program embedded in an HTML document.

Application: Computer software used to perform a distinct function. Also used to describe the function itself.

Application Controls: The transaction and data relating to each computer-based application system. Therefore, they are specific to each such application controls, which may be manual or programmed, are to endure the completeness and accuracy of the records and the validity of the entries made therein resulting from both manual and programmed processing. Examples of application controls include data input validation, agreement of batch controls, and encryption of data transmitted.

Application Layer: The top-most layer in the OSI Reference Model providing such communication service is invoked through a software package. This layer provides the interface between end-users and networks. It allows use of e-mail and viewing Web pages, along with numerous other networking services.

Application Objects: Applications and their components that are managed within an object-oriented system. Example operations on such objects are OPEN, INSTALL, MOVE, and REMOVE.

Application Program Interface (API): A set of calling conventions defining how a service is invoked through a software package. *See also API.*

Architecture: The structure or ordering of components in a computational or other system. The classes and the interrelation of the classes define the architecture of a particular application. At another level, the architecture of a system is determined by the arrangement of the hardware and software components. The terms "logical architecture" and "physical architecture" are often used to emphasize this distinction.

ARCNET: Developed by Datapoint Corporation in the 1970s; a LAN (Local Area Network) technology that competed strongly with Ethernet, but no longer does. Initially a computer connected via ARCNET could communicate at 2.5 Mbps, although this technology now supports a throughput of 20 Mbps (compared to current Ethernet at 100 Mbps and 1 Gbps).

ARP: Address Resolution Protocol. This is a protocol that resides in the TCP/IP suite of protocols. Its purpose is to associate IP addresses at the network layer with MAC addresses at the data link layer.

Array: Consecutive storage areas in memory that are identified by the same name. The elements (or groups) within these storage areas are accessed through subscripts.

Artificial Intelligence (AI): A field of study involving techniques and methods under which computers can simulate such human intellectual activities as learning.

ASP/MSP: A third-party provider that delivers and manages applications and computer services, including security services to multiple users via the Internet or Virtual Private Network (VPN).

Assembler Language: A computer programming language in which alphanumeric symbols represent computer operations and memory addresses. Each assembler instruction translates into a single machine language instruction.

Assembler Program: A program language translator that converts assembler language into machine code.

Assertion: Explicit statement in a system security policy that security measures in one security domain constitute an adequate basis for security measures (or lack of them) in another.

Association-Security-State: The collection of information that is relevant to the control of communications security for a particular application-association.

Asymmetric Cryptosystem: This is an information system utilizing an algorithm or series of algorithms which provide a cryptographic key pair consisting of a private key and a corresponding public key. The keys of the pair have the properties that (1) the public key can verify a digital signature that the private key creates, and (2) it is computationally infeasible to discover or derive the private key from the public key. The public key can therefore be disclosed without significantly risking disclosure of the private key. This can be used for confidentiality as well as for authentication.

479

Asymmetric Key (Public Key):   A cipher technique whereby different cryptographic keys are used to encrypt and decrypt a message.

Asynchronous: A variable or random time interval between successive characters, blocks, operations, or events. Asynchronous data transmission provides variable intercharacter time but fixed interbit time within characters.

Asynchronous Transfer Mode: ATM is a high-bandwidth, low-delay switching and multiplexing technology. It is a data-link layer protocol. This means that it is a protocol-independent transport mechanism. ATM allows very high-speed data transfer rates at up to 155 Mbps. Data is transmitted in the form of 53-byte units called cells. Each cell consists of a 5-byte header and a 48-byte payload. The term "asynchronous" in this context refers to the fact that cells from any one particular source need not be periodically spaced within the overall cell stream. That is, users are not assigned a set position in a recurring frame as is common in circuit switching. ATM can transport audio/video/data over the same connection at the same time and provide QoS (Quality of Service) for this transport.

ATM: *See Asynchronous Transfer Mode.*

Atomicity: The assurance that an operation either changes the state of all participating objects consistent with the semantics of the operation or changes none at all.

Attribute: A characteristic defined for a class. Attributes are used to maintain the state of the object of a class. Values can be connected to objects via the attributes of the class. Typically, the connected value is determined by an operation with a single parameter identifying the object. Attributes implement the properties of a type.

Audio Masking: A condition where one sound interferes with the perception another sound.

Audit: An independent review and examination of system records and activities that test for the adequacy of system controls, ensure compliance with established policy and operational procedures, and recommend any indicated changes in controls, policy, and procedures.

Audit Authority: The manager responsible for defining those aspects of a security policy applicable to maintaining a security audit.

Audit Event Detector Function: A function that detects the occurrence of security-relevant events. This function is normally an inherent part of the functionality implementing the event.

Audit Recorder Function: A function that records the security-relevant messages in a security audit trail.

Audit Trail: A chronological record of system activities that is sufficient to enable the reconstruction, review, and examination of each event in a transaction from inception to output of final results.

Audit Trail Analyzer Function: A function that checks a security audit trail in order to produce, if appropriate, security alarm messages.

Audit Trail Archiver Function: A function that archives a part of the security audit trail.

Audit Trail Collector Function: A function that collects individual audit trail records into a security audit trail.

Audit Trail Examiner Function: A function that builds security reports out of one or more security audit trails.

Audit Trail Provider Function: A function that provides security audit trails according to some criteria.

Authenticated Identity: An identity of a principal that has been assured through authentication.

Authentication: The act of identifying or verifying the eligibility of a station, originator, or individual to access specific categories of information. Typically, a measure designed to protect against fraudulent transmissions by establishing the validity of a transmission, message, station, or originator.

Authentication Certificate: Authentication information in the form of a security certificate which may be used to assure the identity of an entity guaranteed by an authentication authority.

Authentication Exchange: A sequence of one or more transfers of exchange authentication information (AI) for the purposes of performing an authentication.

Authentication Information (AI): Information used to establish the validity of a claimed identity.

Authentication Initiator: The entity that starts an authentication exchange.

Authentication Method: Method for demonstrating knowledge of a secret. The quality of the authentication method, its strength is determined by the cryptographic basis of the key Architecture for Public-Key Infrastructure (APKI) Draft distribution service on which it is based. A symmetric key based method, in which both entities share common authentication information, is considered to be a weaker method than an asymmetric key based method, in which not all the authentication information is shared by both entities.

Authorization: The granting of right of access to a user, program, or process.

Authorization Policy: A set of rules, part of an access control policy, by which access by security subjects to security objects is granted or denied. An authorization policy may be defined in terms of access control lists, capabilities or attributes assigned to security subjects, security objects or both.

Availability: The property of being accessible and usable upon demand by an authorized entity.

Backbone: The primary connectivity mechanism of a hierarchical distributed system. All systems that have connectivity to an intermediate system on the backbone are assured of connectivity to each other.

Backoff: The (usually random) retransmission delay enforced by contentious MAC protocols after a network node with data to transmit determines that the physical medium is already in use.

Backup and Recovery: The ability to recreate current master files using appropriate prior master records and transactions.

Backup Procedures: Provisions make for the recovery of data files and program libraries and for the restart or replacement of computer equipment after the occurrence of a system failure or disaster.

Bandwidth: The difference between the highest and lowest frequencies available for network signals. The term is also used to describe the rated throughput capacity of a given network medium or protocol.

Baseband: A form of modulation in which data signals are pulsed directly on the transmission medium without frequency division and usually utilize a transceiver. In baseband, the entire bandwidth of the transmission medium (cable) is utilized for a single channel. It uses a single carrier frequency and requires all stations attached to the network to participate in every transmission. *See Broadband.*

Basic Service Set (BSS): Basic Service Set is a set of 802.11-compliant stations that operate as a fully connected wireless network.

BBS: *See Bulletin Board System.*

BCP: The newest subseries of RFCs that are written to describe Best Current Practices in the Internet. Rather than specify the best ways to use the protocols and the best ways to configure options to ensure interoperability between various vendors' products, BCPs carry the endorsement of the IESG.

Between-the-Lines Entry: Access obtained through the use of active wire-tapping by an unauthorized user to a momentarily inactive terminal of a legitimate user assigned to a communications channel.

Biometrics: A security technique that verifies an individual's identity by analyzing a unique physical attribute, such as a handprint.

BIOS: The BIOS is built-in software that determines what a computer can do without accessing programs from a disk. On PCs, the BIOS contains all the code required to control the keyboard, display screen, disk drives, serial communications, and a number of miscellaneous functions.

Bit: A binary value represented by an electronic component that has a value of 0 or 1.

Bit Error Rate (BER): The probability that a particular bit will have the wrong value.

Bit Map: A specialized form of an index indicating the existence or non-existence of a condition for a group of blocks or records. Although they are expensive to build and maintain, they provide very fast comparison and access facilities.

Bit Mask: A pattern of binary values that is combined with some value using bitwise AND with the result that bits in the value in positions where the mask is zero are also set to zero.

Bit Rate: This is the speed at which bits are transmitted on a circuit, usually expressed in bits per second.

Bit-stream Image: Bit-streams backups (also referred to as mirror image backups) involve all areas of a computer hard disk drive or another type of storage media. Such backups exactly replicate all sectors on a given storage device. Thus, all files and ambient data storage areas are copied.

Blind Scheme: An extraction process method that can recover the hidden message by means only of the encoded data.

Block Cipher: A method of encrypting text to produce ciphertext in which a cryptographic key and algorithm are applied to a block of data as a group instead of one bit at a time.

Body: One of four possible components of a message. Other components are the headings, attachment, and the envelope.

Bootleg: An unauthorized recording of a live or broadcast performance. They are duplicated and sold without the permission of the artist, composer or record company.

Bote-swaine Cipher: A steganographic cipher used by Francis Bacon to insert his name within the text of his writings.

Bounds Checking: The testing of computer program results for access to storage outside of its authorized limits.

Bridge: A device that connects two or more physical networks and forwards packets between them. Bridges can usually be made to filter packets, that is, to forward only certain traffic.

Broadband: Characteristic of any network that multiplexes multiple, independent network carriers onto a single cable. Broadband technology allows several networks to coexist on one single cable; traffic from one network does not interfere with traffic from another because the conversations happen on different frequencies in the "ether," rather like the commercial radio system.

Broadcast: A packet delivery system where a copy of a given packet is given to all hosts attached to the network (e.g., Ethernet).

Broadcast Storm: A condition that can occur on broadcast type networks such as Ethernet. This can happen for a number of reasons, ranging from hardware malfunction to configuration error and bandwidth saturation.

Brouter: A concatenation of "bridge" and "router" that is used to refer to devices that perform both bridging and routing.

Browser: Short for Web browser, a software application used to locate and display Web pages. The two most popular browsers are Netscape Navigator™ and Microsoft Internet Explorer™. Both of these are graphical browsers, meaning that they can display graphics as well as text. In addition, most modern browsers can present multimedia information, including sound and video, although they require plug-ins for some formats.

Browsing: The searching of computer storage to locate or acquire information, without necessarily knowing whether it exists or in what format.

Brute Force: The name given to a class of algorithms that repeatedly try all possible combinations until a solution is found.

Buffer: A temporary storage area, usually in RAM. The purpose of most buffers is to act as a holding area, enabling the CPU to manipulate data before transferring it to a device. Because the processes of reading and writing data to a disk are relatively slow, many programs keep track of data changes in a buffer and then copy the buffer to a disk. For example, word processors employ a buffer to keep track of changes to files. Then when you save the file, the word processor updates the disk file with the contents of the buffer. This is much more efficient than accessing the file on the disk each time you make a change to the file. Note that because your changes are initially stored in a buffer, not on the disk, all of them will be lost if the computer fails during an editing session. For this reason, it is a good idea to save your file periodically. Most word processors automatically save files at regular intervals. Another common use of buffers is for printing documents. When you enter a Print command, the operating system copies your document to a print buffer (a free area in memory or on a disk) from which the printer can draw characters at its own pace. This frees the computer to perform other tasks while the printer is running in the background. Print buffering is called spooling. Most keyboard drivers also contain a buffer so that you can edit typing mistakes before sending your command to a program. Many operating systems, including DOS, also use a disk buffer to temporarily hold data that they have read from a disk. The disk buffer is really a cache.

Bug: A coded program statement containing a logical or syntactical error.

Bulletin Board System (BBS): A computer that allows you to log on and post messages to other subscribers to the service. To use a BBS, a modem and the telephone number of the BBS is required. A BBS application runs on a computer and allows people to connect to that computer for the purpose of exchanging e-mail, chatting, and file transfers. A BBS is not part of the Internet.

Burn Box: A device used to destroy computer data. Usually a box with magnets or electrical current that will degauss disks and tapes.

Bus: A data path that connects the CPU, input, output, and storage devices.

Business Associate: Under HIPAA, a person who is not a member of a covered entity's workforce (*see* *Workforce*) and who performs any function or activity involving the use or disclosure of individually identifiable health information, such as temporary nursing services, or who provides services to a covered entity which involves the disclosure of individually identifiable health information, such as legal, accounting, consulting, data aggregation, management, accreditation, etc. A covered entity may be a business associate of another covered entity.

Business Continuity Plan (BCP): A documented and tested plan for responding to an emergency.

Business Impact Analysis: An exercise that determines the impact of losing the support of any resource to an organization, establishes the escalation of that loss over time, identifies the minimum resources needed to recover and prioritizes the recovery of processes and supporting systems.

Byte: The basic unit of storage for many computers; typically, one configuration consists of 8 bits used to represent data plus a parity bit for checking the accuracy of representation.

C: A third-generation computer language used for programming on microcomputers. Most microcomputer software products (i.e., spreadsheets and DBMS programs) are written in C.

Cable: Transmission medium of copper wire or optical fiber wrapped in a protective cover.

Cache: Pronounced cash, a special high-speed storage mechanism. It can be either a reserved section of main memory or an independent high-speed storage device. Two types of caching are commonly used in personal computers: memory caching and disk caching. A memory cache, sometimes called a cache store or RAM cache, is a portion of memory made of high-speed static RAM (SRAM) instead of the slower and cheaper dynamic RAM (DRAM) used for main memory. Memory caching is effective because most programs access the same data or instructions over and over. Disk caching works under the same principle as memory caching, but instead of using high-speed SRAM, a disk cache uses conventional main memory. When data is found in the cache, it is called a cache hit, and the effectiveness of a cache is judged by its hit rate.

Callback: A procedure that identifies a terminal dialing into a computer system or network by disconnecting the calling terminal, verifying the authorized terminal against the automated control table, and then, if authorized, reestablishing the connection by having the computer system dial the telephone number of the calling terminal.

Capability: A token used as an identifier for a resource such that possession of the token confers access rights for the resource.

Cardano's Grille: A method of concealing a message by which a piece of paper has several holes cut in it (the grille) and, when placed over an innocent looking message, the holes cover all but specific letters spelling out the message. It was named for its inventor Girolamo Cardano.

Carrier Sense, Multiple Access (CSMA): A multiple-station access scheme for avoiding contention in packet networks in which each station can sense the presence of carrier signals from other stations and thus avoid transmitting a packet that would result in a collision. *See also Collision Detection.*

Central Processing Unit (CPU):   The part of the computer system containing the control and arithmetic logic units.

CERN: European Laboratory for Particle Physics; birthplace of the World Wide Web.

Certificate: A set of information that, at least, identifies the certification authority issuing the certificate, unambiguously names or identifies its owner, contains the owner's public key, and is digitally signed by the certification authority issuing it.

Certification: The acceptance of software by an authorized agent, usually after the software has been validated by the agent or its validity has been demonstrated to the agent.

Certification Authority (CA):   Provides to users a digital certificate that links the public key with some assertion about the user, such as identity, credit payment card number, and such. Certification authorities may offer other services such as time-stamping, key management services, and certificate revocation services. It can also be defined as an independent trusted source that attests to some factual element of information for the purposes of certifying information in the electronic environment.

Certification Path: A chain of certificates between any given certificate and its trust anchor (CA). Each certificate in the chain must be verifiable in order to validate the certificate at the end of the path; this functionality is critical to the usable PKI.

Certification Practices Statement: A statement of the certification authorities practices with respect to a wide range of technical, business, and legal issues that may be used as a basis for the certification authorities contract with the entity to whom the certificate was issued.

Chain of Custody: (1) The identity of persons who handle evidence between the time of commission of the alleged offense and the ultimate disposition of the case. It is the responsibility of each transferee to ensure that the items are accounted for during the time that it is in their possession, that it is properly protected, and that there is a record of the names of the persons from whom they received it and to whom they delivered it, together with the time and date of such receipt and delivery. (2) The control over evidence. Lack of control over evidence can lead to it being discredited completely. Chain of custody depends upon being able to verify that evidence could not have been tampered with. This is accomplished by sealing off the evidence so that it cannot in any way be changed and providing a documentary record of custody to prove that the evidence was at all times under strict control and not subject to tampering.

Chain of Evidence: The "sequencing" of the chain of evidence follows this order: Collection and Identification, Analysis, Storage, Preservation, Presentation in Court, and Return to Owner. Chain of Evidence shows who obtained the evidence, where and when the evidence was obtained, who secured the evidence, and who had control or possession of the evidence.

CHAP (Challenge Handshake Authentication Protocol): Applies a three-way handshaking procedure. After the link is established, the server sends a "challenge" message to the originator. The originator responds with a value calculated using a one-way hash function. The server checks the response against its own calculation of the expected hash value. If the values match, the authentication is acknowledged; otherwise, the connection is usually terminated.

Chat Room: An area of a Web chat service that people can "enter" with their Web browsers where the conversations are devoted to a specific topic; equivalent to a channel in IRC.

Check Digit: One digit, usually the last, of an identifying field is a mathematical function of all of the other digits in the field. This value can be calculated from the other digits in the field and compared with the check digit to verify validity of the whole field.

Checksum: (1) A computed value that depends on the contents of a packet. This value is sent along with the packet when it is transmitted. The receiving system computes a new checksum based on receiving data and compares this value with the one sent with the packet. If the two values are the same, the receiver has a high degree of confidence that the data was received correctly. (2) A checksum of an input data is a value computed by adding together all the numbers in the input data. If the sum of all the numbers exceeds the highest value that a checksum can hold, the checksum equals the modulus of the total (i.e., the remainder that is left over when the total is divided by the checksum's maximum possible value plus 1.) The checksum method is the simplest method of verifying the integrity of digitally transmitted data is the checksum method.

Chosen Message Attack: A type of attack where the steganalyst generates a stego-medium from a message using some particular tool, looking for signatures that will enable the detection of other stego-media.

Chosen Stego Attack: A type of attack when both the stego-medium and the steganography tool or algorithm is available.

CIA: With regard to information security; Confidentiality, Integrity, and Availability

Cipher Disk: An additive cipher device used for encrypting and decrypting messages. The disk consists of two concentric circular scales, usually of letters, and the alphabets can be repositioned with respect to one another at any of the 26 relationships.

Ciphertext: Information that has been encrypted, making it unreadable without knowledge of the key.

Circuit Switching: A communications paradigm in which a dedicated communication path is established between two hosts and on which all packets travel. The telephone system is an example of a circuitswitched network.

CISSP: Certified Information Systems Security Professional

Claim Authentication Information: Information used by a claimant to generate exchange AI needed to 874 authenticate a principal.

Claimant: An entity that is or represents a principal for the purposes of authentication. A claimant includes the functions necessary for engaging in authentication exchanges on behalf of a principal.

Class: An implementation of an abstract data type. A definition of the data structures, methods, and interface of software objects. A template for the instantiation (creation) of software objects.

Cleartext: Data that is not encrypted; plaintext.

Client: A workstation in a network that is set up to use the resources of a server.

Client/Server: In networking, a network in which several PC-type systems (clients) are connected to one or more powerful, central computers (servers). In databases, the term refers to a model in which a client system runs a database application (front end) that accesses information in a database management system situated on a server (back end).

Client/Server Architecture: A local area network in which microcomputers called servers provide specialized service on behalf of the user's computers, which are called clients.

Cloning: The term given to the operation of creating an exact duplicate of one medium on another like medium. This is also referred to as a Mirror Image or Physical Sector Copy.

Closed Network/Closed User Group: These are systems that generally represent those in which certificates are used within a bounded context such as within a payment system. A contract or series of contracts identify and define the rights and responsibilities of all parties to a particular transaction.

Coaxial Cable: A medium used for telecommunications. It is similar to the type of cable used for carrying television signals.

Code Division Multiple Access (CDMA):   A technique permitting the use of a single frequency band by a number of users. Users are allocated a sequence that uniquely identifies them.

Coefficient: A number or symbol multiplied with a variable or an unknown quantity in an algebraic term.

Cold Site: An IS backup facility that has the necessary electrical and physical components of a computer facility, but does not have the computer equipment in place. The site is ready to receive the necessary replacement computer equipment in the event the users have to move from their main computing location to the alternative computer facility.

Collision: This is a condition that is present when two or more terminals are in contention during simultaneous network access attempts.

Collision Detection: An avoidance method for communications channel contention that depends on two stations detecting the simultaneous start of each other's transmission, stopping, and waiting a random period of time before beginning again. *See also Carrier Sense, Multiple Access.*

Color Palette: A set of available colors a computer or an application can display. Also known as a CLUT: Color Look Up Table.

Commit: A condition implemented by the programmer signaling to the DBMS that all update activity that the program conducts be executed against a database. Before the commit, all update activity can be rolled back or canceled without negative impact on the database contents.

Commit Protocol: An algorithm to ensure that a transaction is successfully completed.

Common Business Oriented Language (COBOL):   A high-level programming language for business computer applications.

Common Carrier: An organization or company that provides data or other electronic communication services for a fee.

Common Object Request Broker Architecture (CORBA):   CORBA is the Object Management Group's (OMG) answer to the need for interoperability among the rapidly proliferating number of hardware and software products available today. Simply stated, CORBA allows applications to communicate with one another no matter where they are located or who has designed them.

Communications Security: The protection that ensures the authenticity of telecommunications and that results from the application of measures taken to deny unauthorized persons access to valuable information that might be derived from the acquisition of telecommunications.

Compartmentalization: The isolation of the operating system, user programs, and data files from one another in main storage to protect them against unauthorized or concurrent access by other users or programs. Also, the division of sensitive data into small, isolated blocks to reduce risk to the data.

Compiler: A program that translates high-level computer language instructions into machine code.

Compression: A method of storing data in a format that requires less space than normal.

Compromise: Unauthorized disclosure or loss of sensitive information.

Compromising Emanations: Electromagnetic emanations that convey data and that, if intercepted and analyzed, could compromise sensitive information being processed by a computer system.

Computer Emergency Response Team (CERT): The CERT is chartered to work with the Internet community to facilitate its response to computer security events involving Internet hosts, to take proactive steps to raise the community's awareness of computer security issues, and to conduct research targeted at improving the security of existing systems. The U.S. CERT is based at Carnegie Mellon University in Pittsburgh; regional CERTs are like NICs, springing up in different parts of the world.

Computer Evidence: Computer evidence is a copy of a document stored in a computer file that is identical to the original. The legal "best evidence" rules change when it comes to the processing of computer evidence. Another unique aspect of computer evidence is the potential for unauthorized copies to be made of important computer files without leaving behind a trace that the copy was made. This situation creates problems concerning the investigation of the theft of trade secrets (e.g., client lists, research materials, computer-aided design files, formulas, and proprietary software).

Computer Forensics: The term "computer forensics" was coined in 1991 in the first training session held by the International Association of Computer Specialists (IACIS) in Portland, Oregon. Since then, computer forensics has become a popular topic in computer security circles and in the legal community. Like any other forensic science, computer forensics deals with the application of law to a science. In this case, the science involved is computer science and some refer to it as Forensic Computer Science. Computer forensics has also been described as the autopsy of a computer hard disk drive because specialized software tools and techniques are required to analyze the various levels at which computer data is stored after the fact. Computer forensics deals with the preservation, identification, extraction, and documentation of computer evidence. The field is relatively new to the private sector, but it has been the mainstay of technology-related investigations and intelligence gathering in law enforcement and military agencies since the mid-1980s. Computer forensics involves the use of sophisticated technology tools and procedures that must be followed to guarantee the accuracy of the preservation of evidence and the accuracy of results concerning computer evidence processing. Typically, computer forensic tools exist in the form of computer software.

Computer Fraud and Abuse Act PL 99-474:   Computer Fraud and Abuse Act of 1986. Strengthens and expands the 1984 Federal Computer Crime Legislation. Law extended to computer crimes in private enterprise and anyone who willfully disseminates information for the purpose of committing a computer crime (i.e., distribute phone numbers to hackers from a BBS).

Computer Matching Act Public Law (PL) 100-53:   Computer Matching and Privacy Act of 1988. Ensures privacy, integrity, and verification of data disclosed for computer matching; establishes Data Integrity Boards within federal agencies.

Computer Security: The practice of protecting a computer system against internal failures, human error, attacks, and natural catastrophes that might cause improper disclosure, modification, destruction, or denial-of-service.

Computer Security Act PL 100-235:   Computer Security Act of 1987 directs the National Bureau of Standards (now the National Institute of Standards and Technology [NIST]) to establish a computer security standards program for federal computer systems.

Computer System: An interacting assembly of elements, including at least computer hardware and usually software, data procedures, and people.

Computer System Security: All of the technological safeguards and managerial procedures established and applied to computers and their networks (including related hardware, firmware, software, and data) to protect organizational assets and individual privacy.

Computer-Aided Software Engineering (CASE): Tools that automate the design, development, operation, and maintenance of software.

Concealment Systems: A method of keeping sensitive information confidential by embedding it in irrelevant data.

Concurrent Processing: The capability of a computer to share memory with several programs and simultaneously execute the instructions provided by each.

Condensation: The process of reducing the volume of data managed without reducing the logical consistency of data. It is essentially different than compaction in that condensation is done at the record level whereas compaction is done at the system level.

Confidentiality: A concept that applies to data that must be held in confidence and describes that status or degree of protection that must be provided for such data about individuals as well as organizations.

Configuration Management: The use of procedures appropriate for controlling changes to a system's hardware, software, or firmware structure to ensure that such changes will not lead to a weakness or fault in the system.

Connectionless: The model of interconnection in which communication takes place without first establishing a connection; sometimes (imprecisely) called datagram. Examples include Internet IP and OSI CLNP, UDP, ordinary postcards.

Connection-Oriented: The model of interconnection in which communication proceeds through three well-defined phases: connection establishment, data transfer, and connection release (e.g., X.25, Internet TCP and OSI TP4, ordinary telephone calls).

Console Operator: A person who works at a computer console to monitor operations and initiate instructions for efficient use of computer resources.

Construct: An object; especially a concept that is constructed or synthesized from simple elements.

Contention: Occurs during multiple access to a network in which the network capacity is allocated on a "first come, first served" basis.

Contextual Information: Information derived from the context in which an access is made (e.g., time of day).

Contingency Plans: Plans for emergency response, backup operations, and post-disaster recovery maintained by a computer information processing facility as a part of its security program.

Control: Any protective action, device, procedure, technique, or other measure that reduces exposures.

Control Break: A point during program processing at which some special processing event takes place. A change in the value of a control field within a data record is characteristic of a control break.

Control Totals: Accumulations of numeric data fields that are used to check the accuracy of the input, processing, or output data.

Control Zone: The space surrounding equipment that is used to process sensitive information and that is under sufficient physical and technical control to preclude an unauthorized entry or compromise.

Cookie: A cookie is a piece of text that a Web server can store on a user's hard disk. Cookies allow a Web site to store information on a user's machine and later retrieve it. The pieces of information are stored as name-value pairs.

Cooperative Processing: The ability to distribute resources (i.e., programs, files, and databases) across the network.

Copy: An accurate reproduction of information contained on an original physical item, independent of the original physical item.

Copyright: The author or artist's right to control the copying of his or her work.

CORBA: Common Object Request Broker Architecture, introduced in 1991 by the OMG, defined the Interface Definition Language (IDL) and the Application Programming Interfaces (APIs) that enable client/server object interaction within a specific implementation of an Object Request Broker (ORB).

Corporate Security Policy: The set of laws, rules, and practices that regulate how assets including sensitive information are managed, protected, and distributed within a user organization.

Corrective Action: The practice and procedure for reporting, tracking, and resolving identified problems, in both the software product and the development process. Their resolution provides a final solution to the identified problem.

Corrective Maintenance: The identification and removal of code defects.

Cost/Benefit Analysis: Determination of the economic feasibility of developing a system on the basis of a comparison of the projected costs of a proposed system and the expected benefits from its operation.

Cost-Risk Analysis: The assessment of the cost of potential risk of loss or compromise of data in a computer system without data protection versus the cost of providing data protection.

Counterfeits: Duplicates that are copied and packaged to resemble the original as closely as possible. The original producer's trademarks and logos are reproduced in order to mislead the consumer into believing that they are buying an original product.

Countermeasure: The deployment of a set of security services to protect against a security threat.

Cover Escrow: An extraction process method that needs both the original piece of information and the encoded one in order to extract the embedded data.

Cover Medium: The medium in which we want to hide data; it can be an innocent looking piece of information for steganography or an important medium that must be protected for copyright or integrity reasons.

Covered Entity: The specific types of organizations to which HIPAA applies, including providers, health plans (payers), and clearinghouses (who process nonstandard claims from providers and distribute them to the payers in their required formats: a process that will not be necessary if providers adopt the HIPAA transactions standards)

Covert Channel: A channel of communication within a computer system or network that is not designed or intended to transfer information.

CPRI: Computer-based Patient Record Institute: organization formed in 1992 to promote adoption of healthcare information systems and has created a Security Toolkit with sample policies and procedures (http://www.cpri-host.org).

CPU: The central processing unit; the brains of the computer.

Cracker: The correct name for an individual who hacks into a networked computer system with malicious intentions. The term "hacker" is used interchangeably (although incorrectly) because of media hype of the word hacker. A cracker explores and detects weak points in the security of a computer networked system and then exploits these weaknesses using specialized tools and techniques.

Credentials: Data that is transferred to establish the claimed identity of an entity.

Critical Path: A tool used in project management techniques and is the duration based on the sum of the individual tasks and their dependencies. The critical path is the shortest period in which a project can be accomplished.

Criticality Analysis: An analysis or assessment of a business function or security vulnerability based on its criticality to the organization's business objectives. A variety of criticality may be used to illustrate the criticality.

Cross Certification: Practice of mutual recognition of another certification authority is certificates to an agreed level of confidence. Usually evidenced in contract.

Crossover Error Rate (CER): A comparison metric for different biometric devices and technologies; the error rate at which FAR equals FRR. The lower the CER, the more accurate and reliable the biometric device.

Cryptanalysis: The study of techniques for attempting to defeat cryptographic techniques and, more generally, information security services.

Cryptanalyst: Someone who engages in cryptanalysis.

Cryptographic Algorithm: A method of performing a cryptographic transformation (*see Cryptography*) on a data unit. Cryptographic algorithms may be based on symmetric key methods (the same key is used for both encipher and decipher transformations) or on asymmetric keys (different keys are used for encipher and decipher transformations).

Cryptographic Checkvalue: Information that is derived by performing a cryptographic transformation on a data unit.

Cryptographic Key: A parameter used with a cryptographic algorithm to transform, validate, authenticate, encrypt, or decrypt data.

Cryptography: The study of mathematical techniques related to aspects of information security such as confidentiality, data integrity, entity authentication, and data origin authentication. Cryptography is not the only means of providing information security services, but rather one set of techniques. The word itself comes from the Greek word kryptos, which means "hidden" or "covered." Cryptography is a way to hide writing ("-graphy") but yet retain a way to uncover it again.

Cryptology: The field of study that encompasses both cryptography and cryptanalysis.

Cryptolope: An IBM product which means "cryptographic envelope." Cryptolope objects are used for secure, protected delivery of digital content by using encryption and digital signatures.

Cryptosystem: A general term referring to a set of cryptographic primitives used to provide information security services.

Cybercops: A criminal investigator of online fraud or harassment.

Cybercrime: A criminal offense that involves the use of a computer network.

Cyberspace: Refers to the connections and locations (even virtual) created using computer networks. The term "Internet" has become synonymous with this word.

Cyclic Redundancy Check (CRC): A number derived from a set of data that will be transmitted.

Data: Raw facts and figures that are meaningless by themselves. Data can be expressed in characters, digits, and symbols, which can represent people, things, and events.

Data Classification: Data classification is the assigning a level of sensitivity to data as they are being created, amended, enhanced, stored, or transmitted. The classification of the data should then determine the extent to which the data need to be controlled/secured and is also indicative of its value in terms of its importance to the organization.

Data Communications: The transmission of data between more than one site through the use of public and private communications channels or lines.

Data Contamination: A deliberate or accidental process or act that compromises the integrity of the original data.

Data Definition Language (DDL): A set of instructions or commands used to define data for the data dictionary. A data definition language (DDL) is used to describe the structure of a database.

Data Dictionary: A document or listing defining all items or processes represented in a data flow diagram or used in a system.

Data Diddling: Changing data with malicious intent before or during input to the system.

Data Element: The smallest unit of data accessible to a database management system or a field of data within a file processing system.

Data Encryption Standard (DES): A private key cryptosystem published by the National Institutes of Standards and Technology (NIST). DES is a symmetric block cipher with a block length of 64 bits and an effective key length of 56 bits. DES has been used commonly for data encryption in the forms of software and hardware implementation.

Data Integrity: The state that exists when automated information or data is the same as that in the source documents and has not been exposed to accidental or malicious modification, alteration, or destruction.

Data Item: A discrete representation having the properties that define the data element to which it belongs. *See also Data Element.*

Data Link: A serial communications path between nodes or devices without any intermediate switching nodes. Also, the physical two-way connection between such devices.

Data Link Layer (DLL):   A layer with the responsibility of transmitting data reliably across a physical link (cabling, for example) using a networking technology such as Ethernet. The DLL encapsulates data into frames (or cells) before it transmits it. It also enables multiple computer systems to share a single physical medium when used in conjunction with a media access control methodology such as CSMA/CD.

Data Manipulation Language (DML):   A data manipulation language (DML) provides the necessary commands for all database operations, including storing, retrieving, updating, and deleting database records.

Data Normalization: In data processing, a process applied to all data in a set that produces a specific statistical property. It is also the process of eliminating duplicate keys within a database. Useful as organizations use databases to evaluate various security data.

Data Objects: Objects or information of potential probative value that are associated with physical items. Data objects may occur in different formats without altering the original information.

Data Origin Authentication: The corroboration that the entity responsible for the creation of a set of data is the one claimed.

Data Record: An identifiable set of data values treated as a unit, an occurrence of a schema in a database, or collection of atomic data items describing a specific object, event, or tuple (e.g., the row of a table).

Data Security: The protection of data from accidental or malicious modification, destruction, or disclosure.

Data Set: A named collection of logically related data items, arranged in a prescribed manner and described by control information to which the programming system has access.

Data Warehouse: A collection of integrated subject-oriented databases designed to support the Decision Support function, where each unit of data is relevant to some moment in time. The data warehouse contains atomic data and summarized data.

Database: An integrated aggregation of data usually organized to reflect logical or functional relationships among data elements.

Database Administrator (DBA): (1) A person who is in charge of defining and managing the contents of a database. (2) The individual in an organization who is responsible for the daily monitoring and maintenance of the databases. The database administrator's function is more closely associated with physical database design than the data administrator's function is.

Database Management System (DBMS): The software that directs and controls data resources.

Datagram: Logical grouping of information sent as a network layer unit over a transmission medium without prior establishment of a virtual circuit. IP datagrams are the primary information units in the Internet. The terms "cell," "frame," "message," "packet," and "segment" are also used to describe logical information groupings at various layers of the OSI Reference Model and in various technology circles.

Data-Link Control Layer: Layer 2 in the SNA architectural model. Responsible for the transmission of data over a particular physical link. Corresponds roughly to the data-link layer of the OSI model.

Data-Link Layer: Layer 2 of the OSI reference model. Provides reliable transit of data across a physical link. The data-link layer is concerned with physical addressing, network topology, line discipline, error notification, ordered delivery of frames, and flow control. The IEEE divided this layer into two sublayers: the MAC sublayer and the LLC sublayer. (sometimes called the link layer). Roughly corresponds to the data-link control layer of the SNA model.

DDoS Attacks: Distributed denial of service attacks. These are denial-of-service assault from multiple sources.

Dead Drop: A method of secret information exchange where the two parties never meet.

Deadlock: A condition that occurs when two users invoke conflicting locks in trying to gain access to a specific record or records.

Decipher: The ability to convert, by use of the appropriate key, enciphered text into its equivalent plaintext.

Decipherment: The reversal of a corresponding reversible encipherment.

Decrypt: Synonymous with decipher.

Decrypt/Decipher/Decode: Decryption is the opposite of encryption. It is the transformation of encrypted information back into a legible form. Essentially, decryption is about removing disguise and reclaiming the meaning of information.

Decryption: The conversion through mechanisms or procedures of encrypted data into its original form.

Decryption Key: A piece of information, in a digitized form, used to recover the plaintext from the corresponding ciphertext by decryption.

Dedicated Lines: Private circuits between two or more stations, switches, or subscribers.

Dedicated Mode: The operation of a computer system such that the central computer facility, connected peripheral devices, communications facilities, and all remote terminals are used and controlled exclusively by the users or groups of users for the processing of particular types and categories of information.

Defense-in-Depth: The practice of layering defenses to provide added protection. Security is increased by raising the cost to mount the attack. This system places multiple barriers between an attacker and an organization's business critical information resources. This strategy also provides natural areas for the implementation of intrusion-detection technologies.

Degauss: To erase or demagnetize magnetic recording media (usually tapes) by applying a variable, alternating current (AC) field.

Degree (of a relation):   The number of attributes or columns of a relation.

Delegation: The notation that an object can issue a request to another object in response to a request. The first object therefore delegates the responsibility to the second object. Delegation can be used as an alternative to inheritance.

Delphi: A forecasting method where several knowledgeable individuals make forecasts and a forecast is derived by a trained analyst from a weighted average.

Demodulation: The reconstruction of an original signal from the modulated signal received at a destination device.

Denial of Service (DOS):   The unauthorized prevention of authorized access to resources or the delaying of time-critical operations.

Design: The aspect of the specification process that involves the prior consideration of the implementation. Design is the process that extends and modifies an analysis specification. It accommodates certain qualities including extensibility, reusability, testability, and maintainability. Design also includes the specification of implementation requirements such as user interface and data persistence.

Design and Implementation: A phase of the systems development life cycle in which a set of functional specifications produced during systems analysis is transformed into an operational system for hardware, software, and firmware.

Design Review: The quality assurance process in which all aspects of a system are reviewed publicly.

Dial-Up: Access to switched network, usually through a dial or push-button telephone.

Digimark: A company that creates digital watermarking technology used to authenticate, validate, and communicate information within digital and analog media.

Digital: A mode of transmission where information is coded in binary form for transmission on the network.

Digital Audio Tape (DAT): A magnetic tape technology. DAT uses 4-mm cassettes capable of backing up anywhere between 26 and 126 bytes of information.

Digital Certificates: A certificate identifying a public key to its subscriber, corresponding to a private key held by that subscriber. It is a unique code that typically is used to allow the authenticity and integrity of communication can be verified.

Digital Code Signing: The process of digitally signing computer code so that its integrity remains intact and it cannot be tampered with.

Digital Fingerprint: A characteristic of a data item, such as a cryptographic checkvalue or the result of performing a one-way hash function on the data, which is sufficiently peculiar to the data item that it is computationally infeasible to find another data item that possesses the same characteristics.

Digital Rights Management (DRM): Focuses on security and encryption to prevent unauthorized copying limit distribution to only those who pay. This is considered first-generation DRM. Second-generation DRM covers: description, identification, trading, protection, monitoring, and tracking of all forms of rights usages over both tangible and intangible assets including management of rights holders' relationships. It is important to note that DRM manages all rights, not just those involving digital content. Additionally, it is important to note that DRM is the "digital management of rights" and not the "management of digital rights." That is, DRM manages all rights, not only the rights applicable to permissions over digital content.

Digital Signature: The act of electronically affixing an encrypted message digest to a computer file or message in which the originator is then authenticated to the recipient.

Digital Signature Standard (DSS):   The National Security Administration's standard for verifying an electronic message.

Direct Access: The method of reading and writing specific records without having to process all preceding records in a file.

Direct Access Storage Device (DASD):   A data storage unit on which data can be accessed directly without having to progress through a serial file such as a magnetic tape file. A disk unit is a direct access storage device.

Directory: A table specifying the relationships between items of data. Sometimes a table (index) giving the addresses of data.

Directory Service: A service provided on a computer network that allows one to look up addresses (and perhaps other information such as public key certificates) based upon user-names.

Disaster Notification Fees: The fee a recovery site vendor usually charges when the customer notifies them that a disaster has occurred and the recovery site is required. The fee is implemented to discourage false disaster notifications.

Disc Mirroring: This is the practice of duplicating data in separate volumes on two hard disks to make storage more fault-tolerant. Mirroring provides data protection in the case of disk failure because data is constantly updated to both disks.

Disclosure: The release, transfer, and provision of access to, or divulging in any other manner of information outside the entity holding the information. *See Use, in contrast.*

Discrepancy Reports: A listing of items that have violated some detective control and require further investigation.

Discrete Cosine Transform (DCT):   Used in JPEG compression, the discrete cosine transform helps separate the image into parts of differing importance based on the image's visual quality; this allows for large compression ratios. The DCT function transforms data from a spatial domain to a frequency domain.

Discretionary Access Control (DAC):   A means of restricting access to objects based on the identity of subjects and groups to which they belong. The controls are discretionary in the sense that a subject with certain access permission is capable of passing that permission on to another subject.

Disk Duplexing: This refers to the use of two controllers to drive a disk subsystem. Should one of the controllers fail, the other is still available for disk I/O. Software applications can take advantage of both controllers to simultaneously read and write to different drives.

Disk Mirroring: Disk mirroring protects data against hardware failure. In its simplest form, a two-disk subsystem would be attached to a host controller. One disk serves as the mirror image of the other. When data is written to it, it is also written to the other disk. Both disks will contain exactly the same information. If one fails, the other can supply the user data without problem.

Disk Operating System (DOS): Software that controls the execution of programs and may provide system services as resource allocation.

Diskette: A flexible disk storage medium most often used with microcomputers; also called a floppy disk.

Distinguishing Identifier: Data that unambiguously distinguishes an entity in the authentication process. Such an identifier shall be unambiguous at least within a security domain.

Distortion: An undesired change in an image or signal. A change in the shape of an image resulting from imperfections in an optical system, such as a lens.

Distributed Application: A set of information processing resources distributed over one or more open systems that provides a well-defined set of functionality to (human) users, to assist a given (office) task.

Distributed Component Object Model (DCOM): A protocol that enables software components to communicate directly over a network. Developed by Microsoft and previously called "Network OLE," DCOM is designed for use across multiple network transports including Internet Protocols such as HTTP.

Distributed Computing: The distribution of processes among computing components that are within the same computer or different computers on a shared network.

Distributed Database: A database management system with the ability to effectively manage data that is distributed across multiple computers on a network.

Distributed Environment: A set of related data processing systems in which each system has its own capacity to operate autonomously but has some applications that are executed at multiple sites. Some of the systems may be connected with teleprocessing links into a network with each system serving as a node.

Dithering: Creating the illusion of new colors and shades by varying the pattern of dots in an image. Dithering is also the process of converting an image with a certain bit depth to one with a lower bit depth.

DMZ: Commonly, it is the network segment between the Internet and a private network. It allows access to services from the Internet and the internal private network, while denying access from the Internet directly to the private network.

DNS (Domain Name System, Service or Server): A hierarchical database that is distributed across the Internet and allows names to be resolved to IP addresses and vice versa to locate services such as Web sites and email. An Internet service that translates domain names into IP addresses.)

Domain Name: The name used to identify an Internet host.

Domain Name Server: *See DNS.*

Domain Name System : *See DNS.*

Domain of Interpretation (DOI): The DOI defines payload formats, the situation, exchange types, and naming conventions for certain information such as security policies or cryptographic algorithms. It is also used to interpret the ISAKMP payloads.

Digital Subscriber Line (DSL): A technology that dramatically increases the digital capacity of ordinary telephone lines (the local loops) into the home or office. DSL speeds are tied to the distance between the customer and the telephone company's central office.

Dual Control: A procedure that uses to or more entities (usually persons) operating in concert to protect a system resources, such that no single entity acting alone can access that resource.

Dumb Terminal: A device used to interact directly with the end user where all data is processed on a remote computer. A dumb terminal only gathers and displays data; it has no processing capability.

Dump: The contents of a file or memory that are output as listings. These listing can be formatted.

Duplex: Communications systems or equipment that can simultaneously carry information in both directions between two points. Also used to describe redundant equipment configurations (e.g., duplexed processors).

Dynamic Host Configuration Protocol (DHCP): DHCP is an industry standard protocol used to dynamically assign IP addresses to network devices.

Early Token Release: Technique used in Token Ring networks that allows a station to release a new token onto the ring immediately after transmitting, instead of waiting for the first frame to return. This feature can increase the total bandwidth on the ring. *See also Token Ring.*

Earth Stations: Ground terminals that use antennas and other related electronic equipment designed to transmit, receive, and process satellite communications.

Eavesdropping: The unauthorized interception of information-bearing emanations through methods other than wiretapping.

Echo: The display of characters on a terminal output device as they are entered into the system.

Echo Hiding: Relies on limitations in the human auditory system by embedding data in a cover audio signal. Using changes in delay and relative amplitude; two types of echoes are created that allow for the encoding of 1s and 0s.

EDI: Electronic Data Interchange; computer to computer transactions.

Edit: The process of inspecting a data field or element to verify the correctness of its content.

Electromagnetic Emanations: Signals transmitted as radiation through the air or conductors.

Electromagnetic Interference (EMI): Electromagnetic waves emitted by a device.

Electronic Code Book (ECB): A basic encryption method that provides privacy but not authentication.

Electronic Commerce: A broad concept that covers any trade or commercial transaction that is effected via electronic means; this would include such means as facsimile, telex, EDI, Internet, and the telephone. For the purpose of this book the term is limited to those commercial transactions involving computer to computer communications, whether utilizing an open or closed network.

Electronic Communications Privacy Act of 1986 PL 99-508 (ECPA): Electronic Communications Privacy Act of 1986; extends the Privacy Act of 1974 to all forms of electronic communication, including e-mail.

Electronic Data Interchange (EDI): A process whereby such specially formatted documents as an invoice can be transmitted from one organization to another. A system allowing for intercorporate commerce by the automated electronic exchange of structured business information.

Electronic Data Vaulting: Electronic vaulting protects information from loss by providing automatic and transparent backup of valuable data over high-speed phone lines to a secure facility.

Electronic Frontier Foundation: A foundation established to address social and legal issues arising from the impact on society of the increasingly pervasive use of computers as the means of communication and information distribution.

Electronic Funds Transfer (EFT):   The process of moving money between accounts via computer.

Electronic Journal: A computerized log file summarizing, in chronological sequence, the processing activities and events performed by a system. The log file is usually maintained on magnetic storage media.

Electronic Signature: Any technique designed to provide the electronic equivalent of a handwritten signature to demonstrate the origin and integrity of specific data. Digital signatures are an example of electronic signatures.

Emanation Security: The protection that results from all measures designed to deny unauthorized persons access to valuable information that might be derived from interception and analysis of compromising emanations.

Embedded Message: In steganography, it is the hidden message that is to be put into the cover medium.

Embedding: An integral part of a surrounding whole. In steganography and watermarking, embedding refers to the process of inserting the hidden message into the cover medium.

Encapsulated Subsystem: A collection of procedures and data objects that is protected in a domain of its own so that the internal structure of a data object is accessible only to the procedures of the encapsulated subsystem and that those procedures may be called only at designated domain entry points. Encapsulated subsystem, protected subsystem and protected mechanisms of the TCB are terms that may be used interchangeably.

Encipherment: The cryptographic transformation of data (*see Cryptography*) to produce ciphertext.

Encrypt: To scramble information so that only someone knowing the appropriate secret can obtain the original information (through decryption).

Encrypt/Encipher/Encode: Encryption is the transformation of information into a form that is impossible to read unless you have a specific piece of information, which is usually referred to as the "key." The purpose is to keep information private from those who are not intended to have access to it. To encrypt is essentially about making information confusing and hiding the meaning of it.

Encryption: The use of algorithms to encode data in order to render a message or other file readable only for the intended recipient.

Encryption Algorithm: A set of mathematically expressed rules for encoding information, thereby rendering it unintelligible to those who do not have the algorithm decoding key.

Encryption Key: A special mathematical code that allows encryption hardware/software to encode and then decipher an encrypted message.

End Entity: An end entity can be considered as an end-user, a device such as a router or a server, a process, or anything that can be identified in the subject name of a public key certificate. End entities can also be thought of as consumers of the PKI-related services.

End System: An OSI system that contains application processes capable of communication through all seven layers of OSI protocols. Equivalent to an Internet host.

End-to-End Encipherment: Encipherment of data within or at the source end system, with the corresponding decipherment occurring only within or at the destination end system.

End-to-End Encryption: The encryption of information at the point of origin within the communications network and postponing of decryption to the final destination point.

Enrollment: The initial process of collecting biometric data from a user and then storing it in a template for later comparison.

Enterprise Root: A certificate authority (CA) that grants itself a certificate and creates a subordinate CAs. The root CA gives the subordinate CAs their certificates, but the subordinate CAs can grant certificates to users.

Entrapment: The deliberate planting of apparent flows in a system to invite penetrations.

Error: A discrepancy between actual values or conditions and those expected.

Error Rate: A measure of the quality of circuits or equipment. The ratio of erroneously transmitted information to the total sent (generally computed per million characters sent).

Espionage: The practice or employment of spies; the practice of watching the words and conduct of others, to make discoveries, as spies or secret emissaries; secret watching. This category of computer crime includes international spies and their contractors who steal secrets from defense, academic, and laboratory research facility computer systems. It includes criminals who steal information and intelligence from law enforcement computers and industrial espionage agents who operate for competitive companies or for foreign governments who are willing to pay for the information. What has generally been known as industrial espionage is now being called competitive intelligence. A good deal of information can be gained through "open source" collection and analysis without ever having to break into a competitor's computer. This information gathering is also competitive intelligence, although it is not as ethically questionable as other techniques.

Ethernet: A LAN technology that is in wide use today utilizing CSMA/CD (Carrier Sense Multiple Access/Collision Detection) to control access to the physical medium (usually a category 5 Ethernet cable). Normal throughput speeds for Ethernet are 10 Mbps, 100 Mbps, and 1 Gbps.

Exception Report: A manager report that highlights abnormal business conditions. Usually, such reports prompt management action or inquiry.

Exchange Authentication Information: Information exchanged between a claimant and a verifier during the process of authenticating a principal.

Exchange Type: Exchange type defines the number of messages in an ISAKMP exchange and the ordering of the used payload types for each of these messages. Through this arrangement of messages and payloads security services are provided by the exchange type.

Expert System: The application of computer-based artificial intelligence in areas of specialized knowledge.

Exposure: The potential loss to an area due to the occurrence of an adverse event.

Extensibility: A property of software such that new kinds of object or functionality can be added to it with little or no effect to the existing system.

eXtensible Markup Language (XML): Designed to enable the use of SGML on the World Wide Web, XML is a regular markup language that defines what you can do (or what you have done) in the way of describing information for a fixed class of documents (like HTML). XML goes beyond this and allows you to define your own customized markup language. It can do this because it is an application profile of SGML. XML is a metalanguage, a language for describing languages.

Fail Safe: The automatic termination and protection of programs or other processing operations when a hardware, software, or firmware failure is detected in a computer system.

Fail Soft: The selective termination of nonessential processing affected by a hardware, software, or firmware failure in a computer system.

Fallback Procedures: Predefined operations (manual or automatic) invoked when a fault or failure is detected in a system.

Fall-Through Logic: Predicting which way a program will branch when an option is presented. It is an optimized code based on a branch prediction.

False Acceptance Rate (FAR): The percentage of imposters incorrectly matched to a valid user's biometric. False rejection rate (FRR) is the percentage of incorrectly rejected valid users.

Fast Ethernet: Any of a number of 100-Mbps Ethernet specifications. Fast Ethernet offers a speed increase ten times that of the 10BaseT Ethernet specification, while preserving such qualities as frame format, MAC mechanisms, and MTU. Such similarities allow the use of existing 10BaseT applications and network management tools on Fast Ethernet networks. Based on an extension to the IEEE 802.3 specification. Compare with Ethernet.

FDDI: Fiber Distributed Data Interface. This is a Token Ring type of technology that utilizes encoded light pulses transmitted via fiber optic cabling for communications between computer systems. It supports a data rate of 100 Mbps and is more likely to be used as a LAN backbone between servers. It has redundancy built in so that if a host on the network fails, there is an alternate path for the light signals to take to keep the network up.

Feistal Network: A Feistal network generates blocks of keystream from blocks of the message itself, through multiple rounds of groups of permutations and substitutions, each dependent on transformations of a key.

Fetch Protection: A system-provided restriction to prevent a program from accessing data in another user's segment of storage.

Fiber Distributed Data Interface (FDDI): LAN standard, defined by ANSI X3T9.5, specifying a 100-Mbps token-passing network using fiber optic cable, with transmission distances of up to 2 km. FDDI uses a dual-ring architecture to provide redundancy.

Field Definition Record (FDR): A record of field definition. A list of the attributes that define the type of information that can be entered into a data field.

File Format Dependence: A factor in determining the robustness of a piece of stegoed media. Coverting an image from on format to another will usually render the embedded message unrecoverable.

File Protection: The aggregate of all processes and procedures established in a computer system and designed to inhibit unauthorized access, contamination, or elimination of a file.

File Transfer: The process of copying a file from one computer to another over a network.

File Transfer Protocol (FTP): The Internet protocol (and program) used to transfer files between hosts.

Filter: A process or device that screens incoming information for definite characteristics and allows a subset of that information to pass through.

Finger: A program (and a protocol) that displays information about a particular user or all users logged on a local system or on a remote system. It typically shows full-time name, last login time, idle time, terminal line, and terminal location (where applicable). It may also display plan and project files left by the user.

Finger: The traceroute or finger commands to run on the source machine (attacking machine) to gain more information about the attacker.

Fingerprint: A form of marking that embeds a unique serial number.

Firewall: A system designed to prevent unauthorized access to or from a private network. Firewalls can be implemented in both hardware and software, or a combination of both. Firewalls are frequently used to prevent unauthorized Internet users from accessing private networks connected to the Internet, especially intranets. All messages entering or leaving the intranet pass through the firewall, which examines each message and blocks those that do not meet the specified security criteria. There are several types of firewall techniques:

- Packet filter: Looks at each packet entering or leaving the network and accepts or rejects it based on user-defined rules. Packet filtering is fairly effective and transparent to users, but it is difficult to configure. In addition, it is susceptible to IP spoofing.

- Application gateway: Applies security mechanisms to specific applications, such as FTP and Telnet servers. This is very effective, but can impose performance degradation.

- Circuit-level gateway: Applies security mechanisms when a TCP or UDP connection is established. Once the connection has been made, packets can flow between the hosts without further checking.

- Proxy server: Intercepts all messages entering and leaving the network. The proxy server effectively hides the true network addresses.

Firewall: A device that forms a barrier between a secure and an open environment. Usually the open environment is considered hostile. The most notable open system is the Internet.

Firmware: Software or computer instructions that have been permanently encoded into the circuits of semiconductor chips.

Flame: To express strong opinion or criticism of something, usually as a frank inflammatory statement in an electronic message.

Flat File: A collection of records containing no data aggregates, nested, or repeated data items, or groups of data items.

Foreign Corrupt Practices Act: The act covers an organization's system of internal accounting control and requires public companies to make and keep books, records, and accounts that, in reasonable detail, accurately and fairly reflect the transactions and disposition of company assets and to devise and maintain a system of sufficient internal accounting controls. This act was amended in 1988.

Forensic Examination: After a security breach, the process of assessing, classifying and collecting digital evidence to assist in prosecution. Standard crime-scene standards are used.

Formal Review: A type of review typically scheduled at the end of each activity or stage of development to review a component of a deliverable or, in some cases, a complete deliverable or the software product and its supporting documentation.

Format: The physical arrangement of data characters, fields, records, and files.

Forum of Incident Response and Security Teams (FIRST): A unit of the Internet Society that coordinates the activities of worldwide Computer Emergency Response Teams, regarding security-related incidents and information sharing on Internet security risks.

Fourier Transform: An image processing tool which is used to decompose an image into its constituent parts or to view a signal in either the time or frequency domain.

Fragile Watermark: A watermark that is designed to prove authenticity of an image or other media. A fragile watermark is destroyed, by design, when the cover is manipulated digitally. If the watermark is still intact then the cover has not been tampered with. Fragile watermark technology could be useful in authenticating evidence or ensuring the accuracy of medical records or other sensitive data.

Fragment: A piece of a packet. When a router is forwarding an IP packet to a network with a Maximum Transmission Unit smaller than the packet size, it is forced to break up that packet into multiple fragments. These fragments will be reassembled by the IP layer at the destination host.

Fragmentation: The process in which an IP datagram is broken into smaller pieces to fit the requirements of a given physical network. The reverse process is termed "reassembly."

Frame Relay: A switching interface that operates in packet mode. Generally regarded as the replacement for X.25.

Frequency Domain: The way of representing a signal where the horizontal deflection is the frequency variable and the vertical deflection is the signals amplitude at that frequency.

Frequency Masking: A condition where two tones with relatively close frequencies are played at the same time and the louder tone masks the quieter tone.

Front Porch: The access point to a secure network environment; also known as a firewall.

Front-End Computer: A computer that offloads input and output activities from the central computer so it can operate primarily in a processing mode; sometimes called a front-end processor.

Front-End Processor (FEP):   (1) A communications computer associated with a host computer can perform line control, message handling, code conversion, error control, and application functions. (2) A teleprocessing concentrator and router, as opposed to a back-end processor or a database machine.

Full-Duplex (FDX):   An asynchronous communications protocol that allows the communications channel to transmit and receive signals simultaneously.

Fully Qualified Domain Name (FQDN):   A complete Internet address, including the complete host and domain name.

Function: In computer programming, a processing activity that performs a single identifiable task.

Functional Specification: The main product of systems analysis, which presents a detailed logical description of the new system. It contains sets of input, processing, storage, and output requirements specifying what the new system can do.

Garbage Collection: A language mechanism that automatically deallocates memory for objects that are not accessible or referenced.

Gateway: A product that enables two dissimilar networks to communicate or interface with each other. In the IP community, an older term referring to a routing device. Today, the term "router" is used to describe nodes that perform this function, and "gateway" refers to a special-purpose device that performs an application layer conversion of information from one protocol stack to another. Compare with router.

General-Purpose Computer: A computer that can be programmed to perform a wide variety of processing tests.

Government OSI Profile (GOSIP): A U.S. Government procurement specification for OSI protocols.

Granularity: The level of detail contained in a unit of data. The more there is, the lower the level of granularity; the less detail, the higher the level of granularity.

Graphical User Interface (GUI): An interface in which the user can manipulate icons, windows, pop-down menus, or other related constructs. A graphical user interface uses graphics such as a window, box, and menu to allow the user to communicate with the system. Allows users to move in and out of programs and manipulate their commands using a pointing device (usually a mouse). Synonymous with user interface.

Groupware: Software designed to function over a network to allow several people to work together on documents and files.

Guidelines: Documented suggestions for regular and consistent implementation of accepted practices. They usually have less enforcement powers.

Hacker: A person who attempts to break into computers that he or she is not authorized to use.

Hacking: A computer crime in which a person breaks into an information system simply for the challenge of doing so.

Half-Duplex: Capability for data transmission in only one direction at a time between a sending station and a receiving station.

Handprint Character Recognition (HCR):   One of several pattern recognition technologies used by digital imaging systems to interpret handprinted characters.

Handshake: Sequence of messages exchanged between two or more network devices to ensure transmission synchronization.

Handshaking Procedure: Dialogue between a user and a computer, two computers, or two programs to identify a user and authenticate his or her identity. This is done through a sequence of questions and answers that are based on information either previously stored in the computer or supplied to the computer by the initiator of the dialogue.

Hard Disk: A fixed or removable disk mass storage system permitting rapid direct access to data, programs, or information.

Hardware: The physical components of a computer network.

Hash function/Hashing: A hash function is a mathematical process based on an algorithm that creates a digital representation or compressed form of the message. It is often referred to as the message digest in the form of a hash value or hash result of a standard length which is usually much smaller than the message, but nevertheless substantially unique to it.

Hash Total: A total of the values on one or more fields, used for the purpose of auditability and control.

HDLC (High-Level Data-Link Control):   Bit-oriented synchronous datalink layer protocol developed by ISO. Derived from SDLC, HDLC specifies a data encapsulation method on synchronous serial links using frame characters and checksums.

HDSL: High-data-rate digital subscriber line. One of four DSL technologies. HDSL delivers 1.544 Mbps of bandwidth each way over two copper twisted pairs. Because HDSL provides T1 speed, telephone companies have been using HDSL to provision local access to T1 services whenever possible. The operating range of HDSL is limited to 12,000 feet (3658.5 meters), so signal repeaters are installed to extend the service. HDSL requires two twisted pairs, so it is deployed primarily for PBX network connections, digital loop carrier systems, interexchange POPs, Internet servers, and private data networks. Compare with ADSL, SDSL, and VDSL.

Header: The beginning of a message sent over the Internet; typically contains addressing information to route the message or packet to its destination.

Health Information Clearinghouses: Any public or private entities that process or facilitate processing nonstandard health information into standard data elements (e.g., third-party administrators, pharmacy benefits managers, billing services, information management and technology vendors, and others; HIPAA).

Health Plans: Individual or group plans (or programs) that provide health benefits directly, through insurance, or otherwise (e.g., Medicaid, State Children's Health Insurance Program (SCHIP), state employee benefit programs, Temporary Assistance for Needy Families (TANF), among others.

Healthcare Providers: Providers (or suppliers) of medical or other health services or any other person furnishing healthcare services or supplies, and who also conduct certain health-related administrative or financial transactions electronically (e.g., local health departments, community and migrant health centers, rural health clinics, school-based health centers, homeless clinics and shelters, public hospitals, maternal and child health programs (Title V), family planning programs (Title X), HIV/AIDS programs, among others).

Hertz (Hz): One cycle per second.

Heuristics: The mode of analysis in which the next step is determined by the results of the current step of analysis. Used for decision support processing.

Hexadecimal: A number system with a base of 16.

Hidden Partition: A method of hiding information on a hard drive where the partition is considered unformatted by the host operating system and no drive letter is assigned.

Hierarchical Database: In a hierarchical database, data is organized like a family tree or organization chart with branches of parent records and child records.

High-Level Data-Link Control (HDLC): A protocol used at the data-link layer that provides point-to-point communications over a physical transmission medium by creating and recognizing frame boundaries.

High-Level Language: The class of procedure-oriented language.

Home Page: The initial screen of information displayed to the user when initiating the client or browser software or when connecting to a remote computer. The home page resides at the top of the directory tree.

Honey-Pots: A specifically configured server, designed to attract intruders so their actions do not affect production systems; also known as a decoy server.

Hop: A term used in routing. A hop is one data link. A path from source to destination in a network is a series of hops.

Host: A remote computer that provides a variety of services, typically to multiple users concurrently.

Host: Same as a node. This is a computer (or another type of network device) connected to a network.

Host Address: The IP address of the host computer.

Host Computer: A computer that, in addition to providing a local service, acts as a central processor for a communications network.

Hostname: The name of the user computer on the network.

Hot Site: A fully operational offsite data processing facility equipped with both hardware and system software to be used in the event of disaster.

HTML: *See HyperText Markup Language.*

HTTP: *See HyperText Transport Protocol.*

Hub: A device connected to several other devices. In ARCnet, a hub is used to connect several computers together. In a message-handling service, a hub is used for transfer of messages across the network. An Ethernet hub is basically a "collapsed network-in-a-box" with a number of ports for the connected devices.

Hypertext: Text that is held in frames and authors develop or define the linkage between frames.

HyperText Markup Language (HTML): The specialized language used to insert formatting commands and links in a hypertext document.

HyperText Transfer Protocol (HTTP): A communication protocol used to connect to serves on the World Wide Web. Its primary function is to establish a connection with a Web server and transmit HTML pages to the client browser. The protocol used to transport hypertext files across the Internet.

IAB: Internet Architecture Board. A board of internetwork researchers who discuss issues pertinent to Internet architecture. Responsible for appointing a variety of Internet-related groups such as the IANA, IESG, and IRSG. The IAB is appointed by the trustees of the ISOC.

ICMP: Internet Control Message Protocol. Network layer Internet protocol that reports errors and provides other information relevant to IP packet processing. Documented in RFC 792.

Icon: A pictorial symbol used to represent data, information, or a program on a GUI screen.

ICQ: Pronounced "I Seek You." This is a chat service available via the Internet that enables users to communicate online. This service (users loads the application on their individual computers) allows chat via text, voice, bulletin boards, file transfers, and e-mail.

Identification: (1) The process, generally employing unique machine-readable names, that enables recognition of users or resources as identical to those previously described to the computer system. (2) The assignment of a name by which an entity can be referenced. The entity may be high level (such as a user) or low level (such as a process or communication channel.

Identity-Based Security Policy: A security policy based on the identities or attributes of users, a group of users, or entities acting on behalf of the users and the resources or targets being accessed.

IDS (Intrusion Detection System): An IDS inspects network traffic to identify suspicious patterns that may indicate a network or system attack from someone attempting to break in or compromise a system.

Impersonation: An attempt to gain access to a system by posing as an authorized user.

Implementation: The specific activities within the systems development life cycle through which the software portion of the system is developed, coded, debugged, tested, and integrated with existing or new software.

Incident: An unusual occurrence or breach in the security of a computer system. An event that has actual or potentially adverse effects on an information system. A computer security incident can result from a computer virus, other malicious code, intruder, terrorist, unauthorized insider act, malfunction, and such.

Incomplete Parameter Checking: A system fault that exists when all parameters have not been fully checked for correctness and consistency by the operating system, thus leaving the system vulnerable to penetration.

Independent Basic Service Set Network (IBSS Network): Independent Basic Service Set Network is an IEEE 802.11-based wireless network that has no backbone infrastructure and consists of at least two wireless stations. This type of network is often referred to as an ad hoc network because it can be constructed quickly without much planning.

Inference Engine: A system of computer programs in an expert systems application that uses expert experience as a basis for conclusions.

Infobots: Software agents that perform specified tasks for a user or application.

Information Security Governance: The management structure, organization, responsibility, and reporting processes surrounding a successful information security program.

Information Security Program: The overall process of preserving confidentiality, integrity, and availability of information.

Information Security Service: A method to provide some specific aspect of security. For example, integrity of transmitted data is a security objective, and a method that would achieve that is considered an information security service.

Inheritance: The language mechanism that allows the definition of a class to include the attributes and methods for another more general class. Inheritance is an implementation construct for the specialization relation. The general class is the superclass and the specific class is the subclass in the inheritance relation. Inheritance is a relation between classes that enables the reuse of code and the definition of generalized interface to one or more subclasses.

Initiator: An entity (e.g., human user or computer based entity) that attempts to access other entities.

Initiator Access Control Decision Information: ADI associated with the initiator.

Initiator Access Control Information: Access control information relating to the initiator.

Injection: Using this method, a secret message is put in a host file in such a way that when the file is actually read by a given program, the program ignores the data.

Input Controls: Techniques and methods for verifying, validating, and editing data to ensure that only correct data enters a system.

Instance: A set of values representing a specific entity belonging to a particular entity type. A single value is also the instance of a data item.

Integrated Data Dictionary (IDD): A database technology that facilitates functional communication among system components.

Integrated Services Digital Network (ISDN):   An emerging technology that is beginning to be offered by the telephone carriers of the world. ISDN combines voice and digital network services in a single medium, making it possible to offer customers digital data services as well as voice connections through a single wire. The standards that define ISDN are specified by ITU-TSS.

Integrity: (1) The accuracy, completeness, and validity of information in accordance with business values and expectations. The property that data or information has not been modified or altered in an unauthorized manner. (2) A security service that allows verification that an unauthorized modification (including changes, insertions, deletions, and duplications) has not occurred either maliciously or accidentally. *See also Data Integrity.*

Integrity Checking: The testing of programs to verify the soundness of a software product at each phase of development.

Intellectual Property Identification: A method of asset protection which identifies or defines a copyright, patent, trade secret, and such, or validates ownership and ensures that intellectual property rights are protected.

Intellectual Property Management and Protection (IPMP):   A refinement of digital rights management (DRM) that refers specifically to MPEGs.

Intelligent Cabling: Research is ongoing in this area. The goal is to eliminate the large physical routers, hubs, switches, firewalls, etc. and move these functions (i.e., embed the intelligence) into the cabling itself. Currently this is an electrochemical/neuronic research process.

Interactive: A mode of processing that combines some aspects of online processing and some aspects of batch processing. In interactive processing, the user can directly interact with data over which he or she has exclusive control. In addition, the user can cause sequential activity to initiate background activity to be run against the data.

Interface: A shared boundary between devices, equipment, or software components, defined by common interconnection characteristics.

Interleaving: The alternating execution of programs residing in the memory of a multiprogramming environment.

Internal Control: The method of safeguarding business assets, including verifying the accuracy and reliability of accounting data, promoting operational efficiency, and encouraging adherence to prescribed organizational policies and procedures.

Internet: A global computer network that links minor computer networks, allowing them to share information via standardized communication protocols. The Internet consists of large national backbone networks (such as MILNET, NSFNET, and CREN) and a myriad of regional and local campus networks all over the world. The Internet uses the Internet Protocol suite. To be on the Internet, you must have IP connectivity (i.e., be able to Telnet to or ping other systems). Networks with only email connectivity are not actually classified as being on the Internet. Although it is commonly stated that the Internet is not controlled or owned by a single entity, this is really misleading, giving many users the perception that no one is really in control (no one "owns") the Internet. In practical reality, the only way the Internet can function is to have the major telecom switches, routers, satellite, and fiber optic links in place at strategic locations. These devices at strategic locations are owned by a few major corporations. At any time, these corporations could choose to shut down these devices (which would shut down the Internet), alter these devices so only specific countries or regions could be on the Internet, or modify these devices to allow or disallow or monitor any communications occurring on the Internet.

Internet Address: A 32-bit address assigned to hosts using TCP/IP.

Internet Architecture Board (IAB):   Formally called the Internet Activities Board. The technical body that oversees the development of the Internet suite of protocols (commonly referred to as TCP/IP). It has two task forces (the IRTF and the IETF), each charged with investigating a particular area.

Internet Assigned Numbers Authority (IANA):   A largely government-funded overseer of IP allocations chartered by the FNC and the ISOC.

Internet Control Message Protocol (ICMP):   The protocol used to handle errors and control messages at the IP layer. ICMP is actually part of the IP.

Internet Engineering Task Force (IETF):   The Internet standards setting organization with affiliates internationally from network industry representatives. This includes all network industry developers and researchers concerned with evolution and planned growth on the Internet.

Internet Layer: The stack in the TCP/IP protocols that addresses a packet and sends the packets to the network access layer.

Internet Message Access Protocol (IMAP):   A method of accessing electronic mail or bulletin board messages that are kept on a (possibly shared) mail server. IMAP permits a "client" e-mail program to access remote message stores as if they were local. For example, e-mail stored on an IMAP server can be manipulated from a desktop computer at home, a workstation at the office, and a notebook computer while traveling, without the need to transfer messages of files back and forth between these computers. IMAP can be regarded as the next-generation POP.

Internet Protocol (IP, IPv4): The Internet Protocol (version 4), defined in RFC 791, is the network layer for the TCP/IP suite. It is a connectionless, best-effort, and packet-switching protocol.

Internet Protocol (Ping, IPv6): IPv6 is a new version of the Internet Protocol that is designed to be evolutionary.

Internet Service Provider (ISP): An organization that provides direct access to the Internet, such as the provider that links your college or university to the Net.

Interoperability: The ability to exchange requests between entities. Objects interoperate if the methods that apply to one object can request services of another object.

Intertrust: A company that develops intellectual property for digital rights management (DRM), digital policy management (DPM), and trusted computing systems.

Intrusion Detection: The process of monitoring the events occurring in a computer system or network, detecting signs of security problems.

Investigation: The phase of the systems development life cycle in which the problem or need is identified and a decision is made on whether to proceed with a full-scale study.

Invisible Ink: A method of steganography that uses a special ink that is colorless and invisible until treated by a chemical, heat, or special light. It is sometimes referred to as sympathetic ink.

Invisible Watermark: An overlaid image which is invisible to the naked eye, but which can be detected algorithmically. There are two different types of invisible watermarks: fragile and robust.

IOM: Institute of Medicine: prestigious group of physicians that study issues and advise Congress. The IOM developed a report on computer-based patient records that led to the creation of CPRI. Its most recent popular work is its report on medical errors: To Err is Human: Building A Safer Health System (Washington, DC: National Academy Press, 1999).

IP Address: A unique number assigned to each computer on the Internet, consisting of four numbers, each less than 256, and each separated by a period, such as 129.16.255.0.

IP Datagram: The fundamental unit of information passed across the Internet. Contains source and destination addresses, along with data and a number of fields that define such things as the length of the datagram, the header checksum, and flags to say whether the datagram can be (or has been) fragmented.

IP Security Protocol (IPSec): A protocol in development by the IETF to support secure data exchange. Once completed, IPSec is expected to be widely deployed to implement Virtual Private Networks (VPN). IPSec supports two encryption modes: Transport and Tunnel. Transport mode encrypts the data portion (payload) of each packet but leaves the header untouched. Tunnel mode is more secure since in encrypts both the header and the payload. On the receiving side, an IPSec-compliant device decrypts each packet.

IP Spoofing: IP (Address) Spoofing is a technique used to gain unauthorized access to computers or network devices, whereby the intruder sends messages with an IP source address to pretend that the message is coming from a trusted source.

IRC: Internet Relay Chat. This is a service (you must load the application on your computer) that allows interactive conversation on the Internet. IRC also allows you to exchange files and have "private" conversations. Some major supporters of this service are IRCnet and DALnet.

ISO 17799: ISO 17799 gives general recommendations for information security management. It is intended to provide a common international basis for developing organizational security standards and effective security management practice and to provide confidence in interorganizational dealings.

ISO 9000: A certification program that demonstrates an organization adheres to steps that ensure quality of goods and services. This quality series is comprised of a set of five documents and was developed in 1987 by the International Standards Organization (ISO).

Isolation: The separation of users and processes in a computer system from one another, as well as from the protection controls of the operating system.

ISP: *See Internet Service Provider.*

Iterative Development Life Cycle: A strategy for developing systems that allows for the controlled reworking of parts of a system to remove mistakes or to make improvements based on feedback.

Jargon Code: A code that uses words (esp. nouns) instead of figure or letter-groups as the equivalent of plain language units.

Java: Object-oriented programming language developed at Sun Microsystems to solve a number of problems in modern programming practice. The Java language is used extensively on the World Wide Web, particularly for applets.

Jitter Attack: A method of testing or defeating the robustness of a watermark. This attack applies "jitter" to a cover by splitting the file into a large number of samples, the deletes or duplicates one of the samples and puts the pieces back together. At this point, the location of the embedded bytes cannot be found. This technique is nearly imperceptible when used on audio and video files.

Join: An operation that takes two relations as operand and produces a new relation by concealing the tuples and matching the corresponding columns when a stated condition holds between the two.

Jukebox: Hardware that houses, reads, and writes to many optical disks using a variety of mechanical methods for operation.

Kerberos: Developing standard for authenticating network users. Kerberos offers two key benefits: it functions in a multi-vendor network and it does not transmit passwords over the network.

Kerckhoff's Principle: A cryptography principle that states if the method used to encipher data is known by an opponent, then security must lie in the choice of the key.

Key: In cryptography, a sequence of symbols that controls encryption and decryption. A quantity (number) used in cryptography to encrypt or decrypt information.

Key Generation: The origination of a key or set of distinct keys.

Key Management: The generation, storage, distribution, deletion, archiving, and application of keys in accordance with a security policy.

Key, Primary: A unique attribute used to identify a class of records in a database.

Key/Cryptovariable: Encryption and decryption generally require the use of some secret information, referred to as a key. For some encryption mechanisms, the same key is used for both encryption and decryption; for other mechanisms, the keys used for encryption and decryption are different.

Key2Audio™:   A product of Sony designed to control the copying of CDs by embedding code within the CD that prevents playback on a PC or Mac preventing track ripping or copying.

Knowledge Base: The part of an expert system that contains specific information and facts about the expert area. Rules that the expert system uses to make decisions are derived from this source.

Known-Cover Attack: A type of attack where both the original, unaltered cover, and the stego-object are available.

Known-Message Attack: A type of attack where the hidden message is known to exist by the attacker and the stego-object is analyzed for patterns which may be beneficial in future attacks. This is a very difficult attack, equal in difficulty to a stego-only attack.

Known-Stego Attack: An attack where the tool (algorithm) is known and the original cover object and stego-object are available.

L2F Protocol: Layer 2 Forwarding Protocol. Protocol that supports the creation of secure, virtual, private dial-up networks over the Internet.

Label: A set of symbols used to identify or describe an item, record, message, or file.

LAN: Local Area Network. High-speed, low-error data network covering a relatively small geographic area (up to a few thousand meters). LANs connect workstations, peripherals, terminals, and other devices in a single building or other geographically limited area. LAN standards specify cabling and signaling at the physical and data-link layers of the OSI model. Ethernet, FDDI, and Token Ring are widely used LAN technologies. Compare with MAN and WAN.

LAN Switch: High-speed switch that forwards packets between data-link segments. Most LAN switches forward traffic based on MAC addresses. This variety of LAN switch is sometimes called a frame switch. LAN switches are often categorized according to the method they use to forward traffic: cut-through packet switching or store-and forward packet switching. Multi-layer switches are an intelligent subset of LAN switches. Compare with multi-layer switch. *See also Cutthrough Packet Switching and Store-and-Forward Packet Switching.*

Language Translator: Systems software that converts programs written in assembler or a higher-level language into machine code.

Laser: Light Amplification by Stimulated Emission of Radiation. Analog transmission device in which a suitable active material is excited by an external stimulus to produce a narrow beam of coherent light that can be modulated into pulses to carry data. Networks based on laser technology are sometimes run over SONET.

Laser Printer: An output unit that uses intensified light beams to form an image on an electrically charged drum and then transfers the image to paper.

Latency: In local networking, the time (measured in bits at the transmission rate) for a signal to propagate around or throughput the network. The time taken by a DASD device to position a storage location to reach the read arm over the physical storage medium. For general purposes, average latency time is used. Delay between the time a device requests access to a network and the time it is granted permission to transmit.

Layer 3 Switching: The emerging layer 3 switching technology integrates routing with switching to yield very high routing throughput rates in the millions-of-packets-per-second range. The movement to layer 3 switching is designed to address the downsides of the current generation of layer 2 switches, which are functionally equivalent to bridges. These downsides for a large, flat network include being subject to broadcast storms, spanning tree loops, and address limitations that drove the injection of routers into bridged networks in the late 1980s. Currently, layer 3 switching is represented by a number of approaches in the industry.

LDAP: Lightweight Directory Access Protocol. Protocol that provides access for management and browser applications that provide read and write interactive access to the X.500 Directory.

Leased Line: An unswitched telecommunications channel leased to an organization for its exclusive use.

Least Recently Used (LRU): A replacement strategy in which new data must replace existing data in an area of storage; the least recently used items are replaced.

Least Significant Bit Steganography: A substitution method of steganography where the right-most bit in a binary notation is replaced with a bit from the embedded message. This method provides "security through obscurity," a technique that can be rendered useless if an attacker knows the technique is being used.

Lightweight Directory Access Protocol (LDAP): This protocol provides access for management and browser application that provide read/ write interactive access to the X.500 Directory.

Limit Check: An input control text that assesses the value of a data field to determine whether values fall within set limits.

Line Conditioning: A service offered by common carriers to reduce delay, noise, and amplitude distortion to produce transmission of higher data speeds.

Line Printer: An output unit that prints alphanumeric characters one line at a time.

Line Speed: The transmission rate of signals over a circuit, usually expressed in bits per second.

Linguistic Steganography: The method of steganography where a secret is embedded in a harmless message. *See Jargon Code.*

Load Sharing: A multiple-computer system that shares the work load during peak hours. During nonpeak periods or standard operation, one system can handle the entire load with the others acting as fallback units.

Logging: The automatic recording of data for the purpose of accessing and updating it.

MAC (Media Access Control): *See Media Access Control.*

MAC Address: Standardized data-link layer address ingrained into a NIC that is required for every port or device that connects to a LAN. Other devices in the network use these addresses to locate specific ports in the network and to create and update routing tables and data structures. MAC addresses are 6 bytes long and are controlled by the IEEE. Also known as a hardware address, MAC-layer address, and physical address. Compare with network address.

Machine Language: Computer instructions or code representing computer operations and memory addresses in a numeric form that is executable by the computer without translation.

Madison Project: A code name for IBM's Electronic Music Management System (EMMS). EMMS is being designed to deliver piracy-proof music to consumers via the Internet.

Magicgate: A memory media stick from Sony designed to allow users access to copyrighted music or data.

Mail Relay Server: An e-mail server that relays messages where neither the sender nor the receiver is a local user. The risk exists that an unauthorized user could hijack these open relays and use them to spoof their own identity.

Maintenance: Tasks associated with the modification or enhancement of production software.

Maintenance Programmer: An applications programmer responsible for making authorized changes to one or more computer programs and ensuring that the changes are tested, documented, and verified.

Mandatory Access Control (MAC): MAC is a means of restricting access to data based on varying degrees of security requirements for information contained in the objects.

Masquerade: A type of security threat that occurs when an entity successfully pretends to be a different entity.

Media: The various physical forms (e.g., disk, tape, and diskette) on which data is recorded in machine-readable formats.

Media Access Control (MAC):   Lower of the two sublayers of the data-link layer defined by the IEEE. The MAC sublayer handles access to shared media, such as whether token passing or contention will be used. A local network control protocol that governs station access to a shared transmission medium. Examples are token passing and CSMA. Carrier Sense, Multiple Access.

Megabyte (Mbyte, MB):   The equivalent of 1,048,576 bytes.

Memory: The area in a computer that serves as temporary storage for programs and data during program execution.

Memory Address: The location of a byte or word of storage in computer memory.

Memory Bounds: The limits in the range of storage addresses for a protected region in memory.

Memory Chips: A small integrated circuit chip with a semiconductor matrix used as computer memory.

Menu: A section of the computer program, usually the top-level module: that controls the order of execution of other program modules. Also, online options displayed to a user, prompting the user for specific input.

Message: (1) The data input by the user in the online environment that is used to drive a transaction. The output of transaction. (2) In steganography, the data a sender wishes to remain confidential. This data can be text, still images, audio, video, or anything that can be represented as a bitstream.

Message Address: The information contained in the message header that indicates the destination of the message.

Message Authentication Code (MAC):   Message Authentication Code is a one-way hash computed from a message and some secret data. It is difficult to forge without knowing the secret data. Its purpose is to detect if the message has been altered.

Message Digest: A message digest is a combination of alphanumeric characters generated by an algorithm that takes a digital object (such as a message you type) and pulls it through a mathematical process, giving a digital fingerprint of the message (enabling you to verify the integrity of a given message). An example would be MD5.

Messaging Application: An application based on a store and forward paradigm; it requires an appropriate security context to be bound with the message itself.

Metadata: The description of such things as the structure, content, keys, and indexes of data.

Metalanguage: A language used to specify other languages.

Metropolitan Area Network (MAN): A data network intended to serve an area approximating that of a large city. Such networks are being implemented by innovative techniques, such as running fiber cables through subway tunnels.

Microdot: A detailed form of microfilm that has been reduced to an extremely small size for ease of transport and purposes of security.

Microprocessor: A single small chip containing circuitry and components for arithmetic, logical, and control operations.

Middleware: The distributed software needed to support interactions between client and servers.

Minicomputer: Typically, a word-oriented computer whose memory size and processing speed falls between that of a microcomputer and a medium-sized computer.

Mirror Image Backup: Mirror image backups (also referred to as bit-stream backups) involve the backup of all areas of a computer hard disk drive or another type of storage media (e.g., Zip disks, floppy disks, Jazz disks, etc.). Such mirror image backups exactly replicate all sectors on a given storage device. Thus, all files and ambient data storage areas are copied. Such backups are sometimes referred to as "evidence-grade" backups and they differ substantially from standard file backups and network server backups. The making of a mirror image backup is simple in theory, but the accuracy of the backup must meet evidence standards. Accuracy is essential and to guarantee accuracy, mirror image backup programs typically rely on mathematical CRC computations in the validation process. These mathematical validation processes compare the original source data with the restored data. When computer evidence is involved, accuracy is extremely important, and the making of a mirror image backup is typically described as the preservation of the "electronic crime scene."

Mirrored Site: An alternate site that contains the same information as the original. Mirror sites are set up for backup and disaster recovery as well to balance the traffic load for numerous download requests. Such "download mirrors" are often placed in different locations throughout the Internet.

Mobile Site: The use of a mobile/temporary facility to serve as a business resumption location. They usually can be delivered to any site and can house information technology and staff.

Mode of Operation: A classification for systems that execute in a similar fashion and share distinctive operational characteristics (e.g., Production, DSS, online, and Interactive).

Model: A representation of a problem or subject area that uses abstraction to express concepts.

Modem (Modulator/Demodulator): This is a piece of hardware used to connect computers (or certain other network devices) together via a serial cable (usually a telephone line). When data is sent from your computer, the modem takes the digital data and converts it to an analog signal (the modulator portion). When you receive data into your computer via modem, the modem takes the analog signal and converts it to a digital signal that your computer will understand (the demodulator portion).

Modification: A type of security threat that occurs when content is modified in an unanticipated manner by a nonauthorized entity.

Monitoring Policy: The rules outlining the way in which information is captured and interpreted

Mosaic Attack: a watermarking attack that is particularly useful for images that are distributed over the Internet. It relies on a web browsers ability to assemble multiple images so they appear to be one image. A watermarked image can be broken into pieces but displayed as a single image by the browser. Any program trying to detect the watermark will look at each individual piece and, if they are small enough, will not be able to detect the watermark.

M-trax: An encrypted form of MP3 watermarking technology from MCY Music that protects the music industry and artists from copyright infringements.

Multiple Inheritance: The language mechanism that allows the definition of a class to include the attributes and methods defined for more than one superclass.

Multiprocessing: A computer operating method in which two or more processors are linked and execute multiple programs simultaneously.

Multiprogramming: A computer operating environment in which several programs can be placed in memory and executed concurrently.

Multi-purpose Internet Mail Extension (MIME): The standard for multimedia mail contents in the Internet suite of protocols.

MUSE Project: An initiative which contributes to the continuing development of intellectual property standards. The MUSE project focuses on the electronic delivery of media, embedded signaling systems, and encryption technology with the goal of creating a global standard.

NAK: Negative acknowledgment. Response sent from a receiving device to a sending device indicating that the information received contained errors. Compare with acknowledgment.

NAK Attack: A penetration technique that capitalizes on an operating system's inability to properly handle asynchronous interrupts.

Name Resolution: The process of mapping a name into the corresponding address.

NAT (Network Address Translation): (1) Translation. A means of hiding the IP addresses on an internal network from external view. NAT boxes allow net managers to use any IP addresses they choose on internal networks, thereby helping to ease the IP addressing crunch while hiding machines from attackers. (2) Mechanism for reducing the need for globally unique IP addresses. NAT allows an organization with addresses that are not globally unique to connect to the Internet by translating those addresses into globally routable address space. Also known as Network Address Translator.

Need-to-Know: A security principle stating that an individual should have access only to that needed to perform a particular function.

Negative Acknowledgment (NAK): A response sent by the receiver to indicate that the previous block was unacceptable and the receiver is ready to accept a retransmission.

Network: An integrated, communicating aggregation of computers and peripherals linked through communications facilities.

Network Access Layer: The layer of the TCP/IP stack that sends the message out through the physical network onto the Internet.

Network Access Points (NAPs): (1) Nodes providing entry to the high-speed Internet backbone system. (2) Another name for an Internet Exchange Point.

Network Address: The network portion of an IP address. For a class A network, the network address is the first byte of the IP address. For a class B network, the network address is the first two bytes of the IP address. For a class C network, the network address is the first three bytes of the IP address. In the Internet, assigned network addresses are globally unique.

Network Administrator: The person who maintains user accounts, password files, and system software on your campus network.

Network Information Center (NIC): Originally, there was only one, located at SRI International and tasked to serve the ARPANET (and later DDN) community. Today, there are many NICs, operated by local, regional, and national networks all over the world. Such centers provide user assistance, document service, training, and much more.

Network Layer: The OSI layer that is responsible for routing, switching, and subnetwork access across the entire OSI environment. Think of this layer as a post office that delivers letters based on the address written on an envelope.

Network Propagation System Analysis: A way of determining the speed and method of stego-object (or virus) movement throughout a network.

Neural Network: A type of system developed by artificial intelligence researchers used for processing logic.

Newsgroups: Usually discussions, but not "interactively live." Newsgroups are like posting a message on a bulletin board and checking at various times to see if someone has responded to your posting.

Newspaper Code: A hidden communication technique where small holes are poked just above the letters in a newspaper article that will spell out a secret message. A variant of this technique is to use invisible ink place of holes.

NIC: Network Interface Card. This is the card that the network cable plugs into in the back of your computer system. The NIC connects your computer to the network. A host must have at least one NIC; however, it can have more than one. Every NIC is assigned a MAC address.

NIST: National Institute of Standards and Technology.

Node: A device attached to a network.

Noise: Random electrical signals introduced by circuit components or natural disturbances that tend to degrade the performance of a communications channel.

Non-Discretionary Access Control: A non-discretionary authorization scheme is one under which only the recognized security authority of the security domain may assign or modify the ACI for the authorization scheme such that the authorizations of principals under the scheme are modified.

Non-Intrusive Monitoring: The use on non-intrusive probes or traces to assemble information and track traffic and identity vulnerabilities.

Non-Repudiation: Strong and substantial evidence of the identity of the signer of a message and the message integrity, sufficient to prevent a party from successfully denying the origin, submission or delivery of the message and the integrity of its contents.

Nontransparent Proxy Mode Accelerator: In a Nontransparent Proxy Mode Accelerator, the source addresses of all the packets decrypted by the SSL accelerator have a source address of that SSL accelerator and the client source addresses do not get to the server at all. From the server perspective, the request has come from the SSL accelerator.

NPRM: Notice of Proposed Rulemaking. The publication, in the Federal Register, of proposed regulations for public comment.

NRC: National Research Council. A quasi-governmental body that conducted a study on the state of security in health care: For the Record: Protecting Electronic Health Information (Washington, DC: National Academy Press, 1997).

Null(s): A symbol that means nothing that is included within a message to confuse unintended recipients.

Object Program: A program that has been translated from a higher-level source code into machine language.

Object Request Broker (ORB): A software mechanism by which objects make and receive requests and responses.

Object-Oriented: Any method, language, or system that supports object identity, classification, and encapsulation and specialization. C++, Smalltalk, Objective-C, and Eiffel are examples of object-oriented implementation languages.

Object-Oriented Analysis (OOA): The specification of requirements in terms of objects with identity that encapsulate properties and operations, messaging, inheritance, polymorphism, and binding.

Object-Oriented Database Management System (OODBMS): A database that stores, retrieves, and updates objects using transaction control, queries, locking, and versioning.

Object-Oriented Design (OOD): The development activity that specifies the implementation of a system using the conceptual model defined during the analysis phase.

Object-Oriented Language: A language that supports objects, method resolution, specialization, encapsulation, polymorphism, and inheritance.

Oblivious Scheme: *See Blind Scheme.*

Off-Line Authentication Certificate: A particular form of authentication information binding an entity to a cryptographic key, certified by a trusted authority, which may be used for authentication without directly interacting with the authority.

Offsite Storage: A storage facility located away from the building, housing the primary information processing facility (IPF), and used for storage of computer media such as offline backup data storage files.

OLE: Microsoft's Object Linking and Embedding technology designed to let applications share functionality through live data exchange and embedded data. Embedded objects are packaged statically within the source application, called the "client;" linked objects launch the "server" applications when instructed by the client application. Linking is the capability to call a program, embedding places data in a foreign program.

One-Time Pad: A system that randomly generates a private key, and is used only once to encrypt a message that is then decrypted by the receiver using a matching one-time pad and key. One-time pads have the advantage that there is theoretically no way to "break the code" by analyzing a succession of messages.

On-line Authentication Certificate: A particular form of authentication information, certified by a trusted authority, which may be used for authentication following direct interaction with the authority.

Online System: Applications that allow direct interaction of the user with the computer (CPU) via a CRT, thus enabling the user to receive back an immediate response to data entered (i.e., an airline reservation system). Only one root node can be used at the beginning of the hierarchical structure.

Open Code: A form of hidden communication that uses an unencrypted message. Jargon code is an example of open code.

Open Network/System: Is one in which, at the extremes, unknown parties, possibly in a different state or national jurisdictions will exchange/ trade data. To do this will require an overarching framework which will engender trust and certainty. A user of online services might go through a single authentication process with a trusted third party, receive certification of their public key, and then be able to enter into electronic transactions/data exchanges with merchants, governments, banks, etc., using the certificate so provided for multiple purposes.

Open System: A system whose architecture permits components developed by independent organizations or vendors to be combined.

Open Systems Interconnection (OSI): An international standardization program to facilitate communications among computers from different manufactures. *See ISO.*

OpenMG: A copyright protection technology from Sony that allows recording and playback of digital music data on a personal computer and other supported devices but prevents unauthorized distribution.

Operating System: The various sets of computer programs and other software that monitor and operate the computer hardware and the firmware to facilitate use of the hardware.

Operational Security Information: Transient information related to a single operation or set of operations within the context of an operational association, for example, a user session. Operational security information represents the current security context of the operations and may be passed as parameters to the operational primitives or retrieved from the operations environment as defaults.

Optical Disk: A disk that is written to or read from by optical means.

Optical Fiber: A form of transmission medium that uses light to encode signals and has the highest transmission rate of any medium.

Optical Storage: A medium requiring lasers to permanently alter the physical media to create a permanent record. The storage also requires lasers to read stored information from this medium.

Organizational Security Policy: Set of laws, rules, and practices that regulates how an organization manages, protects, and distributes sensitive information.

OSI 7-Layer Model: The Open System Interconnection seven-layer model is an ISO standard for worldwide communications that defines a framework for implementing protocols in seven layers. Control is passed from one layer to the next, starting at the application layer in one station, and proceeding to the bottom layer, over the channel to the next station and back up the hierarchy.

OSI Reference Model: The seven-layer architecture designed by OSI for open data communications network.

Overwriting: The obliteration of recorded data by recording different data on the same surface.

PABX: Private Automatic Branch Exchange. Telephone switch for use inside a corporation. PABX is the preferred term in Europe, while PBX is used in the United States.

Packet: Logical grouping of information that includes a header containing control information and (usually) user data. Packets are most often used to refer to network layer units of data. The terms "datagram," "frame," "message," and "segment" are also used to describe logical information groupings at various layers of the OSI Reference Model and in various technology circles.

Packet Filtering: Controlling access to a network analyzing the attributes of the incoming and outgoing packets and either letting them pass, or denying them based on a list of rules.

Packet Internet Grouper (PING): A program used to test reachability of destinations by sending them an ICMP echo request and waiting for a reply. The term is used as a verb: "Ping host X to see if it is up."

Packet Switch: WAN device that routes packets along the most efficient path and allows a communications channel to be shared by multiple connections. Formerly called an Interface Message Processor (IMP).

Packet Switching: A switching procedure that breaks up messages into fixed-length units (called packets) at the message source. These units may travel along different routes before reaching their intended destination.

Padding: A technique used to fill a field, record, or block with default information (e.g., blanks or zeros).

Page: A basic unit of storage in main memory.

Page Fault: A program interruption that occurs when a page that is referred to is not in main memory and must be read from external storage.

Paging: A method of dividing a program into parts called pages and introducing a given page into memory as the processing on the page is required for program execution.

PAP (Password Authentication Protocol): Authentication protocol that allows PPP peers to authenticate one another. The remote router attempting to connect to the local router is required to send an authentication request. Unlike CHAP, PAP passes the password and hostname or username in the clear (unencrypted). PAP does not itself prevent unauthorized access, but merely identifies the remote end. The router or access server then determines if that user is allowed access. PAP is supported only on PPP lines. Compare with CHAP.

Parallel Port: The computer's printer port that, in a pinch, allows user access to notebooks and computers that cannot be opened.

Parent: A unit of data in a 1:n relationship with another unit of data called a child, where the parent can exist independently but the child cannot.

Parity: A bit or series of bits appended to a character or block of characters to ensure that the information received is the same as the information that was sent. Parity is used for error detection.

Parity Bit: A bit attached to a byte that is used to check the accuracy of data storage.

Partition: A memory area assigned to a computer program during its execution.

Passive Response: A response option in intrusion detection in which the system simply reports and records the problem detected, relying on the user to take subsequent action.

Passive Wiretapping: The monitoring or recording of data while it is being transmitted over a communications link.

Password: A word or string of characters that authenticates a user, a specific resource, or an access type.

Password Cracker: Specialized securities checker that tests user's passwords, searching for passwords that are easy to guess by repeatedly trying words from specially crafted dictionaries. Failing that, many password crackers can brute force all possible combinations in a relatively short period of time with current desktop computer hardware.

Patchwork: An encoding algorithm that takes random pairs of pixels and brightens the brighter pixel and dulls the duller pixel, and encodes one bit of information in the contrast change. This algorithm creates a unique change, and that change indicates the absence or presence of a signature.

Patent: Exclusive right granted to an inventor to produce, sell, and distribute the invention for a specified number of years.

Payload: The amount of information that can be stored in the cover media. Typically, the greater the payload the greater the risk of detection.

PDA: Personal Digital Assistant. A handheld computer that serves as an organizer for personal information.

Peer-Entity Authentication: The corroboration that a peer entity in an association is the one claimed.

Penetration: A successful unauthorized access to a computer system.

Penetration Testing: The use of special programmer or analyst teams to attempt to penetrate a system to identify security weaknesses.

Perceptual Masking: A condition where the perception of one element interferes with the perception another.

Perfect Forward Secrecy: Perfect forward secrecy means that even if a private key is known to an attacker, the attacker cannot decrypt previously sent messages.

Persistent Object: An object that can survive the process that created it. A persistent object exists until it is explicitly deleted.

PGP: Pretty Good Privacy. Public key cryptography software based on the RSA cryptographic method.

Physical Layer: The OSI layer that provides the means to activate and use physical connections for bit transmission. In plain terms, the physical layer provides the procedures for transferring a single bit across a physical medium, such as cables.

Physical Security: The measures used to provide physical protection of resources against deliberate and accidental threats.

PictureMarc: A DigiMarc application that embeds an imperceptible digital watermark within an image allowing copyright communication, author recognition, and electronic commerce. It is currently bundled with Adobe Photoshop™.

Piggyback Entry: Unauthorized access to a computer system that is gained through another user's legitimate connection.

Piracy (or Simple Piracy):   The unauthorized duplication of an original recording for commercial gain without the consent of the rightful owner; or the packaging of pirate copies that is different from the original. Pirate copies are often compilations, such as the "greatest hits" of a specific artist, or a genre collection, such as dance tracks.

Pixel: Short for Picture Element, a pixel is a single point in a graphic image. It is the smallest thing that can be drawn on a computer screen. All computer graphics are made up of a grid of pixels. When these pixels are painted onto the screen, they form an image.

PKI: Public Key Infrastructure.

Plain Old Telephone System (POTS):   What we consider to be the "normal" phone system used with modems. Does not apply to leased lines or digital lines.

Plaintext: Intelligible text or signals that have meaning and can be read or acted on without being decrypted.

Platform: Foundation upon which processes and systems are built and which can include hardware, software, firmware, and such.

Platform Domain: A security domain encompassing the operating system, the entities and operations it supports and its security policy.

Pointer: The address of a record (or other data grouping) contained in another record so that a program may access the former record when it has retrieved the latter record. The address can be absolute, relative, or symbolic, and hence the pointer is referred to as absolute, relative, or symbolic.

Point-of-Presence (POP):   A site where there exists a collection of telecommunications equipment, usually digital leased lines and multi-protocol routers.

Point-to-Point: A network configuration interconnecting only two points. The connection can be dedicated or switched.

Point-to-Point Protocol (PPP):   The successor to SLIP, PPP provides router-to-router and host-to-network connections over both synchronous and asynchronous circuits.

Polling: A procedure by which a computer controller unit asks terminals and other peripheral devices in a serial fashion if they have any messages to send.

Polymorphism: A request-handling mechanism that selects a method based on the type of target object. This allows the specification of one request that can result in invocation of different methods depending on the type of the target object. Most object-oriented languages support the selection of the appropriate method based on the class of the object (classical polymorphism). A few languages or systems support characteristics of the object, including values and user-defined defaults (generalized polymorphism).

Port: (1) An outlet, usually on the exterior of a computer system, that enables peripheral devices to be connected and interfaced with the computer. (2) A numeric value used by the TCP/IP protocol suite that identifies services and application (e.g., HTTP Internet traffic uses port 80).

Portability: The ability to implement and execute software in one type of computing space and have it execute in a different computing space with little or no changes.

Ports: An interface point between the CPU and a peripheral device.

Presentation Layer: The layer of the ISO Reference Model responsible for formatting and converting data to meet the requirements of the particular system being utilized.

Pretty Good Privacy (PGP):   PGP provides confidentiality and authentication services for electronic mail and file storage applications. Developed by Phil Zimmerman and distributed for free on the Internet. Widely used by the Internet technical community.

Primary Key: An attribute that contains values that uniquely identifies the record in which the key exists.

Primary Service: An independent category of service such as operating system services, communication services and data management services. Each primary service provides a discrete set of functionality. Each primary service inherently includes generic qualities such as usability, manageability and security. Security services are therefore not primary services but are invoked as part of the provision of primary services by the primary service provider.

Principal: An entity whose identity can be authenticated.

Principle of Least Privilege: A security procedure under which users are granted only the minimum access authorization they need to perform required tasks.

Privacy: (1) The prevention of unauthorized access and manipulation of data. (2) The right of individuals to control or influence what information related to them may be collected and stored and by whom and to whom that information may be disclosed.

Privacy Act of 1974:   The federal law that allows individuals to know what information about them is on file and how it is used by all government agencies and their contractors. The 1986 Electronic Communication Act is an extension of the Privacy Act.

Privacy Enhanced Mail (PEM):   Internet e-mail standard that provides confidentiality, authentication, and message integrity using various encryption methods. Not widely deployed in the Internet.

Privacy Protection: The establishment of appropriate administrative, technical, and physical safeguards to protect the security and confidentiality of data records against anticipated threats or hazards that could result in substantial harm, embarrassment, inconvenience, or unfairness to any individual about whom such information is maintained.

Private Key: The private or secret key of a key pair, which must be kept confidential and is used to decrypt messages encrypted with the public key, or to digitally sign messages which can then be validated with the public key.

Private Network: A network established and operated by a private organization for the benefit of members of the organization.

Privilege: A right granted to an individual, a program, or a process.

Privileged Instructions: A set of instructions generally executable only when the computer system is operating in the executive state (e.g., while handling interrupts). These special instructions are typically designed to control such protection features as the storage protection features.

Problem: Any deviation from predefined standards.

Problem Reporting: The method of identifying, tracking, and assigning attributes to problems detected within the software product, deliverables, or within the development processes.

Procedure: Required "how-to" instructions that support some part of a policy or standard, and state "what to do."

Processor: The hardware unit containing the functions of memory and the central processing unit.

Program Development Process: The activities involved in developing computer programs, including problem analysis, program design, process design, program coding, debugging, and testing.

Program Maintenance: The process of altering program code or instructions to meet new or changing requirements.

Programmable Read-Only Memory (PROM): Computer memory chips that can be programmed permanently to carry out a defined process.

Programmer: The individual who designs and develops computer programs.

Programmer/Analyst: The individual who analyzes processing requirements and then designs and develops computer programs to direct processing.

Programming Language: A language with special syntax and style conventions for coding computer programs.

Programming Specifications: The complete description of input, processing, output, and storage requirements necessary to code a computer program.

Protection Ring: A hierarchy of access modes through which a computer system enforces the access rights granted to each user, program, and process, ensuring that each operates only within its authorized access mode.

Protocol: A set of instructions required to initiate and maintain communication between sender and receiver devices.

Protocol Analyzer: A data communications testing unit set that enables a network engineer to observe bit patterns and simulate network elements.

Prototype: A usable system or subcomponent that is built inexpensively or quickly with the intention of modifying or replacing it.

Proxy Server: Proxy server is a server that acts as an intermediary between a remote user and the servers that run the desired applications. Typical proxies accept a connection from a user, make a decision as to whether or not client IP address is permitted to use the proxy, perhaps perform additional authentication, and complete a connection to a remote destination on behalf of the user.

Public Key: In an asymmetric cryptography scheme, the key that may be widely published to enable the operation of the scheme. Typically, a public key can be used to encrypt, but not decrypt or to validate a signature, but not to sign.

Public Key Cryptography: An asymmetric cryptosystem where the encrypting and decrypting keys are different and it is computationally infeasible to calculate one form the other, given the encrypting algorithm. In public key cryptography, the encrypting key is made public, but the decrypting key is kept secret.

Public Key Cryptography Standards: Public Key Cryptography Standards (PKCS) are specifications produced by RSA Laboratories in cooperation with secure systems developers worldwide for the purpose of accelerating the deployment of Public Key Cryptography.

Public Key Encryption: An encryption scheme where two pairs of algorithmic keys (one private and one public) are used to encrypt and decrypt messages, files, and such.

Public Key Infrastructure: Supporting infrastructure, including nontechnical aspects, for the management of public keys.

Purging: The orderly review of storage and removal of inactive or obsolete data files.

Quality: The totality of features and characteristics of a product or service that bear on its ability to meet stated or implied needs.

Quality Assurance: An overview process that entails planning and systematic actions to ensure that a project is following good quality management practices.

Quality Control: Process by which product quality is compared with standards.

Quality of Service (QoS): The service level defined by a service agreement between a network user and a network provider, which guarantees a certain level of bandwidth and data flow rates.

Query Language: A language that enables a user to interact indirectly with a DBMS to retrieve and possibly modify data held under the DBMS.

RADIUS (Remote Dial-In User Service): Database for authenticating modem and ISDN connections and for tracking connection time. Remote authentication dial-in user service Is a protocol used to authenticate remote users and wireless connections.

RAID (Redundant Arrays of Inexpensive Disks): Instead of using one large disk to store data, you use many smaller disks (because they are cheaper). *See Disk Mirroring and Duplexing.* An approach to using many low-cost drives as a group to improve performance, yet also provides a degree of redundancy that makes the chance of data loss remote.

RAM: A type of computer memory that can be accessed randomly; that is, any byte of memory can be accessed without touching the preceding bytes. RAM is the most common type of memory found in computers and other devices, such as printers. There are two basic types of RAM: dynamic RAM (DRAM) and static RAM (SRAM).

RARP (Reverse Address Resolution Protocol): Protocol in the TCP/IP stack that provides a method for finding IP addresses based on MAC addresses. Compare with Address Resolution Protocol (ARP).

Raster Image: An image that is composed of small points of color data called pixels. Raster images allow the representation complex shapes and colors in a relatively small file format. Photographs are represented using raster images.

Read-Only Memory (ROM): Computer memory chips with preprogrammed circuits for storing such software as word processors and spreadsheets.

Reassembly: The process by which an IP datagram is "put back together" at the receiving hosts after having been fragmented in transit.

Reciprocal Agreement: Emergency processing agreements between two or more organizations with similar equipment or applications. Typically, participants promise to provide processing time to each other when an emergency arises.

Recording Industry Association of America (RIAA): A trade group that represents the U.S. recording industry. The RIAA works to create a business and legal environment that supports the record industry and seeks to protect intellectual property rights.

Recovery: The restoration of the information processing facility or other related assets following physical destruction or damage.

Recovery Point Objective (RPO): A measurement of the point prior to an outage to which data are to be restored.

Recovery Procedures: The action necessary to restore a system's computational capability and data files after system failure or penetration.

Recovery Time Objective (RTO): The amount of time allowed for the recovery of a business function or resource after a disaster occurs

Recursion: The definition of something in terms of itself. For example, a bill of material is usually defined in terms of itself.

Redundant Site: A recovery strategy involving the duplication of key information technology components, including data, or other key business processes, whereby fast recovery can take place. The redundant site usually is located away from the original.

Referential Integrity: The assurance that an object handle identifies a single object. The facility of a DBMS that ensures the validity of predefined relationships.

Regression Testing: The rerunning of test cases that a program has previously executed correctly to detect errors created during software correction or modification. Tests used to verify a previously tested system whenever it is modified.

Relational Database: In a relational database, data is organized in two-dimensional tables or relations.

Relying Third Party: The entity, such as a merchant, offering goods or services online that will receive a certificate as part of a process of completing a transactions with the user.

Remanence: The residual magnetism that remains on magnetic storage media after degaussing.

Remote Access: The ability to dial into a computer over a local telephone number using a number of digital access techniques.

Remote Authentication Dial-In User Service (RADIUS): A security and authentication mechanism for remote access.

Remote Procedure Call (RPC): An easy and popular paradigm for implementing the client/server model of distributed computing. A request is sent to a remote system to execute a designated procedure, using arguments supplied, and the result returned to the caller.

Replay: A type of security threat that occurs when an exchange is captured and resent at a later time to confuse the original recipients.

Replication: The process of keeping a copy of data through either shadowing or caching.

Report: Printed or displayed output that communicates the content of files and other activities. The output is typically organized and easily read.

Repudiation: Denying that you did something, or sent some message.

Request for Comments (RFC): The document series, begun in 1969, that describes the Internet suite of protocols and related experiments. Not all (in fact, very few) RFCs describe Internet standards, but all Internet standards are written up as RFCs.

Residual Risks: The risk associated with an event when the control is in place to reduce the effect or likelihood of that event being taken into account.

Residue: Data left in storage after processing operations and before degaussing or rewriting has occurred.

Resource: In a computer system, any function, device, or data collection that can be allocated to users or programs.

Risk: The probability that a particular security threat will exploit a particular vulnerability.

Risk Analysis: An analysis that examines an organization's information resources, its existing controls, and its remaining organization and computer system vulnerabilities. It combines the loss potential for each resource or combination of resources with an estimated rate of occurrence to establish a potential level of damage in dollars or other assets.

Risk Assessment: A process used to identify and evaluate risks and their potential effects

Risk Avoidance: The process for systematically avoiding risk. Security awareness can lead to a better education staff, which can lead to certain risks being avoided.

Risk Mitigation: Some risks cannot be avoided, but they can be minimized or mitigated by putting controls into place to mitigate the risk once an incident occurs.

Risk Transfer: The process of transferring risk. An example can include transferring the risk of a building fire to an insurance company.

Robust Watermark: A watermark that is very resistant to destruction under any image manipulation. This is useful in verifying ownership of an image suspected of misappropriation. Digital detection of the watermark would indicate the source of the image.

Role: A job type defined in terms of a set of responsibilities.

Rollback: (1) Restoration of a system to its former condition after it has switched to a fallback mode of operation when the cause of the fallback has been removed. (2) The restoration of the database to an original position or condition often after major damage to the physical medium. (3). The restoration of the information processing facility or other related assets following physical destruction or damage.

Router: (1) A system responsible for making decisions about which of several paths network (or Internet) traffic will follow. To do this, it uses a routing protocol to gain information about the network, and algorithms to choose the best route based on several criteria known as "routing metrics." (2) A network node connected to two or more networks. It is used to send data from one network (such as 137.13.45.0) to a second network (such as 43.24.56.0). The networks could both use Ethernet, or one could be Ethernet and the other could be ATM (or some other networking technology). As long as both speak common protocols (such as the TCP/IP protocol suite), they can communicate.

RSA: A public key cryptosystem developed by Rivest, Shamir, and Adleman. The RSA has two different keys, the public encryption key and the secret decryption key. The strength of the RSA depends on the difficulty of the prime number factorization. For applications with high-level security, the number of the decryption key bits should be greater than 512 bits. RSA is used for both encryption and digital signatures.

Safeguard: Synonymous with control.

Salt: Salt is a string of random (or pseudo-random) bits concatenated with a key or password to reduce the probability of precomputation attacks.

Sanitizing: The degaussing or overwriting of sensitive information in magnetic or other storage media.

Scalability: The likelihood that an artifact can be extended to provide additional functionality with little or no additional effort.

Scavenging: The searching of residue for the purpose of unauthorized data acquisition.

Scripts: Executable programs used to perform specified tasks for servers and clients.

Search Engine: A program written to allow users to search the Web for documents that match user-specified parameters.

Secrecy: A security principle that keeps information from being disclosed to anyone not authorized to access it.

Secret Key Cryptography: A cryptographic system where encryption and decryption are performed using the same key.

Secure Digital Music Initiative (SDMI): A forum of more than 160 companies and organizations representing a broad spectrum of information technology and consumer electronics businesses, Internet service providers, security technology companies, and members of the worldwide recording industry working to develop voluntary, open standards for digital music. SDMI is helping to enable the widespread Internet distribution of music by adopting a framework that artists and recording and technology companies can use to develop new business models.

Secure Electronic Transaction (SET): The SET specification has been developed to allow for secure credit card and offline debit card (check card) transactions over the World Wide Web.

Secure Operating System: An operating system that effectively controls hardware, software, and firmware functions to provide the level of protection appropriate to the value of the data resources managed by this operating system.

Secure Socket Layer (SSL): A protocol developed by Netscape for transmitting private documents via the Internet. SSL works by using a public key to encrypt data that is transferred over the SSL connection.

Security Association: A security association is a set of parameters which defines all the security services and mechanisms used for protecting the communication. A security association is bound to a specific security protocol.

Security Audit: An examination of data security procedures and measures to evaluate their adequacy and compliance with established policy.

Security Controls: Techniques and methods to ensure that only authorized users can access the computer information system and its resources.

Security Filter: A set of software or firmware routines and techniques employed in a computer system to prevent automatic forwarding of specified data over unprotected links or to unauthorized persons.

Security Kernel: The central part of a computer system (hardware, software, or firmware) that implements the fundamental security procedures for controlling access to system resources.

Security Metrics: A standard of measurement used to measure and monitor information security-related information security activity.

Security Parameter Index (SPI): SPI is an identifier for a security association within a specific security protocol. This means that a pair of security protocol and SPI may uniquely identify a security association, but this is implementation dependent.

Security Program: A systems program that controls access to data in files and permits only authorized use of terminals and other related equipment. Control is usually exercised through various levels of safeguards assigned on the basis of the user's need-to-know.

Seepage: The accidental flow, to unauthorized individuals, of data or information that is presumed to be protected by computer security safeguards.

Semagram: Meaning semantic symbol. Semagrams are associated with a concept and do not use writing to hide a message.

Sensitive Data: Data that is considered confidential or proprietary. The kind of data that, if disclosed to a competitor, might give away an advantage.

Sensitive Information: Any information that requires protection and that should not be made generally available.

Serial Line Internet Protocol (SLIP): An Internet protocol used to run IP over serial lines such as telephone circuits or RS-232 cables interconnecting two systems. SLIP is now being replaced by Point-to-Point Protocol. *See Point-to-Point Protocol.*

Server: A computer that provides a service to another computer, such as a mail server, a file server, or a news server.

Session: A completed connection to an Internet service, and the ensuing connect time.

Session Key: Session key is a randomly-generated key that is used one time, and then discarded. Session keys are symmetric (used for both encryption and decryption). They are sent with the message, protected by encryption with a public key from the intended recipient. A session key consists of a random number of approximately 40 to 2000 bits. Session keys can be derived from hash values.

Session Layer: (1) The OSI layer that provides means for dialogue control between end systems. (2) The layer of the ISO Reference Model coordinating communications between network nodes. It can be used to initialize, manage, and terminate communication sessions.

Shareware: Software available on the Internet that may be downloaded to your machine for evaluation and for which you are generally expected to pay a fee to the originator of the software if you decide to keep it.

Sign a Message: To use your private key to generate a digital signature as a means of proving you generated or certified some message.

Signature (digital):   A quantity (number) associated with a message that only someone with knowledge of your private key could have generated, but which can be verified through knowledge of your public key.

Signature Dynamics: A form of electronic signatures which involves the biometric recording of the pen dynamics used in signing the document.

Simple Network Management Protocol (SNMP):   Provides remote administration of network device; "simple" because the agent requires minimal software.

Simulation: The use of an executable model to represent the behavior of an object. During testing, the computational hardware, the external environment, and even the coding segments may be simulated.

Simultaneous Processing: The execution of two or more computer program instructions at the same time in a multiprocessing environment.

Single Inheritance: The language mechanism that allows the definition of a class to include the attributes and methods defined for, at most, one superclass.

Situation: Situation is a set of all security-relevant information. The decision of an entity on which security services it requires is based on the situation.

Slack Space: The unused space in a group of disk sectors. Or the difference in empty bytes of the space that is allocated in clusters minus the actual size of the data files.

Sniffing: An attack capturing sensitive pieces of information, such as a password, passing through the network.

SNIP: Strategic National Implementation Process (sponsored by WEDI).

Social Engineering: An attack based on deceiving users or administrators at the target site (e.g., a person who illegally enters computer systems by persuading an authorized person to reveal IDs, passwords, and other confidential information).

Socket: A paring of an IP address and a port number. *See Port.*

Softlifting: Illegal copying of licensed software for personal use.

Software: Computer programs, procedures, rules, and possibly documentation and data pertaining to the operation of the computer system.

Software Life Cycle: The period of time beginning when a software product is conceived and ending when the product is no longer available for use. The software life cycle is typically broken into phases (e.g., requirements, design, programming, testing, conversion, operations, and maintenance).

Software Maintenance: All changes, corrections, and enhancements that occur after an application has been placed into production.

Software Piracy: The illegal copying of software.

Source Document: The form that is used for the initial recording of data prior to system input.

Source Program: The computer program that is coded in an assembler or higher-level programming language.

Spam: The act of posting the same information repeatedly on inappropriate places or too many places so as to overburden the network.

Spatial Domain: The image plane itself; the collection of pixels that composes an image.

Specification: A description of a problem or subject that will be implemented in a computational or other system. The specification includes both a description of the subject and aspects of the implementation that affect its representation. Also, the process, analysis, and design that results in a description of a problem or subject that can be implemented in a computation or other system.

Split Knowledge: A security technique in which two or more entities separately hold data items that individually convey no knowledge of the information that results from combining the items. A condition under which two or more entities separately have key components which individually convey no knowledge of the plaintext key that will be produced when the key components are combined in the cryptographic module.

Spoofing: (1) Faking the sending address of a transmission to gain illegal entry into a secure system. (2) The deliberate inducement of a user or resource to take incorrect action.

Spooling: A technique that maximizes processing speed through the temporary use of high-speed storage devices. Input files are transferred from slower, permanent storage and queued in the high-speed devices to await processing, or output files are queued in high-speed devices to await transfer to slower storage devices.

Spread Spectrum Image Steganography: A method of steganographic communication that uses digital imagery as the cover signal.

Spread Spectrum Techniques: The method of hiding a small or narrow-band signal (message) in a large or wide band cover.

SSO: Single Sign-On or Standards Setting Organization.

Standalone Root: A certificate authority that signs its own certificates and does not rely of a directory service to authenticate users.

Standard: Mandatory statement of minimum requirements that support some part of a policy.

Standard Generalized Markup Language (SGML): An international standard for encoding textual information that specifies particular ways to annotate text documents separating the structure of the document from the information content. HTML is a generalized form of SGML.

Standards: A set of rules or specifications that, when taken together, define a software or hardware device. A standard is also an acknowledged basis for comparing or measuring something. Standards are important because new technology will only take root once a group of specifications is agreed upon.

State Transition: A change of state for an object; something that can be signaled by an event.

State Variable: A property or type that is part of an identified state of a given type.

Static Data: Data that, once established, remains constant.

Steering Committee: A management committee assembled to sponsor and manages various projects such as information security program.

Steganalysis: The art of detecting and neutralizing steganographic messages.

Steganalyst: The one who applies steganalysis with the intent of discovering hidden information.

Steganographic File System: A method of storing files in such a way that encrypts data and hides it such that it cannot be proven to be there.

Steganography: (1) The method(s) of concealing the existence of a message or data within seemingly innocent covers. (2) A technology used to embed information in audio and graphical material. The audio and graphical materials appear unaltered until a steganography tool is used to reveal the hidden message.

Stegokey: A key that allows extraction of the secret information out of the cover.

Stego-Medium: The resulting combination of a cover medium and embedded message and a stegokey.

Stego-Only Attack: An attack where only the stego-object is available for analysis.

StirMark: A method of testing the robustness of a watermark. StirMark is based on the premise that many watermarks can survive a simple manipulation to the file, but not a combination of manipulations. It simulates a process similar to what would happen if an image was printed and then scanned back into the computer by stretching, shearing, shifting, and rotating an image by a tiny random amount.

Stream Cipher: An encryption method in which a cryptographic key and an algorithm are applied to each bit in a datastream, one bit at a time.

Strong Authentication: Strong authentication refers to systems that require multiple factors for authentication and use advanced technology, such as dynamic passwords or digital certificates, to verify a user's identity.

Structured Design: A methodology for designing systems and programs through a top-down, hierarchical segmentation.

Structured Programming: The process of writing computer programs using logical, hierarchical control structures to carry out processing.

Structured Query Language (SQL): The international standard language for defining and accessing a relational database.

Subnet: A portion of a network, which may be a physically independent network segment, that shares a network address with other portions of the network and is distinguished by a subnet number. A subnet is to a network what a network is to the Internet.

Subnet Address: The subnet portion of an IP address. In a subnetted network, the host portion of an IP address is split into a subnet and a host portion using an address (subnet) mask.

Subroutine: A segment of code that can be called up by a program and executed at any time from any point.

Substitution: The steganographic method of encoding information by replacing insignificant bits from the cover with the bits from the embedded message.

Substitution-Linear Transformation Network: A practical architecture based on Shannon's concepts for the secure, practical ciphers with a network structure consisting of a sequence of rounds of small substitutions, easily implemented by table lookup and connected by bit position permutations or linear transpositions.

Superclass: A class from which another class inherits attributes and methods.

Supraliminal Channel: A feature of an image which is impossible to remove without gross modifications (i.e., a visible watermark).

Swapping: A method of computer processing in which programs not actively being processed are held on special storage devices and alternated in and out of memory with other programs according to priority.

Symmetric Key Encryption: In symmetric key encryption: two trading partners share one or more secrets, no one else can read their messages. A different key (or set of keys) is needed for each pair of trading partners. Same key used for encryption and decryption.

Synchronous: A protocol of transmitting data over a network where the sending and receiving terminals are kept in synchronization with each other by a clock signal embedded in the data.

Synchronous Optical NETwork (SONET): SONET is an international standard for high-speed data communications over fiber-optic media. The transmission rates range from 51.84 Mbps to 2.5 Gbps.

System: A series of related procedures designed to perform a specific task.

System Analysis: The process of studying information requirements and preparing a set of functional specifications that identify what a new or replacement system should accomplish.

System Design: The development of a plan for implementing a set of functional requirements as an operational system.

System Integrity Procedures: Procedures established to ensure that hardware, software, firmware, and data in a computer system maintain their state of original integrity and are not tampered with by unauthorized personnel.

System Log: An audit trail of relevant system happenings (e.g., transaction entries, database changes).

Systems Analysis: The process of studying information requirements and preparing a set of functional specifications that identify what a new or replacement system should accomplish.

Systems Design: The development of a plan for implementing a set of functional requirements as an operational system.

Systems Development Life Cycle (SDLC): (1) The classical operational development methodology that typically includes the phases of requirements gathering, analysis, design, programming, testing, integration, and implementation. (2) The systematic systems building process consisting of specific phases; for example, preliminary investigation, requirements determination, systems analysis, systems design, systems development, and systems implementation.

TACACS (Terminal Access Controller Access Control System): Authentication protocol developed by the DDN community that provides remote access authentication and related services, such as event logging. User passwords are administered in a central database rather than in individual routers, providing an easily scalable network security solution.

TACACS+: Terminal Access Controller Access Control System Plus is an authentication protocol, often used by remote-access servers or single (reduced) sign-on implementations. TACACS and TACACS+ are proprietary protocols from CISCO®.

TCP Sequence Prediction: Fools applications using IP addresses for authentication (like the UNIX rlogin and rsh commands) into thinking that forged packets actually come from trusted machines.

TCP/IP: Transmission Control Protocol/Internet Protocol is a set of communications protocols that encompasses media access, packet transport, session communications, file transfer, electronic mail, terminal emulation, remote file access, and network management. TCP/IP provides the basis for the Internet. The structure of TCP/IP is as follows:

Process layer clients: FTP, Telnet, SMTP, NFS, DNS

Transport layer service providers: TCP (FTP, Telnet, SMTP), UDP (NFS, DNS)

Network layer: IP (TCP, UDP)

Access layer: Ethernet (IP), Token ring (IP)

Technical Steganography: The method of steganography where a tool, device or method is used to conceal a message (e.g., invisible inks and microdots).

Technological Attack: An attack that can be perpetrated by circumventing or nullifying hardware, software, and firmware access control mechanisms rather than by subverting system personnel or other users.

Telecommunications: Any transmission, emission, or reception of signs, signals, writing, images, sounds, or other information by wire, radio, visual, satellite, or electromagnetic systems.

Teleprocessing: Information processing and transmission performed by an integrated system of telecommunications, computers, and person-to-machine interface equipment.

Teleprocessing Security: The protection that results from all measures designed to prevent deliberate, inadvertent, or unauthorized disclosure or acquisition of information stored in or transmitted by a teleprocessing system.

TEMPEST: The study and control of spurious electronic signals emitted from electronic equipment. TEMPEST is a classification of technology designed to minimize the electromagnetic emanations generated by computing devices. TEMPEST technology makes it difficult, if not impossible, to compromise confidentiality by capturing emanated information.

Temporal Masking: A form of masking that occurs when a weak signal is played immediately after a strong signal.

Test Data: Data that simulates actual data to form and content and is used to evaluate a system or program before it is put into operation.

Texture Block Coding: A method of watermarking that hides data within the continuous random texture patterns of an image. The technique is implemented by copying a region from a random texture pattern found in a picture to an area that has similar texture, resulting in a pair of identically textured regions in the picture.

The Prisoner's Problem: A model for steganographic communication.

Threat Analysis: A project to identify the threats that exist over key information and information technology. The threat analysis usually also defines the level of the threat and likelihood of that threat to materialize.

Threat Monitoring: The analysis assessment and review of audit trails and other data collected to search out system events that may constitute violations or precipitate incidents involving data privacy.

Three-Way Handshake: The process whereby two protocol entities synchronize during connection establishment.

Throughput: The process of measuring the amount of work a computer system can handle within a specified timeframe.

Time Domain: the way of representing a signal where the vertical deflection is the signals amplitude, and the horizontal deflection is the time variable.

Time Stamping: An electronic equivalent of mail franking.

Time-Dependent Password: A password that is valid only at a certain time of day or during a specified time frame.

Timestamping: The practice of tagging each record with some moment in time, usually when the record was created or when the record was passed from one environment to another.

Token Passing: A network access method that uses a distinctive character sequence as a symbol (token), which is passed from node to node, indicating when to begin transmission. Any node can remove the token, begin transmission, and replace the token when it is finished.

Token Ring: A type of area network in which the devices are arranged in a virtual ring in which the devices use a particular type of message called a token to communicate with one another.

Traceroute: (1) A program available on many systems that traces the path a packet takes to a destination. It is mostly used to debug routing problems between hosts. There is also a traceroute protocol defined in RFC 1393. (2) The traceroute or finger commands to run on the source machine (attacking machine) to gain more information about the attacker.

Trademark: A registered word, letter, or device granting the owner exclusive rights to sell or distribute the goods to which it is applied.

Trading Partner Agreement: A contractual arrangement that specifies the legal terms and conditions under which parties operate when conducting transactions by the use of EDI. It may cover such things as validity and formation of contract; admissibility in evidence of EDI messages; processing and acknowledgment of receipt of EDI messages; security, confidentiality, and protection of personal data; recording and storage of EDI messages; operational requirements for EDI (i.e., message standards, codes, transaction, and operations logs; technical specifications and requirements; liability including use of intermediaries and third party service providers; dispute resolution; and applicable law).

Traffic Analysis: A type of security threat that occurs when an outside entity is able to monitor and analyze traffic patterns on a network.

Traffic Flow Security: The protection that results from those features in some cryptography equipment that conceal the presence of valid messages on a communications circuit, usually by causing the circuit to appear busy at all times or by encrypting the source and destination addresses of valid messages.

Traffic Security: A collection of techniques for concealing information about a message to include existence, sender, receivers, and duration. Methods of traffic security include call-sign changes, dummy messages, and radio silence.

Transaction: A transaction is an activity or request to a computer. Purchase orders, changes, additions, and deletions are examples of transactions that are recorded in a business information environment.

Transform Domain Techniques: various methods of signal and image processing (Fast Fourier Transform, Discrete Cosine Transform, and such) used mainly for the purposes of compression.

Transformation Analysis: the process of detecting areas of image and sound files that is unlikely to be affected by common transformations and hide information in those places. The goal is to produce a more robust watermark.

Transmission Control Protocol (TCP): The major transport protocol in the Internet suite of protocols providing reliable, connection-oriented, full-duplex streams.

Transport Layer: (1) The OSI layer that is responsible for reliable end-to-end data transfer between end systems. (2) The layer of the ISO Reference Model responsible for managing the delivery of data over a communications network.

Trojan Horse: A computer program that is apparently or actually useful but contains a trapdoor or unexpected code.

Trust: Reliance on the ability of a system or process to meet its specifications.

Trusted Computer Security Evaluation Criteria (TCSEC): A security development standard for system manufacturers and a basis for comparing and evaluating different computer systems. Also known as the Orange Book.

Trusted Third Party: An entity trusted by other entities with respect to security related services and activities, such as a certification authority.

Tunneling: (1) Tunneling refers to encapsulation of protocol A with protocol B, such that A treats B as though it were a data-link layer. Tunneling is used to get data between administrative domains, which use a protocol that is not supported by the internet connecting those domains. (2) The use of authentication and encryption to set up virtual private networks (VPNs).

Twisted Pair: A type of network physical medium made of copper wires twisted around each other. For example, ordinary telephone cable.

Two-Factor Authentication: The use of two independent mechanisms for authentication; for example, requiring a smart cart and a password.

UDP: User Datagram Protocol. Connectionless transport layer protocol in the TCP/IP stack. UDP is a simple protocol that exchanges datagrams without acknowledgments or guaranteed delivery, requiring that error processing and retransmission be handled by other protocols. UDP is defined in RFC 768.

Uniform Resource Locator (URL): The primary means of navigating the web; consists of the means of access, the Web site, the path, and the document name of a Web resource (e.g., http://www.auerbachpublications.com).

Unshielded Twisted Pair (UTP): A generic term for "telephone" wire used to carry data such as 10Base-T and 100Base-T. Various categories (qualities) of cable exist that are certified for different kinds of networking technologies.

Update: The file processing activity in which master records are altered to reflect the current business activity contained in transactional files.

UPIN: Universal Provider Identification Number, to be replaced by National Provider Identifier under HIPAA

URAC: The American Accreditation HealthCare Commission.

Use: With respect to individually identifiable health information, the sharing, employment, application, utilization, examination, or analysis of such information within an entity that maintains such information. *See Disclosure, in contrast.*

USENET: A facility of the Internet, also called "the news," which allows users to read and post messages to thousands of discussion groups on various topics.

Usenet: A worldwide collection/system of newsgroups that allows users to post messages to an online bulletin board.

User Datagram Protocol (UDP): A transport protocol in the Internet suite of protocols. UDP, like TCP, uses IP for delivery; however, unlike TCP, UDP provides for exchange of datagrams without acknowledgments or guaranteed delivery.

User/Subscriber: An individual procuring goods or services online who obtains a certificate from a certification authority. Since both consumers and merchants may have digital certificates used to conclude a transaction, they may both be subscribers in certain circumstances. This person may also be referred to as the signer of a digital signature or the sender of data message signed with a digital signature.

Validation: The determination of the correctness, with respect to the user needs and requirements, of the final program or software produced from a development project.

Validation, Verification, and Testing: Used as an entity to define a procedure of review, analysis, and testing throughout the software life cycle to discover errors; the process of validation, verification, and testing determines that functions operate as specified and ensures the production of quality software.

Value-Added Network (VAN): A communications network using existing common carrier networks and providing such additional features as message switching and protocol handling.

Vector Image: A digital image that is created through a sequence of commands or mathematical statements that places lines and shapes in a given two- or three-dimensional space.

Verification: (1) The authentication process by which the biometric system matches a captured biometric against the person's stored template. (2) The demonstration of consistency, completeness, and correctness of the software at and between each stage of the development life cycle.

Verify: To determine accurately that: (a) the digital signature was created by the private key corresponding to the public key and (b) the message has not been altered since its digital signature was created.

Verify a Signature: Perform a cryptographic calculation using a message, a signature for the message, and a public key to determine whether the signature was generated by someone knowing the corresponding private key.

Virtual Circuit: A network service that provides connection-oriented service, regardless of the underlying network structure.

Virtual Memory: A method of extending computer memory using secondary storage devices to store program pages that are not being executed at the time.

Virtual Private Network (VPN): (1) A VPN allows IP traffic to travel securely over public TCP/IP network by encrypting all traffic from one network to another. A VPN uses "tunneling" to encrypt all information at the IP level. (2) A secure private network that uses the public telecommunications infrastructure to transmit data. In contrast to a much more expensive system of owned or leased lines that can only be used by one company, VPNs are used by enterprises for both extranets and wide are intranets. Using encryption and authentication, a VPN encrypts all data that passes between two Internet points, maintaining privacy and security

Virus: A type of malicious software that can destroy a computer's hard drive, files, and programs in memory and that replicates itself to other disks.

Virus Signature Files: A file of virus patterns that are compared with existing files to determine if they are infected with a virus. The vendor of the anti-virus software updates the signatures frequently and makes the available to customers via the Web.

Visible Noise: The degradation of a cover as a result of embedding information. Visible noise will indicate the existence of hidden information.

Visible Watermark: A visible and translucent image that is overlaid on a primary image. Visible watermarks allow the primary image to be viewed, but still marks it clearly as property of the owner. A digitally watermarked document, image, or video clip can be thought of as digitally "stamped."

VPN: *See Virtual Private Network.*

WAN (Wide Area Network): Data communications network that serves users across a broad geographic area and often uses transmission devices provided by common carriers. Frame Relay, SMDS, and X.25 are examples of WANs. Compare with LAN and MAN.

Warm Site: A warm site is similar to a hot site; however, it is not fully equipped with all necessary hardware needed for recovery.

Waterfall Life Cycle: A software development process that structures the analysis, design, programming, and testing. Each step is completed before the next step begins.

Watermarking: A form of marking that embeds copyright information about the artist or owner.

Web Crawler: A software program that searches the Web for specified purposes such as to find a list of all URLs within a particular site.

Web Hosting: The business of providing the equipment and services required to host and maintain files for one or more Web sites and to provide fast Internet connections to those sites. Most hosting is "shared," which means that Web sites of multiple companies are on the same server in order to share costs.

Web Server: Using the client-server model and the World Wide Web's HyperText Transfer Protocol (HTTP), Web Server is a software program that serves web page files to users.

WEDI: Workgroup on Electronic Data Interchange.

Whois: An Internet resource that permits users to initiate queries to a database containing information on users, hosts, networks, and domains.

Wiring Closet: A specially designed room used for wiring a data or voice network. Wiring closets serve as a central junction point for the wiring and wiring equipment that is used for interconnecting devices.

Work Factor: The effort and time required to break a protective measure.

Workforce: Under HIPAA, employees, volunteers, trainees, and other persons whose conduct, in the performance of work for a covered entity, is under the direct control of such entity, whether or not they are paid by the covered entity. *See Business Associate, in contrast.*

Worm: With respect to security, a special type of virus that does not attach itself to programs, but rather spreads via other methods such as e-mail.

Wrapper: *See Cover Medium.*

WWW: World Wide Web; also shortened to Web. Although WWW is used by many as being synonymous with the Internet, the WWW is actually one of numerous services on the Internet. This service allows e-mail, images, sound, and newsgroups.

X.400:   ITU-T recommendation specifying a standard for e-mail transfer.

X.500:   The CITT and ISO standard for electronic directory services.

X.509:   A standard that is part of the X.500 specifications that defines the format of a public key certificate.

XDSL: A group term used to refer to ADSL (Asymmetrical Digital Subscriber Line), HDSL (High data rate Digital Subscriber Line), and SDSL (Symmetrical Digital Subscriber Line). All are digital technologies using the existing copper infrastructure provided by the telephone companies. XDSL is a high-speed alternative to ISDN.

Index